Baedeker's
ITALY

HOTEL DELLA SIGNORIA 055-214530 FLORENCE T-W-Th
HOTEL DIANA 06-4751541 ROME FRI 23rd

A SPECTRUM BOOK

PRENTICE-HALL, Inc., Englewood Cliffs, New Jersey 07632

Cover picture: Leaning Tower, Pisa

177 colour photographs
46 maps and plans
1 large road map

Text:
Rosemarie Arnold (History)
Walter R. Arnold (Music)
Monika I. Baumgarten (Italy from A to Z)
Gerald Sawade (Climate)
Christine Wessely (Art)

Editorial work:
Baedeker Stuttgart
English language: Alec Court

Cartography:
Ingenieurbüro für Kartographie
Huber & Oberländer, Munich

Design and layout:
Creativ + Druck (Kolb), Stuttgart

Conception and general direction:
Dr Peter Baumgarten,
Baedeker Stuttgart

English translation:
James Hogarth

© Baedeker Stuttgart
Original German edition

© The Automobile Association
United Kingdom and Ireland

© Jarrold and Sons Ltd
English Language edition Worldwide

Licensed user:
Mairs Geographischer Verlag GmbH & Co.,
Ostfildern-Kemnat bei Stuttgart

Reproductions:
Gölz Repro-Service GmbH,
Ludwigsburg

The name *Baedeker* is a registered trademark

Source of illustrations:

Most of the coloured photographs were provided by
the Italian State Tourist Office, Rome and Frankfurt
am Main. Others:

Allianz-Archiv (p. 330)
Anthony-Verlag, Starnberg (cover picture)
Baedeker-Archiv (p. 133)
Azienda Autonoma di Soggiorno e Cura, Bolzano
   (pp. 54, 79)
Werner Fauser, Stuttgart (p. 149)
Giesse, Milan (pp. 158, 162)
Bildarchiv Hans Huber KG, Garmisch-Partenkirchen
   (pp. 306, 312)
Ulrich Kolb, Winnenden (pp. 209, 278, bottom)
Museo della Civiltà Romana, Rome (pp. 228–229)
Nova Lux, Florence (pp. 36, 113, 114, 117)
Friedrich Schley, Hamburg (p. 134)
Zentrale Farbbild Agentur GmbH (ZEFA), Düsseldorf
   (pp. 331, 333, two)

How to Use this Guide

Europe uses the metric system of measurement. Since
this is the only system you will encounter in your
travels, many of the measurements in this guide are
expressed in metric terms. Conversion is easy.
Multiply metres by 3·3 to get the approximate
dimensions in feet. A kilometre (1000 m) is approxi-
mately 0·62 mile.

The principal towns and areas of tourist interest are
described in alphabetical order. The names of other
places referred to under these general headings can be
found in the very full Index.

Following the tradition established by Karl Baedeker
in 1844, sights of particular interest and hotels and
restaurants of particular quality are distinguished by
either one or two asterisks.

In the lists of hotels b. = beds and SP = swimming
pool. Hotels are classified in the categories shown on
p. 339. A glossary of common geographical, architectural, etc., terms is given on p. 338.

The symbol (i) at the beginning of an entry or on a
town plan indicates the local tourist office or other
organisation from which further information can be
obtained. The initials of these organisations are
expanded on p. 360. The post-horn symbol on a town
plan indicates a post office.
Only a selection of hotels and restaurants can be
given: no reflection is implied, therefore, on establishments not included.

In a time of rapid change it is difficult to ensure that all
the information given is entirely accurate and up to
date and the possibility of error can never be entirely
eliminated. Although the publishers can accept no
responsibility for inaccuracies and omissions they are
always grateful for corrections and suggestions for
improvement.

Printed in Great Britain by Jarrold & Sons Ltd,
Norwich

0-13-055897-4 Paperback
0-13-055905-9 Hard Cover

This guidebook forms part of a completely new series of the world-famous Baedeker Guides to Europe.

Each volume is the result of long and careful preparation and, true to the traditions of Baedeker, is designed in every respect to meet the needs and expectations of the modern traveller.

The name of Baedeker has long been identified in the field of guidebooks with reliable, comprehensive and up-to-date information, prepared by expert writers who work from detailed, first-hand knowledge of the country concerned. Following a tradition that goes back over 150 years to the date when Karl Baedeker published the first of his handbooks for travellers, these guides have been planned to give the tourist all the essential information about the country and its inhabitants: where to go, how to get there and what to see. Baedeker's account of a country was always based on his personal observation and experience during his travels in that country. This tradition of writing a guidebook in the field rather than at an office desk has been maintained by Baedeker ever since.

Lavishly illustrated with superb colour photographs and numerous specially drawn maps and street plans of the major towns, the new Baedeker Guides concentrate on making available to the modern traveller all the information he needs in a format that is both attractive and easy to follow. For every place that appears in the gazetteer, the principal features of architectural, artistic and historic interest are descrlbed, as are its main areas of scenic beauty. Selected hotels and restaurants are also included. Features of exceptional merit are indicated by either one or two asterisks.

A special section at the end of each book contains practical information, details of leisure activities and useful addresses. The separate road map will prove an invaluable aid to planning your route and your travel within the country.

4   Contents

Introduction
to Italy

Visitors to Italy should keep a careful eye on their property and take sensible precautions against theft, particularly in the larger towns. Handbag snatching and the theft of other portable articles of value such as cameras, binoculars, watches and jewelry, as well as more substantial items, including suitcases, are a constant hazard, and particular care should be taken in public places especially shops, cafés and gas stations; even a car slowing down at traffic lights is a possible target for attack. Cars may be broken into, robbed or stolen if left unattended; trailers and minibuses are particularly vulnerable, but even touring coaches and hired cars with Italian registration are not immune.

It is important, therefore, to carry all objects of value – papers, money, travellers' checks, bank and credit cards, keys, etc. – on your person and never to leave them in an unattended car. The glove compartment – and if possible the trunk as well – should be left empty and unlocked. Overnight your car should be kept in a lock-up garage if one is available, preferably with a safety lock or similar device.

The Italian police are always ready to help, but are almost powerless in face of this type of crime, often carried out by organised gangs. After a break-in or robbery by violence they can often do no more than take particulars of the offence (which is in any event an essential part of the procedure for making a claim against your insurance company).

If you lose travellers' checks, a bank card or credit card you should at once inform the bank or other agency concerned by telegram so that they can stop payment.

Lake Garda

**Italy
(Repubblica
Italiana)**

Italy, with a total area of some 301,260 sq. km and a population of over 56 million, is divided into **20 regions** (*regioni*) and **95 provinces** (*province*). Since the national referendum of 2 June 1946, which put an end to the monarchy (the House of Savoy), it has been a democratic **republic** (*Repubblica Italiana*).

Under the 1947 constitution the Italian Parliament, which consists of two chambers, possesses legislative power and is responsible for controlling the executive. The first chamber, the Camera dei Deputati, has 630 members who are elected in a general election held every five years; the members of the second house, the Senato, who number some 320, are elected on a regional basis, also for five years. The President of the Republic, whose functions are mainly of a representative nature, is elected for a seven-year term by both houses of Parliament together with three additional delegates from each region.

The government consists of the Prime Minister (Presidente del Consiglio) and other ministers, who together form the Cabinet (Consiglio dei Ministri). There is a Supreme Court (Corte Costituzionale) responsible for ensuring that the requirements of the constitution are observed.

Italy is a member of the European Community and the North Atlantic Treaty Organisation (NATO).

Lombardy/Lombardia

Bergamo (BG)
Brescia (BS)
Como (CO)
Cremona (CR)
Milan/Milano (MI)
Mantua/Mantova (MN)
Pavia (PV)
Sondrio (SO)
Varese (VA)

Trentino – Alto Adige

Bolzano (BZ)
Trento (TN)

**Venetia/Veneto
(Venezia Euganea)**

Belluno (BL)
Padua/Padova (PD)
Rovigo (RO)
Treviso (TV)
Venice/Venezia (VE)
Verona (VR)
Vicenza (VI)

Friuli – Venezia Giulia

Gorizia (GO)
Pordenone (PN)
Trieste (TS)
Udine (UD)

Piedmont/Piemonte

Alessandria (AL)
Asti (AT)
Cuneo (CU)
Novara (NO)
Turin/Torino (TO)
Vercelli (VC)

**Aosta Valley/
Valle d'Aosta/Val d'Aoste**

Aosta (AO)

Liguria

Genoa/Genova (GE)
Imperia (IM)
La Spezia (SP)
Savona (SV)

Emilia-Romagna

Bologna (BO)
Ferrara (FE)
Forlì (FO)
Modena (MO)
Parma (PR)
Piacenza (PC)
Ravenna (RA)
Reggio nell'Emilia (RE)

Tuscany/Toscana

Arezzo (AR)
Florence/Firenze (FI)
Grosseto (GR)
Livorno (LI)
Lucca (LU)
Massa-Carrara (MS)
Pisa (PI)
Pistoia (PT)
Siena (SI)

Marches/Marche

Ancona (AN)
Ascoli Piceno (AP)
Macerata (MC)
Pesaro-Urbino (PS)

Umbria

Perugia (PU)
Terni (TR)

Latium/Lazio

Frosinone (FR)
Latina (LT)
Rieti (RI)
Rome/Roma (ROMA)
Viterbo (VT)

Abruzzi/Abruzzo

Chieti (CH)
L'Aquila (AQ)
Pescara (PE)
Teramo (TE)

Molise

Campobasso (CB)
Isernia (IS)

Campania

Avellino (AV)
Benevento (BN)
Caserta (CE)
Naples/Napoli (NA)
Salerno (SA)

Apulia/Puglia

Bari (BA)
Brindisi (BR)
Foggia (FG)
Lecce (LE)
Taranto (TA)

Basilicata

Matera (MT)
Potenza (PZ)

Calabria

Catanzaro (CZ)
Cosenza (CS)
Reggio di Calabria (RC)

Sicily/Sicilia

Agrigento (AG)
Caltanissetta (CL)
Catania (CT)
Enna (EN)
Messina (ME)
Palermo (PA)
Ragusa (RG)
Syracuse/Siracusa (SR)
Trapani (TP)

Sardinia/Sardegna

Cagliari (CA)
Nuoro (NU)
Oristano (OR)
Sassari (SS)

Italy has been called the "paradise of travellers", and its manifold attractions continue to draw visitors from far and wide, as they have down the centuries. Few countries offer such a diversity of scenery, from the Alpine peaks with their perpetual covering of snow to the sun-kissed coasts of Sicily; few others possess such a wealth of historical remains, recalling the Roman Empire which extended from Britain to Africa and, in later centuries, the powerful city states of the Middle Ages; and few have such a range of magnificent museums and galleries containing archaeological material, art treasures from all the great periods of history, painting and sculpture which are of central importance in the history of European art. And in addition there are the numerous beautiful resorts which attract thousands of visitors to Italy's coasts and lakes year after year.

To visitors making for the sunny south early in the year **NORTHERN ITALY** may seem no more than a prelude of the real Italy; and indeed there is something of a southern atmosphere about the luxuriant gardens on the shores of the North Italian lakes, with their palms and evergreen magnolias and their abundance of blossom, and in the sheltered valleys of the Adige, the Ticino and the Dora Baltea. This first impression, however, is soon swept away by the undramatic landscape of the Po plain, very different from the accepted picture of Italian scenery, and the bare slopes of the Apennines. Only beyond the Apennines does the traveller encounter the essential features of the Mediterranean landscape, the silver-grey olive-trees and the tall dark cypresses which farther north appear only in specially favoured positions on the southern slopes of the Alps. Still greater is the contrast between the winter cold of the Po plain and the equable climate of the Riviera, sheltered by the coastal hills and warmed by the southern sea.

But the north of the country is much more than a mere prelude to the real Italy. With some 40% of the total area, it houses considerably more than half the population. If the thinly populated Alpine regions and the inhospitable Apennines are excluded, it has a population density of between 200 and 300 to the sq.

kilometre – a figure equalled farther south only in the fertile Campanian plains round Naples. The economic preponderance of northern Italy is strikingly demonstrated by the high proportion it contributes to the national income, based both on its progressive industries and an agricultural output which is unusually high by any standards. Milan, with a population approaching 2 million, is the undisputed economic capital of Italy.

Since the decline of the Roman Empire, northern Italy has outshone peninsular Italy even in the cultural and political fields, if one excepts the inexhaustible tradition of Rome itself and perhaps of Florence. This was made possible by virtue of its geographical role as an intermediary between the Mediterranean world, which still fostered the remnants of ancient culture but which had been reduced to political impotence, and the rising states of central and western Europe. The northward shift in the political and economic centre of gravity from the central Mediterranean to the gateways of the Alps was reflected in the selection of Milan and later Ravenna as capital of the western half of the divided Roman Empire; further evidence of the cultural and political emergence of the north was evinced by the rise to prosperity in subsequent centuries of cities such as Milan, Venice and Genoa, which at various times occupied leading positions in the evolution of the "new" Europe. The Alps are not a barrier to communication; since prehistoric times their valleys have been well populated, and their passes have never served as natural frontiers but rather have formed links binding together territories extending on either side. Accordingly ethnographic and linguistic boundaries in northern Italy do not coincide with the political frontiers. In some areas (Ticino) these boundaries reach beyond the political frontier; in others (Alto Adige) they fall well within it, while in other areas (Aosta valley) mutual infiltration has blurred the lines of division.

The distinctive landscape of northern Italy begins where the closely huddled stone houses in the villages begin to be roofed with slabs of grey gneiss or with interlocking hollow tiles ("monks and nuns"); that is, in the southern Alpine valleys, with the exception of the Alto Adige, where the German-style individual farms and loosely articulated villages of Tirol extend southward over the watershed as far as the *Salorno defile* (Stretta di Salorno). The Tirolean farmhouse, like the houses of the Rhaeto-Romanic population, makes much use of wood in structure and decoration, while the Italians prefer houses built entirely of stone. In northern Italy, therefore, it is less the scenery than the aspect of the settlements, particularly the towns, that is characteristically Italian, though even here there are modifications resulting either from many centuries of contact with neighbouring peoples or from particular local developments (e.g. in Venice).

The division of northern Italy into three parts – the Alpine regions, the Po plain and the Ligurian-Etruscan Apennines – is only a rough approximation based on the pattern of relief: in fact these three areas, externally so different, show an overriding unity in terms both of geological history and of culture. In geological terms the Po plain and its continuation in the northern Adriatic is a marginal depression, still in process of sinking, between the much folded hills of the Apennines and the Southern Alps, which have been steadily rising, and thus increasingly hemming in the intervening depression, since at least the middle Tertiary era. The areas of upthrust on either side competed with one another from the late Tertiary onwards, in varying climatic conditions, in filling in the depression between them: in places the glacial and post-glacial deposits alone reach a depth of over 2000 m. One consequence of this geo-synclinal structure of the Po plain is the abundance of natural gas and oil, worked particularly at Cortemaggiore to the S of Cremona.

It is only rarely possible, on particularly clear days, to glimpse the rugged contours of the Apennines from the southern edge of the Alps, or when descending from the Apennine passes to catch a distant view of the majestic white wall of the Alps, with the **Po plain** extending between them – a wide valley whose floor is covered with gravel terraces desposited by the rivers flowing down from the Alps and Apennines. The later deposits of fine-grained alluvial soil form a relatively narrow strip along the Po and the Adriatic coast at the level of the rivers and sometimes even below them, for in this area the rivers are prevented by high embankments from

spreading their load of sediment over the meadowland in the valley, and accordingly raise the level of their own beds through the soil they carry down, so that at Ferrara, for example, the Po flows at the height of the house roofs. In the lower part of the Po plain the river behaved, even without artificial regulation, as if it were embanked, and the continual increase in the height of its banks displaced the points of inflow of its tributaries and even forced them to run parallel to the main river and flow separately into the Adriatic (Adige, Reno). Something like a third of the Po plain is not drained by the Po itself but by rivers which emerge from the hills as swiftly flowing torrents on beds of white gravel but soon turn into narrow streams flowing tranquilly on their way. In this area the ground-water lies near the surface, emerging in the form of numerous springs (*fontanili*) near the bottom of Pleistocene gravel cones at some distance from the river. The boundary between the higher dry part of the plain and the lower areas at the level of the ground-water is one of the most important divides in the Po plain, separating the foothill areas which lie safely above the flood level from the other land which requires a whole system of embankments and pumps, drainage and regulation works to protect it or to reclaim it from the river.

As a result of its irregular flow and its tendency to silt up and alter its course, the **Po** itself has never been as important as its size might seem to justify. It is significant that in the lower part of its course, below Cremona, no town of any size has developed with the exception of Ferrara; and even Ferrara had bitter experience of the unpredictability of the Po when the embankments burst in the year 1150 and the main arm of the river shifted its bed northward. The *Polésine* in particular – the low-lying area between the lower courses of the Adige and the Po – suffers periodically from breaks in the embankments and devastating floods. Along the Adriatic coast of the Po plain the danger is of being engulfed by sand; for in spite of the continuing tendency of the land to sink, spits of land are being built up all the time on the seaward side, forming a zone of lagoons – half land, half water – which inhibits the development of harbours. The Etruscan city of Spina, once a flourishing port, now lies in a lagoon cut off from the sea below the present water level, the relative rise in which has been unable to stem the extension of the land area. The town of Adria, which at the time of its foundation lay close to and indeed gave its name to the sea, is now 40 km from the mouth of the Po. Similarly the Roman port of Ravenna is now far inland. The road from Ravenna to Comacchio runs for much of the way along the old sea-wall, from which the sea can be seen only occasionally in the far distance. Venice was able to preserve itself from becoming joined to the mainland only by diverting the Brenta. Only the port of Trieste, at the base of the peninsula of Istria, is safe from the danger of silting up, since in general the current sweeps round the Adriatic in a counter-clockwise direction, so that material deposited by the sea does not reach the rocky coast.

In terms of human development the heartland of northern Italy is not the Po plain as a whole, at least not its lower part, but is to be found in the drier but still fertile areas along the edge of the mountains and on the fringes of the mountains themselves. This is shown by the double line of venerable old towns strung along the Via Emilia on the southern margin of the plain and along the N side on the edge of the hills and in the zone of *fontanili*. With only a few exceptions the most active of these towns developed at the points where the roads from the passes met the ancient routes running along the fringes of the hills, usually at some distance from the Po. Only Turin, lying at an altitude of 230 m, and Piacenza grew up at an early stage at bridges over the river. Chief among them all, Milan, lying far out in the fertile Lombard plain but within sight of a magnificent panorama of mountains, succeeded in ancient times in drawing towards itself the roads from the Valtellina, the Ticino valley and the Aosta valley into the Po plain, though in a later period it was unable to prevent the advance of the Swiss Confederation over the important St Gotthard pass to within 35 km of its gates.

Thus the course of human development is determined by the availability of agricultural land and by considerations of situation. It is significant that the great historical regions of northern Italy – Friuli and Venetia, Lombardy and Piedmont, Emilia and Romagna – each include upland territory and an associated area of plain: only Liguria, looking outward

towards the sea, has no stake in the plain. The Po plain was settled and cultivated from the marginal zones to N and S; and it is these areas, the points of origin of the main territorial units of northern Italy, that still attract the modern visitor.

In the areas along the **fringes of the Apennines**, from Romagna to the wine-growing uplands of Monferrato, which geologically must be reckoned as belonging to the Apennine fringes, this is perhaps not immediately evident. The rugged northern slopes of the Apennines, with their wild landscape of soft clays and sandstones cleft by gorges and gullies and distorted by landslides, form a striking background for the cities of Emilia but not one of great scenic magnificence. Only at those points where remains of harder limestones and sandstones have been preserved overlying the clays, as in the crag of San Marino (Monte Titano) and the steeply scarped tabular hill of Bismantova on the road over the Cerreto pass, is there scenery of picturesque grandeur. From the tops of the passes, however, there are magnificent open views of the *Etruscan Apennines*, mountains of medium height with varied but never dramatic contours, formed by flysch sandstones of the early Tertiary, largely bare but with some areas of beautiful beeches and firs (hence the name of the Abetone pass – "Fir-Tree Pass"). The valleys were populated at an early stage: the Etruscan site of Marzabotto (near Vergato), with its large cemeteries, is one of the largest settlements of the pre-Roman period. The most favoured area of settlement from prehistoric times onwards, however, was the Piedmont area on the N side of the hills, with the centres of the Bronze Age Terramare culture near Parma and Bologna and some of the principal sites of the pre-Etruscan Early Iron Age Villanovan culture, named after a suburb of Bologna. Thus the cities of Emilia can look back on an age-old tradition of human settlement.

The military road which the Roman consul Marcus Aemilius Lepidus built in a dead straight line along the foot of the mountains in order to ensure the security of the new province of Gallia Cisalpina was the consequence, not the cause, of the dense settlement of this fertile region, the situation of which made it an area of transit of major importance in all ages. The further period of prosperity enjoyed by the cities of *Emilia* and *Romagna* during the Middle Ages and the Renaissance showed that the advantages of situation were still valid under any political constellation. Art, learning and the crafts flourished at the same time. Bologna was the seat of the oldest, and for centuries the most respected school of law in Europe; Faenza gave its name to the art of faience; Parma, Correggio's native city, was renowned for its incomparable woven goods and its university, founded as early as the 11th c. A flourishing area of *cultura mista*, with intensive fruit-growing and large numbers of vines, draped in garland form from the mulberry-trees and field maples which serve as supports, extends along the Via Emilia and into the valleys of the Apennines.

Farther down in the plain, particularly in Romagna, the visitor will see unusually large and open fields growing industrial crops such as sugar-beet and flax or extensive plantations of poplars. In the lower courses of the unpredictable rivers of the Apennines, particularly the Reno, these mark the areas of former marshland which have been reclaimed for agriculture only in recent times. Even today there are still quite large areas of uncultivable land between the Rimini–Ferrara road and the Po. Farther W there is no "amphibious" area of this kind: the Po flows nearer the edge of the Apennines, and the rivers coming down from them have a sufficient fall. Here Lombardy (province of Pavia) reaches S over the Po into the Apennines. In Piedmont the River *Tánaro*, fed by tributaries from both the Maritime Alps and the Apennines, separates the Tertiary uplands of Monferrato, with their restless contours, from the Ligurian Apennines. With its densely populated hills and well-tended vineyards, which produce the internationally known Asti Spumante and other, mostly sweet, sparkling wines, the *Monferrato* area, which has Turin on its western fringe, has a distinctive character.

The northern edge of the Po plain, with the impressive backdrop of the Alps, shows greater variety of scenery than the southern fringes. Here there is a striking contrast between the calcareous Alps which extend from Gorizia to the E side of Lake Maggiore and the western part of the Alpine fringe, built up of crystalline schists and gneisses, with an entirely different pattern of relief and vegetation cover. No less different is the Alpine foreland which forms the heartland of the regions of Friuli, Venetia, Lombardy and Piedmont. To the E, enclosing the low-lying basin of *Friuli* and extending towards Schio, the mountains rear up almost vertically in places, with bare light-coloured karstic limestone walls rising above the cones of Pleistocene detritus at their base, indented by narrow gorge-like valleys. On the mountains themselves level areas of late Tertiary date (e.g. in the beautiful Bosco del Cansiglio near Vittorio Veneto, in the Monte Grappa area and in the "seven communes" round Asiago) bear witness to the relatively recent upthrust of this region. The Cadore basin, an area of ancient Italian settlement in which Titian was born, extends far into the magnificently structured mountain world of the *Dolomites*, with an old-established Ladin (Rhaeto-Romanic) population distinguished by its characteristic settlement and house forms and, towards the Val Pustería and the Adige valley, a more recently established population of German descent. The Dolomites take their name from the dolomitic rock (a limestone with a high magnesium content) which is predominant here, itself named after the French mineralogist Dolomieu.

The undisciplined rivers with their spasmodic flow emerge from the mountains in beds of light-coloured gravel almost a kilometre wide, still almost on the level of the cones of Pleistocene detritus, some of which have been brought into intensive cultivation only in quite recent times by the installation of irrigation systems. Only at the mouth of the Tagliamento valley is there a wide morainic amphitheatre, but the basin carved out by the Ice Age glacier has been filled up with river gravel. Udine, the capital of Friuli, grew up round an isolated mass of old gravel solidified into conglomerate on which the castle now stands. In this fertile zone of transition maize, tobacco and vines are grown, with fields of sunflowers here and there. The Venetian *terra ferma* is a fertile agricultural region with numerous handsome palaces and villas. Its landscape pattern – found in many parts of the Po plain – of narrow rectangular fields enclosed by irrigation channels and ditches and diversified by vines, mulberry trees, pasture-land and poplars reflects the old Roman "centuriation", the regular field system oriented roughly N–S which is seen at its best between Padua and Mestre — the oldest system of land division in Europe.

The coastal strip to the S of the Trieste–Venice road, between the deltas of the *Isonzo*, the *Tagliamento* and the *Piave*, is still partly occupied by lagoons. Old Roman ports such as Aquileia and Adria now lie some distance inland, replaced by medieval foundations on the coastal spit of land including the charming old episcopal towns of Grado, Caorle and of course *Venice*, with such new-rich upstarts as the rapidly growing resorts of Lignano and Lido di Iésolo.

Between Vicenza and Verona the escarpment is less steep. To the W of the "Schio line", a recent fault line in which the thermal springs of Recoaro emerge, it slopes up gradually and obliquely, cut by valleys famous for their wine (Soave), to the Monti Lessini. In front of the escarpment are the plateau-like *Monti Bérici*, whose limestone quarries supplied most of the foundations of the houses of Venice, and the volcanic *Colli Eugánei*. This isolated range of rounded hills, rising to over 600 m, has all the appearance of a recent volcanic formation: in fact, however, they are the eroded remnants of ancient volcanic rocks, predominantly of submarine origin, and the hot springs of Ábano Terme are to be ascribed to the recent fault already referred to, rather than to volcanic activity which had ceased by the Tertiary era.

The prehistoric settlement of the Piedmont areas, particularly around Este, indicates that the plain N of the Adige was brought under cultivation at an early stage. The dyking and settlement of the *Polésine* area between the Adige and the Po — fertile but subject to flooding — took place much later, probably in post-Roman times.

On the boundary between Venetia and Lombardy, to the W of the Adige, is Lake Garda, marking the beginning of the most beautiful part of the southern Alpine fringes, the region of the **North Italian lakes**. In this area, where the Alps reach their greatest width, the Ice Age glaciers gouged out basins of great depth, the bottoms of which lies far below sea level (Lake Garda – 281 m, Lake Como – 211 m). Here, too, in contrast to the northern fringes of the Alps, the southern situation and low altitude had the result that the

Pleistocene glaciers advanced only a short distance beyond the edge of the mountains; and in consequence the lakes are found not in the Apline foreland but in the fjord-like Alpine valleys themselves, excavated to a great depth by the glaciers. Only *Lake Garda*, the largest of the lakes, extends for a third of its area into the open plain, ringed by a magnificent morainic amphitheatre. The Pleistocene ice-flow of the Adige and Garda glacier split up in the Trento area, and the main mass of ice, instead of following the narrow Adige valley southward, surged over the watershed at Terlago and carved out an asymmetric syncline parallel to the Adige. Thus the Sarca valley and the rift occupied by Lake Garda are like the trough of a wave, with a huge breaker rearing steeply up in the W and a similar rise in the E to the next giant wave, formed by Monte Baldo and Monte Stivo.

The scenic contrast with the lakes of the northern Alpine foreland is striking enough, quite apart from the aspect of the settlements: there the dark carpet of coniferous forest on the slopes of the hills and the lush green meadows on the moraines, here the light-coloured barren-looking rock with its scanty vegetation of gnarled oaks and sub-Mediterranean plants such as the sumach and, in the morainic areas, a patchwork of *cultura mista* with vines and olive-trees.

In the limestone areas the sweet chestnuts so common elsewhere are lacking, but they are found in abundance at those points (e.g. at the N end of Lake Lugano) where crystalline rocks rich in silicic acid interrupt the limestones. In general the vegetation cover of the western lakes is more luxuriant in consequence of the different rocks which begin here, although the olive-trees found on the shores of Lake Garda are less numerous, or indeed altogether absent.

The **plain of Lombardy and Piedmont**, which extends from the edge of the mountains to the Po with a breadth of between 50 and 60 km, is the most fertile part of northern Italy. Here again the rows of poplars, mulberry-trees or willows lining the straight ditches appear to form a forest along the horizon, a forest which perpetually recedes. The division into small rectangular fields still predominates, but there are also increasing numbers of the large *corti*, farms in which the farmhouse, the barrack-like blocks occupied by the farm workers and the farmstead enclose a rectangular courtyard. Stock-farming is more highly developed here than in other parts of the Po plain; it is based on the intensive growing of fodder crops or on grassland farming with the help of irrigation from the *fontanili* (water temperature 8–10 °C – 47–50 °F), which supply a form of natural heating. Visitors from more northerly countries, passing through this area in early spring, when the trees are still bare, are surprised to see the first cutting of hay being taken off the lush irrigated meadowland: there may in fact be as many as eight cuts in the course of the year.

The abundance of water and the gentle slope of the land towards the Po also make possible the cultivation of rice, planted out manually in East Asian fashion in the flooded fields and producing very high yields per acre. The main rice-growing area is between the rivers Ticino and Dora Baltea. S of Vercelli in particular the landscape is dominated in spring by the glittering sheets of water of the paddy-fields, separated by an intricate network of raised embankments, and in summer by the huge green carpets of the ripening grain.

In this part of the Po plain the rivers *Oglio*, *Adda*, *Ticino* and *Sesia* have cut deep into the immense gravel fans of the last two ice ages to a considerable distance from the edge of the mountains. Older gravel deposits, which have weathered a deep red and lie too high on the mountain slopes to permit irrigation, are still covered (particularly at Vauda, N of Turin) with extensive areas of heath – an unusual sight in the densely populated Po plain. Here too the glaciers built up large morainic amphitheatres at the mouths of the valleys; and the Serra at the mouth of the Aosta valley is the highest and most imposing moraine in the whole of the Alps. The glacial basins, however, have been filled up with later gravel deposits, except where (as at Ivrea) the ice-marked rock has been exposed, and now contain no lakes apart from the little Lago de Viverone. The whole of the upper part of the Po plain lies at an altitude of over 200 m. The watershed, which here coincides with the political frontier, moves close to the edge of the mountains. Only the Valle d'Aosta extends more deeply into the mountains, as far as a point immediately below the Mont Blanc group, the highest Alpine massif. This was the route followed by the principal Roman road over the Alps into the province of Gallia Transalpina, and it maintained its importance until the St Gotthard and Brenner passes disputed its authority. The view from Courmayeur of the huge mass of rock and ice rearing up to a height of more than 3000 m above the valley is one of the most magnificent in northern Italy. In the sheltered valley itself, in which the town of Aosta, the Roman Augusta Praetoria Salassorum, nestles within its well-preserved walls, vines grow up to an altitude of 1000 m.

The Ligurian coast, the *Riviera*, is linked with the North Italian plain by easy and much frequented passes but has a character of its own. Looking out towards the sea, it is backed by the sandstone and serpentine hills of the Apennines, large areas of which are covered with the evergreen macchia of the Mediterranean. The steep and rugged coastal area between Sestri Levante and La Spezia has been opened up only in quite recent years by the construction of a road along the coast. In spite of this protective isolation, or perhaps because of it, Savona and above all Genoa, situated at the points where pass routes used since time immemorial reach the coast, developed into major ports, which thanks to their ability to take modern vessels of deep draught have been able to maintain their position and have developed considerable industry. The fame of the Riviera, however, rests on its string of palm-shaded, flower-decked resorts with their girdle of light-coloured villas nestling in the dark-green vegetation on the hillsides. Here visitors will find what they will seek in vain in the rest of northern Italy – the mild air and brilliant light of the South and the deep blue of the sea.

CENTRAL ITALY Begins with the Tuscan **Appennines**, which in spite of their numerous passes at heights of between 900 and 1300 m form an effective geographical barrier between the Italian peninsula proper and the Po plain, with its still sub-Mediterranean climate. The Tuscan Apennines branch off from the Ligurian Apennines without any marked transition and rise to a height of 2165 m in Monte Cimone; but the contours in the region of the watershed are gently rolling upland hills, with only occasional pyramidal peaks rising steeply to greater heights. Geologically this part of the

Apennines consists mainly of the early Tertiary flysch sandstones known as *macigno*, much used in the Renaissance buildings of Tuscany. On the northern scarp they are overlaid by *argille scagliose* ("scaly" clays) coming from the S, which produce a bare and tormented landscape ravined by parallel gullies and subject to landslides (*frane*) in winter. Here and there the clay is in turn overlaid by tabular patches of limestones and sandstones which have survived erosion and at certain points, as in the Rupe Bismantova on the road over the Cerreto pass or the crag of San Marino, produce extraordinary rock formations.

Going over the passes, where some remnants of the once extensive beech and fir forests are still to be seen, the traveller descends through a zone of chestnut-trees and is greeted by those characteristic features of the Mediterranean climate, the olive-trees which pattern the landscape with their silver-grey foliage. The olive does not grow in the Po plain or on the northern slopes of the Apennines, since it requires an average temperature in the coldest months of not less than 4–5 °C (39–41 °F). It first appears in isolated patches in very sheltered positions on the fringes of the Alps, particularly on Lake Garda, but it does not really belong to northern Italy, any more than does the fig.

At Monte Penna, the "rock between the Tiber and the Arno" (Dante), at the foot of which is the little village of La Verna where Michelangelo was born, the Apennines turn S. Their wide eastern slopes are occupied by the **Marches** (*Marche*), a region little frequented by visitors, who usually see it only on their way to Raphael's native town of Urbino, the tiny republic of San Marino or the narrow beaches of the popular resorts on the Adriatic coast.

The central section of the Apennines, beginning somewhere about the southern boundary of Umbria, becomes considerably wider and changes dramatically in character. From a relatively narrow ridge it opens out into the mountain fastnesses of the **Abruzzi**, a region of rugged limestone mountains separated from one another by high plateaux and collapse basins. Its highest peaks, among them Monte Corno (2912 m) in the *Gran Sasso* massif, have in some cases an Alpine aspect as a result of glacial action;

but for the most part the Apennines preserve the conformation of mountains of only medium height, with the limestone peaks rearing up in massive and imposing bulk. The landscape of the Abruzzi, which unlike the Apennines has no overlying surface rocks but shows a relative simple structure of folding and faulting, is reminiscent of the Dinaric mountain ranges of Yugoslavia and Greece. The summits, as in most of the limestone ranges of southern Europe, are completely bare: only in the Abruzzi National Park are there any considerable areas of forest. In addition to glacial features (cirques, moraines) there are numerous karstic forms like poljes (steep-sided depressions with subterranean drainage), dolines (swallow-holes, through which surface water seeps underground), etc. Human settlement is concentrated mainly in deep collapse basins filled with late Tertiary deposits, such as the Sulmona and L'Aquila basins. The plateaux are great tracts of lonely and uninhabited country, the haunt of itinerant shepherds who bring their flocks up here from Apulia in summer. In winter the hills of the Abruzzi are often covered with snow for weeks at a time, and the Campo Imperatore area in the Gran Sasso, brought within easy reach by a cableway, has become a popular winter sports region in the heart of sunny Italy. – Outliers of the calcareous Apennines reach down to the sea in the *Monti Ausoni* at Terracina and the *Monti Aurunci* at Formia and Gaeta, marking out the southern boundary of central Italy. This great arc of hills extending from La Spezia to Terracina, with its open side to the W, encloses the old heartlands of the Italian peninsula, **Tuscany**, **Umbria** and **Latium**. Geologically this whole territory is a single large area of faulting to the rear of what are now the Apennines. As in all Tertiary hills, the direction of the folding and uplift was outwards, in this case towards the Po plain and the Adriatic, while the former Tyrrhenian continent, the detritus from which formed the Apennines, sank down behind the area of folding, leaving only remnants above the surface in the ancient granites and gneisses on the islands of Sardinia, Corsica and Elba. From the area of sea between these islands and the coast of Tuscany the surface deposits overlying the Apennines were thrust up during the Tertiary era.

The *Apuan Alps*, rugged heights which form a kind of Anti-Apennines (a term usually applied in Italy to the whole hinterland of the Apennines with its varied topography), present in their dazzlingly white marble (a Triassic limestone recrystallised under the pressure of the folding movements) a geological window near the area of origin of the overlying rocks of Tuscany.

The products of the faulting to the rear of the Apennines which accompanied the first upthrusts of the hills were the *sub-Apenninic basins of Tuscany and Umbria*, so characteristic of central Italy, which reach deep into the upland regions. During the Pliocene and Quaternary periods they were filled by lakes, the deposits from which can still occasionally be identified, as in the tabular hill of Cerbaie in the Lucca basin or the bizarrely hewn spurs of rock on a terrace in the Valdarno basin. The *Arno* and the *Tiber* captured these basins, one after another, by retrograding erosion; but the Arno, with a shorter course and a steeper gradient, encroached on to the territory of its rival, tapping a river flowing through the Casentino and the Chiana depression into the Tiber and converting it into its own upper course. *Lake Trasimene*, lying in the Chiana depression, long an area of marshland near the watershed between the Arno and the Tiber (which has frequently altered its position since ancient times), is the last of the sub-Apenninic basin lakes not yet captured by the acquisitive rivers.

The fertile and densely populated basins of Tuscany and Umbria, dotted with villages and isolated farms, are excellently situated from the point of view of communications, immediately below the Apennine passes. With their luxuriant *cultura mista* (vines, corn, fruit) and their silver-grey fringes of olive-trees they are in striking contrast to the hills of the Apennines, mostly bare of vegetation, and the other ranges which branch off them. The old-established towns – mainly of Etruscan origin like Arezzo, Perugia, Chiusi and Fiesole (predecessor of Florence) – are built on the high ground above the valley floors, which offered security and freedom from malaria.

The landscape to the S of the lower Arno is very different. In the *Tuscan Uplands*, which rise in the Colline Metallífere

("metal-bearing hills") to over 1000 m, the eye ranges over an apparently formless pattern of rolling mountains, steeply scarped in places but never of genuinely mountainous aspect, which justify the designation of "Anti-Apennines" only in a purely geological sense. In addition to Mesozoic limestones and schists they contain the same sandstones of the early Tertiary era as are found in the northern Apennines. Here, however, they do not form connected chains but are broken up into isolated massifs and mantled in the sandstones and clays of the Pliocene sea in which they once formed an archipelago. The frequent variations in rock type and in altitude produce a very attractive diversity of landscape pattern and scenery. The fertile soil is predominantly devoted to *cultura mista* (olives, vines, corn). This is the land of the *mezzadria*, a share-cropping system with a tradition going back many centuries in which the landlord supplies smallholders, each working a *podere* of between 12 and 24 acres, with arable land, the farmstead, equipment and animals. All over the area, but particularly around the hill towns, conspicuous on their commanding heights, ancient farmsteads, handsome and often palatial villas and churches with their slender campaniles are scattered about the green countryside, variegated by the silver foliage of the olive-trees and by the darker colour and vertical lines of the tall slender cypresses. It is a landscape marked by the labour of men's hands, such as we see depicted in the large 15th c. murals by Ambrogio Lorenzetti in the Palazzo Publico in Siena.

The stony soil of the higher ridges supports meagre stands of oaks and pines and expanses of aromatic Mediterranean heathland (tree heathers, arbutus, cistus, etc.). In the Colline Metallífere and the Chianti mountains this vegetation becomes denser and forms the evergreen Mediterranean macchia (scrub). The landscape becomes different again in the area of Pliocene clays, for example in the area of Volterra or to the S of Siena. Here there are few trees, and the land at all levels is given up to fields of corn which are constantly being eaten away by erosion. Even farmhouses or towns like Volterra which are situated on hills are threatened by deep ravines slashed by erosion, and the good arable soil is constantly being washed off the whitish-grey *biancane* (conical areas of clay soil) by wind and rain.

The strip of land along the coast, the Tuscan *Maremma* (= *maríttima*), has a distinctive character. For centuries this area was shunned as the haunt of malaria, the low-lying ground backing its beautiful curving beaches having reverted to marshland, and its very name became the synonym of a desolate and unhealthy stretch of land. In Etruscan times, however, it was densely populated, the heartland of an empire which extended over half Italy; and the sites of Tarquinia and Vulci, Rosellae and Populonia (N of Piombino), together with the rich Etruscan material recovered at Orbetello, Massa Maríttima and other places, bear witness to the prosperity of the area from the 8th to the 4th c. B.C. Thereafter the Roman system of latifundia, the abandonment of the drainage installations and the consequent spread of malaria condemned it to depopulation for more than 2000 years. It was not until the middle of the 19th c. that the first successful efforts were made to reclaim the marshland by the method known as *colmata* – the channelling into the area of rivers carrying matter in suspension which gradually filled up the marshes. This pioneer work has been crowned in recent years by an effective land reform and the agricultural resettlement work of the Ente Maremma. Visitors travelling over the plains and upland areas between the rivers Cécina and Fiora on the Via Aurelia will now find them dotted with the trim white houses of the new settlers.

The region of **Latium**, to the S, differs in character from Tuscany and Umbria, mainly as a result of volcanic activity in the early Quaternary era. Groups of volcanoes, which became extinct in prehistoric or early historical times, extend from Monte Amiata (1734 m), on the borders of Tuscany, by way of the Monti Volsini, Monti Cimini and Monti Sabatini to the Alban Hills S of Rome, with trains of volcanic tufa running down into the plains between the hills and almost completely covering the older rocks. Circular calderas with steep-sided walls now contain sparkling lakes like lakes Bolsena, Vico, Bracciano, Albano and Nemi. Other old craters, mostly lying at lower levels, have already been breached by erosion, and the surface layers of tufa

have been furrowed by deep gorges and carved into tabular hills as at Tarquinia. The seven hills of Rome are merely the remnants of a layer of tufa which once covered the whole area. In Latium as in Tuscany the coastal regions which were densely populated in Etruscan times (*Tarquinia, Cervéteri*) were for many centuries denuded of their population by the system of latifundia and the malaria-ridden marshes; but here too the traditional view of these areas as a desolate wasteland must now be corrected. The Roman *Campagna* has been largely brought under cultivation, and the Pontine Marshes, now known as the Agro Pontino, have been almost completely drained.

The olives, figs and cypresses of these regions, together with the groves of sweet chestnuts on the slopes of the Apennines, are not yet the vegetation of the real South. Climatically central Italy is an area of transition. It can still be distinctly cool here at Easter, particularly when the *tramontana* blows from the N; and even in April there can be a sudden fall in temperature accompanied by snow and hail. After crossing the Tuscan Apennines, therefore, we find no oranges or lemons except in gardens: it is only when we have gone over the narrow coastal pass below the crag of Terracina, to the S of the former Pontine Marshes, that we encounter the first orange-groves growing unprotected in the open: a sign that we have now reached the real South, with its dry summers and mild winters.

In **SOUTHERN ITALY** the contrast between flourishing and populous cultivated regions and extensive areas of thinly populated and economically backward land, with little to attract tourists, is much more marked than in central Italy. Here too the Apennines form the backbone of the peninsula; but they are now broken up into separate limestone massifs ranging in height between 1500 and 2000 m, which have impressively rugged contours when seen from a distance but have the flattish summits characteristic of upland regions of medium height. The axis of this limestone chain (but not the watershed) lies near the Tyrrhenian Sea, leaving little room for large expanses of land between the mountains and the sea. The watershed lies directly in the sub-Apenninic fault area, so giving rise to the coastal enclaves enclosed on three sides by bare and precipitous rock-faces and rugged foot-hills and bounded on the seaward side by curving beaches, which make up the particular charm of southern Italy. The climate, hot and dry in summer but damp and mild in winter, combines with the rich alluvial soil, much of its fertilised by recent volcanic ash, to produce the most favourable conditions for intensive arable cultivation and a correspondingly high population, particularly in the Fondi plain, in the Campagna of Naples and in the "Conca d'Oro" around Palermo in Sicily.

The **Bay of Naples** and its hinterland can be taken as the prototype of these favoured coastal areas. The recent geological faults bounding this area have given rise to intensive volcanic activity, not yet extinct, in which an earlier and a later phase can be distinguished. To the older phase belongs Monte Somma on *Vesuvius*, the ruined caldera of an earlier Vesuvius much higher than the present volcano. Above its base rises the regular cone of the more recent Vesuvius, whose most violent explosion buried the towns of Pompeii and Herculaneum under masses of ash and lava in A.D. 79. The last major eruption took place in 1944, and today even the famous pine-shaped plume of smoke has disappeared – though this does not mean that the volcano is extinct.

The lower volcanic area of the *Phlegraean Fields* also consists mostly of the ruins of earlier volcanoes, though here too there was a resumption of volcanic activity after centuries of quiescence in the year 1538, when a volcanic cone 140 m high, Monte Nuovo, was formed in the space of two days. At present the Phlegraean Fields are at the solfatara stage. The same can be said of the volcanic island of *Ischia*, the highest point on which is Monte Epomeo (789 m). The last eruption of this volcano was in 1301, and since then only hot sulphur springs, used for medicinal purposes, and emissions of vapour give evidence of the volcanic forces which are still active underground.

This series of volcanoes marking a fault line running from E to W along the N side of the Bay of Naples has its counterpart in a ridge of limestone mountains (Monti Lattari, 1443 m) which runs above a steep-sided fault line with the same orientation on the S side of the bay,

ending in the Sorrento peninsula. Its continuation, also of limestone, is the island of *Capri*. The sun-baked limestone slopes of the *Sorrento peninsula*, with the deposits of volcanic ash from earlier eruptions of Vesuvius, provide excellent conditions for the growing of oranges on the N side and the more delicate lemons on the S side. The Greek name of Naples (Neapolis, "new city") recalls that southern Italy was colonised by Greek settlers in early times (MAGNA GRAECIA). Other evidence of Greek settlement is provided by the nearby temple precinct of Paestum, in the coastal plain of the River *Sele* to the S of Salerno, and the remains of Cumae, the Greek port on the N side of the Phlegraean Fields where the Etruscans, whose power at one stage extended into Campania, were decisively defeated by the Greeks in a naval battle in 474 B.C.

The eastern foreland of the South Italian Apennines contributes new elements to the varied landscape pattern of Italy. In the first place the Apennines draw away from the Adriatic coast, leaving room for wide swathes of marls, clays, sands and sandstones of the Pliocene period, which combine in **Basilicata** to form a charming but melancholy region which drains into the Gulf of Táranto. It lacks the *cultura mista* which gives variety to regions of similar soil in central Italy: here the land belongs to large estates and is occupied by monotonous fields of corn. The few settlements that can claim the status of towns, close-packed huddles of houses on steep-sided hills, are places of considerable poverty and much social deprivation.

Adjoining Basilicata is **Apulia**, a region comparable with no other in Italy and in many respects unique. Its landscape pattern is determined by the horizontal lines of its extensive areas of tubular limestone, which in contrast to the Cretaceous and Jurassic limestones of the Apennines, of similar geological age, have remained unfolded, though sometimes subjected to considerable uplift. The promontory of *Monte Gargano*, the spur of the Italian boot, reaches a height of 1056 m in Monte Calvo, and the Apulian tabular limestones rise in the *Murge*, their highest part, to 680 m. Their meagre soils, with many karstic features, still provide grazing in winter for transhumant flocks of sheep, which formerly travelled to their summer pastures in the Apennines on the broad drove roads known as *tratturi*; the drove roads are still used for this purpose, although many sheep are now carried in lorries or by rail. The lower parts of the Apulian limestone table are very fertile, particularly in those areas where the Tertiary deposits have escaped erosion. Vineyards, almond-groves and extensive plantations of olives (which produce the major part of Italy's exports of olive oil) provide the economic basis of populous towns, whose great problem is shortage of water. This centuries-old difficulty has, however, been largely overcome by the construction of the great Apulian aqueduct, which taps the source of the westward-flowing River Sele, tunnels under the Apennine watershed and conveys the water to the towns and villages on the limestone table through an extensive network of distribution channels. Particularly fertile, with a flourishing and productive system of polyculture, is the coastal strip of territory, the *Terra di Bari* and the *Terra d'Ótranto*. The *Tavoliere*, a large level depression between Monte Gargano and the Apulian limestone table, long served as excellent winter grazing for huge flocks of sheep, but in recent decades its heavy soil has been broken up by mechanised ploughs and converted into a vast expanse of wheatfields.

In the central part of the Murge houses of a very ancient type are found, the *trulli*. These are circular structures built of undressed stone with conical roofs rising in a corbelled vault, the walls often being whitewashed. The effect is particularly picturesque, and quite alien to normal Italian architecture, when several *trulli* are combined in one large complex of buildings. The older part of the little town of Alberobello is built of *trulli*; and they are still being erected in large numbers in the country areas.

The distinctive historical and cultural development of Apulia, the heartland of Norman and Hohenstaufen rule in southern Italy (Foggia in the Tavoliere having been the favourite residence of the Emperor Frederick II), is illustrated by the numerous Romanesque cathedrals dating from this period of greatness and by the proud castles of Frederick II, outstanding among them the unique architectural achievement of Castel del Monte, a hunting lodge built on a lonely and commanding site in the Murge. This great eastward-facing expanse of territory fitted in with Frederick's policies; and he and his sons loved the forests of the region, of whose beauty we can now judge only from the Foresta Umbra. On the Murge only a few gnarled oaks have escaped the attentions of the sheep and the axes of the charcoal-burners.

The most southerly part of the peninsula, **Calabria**, contains two large massifs of granites and gneisses, the *Sila* (1930 m) and the *Aspromonte* range (1958 m), which were thrust up to a considerable height in the Pliocene and to some extent also in the Tertiary era. Geologically they are the counterpart of the ancient rocks which form the core of Sardinia and Corsica. The steep scarps of these mountains leave room only for small coastal plains and sometimes fall directly down to the coast, with no intervening beach; but the summits are gently rounded, sometimes taking the form of high plateaux. Forests of central rather than southern European character, made up of beeches and firs, together with areas of green pasture-land and lakes of some size, most of them created by dams, make up a landscape pattern in which the traveller may feel transported several degrees of latitude northward. The only area of any great fertility, however, is the geologically recent trough through which the little River Crati flows, with Cosenza, the largest town in the region.

The island of **SICILY** (area 25,400 sq. km), separated from the toe of the Italian boot only by the *Strait of Messina*, 3 km wide at its narrowest point (spanned by a power line; bridge planned), is geologically the continuation of the Italian peninsula. The *Monti Peloritani*, extending into the Taormina area, consist of the same gneisses and micaceous schists as the Aspromonte. Along the N coast run the sandstones and argillaceous schists of the *Monti Nébrodi* and the *Madonie*, ranging in height between 1000 and 2000 m, which form the backbone of the island – a kind of Sicilian Apennines. From Palermo to Trápani they are succeeded by Triassic limestones eroded into characteristically shaped hills (Monte Pellegrino, Monte Érice).

Most of the southern part of Sicily consists predominantly of late Tertiary clays and marls, with sheer crags of gypsum, marly limestones and conglomerates rising here and there above them like fortresses. The rest of southern Sicily is occupied by rolling uplands with few trees. In antiquity this area was the granary of Rome, and is still covered with extensive fields of corn. Most of the land belongs to large landowners, producing social tensions which find expression in the occasional acts of violence by the Mafia. In recent years land reform has been successful in establishing independent peasant farmers in Sicily. An important source of income is provided by the sulphur mines of central Sicily. The sulphur is an element in the sedimentary sequence of the Tertiary and is not connected with current volcanic activity on the island, which is more recent than the deposition of the sulphur, being related to crust movements since the end of the Tertiary.

The Strait of Messina and that part of the Tyrrhenian Sea which is enclosed by the Calabrian-Sicilian arc of mountains are an area of faulting of relatively recent date, as is shown by violent earthquakes (Messina) and intensive volcanic activity, extending also to the *Lípari Islands* (Vulcano, Strómboli). This activity was preceded by eruptions in the late Tertiary and early Quaternary era, attested by the volcanic rock, much eroded, of the *Monti Iblei*, which rise to almost 1000 m in south-eastern Sicily.

The principal landmark and the very emblem of Sicily, however, is the mighty cone of **Etna** (3326 m), still known to the local people by its half-Italian, half-Arab name of *Mongibello* (*monte* and *jebel* both meaning mountain). It is a truncated cone between 18 and 20 km in diameter, more impressive for its height than for its form, with a deep crater on the summit. The lava flows which periodically, at intervals of some decades, surge down to destroy the rich farming land at the foot of the volcano have in modern times usually emerged from a *bocca* ("mouth") on the flanks of the mountain. Also characteristic of this type of volcano are the numerous minor cones, like giant warts, which extend far down its slopes, with such names as Monte Rosso, Monte Nero, etc., referring to the blackish, reddish or brown tints of the lava. Etna preserves its covering of snow well into spring (winter sports). A drive in spring from the zone of blossoming almond-trees, vineyards and irrigated fields of early potatoes and vegetables through the girdle of chestnuts and fruit-trees into the desolate expanse of lava and snow above 1800 m is one of the most impressive scenic experiences in Sicily. No less magnificent is the view from Taormina of the smoking cone of Etna rising above the deep blue of the sea in proud isolation, and cut off from the neighbouring heights by deep valleys.

Sicily, like the southern part of the peninsula, was part of the area of Greek settlement known as MAGNA GRAECIA, and the extensive remains of ancient cities, particularly on the S and SE coasts (Selinunte, Agrigento, Gela, Syracuse, etc.), bear witness to the prosperity of the island in that period. Farther N, in a magnificent lonely setting, is the unfinished but still impressive temple of Segesta. Palermo is notable particularly for remains dating from the Arab, Norman and Hohenstaufen periods.

In Sicily the Mediterranean climate with its dry summers and mild winters reaches its fullest expression. On the coast the temperature in January remains consistently above 10 °C (50 °F); and the months of June to August are practically rainless. It is not surprising, therefore, that the wine, particularly on volcanic soil, is very sweet. But although Goethe called Sicily the "key to everything" it is not the key to the whole of Italy. It has a very distinctive character in terms of landscape, in the serious and proud disposition of its people – still beset by unsolved social problems – and in the divergent course of its history.

This can be said also of the island of **SARDINIA** (area 24,000 sq. km), which in consequence of its remoteness and its relative lack of historic old buildings has only recently been opened up to tourists, although it has excellent roads and unexpectedly impressive natural beauties. Its landscape and scenery are quite different from anything to be seen in the Italian peninsula. The island consists almost exclusively of Palaeozoic granites, gneisses and crystalline schists and ancient volcanic deposits, which build up into a varied landscape of hills and mountains reaching their highest point in the *Gennargentu* massif (1834 m). The shy moufflon (mountain sheep) is still found on the hill pastures which have been largely deforested by the hand of man. The low-lying coastal areas, in particular the *Campidano depression* which extends from Cagliari to the Gulf of Oristano, are or were marshy and the fear of malaria – now mercifully eradicated – spread throughout the island. As a result, however, Sardinia – the second largest island in the Mediterranean – has one of the lowest population densities in Italy. Yet it has many attractions which are now drawing increasing numbers of visitors: its lonely uplands, its beautiful beaches of light-coloured sand, still not crowded even at the better known resorts (Costa Smeralda, etc.), and its thousands of *nuraghi*, the conical round towers of the Stone Age and early Bronze Age which are so characteristic of Sardinia.

Population

The 56 million inhabitants of Italy, including 520,000 Friulians (among them 30,000 Ladins), 260,000 German-speakers in the Alto Adige, 53,000 Slovenes and small French and Albanian minorities, are almost exclusively of the Roman Catholic faith. The devoutness of the population, often naive in form, has had marked influence on the social structure of the country. The family bond is in general stronger than in other European countries, although the traditional role of women is now increasingly being called into question (provision for divorce introduced 1970).

The contrast between the developed north and the underdeveloped south is reflected in social differences: for example the birth rate in the south (with its maximum in Naples) is considerably higher than in the north. The density of population in the south, with the exception of the conurbations round Rome and the Bay of Naples, is lower than in the north, as is the proportion of the population living in towns. The north is also better provided with educational institutions, including ancient and famous universities, than the south; and this makes it more difficult to train the skilled labour which is so urgently needed for the development of the "Mezzogiorno".

Climate

As a result of its great extent from N to S and the great mountain barriers which break up its territory, Italy is a country of **great climatic diversity**. The N, with the Alps, which climatically belong predominantly to central Europe, and the Po plain, cut off from the Mediterranean by the Apennines, has a continental climate with relatively warm summers and cold winters (Milan average annual temperature 13 °C (55 °F), January 1·9° (35·4°), July 24° (75°), measured at alt. 147 m (482 ft); in the Alps about 0·7° (1°) less per 100 m of altitude in summer, 0·4° (0·7°) less in winter). The northern Adriatic has little moderating influence (Venice annual 13·4 °C (56 °F), January 3·5° (38°), July 24° (75°); Trieste annual 14·3° (58°), January 4° (39°), July 23·5° (74°). – The *bora*, a cold wind blowing down from the karstic hills on to the warm Adriatic, is feared for its occasionally destructive effects. Only around the North Italian lakes, lying below the Alps and sheltered from the N winds, is there a sub-tropical climate oasis with a lush growth of vegetation (Pallanza annual 13·4 °C (56 °F), January 3·5° (38°), July 24·5° (76°); Salò on Lake Garda, annual 13·2° (55°), January 3·5° (38°), July 23° (73°)). In winter and spring the *ora*, a cold S wind, blows over Lake Garda, then relatively warm, about midday during good weather. A number of sheltered valleys within the Alps, such as the Aosta valley, the wine-growing Valtellina and the upper Adige valley, are also climatically favoured (Bolzano, alt.

265 m (869 ft), annual 12·4 °C (54 °F), January 1·5° (34·7°), July 22·5° (72°).

The boundary between the continental climate and the Mediterranean climate, with its warm dry summers and sometimes rainy winters, is formed by the *Apennines*. On the Riviera, sheltered as it is from the cold N winds, the influence of the Mediterranean is particularly marked (San Remo annual 16·4 °C (61 °F), January 10° (50°), July 23·5° (74°); Alassio July 25° (77°)). Similar winter temperatures are found only much farther S, while summer temperatures rise relatively little towards the S (Florence annual 14·4 °C (58 °F), January 5° (41°), July 24° (75°); Rome annual 15·6° (60°), January 7° (44°), July 25° (77°); Naples annual 16·3° (61°), January 8° (46°), July 24° (75°); Syracuse annual 17·8° (64°), January 11° (51°), August 26° (79°); Cagliari annual 17° (62°), January 9° (48°), July 25° (77°)). In mountainous regions like the Abruzzi, and even far to the S in Calabria, in the Sila hills with their coniferous forests, the climate is similar to that of central Europe, though with little rain in summer.

The **surface temperature of the sea** ranges between 5 and 10 °C (41 and 50 °F) in winter in the northern Adriatic and between 12 and 13° (53 and 55°) in the southern Adriatic and the other seas round Italy. The following are some typical temperatures for the months April to October:

April	Trieste 11·7 °C (53 °F); Grado, Rimini and Viareggio 16° (60°); Bari 20° (68°).
May	Trieste 15·8° (60°); Rimini and Capri 18° (64°); Taormina 18·3° (65°); Bari 22° (71°).
June	Capri and Cagliari 20° (68°); La Spezia 23·4° (74°); Bari 25° (77°); Rimini 26° (79°).
July	Capri and San Remo 24·8° (76°); Grado 25·5° (78°); Bari 27° (81°); Rimini 30° (86°).
August	Viareggio 23·2° (74°); Trieste and Taormina 24° (75°); Rimini and Bari 28° (82°).
September	San Remo and Anzio 22·8° (73°); Rimini and Bari 25° (77°); Elba 25·5° (78°).
October	Anzio 18° (64°); Taormina 18·4° (65°); San Remo 19·6° (67°); Rimini and Palermo 22·2° (72°).

Within the Alps **rainfall** and snow are distributed throughout the year, with a marked minimum in winter (Cortina d'Ampezzo annual average 1252 mm (49¼ in), February 45 mm (1¾ in), July 140 mm (5½ in)). Rain falls in spring and autumn on the southern fringes of the Alps, again with a minimum in winter (Trento annual 1019 mm (40 in), January 50 mm (2 in), May 98 mm (3¾ in), July 92 mm (3½ in), October 115 mm (4½ in)). There is more rain in the Po plain, with minima in winter and summer and often long periods of cool damp fog in winter (Milan annual 997 mm (39¼ in), February 58 mm (2¼ in), May 98 mm (3¾ in), August 70 mm (2¾ in), October 112 mm (4½ in)), and still more in central Italy, with a marked minimum in summer (Florence annual 830 mm (32¾ in), February 55 mm (2¼ in), April 73 mm (3 in), July 33 mm (1¼ in), November 102 mm (4 in)). S of Florence the summer becomes steadily drier (1–2 months without rain), autumn and winter steadily wetter, with frequent thunder showers and occasionally the *scirocco*, an enervating warm and moist S wind which is the harbinger of a cyclone (Rome annual 821 mm (32¼ in), January 82 mm (3¼ in), July 16 mm (½ in), October 120 mm (4¾ in)). In Apulia, Calabria, Basilicata, Sardinia and Sicily the rain falls mainly in winter, with little precipitation in summer (4–5 dry months) and practically none at all at the height of summer (Syracuse annual 529 mm (20¾ in), January 93 mm (3¾ in), July 5 mm (¼ in)). – With heavier rainfall than in more northerly parts of Europe, there are fewer days on which rain actually falls (c. 40–120 days in the year).

History

From prehistoric and early historical times to the establishment of Roman rule (*c.* 600000 to 400 B.C.). – The name of ITALIA (Lat. *vituli*, bull-calves, sons of the bull god) was first applied by the Greeks to the SW tip of the peninsula; it was extended only in Roman Imperial times to mean the whole territory as far as the Alps. The names of the original inhabitants have sometimes been preserved in the names of regions and districts. Italy was already occupied by man in the *Old Stone Age.*

1800–1600 Early Metal Age in northern Italy: **Remedello culture** (copper daggers), named after the site near Brescia where they were found.

1600–1200 *Bronze Age:* **Terramare culture** (Italian *terramara* = earth mound) in northern Italy, with fortified villages of pile dwellings.

1200 onwards Migrations of Indo-European peoples coming from the N. The **Italic peoples** break up into the Latin group, to which the *Romans* belong, and the Umbro-Sabellian group, to the main branch of which, the *Oscans*, the *Samnites* of Campania belong. Other Oscan tribes later move S into southern Italy and Sicily.

1000 onwards An Illyrian people, the **Veneti**, move into Venetia.

1000–500 The Iron Age **Villanovan culture**, developed by an Indo-European people (named after the site near Bologna where the discovery was made).

900–500 The **Etruscans**, apparently coming from Asia Minor, move into Etruria (Tuscia, Tuscany), Campania and the Po plain. *Confederation of 12 cities* on the Ionian model; active trade, centred on Felsina (Bologna), with central and northern Europe; highly developed cult of the dead (cemeteries). The Etruscans bring to Italy the culture and art of Greece and Asia Minor, technology and administrative skills – all taken over by the Romans.

After 800 Establishment of naval bases in western Sicily and Sardinia by the **Phoenicians** in order to protect their sea trading routes in the western Mediterranean.

750–550 The **Greeks** establish colonies in southern Italy and Sicily (MAGNA GRAECIA) – Kyme (Cumae), Neapolis (Naples), Kroton (Crotone), Taras (Taranto), Akragas (Agrigento), Syracuse and many more. Conflicting commercial interests lead to wars with the Carthaginians and Etruscans. – Development of the Latin alphabet from the Greek alphabet.

600–400 Building of temples in Magna Graecia (remains at Segesta, Selinunte, Agrigento, Paestum, etc.).

485–467 Tyrannies of *Gelo* and *Hiero I* in Syracuse, now the dominant power in the western Greek territories. *Aeschylus* and *Pindar* at Hiero's court.

Italy under Roman rule (753 B.C. to A.D. 476). – Rome, at first merely a city state, wins control, in spite of the resistance of the Italic peoples, of the whole of the Italian mainland, then of the islands, and finally of western Europe and the East. Under Roman generals and later under the Emperors, ruling with absolute power, the *Roman Empire* is held together and defended for centuries against attacks by neighbouring peoples. The spread of Christianity and urban culture provide the basis for the cultural development of western Europe.

753 *Legendary foundation of Rome* (probably from the Etruscan *Rumlua*) by Romulus, a descendant of the Trojan Aeneas. (Settlement on Palatine as early as *c.* 900.)

600–510 Rome is ruled by the Etruscan *Tarquins* until the establishment of the **Republic** (510).

About 400 The **Celts** invade northern Italy. The Romans are defeated in the battle of the River Allia (387–386).

396–280 Rome conquers central Italy and ensures control of its territory by the building of military roads and the foundation of military colonies. Latinisation of the Italic peoples.

About 378 Rebuilding of Rome after its destruction by the Gauls and erection of walls round the seven hills.

312 Construction of the Via Appia, a military road to Capua, later extended to Brundisium (Brindisi).

About 300 to 146 Extension of Roman rule to northern Italy, southern Italy and Sicily. In the three **Punic Wars** Carthage is defeated and its dominant role in the western Mediterranean taken over by Rome.

229–64 By conquering Macedonia, Greece and Asia Minor, Rome gains control of the eastern Mediterranean.
Exploitation of the provinces, use of slave labour, development of a monetary economy, increased Hellenistic influence (assimilation of Greek and Oriental culture), increasing luxury of the ruling classes.

220 Construction of the Via Flaminia (Rome to Rimini); continued to Placentia (Piacenza) in 187.

133–30 **Civil wars**, caused by increasing impoverishment of the peasants, and slave risings reveal grave shortcomings in the state.

113–101 Wars against **Cimbri** and **Teutones**.

58–51 **Caesar** conquers Gaul.

45 Caesar becomes sole ruler (murdered 14 March 44): *end of Republic.*

30 B.C.–A.D. 14 **Augustus** establishes the **Empire** (*Principate*) and maintains peace both internally and externally (Pax Augusta). Cultural flowering (Virgil, Horace, Ovid) and much building activity in Rome. The Empire is romanised.

A.D. 14–395 The **Roman Empire** reaches its greatest extent.

64 Burning of Rome. *Nero* initiates the *first persecution of Christians.*

79 Pompeii and Herculaneum are destroyed in a great eruption of Vesuvius.

220 onwards Arabs, Germans, Persians and others attack the frontiers of the Roman Empire.

303 Last and greatest persecution of Christians under *Diocletian.*

313 **Constantine the Great** grants religious freedom to Christians (Edict of Milan).

330 Constantine makes Byzantium capital of the Roman Empire under the name of Constantinople.

About 375 The **Huns** burst into Europe: beginning of the great migrations.

391 *Theodosius* makes *Christianity the state religion.*

395 Division of the Empire by Theodosius into the **Western Roman Empire** (capital Ravenna) and the Eastern Roman Empire.

410 The **Visigoths** led by *Alaric* take Rome.

452 Devastation by the Huns in the Po plain.

455 Sack of Rome by the **Vandals** led by *Gaiseric*.

476 *Romulus Augustulus*, the last Western Roman Emperor, is deposed by the Germanic general *Odoacer*.

Italy in the early Middle Ages and under the German Emperors (493–1268).

– The *great migrations* of the Germanic peoples have a profound effect on the development of western and southern Europe. In spite of the Great Schism (1045) Byzantium remains in contact with the West, on which it exerts a strong influence, through its possessions in southern Italy. The attempts of German kings and emperors to re-establish the unity of Italy founder mainly on the resistance of the Papacy: the *Investiture Conflict*.

493–526 *Theodoric the Great*, with the authority of the Eastern Roman Emperor, founds an **Ostrogothic kingdom** in Italy, with Ravenna, Pavia and Verona as capitals.

535–553 *Justinian* makes Italy a province (exarchate) of the Eastern Roman Empire.

568–774 **Lombard kingdom** in northern Italy (Lombardy: capital Pavia). Tuscia, Spoleto and Benevento become Lombard duchies.

754–756 The Carolingian king *Pepin* defeats the Lombards and compels them to recognise Frankish suzerainty. The Exarchate of Ravenna and the Pentapolis (Ancona, Rimini, Pesaro, Fano and Senigallia) are handed over to the Pope.

773–774 **Charlemagne** conquers the Lombard kingdom and unites it with the *Frankish kingdom*; the duchies, with the exception of Benevento, become Frankish marquisates.

800 Charlemagne is crowned Emperor in Rome.

827 The **Magyars** move into the Po plain for the first time.

827–901 The **Saracens**, coming from Tunisia, conquer Sicily, which becomes an independent emirate in 948 and enjoys a great cultural flowering (capital Palermo).

887–1013 Fighting between native and Frankish nobles for the Lombard crown.

899 The Magyars plunder northern Italy.

951 The German emperor, **Otto the Great**, is appealed to for help by *Adelheid*, widow of the Lombard king, and gains control of northern Italy. Beginning of German intervention in Italian affairs.

962 Otto I is crowned Emperor in Rome.

951–1268 Italy ruled by the German emperors. Perpetual conflicts with the Popes, native rulers and the towns. Formation of two parties – the *Ghibellines*, who support the Emperor, and *Guelfs*, who support the Pope.

982 The Arabs inflict an annihilating defeat on *Otto II* at Cotrone.

1000–1200 Southern Italy and Sicily are joined by the **Normans** into a new kingdom. Although this puts an end to Byzantine and Arab rule their cultural influence continues.

1059 The Pope invests the Norman duke *Robert Guiscard* with southern Italy and Sicily (not yet conquered).

1076–1122 In the *Investiture Conflict*, the decisive confrontation between the Empire and the Papacy, the Pope breaks free of the influence of the Emperor and turns to the rising new Romance states.

1077 The excommunicated Emperor *Henry IV* travels to *Canossa* as a penitent and humbles himself before the Pope.

About 1110 Foundation of a medical school in Salerno.

1119 Foundation of the first university in Europe at Bologna.

1130 After the union of southern Italy and Sicily *Roger II* is crowned king in Palermo. Heyday of the Norman-Saracen culture.

1154–77 *Frederick I* **Barbarossa** tries to secure recognition of his suzerainty from the Lombard towns, but after a defeat at Legnano in 1176 is compelled to recognise their privileges. He becomes reconciled with Pope Alexander III in 1177.

1186 *Henry IV* marries *Constance*, heiress of the Norman kingdom. The struggle between the Emperor and the Pope is exacerbated by the encirclement of the Papal possessions by the Hohenstaufens.

1194–1268 Southern Italy and Sicily under **Hohenstaufen** rule.

1212–50 **Frederick II**, crowned Emperor in Rome in 1220, makes the Norman kingdom a rigidly organised absolutist state and a base of Imperial power; conflicts with the Papal and Lombard party. – Art and learning are fostered.

1222 Foundation of Padua University (and of Naples University in 1224).

From the emergence of independent city states during the Renaissance to the periods of Spanish, Austrian and French rule (1250–1815).

– In a politically fragmented Italy *city states* are established, and later also princely states, which rise to great intellectual, cultural and economic importance in Europe and come into conflict with the neighbouring great powers.

From 1250 *Rise of independent states* in Italy. The republican constitutions of the towns give place, following internal party strife, to rule by **Signorie**. Through the conquest of neighbouring towns a number of larger units are formed: In **Milan** the *Viscontis* come to power, and Giangaleazzo Visconti purchases the ducal title. After 1450 the city is ruled by the *Sforzas*. – **Verona** is ruled by the *Della Scala* (Scalinger) family. *Dante*, banished from Florence, lives at their court. In 1387 the Scaligers lose the whole territory to the Viscontis of Milan. – **Mantua** is ruled by the *Gonzaga* family. – **Venice** achieves naval superiority over Genoa and a commanding position in the Levantine trade. In the 13th c. it establishes trading stations in the Peloponnese, Crete, Cyprus and elsewhere, and in 1339 begins to expand on to the Italian mainland. Venice is ruled by a strictly aristocratic constitution; the Doge is elected for life. – From 1050 onwards **Piedmont** is ruled by the Counts (from 1416 Dukes) of *Savoy*. – The aristocratic republic of **Genoa** develops into an important commercial city, and in 1284 gains possession of Sardinia, Corsica and Elba. – From 1264 onwards **Ferrara** is ruled by the *Este* family. –

Florence, an important commercial city and the home of large banking houses, acquires a democratic constitution in 1282. Around 1400 the *Medici* rise to prominence and, as ruling princes, to great political influence.

About 1250 to 1600 *Humanism and the Renaissance.* Italian humanists (Dante, Petrarch, Boccaccio, etc.) rediscover ancient literature, which becomes a stimulus to literature and learning. The Renaissance, concerned with this world rather than the next, finds its principal expression in painting and architecture, but also in science and learning, which now break free from theology.

Increasing wealth of cities and ruling princes; luxurious and often unprincipled life of eccesiastical and lay rulers; patronage of the arts (Florence, Rome).

From the end of the 16th c. onwards the **Renaissance** spreads to all the courts and great commercial cities of Europe (painters, sculptors and architects, among them Giotto, Raphael, Michelangelo, Leonardo da Vinci, etc.).

1268–1442 Naples ruled by the house of **Anjou**.

1282 "*Sicilian Vespers*": murder or expulsion of all the French in Palermo, and later in the whole of Sicily. The kingdom of *Charles of Anjou* (1265–85) is reduced to Naples.

1282–1442 Sicily is ruled by the house of **Aragon**.

1310–1452 Last campaigns of the German Emperors in Italy.

1347 Unsuccessful attempt by *Cola di Rienzo* to re-establish the Roman Republic.

About 1350 Milan becomes the most powerful city state in northern Italy.

1378–81 *War of Chioggia*, a naval war between Genoa and Venice for supremacy in the Mediterranean. Venice is victorious and further extends its influence in the East; Genoa turns towards the West.

1442–1504 The Aragonese rulers of Sicily succeed in reuniting it with the kingdom of Naples.

1494 In Florence, after the temporary expulsion of the Medici, the Dominican prior *Savonarola* establishes a republic. In 1498 he is burned as a heretic.

1494–1556 The **French** attempt, without success, to establish their supremacy in Italy.

1504–1713 Sicily is ruled by the **Spanish Habsburgs**. A number of risings are repressed by the Spanish viceroys.

1515 *Francis I* of France takes Milan.

1521–44 The Emperor **Charles V** fights four wars with Francis I, who is taken prisoner at Pavia in 1525.

1527 In the *Sacco de Roma* Rome is plundered by Charles V's troops.

1540 Charles V gives his son *Philip II* the duchy of Milan, which remains a possession of the Spanish crown until 1700 and together with the kingdom of Naples and Sicily maintains Spanish influence in Italy.

1569 *Cosimo dei Medici*, Duke of Florence, becomes Grand Duke of Tuscany.

1633 *Galileo* is compelled by the Roman Inquisition to recant his acceptance of the Copernican picture of the Universe.

1703–37 Mantua (1703), Lombardy (1714) and Tuscany (1737) fall into the hands of the **Austrian Habsburgs**.

1718 After the Turkish War (1714–18) Venice loses its possessions in the Levant and with them its leading position in trade with the East.

1718–20 *Victor Amadeus II*, Duke of Savoy, receives Sardinia and along with it the title of king.

1719 Herculaneum, buried by the eruption of Vesuvius in A.D. 79, is rediscovered. Excavations at Herculaneum in 1737, at Pompeii in 1748.

1735–1806 The **Bourbons** in Naples and Sicily. From 1735 onwards Charles of Bourbon carries through reforms based on the principles of the *Enlightenment*.

About 1750 A new *national consciousness* comes into being in Italy, preparing the way for the liberation and unification movement of the 19th c.

1768 Genoa sells Corsica to France.

1783 Severe earthquake in Messina.

1796 **Bonaparte's Italian campaign**.

1797 Establishment of the *Cisalpine Republic* (Milan, Modena, Ferrara, Bologna, Romagna) and the *Ligurian Republic* (Genoa).

1798 *Tiberine Republic* (Rome).

1800 *Napoleon* defeats the Austrians at Marengo.

1805 **Napoleon becomes King of Italy**; the Ligurian Republic is incorporated in France.

1806 *Joseph*, Napoleon's brother, becomes King of Naples, followed in 1808 by his brother-in-law *Murat*. The king of Sicily, *Ferdinand IV*, is supported by Britain.

1814–15 **Congress of Vienna**, presided over by Prince *Metternich* (Austria). The former petty states are re-established.

From the Risorgimento to the end of the First World War (1815–1919). – The Napoleonic era had strengthened the newly awakened national consciousness, but it is left to Cavour to bring the idea of the independent national state within sight of realisation. After achieving reunification Italy, like other national states, seeks to promote its imperialistic interests.

1816 Ferdinand IV unites Naples and Sicily in the **Kingdom of the Two Sicilies** and henceforth styles himself *Ferdinand I*.

1820–32 Austrian troops suppress several risings against reactionary governments. The secret society of the Carbonari ("Charcoal-Burners") and the underground republican movement of Giovine Italia ("Young Italy") founded by *Mazzini* in Marseilles lead the fight for unification and liberation.

1847 The newspaper which gives its name to the whole unification movement, "**Il Risorgimento**", appears in Turin.

1848–49 *Revolution* in Italy and Sicily, of which King *Charles Albert of Sardinia* puts himself at the head. After the victory of the Austrian Field-Marshal Radetzky at Custozza and Novara he abdicates in favour of his son *Victor Emmanuel II*.

1859–60 The process of reunification begins with a rapprochement with France initiated by Count *Cavour*.

1859 The allied army of Sardinia and France defeats Austrian forces at Magenta and Solferino. Austria loses Lombardy to Napoleon III, who cedes it to Sardinia in exchange for Nice and Savoy.

1860 Expulsion of the ruling princes from the states of central and northern Italy. *Garibaldi* and his irregular forces defeat the Bourbons and occupy the States of the Church. Plebiscites all over the country declare for union with Sardinia.

1861 *Victor Emmanuel II* becomes king. The first capital of the **Kingdom of Italy** is Florence.

1866 **War with Austria.** In spite of defeats at Custozza and Lissa, Venice is incorporated into Italy by negotiation. – Mazzini puts forward Italian claims to Istria, Friuli and South Tirol ("Italia Irredenta", "Unrecovered Italy").

1870 *Rome* is occupied by Italian troops and becomes *capital of Italy*. The Pope retains sovereignty over Vatican City.

1878 Under *Umberto I* Italy became a great power.

1882 Italy forms the *Triple Alliance* with Germany and Austria-Hungary.

1882–83 Foundation of the Italian Socialist Party.

1887–89 **War with Abyssinia.** Italy gains the colonies of Eritrea and Italian Somaliland.

1900 Treaty defining Italian and French spheres of interest in Morocco and Tripoli.

1911–12 **War with Turkey.** Italy annexes Cyrenaica, Tripoli and the Dodecanese, including Rhodes.

1912 Introduction of universal suffrage.

1914 After the outbreak of the First World War Italy declares its neutrality (3 August).

1915–18 Italy in the **First World War.**

1915 Secret treaty of London: Italy's colonial and irredentist claims are guaranteed by Britain and France (26 April). Italy declares war on Austria-Hungary (23 May) and Germany (28 August 1916).

1915–17 Austrian and German troops defend the Isonzo line in 11 battles, and in the twelfth battle of the Isonzo (Oct.–Dec. 1917) break through at Caporetto and reach the Piave.

1918 Italian counter-offensive: collapse of the Austro-Hungarian front at Vittorio Veneto.

1919 Treaty of Saint-Germain-en-Laye (10 September): Italy receives South Tirol as far as the Brenner, Istria (apart from Fiume) and a number of Dalmatian islands.

From the end of the First World War to the present day. – After the First World War Italy seeks to acquire further territory by an expansionist policy and to overcome the "crisis of democracy" by a new ideology, *Fascism*. Although it fights in the *Second World War* on the side of the Allies from 1943 onwards it has to bear the consequences of the power politics of the Fascist period. After the war the new *Republic of Italy* is rent by ideological conflicts and faced with grave economic and social problems. Internal political developments are influenced by the numerous parties with their varying relationships and alliances.

1919–21 *Mussolini* forms "fighting groups" (*fasci di combattimento*); growing influence of the Fascists; attacks on Communists, with open violence.

1922 *"March on Rome"*: Mussolini is granted dictatorial powers by Parliament; the Fascists gradually take over the government.

1923 Beginning of a rigorous policy of assimilation in Alto Adige (South Tirol).

1924 Fiume falls to Italy.

1926 British-Italian agreement on Abyssinia, which is divided into economic spheres of interest. Treaty of friendship with Spain.

1931 Measures of state control to deal with the *economic crisis*; development of agriculture.

1933 Treaty of friendship with the Soviet Union.

1934 "Roman Economic Protocol" between Italy, Austria and Hungary. – First meeting between Mussolini and *Hitler* in Venice.

1935–36 *Italian invasion of Abyssinia* and annexation of the whole country.

1936 Establishment of the "Rome-Berlin Axis" in a treaty with Germany. Italian troops support Franco in the Spanish Civil War.

1937 Italy leaves the League of Nations (of which it had been a founder member in 1919).

1939 *Occupation of Albania* (April). Military alliance with Germany (the "Pact of Steel").

1939–45 Second World War. Mussolini attempts to mediate, without success; Italy at first remains "non-belligerent".

1940 Italy declares war on France and Britain (10 June). Italian-French armistice signed in Rome (24 June). Three-power pact with Germany and Japan (27 September).

1941 Military failures in N Africa; Abyssinia is lost.

1943 Surrender of Italian forces in N Africa (13 May). *Allied landings in Sicily* (10 July). Fall of the Fascist regime; Mussolini is arrested (24 July). Formation of a new government under *Badoglio*, who signs an armistice with the Allies (3 September) and declares war on Germany (13 October). Rival government established by Mussolini (freed by a German commando group), who continues the war against the Allies.

1945 Surrender of German forces in Italy (28 April). Mussolini is shot by partisans. The Democrazia Cristiana (Christian Democrat party) forms a government, led by de Gasperi (until 1953).

1946 King Victor Emmanuel III abdicates. Plebiscite in favour of a **Republic** (18 June).

1947 Treaty of Paris: Italy cedes the Dodecanese to Greece and Istria to Yugoslavia; Trieste becomes a free state. Italy renounces its colonies.

1948 A new democratic constitution comes into force. Economic and social disparities between the well-developed North of Italy and the underdeveloped South. After the economic difficulties of the immediate post-war period (Marshall Aid) there is an economic resurgence. Italy joins the Western powers, becoming a founder member of NATO (1949), the European Coal and Steel Community (1951), the European Economic Community (1957), etc.

1950 Partial expropriation of large landowners, with compensation, under the Sila Law.

1953 The Christian Democrat party loses its absolute majority; thereafter frequent changes of government.

1954 The free state of Trieste is divided between Italy and Yugoslavia.

From 1957   Rapid increase in movement from the South to the industrial regions of northern Italy or to other countries.

1960   Summer Olympic Games in Rome.

1963   Moro (DC) forms the first Centre-Left government. The latent governmental crisis remains unresolved.

1966   Catastrophic floods in northern and central Italy.

1969   Self-government for the Alto Adige (South Tirol: not yet fully in effect).

From 1970   Increased contacts with East European and Balkan states.

1972   Government of the Centre.

1973   Centre-Left government. Domestic political crisis: balance of payments deficit, inflation, economic crisis.

From 1974   The world-wide *energy crisis* and the economic *recession* hit Italy particularly hard: increasing unemployment, high inflation, foreign debts, etc. New economic programme, frustrated by increasingly acute domestic political crisis, party strife, numerous strikes and acts of terrorism, corruption scandals and kidnappings accompanied by ransom demands.

1975   Final settlement of the Trieste problem. – Great gains by the Communist Party (PCI) in regional, provincial and municipal elections.

1976   Severe earthquake in the provinces of Udine and Pordenone in Friuli (6 May). – Minority DC government, dependent on Communist support (June). – Escape of poisonous gas cloud at Seveso, near Milan (10 July).

1977   Heavy destruction in street fighting with demonstrating students (13 March). – Parliament approves a programme of economic reform, stepping-up of internal security, educational and press policy and regionalisation (16 July). – Violent political reactions after a former SS officer named Kappler escapes from the Roman military prison (15 August).

1978   *Moro*, chairman of the DC party and a former Prime Minister, is kidnapped on 13 March by members of the "Red Brigades" and found murdered 54 days later. Tightening-up of the laws against terrorism (March). – Political crisis following the resignation of President *Leone* (15 June); an 81-year-old Socialist, *Pertini*, is elected to succeed him (8 July).

Art

The Italian peninsula, like the rest of the Mediterranean world, has been occupied by man since the remotest times, and over this long period Italy has accumulated an almost incalculable store of art treasures. In spite of serious difficulties the Italian authorities have considerable achievements to their credit in the preservation, study and presentation of these treasures.

Remains of the *Stone Age* are to be found particularly in Sicily and northern Italy, and the museums of Florence, Bologna, Turin, Milan and many smaller towns have much valuable material dating from this period, including domestic utensils, weapons and articles buried in graves from the settlements of pile-dwellings on the North Italian lakes. – Remains of buildings, chambered tombs and standing stones belonging to the *Megalithic culture* can be seen at Táranto and on the islands of Lampedusa and Pantelleria. On Sardinia there are the curious round towers known as *nuraghi*, and on both Sardinia and Sicily there are remains of the Iberian Beaker people.

During the *Bronze Age* Italy appears to have had links with the Creto-Mycenaean culture, as is shown, for example, by finds from Ascoli Piceno. The *Terramare culture* which came to Italy from Illyria can be ascribed with reasonable certainty to the original Italic population (urn burials). The *Villanovan culture* (Umbrians, Latins) which developed out of the Terramare, an Iron Age culture which flourished in the Po plain and central Italy (900–400 B.C.), produced the characteristic situla, a kind of bucket with rich figured decoration which attained its finest form about 500 B.C. – The best place to study the cultures of the prehistoric and early historical periods is the Museo Preistorico ed Etnografico Luigi Pigorini in Rome.

From the 8th to the 5th c. B.C. the **Etruscans** (Latin *Tusci* or *Etrusci*) occupied a dominant position in central and northern Italy (Cato: "Almost the whole of Italy was under the rule of the Etruscans"). In addition to numerous local centres there was a confederation of 12 cities to which Velathri (Volterra), Arretium (Arezzo), Curtuns (Cortona), Perusia (Perugia), Chamars/Clevsin/Clusium (Chiusi), Rusellae (Roselle), Vatluna (Vetulonia), Volsinii (Orvieto), Vulci, Tarchuna/Tarquinii (Tarquinia), Caere (Cerveteri) and Veii (Veio) belonged. (The membership of the league seems to have varied from time to time.) The Etruscans appear to have been a non-Indo-European people of advanced culture who came to Italy from the East. The magnificent works of art they produced are mostly known to us from their tombs (sarcophagi with life-size recumbent terracotta figures from the Banditaccia cemetery, Cerveteri; wall paintings, in a realistic style showing Greek influence, in chamber tombs at Tarquinia and elsewhere). The famous she-wolf in the Capitoline Museum is also Etruscan work. In architecture the Etruscans had mastered the structure of the true arch and the technique of the barrel vault. Their arts and crafts are represented by an abundance of objects of high quality to be seen in the Archaeological Museum in Florence, the Villa Giulia in Rome and museums in Cerveteri, Chiusi, Tarquinia, Veii, Volterra and many other towns.

Between the 8th and 5th c. B.C. more than 40 Greek colonies were founded in Sicily and southern Italy (Greek *Megale Hellas*, Latin *Magna Graecia*), including Zankle (Messina), Tauromenion (Taormina), Katana (Catania), Syrakousai (Syracuse), Akragas (Agrigento), Selinus (Selinunte), Segesta, Taras (Taranto), Poseidonia (Paestum) and Neapolis (Naples). Unlike the Etruscans, who used wood and terracotta, the **Greeks** constructed their monumental buildings in marble. The most impressive demonstration of their skill is provided by the

An Etruscan tomb – Ipogeo dei Volumni, Perugia

Etruscans
and
Greeks
in
Italy

Megale
Hellas

Magna
Graecia

● Etruscan Centres	● Greek Foundations
1 **Arretium** (Arezzo)	13 **Neapolis** (Naples)
2 **Velathri** (Volterra)	14 **Poseidonia** (Paestum)
3 **Curtuns** (Cortona)	15 **Metapontion** (Metaponto)
4 **Perusia** (Perugia)	16 **Taras** (Taranto)
5 **Chamars/Clevsin/Clusium** (Chiusi)	17 **Kroton** (Crotone)
6 **Rusellae** (Roselle)	18 **Zankle** (Messina)
7 **Vatluna** (Vetulonia)	19 **Tauromenion** (Taormina)
8 **Volsinii** (Orvieto)	20 **Katana** (Catania)
9 **Vulci** (Vulci)	21 **Syrakousai** (Syracuse)
10 **Tarchuna** (Tarquinia)	22 **Akragas** (Agrigento)
11 **Caere** (Cerveteri)	23 **Selinus** (Selinunte)
12 **Veii** (Veio)	24 **Segesta**

temple precinct of Paestum. The Paestum temples, magnificent examples of Doric architecture (metopes from the Temple of Hera in the Paestum museum), together with the temples of Selinunte and Segesta and the theatres of Syracuse, Catania, Segesta and above all Taormina, give a powerful impression of the beauty, power and nobility of ancient Greek architecture.

Only a few examples of Greek sculpture from southern Italy have been preserved, including the metopes from Selinunte (in the Museo Nazionale, Palermo), a bronze statue of Apollo from Pompeii (in the National Archaeological Museum, Naples), a Medusa head (in the Museo delle Terme, Rome) and the famous Laocoön group (in the Museo Pio-Clementino in the Vatican). Terracotta sculpture is better represented, with numerous examples in various museums in southern Italy.

Greek painting is known only from the work of the vase-painters (particularly the black-figure type) and the Hellenistic wall paintings of Pompeii in a later period.

Between 400 and 200 B.C. the **Romans** became masters of Italy. Originally a people of farmers and warriors, they assimilated the art and culture of the territories they conquered – first of the Etruscans, later of the Greeks and finally of the East. The remains of Roman buildings can still be seen all over Europe, western Asia and North Africa, and a vivid impression of Roman life is provided by the remains, excavated from the 18th c. onwards, of the towns of Pompeii and Herculaneum which were buried under layers of lava, ashes and cinders by an eruption of Vesuvius in A.D. 79. Imposing examples of Roman architecture can also be seen in Rome (Forum Romanum, etc.), in spite of later destruction and rebuilding. Perhaps the main Roman contribution to western architecture was the development of the method of vaulted construction which they took over from the Etruscans. Roman industrial and commercial buildings can be seen in the excavations of Ostia, the port of ancient Rome.

The centre of any Roman town was the **forum**, which served as a market, a meeting-place and a political arena. The Roman **temple**, which like its Etruscan counterpart is built on a platform, differs from the Greek temple in having only a single entrance; the cella is usually preceded by an open hall (as in the temple of Fortuna Virilis in Rome). Another important feature of a Roman town was the **basilica** (lawcourt), a long pillared hall with the entrance on one of the side walls: a structure which developed into the early Christian churches of basilican type.

The **baths** (*thermae*) were equipped with cold, warm and hot installations and were often large and extravagantly luxurious. The church of Santa Maria degli Angeli in Rome, built by Michelangelo, incorporates the *tepidarium* (warm bath) of the Thermae of Diocletian.

The **palaces** of the Roman Emperors were large architectural complexes with barrel vaulting and domes, richly decorated with frescoes, mosaics and festoons and articulated by columns.

The Roman **theatre** developed out of its Greek forerunner. The auditorium forms a semicircle, and the stage wall becomes an elaborate architectural structure. Alongside the theatre there developed the amphitheatre, oval in plan, with seating for many thousands of spectators (Colosseum in Rome; Arena in Verona).

The **triumphal arch** was originally a gateway erected for the ceremonial entry of victorious troops, but developed into an elaborate structure, richly decorated with sculpture, commemorating the victories of Roman emperors (Arches of Constantine, Septimius Severus and Titus in Rome). Triumphal *columns* served a similar purpose (Trajan's Column, Rome).

Roman **aqueducts** were masterpieces of engineering which carried water into the towns from many kilometres away, often on a long series of towering arches. The **roads** and **bridges** are also impressive demonstrations of Roman technical skill.

The **houses** of wealthy Romans were built round an open inner courtyard, the *atrium*, and entered through a hall or *vestibulum*. Along the sides of the house were private apartments, together with a pillared courtyard, a dining room, corridors and a garden. The interior was richly decorated with frescoes, mosaics and sculpture (often copies of Greek originals): good examples in Pompeii.

Roman sculpture is largely based on Greek models, but in the portrait sculpture of the Republican period achieves a remarkable degree of realism. Under the Empire the most imposing form of portrait sculpture, the equestrian statue, came to the fore; the only surviving example is the figure of Marcus Aurelius (A.D. 179) on the Capitol in Rome. – Sculptured reliefs were also used to depict great historical events (Trajan's Column and the Ara Pacis in Rome). Roman painting shows Hellenistic influence. – The wall paintings of which numerous examples can be seen in Pompeii show great diversity of style, realistic and almost impressionistic grotesques alternating with trompe-l'œil architecture, classical Greek themes, gay bucolic scenes and heroic legends. Mosaics were also used for the decoration of walls and floors (pavement mosaic of "Alexander's Battle" in Pompeii, A.D. 50).

In architecture the **early Christian period** developed the basilican church out of the Roman law-court. The nave, which probably had a flat roof, was usually divided into three or five aisles, the central aisle being as a rule higher than the others; the W end faced on to the street, and there was a semicircular apse at the E end. Externally the basilicas were plain brick buildings, but the interiors were usually sumptuously decorated, showing Byzantine influence. From the 7th c. onwards there was usually a separate bell-tower. A small circular baptistery served for adult baptism.

Under the Emperor Justinian (527–565) churches began to be built also on a centralised plan, the model for this new type being Hagia Sophia in Constantinople. The central feature was the space under the dome, with four barrel-vaulted wings opening off it in the form of a cross. These might also be domed, as in St Mark's in Venice (begun 830).

Ravenna now became an important political and artistic centre, and it still preserves magnificent examples of early Christian and Byzantine art and architecture, such as the basilicas of Sant'Apollinare in Classe and Sant'-Apollinare Nuovo, the Mausoleum of Galla Placidia and the Baptistery of the Orthodox (both on a centralised plan), and the church of San Vitale, an octagonal structure with a central dome supported on piers. The rows of columns are now spanned by arcades in the Byzantine fashion.

The great achievement of this period in the artistic field was the mosaic decoration of the churches. Byzantine art, subject to strict hierarchical rules, evolved a series of formal stereotypes, with no sense of space or perspective, which were set on a golden ground, the symbol of heaven (San Vitale, Sant'Apollinare Nuovo, Mausoleum of Galla Placidia, all in Ravenna).

Mention should also be made of the Roman catacombs – underground burial-places constructed on several levels with an extensive system of corridors and passages and frequently decorated with paintings of Christian motifs.

Christian sculpture began by following pagan models – sarcophagi with carved decoration, figures of Christ as a young man (e.g. the "Good Shepherd", a marble statuette of the 3rd c. A.D. in the Vatican Museum, Rome).

The *great migrations* from A.D. 400 onwards brought a series of Germanic peoples into Italy – Goths,. Vandals, Lombards. The tomb of the Ostrogothic king Theodoric the Great (*c.* 456–526) in Ravenna, a circular structure roofed with a single massive slab of stone, is one of the very few surviving examples of Germanic architecture in stone, though it was undoubtedly based on Roman and Eastern models.

Romanesque architecture developed out of early Christian architecture in the 11th c., with variations in style in different regions. At first Rome remained backward in this field, while the cities of Tuscany vied with one another in building churches in the new style. An early example was San Frediano in Lucca (1112–47), a basilica of rather old-fashioned stamp. About 1050 a new type of façade, with inlaid marble decoration, came into vogue (San Miniato, Florence; pillared arcades of Pisa and Lucca Cathedrals). Pisa Cathedral (begun 1063), with its massive transepts, is the most imposing building of this period.

The Lombard churches of northern Italy show German and Burgundian influence. They are mostly basilicas with groined vaulting and richly articulated façades (Sant'Ambrogio, Milan; San Zeno, Verona; cathedrals of Piacenza, Módena, Parma and Ferrara).

In Apulia many fine churches (Barletta and Trani cathedrals; pilgrimage church of San Nicola and Cathedral, Bari; Bitonto Cathedral) were built in the Apulian Romanesque style, which shows a mingling of Byzantine, Lombard, Norman and even Saracen influences.

In Sicily the Norman influence was less strongly felt than in Apulia, but there are a number of notable buildings of this period in Palermo – the church of San Giovanni degli Eremiti, a building of rather Oriental aspect with its five tall red domes; the Martorana, a beautiful church with excellent Byzantine mosaics; San Cataldo, a Byzantine domed church of 1161; and the Capella Palatina, built by Roger II in 1132–40, with superb mosaic decoration which makes it surely the finest of all royal chapels. Monreale Cathedral (c. 1180) is the largest Norman building in Sicily, with a magnificent choir; adjoining it is the largest and most beautiful cloister in the Italian Romanesque style.

The secular architecture of this period has also some fine buildings to its credit – in northern Italy, for example, the castles in the valley of the Dora Baltea and at Canossa, Cannero and Prato, and the defensive towers built by noble families in the towns (e.g. in Bologna). The 13 towers of San Gimignano and its picturesque town walls are particularly impressive. In central and southern Italy there are also handsome palaces (Palazzo dei Normanni, Palermo; the Cuba and Zisa, showing Saracen influence) and town halls (Orvieto).

Romanesque sculpture long remained under strong Byzantine influence. From the end of the 11th c. onwards the casting of bronze doors with relief decoration reached a consummate degree of skill (San Zeno, Verona; door by Barisanus, Trani Cathedral; doors of Amalfi, Atrani and Salerno cathedrals; door by Bonannus, Pisa Cathedral, 1180).

Sculpture in stone enjoyed a great flowering together with architecture, and Lombard sculptors in particular produced work of the highest standard. The first to undertake large figures was Wiligelmus, who carved the scenes from Genesis on the façade of Módena Cathedral about 1100. About 1135 Master Nicolò was working on the doorways of Ferrara and Verona cathedrals.

The leading sculptor of the High Romanesque period in northern Italy was *Benedetto Antelami*, among whose principal works are the "Descent from the Cross" in Parma Cathedral, the bishop's throne in the choir and the outer walls and doorway of the baptistery. French and above all Provençal influences can be detected in his work.

There were also notable sculptors in Tuscany, like *Guidetto* and *Guido Begarelli* of Como (font in Baptistery, Pisa). In Rome the group known as the *Cosmati* (from the name Cosmas borne by some of its members) worked on the decoration of churches and convents, evolving the distinctive style called Cosmatesque.

In southern Italy the busts from the Volturno Gate of Capua (now in the Campanian Provincial Museum, Capua) are particularly notable. The Apulian churches also have rich sculptured decoration (bishop's thrones at Canossa and Bari; pulpit, Bitonto).

Romanesque sculpture reaches its final culmination in the work of *Nicola* **Pisano** (1225–78), the first artistic personality of the Middle Ages with whom we have any real acquaintance, who bases himself on ancient models (marble pulpit in the Baptistery, Pisa, 1260; marble pulpit in Siena Cathedral, 1268; fountain in front of Perugia Cathedral).

The painting of the Romanesque period is dominated by Byzantine influence (the *maniera greca*); and the mosaics of Venice and those produced in Sicily in the 12th c. are still wholly within the Byzantine tradition. The leading master of Romanesque painting, who towards the end of the 13th c. sought to break away from the old rigid tradition and thus prepared the way for Giotto, was *Giovanni Cimabue* (mentioned in 1272 and 1301–02; "Madonna Enthroned with Angels", Uffizi, Florence).

Italy now entered the **Gothic** period, at a time when French Gothic had already passed its peak. The older traditions, however, were never entirely forgotten; reflected in countless buildings which still survive, the inheritance from the East (*maniera bizantina* or *maniera greca*) made its way into Europe by way of Italy. Alongside all these various influences, however, there now began to emerge new and distinctively Italian creative forces which were to extend their influence over the whole of Europe.

Italian art first begins to show distinctive national characteristics in the age of Dante, at the end of the 13th c. Thereafter the centuries are known by the following names:

Duecento	=	13th century
Trecento	=	14th century
Quattrocento	=	15th century
Cinquecento	=	16th century
Seicento	=	17th century
Settecento	=	18th century
Ottocento	=	19th century
Novecento	=	20th century

The art of the late Middle Ages (*Trecento*, 14th c.), the *stile gotico*, was introduced into Italy mainly by the mendicant orders; but the Italian sense of form soon displaced the Burgundian influence (Santa Croce, Florence, begun by Arnolfo di Cambio in 1295, still without vaulting). Particularly notable are the double church in Assisi (upper church completed 1253, the earliest Gothic church in Italy), Sant'Anastasia in Verona and, in Venice, the Dominican church of Santi Giovanni e Paolo (1330–90) and the Franciscan church of Santa Maria Gloriosa dei Frari (1330–1470). Italian taste, however, was against the excessive reduction of the wall surfaces; the horizontals were still stressed, as they had been in Romanesque architecture, and the façades of cathedrals were lavishly encrusted with decoration.

The cathedrals erected at municipal expense became steadily more sumptuous as each town sought to outdo the other (Siena, Florence, Bologna). The Duomo in Florence, a three-aisled structure with a triple-apsed choir which was probably begun by Arnolfo di Cambio in 1296, the dome being added later by Brunelleschi, is the most impressive of these cathedrals, exceeded in size and massiveness only by Milan Cathedral, a cruciform church begun in 1386. The radiant exterior, with its 135 pinnacles and 2300 marble statues, is in striking contrast to the rather dark interior with its 52 massive piers and its huge windows.

Secular Gothic architecture continues the tradition of Romanesque with a strict sense of form. Huge Gothic public buildings and palaces were now built in towns (Palazzo Vecchio, Florence; Palazzo Pubblico, Siena; Scaliger castles in Verona and Sirmione; Gonzaga Palace, Mantua; Este Palace, Ferrara; Doges' Palace and Ca' d'Oro, Venice), and the houses of patrician families steadily increased in comfort and luxury.

Romanesque and Gothic features are combined in the Hohenstaufen castles in Apulia. Castel del Monte near Foggia (built about 1240), a polygonal structure crowning an isolated hill, is particularly impressive; it is said to have been designed by the Emperor Frederick II himself, who paid frequent visits to the region for relaxation or hunting. Other important Hohenstaufen buildings are the castles of Gioia del Colle and Lagopésole and Frederick II's castle at Lucera, of which only fragments survive, though sufficient to show the monumental character of the original palace.

Gothic sculpture established itself only towards the end of the 13th c. Its greatest master was *Giovanni Pisano*, son of Nicola (pulpits in Sant'Andrea, Pistoia, and Pisa Cathedral; Madonna in Scrovegni Chapel, Padua). *Andrea Pisano* continued Giovanni's rhythmically flowing style (oldest of the three bronze doors of the Baptistery, Florence). Other sculptors of the period were *Andrea di Cione*, known as *Orcagna* (d. about 1368 in Florence), who was also active as an architect and painter (tabernacle in Or San Michele, Florence, 1348–59), and *Tino di Camaino* (Gothic tombs of the Anjou family in Santa Chiara, Naples).

In the 14th c. the practice of erecting huge monuments to the dead came into vogue (equestrian figures of Paolo Savelli, 1405, in the Frari church, Venice; Scaliger tombs in San Francesco cemetery, Verona).

In the field of Gothic painting the work of **Giotto** (*Giotto di Bondone, c.* 1266–1337) marked a great advance. Although influenced by Cimabue and *Duccio di Buoninsegna* ("Maestà", the Madonna enthroned with angels, 1308–11; now in Cathedral Museum, Siena), in whom reminiscences of the *maniera greca* can still be detected, Giotto took the decisive step which provided the basis for the whole of modern painting.

Painting now acquired, as sculpture had done at an earlier stage, the ability to depict spiritual events; and Giotto, breaking away from the constraints of Byzantine iconography, was able to give his Biblical scenes a new form and a new content. His principal works are the overwhelming cycle of scenes in the Scrovegni Chapel in Padua, freed only a few years ago from later over-paintings, and the frescoes in the two choir chapels in Santa Croce, Florence (unfortunately much repainted). In Florence the school of Giotto remained active throughout the whole of the 14th c. (series of frescoes in Santa Croce, Santa Maria Novella and the Cappella degli Spágnoli by Andrea da Firenze; frescoes in Campo Santo, Pisa).

A distinctive school also developed at the Visconti court in Milan around 1500 (Zavattari and Giovannino de' Grassi, Casa Borromeo, Milan; pictures of the Months in the Torre dell'Aquila, Castello, Trento).

The **Renaissance** (Italian *Rinascimento*) was literally a rebirth of the spirit of antiquity. While the Middle Ages had seen the purpose of life in overcoming the terrestrial world and preparing for the world beyond, man now began, in a return to the attitudes of antiquity, to discover himself and the world as independent entities in their own right and to seek his tasks in the world here below. The metaphysical orientation of Gothic, concerned only with the world to come, was no longer adequate: the new conception of the beauty of the world, the joys of life and the freedom of the spirit demanded quite new forms of expression. There was no smooth transition as there had been between Romanesque and Gothic, but a sudden break. The master craftsman of the past now became an artist, who was no longer content to take second place to his work. He was now an individual artistic personality putting his work before a critical public, not a devout community of believers.

The architects of the *Quattrocento* (15th c.) were the first to adopt the new style modelled on the architectural forms of antiquity. *Filippo* **Brunelleschi** (1377–1446) was the pioneer of the early Renaissance, using new techniques in building the dome of Florence Cathedral, the churches of San Lorenzo and the Santo Spirito and the Pazzi Chapel.

Leon Battista Alberti (1404–72), an artistic personality of universal scope and author of an interesting treatise on architecture, began the church of Sant'Andrea in Mantua in the last year of his life: forward-looking in its conception of space, it ranks with the church of San Francesco in Rimini as his finest achievement.

The indebtedness of the new period to classical art was particularly evident in the field of sculpture. The range of subject-matter was now extended to take in secular themes, and mythology and contemporary history alike supplied subjects for artistic treatment. The study of anatomy enabled artists to depict the human body in a new way. Portrait sculpture now also developed, producing realistic representations of the sitters who commissioned them. Medieval symbolism gave place to delineations of actual people, the world of spiritual forces to visible down-to-earth reality.

Lorenzo Ghiberti (1378–1455), painter and sculptor, created the second and the famous third door (the Porta del Paradiso) of the Baptistery in Florence. Other major works were the reliefs on the font in San Giovanni, Siena, and the bronze figures of Or San Michele, Florence.

Donatello (*Donato de Bardi*, 1368–1466) is generally regarded as the leading figure of the early Renaissance. A pupil of Ghiberti's, he produced both marble sculpture (Duomo, Florence) and bronze statues ("David", c. 1430; in the Bargello, Florence). One of his most powerful works is the equestrian statue of Gattamelata in Padua; other major works are "Judith and Holofernes" (in front of the Palazzo Vecchio, Florence), the first free-standing sculptured group of modern times, and "St George", also in Florence.

Andrea del Verrocchio (1436–88) worked mainly for the Medici in Florence ("David", 1465; bronze group, "Christ and Thomas", Or San Michele), but also created the equestrian statue of the condottiere Bartolommeo Colleoni in Venice – less massive than Donatello's Gattamelata but livelier and tauter.

Luca della Robbia (1399–1482) was the third of the great masters of the early Renaissance in Florence. He applied the techniques of faience to larger works of sculpture and produced a whole series of majolica pieces (figures of the Madonna).

Early Renaissance painting began with the work of *Masaccio* (Tommaso di Giovanni di Simone Guidi), who died young (1401–28). He painted the frescoes in the Brancacci Chapel of Santa Maria del Carmine and the "Virgin with St Anne" in the Uffizi.

Andrea Mantegna (1431–1506) was the leading North Italian painter of the Quattrocento. His pictures, works of high seriousness and rigour, depict plastic bodily forms with almost exaggerated clarity, achieving a very characteristic effect of depth by the use of perspective, with drastic foreshortening (altarpiece, San Zeno, Verona; "St Sebastian", Museo Nazionale, Florence; Camera degli Sposi in the Castello in Mantua, with the first group portrait and the first trompe-l'œil ceiling painting in the history of art; "Madonna della Vittoria", Louvre, Paris).

Fra Angelico (*Fra Giovanni da Fiesole*, 1387–1455) created works of an exclusively religious character, deeply devout and peopled with graceful angel figures (frescoes in the monastery of San Marco, Florence).

Piero della Francesca (*c.* 1420–92) was the Quattrocento's great master and teacher of perspective. Among his principal works are the votive picture of Sigismondo Malatesta (in San Francesco, Rimini), the portrait of Federigo da Montefeltro (Uffizi, Florence), the "Resurrection" in Urbino and the "Adoration of the Child" in the National Gallery, London.

The Florentine *Sandro* **Botticelli** (1444–1510) worked during the most brilliant period of the Medici. A kind of dreamy melancholy hangs over his graceful youths and maidens, and there is a touch of the same feeling even in his pagan mythological pictures ("Spring", "Birth of Venus", both in the Uffizi, Florence).

Fra Filippo Lippi (1406–69), a Carmelite monk working in Florence, painted pictures transfiguring Biblical scenes by the depiction of secular and terrestrial beauty. His work is filled with fresh sincerity and love of nature ("Coronation

of the Virgin", Uffizi; "Annunciation", San Lorenzo, Florence; frescoes in Spoleto Cathedral).

Domenico Veneziano (*c.* 1400–61) worked in Venice, where painting was concerned primarily with brilliance of colour and delicacy of sentiment. In his "Sacra Conversazione" the Madonna is surrounded by a group of saints.

The **High Renaissance** falls into the first half of the *Cinquecento* (16th c.). One of its great masters was *Donato* **Bramante** (1444–1514), the clarity and harmonious beauty of whose buildings is best seen in his plan for the new St Peter's in Rome, a centralised structure in the form of a Greek cross. He did not live to complete the building, which was continued by Michelangelo and crowned with a mighty dome.

Michelangelo *Buonarroti* (1475–1564), a universal genius and one of the greatest artistic personalities of a time rich in geniuses, was the leading master of the High Renaissance. A pupil of Ghirlandaio's, he worked as architect, painter and sculptor, and in addition made a name for himself as a poet with his sonnets. Among the works he produced in Florence were his "David" (Accademia), the mausoleum of the Medici in San Lorenzo (Sagrestia Nuova) and the staircase of the Biblioteca Laurenziana.

Michelangelo's "Pietà" (St Peter's, Rome)

Summoned to Rome by Pope Julius II, he worked on Julius's tomb (figure of Moses, "Fettered Slave" and "Dying Slave"), which remained unfinished, completed the building of St Peter's and painted the magnificent cycle of frescoes in the Sistine Chapel. With the "harmony" and "power" (Michelangelo's watchwords) of his work he moved beyond the High Renaissance and prepared the way for the Baroque.

The second universal genius (*"uomo universale"*) of the High Renaissance was **Leonardo da Vinci** (1452–1519), sculptor, architect, painter, scientist and constructor. Working at the Sforza court in Milan, in Florence, in Rome and finally for Francis I in France, he was the richest incarnation of the universal man of the Renaissance. In him art and science were fused to form a unity, and his achievements in the field of natural science alone would entitle him to a leading place in the history of human intellectual development. Among his greatest works are the "Virgin of the Rocks", the "Virgin and Child with St Anne and the Infant St John" and the "Gioconda" (Mona Lisa), all in the Louvre, and his "Last Supper", a mural (unfortunately much damaged) in the monastery of Santa Maria delle Grazie in Milan. A unique insight into his methods of working is given by his drawings and studies, in a great variety of different techniques.

The name of **Raphael** (*Raffaello Santi*, 1483–1520) calls up the image of a serene artist, beloved of gods and men, the painter of charming Madonnas ("Madonna della Sedia", Madonna Tempi, Sistine Madonna). In Rome he decorated the "Stanze" in the Vatican with wall and ceiling paintings, worked as an architect and directed excavations of ancient Rome.

Another important painter of the High Renaissance was *Giovanni Bellini* (1430–1516), who sought to achieve simplicity, grandeur and clarity. His Madonnas are built up symmetrically, in the form of a pyramid (*figura piramidale*). One of his principal works is an altarpiece, "Madonna Enthroned with Saints", in San Zaccaria in Venice. Among his pupils were Giorgione, Palma Vecchio and Titian. – *Vittore Carpaccio* (*c.* 1460–*c.* 1526) was a master of the narrative

picture and a vivid portrayer of the Venice of his day ("Miracle of the Cross"; scenes from the life of St Ursula, Accademia, Venice).

In Venice **Giorgione** (*Giorgio da Castelfranco*, 1478–1510) continued the tradition of Bellini and became the founder of the Venetian school of High Renaissance painting ("Three Philosophers", "Tempesta", "Sleeping Venus").

The neo-classical architecture of the **Late Renaissance**, exemplified by the work of *Andrea* **Palladio** (1508–80), provided models for the whole of Europe. Palladio was both a practical architect and an architectural theorist, author of "Quattro libri dell'architettura", and his return to the styles of ancient Rome was of major importance to the development of architecture. His principal works were the Basilica and the Palazzo Chiericati in Vicenza and the churches of San Giorgio Maggiore and the Redentore in Venice. A new type of building now developed in Italy, the *palazzo*, successor to the old castles built in towns in the Middle Ages (Palazzo Pitti and Palazzo Rucellai, Venice; Cancelleria and Palazzo dei Conservatori, Rome).

The great master of Venetian painting, already belonging to the Late Renaissance, was **Titian** (*Tiziano Vecellio*, 1477–1576), whose work in many ways looks forward to the Baroque ("Assunta" in the Frari church, Venice; "Worship of Venus" and "Bacchanal", both in the Prado, Madrid; portraits of Charles V, seated and on horseback; "Danaë", "Nymph and Shepherd", "Jacopo da Strada").

Palma Vecchio (1480–1528) also worked in Venice. His favourite theme was the "Sacra Conversazione" (altarpiece in Santa Maria Formosa, Venice). – **Tintoretto** (*Jacopo Robusti*, 1518–94), all of whose work was done in Venice, stood at the point of transition to the Mannerist and Baroque style (wall and ceiling paintings in Scuola di San Rocco, Venice; "Paradise", Sala del Maggior Consiglio, Doges' Palace, Venice).

Mannerism, the style which flourished in the second half of the 16th c., between the late Renaissance and the early Baroque period, was characterised by its delight in the unusual and bizarre: it loved allegory and metaphor and the extravagantly complex, corkscrew-like movement of the *figura serpentina*. Leading representatives of this period were the painters *Parmigianino* (Francesco Mazzola, 1503–40) and *Giuseppe Arcimbolda* (1527–93), who worked in Prague as court painter to Rudolf II, and *Giovanni da Bologna* (1529–1608), the most notable sculptor of the late Mannerist period. Mannerism achieved some of its most remarkable effects in the field of landscape gardening, in which natural scenery, architecture and grotesque sculpture in classical style were combined to produce startling results (e.g. in the Parco dei Mostri at Bomarzo, between Terni and Viterbo).

The age of **Baroque** was marked in architecture by the emergence of a new type of church. The rectangular nave now increasingly gave place to a centralised plan, crowned by a dome. An intermediate position is occupied by the Jesuit church of the Gesù in Rome, erected by *Giacomo Vignola* (1507–73). *Carlo Maderna* (1556–1629) lengthened St Peter's by the addition of a basilican nave (*c.* 1610).

In the *Seicento* (17th c.) the most influential Baroque architect and sculptor was *Giovanni Lorenzo* **Bernini** (1598–1680), who was responsible for the semicircular colonnades in St Peter's Square in Rome and the magnificent fountains in the Piazza Barberini (Triton Fountain) and Piazza Navona (Four Rivers Fountain). Among his other works of sculpture are his "Apollo and Daphne" (Villa Borghese, Rome), the tomb of Pope Urban VIII in St Peter's and "Santa Teresa" (Santa Maria della Vittoria, Rome).

Contemporary with Bernini was *Francesco Borromini* (1599–1667), a master of the flowing lines and curves characteristic of the High Baroque, whose work at first encountered violent opposition (San Carlo alle Quattro Fontane, Rome). – *Guarino Guarini* (1624–83) worked in a similar style, mainly in Turin. *Baldassare Longhena* (1604–82) worked in Venice (Palazzo Pesaro, Palazzo Rezzonico).

An early representative of Baroque painting was *Paolo* **Veronese** (*P. Caliari*, 1528–88), a master of illusionist painting who marshals large numbers of figures in lively attitudes of rather theatrical effect.

Michelangelo da **Caravaggio** (*M. Meristi*, 1573–1610) was the initiator of the realistic chiaroscuro painting which was to be so influential in the whole of European painting; his concern was to achieve a plastic modelling of his figures in a setting which was often merely hinted at.

Annibale Carracci (1560–1609) painted frescoes on themes from ancient mythology in the Palazzo Farnese in Rome and was also a considerable landscape painter (idealistic landscapes, often with mythological figures). *Domenichino* (Domenico Zampieri, 1581–1641) and *Guido Reni* (1575–1642) were two of Carracci's principal pupils. Other painters of this period were *Guercino* (Giovanni Francesco Barbieri, 1591–1666), *Pietro da Cortona* (1596–1669), the great master of illusionist ceiling painting (Palazzo Barberini and Palazzo Pamphili, Rome; Palazzo Pitti, Florence) and two other exponents of this art, *Andrea del Pozzo* (ceiling paintings in San Ignazio, Rome, 1685) and *Giovanni Battista* **Tiépolo** (1696–1770), both of whom also worked outside Italy.

Two artists of the period who worked in Naples were the Spanish painter Jusepe de Ribera, known as *Lo Spagnoletto* (1588–1652), and *Salvatore Rosa* (1615–73), a painter of very distinctive style who specialised in wild and rugged landscapes and battle scenes teeming with life and activity.

In the *Settecento* (18th c.) the leading place in Italian painting was taken by Venice. The principal masters of the **Rococo** period, in addition to Tiepolo (frescoes in the Villa Vilmarana, Vicenza; numerous altars and frescoes in Venice), were *Giovanni Battista Piazzetta* (1682–1754), the two **Canalettos**, *Antonio Canale* (1697–1768) and *Bernardo Bellotto* (1720–80), who painted views (*vedute*) of great architectural exactness (Canale of Venice, Bellotto of Vienna, Warsaw and Dresden), *Francesco Guardi* (1712–93), who painted lively scenes of Venetian life and festivals, and the woman painter *Rosalba Carriera* (1675–1757), who specialised in charming pastel portraits and miniatures.

In parallel with the characteristic painting of the Rococo period there was a neoclassical school of artists who devoted themselves to depicting the excavations of Pompeii and Herculaneum (which began in the first half of the 18th c.) and to romantically idealised pictures of the ruins of ancient Rome. The leading member of this group was *Giovanni Battista Piranesi* (1720–78), an architect and engraver working in Rome, who also produced eerie and grotesque architectural fantasies ("Prisons", 1745).

In this period the architect *Filippo Juvara* (1678–1736) built some notable palaces and churches in Piedmont. The 18th c. also saw the emergence in Italy of **Neo-Classicism**, the principal exponent of which was *Antonio* **Canova** (1757–1822). His tomb of Pope Clement XIV in Rome (1783–87) was a work of epoch-making significance, but perhaps his best-known work is the statue of Pauline Borghese (Villa Borghese, Rome, 1807).

In the *Ottocento* (19th c.) Italian architecture lived on the traditions of a great past (various brands of Historicism). *Giuseppe Piermarini* (1734–1808) was a typical representative of the neo-classical school of architecture which looked to antiquity for its models. Among the buildings he designed was Milan's great opera-house, La Scala. A master of neo-classical town planning was *Giuseppe Valadier*, who laid out the Piazza del Popolo in Rome. These trends appealed to the Fascist regime which rose to power after the First World War, and it was only with the formation of the group of architects known as *Gruppo 7* in 1927 that Italian architecture began to break out of its eclectic fossilisation.

The painting of the 19th c. was of purely local importance: as in the rest of Europe it was committed to the ideas of **Historicism**. Only *Giovanni Segantini* achieved international reputation as a Neo-Impressionist and Symbolist. The graphic artist *Alberto Martini* (1876–1954) also merits mention.

At the beginning of the *Novecento* (20th c.) the **Futurists** called for a break with tradition. Leading representatives of this movement were *Carlo Carrà* (1881–1966), *Umberto Boccioni* (1882–1916) and *Luigi Russolo* (1885–1947).

Giorgio de **Chirico** (1880–1978), regarded by many as the leading contemporary painter, founded the school of *pittura metafisica*, which came to an end about 1920. Its objectives were thereafter pursued by the Surrealists.

Giorgio Morandi (1890–1964) came under the influence of French Cubism at an early stage and was then associated with de Chirico for a time before evolving a very individual style of great clarity and purity. *Mario Sironi* (1885–1961) sought to find common ground between *pittura metafisica* and Cubism/Futurism. The painter and sculptor *Amedeo* **Modigliani** (1884–1920) worked principally in Paris, where he came under the influence of Cézanne and the Cubists.

After the Second World War there was a great industrial building boom (Olivetti building, Ivrea, 1948–50), and the Neo-Liberty architectural style, using Art Nouveau detailing, came to the fore (R. Gabetti, A. d'Isola). Some of the leading Italian industrial firms including Olivetti, Pirelli and Fiat promoted the development of modern architecture and industrial design (Pirelli building, 1955–58; and Torre Velasca, 1957, in Milan; car design, office machinery, furniture, lamps, etc.).

Pier Luigi **Nervi** (1891–1979), one of the leading architects of the 20th c., was a representative of "rationalist" architecture and has had great influence on whole generations of artists. He was one of the first to use reinforced concrete in architecture. He built exhibition halls (Turin, 1950 and 1961), sports stadia (Stadium, Florence, 1930–32; Large and Small Sports Palaces and Stadium for the Summer Olympics in Rome, 1956–59), airport terminals and office blocks (UNESCO, Paris, 1953–57).

In our own day Italian sculpture has at last produced successors to Canova in the persons of *Marino* **Marini** (b. 1901), famous for his horses and riders, and *Giacomo* **Manzù** (b. 1908), who returned to an older theme with his bronze doors decorated with reliefs (door of Salzburg Cathedral, 1959; Porta della Morte, St Peter's, Rome, 1964).

After 1945 **abstract painting and sculpture** came to the fore in Italy as in other Western countries, in a great range of variations (Tachism, Montage, "Lyrical Abstraction"). Leading exponents of non-representational painting are *Giuseppe Santomaso* (b. 1907), *Afro Basaldella* (b. 1912) and *Emilio Vedova* (b. 1919). In the field of sculpture there are a variety of trends, represented by *Fausto Melotti* (b. 1901), *C. Capello, P. Consagra* and the brothers *A.* and *G. Pomodoro* among others. The ingenious *Piero Manzoni* (1933–63) finally declared the whole earth to be a work of art and set himself up on a pedestal to become a forerunner of Concept Art (1962).

A central figure, at the intersection of the most varied artistic trends, was the painter and sculptor *Lucio* **Fontana** (1899–1968), who developed the theory of "Spatialism". *Antonio Corpora* (b. 1909) and other Italian artists became associated with the Ecole de Paris. Among painters of the younger generation are *Enrico Castellani* (b. 1930), *Lucio del Pezzo* (b. 1933), *Michelangelo Pistoletti* (b. 1933), *Agostino Bonalumi* (b. 1935), *Gino Marotta* (b. 1935), *Giuseppe Spagnulo* (b. 1936), *Mario Ceroli* (b. 1938), *Ugo La Pietra* (b. 1938), *Giulio Paolini* (b. 1940) and *Gianni Piacentino* (b. 1945).

As "objective artists" of the Arte Povera school *Mario Merz* (b. 1925), *Giovanni Anselmo* (b. 1934), *Alighiero Boetti* (b. 1940), *Piero Gilardi* (b. 1942) and *Gilberto Zorio* (b. 1944) have made a name for themselves.

Finally mention should be made of the Italian school of **Photorealism**, represented by *Gianni Bertini* (b. 1922), *Vincenzo Agnetti* (b. 1926), *Carlo Massimo Asnaghi* (b. 1927), *Luca Patella* (b. 1934), *Mario Schifano* (b. 1934), *Antonio Paradiso* (b. 1936), *Aldo Tagliaferro* (b. 1936), *Franco Vaccari* (b. 1936), *Bruno di Bello* (b. 1938), *Ketty La Rocca* (b. 1938), *Luigi Ontani* (b. 1943), *Elio Mariani* (b. 1943) and *Claudio Parmiggiani* (b. 1943).

Music

Among all the countries of the West the Italian peninsula has the richest inheritance of vocal music from the early Christian period, with large stores of *early liturgical music* (Milan, Rome, Benevento). The medieval neums (an early form of musical notation) have not yet been satisfactorily deciphered, but nevertheless reflect, in their short-paced melodic structure, a national characteristic and probably also the influence of the folk music of southern Italy. This early music was supported by the theoretical writings of *St Augustine* ("De musica", 387–389) and *Boëthius* ("De institutione musicae", *c.* 500). The father of western church singing was *St Ambrose*, bishop of Milan in the 4th c., who introduced the Ambrosian Liturgy still used in parts of northern Italy. This was the foundation on which Pope *Gregory the Great* developed *Gregorian chant* at the end of the 6th c.

In the 11th c. *Guido of Arezzo* (992–1050) devised a new system of musical notation, the origin of the system still used today.

The origins of unison liturgical singing (plainsong) are closely bound up with folk music, Greco-Roman and Jewish traditions. The folk music, which was for long repressed by the Church, enjoyed a revival between the 11th and 13th c. in the form of *laudi* and *ballati*.

At the beginning of the 14th c. the stylistically more refined art of the *Renaissance* developed in Italy, facilitated by the increasing importance of Italian as a literary language (Dante, Petrarch, Boccaccio). Forms like the *caccia*, the ballade and the madrigal sought to give expression to the new spirit, the most notable figures in this field being *Jacopo da Bologna* (14th c.), *Batilinus of Padua* (*c.* 1400) and above all the poet and organist *Francesco Landino* (1325–97), the leading representative of the Florentine "Ars Nova".

Dutch and Flemish composers, among them *Johannes Ciconia* (1335–1411), *Guillaume Dufay* (*c.* 1400–74) and *Heinrich Isaac* (1450–1517), dominated musical life at the Italian princely courts in the 15th and early 16th c. In addition to the madrigal, the main form of secular music, and the motet and mass in religious music a number of forms derived from folk music also came into vogue – the *frottola*, the villanelle, the *villota*, the laud and, from the late 15th c., the *canti carnascialeschi*.

In the 16th c. differences began to arise between the musical centres of Venice and Naples on the one hand and Rome on the other. In the Papal chapel in Rome there grew up a *Roman school*, the most famous representative of which was *Giovanni Pierluigi* **Palestrina** (1525–94). In his contrapuntally perfect masses, motets and other works he brought *a cappella* polyphony to a pitch of perfection which marked one of the peaks of Roman Catholic Renaissance *church music*. In Venice *Andrea Gabrieli* (1515–86) and his nephew *Giovanni Gabrieli* (1557–1612) wrote music for several choirs (*canzoni*, sonatas; 3–22 voices), which provided a basis for the development of independent orchestral and chamber music.

A group of poets (O. Rinuccini, 1562–1621, and others), musicians (D. di Cavalieri, 1550–1602; J. Peri, 1561–1633; etc.) and humanist scholars who met in the houses of counts Bardi and Corsi in Florence (the "Camarata fiorentina") were concerned to renew ancient tragedy with their music and to achieve a harmonious relationship between words and music. This gave rise in the 16th c. to *solo singing* with a basso continuo accompaniment.

The first operas were now composed by *Jacopo Peri* ("Dafne", 1594) and *Giulio Caccini* ("Euridice", 1600).

With the Baroque began a period which was of the greatest importance for the development of music throughout Europe right down to the 20th c. In the work of *Claudio* **Monteverdi** (1567–1643) the *opera* had its first flowering ("L'Incoronazione di Poppea", "Orfeo"). He brought opera out of its original narrow aristocratic milieu and made it available to a wider public, a change reflected in the opening of the first opera-house in Venice in 1637. Among Venetian operatic composers were *Francesco Vacalli* (1602–76) and *Marc'Antonio Cesti* (1623–69). Opera also developed in Rome and Naples. Recitative and the *da* *capo* aria now evolved. The work of the leading representatives of *opera seria*, like *Alessandro* **Scarlatti** (1660–1725), *Leonardo Vinci* (1690–1730) and *Leonardo Leo* (1694–1744), influenced foreign operatic composers like Handel, Gluck and Mozart. *Opera seria*, however, soon degenerated into sterility, since it increasingly developed into virtuoso concert opera, in which the voices of the castrati and the ingenious stage machinery were more important than the content and the musical and dramatic expression.

From Naples and Rome *opera buffa* set out on its victorious progress through Europe. The works of *Giovanni* **Pergolesi** (1710–36: "La Serva Padrona"), *Giovanni Paisiello* (1740–1816: "The Barber of Seville") and *Domenico Cimarosa* (1749–1801: "The Secret Marriage") are still performed today.

Along with opera the *oratorio* and the *cantata* also developed (G. Carissimi, 1605–74; A. Stradella, 1641–82).

The *instrumental music* of the 17th c. also evolved an expressive virtuoso style and a variety of new forms (sonata, concerto grosso, overture, suite, concerto with soloist). For long the keyboard instruments (organ, harpsichord) took pride of place, and *Girolamo Frescobaldi* (1583–1643) wrote numerous compositions for these instruments (*canzoni*, partitas, toccatas, etc.). From about 1650, however, the Italian tradition of violin-playing was established, beginning with *Arcangelo Corelli* (1653–1713) and fostered by the violin-making skill of the Amati, Stradivari and Guarneri families. The works of *Antonio* **Vivaldi** (*c.* 1678–1741), *Domenico Scarlatti* (1685–1757), *Giuseppe Tartini* (1692–1770), *Luigi Boccherini* (1743–1805) and *Muzio Clementi* (1752–1843), which gave a prominent place to stringed instruments, promoted the development of instrumental music as an independent form. In the 19th c. *Niccolò Paganini* (1782–1840) carried the virtuoso violin concerto to a peak of perfection.

In the Italian music of the 19th c. *opera* played a central part. The best-known operatic composers in the first half of the century were *Gaetano Donizetti*

(1797–1848: "L'elisir d'amore", "Lucia di Lammermoor", "Don Pasquale"), *Vincenzo Bellini* (1801–35: "Norma", "La Sonnambula") and *Gioacchino Rossini* (1792–1868: "The Barber of Seville", "William Tell", "The Thieving Magpie").

Giuseppe **Verdi** (1813–1901), whose early works (particularly "Nabucco") were very much in tune with the aspirations of the Risorgimento, was the outstanding Italian artistic personality in the second half of the 19th c. The operas he composed between 1851 and 1853 ("Rigoletto", "Il Trovatore" and "La Traviata") made him famous in Italy, but it was only with his late works ("Don Carlos", 1867; "Aida", 1871; "Otello", 1887; "Falstaff", 1893) that he achieved international recognition and became accepted as one of the world's great operatic composers. – Other composers who worked in Verdi's shadow were *Arrigo Boito* (1842–1918: "Mefistofele"), *Umberto Giordano* (1867–1948: "Andrea Chénier") and *Amilcare Ponchielli* (1834–96: "La Gioconda").

The opera "Cavalleria Rusticana" by *Pietro Mascagni* (1863–1945) was seen as the first work in the style known as Verismo (musical naturalism), another representative of which was *Ruggiero Leoncavallo* (1858–1919: "Pagliacci"). The works of *Giacomo* **Puccini** (1858–1924: "La Bohème", "Tosca", "Madame Butterfly", "Gianni Schicchi", "Turandot") formed the last great high point of Italian opera. – *Ermanno Wolf-Ferrari* (1876–1948: "I Quattro Rusteghi") returned to the tradition of *opera buffa*.

The Italian folk song now spread over the world, with such popular titles as "O Sole mio".

In the 20th c. instrumental music once again came into its own. The compositions of *Ottorino Respighi* (1879–1936) are notable for their rich musical colour. *Ildebrando Pizzetti* (1880–1968), *Gian Francesco Malipiero* (1882–1973) and *Alfredo Casella* (1883–1947) sought to achieve a synthesis between traditional and modern music.

Goffredo Petrassi (b. 1904), *Luigi Dallapiccola* (1904–75), *Mario Peragallo* (b. 1910), *Bruno Maderna* (1921–73), who was the first to combine tape-recorded and instrumental music, and *Luigi Nono* (b. 1924) largely follow the compositional principles of the modern Western European school (12-tone music, serialism, punctualism).

The problem of Italy's Fascist past is reflected in the opera "La Speranza" (1970) by *Franco Mannino* (b. 1924). – Since 1956 Milan Radio has had a special studio for electronic music, directed by *Luciano Berio* (b. 1925).

Economy

Italy is made up of two very different economic spheres. *Northern Italy* is an industrial region with excellent communications and a flourishing economy, while *Southern Italy*, the *Mezzogiorno*, with a backward development and system of communications, is almost purely agricultural, with low yields per acre and only a few developing industrial centres – around Rome and Bari and in southern and eastern Sicily. One of the poorest regions in Europe is Sardinia, whose inhabitants live almost exclusively from pastoral farming, fishing and in quite recent years tourism.

Italy is ill provided with minerals. In addition to natural gas and the oil which has recently been discovered in the Po plain there are modest quantities of iron ore and mercury in Tuscany, the old-established marble quarries of Carrara and the now declining industry of sulphur extraction in Sicily, the Marches and Emilia. The coal of Sardinia is barely economic to work and not suitable for industrial use. Most of the raw materials Italy needs have to be imported in large quantities, and a major part is therefore played by the various processing industries, mostly established in northern Italy, where they have the advantage of good communications and transport facilities as well as local sources of power (hydroelectric power from the Alps, natural gas from the Po plain), supplemented by imports of oil from North Africa.

The metal-working industries (car manufacture, engineering) in the north-western part of the Po plain have an international reputation, and Italian textiles (silkworm culture in Venetia, fashion goods in Milan), shoes and chemical products are also famous. Other major industries are publishing and printing, styling and design, and the tourist industry, the main centres of which are also in the north (Adriatic coast, Riviera, Alps).

A high degree of mechanisation and the development of progressive co-operative methods have made the Po plain one of Italy's leading agricultural regions, producing wheat, rice and maize as well as most of the country's meat and milk (65% of the total Italian stock of cattle). At the foot of the Alps the main products are fruit (apples, peaches and walnuts in the Alto Adige and the Adige valley) and wine; at high altitudes there are pastoral farming, forestry and tourism (with both summer resorts and winter sports centres).

The Apennines are economically almost undeveloped, and little use is made of their extensive tracts of forest. The pastoral economy of the upland regions is interrupted in the basins of Tuscany and Umbria by Mediterranean *cultura mista* (corn, pulses, fruit, olives, wine). From Tuscany comes the famous Chianti wine.

In spite of the predominance of agriculture in the South, yields fall far below the land's potential as a result of inefficient farming methods on family holdings which are mostly of very small size. The most productive crops are the citrus fruits grown in terraced plantations on the volcanic soil round Vesuvius and Etna.

Fishing is only of regional significance, and the fishing fleet is in need of modernisation. The catches are insufficient to meet the demand and have to be supplemented by imports.

The reduction of the economic disparity between the northern and southern parts of the country and the drift of population from the South to northern Italy, the highly industrialised countries N of the

Alps and overseas have presented Italy with grave problems; and these problems are also the concern of Italy's partners in the European Community. Various development programmes have been initiated, designed to attract new industries by improvement of the infrastructure, tax concessions and financial assistance from the Cassa per il Mezzogiorno. Holding companies have been set up to be responsible for the provision of power supplies (ENI, Ente Nazionale Idrocarburi) and state control of the main key industries and communications (IRI, Istituto per la Ricostruzione Industriale). The great efforts which have been made to develop the economy of the Mezzogiorno, however, have not been as successful as was hoped; and frequent strikes have done grave harm to the economy of the country as a whole and to the industrial development of southern Italy in particular.

More than 90% of Italian firms have fewer than ten employees – a great number of small businesses supplying a small number of large concerns, mainly in the N. The broad band of efficient firms of medium size which is found in other European countries is almost entirely lacking in Italy.

Italy ranks among the ten most export-oriented countries in the world. Its principal trading partners are the EEC countries and North America; its main exports are motor vehicles and machinery (35%), textiles and shoes (20%), agricultural produce and flowers. In addition the tourist trade is a major earner of foreign currency, though increasingly exposed to competition from countries with a lower cost of living. The main import is oil from Algeria and Libya. A large gas pipeline to run from Sicily under the Strait of Messina into Calabria and on to La Spezia is at present under construction.

With some 285,000 km of national trunk roads and 5500 km of motorways, the Italian road network is one of the best in Europe. The Autostrada del Sole ("Motorway of the Sun") runs down the whole country from N to S, providing a magnificent through route for long-distance traffic. The quite substantial toll charges on the motorways, however, lead many motorists to prefer the cheaper but more troublesome journey on the overcrowded national highways; and the reduced toll revenues are no longer sufficient to cover the running costs of the motorways.

Italy's 20,000 km of railway lines serve all towns of any size, extending all the way down to Sicily. There is, however, the same tendency as in other countries for both passenger and goods traffic to switch from rail to road.

The state-owned national airline, *Alitalia*, is equipped with modern aircraft and flies all over the world. Domestic air services are provided by the *Itavia* and *Alisarda* companies.

Italy has a merchant shipping fleet with a considerable tonnage of relatively new vessels. The major ports of Genoa, Venice, Trieste, Naples, Livorno, Palermo and Augusta handle a large volume of traffic, including in particular the country's extensive imports of oil. Inland navigation is of little consequence.

Italy
A to Z

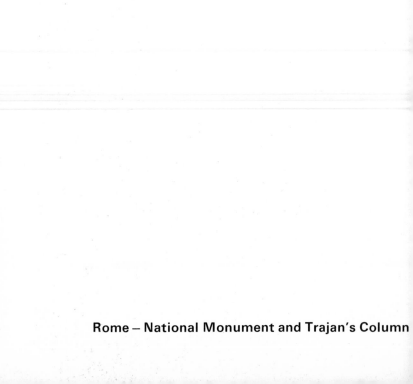

Rome – National Monument and Trajan's Column

Abruzzi

ⓘ **EPT L'Aquila**, Piazza S. Maria de Paganica,
I-67100 L'Aquila (AQ);
tel. (0862) 2 51 40–9.
EPT Chieti, Via B. Spaventa 29 (Palazzo INAIL),
I-66100 Chieti (CH);
tel. (0871) 6 52 31–2.
EPT Pescara, Via Fabrizi 171–3,
I-65100 Pescara (PE);
tel. (085) 2 27 07.
EPT Teramo, Via del Castello 10,
I-64100 Teramo (TE);
tel. (0861) 5 13 57.

The Abruzzi, the highest and wildest part of the Apennines, cover an area of 10,794 sq. km in eastern Central Italy, extending from the watershed of the Central Apennines to the Adriatic and taking in the four provinces of L'Aquila degli Abruzzi, Pescara, Chieti and Teramo. They are bounded on the N by the Marche, on the W by Latium and on the SE by Molise, with which they have been combined since 1963 to form the administrative unit of Abruzzi e Molise.

Gran Sasso d'Italia

The topography of the Abruzzi is dominated by three mighty mountain chains, the most easterly and highest of which contains the highest peaks in the peninsula, in the *Gran Sasso d'Italia group (Corno Grande, 2914 m). Between these chains lie the central uplands of the Abruzzi, in which the longitudinal valley of the Aterno, the high valleys of L'Aquila and Sulmona and the wide and fertile Fucino basin form substantial indentations. The north-eastern part, beyond the Gran Sasso massif, is occupied by an

upland region traversed by numerous rivers which slopes down gradually towards the Adriatic. Along the coast are a string of attractive seaside resorts.

With the exception of certain areas, particularly in the S and in the lower-lying regions, the Abruzzi are sparsely wooded and infertile, with much karstic terrain, a harsh climate and an abundance of snow. Arable farming is possible only in the valleys and depressions, particularly in the Fucino basin; the upland regions are good only for grazing. The population of 122,000 is concentrated in the towns of L'Aquila, Teramo, Pescara, Sulmona and Avezzano; the rest is only thinly settled. The revenue from agriculture has been supplemented in more recent years by the rapid development of tourism, particularly in the Gran Sasso, which has been equipped with facilities for winter sports (cableway to Campo Imperatore, 2130 m).

The southernmost part of the Abruzzi is occupied by the *Abruzzi National Park (Parco Nazionale d'Abruzzo) with its beautiful beech forests. The park, covering an area of some 74,000 acres in the valley of the upper Sangro and its numerous side valleys, is ideally suited for walkers and climbers with its network of footpaths and its mountain huts. It was established in 1921 as a nature reserve to protect the landscape, flora and fauna of the Abruzzi. Among the mountain creatures which can still be encountered here are the Abruzzi brown bear (Ursus arctos marsicanus), the Abruzzi chamois (Rupicapra rupicapra ornata), the Apennine wolf (Canis lupus italicus) and the golden eagle.

The central point of the park is the village of Pescasséroli in the Sangro valley (alt. 1167 m; *Grand Hotel del Parco, I, 236 b., SP), which is frequented both by summer holidaymakers and winter sports enthusiasts (enclosures in which animals can live in natural surroundings, botanic garden, museum on the natural history of the park). The philosopher Benedetto Croce (1866–1952) was born here. 5 km SE is the village of Opi, starting point for the very rewarding climb of Monte Marsicano (2242 m).

In the northern Abruzzi is the provincial capital of **Téramo** (alt. 265 m; pop. 25,000; hotels: Michelangelo, II, 250 b.,

SP; Sporting, II, 105 b., SP; Abruzzi, II, 81 b.; etc.). In the centre of the town is the Piazza Orsini, with the Town Hall, the *Bishop's Palace* and the cathedral (12th c., restored 1932; Romanesque doorway of 1332), which contains a silver altar frontal by Nicola da Guardiagrele (1433–48). SE of the cathedral are the remains of a Roman amphitheatre. – The W front of the cathedral faces on to the Piazza dei Martiri della Libertà, from which the Corso San Giorgio, the town's main street, runs to the municipal park (small local museum).

In the NW corner of the *Fucino basin* (Piana del Fucino, alt. 655–670 m), once Italy's largest lake, which was drained in 1875, is **Avezzano** (alt. 698 m; pop. 30,000; hotels: Nuova Italia, II, 110 b.; Principe, II, 90 b.; etc.). The town was almost completely destroyed by an earthquake in 1915 in which 30,000 people lost their lives. – An interesting excursion can be made to *Albe* (7 km N), with the remains of the strongly fortified ancient town of **Alba Fucens**, which belonged to the Aequi (massive town walls, baths, amphitheatre, basilica); 11th c. Romanesque church built into a temple of Apollo.

Above the Pescara valley, in a situation affording extensive views, is **Chieti** (alt. 330 m; pop. 55,000; hotels: Grande Albergo Abruzzo, II, 90 b.; Sole, II, 75 b.; etc.), capital of the province of the same name and the see of an archbishop. In Piazza Vittorio Emanuele are the Town Hall (collection of pictures) and the Gothic cathedral of San Giustino, with a Baroque interior. From the back of the Town Hall the town's principal street, Corso Marrucino, runs SW, passing near a group of three temples of the 1st c. A.D. (to right), to the municipal park and the Villa Comunale (*views). In the Villa Comunale is the *National Museum of Antiquities (Museo Nazionale di Antichità), with a remarkable collection of prehistoric and Roman material. – Just below Strada Marrucina, which flanks the E side of the Town Hall, is a large rock-cut Roman cistern, with the remains of the baths which it supplied.

On the Adriatic coast, astride the River Pescara, which reaches the sea here, is the provincial capital of **Pescara** (alt. 6 m; pop. 120,000; hotels: *Esplanade, I, 278 b.; *Singleton, I, 132 b.; *Carlton, I, 101 b.; Regent, II, 254 b.; Plaza Moderno, II, 160 b.; Astoria, II, 116 b.; Ambra, III, 100 b.; etc.). The town was badly damaged during the Second World War but has been rebuilt on an impressive scale. In Piazza dei Vestini, on the left bank of the river, is the imposing Palazzo della Prefettura. 0·5 km S, on the other side of the river, is the Templo della Conciliazione, built 1935–38 to commemorate the Lateran treaties. – There are bathing beaches in the resorts N and S of the town.

Along the Adriatic coast is a whole series of resorts, some of them with very beautiful beaches – from N to S *Martinsicuro, Alba Adriática, Tortoreto Lido* (5 km W, the little medieval town of *Tortoreto Alto*), *Giulianova Lido, Roseto degli Abruzzi* (formerly Rosburgo), *Pineto* (11 km W, the little town of *Atri*, with a Gothic cathedral containing fine frescoes), *Silvi Marina, Montesilvano, Francavilla al Mare, Ortona* (ruined castle with fine *views), *San Vito Chietino* (12 km SW, the walled town of *Lanciano*, with a cathedral dating from 1227), *Fossacésia Marina* (near which is the Romanesque basilica of San Giovanni in Vénere, 8th–13th c.) and *Vasto*, with several interesting churches and, in the cathedral square, the Palazzo d'Avalos.

Agrigento

Region: Sicilia. – Province: Agrigento (AG).
Altitude: 326 m. – Population: 50,000.
Post code: I-92100. – Dialling code: 0922.
(i) **AA**, Piazzale Roma;
    tel. 2 04 54.
EPT, Viale della Vittoria 255;
    tel. 2 69 26.
ACI, Via San Vita 25;
    tel. 2 65 01.
TCI, Piazza Vittorio Emanuele;
    tel. 2 03 91.

HOTELS. – *Jolly dei Templi*, 5 km SE on S.S. 115, Villaggio Mosè, I, 292 b., SP; *Villa Athena*, in the temple area, I, 56 b., SP; *Akrabello*, 6 km SE at Parco Angeli, II, 220 b., SP; *Della Valle*, Via dei Templi 94, II, 164 b.; *Belvedere*, Via San Vito 20, III, 63 b.; etc.

Agrigento, one of the most beautifully situated towns in Sicily, half way along the S coast, is one of the island's principal tourist attractions with its magnificent ruined ⁕⁕temples. The skyline of the town itself, however, has been drastically changed by the tall blocks of new

housing developments, particularly on the S side of the old town.

HISTORY. – Agrigento was founded in 582 B.C., under the name of *Akragas*, by settlers from the Greek colony of Gela, 80 km SE. Magnificently situated on a ridge between the rivers *Akragas* (the modern *San Biagio*) and *Hypsas* (*Santa Anna*), it was celebrated by Pindar as "the fairest city of mortal men". On the N side of the hill, now occupied by the modern town, was the acropolis, and the ancient city lay to the S of this on land sloping down gradually towards the sea, on the site now marked by the extensive remains of its walls and temples. The town was mostly ruled by tyrants, one of whom, *Phalaris* (c. 549 B.C.), was notorious for his cruelty: he is said to have sacrificed his enemies to Zeus Atabyrios by roasting them in a brazen bull. Akragas rose to wealth and power, at first by war and later by trade with Carthage, and some of its citizens lived in princely state. It reached its peak of prosperity as a free state under the leadership of *Empedocles* (who died c. 424 B.C.), but soon afterwards (406 B.C.) succumbed to the Carthaginians. The town was plundered, its art treasures carried off to Carthage and the temples set on fire. – As the Roman *Agrigentum* (from 210 B.C.) the town was a place of no consequence. In 828 it was taken by the Saracens and grew to rival Palermo. In 1086 the Norman ruler *Roger I* established a bishopric here which developed during the Middle Ages into the richest in Sicily. Until 1927 the town was known by its Saracenic name of *Girgenti*. – Agrigento was the birthplace of the dramatist *Luigi Pirandello* (1867–1936).

SIGHTS. – At the NW corner of the old town, a huddle of narrow winding streets, is the **Cathedral**, built on the foundation of a temple of Jupiter of the 6th c. B.C. It was begun in the 11th c., enlarged in the 13th and 14th c. and largely remodelled in the 16th–17th c. A landslip in 1966 caused considerable damage, now mostly made good. At the end of the N aisle is the *Capella de Marinis*, with the tomb of Gaspare de Marinis (1492). In the S transept is the Cappella de S. Gerlando, with a fine Gothic doorway, which contains a silver reliquary (1639) with the remains of S. Gerlando, first bishop of Agrigento. From the unfinished campanile (14th c.) there are fine *views. W of the cathedral is the *Diocesan Museum*.

To the S of the old town, in Piazza Pirandello, is the *Museo Civico* (Civic Museum) (medieval and modern art, pictures by Sicilian artists).

The principal street of the town is the busy *Via Atenea*, which runs E from the Piazza del Municipio to the Piazzale Roma. 1·5 km farther E, in a private garden, is the **Rupe Atenea** (Rock of Athena, 351 m), from which there are extensive views.

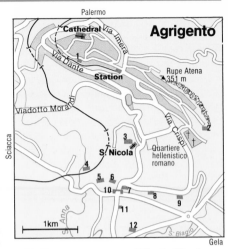

1 Civic Museum
2 Temple of Ceres and Proserpine
3 Archaeological Museum
4 Temple of Vulcan
5 Temple of Castor and Pollux
6 Temple of Zeus
7 Temple of Hercules
8 Temple of Concord
9 Temple of Juno
10 Porta Aurea
11 Tomb of Theron
12 Temple of Aesculapius

The temples are reached by following the signposted *Passeggiata archeologica*, which runs SE along *Via Crispi* from Piazza Marconi (railway station), immediately S of the Piazzale Roma. – In 1 km a road goes off on the left to the *cemetery*, at the SE corner of which are remains of the Greek town walls. From here it is 0·5 km E on the stony ancient road to the *Temple of Ceres and Proserpine* (*Tempio di Demetra*), standing on high ground; originally built about 470 B.C., it was converted by the Normans into the little *church of San Biagio*. To the E, below the terrace, is a *cave sanctuary of Demeter* (c. 650 B.C.).

Soon afterwards another road branches off Via Crispi on the left to the Temple of Juno Lacinia and the road to Gela (S.S. 115). In another 0·5 km a recently excavated section of the *Greco-Roman city* (4th c. B.C. to 5th c. A.D.: fine wall paintings and mosaic pavements) is passed on the left, and 300 m beyond this, on the right, is the **National Archaeological Museum** (*Museo Archeologico Nazionale*), with prehistoric material, ancient sarcophagi, vases, coins and architectural fragments; particularly fine is a marble statue of an *ephebe (c. 490 B.C.). Immediately S of the museum is the little Gothic *church of San Nicola* (13th c.; fine doorway), which contains an ancient marble *sarcophagus carved with scenes from the story of Phaedra and Hippolytus. Close to the church, to the W, are the so-called *Oratory of Phalaris* and an almost square *cella*, the tomb of a Roman matron (1st c. B.C.).

1 km beyond San Nicola the road reaches the entrance to the enclosed **Temple Area** (freely open at all times). To the right is the Temple of Zeus; to the left, near the S wall of the ancient city, the so-called **Temple of Hercules** (*Tempio di Ércole*, 6th c. B.C.), with eight columns on the S side (out of the original 38) which were re-erected in 1923.

From the Temple of Hercules a new road runs E past the *Villa Aurea* (offices of the Temple Area administration; temporary exhibitions) to the Doric ****Temple of Concord** (5th c. B.C.; converted into a church in the Middle Ages), with all its 34 columns still standing, which ranks with the Theseion in Athens as the best preserved ancient temple.

Some 700 m farther E, magnificently situated above a steep escarpment at the SE corner of the ancient city, near the road to Gela, is the so-called ****Temple of Juno Lacinia** (second half of 5th c. B.C.), a classic example of the Doric style. The temple, actually dedicated to Hera, has 25 complete columns standing and nine others partly re-erected.

Between the temples of Hercules and Zeus is the *Porta Aurea* or harbour gate, through which passes the road to *Porto Empédocle* (10 km SW; pop. 20,000) and the ancient port, which lay due S at the mouth of the River San Biagio. Outside the Porta Aurea is the so-called **Tomb of Theron** (*Tomba di Terone*), the remains of a tower-like Roman mausoleum.

NW of the Porta Aurea are the ruins of the unfinished **Temple of Zeus** (*Tempio de Giove Olimpico*, 5th c. B.C.), the largest temple of Greek antiquity, 113 m long (Temple G at Selinunte 111 m; Artemision, Ephesus, 109 m; Parthenon, Athens, 70 m). The entablature was probably supported by the huge Telamones or Atlas figures whose remains were found on the site; one of them, restored (lying on the ground), measures 7·75 m ("il Gigante").

W of the Temple of Zeus is the **Temple of Castor and Pollux** (*Tempio de Castore e Polluce*) or Temple of the Dioscuri, four

Temple of Castor and Pollux, Agrigento

columns of which have been re-erected. A little way N is the *Sanctuary of the Chthonic Divinities* (Santuario delle Divinità Ctonie, 6th c. B.C.), a unique cult place dedicated to the divinities of the underworld (probably Demeter and Persephone). The remains of 12 altars and eight small temples in the form of treasuries have been excavated.

Farther to the NW, beyond the railway, are remains of the so-called *Temple of Vulcan* (*c.* 470 B.C.), from which there is a view of the main range of temples.

Alto Adige (South Tirol)

Region: Trentino/Alto Adige. – Province: Bolzano (BZ).

ⓘ **EPT Bolzano**, Piazza Walther 77, I-39100 Bolzano (BZ); tel. (0471) 2 69 91.

The *Alto Adige (Upper Adige), in the extreme N of Italy, is an area of very distinctive character which has retained much of its individuality in spite of its development into a popular holiday and tourist region. The population includes a majority of German-speakers, to whom it is South Tirol (Südtirol), and the place-names have usually two forms, Italian and German. The situation of Alto Adige on the southern fringe of the Alps gives

it a varied range of topography and scenery, from the eternal snow of the great glaciated peaks of the Central Alps and the Ortles (Ortler) group (3902 m) to the Mediterranean climate and the vineyards of the Bolzano (Bozen: alt. 265 m) and Merano (Meran) areas.

The geological structure is determined by the girdle of ancient Alpine rocks (gneisses, granites, schists and quartz phyllites) in the N and W, the considerable area of dolomitic limestone crags in the E and the great spread of porphyries round Bolzano in the S, extending far into the neighbouring Trentino.

Extending S from the Résia (Reschen) pass on the frontier with Austria is the upper Adige (Etsch) valley, which from here to Merano is known as the Val Venosta (Vintschgau), with the most massive peaks (c. 3000 m) of the Eastern Alps. At Merano the Val Passiria (Passeiertal) branches off and runs N to the Passo di Monte Giovo (Jaufenpass, 2094 m). Beyond this is Vipiteno (Sterzing) in the Isarco (Eisack) valley, which descends from the Brenner and some distance farther S is joined by the Pustería (Puster) valley.

Between the Valtellina, the Val Venosta and the upper Noce valley (Val di Sole and Val di Non) extends the Ortles (Ortler) group, a range of mainly crystalline rocks but with its highest peaks, Ortles (Ortler, 3902 m) and the majestic Gran Zebrù (Königsspitze, 3859 m), built up from Triassic limestones. On the N side of the range are the Solda (Sulden), Martello (Martell) and Último (Ulten) valleys, on the W the Valfurva and on the S the Péio and Rabbi valleys, all much glaciated in the upper reaches. To the S of the Passo di Tonale (1883 m), bounded on the W by the Oglio valley (Val Camónica) and on the E by the Sarca valley, is the Adamello-Presanella group (Cima Presanella, 3556 m; Monte Adamello, 3554 m), consisting mainly of tonalites, through which runs the wild Val di Génova with its waterfalls.

Along the E side of the Ortles and Adamello-Presanella groups run the Valli Giudicarie (the middle valley of the Sarca and upper valley of the Chiesa or Chies),

one of the most striking fault lines in the Alps. To the E of this line the land has sunk 200 m in places, so that here, in contrast to the crystalline Central Alps, the substance of the mountains is made up of Triassic and Jurassic dolomites and limestones. The best-known range is the dolomitic Brenta group (Cima Tosa, 3173 m), which in spite of its geographical separation from the main Dolomites E of the Adige ranks equal with them in the magnificence of its mountain scenery. A parallel chain to the E, with Monte Roén (2116 m) towards its northern end, falls down in sheer limestone walls to the morainic uplands on the upper Adige in the N and the wide Adige valley, covered with later fluvial deposits, farther S.

S of the Pustería valley and to a lesser extent in the north-eastern Sarentine Alps (Sarntaler Alpen) is a zone of quartz phyllites, mainly dark coloured. In Rasciesa (Raschötz, 2283 m) and the southern Sarentine Alps this is overlaid by the Bolzano porphyries, hard reddish volcanic rocks of the Permian period. This porphyry zone, extending S as far as the Trento region and reaching its highest point in the Lagorai chain (Cima de Cece, 2772 m) near Predazzo, is slashed by gorge-like valleys, notably the Val d'Ega (Eggental) at Bolzano and the Tires valley (Tierser Tal). The infertile porphyry has been covered, particularly on the Renón (Ritten) by old moraines, which have been eroded by heavy rain, leaving the famous "earth pillars" capped by their protective boulders. – The porphyries combine with melaphyres and sandstones of the late Permian, soft schists, clays and variegated marls of the Lower Triassic and intrusions of dark-coloured lavas and volcanic tuffs to form the undulating basement formation, covered with beautiful Alpine meadows and coniferous forests, of the Dolomites (see p. 103).

The CLIMATE of the region reflects its geographical diversity, ranging from the Alpine conditions of the mountain valleys with their abundance of snow through the normal European climate of the intermediate areas to the Mediterranean type, with mild winters and sometimes very hot summers, of the wide valleys of the Adige and the Isarco with their southern exposure and their sheltered situation, protected from the N winds by the mountains. The Val Venosta in the W of the region has the reputation of being the driest valley in the Eastern Alps; its upper reaches have an Alpine climate, but its lower course approximates to the climatic pattern of Merano.

The FLORA and FAUNA vary according to the climate. Differences in the Alpine flora reflect differences in the subsoil – ancient rocks or dolomitic limestones – and the *Alpe di Siusi* (Seiser Alm) offers a famous example of this diversity. The flora of the south is characterised by the zone of downy oaks, interspersed with some evergreen species, which reaches up from Lake Garda and by the famous parks and gardens of Bressanone, Bolzano and Merano, in which olives, holm-oaks and winter jasmine flourish as well as various exotic species. These climatic islands were used for wine-growing at a very early period, in pre-Roman times, and the vine now extends as far N as Bressanone and Silandro (Schlanders) and to an altitude of around 800 m. No less famous than the wines of the Alto Adige are the fruit grown in the valleys, and the blossoming orchards are one of the great sights of the region at Easter. – The animals and fishes of the Alto Adige have maintained their numbers as a result of statutory regulation, and there are one or two notable representatives of typically southern fauna like the green lizard, the cicada and the praying mantis.

All Alpine species of plants and shrubs are statutorily protected in the Alto Adige. The uprooting of plants and the breaking off of parts of plants are prohibited, but it is permissible to pick up to 10 flowers (i.e. flower stems) per person per day.
The picking of any plants or parts of the following is **strictly prohibited** on pain of a substantial fine:
Yellow Alpine anemone (*Anemone alpina* L., subsp. *sulphurea*)
Lady's slipper (*Cypripedium calceolus* L.)
Common mezereon (*Daphne mezereum* L.)
Garland flower (*Daphne cneorum* L.)
Striated mezereon (*Daphne striata* Tratt.)
Fire lily (*Lilium bulbiferum* L.)
Martagon lily (*Lilium martagon* L.)
Spring snowflake (*Leucojum vernum* L.)
Poet's narcissus (*Narcissus poeticus* L.)
White water-lily (*Nymphaea alba* L.)
Yellow water-lily (*Nuphar lutea* L.)
Bulrush (*Typha latifolia* L.)
Lesser bulrush (*Typha angustifolia* L.)
Dwarf bulrush (*Typha minima* Hoppe)
Burning bush (*Dictamnus albus* L.)
Peony (*Paeonia officinalis* L.)
Auricula (*Primula auricula* L.)
Devil's claw (*Phyteuma comosum* L.)
Edelweiss (*Leontopodium alpinum* Cass.)

The population of the Alto Adige is mixed, consisting of Germans, Italians and Ladins, the descendants of the original Rhaeto-Romanic inhabitants; and, lying as it does on one of the great European transit routes from north to south, it has suffered many vicissitudes in the course of its history, from the time of the great migrations to the present day.

The German-speaking population of 260,000 have German schools, they can develop their cultural life freely, and their language has equal status with that of the 137,000 Italians, who live chiefly in the towns. The culture and language of the Ladins, some 15,000 in number, are also protected. Each linguistic group is entitled to a proportionate share of posts in the government service. It must be added, however, that since the violent confrontations of the 1960s only a measure of détente has been achieved, and that the Catholic inhabitants of the region (some 85% of whom belong to the middle-class South Tirol People's Party, the remainder to various socialist splinter groups) do not yet enjoy all the rights to which they are statutorily entitled.

HISTORY. – This begins with the finds of Neolithic material in the S of the region and Bronze Age material in the Alpine territory. The indigenous population, known to the Romans as *Rhaetians* but subject also to Celto-Illyrian, Ligurian and Etruscan influences, were incorporated in the Roman Empire by Augustus in 15 B.C. and over the course of half a millenium were Romanised, at least in language. During the period of the great migrations this relatively thinly settled region, occupied by peoples who were now known as *Rhaeto-Romanic*, saw the passage of the invading Goths and Lombards, but the first invaders to settle here were the *Bajuwari*, who had occupied the whole of the region by the end of the 6th c., making it a purely German-speaking area, along the fringes of which (the Dolomite valleys, the Val Venosta) the Rhaeto-Romanic population have contrived to survive down to modern times, preserving at least in part their language and their way of life as in the Val Gádera (Gadertal) and Val Gardena (Gröden).

The Alto Adige then became a part of the Frankish kingdom, and at the beginning of the 11th c. passed into the hands of the prince-bishops of Trento and Bressanone, whose lay governors, principally the *Counts of Tirol*, sought to unite their territories. These territories, lying on both sides of the Brenner, fell into the hands of the Habsburgs in 1363 and remained Austrian until 1918, with a short interruption during the Napoleonic period (Andreas Hofer's successful rising and subsequent defeat). Thereafter South Tirol became Italian against its will and was subjected to a process of denationalisation under Fascist rule. After the Second World War, under the Treaty of Paris, the region was granted a substantial measure of self-government.

The vicissitudes of history are reflected in the **art and architecture** of the region, with examples of Romanesque (Val Venosta, San Cándido Cathedral), a rich range of Gothic (frescoes, altars with side panels) and major works of Renaissance and Baroque architecture. The Alto Adige is also notable for its numerous fortified castles.

A short TOUR OF ART AND ARCHITECTURE can properly begin in the Val Venosta, which has monuments dating back to the early days of Christianity in this region, such as the crypt of *Monte Maria* (Marienberg) abbey, the Carolingian church of San Benedetto in *Malles* (Mals), numerous other churches in the valley which now stand empty, and above all San Prócolo at *Naturno* (Naturns), with the oldest surviving wall paintings in German-speaking

Castel Róncolo (Burg Runkelstein), near Bolzano

territory. Other fine examples of Romanesque architecture which must be seen are the doorways in *Castel Tirolo* (Schloss Tirol) with their carved bestiary and the completely preserved cathedral at *San Cándido* (Innichen) in the Val Pusteria.

Bolzano (Bozen) offers fine examples of Gothic, in particular its late Gothic cathedral and the altar by Michael Pacher (Coronation of the Virgin) in the old parish church of Gries. There is much of interest to be seen also in Bolzano Museum and the Diocesan Museum in *Bressanone* (Brixen). Both of these museums also contain Baroque pictures, while some of the finest painting to be found in the Alpine countries can be seen in the famous cloisters of the Franciscan and Dominican monasteries in Bolzano and in those of *Novacella* (Neustift) and above all Bressanone.

The Alto Adige is poor in major buildings of the Baroque period, apart from the beautiful church at *Dobbiaco* (Toblach) in the Val Pusteria. The finest Baroque palace in the region, *Castello Mareta* (Wolfsthurn), lies in the Val Ridanna, a remote side valley near Vipiteno.

Folk art and traditions. – Pending the opening of the folk museum which is planned at Teodone (Dietenheim), near Brunico (Bruneck), the finest examples of the handicrafts of the Alto Adige are to be seen in the Folk Museum in Innsbruck (Austria). Other old traditions are represented by the numerous local *bands* with their smart traditional *costumes*. The beautiful old peasant costumes are still worn in the Val Sarentina, during the ordinary working week and not merely on special occasions. The Corpus Christi procession of Castelrotto (Kastelruth) is famous, and many towns and villages, particularly in the mountain valleys, still have impressive *processions* which show a characteristic combination of genuine piety with attachment to traditional practices.

The **economy** of the region still depends mainly on the vigour and energy of its farming population (the limit of settlement being as high as 1950 m). Industry is almost entirely confined to firms of

medium size, except in Bolzano. For the last 20 years or so *tourism* has also made a major contribution to the economy. The road and rail route over the Brenner and through the Isarco and Adige valleys is the most important N–S link in the Eastern Alps. The wide stretch of the Adige valley between Merano and the Salorno defile is also of great economic importance as the main area of production of the region's high-quality *fruit* (particularly apples and pears) and its renowned *wines*.

Wines of the Alto Adige. – The wine-producing region extends from the Isarco valley in the N to the Salorno defile in the southern Adige valley, taking in part of the Val Venosta to the W and part of the Rienza valley to the E. It is divided into six main areas – the Isarco valley, the Val Venosta, the area round Merano, the Bolzano basin, the Upper Adige and the Adige valley. The total area under vines is over 14,826 acres, which produce some 70,000,000 litres of wine annually (85% red, 15% white). About four-fifths of the output is exported, mainly to Switzerland, Germany and Austria.

The earliest evidence of wine-making in the region dates back to the 5th c. B.C. The wines of Rhaetia were well known to the Romans, and Augustus and Tiberius praised them greatly. During the Roman period the wine-producers of the Adige valley were already storing their wine in wooden casks, in contrast to the Mediterranean region which used amphoras or animal skins. The vineyards of "Bauzena" (Bolzano) are first mentioned in the records in the 9th c. After the draining of the Adige valley in the 19th c. there was a great expansion of wine-growing.

Well-known quality wines are *Santa Maddalena* (St Magdalener: ruby-red, full-bodied, velvety), grown on the hillsides of the Bolzano basin; *Merano* (Burggräfler: ruby-red, strong, well rounded); and *Lago di Caldaro* (Kalterersee: light red to ruby-red, light, harmonious).

Winter on the Alpe di Siusi (Seiser Alm)

A characteristic feature of vine-growing in the Alto Adige is the use of "pergolas" – wooden frameworks on which the vines grow, enabling large quantities of grapes to be produced in a relatively small area. The largest vine in Europe can be seen at Prissiano. – The wine is pressed with an ancient type of wine-press known as the "torkel". At the time of the vintage (September–October) the local people like to visit the wine-cellars and wine-shops to taste the new wine, accompanying it with walnuts, roast chestnuts and home-made bread.

The "Alto Adige wine route" (Südtiroler Weinstrasse), 30 km long, runs down the W side of the Adige valley from Castle Firmiano ((Sigmundskron), W of Bolzano, to Frangarto, Cornaiano (Girlan), Appiano (Eppan: with San Michele/St Michael, San Paolo/St Pauls and Missiano/Missian; continuation northward to Nalles/Nals planned), *Caldaro* (Kaltern), *San Giuseppe* (St Josef), *Termeno* (Tramin), *Cortaccia* (Kurtatsch), *Magrè* (Margreid), *Cortina all'Adige* (Kurtinig: possible continuation via Rovere della Luna to Mezzocorona) and *Salorno* (Salurn), on the left bank of the Adige.

The Bolzano area has the greatest concentration of *commerce* and *industry* (Bolzano Trade Fair; metal-working, particularly iron, aluminium and magnesium; engineering, vehicle manufacture; chemicals, textiles, leather goods, woodworking, canning). Merano has chemical plants (artificial fertilisers, etc.). There are numerous smaller industrial and craft establishments in the Isarco valley (Bressanone), Val Pusteria (Brunico) and the Val Venosta. Lasa (Laas), near Silandro, is famous for its *marble quarries*. In the Val Venosta and the Isarco valley there are a number of *hydroelectric stations* harnessing the power of the mountain streams. Corn-growing is steadily declining in favour of fodder crops (maize) and seed potatoes. In this region *forestry* is an important activity, while the extensive Alpine meadows provide pasture for *cattle* (particularly dairy cows); the numbers of sheep and goats, however, are falling. Haflinger horses (named after a village near Merano) are prized both as working and as riding animals. In the Val Gardena there are numerous woodcarvers; the Valle Aurina (Ahrntal) produces carved masks and pillow lace.

One of the main pillars of the economy is now **tourism**, promoted by the incomparable beauty of the scenery, the excellent snow conditions in the high valleys in winter and the favourable climate. The region is well equipped for the tourist trade, with important main railway lines, the Brenner motorway and a network of other good roads (bus services) leading to the remotest corners, as well as excellently engineered hill roads, originally built for military purposes during the First World War, which offer extensive views; together with numerous funiculars, ski-lifts and other recreational facilities, a dense system of way-marked footpaths, and routes for climbers and ample accommodation for visitors, ranging from modestly priced rooms in private houses to first-class hotels offering every amenity.

Amalfi

Region: Campania. – Province: Salerno (SA).
Altitude: 0–11 m. – Population: 6400.
Post code: I-84011. – Dialling code: 089.
(i) **AA**, Corso Roma 19;
    tel. 87 11 07.

HOTELS (some closed in winter). – *Excelsior Grand Hotel*, 4 km SW on the road to Agerola, I, 163 b., SP; *Cappuccini Convento*, I, 83 b.; *Santa Catarina* (with annexe), I, 111 b., SP; *Luna e Torre Saracena*, beautifully situated in an old monastery, I, 74 b., SP; *La Bussola*, II, 100 b.; *Dei Cavalieri*, II, 95 b., no rest.; *Caleidoscopio*, 2 km SW in Lone, II, 65 b., SP; *Aurora*, II, 61 b.; *Miramalfi*, II, 83 b., SP; etc. – IN RAVELLO: *Palumbo*, I, 60 b.; etc.

EVENTS. – *Exhibition of ship models* in alternate years.

*Amalfi, clinging to the rocky S coast of the Sorrento peninsula at the mouth of a deep gorge running into the Gulf of Salerno, is one of the most beautifully situated and most popular holiday resorts in Italy, particularly favoured by the people of Naples.

HISTORY. – Legend has it that the town was founded by Constantine the Great. It first appears in the records in the 6th c., and in 987 it became the see of an archbishop. During the Middle Ages it was an independent state with a population of some 50,000, ruled by self-appointed dukes who later became hereditary. In 1077 it was incorporated by Robert Guiscard in the Norman kingdom, and thereafter rose to great wealth and influence through its active trade with the East. As a sea power it came into conflict with Pisa and Genoa. Amalfi's code of maritime law, the Tabulae Amalfitanae, prevailed throughout the whole of the Italian Mediterranean from the 13th to the 16th c. The invention of the ship's compass is attributed to a citizen of Amalfi, *Flavio Gioia* (1302).

SIGHTS. – From the **Harbour** (boat services to and from Salerno, Positano and Capri in summer) it is a short distance by way of *Piazza Flavio Gioia* to the *Town Hall* (modern mosaic on façade), in the Corso Roma. To the S is the beach, to the N the little *Piazza del Duomo*, from which a flight of 62 steps leads up to the cathedral. – The **Cathedral** of Sant'Andrea, in Lombard Romanesque style, was built in 1203 (campanile 1180–1276). The fine *portico*, with pointed arches, was completely rebuilt in 1865. On the W front (restored 1890, with a modern mosaic gable) is a bronze door cast in Constantinople in 1066. The crypt contains the remains of the Apostle St Andrew, brought here in the 13th c. In the portico (to left) is the entrance to the *Chiostro del Paradiso* (Cloister of Paradise, 1266–68), which contains a small archaeological museum (admission fee).

500 m W of the cathedral, high above the town (also reached by lift from the coast road), is the former **Capuchin monastery**, now a hotel, with a beautiful cloister and fine *views of the town, with Castello Pontone towering above it on the E.

SURROUNDINGS. – There is an attractive trip by motorboat (15 minutes) to a stalactitic cave, the ***Grotta di Amalfi**, also known as the *Grotta di Smeraldo* or *Grotta Verde*, 4 km W of the town at Capo Conca (admission fee).

The coast at Amalfi

1 km E of Amalfi on the coast road, beyond the **Capo di Amalfi** (watch-tower), is the little town of **Atrani** (alt. 12 m), picturesquely situated at the mouth of a rocky gorge, the Gola del Dragone. In the piazza, in the lower part of the Atrani, is the 10th c. church of San Salvatore, with Byzantine bronze doors cast in Constantinople in 1087.

From the E side of Atrani a road (5 km) winds up through orange-groves, with two sharp bends, to **Ravello** (alt. 374 m), an old hill town in a superb **situation above Amalfi coast. Founded during the Norman period, it rose to great prosperity under the Anjou dynasty in the 13th c., when it had a population of 36,000 and possessed 13 churches, four monastic

houses and numerous palaces. – In the centre of the town is the Romanesque *cathedral of San Pantaleone (begun in 1086, remodelled in Baroque style), with fine bronze doors (covered externally with wooden doors) by Barisanus of Trani (1179). It contains a marble *pulpit with a mosaic ground by Niccolò da Foggia (1272) and an ambo (pulpit) of 1131. In the choir is a bishop's throne decorated with mosaic; to the left is the Cappella di San Pantaleone, in which some of the saint's blood is preserved. – SE of the cathedral is the *Palazzo Rufolo (admission fee), in Saracenic style (11th c.), with a charming little pillared courtyard. The beautiful garden with its outlook terrace (alt. 340 m) provided Wagner in 1880 with the model for Klingsor's enchanted garden (Wagner Festival at end of June). – From the cathedral it is 8 minutes' walk – first S through an arcade, then up through the portico of the church of San Antonio (Romanesque cloister) and past the church of Santa Chiara (view) – to the Palazzo Cimbrone (admission fee). An avenue runs through the beautiful park to the * *Belvedere Cimbrone, from which there are incomparable views of the Amalfi coast. – 200 m NE of the cathedral is the church of San Giovanni del Toro (11th c.; remodelled in Baroque style and modernised), with a mosaic pulpit (c. 1175) adorned with Persian majolica. On the pulpit steps and in the crypt are frescoes of scenes from the life of Christ.

Ancona

Region: Marche. – Province: Ancona (AN).
Altitude: 16 m. – Population: 110,000.
Post code: I-60100. Dialling code: 071.
(i) **AA**, Via Thaon di Revel;
    tel. 20 13 48.
    Information office at the harbour;
    tel. 20 11 83.
    EPT, Via M. Marini 14;
    tel. 2 36 39.
    Information office at station;
    tel. 2 88 85.
    ACI, Corso Stamira 78;
    tel. 5 53 35.

HOTELS. – *Grand Hotel Palace*, Lungomare Vanvitelli 24, I, 69 b.; *Grand Hotel Passetto*, Via Thaon di Revel 1, 75 b.; *Jolly Miramare*, Rupi di Via XXIX Settembre 14, I, 130 b.; *Grand Hotel Roma e Pace*, Via G. Leopardi 1, 138 b.; *Fortuna*, Piazza Stazione 15, 99 b.; *Moderno*, Via G. Bruno 1, 68 b.; etc. – *Motel Agip*, 6 km W in Palombina Nuova, III, 102 b. – CAMPING SITE.

EVENTS. – International *Angling and Water Sports Fair* (June–July).

Ancona is the most important town in the Marche region and the capital of its province, picturesquely situated between the Colle Astagno and Colle Guasco on the Italian Adriatic coast.

As an important traffic junction (rail junction; airport 13 km W at Falconara) and a developing naval and commercial port (ferry services to Yugoslavia and

Greece) with a long tradition, the town has enjoyed a considerable economic upswing in recent years (shipment of corn; petrochemicals at Falconara Maríttima; shipbuilding, particularly tankers). During the last war Ancona suffered heavy damage, and the part of the old town around the harbour was completely destroyed. Since the war new districts have been developed to the E of Ancona.

HISTORY. – Ancona was founded by refugees from Syracuse about 390 B.C. under the name of *Dorica Ancon* (from the Greek word for a bend or curve, after the shape of the promontory on which the town was built). In the 3rd c. B.C. it became a Roman colony, and in the reigns of Caesar and Trajan it was fortified and developed into a naval base. Although it was presented to the Pope by Charlemagne in 774 and at the end of the 16th c. was formally incorporated in the Papal States, the town contrived in practice to maintain its independence throughout the Middle Ages. – Ancona has been the seat of a bishop since 462.

Arch of Trajan, Ancona

SIGHTS. – The hub of the town's traffic is the *Piazza della Repubblica*, on the W side of which is the **Harbour**, an oval basin 800–900 m in diameter, the northern part of which is of Roman origin. At the E end of the northern breakwater is the **Arch of Trajan** (Arco di Traiano), a marble triumphal arch with an inscription recording that it was erected in A.D. 115 in honour of the Emperor Trajan and his wife and sister. Along the breakwater to the W is the 18th c. *Arco Clementino*. At the S end of the harbour is the former Lazaretto, built in 1773 on a pentagonal bastion. Adjoining it is the *Porta Pia* (1789). To the NW are the modern port installations.

From the Piazza della Repubblica a street on the right leads past the *Theatre* (1827) into the elongated *Piazza del Plebiscito*.

At the E end of this square, approached by a flight of steps, is the Baroque *church of San Doménico* (18th c.). To the W is the *Loggia dei Mercanti* (Exchange), a late Gothic building with a façade by Giorgio da Sebenico (1454–59), adjoining which is the beautiful *Palazzo Benincasa* (15th c.). From here a street on the right leads to the 10th c. *church of Santa Maria della Piazza*, with an over-decorated façade of 1210. – Farther N, in the *Piazza San Francesco*, is the *church of San Francesco delle Scale*, with a richly decorated Gothic doorway by Giorgio da Sebenico (1455–59).

From the Piazza San Francesco *Via Pizzecolli* runs N to the 18th c. *church of the Gesù* (view) and the 13th c. *Palazzo Comunale* or *Palazzo degli Anziani*, standing high above the sea, which contains the small *municipal picture collection* (works by Titian, Lotto, Crivelli, etc.). A little way N is the *Palazzo Ferretti* (16th c.), which houses the **Museo Nazionale delle Marche** (prehistoric and Roman material). – From here we can walk up a flight of steps or drive up a winding *panoramic road* built after the destruction of the harbour district to the top of Monte Guasco (extensive views), on which is the *Cathedral of San Ciriaco, a domed cruciform church (12th c.; façade 13th c.) in Byzantine-Romanesque style, built on the site of a temple of Venus. In the crypt is the small *Museo del Duomo*, a notable feature of which is an early Christian sarcophagus with carved decoration belonging to Flavius Gorgonius, a praetorian prefect (4th c.).

SURROUNDINGS. – There is an attractive drive S on the beautiful coast road to the *church of Santa Maria di Portonova* (11th c.) and on from there by way of **Monte Conero** (572 m: *views) and the picturesque village of *Sirolo* to the little seaside resort of *Numana*.

Aosta

Autonomous region of Valle D'Aosta (AO).
Altitude: 583 m. – Population: 40,000.
ⓘ **AA**, Piazza E. Chanoux 3;
tel. 4 05 26.
ACI, Piazza Roncas 7;
tel. 4 02 41.

HOTELS. – *Valle d'Aosta*, I, 204 b.; *Corona e Posta*, II, 118 b.; *Europe*, II, 97 b.; *Turin*, II, 89 b.; *Norden*, II, 88 b.; *Jockey*, II, 83 b.; *Ambassador*, II, 81 b.; *Roma*, II, 57 b.; *Splendor*, III, 100 b.; *Bus*, III, 68 b.; *Gran Paradiso*, 54 b.; etc.

The old Savoy town of Aosta (French Aoste), capital of the autonomous region, largely French-speaking, of Valle d'Aosta, lies in a fertile valley at the confluence of the Buthier and the Dora Báltea, ringed by an imposing circle of mountains, with Grand Combin, to the N, rising to 4317 m.

The town, which has been a place of importance from time immemorial as the gateway to the Great and Little St Bernard passes, was originally built as the Roman fort of *Augusta Praetoria Salassorum* soon after 25 B.C., and its plan still reflects the regular layout of the Roman station. It preserves numerous important monuments dating from the Roman and medieval periods. It is still an important traffic junction at the meeting of the access roads to the Mont Blanc tunnel and the Great St Bernard pass, and also has a not inconsiderable ironworking industry.

SIGHTS. – The old town is still surrounded by well-preserved **Roman town walls** which form a rectangle 724 by 572 m, with 20 towers. The E gate or *Porta Praetoria*, originally three-arched, lies some 2·5 m below the present street level, with a spacious court to the rear. Close by is the square tower of a medieval castle which belonged to the Lords of Quart. A few paces to the NW is the stage wall, 22 m high, of the *Roman theatre*. – 400 m E of the Porta Praetoria is the *Arch of Augustus*, with ten Corinthian pilasters. A little way NW is the former **collegiate**

church of **Saint-Ours** (originally 10th c., remodelled in late Gothic style at the end of the 15th c.), with 11th c. frescoes. In front of it is a handsome campanile (*c.* 1150), partly built of Roman hewn stones. On the S side of the church is a Romanesque cloister (1133), with fine carved capitals.

In the centre of the town, at the point where the two principal roads of the Roman fort crossed, is the market square, the *Piazza Chanoux*, with the *Town Hall*. To the NW is the **Cathedral** (15th–16th c.), with a Renaissance façade (*c.* 1552; porch added 1837). The treasury (not open to the public) contains an ivory *diptych of the consul Probus (406). On the W side of the Cathedral are remains of the *Roman forum*.

SURROUNDINGS. – S of Aosta is *Les Fleurs* (1367 m), which can be reached by cableway or by road (11 km). From here there is a cabin cableway to the *Conca de Pila* (1800 m); then chair-lift to the **Lac de Chamolé** (2312 m).

There is a very fine excursion (34 km) NW from Aosta on S.S. 27 up the Vallée du Grand St-Bernard to the **Great St Bernard** pass (2469 m: small lake), between the Mont Blanc massif and the Valais Alps. The pass, now marking the Italian-Swiss frontier, has been used since Roman times. (There is also a *road tunnel, 5828 m long, between St-Rhémy and Bourg St-Bernard on the Swiss side.) In Swiss territory is the famous hospice founded by St Bernard (d. 1081).

Aosta Valley

Ufficio Regionale per il Turismo Valle d'Aosta,
Piazza E. Chanoux 3, I-11100 Aosta (AO); tel. (0165) 3 56 55.

The autonomous region of the *Aosta valley (Italian Valle d'Aosta, French Val d'Aoste) occupies an area of 3262 sq. km in the deeply slashed valley of the Dora Báltea and its beautiful side valleys. Set amid magnificent mountain scenery at the foot of the Mont Blanc massif and surrounded by the highest summits of the Alps, it ranks high among the regions of Italy for scenic beauty and grandeur.

The valley, important since ancient times as the access route to two of the principal Alpine passes, the Great and Little St Bernard, was guarded throughout its length by a string of castles and other

Roman theatre, Aosta

fortified buildings, often very picturesquely situated. The beautiful scenery and the excellent snow to be found at the higher altitudes even in summer have promoted the development of a flourishing tourist trade. Other major sources of revenue are wine-growing at the lower levels, pasturing and a certain amount of industry. The region has a population of 110,000, mostly French-speaking.

The valley was strongly fortified by the Romans and by successive inhabitants. In 1191 it became part of Savoy, and together they passed temporarily to France in the early 19th c. and later to Piedmont. When it was incorporated in Italy in 1869 the French-speaking population resisted the threat of Italianisation in language and culture, and the growth of separatist feeling finally led to the recognition of the valley's special status as an autonomous region in 1948.

UP THE AOSTA VALLEY from Pont-St-Martin to Entrèves (94 km). – The road from Turin, S.S. 26 (also the A 5 motorway) enters the Valle d'Aosta region at **Pont-St-Martin** (alt. 345 m), where the River *Lys*, coming from the N, flows into the Dora Baltea. From here an attractive detour (34 km) can be made up the *Valle di Gressoney*, following the deeply indented course of the Lys, with numerous dams. The road passes through the village of *Issime* (14 km; alt. 939 m; Hotel Mont Nery, III, 72 b.), founded by German-speaking settlers from the Valais in the 13th c., and the little holiday resort of *Gressoney-St-Jean* (14 km; alt. 1385 m; Hotel Lyskamm, II, 39 b.; etc.), and comes to **Gressoney-la-Trinité** (alt. 1627 m; Hotel Busca-Thedy, II, 16 b.; etc.), from which there is a chair-lift to *Punta Jolanda* (2333 m; upper station 2247 m) and also a cabin cableway to *Lago Gabiet* (2367 m; upper station 2342 m). This is a good base for climbing in the **Monte Rosa** range, particularly for the ascent (6–7 hours; guide required) of the *Pointe Dufour* (4634 m), the highest peak in the Monte Rosa group. A chair-lift to *Colle Bettaforca* is under construction.

The main road continues from Pont-St-Martin up the Aosta valley, which becomes steadily narrower. Beyond *Donnaz* (alt. 322 m) the massive *Fort Bard* (11th c.) is seen on a hill on the right (alt. 391 m). – 10 km: *Arnaz* (alt. 412 m), with a ruined castle high above it (634 m).

Beyond this, on the right bank of the Dora, is the *castle of Issogne* (1480), with an interesting interior. – 4 km: **Verrès** (alt. 368 m; Hotel Stazione, III, 67 b.; etc.), with an old castle, the *Rocca* (1390), picturesequely situated on a rocky hill.

From Verrès there is a rewarding excursion (27 km N) up the valley of the River Evançon, the *Valle di Challant*. The road passes through the summer holiday resort of **Brusson** (16 km; alt. 1332 m; hotels: Brusson, IV, 79 b.; Aquila, IV, 55 b.; Italia, in Pasquier, III, 105 b.; etc.), in the lower part of the valley, and comes to **Champoluc** (11 km; alt. 1570 m; hotels: Anna Maria, II, 34 b.; Breithorn, III, 114 b.; Moderne, III, 115 r.; Alpi Rosa, III, 82 b.; etc.), the principal place in the upper part of the valley, which is known as the *Val d'Ayas*. This is also a popular holiday resort, with views of the twin mountains *Castor* (4230 m) and *Pollux* (4094 m) and the *Breithorn* (4171 m), S of the Matterhorn. Cabin cableway to *Crest* (1974 m), then chair-lift to 2500 m.

Beyond Verrès the main road continues up the Aosta valley, passing the castle of *Montjovet*, and then runs through the picturesque *Montjovet defile*, beyond which we get our first glimpse of Mont Blanc. – 12 km: **St-Vincent** (alt. 575 m; hotels: *Billia, L, 250 b., SP; Elena, II, 84 b.; Du Parc, II, 83 b.; Leon d'Oro, III, 81 b.; Posta, III, 70 b.; etc.), a popular summer holiday resort with a casino and mineral springs (recommended for stomach disorders). Beyond this, loftily perched on the left, is the castle of *Ussel* (c. 1350). – 3 km: **Châtillon** (alt. 549 m; pop. 4000; hotels: Rendez-Vous, III, 46 b.; Marisa, II, 45 b.; etc.), with a handsome castle.

From Châtillon there is an attractive drive (27 km N) up the *Val Tournanche*, through which the River *Marmoire* (Italian *Mármore*) flows down from the Matterhorn. The road runs through *Antey-St-André* (7 km; alt. 1080 m; hotels: Filey, III, 72 b.; Beau Séjour, III, 68 b.; Matterhorn-Favre, III, 51 b.; etc.), beyond which the Matterhorn comes into sight, and *Buisson* (4 km; alt. 1128 m; cable E to the *Chamois*, 1818 m, and from there chair-lift to *Lago de Lod*, 2015 m), and comes to **Valtournanche** (7 km; 1524 m; hotels: Tourist, II, 63 b.; Montana, II, 58 b.; Bich, III, 55 b.; Delle Alpi, III, 42 b.; Meynet, III, 31 b. – all in the main village, Paquier), which is popular both with summer visitors and winter sports enthusiasts (chair-lift E to the *Alpe Chanlève*, 1850 m; cableway to *Monte Molar*, 2484 m/2244 m). The road then continues through a gorge, just before which a footpath goes off (10 minutes' walk) to the *Gouffre des Busserailles*, 104 m long and 35 m deep (waterfall; admission fee), and comes to **Breuil** or **Cervina** (alt. 2046 m; hotels: Residence Cielo Alto, I, 172 b., SP; Cristallo, I, 149 b.,

SP; Plein Soleil, II, 164 b.; Petit Tibet, II, 110 b.; Petit Palai, II, 100 b.; President, II, 80 b.; Breuil, II, 76 b.; Europa, II, 75 b.; Hermitage, II, 64 b.; Planet, III, 60 b.; Marmore, III, 82 b.; Giomein-Monte Cervino, III, 72 b.; Edelweiss, III, 64 b.; etc.), a winter sports resort which is also popular in summer (bobsleigh run 1540 m long to the Lac Bleu). The setting is magnificent, with the mighty triangular peak of the **Matterhorn (Monte Cervino, 4482 m; the climb, with guide, takes 12 hours) rearing up to the N and the rock wall of the *Grandes Murailles* (3872 m) to the W. From Breuil there is a cableway E to the *Plan Maison* (2548 m; Hotel Lo Stambeco, II, 94 b.) and from there NE to the *Furggen* ridge (3488 m), or alternatively E, either direct or via *Cime Bianche* (2823 m), to the *Plateau Rosà* (3472 m). 1 km N of the Plateau Rosà is the *Theodule pass* (3322 m; mountain hut, 68 b.), with magnificent *views, extending also into the Zermatt valley.

Castle of St Pierre, Aosta valley

Beyond Châtillon the Aosta valley road affords open views of the fertile valley and the mountains around Aosta, with the three-peaked Rutor in the background. Farther on, above the mouth of the *Val de Clavalité* or *Val de Fénis*, in which the snowy peak of Tersiva can be seen, the mighty castle of *Fénis (1330, with later additions) can be seen on the left; beautiful 15th c. courtyard (wall paintings), 14th c. frescoes. – 12 km: *Nus* (alt. 535 m), at the mouth of the *Vallée de St-Barthélemy*, with a ruined castle. On the slope above is the village of *St-Marcel* (631 m), at the mouth of the valley of the same name. – 12 km: **Aosta** (see p. 57).

The road to the Mont Blanc Tunnel continues up the valley of the Dora Báltea beyond Aosta. – 6 km: *Sarre* (alt. 631 m), with a castle of 1710. From here there is a pleasant detour (28 km S) up the *Val de Cogne*. The road runs past the castle of *Aymavilles* with its four towers (16th–17th c., restored) and up the monotonous valley at a great height above the ravine of the roaring *Grand' Eyvie*. Far below can be seen Pont d'El, with a Roman *aqueduct of the Augustan period, 120 m above the stream. The road then continues to **Cogne** (alt. 1534 m; hotels: Grivola, II, 98 b.; Bellevue, II, 85 b.; Roccia Viva, II, 47 b.; Château Royal, III, 30 b.; etc.), the chief town in the valley which is popular both as a summer and a winter resort (iron mine; tunnel 6 km long on mine railway to Aosta). From here there is a beautiful view to the S of *Gran Paradiso* (4061 m: the climb by way of Valsavaranche takes 17 hours, with guide) and to the NW of Mont Blanc. Lift to *Mont Cuc* (2075 m). Cogne is a good centre for climbers and hill walkers, and particularly for expeditions in the *Gran Paradiso National Park

(Parco Nazionale del Gran Paradiso, 600 sq. km; many ibexes), which takes in the northern *Graian Alps*.

Beyond Sarre the road continues past the castles of *St-Pierre* (14th c.) and *Sarriod de la Tour* (14th c.) and the *Tour Colin* (13th c.). It then passes the mouths of the *Val de Rhême* and *Val Grisanche*, which run S to the French frontier, and enters the wild defile of *Pierre Taillée* (waterfalls). Beyond this, on the hillside to the right, is the village of *La Salle* (alt. 1001 m), with the ruined 13th c. castle of *Châtelard* (1171 m). Ahead can be seen the towering mass of Mont Blanc. – 22 km: **Morgex** (alt. 920 m; hotels: Grivola, III, 45 b.; Tête d'Arpy, III, 29 b.; etc.). – 4 km: **Pré-St-Didier** (alt. 1000 m; hotels: Monte Bianco, II, 82 b.; Crammont et des Alpes, II, 27 b.; Edelweiss, III, 71 b.; etc.), a picturesquely situated village with an arsenical chalybeate spring (33 °C – 91 °F) at the point where the *Thuile* forces its way through precipitous cliffs into the Dora valley.

At Pré-St-Didier S.S. 26 leaves the Aosta valley and runs SW to **La Thuile** (10 km; alt. 1441; Hotel Kristal, II, 46 b.; etc.), the starting point for the climb of the much-glaciated *Rutor* (3486 m; 7–8 hours, with guide, passing the *Rutor Falls, alt. 1934 m). From *Golette* (1496 m; hotels: Antares, II, 64 b.; Miravidi, III, 50 b.; etc.) there is a cableway SW to *Les Suches* (2175 m; mountain hut), and from there a chair-lift to *Mont Chaz-Dura* (2581 m). – The road then continues for another 13 km, with many bends and magnificent retrospective views, to reach the French frontier at the little *Lac Verney* and the **Little St Bernard Pass** (2188 m). (Until 1947 the frontier was 2 km farther S.)

Beyond Pré-St-Didier the Aosta valley road passes below the village of *Verrand* (1263 m), in a situation commanding panoramic views, and comes in 5 km to **Courmayeur** (alt. 1224 m; hotels: Royal,

I, 155 b., SP; Pavillon, I, 70 b., SP; Moderno, I, 56 b.; Palace Bron, I, 45 b.; Ange et Grand Hôtel, II, 89 b.; Majestic-Parigi, II, 80 b.; Cresta et Duc, II, 70 b.; Del Viale, II, 55b.; Centrale, II, 54 b.; Svizzero, III, 51 b.; Edelweiss, III, 50 b.; etc.), a major tourist centre at the foot of the Mont Blanc massif. Mineral springs (chalybeate), with spa establishment; Alpine Museum. A chain of cableways leads up to the *Plan Chécrouit* (1697 m), from there to the *Col Chécrouit* (2256 m), then to the *Cresta de Youla* (2624 m) and finally to the *Testa d'Arp* (2755 m). There is also a cableway to the *Pré de Pascal* (1912 m) and a new cabin cableway to the Val Vény.

4 km beyond Courmayeur is *Entrèves (alt. 1306 m; hotels: Des Alpes, I, 116 b.; Aiguille Noire, III, 41 b.; etc.), a magnificently situated village with open views of Mont Blanc to the NW and the Dent du Géant (4014 m) and Grandes Jorasses (4206 m) to the NE. There is an even finer prospect from the pilgrimage church of *Notre-Dame de la Guérison* (1486 m), 2 km W, which affords a striking close view of the Brenva glacier. From *La Palud*, 1 km NE (hotels: Astoria, III, 56 b.; Vallée Blanche, III, 43 b.; etc.), there is a very attractive **drive (15 km; 1½ hours, with three cableways) by way of the *Pavillon du Mont Fréty* (2130 m) and the *Rifugio Torino* (3322 m; *view), below the *Col du Géant* (3369 m), then by the *Punta Helbronner* (3462 m; passport control), to the *Gros Rognon* (3533 m) and the *Aiguille du Midi* (3842 m), and so on to Chamonix.

**Mont Blanc (Italian *Monte Bianco*, 4807 m), the highest peak in the Alps, over which the Italian-French frontier runs, was first climbed in 1786 by Jacques Balmat of Chamonix and the village doctor, Michel Paccard. In the following year it was climbed again by the Geneva scientist Horace-Bénédict de Saussure, accompanied by Balmat and 16 porters. The climb (with a guide) takes 10–12 hours; the best starting point is Les Houches, 10 km SW of Chamonix.

Traffic through the Alps has been greatly facilitated by the construction of the *Mont Blanc Tunnel (*Galleria del Monte Bianco*: begun 1958, boring completed 1962, opened to traffic 16 July 1965). The tunnel begins at Entrèves (alt. 1381 m) and ends 11·6 km farther N at an altitude of 1274 m above the hamlet of *Les Pèlerins*, near Chamonix. The width of the carriageway is 7 m, the total width including walkway and buffer strip 8·15 m, the greatest height 5·98 m. The tunnel, which is open throughout the year, shortens the journey from Italy to western Switzerland and central and northern France by several hundred kilometres during the period from October to June when the high Alpine passes are closed.

Apennines

The Apennines (from the Celtic word *pen*, "mountain") are the mountain range 1400 km long and between 30 and 150 km wide, which extends in a long arc down the whole length of the Italian peninsula from the Alps in the Ligurian Gulf to the SW tip of Calabria and continues into Sicily.

As a result of late folding during the early Tertiary period the outer side of the range facing the Po plain and the Adriatic has a more gradual slope, composed of sedimentary rocks, while the inner side, in consequence of later collapses, slopes down in a steeper scarp to the sea and the basins of Tuscany, Umbria and eastern Latium. The *Northern Apennines*, reaching their highest point in Monte Cimone (2165 m), and the *Central Apennines* have regular slopes and continuous summit ridges which are crossed by a series of traffic routes at heights of between 650 and 1300 m. The rocks are mainly of Cretaceous and Tertiary date, There are large expanses of sandstones and schists, clays and marls, with rounded summits and gentle slopes which show little variation, though when soaked with rain they are very vulnerable to landslides (*frane*). Sharper contours are produced by the dolomites and limestones, which have weathered into rugged and contorted karstic land-forms, particularly in the *Monti Sibillini* (2478 m) and the wild **Abruzzi** (see p. 48), which reach their highest point in the Gran Sasso d'Italia (2914 m). The lower *Neapolitan Apennines*, abutting at their northern end of the

The Aveto valley in the Northern Apennines

Abruzzi, and the *Lucanian Apennines* run into the *Calabrian Apennines*, in which the landscape pattern from the Crati valley onwards is formed by ancient rocks (granites, gneisses and micaceous schists). In this area are the *Sila* (1930 m) and *Aspromonte* (1958 m) ranges with their beautiful forests of deciduous and coniferous trees, reminiscent of the upland regions of central Europe.

The CLIMATE of the Apennines is relatively harsh at higher altitudes. Rainfall in the Northern Apennines is high, while in the lower-lying areas the aridity of the Mediterranean climate predominates. At the foot of the hills there are numerous mineral springs.

At the foot of the Apennines the FLORA is of Mediterranean type, with edible chestnuts and fruit-trees. Above this is a zone of open forests, with beeches predominating at the lower levels and conifers higher up. Long human occupation, however, has destroyed much of the original forest cover, which has been replaced over large areas by an evergreen macchia. In consequence there is an almost total absence of the larger fauna, and the flow of the rivers is irregular. At heights above 1800 m the slopes are covered with carpets of stones and scree.

Within the mountainous areas SETTLEMENT is confined to the basins and valleys. The main occupations are stock-farming (goats and sheep), some modest arable farming and forestry.

Apulia/Puglia

(i) **EPT Bari**, Piazza Roma 33 A,
I-70100 Bari (BA);
tel. (080) 25 86 76.
EPT Brindisi, Piazza Dionisi,
I-72100 Brindisi (BR);
tel. (0831) 2 19 44.
EPT Foggia, Via Senatore Emilio Perrone 17,
I-71100 Foggia (FG);
tel. (0881) 2 31 41.
EPT Lecce, Via Monte San Michele 20,
I-73180 Lecce (LE);
tel. (0832) 5 41 17.
EPT Taranto, Corso Umberto 115,
I-74100 Taranto (TA);
tel. (099) 2 12 33.

The region of Apulia (in Italian Puglia or Puglie) in SE Italy consists of the provinces of Bari, Brindisi, Foggia, Lecce and Taranto and covers an area of 19,347 sq. km E of the Apennines between the spur (the Gargano hills) and the heel (the Salentine peninsula) of the Italian boot.

The northern part of the region is occupied by the plain round Foggia, the *Tavoliere di Puglia*, at the E end of which

are the limestone hills of the *Gargano* promontory (Monte Calvo, 1056 m). In the centre is the karstic limestone plateau, with numerous caves and swallow-holes, of the *Murge* (altitude up to 680 m), which merges in the S into the varied terrain, partly flat and partly hilly, of the *Salentine peninsula* (up to 200 m).

Apulia is a purely agricultural region, its main crops being wheat on the Tavoliere, tobacco around Lecce, vegetables on the coast, together with grapes (wine and eating), almonds and olives. The itinerant grazing economy which once played an important part is now confined to a few karstic hill regions. Large-scale water supply schemes like the 360 km long Acquedotto Pugliese, which is carried through the Apennines in a tunnel, have promoted considerable development of agriculture in this very dry but fertile country. In recent years a certain amount of industry, particularly petrochemicals, has been established in the coastal areas.

HISTORY. – In ancient times the name of Apulia was confined to the Gargano hills. The region was conquered by the Romans in 317 B.C. and together with Calabria became Regio II, which played an important part in Roman trade with the East. After the fall of the Empire Apulia passed into the hands of the Ostrogoths and later the Byzantines, and in 568 part of it was occupied by the Lombards. Robert Guiscard conquered it for the Normans from 1141 onwards and was granted Apulia as a fief by Pope Nicholas II. Under Roger II it was united with the kingdom of Naples and Sicily, and enjoyed a period of high prosperity under the Staufen dynasty. Foggia was a favourite residence of Frederick II, who left behind him a whole series of fine buildings and works of art, foremost among them the Castel del Monte.

Every tourist should visit the ****Trulli country**, an area of some 100 sq. km in the Murge region containing thousands of the curious dwellings called *trulli* – small round stone-built houses, often linked together in groups, with conical roofs formed of overlapping courses of stone (cf. the *nuraghi* of Sardinia).

The area takes in the communes of **Alberobello** (alt. 416 m; pop. 10,000; hotels: Dei Trulli, I, 54 b.; Astoria, II, 89 b.; etc.), a picturesque little town with over 1000 *trulli* in the *Zona Monumentale, including the church of Sant'Antonio, built in *trullo* form, and the two-storey Trullo Sovrano in the N of the town, the largest in Alberobello; **Locorotondo** (alt. 410 m; pop. 11,000; Hotel Valle d'Itria, III, 28 b.), which is circular in plan; **Martina Franca** (alt. 431 m; pop. 40,000; Hotel

Trulli at Fasano (Apulia)

San Michele, II, 53 b., SP; etc.), with charming Baroque buildings, the 12th c. Palazzo Ducale and the collegiate church of San Martino (18th c.); **Cisternino** (alt. 393 m; pop. 11,000; Hotel Aia del Vento, II, 48 b.); and **Fasano** (alt. 111 m; pop. 30,000; Motel Rosa, II, 32 b.; etc.). – Between Locorotondo and Martina Franca is the *Valle d'Itria*, also with numerous *trulli*.

To the N of the trulli region, 15 km SW of the port of **Monópoli** (alt. 9 m; pop. 37,000; Hotel Monopoli, IV, 15 b.; etc.), which has an 18th c. cathedral, are the **Grotte di Castellana**, which rank with the Postojna caves in Yugoslavia as the finest stalactitic caves in Europe (conducted tour; Hotel Vittoria, II, 30 b.; Autostello ACI, II, 12 b.; etc.). The caves have a total length of 1·2 km – much more if the various ramifications are included. Access is by means of a lift. The finest of the caves is the *Grotta Bianca* (special conducted tours), unsurpassed in Europe for its perfect condition and its profusion of stalactites and stalagmites. Above the caves is an outlook tower (28 m high, 170 steps); Cave Museum.

Castel del Monte: see p. 70.

L'Aquila

Region: Abruzzi. – Province: L'Aquila (AQ).
Altitude: 615–721 m. – Population: 61,000.
Post code: I-67100. – Dialling code: 0862.
(i) **AA**, Piazza Santa Maria di Paganica 5; tel. 2 51 49.

HOTELS. – *Grand Hotel e del Parco*, I, 172 b.; *Duca degli Abruzzi*, II, 152 b.; *La Cannelle*, II, 116 b., SP; *Italia*, III, 54 b.; etc. – *Motel Amiternum*, II, 115 b.; *Gran Panorama*, II, 95 b.

L'Aquila, surrounded by the mighty limestone heights of the Abruzzi, is a busy town, capital of the Abruzzi and of the province of L'Aquila. It was founded about 1240 by the Hohenstaufen emperor Frederick II, and is still surrounded by its 14th c. walls. Its handsome buildings bear witness to the wealth brought to the town by the wool trade. It is the see of an archbishop.

SIGHTS. – In the centre of the town is the spacious *Piazza del Duomo*, on the W side of which is the cathedral of San Mássimo (13th c.; several times destroyed by earthquakes and rebuilt; it contains (to the right of the entrance) a monumental effigy of Cardinal Agnifili (1480). To the N is the little church of *San Giuseppe*, with the tomb of the Camponeschi family (1412, by "Walter of Germany"). Also N of the cathedral, in Piazza del Palazzo, is the former *Palace of Margaret of Parma* (1573; campanile), now occupied by the Court of Appeal.

SE of Piazza del Palazzo is the porticoed street intersection known as the *Quattro Cantoni*, in the Corso Vittorio Emanuele II, the town's principal street. From here Via San Bernardino leads to the **church of San Bernardino di Siena** (1452), with a handsome façade of 1527, which contains the saint's marble tomb (1500–05). From San Bernardino we descend to the piazza, follow Via Fortebraccio straight ahead and continue through the *Porta Bazzano* to the magnificent church, formerly belonging to the Celestine order, of *Santa Maria di Collemaggio, founded about 1280 by Pietro da Morrone, who was crowned here as Pope Celestine V in 1294; it has a Baroque interior, with the Pope's Renaissance tomb (1517) and wall paintings by Ruter, a pupil of Rubens, depicting his life and deeds.

Castello, L'Aquila

In the NE of the town is the *Parco del Castello* (*views of the Aterno valley and the Gran Sasso and Maiella range), with a beautiful *Fontana Monumentale*. On the E side of the park is the **Castello**, built by the Spaniards in 1534, which now houses the *Museo Nazionale d'Arte Antica e Moderna* (entrance on E side), notable particularly for its collection of Abruzzi majolica (17th–18th c.) from Castelli.

At the foot of the hill on the W side of the town, near the station and just inside the *Porta Rivera*, is the *Fontana delle Novantanove Cannelle* (1272, with later restoration), with sides of red and white marble from which the water spouts through 99 different masks.

SURROUNDINGS. – The most rewarding trip from L'Aquila is to the **Gran Sasso d'Italia** (48 km). The road passes the *cemetery*, with the convent church of *Santa Maria del Soccorso* (early Renaissance), and then continues via the village of *Assergi* (alt. 870 m; church of Santa Maria Assunta, with a 15th c. façade, a Gothic rose window and a 12th c. crypt), on the SW slopes of the Gran Sasso group, to *Fonte Cerreto* (alt. 1105 m; Albergo Fiordigigli, II, 108 b., etc.), starting point of the cableway to the Gran Sasso d'Italia (3240 m long; 16 minutes). A panoramic road (27 km) leads to the upper station of the cableway (2130 m), on the western edge of the **Campo Imperatore** (1600–2200 m; Albergo Campo Imperatore, III, 87 b.), a high valley 20 km long and up to 5 km wide which is an excellent walking and climbing centre and a popular winter sports area. Near the cableway station are the modern chapel of the *Madonna della Neve* and a new *observatory*. 45 minutes' climb above the hotel, on the Portelle ridge, is the *Rifugio Duca degli Abruzzi* (2381 m; *views). from which it is another 3½–4 hours' climb to the *Corno Grande* or *Monte Corno* (2914 m), the highest peak in the *Gran Sasso d'Italia, the most elevated mountain range in the Italian peninsula, with sheer rock walls like those of the Calcareous Alps. From the summit there are magnificent *views extending over the whole of Central Italy to the Adriatic in the E and over the Sabine hills and on clear days as far as the Tyrrhenian Sea in the W.

From L'Aquila to Avezzano (62 km). – The road winds up the NE slopes of *Monte d'Orce* (2206 m), with many bends and fine retrospective *views, and continues through the wide high valley between *Monte Velino* on the right and *Monte Sirente* on the left, with a number of villages which are popular summer and winter resorts (climbing in the Velino and Sirente groups). It then winds its way downhill, with attractive views ahead of the little town of *Celano* (alt. 880 m; pop. 11,000) with the ruins of a Romanesque and Gothic church; castle, 1392–1451 on its hill, and the wide Fucino basin. – From Celano an excursion can be made to a wild gorge, the *Gole di Celano*: 1·5 km S on the road to Sulmona and the Abruzzi National Park, then a footpath on the left (15 minutes).

Aquileia

Region: Friuli-Venezia Giulia.
Province: Udine (UD).
Altitude: 3 m. – Population: 3000.
Post code: I-33051. – Dialling code: 0431.
ⓘ **EPT Udine**, Piazza Venerio 4;
　I-33100 Udine (UD);
　tel. (0432) 5 42 05.

HOTELS. – *Aquila Nera*, IV, 35 b.; etc. – CAMPING SITE.

Aquileia, in the Isonzo delta, now a town of little importance, can look back on a long history. Founded by the Romans in 181 B.C. as a defensive post against the Celts, it became one of the great cities of ancient Italy, a major trading centre in the Gulf of

Trieste and from the 6th c. the seat of a Patriarch.

SIGHTS. – The most important monument of this great past is the *Cathedral, built at the beginning of the 11th c. on the site of an earlier church and remodelled in Gothic style at the end of the 14th c. It has a fine interior, with a mosaic pavement from the original church (4th c.), a handsome Renaissance pulpit, remains of 11th c. frescoes in the apse and a Renaissance gallery; crypt, with superb *frescoes. At the main entrance is an Easter Sepulchre (11th c.), and close by is the entrance to the *Cripta degli Scavi (3rd c. A.D.: mosaics). From the 73 m high tower (11th and 14th c.) there are far-ranging views. – From the military cemetery behind the chancel of the cathedral the Via Sacra, lined by cypresses, runs 700 m N to the recent *excavations of the *Roman river harbour.* A little way NE is the *Museo Paleocristiano* (Early Christian Museum), to the W the *Forum* (partly reconstructed). – To the W of the cathedral are the meagre remains of an *amphitheatre,* the Roman *street of tombs,* a Roman *mausoleum* (rebuilt) and a number of partly excavated *oratories* with well-preserved *mosaic pavements. – SW of the cathedral is the *Museo Archeologico,* containing Roman material recovered by excavation, some of it displayed in the courtyards (many pyramidal ash-urns).

Roman forum, Aquileia

SURROUNDINGS. – 11 km S of Aquileia, on the spit of land S of the lagoon, is the popular seaside resort of **Grado** (alt. 2 m; pop. 10,000; hotels: Astoria Palace, I, 329 b., SP; Fonzari, II, 176 b.; Tiziano Palace, II, 151 b.; Parco alla Salute, II, 146 b.; Bellevue, II, 142 b.; Savoy, II, 132 b., SP; Saturnia, II, 114 b.; Argentina, II, 93 b.; Touring, II, 91 b.; Al Bosco, II, 85 b.; Friuli, II, 71 b.; Plaza, II, 81 b.; Terme, II, 75 b.; Ariston, II, 75 b.; Adria, III, 114 b.; Diana, III, 111 b.; Ville Bianchi, III, 96 b.; etc.). Half way along the spit of land is the little fishing port; to the N lies the harbour canal, to the E, along the beautiful sandy beach (3 km long: hot sand baths), is the hotel and villa quarter, with a freshwater swimming pool. Grado came into being as the resort of Roman Aquileia, and enjoyed a period of great prosperity when the Patriarch of Aquileia fled here in 568 to escape the Lombards. The *Cathedral of Sant'Eufemia was built during this period, with a mosaic pavement, a Romanesque pulpit and a Venetian silver frontal (Venetian, 1372) on the high altar. To the left of the cathedral is the Baptistery (6th c.), and beyond this the church of Santa Maria delle Grazie, with a mosaic pavement.

Arezzo

Region: Umbria. – Province: Arezzo (AR).
Altitude: 256–296 m. – Population: 40,000.
Post code: I-52100. – Dialling code: 0575.
ⓘ **EPT,** Piazza Risorgimento 116;
tel. 2 08 39.
ACI, Viale L. Signorelli 24 A;
tel. 2 32 53.
ICI, *Saturnia Tours,* Via Roma 9;
tel. 2 56 46.
Information office, Via Guelfa 8;
tel. 2 82 38

HOTELS. – *Minerva,* II, 139 b.; *Continentale,* II, 138 b.; *Graverini,* II, 100 b.; *Da Cecco,* II, 83 b.; *Europa,* II, 81 b.; *Astoria,* II, 53 b.; *Etruria,* III, 45 b.; etc.

EVENTS. – *Medieval jousting* in June and September.

The provincial capital Arezzo, the Roman Arretium, lies in eastern Tuscany some 80 km SE of Florence.

Arezzo was the birthplace of Maecenas (d. 8 B.C.), the friend of Augustus and patron of Virgil and Horace; Petrarch (1304–74), Italy's greatest lyric poet and the father of humanism; the brilliant and notorious satirical poet Pietro Aretino (1492–1556); and probably also Guido Monaco or Guido of Arezzo (Aretinus, c. 990–1050), inventor of our system of musical notation. – The town is also a centre of the antiques trade.

SIGHTS. – In the centre of the town is the **church of San Francesco,** founded in 1322, with *frescoes (painted between 1452 and 1466: scenes from the legend of the Cross) by Piero della Francesca, who was noted for his mastery of perspective and chiaroscuro.

From San Francesco we go SE along Via Cavour and then turn left up the Corso Italia to reach the Romanesque *church of Santa Maria della Pieve (11th–

13th c.), with a late Romanesque façade and a tower completed in 1333, both by Marchionne. To the E of the church is the picturesque *Piazza Grande*, scene of the Giostra del Saracino, the medieval joust performed on the first Sunday in June and September. On the W side of the square is the beautiful *Palazzo della Fraternità dei Laici* (1375–1460), on the N side the *Palazzo delle Logge* (1573). – Behind the Logge, in Corso Italia, is the *Palazzo Pretorio* (1322), its façade decorated with the coats of arms of former mayors. – From here it is only a short way, skirting a beautiful park, the *Passeggio del Prato*, to Via dell'Orto, with *Petrarch's birthplace* (on left), and beyond this the *Palazzo Comunale* (Town Hall, 1533), decorated with numerous coats of arms.

Opposite the Town Hall is the *Cathedral, a Gothic building (begun 1277) with a modern façade (1900–14). On the high altar is the Arca di San Donato, the marble tomb of St Donatus (1369–75). At the E end of the N aisle is the tomb of Guido Tarlati, a warlike bishop of Arezzo (d. 1327).

Some 500 m NW of the cathedral, in Via Garibaldi, is the *Museum of Medieval and Modern Art* (closed Sunday afternoon and Monday), with an important collection of vases and a picture gallery (altarpiece by Luca Signorelli, 1520).

Ascoli Piceno

Ascoli Piceno

Region: Marche. – Province: Ascoli Piceno (AP).
Altitude: 153 m. – Population: 55,000.
Post code: I-63100. – Dialling code: 0736.
(i) AA, Via del Trivio;
   tel. 5 30 45.
   EPT, Corso Mazzini 229;
   tel. 5 11 15.
   ACI, Viale Indipendenza 38 A;
   tel. 5 13 52.
   TCI, Viaggi Brunozzi, Piazza Arringo 33;
   tel. 5 04 60.

HOTELS. – *Marche*, I, 60 b.; *Castelli*, II, 65 b.; *Gioli*, II, 54 b.; *Nuova Posta*, III, 70 b.; *Tornasacco*, III, 65 b.; *Piceno*, III, 62 b.; etc. – YOUTH HOSTEL, 40 b.

EVENTS. – *Jousting* in August.

The provincial capital of Ascoli Piceno, the Roman Asculum Picenum, lies in the southern Marches at the confluence of the rivers Castellano and Tronto, surrounded on three sides by massive mountain ranges. **It has interesting Roman remains and many handsome pre-Renaissance buildings. – The painter and architect Cola Filotesio dell'Amatrice worked here between 1519 and 1542.**

SIGHTS. – The hub of the town's traffic is the picturesque *Piazza del Popolo*, in which the "Torneo Cavalleresco della Quintana", a medieval joust, is held on the first Sunday in August. In this square is the *Palazzo dei Capitani del Popolo* (12th–13th c., remodelled in 16th c.), which houses the Museo Civico. On the N side of the square, here traversed by the Corso Mazzini, the town's principal street, is the Gothic hall-church of *San Francesco* (1262–1371), with a Lombard-style doorway guarded by stone lions and the crenellated *Loggia dei Mercanti* (c. 1500). On the N side are two beautiful cloisters.

SE of the Piazza del Popolo is the *Piazza dell'Arringo*, in which stands the massive **Palazzo Comunale** (Town Hall, 1683–1745), with a valuable *collection of pictures* (works by Cola dell'Amatrice, Crivelli, Titian, etc.) and a *cope presented to the cathedral by Pope Nicholas IV in 1288. – On the E side of the square is the **Cathedral** of Sant'Emidio, originally an early Romanesque building, with a Gothic nave of hall-church type and a façade (1532) attributed to Cola dell'-Amatrice. In the large chapel in the S aisle is an altarpiece by Crivelli (1473). Adjoining the cathedral, to the left, is the early Romanesque baptistery.

From the Piazza dell'Arringo the Corso Vittorio Emanuele runs E past the *municipal park* to a medieval bridge over the Castellano, the *Ponte Maggiore*, with a view to the left of the Monte dell'Ascensione (1103 m) and to the right of the *Ponte di Cecco*, a two-arched Roman bridge dating from the late Republic (restored after destruction in the last war). Close by is the picturesque *Forte Malatesta* (1348).

300 m NW of the Piazza del Popolo are the Romanesque *church of Santi Vincenzo e Anastasio* (12th c.), with an unusual façade of 64 square compartments, and the *church of San Pietro Mártire* (14th c.). – The picturesque Via di Solestà leads farther NW to the *Ponte di Solestà*, a Roman bridge over the Tronto. A little way SW is the *Palazzetto Langobardo* (10th c.?), now a youth hostel, and adjoining it the *Torre Ercolani*, a tower 40 m high, once the stronghold of a noble family.

At the W end of the Corso Mazzini, in the Piazza di Cecco, is the *Porta Gémina*, a double gate through which in Roman times the Via Salaria entered the town. – Above the town to the SW is the *Santissima Annunziata church*, from which there are fine views. There is an even more extensive prospect from the 16th c. *Fortezza Pia*, farther to the W.

SURROUNDINGS. – A road runs S from Ascoli Piceno and winds its way (many good views) up to the *Colle San Marco* (694 m; Hotel Roxy Miravelle, II, 67 b.; etc.), from which there are magnificent views. 5 km farther S, beyond the *Rifugio Paci* (905 m), is *San Giacomo* (1105 m), starting point of the cableway up the *Montagna dei Fiori (Monte Piselli*, 1676 m). From the summit there are magnificent views, extending on a clear day as far as the Dalmatian coast of Yugoslavia.

Assisi

Region: Umbria. – Province: Perugia (PU).
Altitude: 403–500 m. – Population: 6000.
Post code: I-06081. – Dialling code: 075.
(i) **AA**, Piazza del Comune 12;
tel. 81 25 34.
TCI, *Mavitur*, Via Frate Elia 1 B;
tel. 81 23 77.

HOTELS. – *Giotto*, II, 126 b.; *Subasio*, II, 120 b.; *Il Castello*, II, 108 b.; *San Francesco*, II, 90 b.; *Windsor Savoia*, II, 63 b.; *Fontebella*, II, 62 b.; *Dei Priori*, II, 50 b.; *Umbra*, II, 48 b.; *Europa*, III, 114 b.; *San Pietro*, III, 79 b.; etc. – CAMPING SITE.

Assisi, the ancient Umbrian city of Asisium, has a magnificent *situation on artificial terraces on an outlier of Monte Subasio, SE of Perugia. It owes its fame to St
Francis, born here in 1182, the son of a wealthy merchant, who after spending his early years in a life of pleasure and dissipation devoted himself to the service of the poor and the sick, founded the Franciscan order and died in 1226 in poverty and abstinence. With its well-preserved *medieval streets and houses and its treasures of art and architecture Assisi is one of Italy's great tourist sights.

SIGHTS. – The **Franciscan convent** with its massive substructures is a conspicuous sight on the edge of the hill at the NW end of the town. Building began soon after the saint's death; the courtyard and the external passage (from which there are magnificent views) were renewed by Pope Sixtus IV (1471–84). The great ****church** built over St Francis's tomb is two-storeyed. The dark lower church has squat late Romanesque vaulting (1228–53) and a vestibule added in 1488; the upper church, completed in 1253, is Italy's earliest Gothic church. Both churches are decorated with famous *frescoes (*c.* 1320–30) – in the choir of the upper church and in the transepts frescoes of the school of Cimabue, in the nave 28 scenes from the life of St Francis by Giotto and his pupils. In the crypt, built in 1818 and enlarged in 1925–32, is a stone sarcophagus containing the saint's remains. In the large cloister is the *treasury*.

Basilica di San Francesco, Assisi

Leaving the lower church, we follow Via San Francesco (to left). This street and its continuation lead up to the town's main square, the *Piazza del Comune*, on the site of the Roman forum. On the left is the portico of the ***Temple of Minerva**, perhaps dating from the Augustan period, now the *church of Santa Maria della Minerva*. At the far end of the square, on the right, is the *Palazzo Comunale* or

Palazzo dei Priori (Town Hall, 14th c.), with the municipal *picture gallery*. To the S, on a lower level, is the *Chiesa Nuova* (1615), a small church on a centralised ground plan, on the site of St Francis's birthplace.

From the Piazza del Comune the Via di San Rufino runs E to the **Cathedral** of San Rufino (12th–13th c.), with a beautiful façade. – S of the cathedral, in Piazza Santa Chiara, is the Gothic **church of Santa Chiara** (1257). Under the high altar is the open tomb of St Clare (d. 1253), the enthusiastic disciple of St Francis who founded the order of Clarissines or Poor Clares.

From the Piazza di San Rufino the old Via Santa Maria delle Rose leads up to the **Rocca Maggiore**, high above the town, a castle (rebuilt by Cardinal Albornoz in 1365) in which the Emperor Frederick II spent some time in his youth (panoramic views).

SURROUNDINGS. – 2 km SE of the town centre is the little **convent of Santo Damiano** (alt. 305 m), founded by St Francis, of which St Clare was the first abbess. On the small terrace, gay with flowers, in front of the convent, St Francis is said to have composed his famous "Canticle of the Sun". – 5 km S on S.S. 75, near the railway station, is the village of **Santa Maria degli Angeli** (alt. 218 m), with the **church* of the same name. This is a massive domed structure in Renaissance style, built between 1569 and 1630 over St Francis's oratory, the Portiúncula, and the cell in which he died. The nave and choir were re-erected after an earthquake in 1832 and provided with a new façade in 1925–28. To the E of the sacristy is a small garden, in which it is said the roses have been thornless since a famous act of penance by the saint. Adjacent is the *Cappella delle Rose*, with frescoes by Tiberio d'Assisi (1518) depicting scenes from the saint's life. – 4 km E of Assisi, charmingly situated in a small wood of holm-oaks above a ravine between the bare rock faces of Monte Subasio, stands the **Éremo delle Cárceri** (alt. 791 m), a hermitage to which St Francis retired for devotional exercises. The buildings date from the 14th c. Visitors are also shown the saint's rock-bed. From here it is an hour and a half's climb to the broad ridge of *Monte Subasio* (1290 m), which commands extensive views.

Asti

Region: Piemonte. – Province: Asti (AT).
Altitude: 125 m. – Population: 80,000.
Post code: I-14100. – Dialling code: 0141.
ⓘ **EPT**, Piazza Alfieri 34;
tel. 5 03 57.
    ACI, Piazzale Medici 21–22;
    tel. 5 35 34.
    ICI, *Viaggi Ecclesia*, Corso Dante 3;
    tel. 5 36 81.

HOTELS. – *Salera*, I, 98 b.; *Aleramo*, II, 68 b.; *Palio*, II, 54 b.; *Rainero*, II, 54 b.; *Hasta*, II, 45 b., SP; *Lis*, II, 44 b.; *Reale*, III, 49 b.; etc.

Asti, the Roman Asta, the seat of a bishop since 932 and one of the most powerful of the city-republics of northern Italy in the Middle Ages, lies in the valley of the Tárano, in a fertile wine-growing area which is particularly renowned for its sparkling wine, Asti Spumante.

SIGHTS. – At the E end of the *Corso Vittorio Alfieri*, the town's principal street, are the Romanesque **baptistery of San Pietro** (12th c.) and the *church of San Pietro in Consavia* (1467; beautiful terracottas and cloister), now part of the *Archaeological Museum* (closed Mondays). – Near the *Town Hall* is the Romanesque and Gothic **church of San Secondo* (13th–15th c.; crypt). – Towards the western end of the main street is the *Palazzo Alfieri* (museum), with the room in which the dramatist Vittorio Alfieri (1749–1803) was born. – Nearby is the **Cathedral** (brick façade, Romanesque campanile of 1266), built 1309–48 on the site of an earlier church. The S doorway is decorated with statues; the spacious interior contains Baroque paintings. On the N side is the Romanesque *baptistery of San Giovanni*, with a crypt (9th c.). – There are a number of old tower-houses belonging to noble families, among them the *Torre Troiana* and the *Torre dei Conentina*.

Bari

Region: Puglia. – Province: Bari (BA).
Altitude: 4 m. – Population: 360,000.
Post code: I-70100. – Dialling code: 080.
ⓘ **EPT**, Piazza Roma 33 A;
tel. 25 86 76.
    ACI, Via Ottavio Serena 26;
    tel. 33 13 54.
    TCI, Via Melo 259;
    tel. 36 51 40.
    CIT, Via Principe Amedeo 92;
    tel. 21 35 52.

HOTELS. – *Palace*, Via Lombardi 13, I, 336 b.; *Jolly*, Via G. Petroni, I, 322 b.; *Casa dello Studente*, Largo Fraccacreta 2, II, 363 b.; *Ambasciatori*, Via Omodeo 51, II, 333 b., SP; *Grand Hotel e d'Oriente*, Corso Cavour 32, II, 282 b.; *Windsor Residence*, Via Mauro Amoruso 62/7, II, 250 b., SP; *Astoria*, Via Bozzi 59, II, 204 b.; *Leon d'Oro*, Piazza Roma 4, II, 198 b.; *Victor*, Via Nicolai 71, II, 146 b.; *7 Mari*, Via Verdi 60, II, 144 b.; *Boston*, Via Piccinni 155, II, 111 b.; *Europa*, Via Oberdan 64, III, 91 b.; *Roma*, Piazza Roma 45, III,

81 b.; *Corona*, Via Sparano 15 A, III, 67 b.; etc. – YOUTH HOSTEL in Palese, Via Nicola Massaro 33, 194 b. – CAMPING SITE.

RESTAURANTS. – *La Pignata*, Via Melo 9; *Marc'Aurelio*, Via Fiume 1; *La Sirenetta al Mare*, Longomare Imperatore Traiano 52, 6 km outside town; etc.

EVENTS. – *Fiera del Levante* (Levant Fair), annually in September.

Known as the "gateway to the East" by virtue of its trade with the Eastern Mediterranean, the port of Bari is the chief town of the region of Apulia and the province of Bari, the largest city in Apulia and the second largest in southern Italy after Naples. It is an important industrial and commercial centre (petrochemicals, shipbuilding; site of Italy's first atomic power station), the see of an archbishop and possesses a university and a naval college.

Old Harbour, Bari

The picturesque old town, with its narrow winding streets, frequently spanned by arches, lies to the N, on a promontory between the old and new harbours. To the S is the spacious and regularly planned new town, which has developed considerably since 1930, when the Levant Fair was first held here. – The airport is 9 km W of the town at Palese.

HISTORY. – The ancient town of *Barium* was a place of no particular importance. Later the Byzantines made it their main base in southern Italy until its capture by Robert Guiscard in 1071. From 1324 it was an almost independent fief, which finally passed to the kingdom of Naples in 1558.

SIGHTS. – The central feature of the NEW TOWN is the palm-shaded Piazza Umberto I, on the W side of which are the University, with a well-stocked *Library* (160,000 volumes), and the interesting *Museo Archeologico Nazionale* (closed Mondays; move to Piazza San Pietro in the old town is planned), the leading collection of Apulian antiquities. – From the N side of the square the new town's principal traffic artery, *Via Sparano*, coming from the station, runs N past the modern church of San Fernando into the busy Corso Vittorio Emanuele II, which separates the new town from the old. 100 m along this to the left is the *Piazza della Libertà*, the hub of the city's traffic. On the right is the *Prefecture*, on the left the Town Hall, which also accommodates the *Teatro Piccinni*. – From the E end of

the Corso Vittorio Emanuele II the Corso Cavour, lined with handsome buildings, leads S towards to station, passing the *Teatro Petruzzelli*, one of the largest theatres in Italy. – The E end of the Corso Vittorio Emanuele II is also the starting point of the *Lungomare Nazario Sauro, a magnificent seafront promenade which runs SE past the Old Harbour. 1 km along this, on the right, is the Palazzo della Provincia, headquarters of the provincial administration, which contains the provincial *picture gallery* (mainly older pictures of Bari and the surrounding area; also works by Bellini, Vivarini, Veronese, Tintoretto, etc.).

In the centre of the OLD TOWN is the *Cathedral of San Sabino, originally built 1170–78, with considerable remains of Norman ornament. In the crypt is an elaborately adorned painting of the Virgin from Constantinople. The archives contain two parts of a large *exsultet roll (the Catholic Easter liturgy) of the 11th c. – A little way N of the cathedral is the *church of San Nicola, a large pilgrimage church (begun in 1087 but not completed until the 13th c.) which is one of the finest achievements of Romanesque architecture in Apulia.

INTERIOR. – Above the high altar is a 12th c. *tabernacle, and to the right of the altar is a "Madonna with Saints" by Vivarini (1476). In the apse is the tomb (1593) of Bona Sforza (d. 1558), wife of King Sigismund II of Poland and last duchess of Bari. The *crypt*, with 26 different columns, contains a silver altar (1684), under which is a vault containing the remains, brought here from Myra in Lycia (Asia Minor), of the very popular *Saint Nicholas of Bari* (c. 350), patron of seamen, prisoners and children (principal feast 8 May). The crypt also contains the *episcopal throne of Bishop Elia (1098), with fine carved decoration. – The church has a valuable *treasury*.

Beside San Nicola is the little *church of San Gregorio* (11th c.), with richly decorated windows.

To the W of the old town is the **Castello**, begun by Frederick II in 1233, converted into a palace by Bona Sforza in the 16th c. and later used as a prison and signal station. It now houses an interesting *Museum* with copies of Apulo-Norman sculpture (special exhibitions from time to time). – From the Castello the wide Corso Vittorio Veneto runs W past the **Great Harbour** (or New Harbour) to the grounds of the Levant Fair, 2·5 km away on the seafront.

SURROUNDINGS. – 15 km SW of Bari is the little town of **Bitetto** (alt. 139 m; pop. 7000), with a beautiful 14th c. cathedral. – From here it is another 29 km SW over the *Murge* plateau to **Altamura** (alt. 473 m; pop. 45,000; Autostello, III, 23 b.), still partly surrounded by its old walls, with an imposing *cathedral (begun in 1231, during the reign of Frederick II; renewed in the 14th and 16th c.). Richly decorated doorway (1312) on main front; pulpit and bishop's throne (16th c.); beautifully carved choir-stalls (1543). – 11 km E of Altamura is **Gravina di Puglia** (alt. 350 m; pop. 33,000; Hotel Peucezia, II, 62 b.), picturesquely situated above a deep gorge (*gravina*), with a 15th c. cathedral (choir-stalls), the church of Santa Sofia (tomb of a duchess of Gravina, 1518) and a municipal museum. Immediately outside the town, in the gorge, is the rock-hewn church of San Michele, with remains of Byzantine painting, and there is another rock-hewn church beyond the viaduct. On a hill N of the town are the ruins of a Hohenstaufen castle.

17 km W of Bari is **Bitonto** (alt. 118 m; pop. 38,000; hotels: S.1, II, 30 b.; Nuovo, III, 60 b.; etc.), with well-preserved town walls. In the centre of the old town is the *cathedral (*c.* 1200), perhaps the finest example of Apulian Romanesque architecture. Particularly beautiful are the richly decorated main doorway and the delicate pillared gallery on the S side; two fine pulpits. Under the church is a crypt with 24 columns. – E of the cathedral is the Palazzo Sylos-Labini, with a Renaissance courtyard (1500).

Barletta

Region: Puglia. – Province: Bari (BA).
Altitude: 15 m. – Population: 80,000.
Post code: I-70051. – Dialling code: 0883.
(i) **AA**, Piazza Roma;
tel. 31 13 73.

HOTELS. – *Helios Residence*, II, 144 b., SP; *Vittoria*, II, 53 b.; *Artu*, II, 50 b.; *Royal*, II, 42 b.; *Savoia*, III, 29 b.; etc.

The busy port of Barletta, one of the principal towns of Apulia, lies on the coast of the Adriatic between Foggia and Bari.

SIGHTS. – At the junction of Corso Vittorio Emanuele and Corso Garibaldi, one of Barletta's busiest traffic inter-sections, is the **church of San Sepolcro** (12th c.), an early Gothic church on the Burgundian model, with a rich trea-sury. In front of the church is a *bronze statue*, over 5 m high, of a Byzantine emperor (perhaps Valentinian I, d. 375), the finest piece of colossal sculpture in bronze that has come down to us from ancient times. – NE of the church is the *Municipal Museum*, with a picture gallery.

A little way to the NE, at the end of the narrow Via del Duomo, the continuation of the Corso Garibaldi, is the *Cathedral of Santa Maria Maggiore. The W end and campanile are Romanesque (1147–92), the rest of the nave and the choir Gothic (14th c.). The church contains the tomb of a count of Barby and Mühlingen (d. 1566), with an inscription in German, and a fine pulpit and tabernacle (both 13th c.).

Castel del Monte

– Beyond the cathedral is the massive **Castello**, originally built by the Hohen-staufens in the 13th c., with four bastions added in 1537. – NW of the cathedral is the *church of Sant'Andrea*, with a Romanesque doorway (13th c.). – On the promontory N of the town is the *Porta Marina* (1751). To the E of this is the *harbour*, to the W the *bathing beach*.

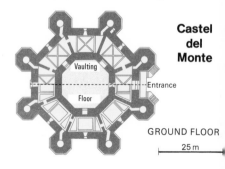

Castel del Monte

Vaulting

Floor

Entrance

GROUND FLOOR
|— 25 m —|

SURROUNDINGS. – The most rewarding excursion within easy reach of Barletta is to **Castel del Monte**, 30 km S. The road comes first (12 km) to **Andria** (alt. 151 m; pop. 78,000; Hotel Parco Vecchia Masseria, III, 34 b.; etc.) once a favourite residence of the Emperor Frederick II. In the crypt of the cathedral are the tombs of his second and third wives, Iolanthe of Jerusalem (d. 1228) and Isabella of England (d. at Foggia 1241). The church of Sant'Agostino has a fine doorway (13th c.).

From Andria it is another 18 km S to the****Castel del Monte** (alt. 540 m; closed Mondays; Ostello di Federico, III, 10 b.), the most imposing Hohenstaufen castle in Italy, built about 1240 as a hunting lodge for Frederick II, probably to his own design. The massive limestone structure, in early Gothic style, is an exact octagon, ringed by eight towers and with eight rooms of the same size on each floor; these originally had rich marble decoration; there is a beautiful inner courtyard. The rooms on the upper floor, which have particularly fine windows, are believed to have been the emperor's apartments. Later the castle served as the prison of the sons of Count Manfred (Frederick's grandsons). From the roof there are fine views, extending as far as Monte Gargano.

There is an attractive drive W from Castel del Monte (21 km) to **Minervino Murge** (alt. 445 m; pop. 20,000), splendidly situated on the highest part of the Murge and commanding extensive views. It has a castle and a small cathedral. In a park outside the town is a large war memorial, the Faro Votivo ai Caduti. From the N side of the park there are views of the town and surroundings. – 16 km N of Minervino is **Canosa di Puglia** (alt. 154 m; pop. 40,000), built on the site of the important Roman town of *Canusium*. There are remains of Roman walls, a town gate (to the W, outside the modern town) and the ruins of an amphitheatre of some size. The principal church, San Sabino, contains 18 ancient columns; in the choir is a marble bishop's throne supported by elephants (by Romualdus, 1078–89), in the nave a marble pulpit of c. 1120. In the court to the S (entered from the S aisle) is the *chapel, with a massive bronze door by Rogerius of Melfi, where Prince Boemond of Taranto (d. 1111), ruler of the Latin principality of Antioch is buried. – From Canosa it is 22 km NE back to Barletta. About half way there, off the road to the left, is the cemetery of the ancient town of *Cannae*, where Hannibal defeated a Roman army in 216 B.C. (museum; medieval cemetery of the 9th–11th c.).

Basilicata (Lucania)

ⓘ **EPT Potenza**, Via Alianelli 4,
I-85100 Potenza (PZ);
tel. (0971) 2 18 12.
EPT Matera, Piazza Vittorio Veneto 19,
I-75100 Matera (MT);
tel. (0835) 2 11 88.

The southern Italian region of Basilicata or Lucania, consisting of the provinces of Potenza and Matera, occupies 9992 sq. km of mountains and table-land, most of it in the southern Neapolitan Apennines. Bounded on the N by Apulia, on the S by Calabria and on the W by Campania, it is open to the Tyrrhenian Sea in the Gulf of Policastro and to the Ionian Sea in the Gulf of Táranto. In spite of the relatively fertile soil, which yields wheat, maize, wine, olives and edible chestnuts, many of the 600,000 inhabitants of the region still live in great poverty.

HISTORY. – A number of Greek colonies were established on the coast of the Ionian Sea in the 8th and 7th c. B.C., and the area was later Romanised, becoming Regio III of the Roman Empire. Throughout its history, however, Basilicata remained an area of little consequence, broadly sharing the destinies of neighbouring regions.

Potenza (alt. 823 m; pop. 60,000; hotels: Tourist, II, 154 b.; Grande Albergo, II, 98 b.; Park, II, 70 b.; San Michele, III, 48 b.), capital of the more westerly province, lies above the River *Basento* on a ridge between two valleys. It suffered severe damage in an earthquake in 1857 and again during the Second World War, but has since largely been rebuilt. In the centre of the old town, on the main street (Strada Pretoria), is Piazza Matteotti. To the NE stands the 18th c. cathedral. At the W end of the Strada Pretoria (to right) rises the Romanesque church of San Michele (11th c.). – Below the old town, to the N, lies the district of Santa Maria, with the important *Museo Provinciale Lucano* (finds from tombs, architectural fragments from the temple of Apollo Lyceus at Metaponto).

EXCURSION from Potenza. – Take the road which runs N via *Castel Lagopésole* (alt. 756 m), with a *castle in Gothic style built by Frederick II about 1242 on an eminence (829 m) W of the former lake from which the place takes its name. Beyond this, 51 km from Potenza, is **Rionero in Vulture** (alt. 662 m; pop. 15,000). From here it is 6 km NW to ***Monte Vulture** (1330 m; cableway), an extinct volcano visible from all over Apulia, its crater covered with a

On Monte Vulture

dense growth of beech forest. – 10 km W of Rionero are two small lakes, the Laghi di Monticchio (alt. 652 m; depth 35–38 m; Hotel Casina ai Laghi, III, 10 b.), on the smaller of which are the former Capuchin monastery of San Michele and a hydroelectric station. Between the two lakes are the ruins of the abbey of San Ippólito. 7 km away, on the western slopes of Monte Vulture, is the little spa of Monticchio Bagni (alt. 540 m).

From Rionero the road continues N (9 km) to Rapolla (alt. 438 m; pop. 5000; Hotel Terme Ala, III, 120 b.), from which a detour can be made to *Venosa (alt. 415 m; pop. 12,000), an ancient Samnite town, later (291 B.C.) a Roman colony (Venusia) and the birthplace of the poet Horace. Excavation has brought to light considerable remains of the town dating from the Imperial period. Stones from the amphitheatre were used in the construction of the church of the Santissima Trinità, founded in 1046, which is situated to the NE of the present town. The church was intended by Robert Guiscard (d. 1085) as a family burial place, but remained unfinished. It contains 11th c. frescoes, the tomb of Robert Guiscard's wife and Roman inscriptions and fragments of sculpture. To the N, on the road to the station, are Jewish catacombs (4th–5th c.), with inscriptions in Hebrew, Latin and Greek. In the centre of the town stands a 15th c. castle.

6 km NW of Rapolla, on a much-eroded lateral crater of Monte Vulture, is Melfi (alt. 531 m; pop. 20,000; Hotel Cemaca, III, 68 b.; etc.), the market town of an extensive wine- and olive-growing area. It has a 12th c. cathedral (modernised 1851). Adjoining the cathedral is the former Archbishop's Palace, which contains a magnificent Roman *sarcophagus (A.D. 165–170) from Rapolla. Above the town is a Norman castle (1270–80; restored).

The chief town of the more easterly province of Basilicata is Matera (alt. 401 m; pop. 45,000; hotels: President, II, 116 b., SP; De Nicola, II, 122 b.; Italia, III, 46 b.; etc.), the former capital of the whole region and see of an archbishop, in a remarkably picturesque *situation above the rocky gorge of the River Gravina. The houses, many of them hewn from the rock, are built in tiers on the hillside. On the highest point of the old town is the 13th c. cathedral: chapel decorated with sculpture, 16th c. crib (Nativity group). To the S of the cathedral is the church of San Francesco (paintings by Vivarini in the apse). – NW of San Francesco, past the old church of San Domenico, is the Romanesque church of San Giovanni Battista (13th c.). S of San Francesco, in Via Ridola, is the Museo Ridola (prehistoric material from the surrounding area). – The Strada Panoramica runs along the top of the gorge past the church of San Pietro Caveoso to the church of Santa Maria de Idris (Byzantine frescoes), on the rocky hill of Montorrone.

Near the NW coast of the Gulf of Taranto is Metaponto, with the remains of the famous Greek city of Metapontion, the Roman Metapontum. The town, probably founded by Achaean settlers at the beginning of the 7th c., became in the 6th c. a centre of Pythagorean teaching, the home of the great mathematician and philosopher Pythagoras, who is said to have died here in 497 B.C. at the age of 90. To the N of the town are the *Távole Palatine, the remains of a Doric temple, with 15 of the original 32 columns still standing. The *Antiquarium can display at any one time only a selection of the rich store of finds recovered in the excavations of recent years. Most of the material comes from the sacred precinct containing the remains of four large temples, which probably collapsed when they were undermined by rising ground-water in the 3rd c. A remarkable feature of the area is the carefully planned layout of the fertile plain, with regular field boundaries, roads and water channels and more than 300 Greek farmsteads, 11 of which have been excavated. The theatre (3rd c. B.C.), the walls of which were pulled down and the stones removed at an early period, had a semicircular cavea and Doric columns, anticipating some of the main features of the Roman theatre.

Benevento

Region: Campania. – Province: Benevento (BN).
Altitude: 135 m. – Population: 60,000.
Post code: I-82100. – Dialling code: 0824.
ⓘ EPT, Via Nicola Sala 31;
   tel. 2 19 60.
   ACI, Via Salvator Rosa 24–26;
   tel. 2 15 82.

HOTELS. – President, Via Perasso 1, I, 113 b., SP; Italiano, Viale Principe di Napoli 137, II, 120 b.; Traiano, Viale dei Rettori 9, III, 38 b.; etc.

Benevento, chief town of its province and the economic and communications centre of the fertile Benevento basin, is situated on a flat-topped hill between the rivers Sábato and Calore.

HISTORY. – The town was originally called Maleventum, but after the "Pyrrhic victory" of King Pyrrhus of Epirus over the Romans in 279 B.C. and the establishment of a Roman military colony in 268 it was given the more auspicious name of Beneventum. Situated at the junction of the Via Appia with four

Roman theatre, Benevento

other Roman roads, it developed into one of the most important towns in southern Italy, and from the 6th to the 11th c. was the seat of powerful Lombard dukes. Thereafter the town belonged to the Papal State (with a short interruption under Napoleon) until it became part of Italy in 1860. It has been the see of an archbishop since 969.

SIGHTS. – The town's principal street, running from NW to SE, is the *Corso Garibaldi*, in which stands the **Cathedral** (founded *c.* 1200), which was completely destroyed in 1943 apart from the façade and the campanile but has since been rebuilt. – SW of the cathedral are the remains of a *Roman theatre* (2nd c. A.D.). – Another 500 m SW is the *Ponte Leproso*, still incorporating part of the Roman bridge which carried the Via Appia over the Sabato.

E of the cathedral along Corso Garibaldi is the *Town Hall*, beyond which (to the left, along Via dell'Arco di Traiano) rises the *Arch of Trajan* or *Porta Aurea*, dedicated by the senate and people of Beneventum to the "best of princes" in A.D. 114 in anticipation of his return from the Parthian wars. The arch, built of Greek marble, stands 15·5 m high and is excellently preserved. One of the finest of its kind, it is decorated with reliefs glorifying the emperor.

Farther E along Corso Garibaldi is Piazza Santa Sofia (officially Piazza Matteotti), where stands the *church of Santa Sofia*, a circular structure of the Lombard period (732–74) with a 13th c. doorway. Adjoining the church is the beautiful cloister of a former convent of Benedictine nuns, now housing the interesting *Museo del Sannio* (Museum of Samnium: closed Sunday afternoons and Mondays), which contains a very fine prehistoric and early historical department (including Egyptian as well as Greco-Roman sculpture), a rich coin collection and medieval and modern pictures. – Still farther E, in Piazza IV Novembre, are a 14th c. castle, the *Rocca dei Rettori*, which contains the historical section of the Museo del Sannio, and the beautiful *municipal park* (views).

Bergamo

Region: Lombardia. – Province: Bergamo (BG).
Altitude: 247–368 m. – Population: 130,000.
Post code: I-24100. – Dialling code: 035.
ⓘ **EPT**, Viale Vittorio Emanuele 4;
tel. 24 22 26.
ACI, Via Angelo Maj 16;
tel. 24 76 21.

HOTELS. – *Grand Hotel Moderno*, Viale Papa Giovanni XXIII 106, I, 160 b.; *Excelsior San Marco*, Piazzale della Repubblica 6, I, 139 b.; *Arli*, Largo Porta Nuova 12, II, 80 b.; *Città dei Mille*, Via Autostrada 3, II, 66 b.; *Del Moro*, Largo Porta Nuova 6, II, 38 b.; *Piemontese*, Piazzale G. Marconi 11, III, 88 b.; *Cappello d'Oro*, Viale Papa Giovanni XXIII, III, 84 b.; *Commercio*, Viale T. Tasso 88, III, 58 b.; etc. – YOUTH HOSTEL: Viale Galileo Ferraris 1, 100 b.

RESTAURANT. – *Taverna del Colleoni*, Piazza Vecchia 7.

The provincial capital of Bergamo, picturesquely situated at the foot of the Bergamo Alps between the rivers Brembo and Serio, consists of an old town of narrow winding streets on a hill, defended by bastions erected between 1561 and 1592, and a lower town extending out on to the plain with modern buildings and busy industries (textiles, cement, printing).

HISTORY. – Originally a Gallic settlement and recorded in 200 B.C. as the Roman *Municipium Bergomum*, the town achieved no great importance until the Lombard period. In 1167 it became a member of the Lombard league of towns; then in 1264 it passed uder the control of Milan, and from 1428 to 1797 it belonged to Venice.

SIGHTS. – The centre of the LOWER TOWN (*Città Bassa*, alt. 247 m) is the *Piazza Matteotti* (gardens, monuments), adjoining which on the NW is the imposing *Piazza Vittorio Véneto*, with the *Torre del Caduti*, a war memorial. On the SE side of Piazza Matteotti are the twin neo-classical gatehouses of the *Porta Nuova* (*view of the upper town), from which the wide Viale Papa Giovanni XXIII runs SE to the station. This street and the Viale Vittorio Emanuele II, which leads NW from the Piazza Vittorio Veneto to the upper town, form Bergamo's principal traffic artery.

E of Piazza Matteotti, in the busy street called the Sentierone, stands the *Teatro Donizetti*, and in the Piazza Cavour on its E side is a monument to the Bergamo-born composer *Gaetano Donizetti* (1797–1848). – At the NE end of the

Upper town, Bergamo

- -

Sentierone is the church of San Bartolomeo (17th c.; façade 1901). Fine choir-
stalls; behind the high altar Lorenzo
Lotto's *"Madonna with Ten Saints"
(1516), one of his chief works.

From San Bartolomeo Via Torquato Tasso
runs NE to the church of the Santo
Spírito, which has a "Madonna with
Four Saints" by Lotto. – A short distance
N, in the steep Via Pignolo, is the little
church of San Bernardino in Pignolo, with
a *"Madonna Enthroned" by Lotto
(1521) in the choir. Higher up are a
number of palaces with beautiful Early
Renaissance courtyards. – In Via Santo
Tommaso, which goes off Via Pignolo on
the right, is the Accademia Carrara,
with a fine *picture gallery (works by
Lorenzo Lotto, Palma Vecchio, Moroni,
Carpaccio, Jacopo and Giovanni Bellini,
Mantegna, Romanino, Tiepolo, Titian,
Veronese, Raphael, Botticelli, Signorelli,
Crivelli, as well as Dürer, Cranach, Ru-
bens, Van Dyck and Clouet). – From the
Accademia Carrara a stepped lane leads
up to the Porta San Agostino.

From Piazza Vittorio Veneto the Viale
Vittorio Veneto runs NW and then NE past
the lower station of the funicular and
through the Porta San Agostino into the
UPPER TOWN (Città Alta, alt. 325–68
m). From the gate we keep straight ahead,
past the church of San Agostino on the
right, and then bear left and continue
steeply uphill on the Via di Porta Dipinta,
past the beautiful churches of San Michele al Pozzo Bianco and Sant'Andrea,
to the Piazza Mercato delle Scarpe, with
the upper station of the funicular on the
left. – From here Via Rocca, to the right,
ascends to the Rocca (12th–15th c.),
with the Museo del Risorgimento and the
church of Santa Eufemia. From the castle

keep and the adjoining Parco della
Rimembranza there are very fine *views.

From the Piazza Mercato delle Scarpe the
narrow Via Gombito, in which is a
patrician tower-house, the Torre di Gombito (c. 1100), leads to the *Piazza
Vecchia, which together with the neighbouring Piazza del Duomo forms the
architecturally impressive centre of the
upper town. Between the two squares is
the Palazzo dẹlla Ragione or Broletto
(largely rebuilt 1513), with an open
colonnade. Adjoining it is the tall Torre
Civica (lift). On the N side of the Piazza
Vecchia is the Palazzo Nuovo (Municipal
Library), in late Renaissance style, and on
the W side of the square the Università di
Lingue.

In the Piazza del Duomo the *church of
Santa Maria Maggiore, begun in 1137
as a Romanesque basilica, has a stepped-
back tower over the crossing and a
picturesque choir. On the S and N sides
are doorways guarded by lions, with
beautiful Gothic canopies (1351 and
1360). Fine 16th c. choir-stalls. – Adjoining the church is the *Cappella Colleoni,
in early Lombard Renaissance style, with
a lavishly decorated marble façade, built
1470–76 to house the tomb of Bartolomeo Colleoni. Tombs of Colleoni and
his daughter Medea (d. 1470), both by
Amadeo; ceiling paintings by Tiepolo
(1732). – To the right of the chapel is the
Baptistery (1340), originally in Santo
Mario Maggiore, which was re-erected
here in 1898. Opposite it is the Cathedral
of Sant'Alessandro (1459; choir 1560;
dome and façade modern), with good
pictures by Tiepolo and Bellini.

From the Piazza Vecchia the narrow
Via Colleoni runs NW to the Citadel
with museums of natural science and
archaeology. Beyond it is the Porta
Sant'Alessandro (funicular to viewpoint
on Colle San Vigilio, 5 minutes), from
which Viale delle Mura leads round the
walls (fine views) to the Porta San
Giácomo, the handsomest of the town
gates, and so back to the Porta San
Agostino.

SURROUNDINGS. – 24 km N, in the Bergamo Alps
is the spa of San Pellegrino Terme (alt. 355 m
hotels: Grand, I, 168 b.; Terme, I, 87 b.; Excelsior, II
107 b.; Bigio, II, 68 b.; etc.), which also attract
visitors because of its beautiful situation in the
Wooded Brembo valley and its equable climate. It

widely renowned alkaline mineral water (recommended for gout and stomach, liver and urinary disorders) comes from three springs (27 °C – 81 °F) on the right bank of the Brembo. Pump room, Kursaal, casino, theatre. From the Kursaal a funicular runs up in 10 minutes to *San Pellegrino Vetta* (750 m: restaurant). – There are many other attractive trips in the **Bergamo Alps**, to the N of the town.

RESTAURANTS. – *Al Papagallo*, Pi
Al Cantoncino (*Al Cantunzein*), P
Don Chisciotte-Sancio Pancia, Via
Grassilli, Via dal Luzzo 3; *Roste*
Nazario Sauro 19; *Sampieri*, Via Sampieri
Galli D'Oro, Via Stalingrado 42; *Diana*, Via Indipendenza 24; *Guido*, Via Andrea Costa 34; *Nerina*, Piazza Galileo 6; *Antico Brunetti*, Via Caduti di Cefalonia 5; *Nettuno*, Via Laura Bassi 1 – 2.

Bologna

Region: Emilia-Romagna. – Province: Bologna (BO).
Altitude: 50 m. – Population: 500,000.
Post code: I-40100. – Dialling code: 051.
ⓘ **EPT**, Via Leopardi 1;
tel. 23 74 14.
Information offices at stations and on motorways to S and E.
ACI, Via Marconi 7;
tel. 27 69 91.

HOTELS. – *Royal Hotel Carlton*, Via Montebello 8, L, 468 b.; *Grand Hotel Majestic Baglioni*, Via dell'-Indipendenza 8, L, 189 b.; *Eurocrest*, Piazza della Constituzione, I, 271 b., SP; *Elite*, Via A. Saffi 36, I, 269 b.; *Jolly Hôtel de la Gare*, Piazza XX Settembre 2, I, 224 b.; *Internazionale*, Via dell'Indipendenza 60, I, 210 b.; *Garden*, Via delle Lame 109, I, 142 b.; *Milano Excelsior*, Via Pietramellara 51, I, 29 b.; *Alexander*, Via Pietramellara 45, II, 203 b.; *Palace*, Via Montegrappa 9, II, 161 b.; *Roma*, Via d'Azeglio 9, II, 133 b.; *Motel Agip*, Via M.E. Lepido 203, II, 120 b.; *San Donato*, Via Zamboni 16, II, 91 b.; *Europa*, Via C. Boldrini 4, II, 86 b.; *Maggiore*, Via Emilia Ponente 62, II, 86 b.; *Cristallo*, Via San Giuseppe 5, II, 57 b.; *Metropolitan*, Via dell'Orso 6, II, 57 b.; etc. – YOUTH HOSTEL in Pescarola, Via Cà Bianca 32, 188 b. – Two CAMPING SITES.

The old capital of Emilia, situated in the fertile Upper Italian plain under the northern end of the Apennines, is one of the oldest towns in Italy, the seat of an archbishop and of an ancient and famous university. It has a character all its own, with its long arcaded streets (total length 35 km), its brick-built palaces, its numerous old churches, its curious leaning towers and the remains of its 8 km circuit of 13th and 14th c. walls. A considerable programme of clearance and improvement is under way. Bologna is also famous for its culinary specialities, chief among them meat sauce "à la bolognese" and Bologna sausage.

Bologna's principal industries are the manufacture of pasta and sausages (particularly mortadella), shoe manufacture, chemicals, engineering, precision instruments and publishing. – The airport is at Borgo Panigale, 7 km NE.

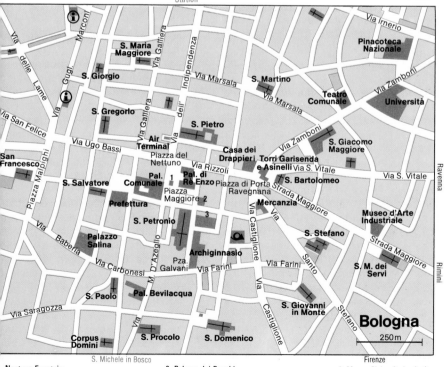

| Neptune Fountain | 2 Palazzo dei Banchi | 3 Museo Civico Archeologico |

HISTORY. – The town, known to the Etruscans as *Felsina*, became a Roman colony in 189 B.C. under the name of *Bononia* (the city centre still shows the regular layout of a Roman camp). It was declared a free city by the Emperor Henry V in 1116, and thereafter became a member of the Lombard League and took an active part in the struggle against the Hohenstaufens. The Imperial School of Bologna, which is said to have been in existence as early as the 5th c., became a university in the 13th c. – the oldest in Europe – and attracted students from many lands; in the 14th c. it pioneered the teaching of human anatomy. The noble families of the town, who were in constant conflict with the Papacy, managed to assert their authority in the 14th c., but in 1506 Pope Julius II was able to incorporate the town in the Papal State. In 1530 Charles V was crowned Emperor here – the last Imperial coronation on Italian soil. In 1796 the town was incorporated in Napoleon's Cisalpine Republic. In 1815 it reverted to Papal rule, and in 1860 finally became part of a united Italy. During the last war there was heavy fighting near Bologna, which suffered considerable damage, now largely made good.

ART. – The characteristic feature of the *architecture* of Bologna is the use of brick. The first buildings of any consequence date from the Gothic period (San Petronio). The Renaissance and Baroque are abundantly represented, outstanding among local architects being *Fioravante Fioravantini* (d. after 1430) and his son *Rodolfo*, known as *Aristotele* (d. 1486), *Pellegrino Tibaldi* (d. 1597) and *Sebastiano Serlio* (1475–1522), one of the great architectural theorists of the late Renaissance. Serlio's school of theatre architects and painters achieved an international reputation in the 17th and 18th c. through the work of the *Bibiena* family of Tuscany, laying the foundations of modern stagecraft. – *Sculpture* was practised mainly by artists from other parts of Italy. *Michelangelo* worked in San Domenico in 1494. – In *painting*, the first artist to attain more than local fame was *Francesco Francia* (1450–1517). Later the academy founded by *Lodovico Carracci* (1555–1619) and carried on by *Annibale* and *Agostino Carracci* fostered the school known as Eclecticism, whose leading representatives were *Guido Reni* (1575–1642), *Domenichino* (1581–1668) and *Guercino* (1581–1666).

SIGHTS. – The life of the town centres round two adjoining squares (both pedestrian precincts), the *Piazza Maggiore* and the *Piazza del Nettuno*. In the Piazza del Nettuno is the *Neptune Fountain* (by Giovanni Bologna, 1563–67).

From the Piazza del Nettuno the busy Via Rizzoli runs E to the Piazza di Porta Revegnana, with the famous leaning towers (see below), and another busy shopping street, Via dell'Indipendenza, leads N to the station. In this street, on the right, is the **Cathedral** of San Pietro (the *Metropolitana*), founded in 910, with a choir by Tibaldi (1575) and a nave remodelled in Baroque style (1605 onwards). Immediately E of the choir is the *Archbishop's Palace*. – Parallel to the Via dell'Indipendenza on the W is Via Galleria, with many old aristocratic mansions.

The W side of the Piazza del Nettuno and Piazza Maggiore is occupied by the **Palazzo Comunale** (Town Hall), an extensive Gothic building begun in 1290 and largely rebuilt in 1425–30. Above the main entrance (1548) is a bronze statue (1580) of Pope Gregory XIII, a native of Bologna. On the second floor is the *Municipal Art Gallery* (closed Tuesdays). – Opposite the Palazzo Comunale is the Gothic *Palazzo di Re Enzo* (restored 1905), in which Enzo, the poet son of Frederick II, was kept prisoner from 1249 to 1272. – On the N side of the Piazza Maggiore is the former *Palazzo del Podestà* (1201; rebuilt 1492–94 in early Renaissance style; tower 1263–68).

The S side of the Piazza Maggiore is dominated by *San Petronio, the largest church in Bologna, which is dedicated to the town's patron saint. Begun in 1390 in emulation of other large Gothic churches of the day, it was not completed according to the original plan, work being suspended about 1650 after the construction of the nave (117 m long, 48 m wide, 40·4 m high). The sculpture on the main doorway of the unfinished façade is by Jacopo della Quercia (1425–38). The interior ranks as the supreme achievement of Gothic architecture in Italy. An unusual feature is the meridian line set into the pavement. To the left of the choir is the *Museo di San Petronio.*

To the E of San Petronio, in Via dell'Archiginnasio (No. 2), stands the *Museo Civico Archeologico** (closed Mondays), with a collection of prehistoric and Etruscan material from the surrounding area, and other antiquities; the museum has the finest Egyptian department after those of Turin and Venice (Rooms III–V). The Greek department (Room VI) contains a *head of Athena Lemnia (copy of a work by Phidias, 5th c. B.C.).

From the Museum the Via dell'Archiginnasio, with the *Portico del Pavaglione* and its numerous shops, runs S to the Piazza Galvani, where stands a marble statue of the Bologna-born physiologist *Luigi Galvani* (1737–98), discoverer of the "Galvanic discharges" (though he himself interpreted them wrongly). On the left is the *Archiginnasio* (1562–63), until 1803 occupied by the university (with the old anatomy lecture-room, the Teatro Anatomico) and now housing the Municipal Library (600,000 volumes). – To the SW, in Via d'Azeglio, is the *Palazzo Bevilacqua* (1481–84), in early Florentine Renaissance style, with a magnificent courtyard. – From here Via Marsili leads to the Piazza San Domenico, in which are two columns bearing statues of St Dominic and the Virgin and the Gothic tombs of two learned lawyers, Rolandino Passagieri (d. 1300) and Egidio Foscherari. On the S side of the square is the **church of San Domenico** (begun *c.* 1235; façade unfinished), with an interior remodelled in Baroque style. In the S aisle is the *tomb of St Dominic (d. in Bologna 1221), a marble sarcophagus with carving by Niccolò Pisano and Fra Guglielmo (1267); cover by Nicolò dall'Arca (d. 1494; the angel on the right, the figure of St Petronius on the cover and the youthful St Proculus (to rear) are early works by Michelangelo (1494). Fine intarsia (mosaic woodwork) choir-stalls (1528–50). To the left of the choir, between the first and second chapels is a wall monument to King Enzo ("Hencius Rex", d. 1271; restored 1731). In the sacristy is the *Museo San Domenico.*

From the Piazza del Nettuno Via Rizzoli runs E to the *Piazza di Porta Ravegnana*, on the S side of which is the beautiful Gothic **Mercanzia** (1384), home of the Chamber of Commerce. In the middle of the square are the ***Leaning Towers**, two

The Leaning Towers, Bologna

plain brick towers, originally built for defensive purposes, which have become a landmark and an emblem of the city. The *Torre degli Asinelli* (1119; 498 steps), 97·6 m high, leans 1·23 m from the vertical; the *Torre Garisenda* (begun 1110), 48 m high, is 3·22 m aslant.

From the Piazza di Porta Ravegnana five streets radiate to the gates on the E side of

the town – Via Castiglione, Via Santo Stefano, Strada Maggiore, Via San Vitale, Via Zamboni. – In Via Santo Stefano is the basilica of **Santo Stefano**, a complex of eight buildings of which three have frontages on the street – the *church of the Crocifisso*, now the principal church, originally Romanesque but rebuilt in 1637, with an external pulpit (12th c.) and a crypt (1019); the *church of San Sepolcro*, an octagonal building on a centralised plan containing the tomb of St Petronius; and the Romanesque *church of Santi Vitale e Agricola* (founded 4th c.; present building 1019; façade 1885), with the 13th c. *Chiesa della Trinità.* Behind San Sepolcro is the *Cortile di Pilato,* a pillared courtyard of 1142 (marble basin, 741), adjoining which is a two-storey *cloister; museum. – In Strada Maggiore, immediately left, is the *church of San Bartolomeo* (1530; interior 17th c.). Farther along, on the right (No. 19), is *Casa Isolani,* a 13th c. aristocrat's mansion with a projecting upper storey supported on oak beams. Opposite (No. 24) is the *Palazzo Sampieri,* with admirable frescoes from the story of Hercules by the Carraccis and Guercino. Next door (No. 26) is the house of the composer *Gioacchino Rossini,* who lived mostly in Bologna between 1825 and 1848 (commemorative tablet). At No. 44 is the **Palazzo Davia-Bargellini** (1661), with a *Picture Gallery* and *Museum of Industrial Art* (closed Tuesdays). Almost opposite is the church of **Santa Maria dei Servi** (begun 1383), with a beautiful portico. – Some 500 m SE of the church, in Piazza Carducci, is the *Casa di Carducci,* which belonged to Giosuè Carducci (1835–1907), the most popular Italian poet of the 19th c.; to the right, on the town walls, is a monument to the poet (1928).

In the Via Zamboni (No. 13) is the *Palazzo Malvezzi-Médici* (1560), now the headquarters of the provincial administration. Farther along, on the right, is the **church of San Giacomo Maggiore** (1267; rebuilt *c.* 1500), which contains the *tomb of the jurist Antonio Bentivoglio (d. 1435), by Jacopo della Quercia. To the left of this, in the Cappella Bentivoglia, is a *"Virgin Enthroned" by Francesco Francia. The *Oratory of Santa Cecilia,* with beautiful frescoes by Lorenzo Costa, Francesco Francia and their pupils (1504–06), adjoins the church. Farther along Via Zamboni, on the left, stands the

Teatro Comunale (opera-house), 1756– 63). On the opposite side of the street is the former *Palazzo Poggi*, with a façade and ceiling paintings by Pellegrino Tibaldi (1569), which has been occupied since 1803 by the **University** (with some 40,000 students). Farther NE is situated the finely planned University City.

To the N of the university, in Via delle Belle Arti (No. 56), is a former Jesuit college which now houses the *Pina-coteca Nazionale* (closed Mondays), with some of the best works of Bolognese painters of the 15th–19th c., the 17th c. being particularly well represented. Outstanding among other works are a *"Madonna with Saints" by the Ferrarese artist Francesco del Cossa, one of his finest works, and a masterpiece by Raphael, **"St Cecilia". There are also pictures by Venetian masters including Tintoretto, Palma il Giovane, Cima da Conegliano and Vivarini. – At the W end of the Via delle Belle Arti stands the Carmelite *church of San Martino* (Gothic, 1313), which contains (first chapel on left) a "Madonna with Saints" by Francesco Francia.

In Piazza Malpighi, to the W of the town centre, is the **church of San Francesco**, built 1236–63 on the model of French churches, with a tower built 1397–1405. It contains a large Gothic marble altar (1388) and the tombs of three 13th c. jurists. – 500 m SE, in the *Palazzo Salina* (Via Barberia 13), we find the *Textile Museum*.

SURROUNDINGS. – 1 km from the Porta San Mámolo, on the S side of the town, at the end of Via Cadivilla, stands the former convent of **San Michele in Bosco** (alt. 134 m), now an orthopaedic hospital (*view). – 1·5 km W of Porta Sant'Isaia, on the site of an Etruscan cemetery, is the **Certosa** (founded 1333; used as a cemetery since 1801), with old and new cloisters and magnificent colonnades. – Also to the W of the Porta Sant'Isaia is the *Stadio Comunale*, which can accommodate 50,000 spectators.

500 m W of the Porta Saragozza, the SW town gate, begins a colonnade of 666 arches, 3·5 km long, which extends by way of *Meloncello* (where a branch goes off to the Certosa) to the *Monte della Guardia* (reached also by cableway and a motor road), with the pilgrimage *church of the **Madonna di San Luca**: beautiful *views, as far as the Adriatic and the Apennines and in clear weather the Alps.

Bolzano

Region: Trentino-Alto Adige. – Province: Bolzano (BZ).
Altitude: 265 m. – Population: 107,000.
Post code: I-39100. – Dialling code: 0471.
(i) **AA**, Piazza Walther 28;
    tel. 2 56 56.
    ACI, Corso Italia 19 A;
    tel. 3 00 03.
    CIT, Piazza Walther 11;
    tel. 2 15 16.

HOTELS. – *Park Hotel Laurin*, Via Laurino 4, I, 180 b., SP; *Grifone-Greif*, Piazza Walther 7, II, 210 b., SP; *Alpi*, Via Alto Adige 35, II, 162 b.; *Città-Stadthotel*, Piazza Walther 21, II, 167 b.; *Luna-Mondschein*, Via Piave 15, II, 135 b.; *Scala-Stiegl*, Via Brennero 11, II, 100 b.; *Metropol*, Via Rosmini 14, III, 66 b.; *Figl*, Piazza del Grano 9, III, 32 b.; *Cappello di Ferro-Eisenhut*, Via Bottai 21, III, 79 b. – IN GRIES: *Reichrieglerhof*, on the hill of Guncinà (Guntschnaberg), II, 46 b., SP; *Posta-Post*, III, 120 b.; *Gurhof*, III, 42 b. – CAMPING SITES: Via San Maurizio 83 and 93; Via Beato Arrigo 11.

RESTAURANTS. – In most hotels; also *Pircher-Grill*, Via Merano 52; *Caterpillar*, Via Castel Flavon 109 (S of the Isarco); *Da Cesare*, Via Perathoner 17; *Chez Frédéric*, Via Armando Diaz 12.

DANCING. – *Blow Up*, Via Rovigo 15; *Burgtaverne*, Via dei Portici 51.

SPORT and RECREATION. – Lido open-air and indoor baths, Viale Trieste; open-air pool on Monte Vírgolo; baths with sauna; tennis; bowling; *bocce* (Italian bowls); mini-golf; riding school in San Giácomo, 5 km S; climbing school; keep-fit track, Colle.

WINTER SPORTS. – Ice-rink in Palazzo della Fiera; skiing on Renon, at San Genesio and at Colle.

CABLEWAYS. – N to *Soprabolzano* (Renon) and *San Genesio*; S to *Vírgolo* (453 m; restaurant, open-air swimming pool, tennis) and *Colle* (1126 m; with the little resorts of *Col di Villa* (1140 m; keep-fit trail, ski-lifts) and *Col dei Signori* (1180 m).

EVENTS. – *Municipal Theatre*, Piazza Gries; *Walther von der Vogelweide House of Culture*, Via Crispi (near station), with theatre and congress hall; cinemas; concerts; exhibitions and conferences; artistic, cultural and sporting events, particularly during the *Bolzano Spring Festival* (mid April to mid June) performances by folk groups in Piazza Walther) *Bolzano Wine-Tasting* (Mar. or Apr.); Ferruccio Busoni International Piano Competition (Aug.– Sept.); Mendola International Car Race (at Appiano) *International Trade Fair* (Sept.); International Alpine Agricultural Show (end of Oct. in alternate years: next in 1981); wine-tasting trips at vintage time (mid Oct. to beginning of Nov.).

Bolzano (in German Bozen), capital of the autonomous province of Bolzano and the chief commercial, industrial and tourist centre of the mainly German-speaking region of Alto Adige (Südtirol), lies in a fertile basin at the junction of the river Isarco (Eisack), coming from the

Bolzano and the Catinaccio group

Brenner, with the Talvera (Talfer), coming from Val Sarentina. The Isarco, thus reinforced, flows into the Adige (Etsch) to the SW of the town. The background to the E is formed by the magnificent *Catinaccio group, with the Torri del Vaiolet, typical Dolomite peaks.

Situated at the intersection of important through routes and at the starting point of popular mountain roads, Bolzano has a busy transit traffic, but its convenient situation and beautiful surroundings also make it an excellent base from which to explore the region.

The old town, lying within the confluence of the Talvera and the Isarco, suffered considerable damage from air attacks during the Second World War but has nevertheless preserved its character almost intact. With its handsome Renaissance and Baroque buildings, its picturesque oriel windows, inner courts and staircases, it is a typical Germanic town. To the W of the Talvera are Italian residential districts. S of the Isarco is Bolzano's industrial zone.

HISTORY. – Bolzano was the Roman *Bauzanum*. In 680 it was taken by the Lombards and in 740 by the Franks, and later became the seat of Bavarian lords of the marches. For a time it belonged to the bishopric of Trent, which was compelled to cede it to the count of Tirol in the 13th c. It came under Habsburg rule in 1363, and thereafter shared the destinies of Tirol until 1919, when it passed to Italy. In 1948 the provinces of Bolzano and Trento were formed into the autonomous region of Trentino-Alto Adige, and German was granted the status of a second official language in the province of Bolzano. – Since 1964 Bolzano has been the headquarters of the bishopric of Bolzano and Bressanone, in which the communes in Bolzano province previously belonging to the diocese of Trento were also incorporated.

SIGHTS. – The central feature of the town is the **Piazza Walther** (Waltherplatz),

named after the German minnesinger Walther von der Vogelweide (*c.* 1170–1230). The monument to the poet which previously stood in the square was moved in 1935 to the Rosegger Park, 500 m SW, but is to be returned to its former position. At the SW corner of the square is the Gothic **parish church** (14th–15th c.), which, like its counterpart in Bressanone, has the status of a cathedral. It has an elegant tower 65 m high (1504–09) and a Lombard doorway; fine interior, with a late Gothic pulpit (1513–14) decorated with carved reliefs and frescoes of the 14th–15th c. – To the W is the Gothic **Dominican church** (13th–14th c.; rebuilt after war damage), with late 14th c. frescoes. In the adjoining *St John's Chapel* are *frescoes of the school of Giotto (1330–50), including a fine "Triumph of Death". The *cloister* of the former Dominican monastery (now the Conservatoire) has frescoes by Friedrich Pakker and other artists. – To the SE is the **Capuchin church** (1680; monastery 1599–1602).

To the N of Piazza Walther is the arcaded *Via dei Portici* (Laubengasse), the town's principal shopping and commercial street (pedestrian precinct), with fine 17th c. town houses. The handsome *Palazzo Mercantile* (1708–27: now the Chamber of Commerce), on the S side of the street, is the only example of an Italian palazzo in Bolzano (fine hall for conferences, etc.)

At the E end of Via dei Portici in a small square stands the *Town Hall*, a building in Baroque style erected in 1907; at its W end is the Piazza delle Erbe, with a *Neptune Fountain* (1777). A little way N

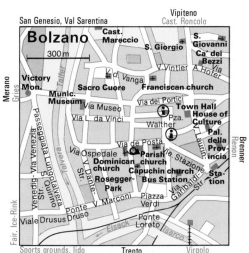

of the Piazza delle Erbe is the *Franciscan monastery*, with a **church** (13th–15th c.), restored after severe war damage, and a late Romanesque *cloister* (14th c.) which is now used for concerts. The fine late Gothic *altar of carved wood (by Hans Klocker, c. 1500) which formerly stood in the church is at present kept in the monastery. – Farther NE stands the late Gothic *church of the Teutonic Order* (Deutschhauskirche), San Giorgio.

From the Piazza delle Erbe the Via del Museo runs W to the **Municipal Museum** (closed Sundays), with archaeological material, peasant house interiors, traditional costumes, folk art and works by local artists.

From the *Lungotálvera Bolzano*, which begins at the Municipal Museum and follows the E bank of the Talvera for 1300 m, there are fine *views of Monte Sciliar and the Catinaccio group. A little way along this promenade, on the right, is **Castel Mareccio** (Schloss Maretsch, 13th–16th c.), with five towers. At the N end of the promenade is the 17th c. *Castel Sant'Antonio* (Schloss Klebenstein), and above it on a precipitous porphyry crag the 13th c. *Castel Roncolo (Schloss Runkelstein: alt. 361 m), with interesting frescoes of the 14th–16th c. – Passeggiata del Guncinà and Passeggiata Sant'Osvaldo: see below under *Surroundings*.

To the W of the Talvera extends the predominantly Italian NEW TOWN. Just beyond the Talvera Bridge is a large triumphal arch, the *Victory Monument* (Monumento della Vittoria, 1928). To the left is the Viale Venezia, which runs S to the *Lido* (open-air and indoor swimming pools and other sports facilities), 1 km away. A little way W of this are the grounds of the **Bolzano Trade Fair**, with the *Palazzo della Fiera* (at present an ice-rink). From here the Corso Italia runs N past the massive *Law Courts* to the Piazza Mazzini, where it meets the *Corso Libertà*, a street which runs W, lined by tall arches, from the Victory Monument and continues to the main square of Gries.

The suburban district of GRIES (alt. 273 m), which was incorporated in Bolzano in 1925, lies at the foot of the hill of Guncinà (Guntschnaberg) and was formerly a popular winter resort noted for its mild

climate. The old central area is surrounded by numerous villas set in trim gardens.

On the E side of the main square of Gries is a *Benedictine monastery*, originally built as a castle, with a beautiful **church** in late Rococo style (1769–78: *ceiling paintings and altarpieces by Martin Knoller). To the NW stands the *Old Parish Church* (Gothic, 15th–16th c.), with a beautifully carved *altarpiece by Michael Pacher.

SURROUNDINGS. – To the N of the Old Parish Church in Gries is the beginning of the *Passeggiata del Guncinà*, an attractive path which winds its way up the hill and ends at the Reichrieglerhof hotel (45 minutes). The hotel can also be reached by road (3·5 km) from the Victory Monument by way of Via Cadorna and Via Miramonti. From here a steep paved footpath descends into the valley past the *Torre di Druso* (Gescheibter Turm) to the upper bridge over the Talvera (20 minutes). Beyond the bridge are *Castel Sant'Antonio* and the beginning of the *Passeggiata Sant'Osvaldo*, which climbs through the vineyards, affording fine views, to a height of 400 m and then runs down past the picturesque wine village of *Santa Maddalena* to the suburban district of *Rencio* on the road to the Brenner (1¼ hours).

The best view of Bolzano and the surrounding area is from the *Vírgolo (Virgl, 453 m: restaurant), which can be reached by cableway from the right bank of the Isarco, 0·5 km S of the Piazza Walther, or on foot on a mule-track (30 minutes).

Another attractive walk (1–1½ hours) is to **Colle** (Kohlern, 1126 m; also accessible by cableway), with *views of the Sciliar and Catinaccio groups. E of the little summer resort of *Col di Villa* (Bauernkohlern, 1140 m) another small resort, *Col dei Signori* (Herrenkohlern, 1180 m) can be reached on foot in ½ hour.

A little way N of the upper bridge over the Talvera is a cableway up to **San Genesio Atesino** (Jenesien, 1080 m; also reached on a narrow mountain road), a village which is a popular health resort, with magnificent *views of the Dolomites.

NE of Bolzano is the *Renón (Ritten), an extensive porphyry plateau lying between the Talvera and the Isarco, reached by an excellent road (17 km) from Bolzano. – 12 km: *Áuna di Sotto* (Unterinn, 908 m), where a narrow road (5 km) branches off, past the little *Lago di Castro*, to **Soprabolzano** (Oberbozen, 1220 m), which can also be reached by cableway from Bolzano (replacing the rack railway which operated 1907–66); tram from Soprabolzano to Collalbo (5·4 km). – 5 km: **Collalbo** (Klobenstein, 1190 m), which, like Soprabolzano, is a popular summer resort, with superb *views of the Dolomites. To the N, in the Fosco gorge beyond *Longomoso*, are interesting *earth pyramids which are reached in ½ hour.

Over the Passo di Pennes to Vipiteno (67 km: gradients of up to 13%). – A beautiful run on an excellently engineered road. Leave Bolzano by way of Via Castel Roncolo and Via Beato Arrigo; then past Castel Sant'Antonio (on left: road to San Genesio cableway), and below Castel Roncolo (on right) over the Talvera to join the road which comes in from Gries on the left. Continue N on this road, passing on the right a covered wooden bridge carrying an old road over the river, and beyond this, in the valley, the old moated *Castel Novale* (Schloss Ried); then up the *Val Sarentina* (Sarntal), which narrows in places into a gorge between sheer walls of porphyry, with 24 tunnels. The road passes the extensive ruins of *Castel Sarentino* (Schloss Rafenstein, 16th c.: alt. 692 m) on the left and *Castel Vanga* (Schloss Wangen) on the right. Soon afterwards *Monte San Giovanni*, a massive porphyry crag 230 m high, with the old *church of San Giovanni*, can be seen ahead. – 10 km: *Locanda alla Posta* (Gasthaus zur Post Halbweg). The road continues up the valley, which here widens out. – 5 km: *Ponticino* (Bundschen-Dick, alt. 923 m: inn), with houses built for workers in the hydroelectric power station. – 1 km farther on, on the right, is the *Pino* inn, and soon afterwards (on left, lower down) the little spa of *Bagni di Serga* (Bad Schörgau: chalybeate water). – 4 km: **Sarentino** (Sarnthein, alt. 981 m), the chief place in the valley, a beautifully situated little town which is a favourite summer holiday resort. Two castles of *Regino* (Reineck, 13th c.) and *Kränzelstein*. The little church of San Cipriano contains over-painted 16th c. frescoes. Picturesque local costumes worn on Sundays.

The road continues up the Val Sarentina. – 3 km: **Campolasta** (Astfeld, alt. 1023 m), a pretty village at the junction of two valleys – to the right the Valdurna, with the village of the same name, situated on the beautiful *Lago di Valdurna* (12 km: alt. 1568 m; inn); to the left the pretty *Val di Pennes*. Going up the Val di Pennes, the road climbs gradually, coming in 9 km to the Alpenrose inn (on left). It then continues past a reservoir and the modest Edelweiss inn, running along the slope of the hillside. – 18 km: **Pennes** (Pens, alt. 1459 m), a straggling village, with a church, which is the chief place of the valley. The road then climbs more steeply up the bare hillside, with three sharp bends: to the left is the *Corno Bianco* (Weisshorn, 2705 m). – 10 km: **Passo di Pennes** (Penser Joch, 2211 m), with magnificent views, particularly of the peaks in the Ötz and Stubai valleys (Zuckerhütl, 3507 m). – Beyond the pass the road descends (gradient of 10%), at first high up on the bare slopes above the Val di Dosso (Eggertal). In 8 km, below the Schönblick inn, it comes to the hamlet of *Dosso* (Egg), with a chapel. It then runs down through forest country, with picturesque glimpses of the Isarco valley (Vipiteno, Burg Sprechenstein). Then a steep descent (13%) into the Isarco valley, joining the road from the Passo di Monte Giovo shortly before reaching the parish church of Vipiteno. – 17 km: **Vipiteno** (Sterzing, alt. 948 m).

Bordighera

Region: Liguria. – Province: Imperia (IM).
Altitude: 5 m. – Population: 12,000.
Post code: I-18012. – Dialling code: 0184.
(i) **AA**, Via Roberto 1;
tel. 2 15 80.

HOTELS. – *Grand Hotel del Mare*, I, 231 b., SP; *Grand Hotel Cap Ampelio*, I, 160 b., SP; *Jolanda*, I, 86 b.; *Florida*, II, 139 b.; *Continentale*, II, 132 b.; *Belvedere Lombardi*, II, 126 b.; *Miramare*, II, 81 b.; *Excelsior*, II, 71 b.; *Martinelli*, II, 66 b.; *Colibri*, II, 64 b.; *Residence Mimosa*, II, 60 b.; *Centro*, II, 56 b.; *Splendid*, II, 48 b.; *Astoria*, II, 42 b.; *Garden*, II, 40 b.; *Della Punta*, II, 36 b.; *Britannique e Jolie*, III, 90 b.; *Parigi*, III, 59 b.; *Villa Elisa*, III, 57 b.; etc. – CAMPING SITE.

Bordighera from Monte Nero

The little town of Bordighera, charmingly situated on the Riviera di Ponente near the French frontier, has long been a popular health resort and in more recent times has become equally popular as a seaside resort.

Bordighera consists of the picturesque old town (Città Vecchia), high above *Capo Sant'Ampelio*, and the newer districts W of the cape. It is famed for the date-palms (*Phoenix dactylifera*) which flourish here, though the dates seldom ripen sufficiently to be edible. Large quantities of branches are supplied to Roman Catholic churches for Palm Sunday and to Jewish communities for the Feast of Tabernacles. Flower-growing is also a considerable local industry.

SIGHTS. – The main traffic artery of Bordighera is Via Vittorio Emanuele, in which are the *theatre* and the *Chiesa di Terrasanta*. From this street various side streets climb up to the Via Romana (the ancient *Via Aurelia*), from which there are charming views of beautiful palm-gardens. The Via Romana ends in the W at the *Rio Borghetto*, in the E at the *Spianata del Capo*, on top of the promontory, from which there are magnificent *views – of the Ospedaletti bay to the NE and Ventimiglia, the Côte d'Azur and the peaks of the Maritime Alps, usually snow-capped, to the W. At the foot of the cliff-fringed promontory is a seafront promenade, the Lungomare Argentina.

Just N of the Spianata del Capo is the old town, a huddle of narrow winding streets, still with the old town gates. From here the Via dei Colli runs W above the little town, affording superb views.

In the outlying district of *Arziglia*, to the E, near the mouth of the Sasso valley and the Kursaal, are the *Vallone Gardens* (private property), laid out by a German gardener named Ludwig Winter (d. 1912). – 1·5 km farther E, on the road to Ospedaletti, is the *Madonna Garden*, also laid out by Winter (and also private property).

SURROUNDINGS. – From the Via dei Colli a road runs N above the Sasso valley to (3 km) the fortress-like village of **Sasso**, situated on the summit of a hill (220 m). 8 km farther on is the little village of *Seborga* (alt. 513 m), which commands extensive views.

Brescia

Region: Lombardia. – Province: Brescia (BS).
Altitude: 149 m. – Population: 220,000.
Post code: I-25100. – Dialling code: 030.
EPT, Corso Zanardelli 34;
   tel. 4 34 18.
ACI, Via XXV Aprile 16;
   tel. 4 05 61.

HOTELS. – *Vittoria*, Via Dieci Giornate 20, I, 89 b.; *Ambasciatori*, Via Crocifissa di Rosa 92, II, 106 b.; *Igea*, Viale Stazione 15, II, 98 b.; *Ascot*, Via Luigi Apollonio 72, II, 77 b.; *Italia*, Via Gramsci 11, II, 68 b.; *Moderno Gallo*, Via Trieste 10, II, 43 b.; etc. – *Motor Hotel*, Viale Bornata 22, II, 76 b.; *Industria*, Via Orzinuovi 58, III, 105 b.; *Agip*, Viale Bornata 42, III, 57 b.

RESTAURANTS. – *La Sosta*, Via San Martino della Battaglia 20; *Augustus*, Via Laura Cereto 8; etc.

The provincial capital of Brescia, second in importance only to Milan among the towns of Lombardy, is attractively situated below two foothills of the Brescian Alps, on one of which is the Castello. The picturesque old town, surrounded by gardens, has Roman remains dating from the early Empire and handsome Renaissance buildings.

Following heavy damage during the Second World War some parts of the town have been rebuilt with wider streets and larger squares. The town's industries include textiles and hardware (one notable product being shotguns), and it is also an important market centre for the agricultural produce of the fertile surrounding area.

HISTORY. – The ancient *Brixia* became a Roman colony in the time of Augustus under the name of *Colonia Augusta Civica* and rose to prosperity as a result of its situation on the road which ran from Bologna through the Alps by way of the Splügen pass. During the Middle Ages it was an active member of the Lombard league of towns. From 1427 to 1797 it

belonged to Venice. – Brescia produced two notable painters – *Alessandro Bonvicino*, known as *Il Moretto* (1498–1555), whose colouring vies with that of the Venetians, and *Girolamo Romano*, known as *Il Romanino* (c. 1485–1559). Their works are well represented in the town's churches and in the Pinacoteca.

SIGHTS. – In the Piazza del Duomo is the cathedral, the **Duomo Nuovo** (17th c.; central dome 1825). On its S side is the **Rotonda** or *Duomo Vecchio*, a massive circular structure crowned by a dome (11th–12th c.) containing works by Moretto and Romanino. Beneath the transept lies the *Basilica di San Filastrio*, the remains of a pillared basilica of the Lombard period. – To the N of the Duomo Nuovo is the **Broletto** (1187–1250), the old Town Hall, now housing the Prefecture, with the Torre del Popolo.

To the W of the Piazza del Duomo is the *Piazza della Vittoria*, the town's central square (rebuilt 1933). Behind the Post Office lies the *Piazza della Loggia*, one of the most picturesque squares in northern Italy. On its W side is the superb **Loggia* (Town Hall), begun in Early Renaissance style (1492–1508) and completed between 1526 and 1574 (windows by Palladio). On the E side, above a palatial façade, rises the *Torre dell'Orologio* (Clock-Tower, 1552). On the S side is the *Monte di Pietà*, with a beautiful Early Renaissance loggia (end of 15th c.).

From the Broletto steps lead up to the **Castello**, an old stronghold of the Visconti family, surrounded by a park

1 Duomo Nuovo	6 Santa Madonna dei Miracoli
2 Duomo Vecchio (Rotonda)	7 Santi Nazaro e Celso
3 Monte de Pietà	8 Tempio Capitolino
4 Loggia (Town Hall)	Museo Romano
5 San Giovanni Evangelista	9 Museo dell'Età Cristiana

(zoo, museums, observatory); fine views. A tunnel, the *Galleria Tito Speri*, under the castle hill leads to the developing district of Borgo Trento.

From the Broletto the *Via dei Musei*, once the Via Aemilia, the main street of the Roman town, runs E to the **Tempio Capitolino**, a Corinthian temple built in A.D. 72, in the reign of Vespasian, and dedicated to Jupiter, Juno and Minerva, with a pronaos of eight columns and three cellas. The temple (closed Mondays) contains a collection of Roman inscriptions. Behind it is the **Museo Romano** (also closed Mondays), with Roman material from Brescia and the surrounding area, including a bronze statue, almost 2 m high, of a winged *Victory, dating from the period of construction of the temple. – Farther E, in Via Piamarta, is the **Museo dell'Età Cristiana** (Museum of Christian Antiquities: closed Mondays), in the early medieval *convent church of Santa Giulia*, with carved ivories of the 3rd–5th c. and a gold cross which belonged to the Lombard king Desiderius (8th c.). Immediately E of this is the 9th c. *church of San Salvatore*, which has a beautiful crypt (42 columns).

In the Corso Martiri della Libertà, to the SW of the town, is the little *church of the Madonna dei Mirácoli* (restored), with an elegant Early Renaissance vestibule (1487–1508) and an impressive interior. – To the SW of this stands the church of *Santi Nazario e Celso* (1780), with altarpieces by Moretto and a "Resurrection" by Titian behind the high altar. To the N is the Gothic *church of San Francesco* (1254–65), with an altarpiece by Romanino on the high altar and a beautiful Gothic cloister.

NW of the Piazza della Vittoria is the *church of San Giovanni Evangelista*, with paintings by Moretto and Romanino, and farther W, at the end of Via Capriola, the former *convent church of Santa Maria delle Grazie* (begun 1522), with a sumptuous interior (cloister, pilgrimage chapel).

The life of the town centres on the *Corso Zanardelli*, to the S of the Piazza del Duomo. On its N side, behind some houses, is the *Teatro Grande* (18th c.), with a handsome auditorium and foyer.

500 m SE, in Piazza Moretto, is the *Pinacoteca Tosio Martinengo** (closed Mondays), with fine works by Moretto, Romanino, Lotto, Vincenzo Foppa, Raphael and other masters. It has a department of modern art at Via dei Musei 81B.

SURROUNDINGS. – 13 km E of Brescia, a road with many bends and magnificent views leads to **Monte Maddalena** (875 m), from which there is a panoramic * prospect extending as far as Monte Rosa. – Other attractive trips from Brescia are to **Lake Garda** (see p. 122), to the E, and *Lake Iseo, to the NW.

Brindisi

Region: Puglia. – Province: Brindisi (BR).
Altitude: 11 m. – Population: 85,000.
Post code: I-72100. – Dialling code: 0831.
(i) **EPT**, Piazza Dionisi;
tel. 2 19 44.
ACI, Viale Liguria;
tel. 8 29 49.

HOTELS. – *Internazionale*, Lungomare Regina Margherita 26, I, 138 b.; *Jolly*, Corso Umberto I, I, 113 b.; *Mediterraneo*, Viale Liguria 70, II, 113 b.; *Barsotti*, Via Cavour 1, II, 84 b.; *Corso*, Corso Roma 83, II, 68 b.; *Regina*, Via Cavour 5, II, 63 b.; *L'Approdo*, Via del Mare 54, II, 37 b.; *La Rosetta*, Via San Dionisio 2, III, 57 b.; etc. – YOUTH HOSTEL in Casole, Via Nicola Brandi 2, 68 b.

The port of Brindisi, the Roman Brundisium, lying at the head of a wide inlet on the E coast of Apulia, has been since ancient times an important centre of trade with the Eastern Mediterranean, and it was used by the Crusaders as a naval base. The poet Virgil died here in 19 B.C. on his way back from Greece.

The sheltered *Inner Harbour* consists of two arms – to the W the *Seno di Ponente*, 600 m long, with long quays and a bathing beach, and to the E the *Seno di Levante*, 450 m long, in which very large vessels can berth. A channel 525 m long connects both arms with the *Outer Harbour*, the entrance to which is divided into two by the islet of Sant'Andrea, with a 15th c. fort. – Brindisi is the see of an archbishop and has active industries. – Airport 6 km NE.

SIGHTS. – The life of the town centre on the *Piazza del Popolo* and the adjoining *Piazza della Vittoria*, in which is the Head Post Office. To the S of the Piazza del Popolo stands the *church of Santa Lucia*, with a Byzantine crypt and catacombs. – From the Piazza del Popolo the Via Garibaldi runs NE to the Piazza Vittorio Emanuele, which overlooks the Seno di Levante. On the right is the *Marine Station* (ferry services to Greece). The Viale Regina Margherita, to the left, leads to a *marble column*, 19 m high, marking the end of the Via Appia (constructed from 312 B.C. onwards), the "Queen of Roads", which ran from Rome via Taranto to Brindisi.

SW of the column is the **Cathedral** (18th c.), and adjoining it (to left) the *Museo Archeologico Provinciale*, with medieval sculpture, Roman portrait statues, etc. Facing the museum, to the W, stands the 13th c. *Casa Balsamo*, with a richly decorated balcony. Farther SW is the former *baptistery of San Giovanni al Sepolcro* (11th c.), and beyond this the Norman *church of San Benedetto* (*c.* 1100), with a Byzantine side doorway and a cloister (fine relief carving).

Castello Svevo, Brindisi

Some 500 m W of the cathedral, above the Seno di Ponente, is the **Castello Svevo** (not open to the public), built by Frederick II in 1233, with massive round towers.

SURROUNDINGS. – There is a pleasant boat trip of a few minutes from Viale Regina Margherita across the Seno di Ponente to the *Monumento al Marianaio d'Italia*, a naval war memorial (1933) in the form of a ship's rudder, 40 m high (lift; fine *views from top). – 1·5 km NW of this (3 km from Brindisi) is the former *convent church of Santa Maria del Casale* (1322), with a beautiful doorway and fine frescoes.

Cagliari

Region: Sardegna. – Province: Cagliari (CA).
Altitude: 10 m. – Population: 230,000.
Post code: I-09100. – Dialling code: 070.
ⓘ **EPT**, Piazza Deffenu 9;
　　tel. 65 19 46.
　　Information office, Piazza Matteotti 1.
　　ACI, Via Enrico Carboni Boi 2;
　　tel. 49 19 50.

HOTELS. – *Jolly Regina Margherita*, I, 191 b., SP; *Mediterraneo*, II, 256 b.; *Moderno*, II, 139 b.; *Sardegna*, II, 119 b.; *Italia*, III, 192 b.; etc.

EVENTS. – *Sagra di San Efisio* (beautiful traditional dress) on 1 May; *Santa Maria di Bonaria* (patronal festival) on 24 April.

Cagliari (in Sardinian Casteddu), capital of the autonomous region of Sardinia, the island's principal port and commercial centre, a university town and the see of an archbishop, lies on the S coast of the island in the wide Gulf of Cagliari.

The oldest part of the town, which was founded by the Phoenicians and became the Roman *Carales*, is known as the *Castello* (Sardinian *Castedd'e susu*). It clings picturesquely to the slopes of a precipitous hill, around the foot of which are the newer districts and suburbs of the town. To W and E are two large lagoons, the *Stagno di Cagliari* and the *Stagno di Molentargius*, with extensive salt-pans.

SIGHTS. – The tree-shaded Via Roma runs along the harbour quay, with the *railway station* and the modern **Town Hall** (two towers; in the interior murals by F. Filgari) at its NW end. From the Town Hall the wide *Largo Carlo Felice* goes NE, gently uphill, to Piazza Yenne, from which the busy Corso Vittorio Emanuele runs NW. – Via G. Manno, a shopping and commercial street popularly known as the *Costa*, descends SE from Piazza Yenne to the Piazza della Costituzione. Off the Via Garibaldi, which begins here, is the *church of San Domenico*, with a beautiful cloister. – Farther E, in the wide Via Dante, is the *church of Santi Cosma e Damiano* (founded in the 5th c., enlarged in the 11th–12th c.), the oldest Christian building on the island.

From the Piazza della Costituzione the beautiful *Viale Regina Elena*, affording fine views, runs N below the sheer E side of the old bastion to the *Giardino Pubblico*.

Cagliari

A flight of marble steps, the *Passeggiata Coperta*, climbs to the *Bastione San Remy (officially *Terrazza Umberto I*), a magnificent terrace (views) laid out on the medieval bastions (which are preserved in part). Higher up, to the N, is the *Bastione Santa Caterina*, which also commands extensive views. From here Via dell'Università leads NW to the *University* (founded 1956: good library) and the massive *Torre dell'Elefante* (1307). – From the Bastione San Remy we pass through the gate of the old *Torre dell'Aquila* into the narrow Via Lamarmora, the main street of the old town, which runs N along the steep hillside, linked with parallel streets to right and left by steep lanes or dark archways and flights of steps. Half way along is the terraced Piazza del Palazzo, above the E side of which is the **Cathedral** of Santa Cecilia, built by the Pisans in 1312, with beautiful old doorways in the transepts. Inside, on either side of the entrance, are the two halves of a *pulpit from Pisa Cathedral which was presented to Cagliari in 1312. This masterpiece of 12th c. Pisan sculpture (by Master Guillelmus) is decorated with New Testament scenes. There are a number of tombs in the crypt of the cathedral.

At the N end of Via Lamarmora is the Piazza dell'Indipendenza, in which are the *Torre San Pancrazio* (1305: view) and the ***Museo Nazionale Archeologico** (closed Mondays), with Punic, Greek and Roman material as well as the largest collection of Sardinian antiquities. Of particular interest in Room 1 are the *bronzes found in the *nuraghi* (dolmens).

They are of crude and primitive workmanship but have a distinctive character. On the upper floor are pictures of the 14th to 18th c.

From the museum, Viale Buon Cammino runs N through the outer courtyard of the Citadel and along the ridge of the hill. In 500 m a road leads down on the left to the Roman **Amphitheatre** (88·5 by 73 m; arena 50 by 34 m), constructed in a natural depression in the rock, which is now used as an open-air theatre. SW of the amphitheatre is the *Botanic Garden* (closed Mondays), with luxuriant southern vegetation.

SURROUNDINGS. – There is an attractive trip (7 km SE), passing close to *Monte Sant'Elia* (139 m: view) and the extensive *Molentargius* salt-pans, to the **Spiaggia di Poetto**, Cagliari's popular bathing beach, which extends for 10 km along the *Golfo di Quartu*. – From here it is possible to continue for another 50 km to the SE tip of the island. The road traverses an extensive agricultural development area; then beyond the hamlet of *Flúmini* a beautiful stretch of road keeps close to the coast through beechwoods, passing many old watch-towers and *nuraghi*, to *Capo Carbonara*, the extreme south-easterly point of Sardinia (views), with the *Torre Santa Caterina* (17th c.: alt. 115 m). Nearby is the *Fortezza Vecchia* (17th c.).

Another rewarding excursion is a tour of the *Iglesiente*, the hilly region in the SW of the island. – Leave Cagliari on S.S. 195, which runs SW along the spit of land between the *Stagno di Cagliari* and the sea and past the large S. Gilla salt-pans. At the village of *Sarroch* (20 km) is a very characteristic *nuraghe*. 7 km farther on is *Pula*, from which a road leads S (4 km) to the remains of the Phoenician and later Roman town of **Nora**, on a narrow peninsula (forum, amphitheatre, temples, foundations of villas, well-preserved mosaic pavements). – After some time the road leaves the coast. 38 km from Pula it crosses a pass (301 m), with the *Nurag de Musu*, and comes in another 14 km to the attractively situated little town of **Teulada** (alt. 63 m), chief place of the southern part of the Iglesiente, known as *Sulcis*. – 36 km from Teulada S.S. 195 joins S.S. 126 at *San Giovanni Suergiu*.

From San Giovanni Suergiu there is an interesting excursion (11 km SW) to the volcanic island of **Sant'Antíoco** (alt. 15 m; pop. 11,000; Hotel La Fazenda, III, 60 b.; etc.). On either side of the castle is a well-preserved Phoenician cemetery (*c.* 550 B.C.), with a small museum. Many of the tombs – sometimes enlarged by knocking down party walls – are occupied as dwellings. 9 km NW of Sant'Antioco is *Calasetta* (alt. 29 m; Hotel Stalla del Sud, III, 100 b., SP; etc.), a little place of rather Oriental appearance which was originally established by settlers from Carloforte, on the neighbouring island of San Pietro, who, like the inhabitants of that island preserved the language and costumes of Genoa; there are boats to Carloforte ($\frac{1}{2}$ hour) several times daily.

Beyond San Giovanni Suergiu the tour of the Iglesiente continues N of S.S. 126, which comes in 6 km to **Carbonia** (pop. 35,000; Hotel Centrale, IV, 57 b.), a new town founded in 1938 in the middle of the

Sardinian coalfield. In another 11 km a road branches off on the left to the little ports of *Portoscuso* (tuna fishing) and *Portovesme*, from which there are boats (including car ferries) several times daily (¾ hour) to **Carloforte** (alt. 10 m; pop. 8000; Hotel Riviera, III, 45 b.), the chief place on the island of **San Pietro** (area 52 sq. km). Carloforte was founded in 1736 by Genoese settlers from an island off Tunisia which had been in Genoese hands since the 13th c., and their descendants still preserve their distinctive language and costume. – An interesting trip (though not for the faint-hearted) is a visit to the **tuna-fishing grounds** (*tonnare*) off the northern tip of the island near the little *Isola Piana* and Portoscuso during the tuna season (May and early June). The tuna grows to a length of 2–4 m and a weight of 150–300 kg (330–661 lb); canned in oil the fish are much prized in Italy. It lives mainly in the Mediterranean, moves E in spring to spawn, travelling in dense shoals which are often accompanied by sharks, and is caught in large nets and rather messily killed off the coasts of Sardinia and Sicily. Thousands of people are employed during the season on the catching, cutting up, cooking and canning of the fish.

13 km beyond the turning for Portoscuso and Portovesme is *Iglesias* (alt. 190 m; pop. 23,000; Hotel Artu, III, 31 b.), an old episcopal town in the centre of the Iglesiente which still preserves remains of its medieval walls and has a Mining Academy (museum). In the Piazza del Municipio is the cathedral built by the Pisans in 1285, and to the S of the square is the medieval church of San Francesco. Above the town to the E is the Castello Salvaterra.

From Iglesias it is 56 km E on S.S. 130 to Cagliari. Shortly before reaching the town the necropolis of ancient *Carales* can be seen in the limestone cliffs on the left of the road, with Punic and Roman tomb chambers hewn from the rock in vertical shafts.

Calabria

Provinces: Catanzaro, Cosenza and Reggio di Calabria.

ⓘ **EPT Catanzaro**, Via F. Spasari,
I-88100 Catanzaro (CZ);
tel. (0961) 2 98 23.
EPT Cosenza, Via Tagliamento 15,
I-87100 Cosenza (CS);
tel. (0984) 2 78 21.
EPT Reggio di Calabria, Via C. Colombo 9,
I-89100 Reggio di Calabria (RC);
tel. (0965) 9 84 96.

The region of Calabria, consisting of three provinces with a total population of some 2 million, occupies the toe of the Italian boot. Occupying an area of 15,080 sq. km in the SW of the peninsula, it lies between the Ionian and Tyrrhenian seas. It is traversed by the Calabrian Apennines – three massive ranges of granite and gneiss heights belonging to an ancient mountain rump. In the N is the Sila (Botte Donato, 1930 m) and in the S the Aspromonte

Verbicaro and the Catena Costiera

range (Montalto, 1958 m), separated by an expanse of low-lying land, once marshy and malaria-ridden, which is caught between the Golfo di Squillace in the E and the Golfo di Santa Eufemia in the W. Along the W coast of northern Calabria, separated from the Sila by the fertile Crati valley, extends the Calabrian Coastal Chain (Catena Costiera), falling down to the sea in precipitous cliffs.

The lower uplands are covered with dense mixed forests of beeches and pines (representing about 40% of the total area of Calabria), which give the landscape an almost Central European character. There are no beaches along the coasts, which are much indented by bays and coves. The region has been frequently devastated by violent earthquakes, particularly along the Strait of Messina.

Economically Calabria is one of the most underdeveloped parts of Italy. The overwhelming majority of the population live by agriculture. In the fertile low-lying land a mixed agriculture of Mediterranean type predominates, producing wheat, olives, citrus fruit, wine and figs; at the higher levels only pasturing is possible. The only minerals of any consequence are rock salt (at Lungro) and sulphur (at Strongoli). A number of dams in the Sila range supply electric power for the recently developed industrial area around Crotone.

HISTORY. – In ancient times the name of Calabria was given to the Salentine peninsula, the "heel" of Italy between the Gulf of Taranto and the Adriatic, which was occupied by the Iapyges and conquered by Rome in 272 B.C. Present-day Calabria was then the land of the Bruttii, and formed part of Magna Graecia from the 8th c. until it was occupied by Rome during the second Punic War. After the fall of the Ostrogothic kingdom it passed to Byzantium and was given the name of Calabria after the loss of the Salentine peninsula. In the 9th and 10th c. Calabria suffered repeated Saracen raids. It was conquered by the Normans in 1060, and later became part of the kingdom of Naples until its union with Italy in 1860.

The capital of the region is **Catanzaro** (alt. 343 m; pop. 45,000; hotels: Grand, II, 159 b.; Sant'Antonio, II, 128 b.; Albergo Moderno, II, 90 b.; Guglielmo, II, 73 b.; Diana, II, 69 b.; Casalbergo, III, 244 b.; etc. – Motel Agip, II, 152 b.), the see of an archbishop, beautifully situated on a plateau which falls away to the S, E and W. In the centre of the town are the cathedral (rebuilt after its destruction during the Second World War) and the church of San Domenico (good pictures and sculpture). There are very fine views from Via Bellavista, on the S side of the town, and the municipal gardens to the E. – 13 km S of Catanzaro, on the coast of the Ionian Sea between the mouths of the rivers Corace and Fiumarella, is the port and seaside resort of *Catanzaro-Lido* (alt. 5 m; hotels: Palace, II, 165 b.; Niagara, II, 90 b.; Lido, II, 45 b.; Stillo, II, 36 b.; King, III, 21 b.).

17 km E of Catanzaro, in a delightful setting, is the little town of **Tiriolo** (alt. 690 m; pop. 5000; Hotel Calabrese, IV, 12 b.; Autostello ACI, III, 10 b.), renowned for the beautiful costumes of its women and for its embroidery and lace. Above the town to the NE (½ hour's climb) is *Monte di Tiriolo* (838 m: *view), with a ruined castle.

34 km NW of Catanzaro, in a gorge near the coast and on the hillside above, is **Paola** (alt. 94 m; pop. 9000; Hotel Duemila, IV, 15 b.), with its port of *Paola Marina* (hotels: Giulia, II, 160 b.; Terminus, II, 108 b.; Alhambra, II, 80 b.; L'Ostrica, III, 39 b.; etc.). – 1·5 km NW of Paola is the convent of San Francesco di Paola (1416–1507, born in Paola, founder of the mendicant order of the Minims). The convent was built straddling a gorge in the 15th c. and enlarged in the 17th. – There is also an attractive drive from Paola (17 km) to the *Passo Crocetta* (979 m: *view).

In the fertile Crati valley in NW Calabria lies **Cosenza** (alt. 240 m; pop. 100,000; hotels: Jolly, I, 108 b.; Imperiale, II, 99 b.; Centrale, II, 80 b.; Mondial, III, 80 b.; Nuovo Excelsior, III, 76 b.; Alexander, III, 76 b.; etc.), once capital of the Bruttii (*Cosentia*), now a provincial capital and the see of an archbishop. The Visigothic leader Alaric died in Cosentia in A.D. 410 and was buried with his treasure in the bed of the River Busento. The handsome new town lies to the NW; the old town with its narrow winding streets is built on the slopes of the castle hill and the tongue of land within the confluence of the Crati and the Busento. In the winding main street, Corso Telesio, is the early Gothic cathedral (consecrated 1222), in which the unhappy Hohenstaufen king Henry VII was buried in 1242; in the N transept is the tomb of Isabelle, wife of Philip III of France, who died in Cosenza in 1271. – From the municipal gardens on the S side of the old town a footpath climbs NW to the Castello (alt. 385 m: view), with walls 3 m thick which nevertheless were not strong enough to withstand the frequent earthquakes (particularly severe in 1783 and 1905).

From Cosenza a very rewarding trip can be made into the *Sila range. This consists of three parts – the main range, *Sila Grande*; the *Sila Piccola* to the S; and along the northern edge of the range the *Sila Greca*, named after the Albanians of the Greek Orthodox faith who have been settled there since the 15th c. The Sila is a plateau-like massif of ancient rocks with a total area of 3300 sq. km and an average height of 1300–1400 m, rising to 1930 m in Botte Donato, which presents a precipitous face to the Crati valley but falls away gradually towards the Gulf of Taranto. Its extensive forests of chestnuts, beeches, oaks, black spruces and pines are still inhabited by wolves as well as by numerous black squirrels. Since 1927 the rivers have been harnessed to provide electricity by the construction of dams which form large artificial lakes; one of the most attractive of these is *Lago Arvo (alt. 1280 m). On the high plateaux, with their extensive areas of grazing, the trim houses of the new settlers who have been

Capo Vaticano

Women of Rossano in local costume

established here under the government's land reform form a striking contrast to the wretched cottages of the past. – In the N of the Sila Greca, picturesquely situated on a hillside a few kilometres from the sea, is **Rossano** (alt. 297 m; pop. 24,000; Hotel Scigliano, III, 45 b.; etc.), once capital of Calabria and still the see of an archbishop. On a crag to the SE of the town is the church of San Marco, a church of Byzantine type on a centralised plan, with five domes, dating from the Norman period. The archiepiscopal library contains a valuable 6th c. Gospel manuscript. From the terrace half way along Via Garibaldi there is a very fine *view of Monte Pollino and the Apulian plain.

32 km NW of Rossano, in the lower course of the Crati, not far from the sea, are the remains of the ancient city of **Sybaris**, founded in 709 B.C. by Achaeans, which became proverbial for its luxury but was destroyed in 510 B.C. by the people of Croton. Systematic excavations have been carried out here since 1960 by Milan Technical College and Pennsylvania University.

On the E coast of northern Calabria is the port and industrial town of **Crotone** (alt. 43 m; pop. 52,000; hotels: Casarossa, II, 364 b., SP; Tiziana, II, 346 b., SP; Costa Tiziana, II, 220 b.; Bologna and de la Ville, II, 128 b.; Capitol, II, 114 b.; Jorno, III, 55 b.; etc.), in antiquity the famous Achaean colony of *Croton*, founded in the 8th c.

B.C., which was ruled in the 6th c. by Pythagoras and his disciples. In the Castello is the Museo Civico, with prehistoric and classical material; from the tallest tower there are very fine views.

From Crotone an interesting excursion can be made (11 km) to **Capo Colonna** which has the remains of a temple of Hera Lacinia. The rounding of this cape by the Romans in 282 B.C. led to the outbreak of the Pyrrhic War. In 203 B.C. Hannibal sailed from here, leaving a record of his deeds in the temple.

The principal town of southern Calabria is **Reggio di Calabria** (see p. 210). – 24

The Castello, Scilla

km N, in a charming *situation, is the little town of **Scilla** (alt. 73 m; pop. 7000), with a picturesque castle rearing above it. This was the ancient *Scylla*. It was destroyed by an earthquake in 1908 but subsequently rebuilt. – The rock of **Scylla**, represented in the "Odyssey" as a roaring and devouring marine monster (the upper part a beautiful virgin and the lower a monster with a wolf's body and a dolphin's tail), is depicted by ancient writers as combining with **Charybdis** on the opposite shore to form a hazardous passage for all shipping – no doubt reflecting the dangerous eddies produced by the action of wind and tide in these straits. – 9 km SW of Scilla is **Villa San Giovanni** (alt. 38 m; pop. 11,000; hotels: Piccolo, I, 128 b.; Cotroneo, III, 58 b.; etc.), from which there is a ferry across the **Strait of Messina** (here 4 km wide) to Sicily. There are plans to build a bridge.

On the E coast of southern Calabria, 3 km S of the resort of **Locri** (alt. 3 m; pop. 10,000; hotels: Rachel, II, 185 b.; Teseyon, II, 95 b.; Demaco, II, 47 b.; etc.), are the remains of the ancient Greek city of *Lokroi Epizephyrioi* (signposted "Scavi di Locri"), famous for the code of laws compiled by Zaleucus. Near the coast road are the foundations of a temple rebuilt in Ionic style in the 5th c. B.C., and on the hill of *Mannella*, to the N of the excavation site, are remains of the town walls. There are also a theatre, a Doric temple and an extensive pre-Greek and Greek cemetery.

Campania

Provinces: Avellino, Benevento, Caserta, Napoli and Salerno.

(i) **EPT Avellino**, Via Due Principati 5,
I-83100 Avellino (AV);
tel. (0825) 3 51 69.
EPT Benevento, Via N. Sala 31,
I-82100 Benevento (BN);
tel. (0824) 2 19 60.
EPT Caserta, Piazza Dante 33,
I-81100 Caserta (CE);
tel. (0823) 2 11 37.
EPT Napoli, Via Partenope 10A,
I-80100 Napoli (NA);
tel. (081) 40 62 89.
EPT Salerno, Via Velia 15,
I-84100 Salerno (SA);
tel. (089) 22 43 22.

The region of Campania, comprising the five provinces of Avellino, Benevento, Caserta, Naples and Salerno, **with a total population of some 5·2 million, covers an area of 13,595 sq. km extending from the Neapolitan Apennines (Monte Cervati, 1809 m) to the coast of the Tyrrhenian Sea, here much indented (gulfs of Gaeta, Naples, Salerno and Policastro). It is a fertile low-lying region, well watered by the rivers Garigliano, Volturno and Sele, on which volcanic activity in historical and modern times (Vesuvius) has also left its mark.**

Lacco Ameno, Ischia

The extraordinary fertility of the soil, the mild climate and the availability of water earned the region the name of "Campania Felix" in ancient times. It has long been one of the most densely populated parts of Italy and is intensively cultivated (wheat, citrus fruits, wine, vegetables, fruit, tobacco).

The original inhabitants were an Italic people, the Osci. In the 8th c. a number of Greek colonies (Kyme, Dikaiarchia, Neapolis) were established on the coast. At the end of the 6th c. Campania was occupied by the Etruscans; in 430 B.C. it was captured by the Samnites, and in 344 B.C. by the Romans. Under the Empire it was much favoured by aristocratic and prosperous Romans as a place of residence, and the wealth and ostentation of this period has been preserved for us in the ruins of Herculaneum and Pompeii. In the early medieval period Campania was divided into Lombard and Byzantine spheres of influence, but was reunited by the Normans in the 11th c. and thereafter passed to the kingdom of Sicily and the joint kingdom of Naples and Sicily.

The most important towns in the region are **Naples** (see p. 168) and **Salerno** (see p. 254). Half way between them, surrounded by hills containing numerous villages, is the attractively situated little town of **Cava de' Tirreni** (alt. 196 m; pop. 20,000; Hotel Victoria, II, 76 b.; etc.), a popular holiday resort. On the hills round the town are slender round towers, many of which are still used to trap wild pigeons in October, the birds being attracted by small white stones thrown from the towers and are then caught in nets. – 2·5 km SE from Cava is *Alessia* (alt. 270 m), from which it is a 45 minutes' walk up *Monte San Liberatore* (462 m), perhaps the finest viewpoint in the Gulf of Salerno. – 3·5 km SW of Cava, on the River Selano, is the Benedictine abbey of *La Trinità della Cava, founded in 1011. The present buildings date mostly from the late 18th c. The church contains marble and mosaic altars, tombs of the earliest abbots and a 12th c. marble pulpit. Other notable features are the chapter-house (16th c.), the Romanesque cloister (small museum), the crypt, a picture gallery and the abbey archives.

Campania is also notable for its ancient sites. In addition to **Pompeii** (see p. 201), **Herculaneum** (p. 131) and **Paestum** (p. 183) there is the interesting Roman site of **Velia**, once a popular resort of the Roman aristocracy, which has the remains of a number of villas and town gates. 5 m beneath the Roman city were found remains of the Greek town of **Elea**, including some fine pieces of statuary. The Greek town was founded in 536 B.C. by Phocaeans who had been driven out of their original settlement at Alalia on Corsica. Between about 540 and 460 B.C. this was the home of the famous Eleatic school of philosophy led by Xenophanes, Parmenides and Zeno, and the town also had a noted school of medicine. At that time Elea probably had a population of 40,000, and its walls had a total length of 6 km, later extended to 7 km. The excavation of the ancient city (under which earlier remains dating from the 8th c. were found) is still in progress, and it is planned to build a museum. – On a hill to the N of the site excavations have brought to light the foundations of a temple of the 5th c. B.C. which was destroyed during the construction of the medieval castle, together with remains of a square tower of the 4th c. B.C., three smaller temples, a sacrificial altar, several dwelling-houses (2nd c. B.C.) and the road from the acropolis to the harbour.

In northern Campania, at the village of *Roccamonfina* on the eastern slopes of the volcano of the same name, are considerable remains of the ancient city of *Cales*, which was captured from the Greeks in 335 B.C. during the Romans' victorious campaign in southern Italy and later developed into an important trading centre. Excavations have so far revealed remains of baths (1st c. B.C.), the forum, dwelling-houses of the 8th c. B.C., a Christian cemetery and a 5th c. church. The town was destroyed by the Saracens in A.D. 879.

Campania has numerous seaside resorts, some of them very elegant and fashionable, particularly in the bays of Naples and Salerno. Farther S is the select resort of **Palinuro** (alt. 75 m; hotels: Saline, I, 80 b., SP; San Paolo, II, 71 b., SP; Gabbiano, II, 68 b., SP; Rizzo, II, 56 b.; Santa Caterina, II, 56 b.; La Conchiglia, II, 46 b.; Eden, II, 44 b.; La Torre, II, 41 b.; Elea, III, 42 b.; etc.; holiday village of Club Méditerranée, 2 km N), with excellent facilities for all kinds of water sports. To the W of the town is the *Grotta Azzurra* ("Blue Grotto"), which is accessible only by boat. – 2·5 km SW is *Capo Palinuro* (alt. 203 m; lighthouse), the S side of which falls sheer down to the sea. Here too are several caves accessible only from the sea.

Campanian pottery

From the Salerno–Messina motorway (A 3) an attractive detour can be made by way of the little town of *Auletta* (alt. 280 m; Hotel Universo, III, 22 b.; etc.), below the N side of the *Monti Alburni* (1742 m), to the stalactitic *Grotta di Pertosa, a cave system 2250 m long. Farther S, just outside **Padula** (alt. 698 m; pop. 7000), is the *Certosa di San Lorenzo*, originally founded in 1308, a massive building, mostly dating from the 17th and 18th c., with three beautiful arcaded courtyards and a large external staircase by Vanvitelli.

Marina Grande, Capri

Capri

Region: Campania. – Province: Napoli (NA).
Area: 10·5 sq. km. – Population: 12,000.
Post code: I-80073. – Dialling code: 081.
(i) **AA**, Piazza Umberto I;
  tel. 8 37 06 86.
  CIT, Via Vittorio Emanuele 25;
  tel. 8 37 04 66.

HOTELS. – *Quisisana e Grande, L, 229 b., SP; *Tiberio Palace, I, 172 b.; La Palma, I, 143 b.; Regina Cristina, I, 107 b., SP; Luna, I, 94 b., SP; Residence Punta Tragara, I, 77 b., SP; La Scalinatella, I, 53 b.; Calypso, I, 14 b.; La Residenza, II, 146 b., SP; La Pineta, II, 83 b., SP; La Floridiana, II, 62 b.; Semiramis, II, 61 b.; Gatto Bianco, II, 54 b.; La Pergola, II, 49 b.; Nuovo Reale, II, 48 B.; Villa delle Sirene, II, 47 b.; Villa Igea, II, 45 b.; Villa Margherita, II, 45 b.; Capri, II, 40 b.; Pagano Vittoria e Germania, III, 107 b.; Villa Pina, III, 88 b., SP; etc. – IN MARINA GRANDE: Excelsior Parco, II, 53 b.; Metropole, III, 35 b.; etc.

BOAT SERVICES. – Regular service several times daily from *Naples* in 1 hour 20 minutes (taking car not worth while: use prohibited in summer); also hydrofoil service (½ hour). – Also services from *Sorrento*, *Positano, Amalfi* and *Ischia*.

The island of * *Capri, lying off the tip of the Sorrento peninsula on the S side of the Bay of Naples, is one of the most beautiful and most visited of the islands in the Tyrrhenian Sea. In Roman times, when it was known as Caprae, it was a favourite resort of the emperors Augustus and Tiberius.**

The island, 6 km long and between 1 and 2·5 km wide, has rugged limestone crags rising to a height of 589 m above the sea. The only places of any size are the picturesque little towns of Capri and Anacapri. The island has a rich flora of some 800 species, including the acanthus, whose leaves form the characteristic ornament of Corinthian capitals.

The regular boats land their passengers in the picturesque port of *Marina Grande*, on the N coast of the island. From here a funicular (5 minutes), a stepped footpath (½ hour) and a road (3 km) lead up to the town of **Capri** (alt. 138 m; pop. 8000), the island's capital, situated on a saddle between the hills of *Il Capo* to the E, *Monte Solaro* to the W, *San Michele* to the NE and *Castiglione* (ruined castle) to the SW. The central feature of the town is the little Piazza Umberto I ("the Piazza" for short), at the top of the funicular from Marina Grande. From here it is a 5 minutes' walk past the steps leading up to the church of Santo Stefano (1683) and along the main shopping street to the *Certosa* (founded 1371, restored 1933), a former Carthusian house, with the church of San Giacomo (Gothic doorway; 12th c. frescoes) and two cloisters (access to *viewpoint). – From the Hotel Quisisana, half way along the road to the Certosa, it is a 15 minutes' walk to the terrace on *Punta Tragara*, the SE promontory of the island, which commands a picturesque view of the S coast and the three stacks known as the *Faraglioni*.

From Capri a very attractive footpath, the "Via Tiberio" (¾ hour), runs NE to the promontory of *Il Capo*. Immediately beyond a gateway is the rock known as the *Salto di Tiberio* (297 m) from which legend has it that the tyrannical Emperor Tiberius had his victims thrown into the sea (*view). To the right are the substructures of an ancient *lighthouse*. – Beyond this are the extensive remains of the *Villa de Tiberio or Villa Jovis, rising in terraces to the top of the hill, in which Tiberius is said to have lived from A.D. 27 until his death in 37. On the adjoining promontory is the *chapel of Santa Maria di Soccorso*, with a conspicuous figure of the Virgin; magnificent *views. – From the Villa di Tiberio a footpath to the right leads in 15 minutes to the *Arco Naturale, a natural archway in the rock (*view), from which steps run down to the *Grotta di Matromania*, perhaps a sanctuary of the

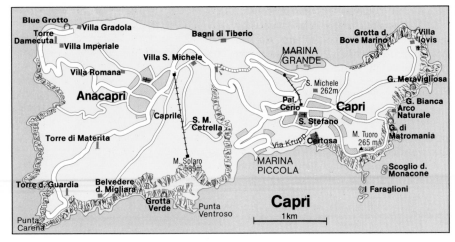

nymphs. From the cave a *footpath (¾ hour) runs along above the sea, with views of the *Scoglio del Monacone*, a rocky islet, and the *Faraglioni*, and so back to Punta Tragara.

SW of Capri is the little harbour of **Marina Piccola**, reached by a wide footpath, the *Via Krupp, laid out by the German industrialist Friedrich Krupp. The path begins W of the Certosa and runs below the beautiful *Parco Augusto* (*terrace with fine views) and round the steep-sided Castiglione to join (15 minutes) the road from Capri, on which it is another 10 minutes' walk to the harbour.

Anacapri, in the W of the island, is reached either by a beautiful *road (3·5 km: bus service) which winds its way up the rocky slope from the town of Capri or on an ancient flight of 960 steps which leads up from Marina Grande to the viewpoint of *Capodimonte, 10 minutes' walk E of the town. Above the viewpoint is the *Castello di Barbarossa*, the ruins of a castle destroyed by the pirate Khaireddin Barbarossa in 1544. On the slopes of Capodimonte is the conspicuous *Villa San Michele*, home of the Swedish doctor and author Axel Munthe (1857–1949). – *Anacapri (alt. 286 m), a little town of almost Oriental aspect, straggles over the plateau, surrounded by vineyards. The church of San Michele has a fine majolica pavement (1761). In the Piazza is the town's principal church, Santa Sofia. – Half an hour's walk SW of the town is the viewpoint of *Migliara*, 300 m above the sea.

From Anacapri a chair-lift (12 minutes) and a footpath (1 hour) lead up to the top of **Monte Solaro** (598 m: restaurant), to the SE, the highest point on the island, from which on clear days there are magnificent **views extending as far as the Abruzzi.

3 km NW of Anacapri, in the steep cliffs on the N coast of the island, is one of Capri's great tourist attractions, the **Blue Grotto** (*Grotta Azzurra*), which can be reached either by boat from Marina Grande or by the Via Pagliaro (3 km) from Anacapri. This, the most famous of Capri's caves, was carved out of the rock in prehistoric times by the constant battering of the sea, and as a result of the sinking of the land is now half filled with water. The entrance, only 1·75 m high, can be negotiated only by small boats when the sea is calm. The cave is 54 m long, 30 m wide and 15 m high, with 16 m depth of water. When the sun is shining it is filled with an extraordinary blue light (at its best from 11 a.m. to 1 p.m.).

Another very attractive excursion is a *boat trip round the island (1½–2 hours by motorboat, 3–4 hours by rowing-boat), which allows visitors to see the other caves round the coasts of Capri. The finest are the *Grotta Bianca* and the *Grotta Meravigliosa* above it (on the E coast near the Arco Naturale), the *Grotta Verde* at the foot of Monte Solaro, the *Grotta Rossa* and the green *Grotta del Brillante*.

Carrara

Region: Toscana. – Province: Massa-Carrara (MS). Altitude: 100 m. – Population: 70,000. Post code: I-54033. – Dialling code: 0585.

ⓘ **EPT**, Piazza 2 Giugno 14; tel. 7 06 68.
  TCI, *Viaggi Sara*, Via Roma 22; tel. 72 21 92.

HOTELS. – *Michelangelo*, II, 54 b.; *Da Roberto*, III, 21 b.

The busy town of Carrara, in a valley in the Apuan Alps only a few kilo-metres from the Ligurian Sea, is

famous for the 400 *marble quarries around the town which provide employment for most of its population. The stonemasons' workshops are of great interest.

SIGHTS. – In the N of the town is the **Cathedral** of Sant'Andrea (13th c.), with a fine Romanesque and Gothic façade and a Romanesque interior. To the S, in Via Roma, the town's principal street, is the *Accademia di Belle Arti* (closed Sundays), with pictures and marble sculpture, both ancient and modern. – 0·5 km W of the cathedral is the *church of the Madonna delle Grazie*, with sumptuous marble decoration.

SURROUNDINGS. – Every tourist should visit the *marble quarries (cave)* in the three valleys which meet at Carrara, the *Colonnate, Fantiscritti* and *Torano* valleys. They can be reached on reasonably good minor roads. The quarries were already being worked in Roman times, but achieved their widest fame through Michelangelo, who greatly prized the marble of Carrara. Particularly impressive are the quarries at *Piastre* (4 km E), which yield the fine *marmo statuario*.

7 km SE of Carrara is **Massa** (alt. 65 m; pop. 63,000; Hotel Annunziata, III, 63 b.; etc.), chief town of the province of Massa-Carrara, which also has large marble quarries. The former Palazzo Ducale, a handsome Baroque building of 1701, now houses the Prefecture. Church of San Francesco. 15 minutes NE is the massive Castello (15th–16th c.: *view). – 11 km farther SE is **Pietrasanta** (alt. 20 m; pop. 26,000; hotels: Azzurro, III, 45 b.; Italia, III, 36 b.; Palagi, III, 30 b.; etc.), beautifully situated among hills. – 4 km SW is *Pietrasanta Marina*, one of the principal resorts of the Versilia region, with numerous good hotels, the 14th c. cathedral of San Martino (fine pulpit) and an imposing ruined castle.

Caserta

Region: Campania. – Province: Caserta (CE).
Altitude: 68 m. – Population: 65,000.
Post code: I-81100. – Dialling Code: 0823.
ⓘ **EPT**, Corso Triesta/Piazza Dante;
tel. 2 11 37.
ACI, Via Nazario Sauro 10;
tel. 2 12 34 and 2 14 42.

HOTELS. – *Jolly*, I, 147 b.; *Europa*, I, 114 b.; *Centrale*, II, 77 b.; *Vittoria*, III, 42 b.; etc.

The modern provincial capital of Caserta, situated at the foot of the Monti Tifatini in the northern part of the Campanian plain, was the Versailles of the Bourbon rulers of Naples.

SIGHTS. – Opposite the station is the former *Royal Palace (253 m long, 41 m high), a magnificent Baroque residence in the manner of Versailles built by Luigi Vanvitelli for King Charles III of Naples and Sicily from 1752 onwards. During the Second World War it was the headquarters of the Allied Mediterranean Command, and the document of surrender of the German forces in Italy was signed here on 29 April 1945. The interior, with its well-preserved decoration and furnishings, forms a museum of the Bourbon dynasty which ruled the kingdom of the Two Sicilies (1734–1860). Particularly fine are the Grand Staircase (116 steps), the Cappella Reale, the Royal Apartments and the Theatre. Behind the palace is the *Park, with magnificent fountains and cascades, adorned with statues. From the terrace beyond the beautiful English Garden (45 minutes' walk N of the palace) there are very fine views. – 10 km NE of Caserta is the dilapidated village of *Caserta Vecchia* (alt. 410 m), originally founded by the Lombards, with the castle of the counts of Caserta and a cathedral (12th–13th c.) in the Normano-Sicilian style.

Fountain of Ceres in park of Royal Palace, Caserta

SURROUNDINGS. – From Caserta there is an interesting trip (7 km W) to the developing town of **Santa Maria di Capua Vétere** (alt. 30 m; pop. 30,000), on the site of the ancient capital of Campania, *Capua*, which was originally founded by the Etruscans. As the centre of this fertile region Capua became a wealthy and powerful city renowned for its luxury, but after its destruction by the Saracens in the 9th c. the town was moved to its present-day site (see below). In the NW of the town is the *Amphitheatre, built in the reign of Augustus (1st c. A.D.) and restored by Hadrian, which was the largest in Italy until the building of the Colosseum in Rome (170 m long, 140 m across). Under the arena (76 m long, 46 m across) are well-preserved substructures (passages, cages for wild beasts). – 0·5 km S, in an underground passage, is a *mithraeum (2nd A.D.), a shrine of the Persian god of light Mithras, richly decorated with paintings. – 0·5 km farther SE is the cathedral of Santa Maria Maggiore, with columns from the amphitheatre.

5 km NW of the ancient city, in a bend of the River Volturno, is the modern town of **Capua** (alt. 25 m; pop. 19,000; hotels: Mediterraneo, II, 72 b., SP; Capys, III, 36 b.), the see of an archbishop, built on the site of the ancient *Casilium* after the destruction of Roman Capua by the Saracens in the 9th c. and held for many years by Norman rulers. In the centre of the town, near the Volturno, is the cathedral, rebuilt after its destruction during the Second World War, the only parts which survived unscathed being the campanile and the 11th c. forecourt with its ancient columns. Nearby is the *Campanian Provincial Museum, the most important archaeological museum in Campania after the National Museum in Naples. – 5 km E, on the western slopes of *Monte Tifata* (604 m), stands the village of *Sant'Angelo in Formis*, with a Romanesque *basilica built in 1058 on the site of a temple of Diana Tifatina. The beautiful portico has Oriental pointed arches. The church contains ancient marble columns and fine frescoes of the school of Montecassino (11th c.).

Catania

Region: Sicilia. – Province: Catania (CT).
Altitude: 38 m. – Population: 400,000.
Post code: I-95100. – Dialling code: 095.
(i) **EPT**, Largo Paisiello 5;
     tel. 31 21 24.
     Information offices at station and Fontana Rossa airport, 4 km S.
     ACI, Via Etnea 28;
     tel. 31 78 90.

HOTELS. – *Excelsior*, Piazza G. Verga, I, 240 b.; *Jolly Trinacria*, Piazza Trento 13, I, 199 b.; *Central Palace*, Via Etnea 218, I, 178 b.; *Costa*, Via Etnea 551, II, 304 b.; *Bristol*, Via Santa Maria del Rosario 9, II, 107 b.; etc. – *Motel Agip*, 4 km S on S.S. 114, III, 87 b. – Two CAMPING SITES.

EVENTS. – *Feast of St Agatha* (3–5 Feb.), with processions; *Agricultural Show* (Feb.).

Catania, capital of its province, the see of an archbishop and a university town, lies half way along the flat eastern coast of Sicily to the SE of Mt Etna. It is Sicily's second largest town after Palermo and one of the most important ports in Italy, shipping the produce of the wide and fertile Piana di Catania, the principal grain-growing region in Sicily.

Catania is a town of imposing modern aspect, having been almost completely rebuilt, with long straight streets, after a devastating earthquake in 1693. The wealth of the city is demonstrated by its handsome Baroque churches and large aristocratic mansions, frequently rebuilt after earthquake damage.

HISTORY. – *Katana* was founded about 729 B.C. by Greek settlers from Naxos, and was one of the first places on the island to be taken by the Romans (263

B.C.). Under Roman rule it grew into one of the largest towns on Sicily, but during the early medieval period it declined into insignificance, recovering its prosperity only in the 14th c. under Aragonese rule. The 1693 earthquake, which affected the whole of Sicily, was particularly destructive in Catania.

SIGHTS. – The central feature of the town is the beautiful *Piazza del Duomo*, in the centre of which is a fountain with an ancient *elephant*, carved from lava, and bearing a granite Egyptian obelisk. On the E side of the square rises the 18th c. **Cathedral** (choir apses and E wall of transept 13th c.). In the interior (by the second pillar on the right) lies the tomb of the composer Vincenzo Bellini (1801–35), a native of Catania. To the right, in front of the choir (beautiful choir-stalls), is the chapel of St Agatha, with the tomb of the Spanish viceroy Acuña (d. 1494). – Across the street from the cathedral, to the N, stands the *Abbey of Sant'Agata*, with a Baroque church. – SE of the Piazza del Duomo, beyond the railway viaduct, lies the **Harbour**.

0·5 km SW of the Piazza del Duomo, in Piazza Federico di Svevia, is the **Castello Ursino**, lying close to the sea, which was built for Frederick II about 1240 and later, in the 14th c., became the residence of the kings of Aragon. Thereafter it served as a prison and as barracks, and since 1934 has housed the *Museo Civico*, with the fine municipal collection.

From the SW corner of the Piazza del Duomo the busy Via Garibaldi runs past the Piazza Mazzini, surrounded by 32 ancient columns, to the *Porta Garibaldi*

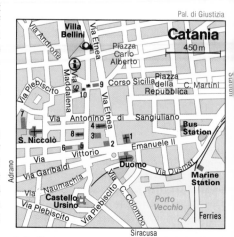

1 Sant'Agata	6 Ancient Theatre
2 Town Hall	7 Observatory
3 University	8 San Benedetto
4 Collegiate Church	9 Amphitheatre
5 Bellini Museum	10 San Carcere

Roman theatre, Catania

(1768). To the N, in Via Vittorio Emanuele, a wide street 3 km long, is the
Piazza San Francesco, with the *Bellini
Museum*, in the house in which Bellini
was born. Immediately to the W (entrance
from the Via Teatro Greco) stands the
Ancient Theatre (*Teatro Romano*), on
Greek foundations, most of it now underground. On its W side is the *Odeon*, a
small and well-preserved Roman theatre
for rehearsals and musical competitions.

In Via Crociferi, which runs N from the
Piazza San Francesco, are two churches
with Baroque façades, *San Benedetto*
and the *Jesuit church* (on left). – 0·5 km
W, in Piazza Dante, is the former
Benedictine **monastery of San Nicolò**
(founded 1518, rebuilt 1735), used from
1866 as a barracks and a school. The
church, with an unfinished façade, is a
massive Baroque structure, the largest in
Sicily. From the lantern of the dome
(internal height 62 m) there are extensive
*views. There are also fine views from the
Observatory which adjoins the church on
the NW.

From the Piazza del Duomo **Via Etnea**,
the town's wide principal street, runs N for
3 km, interrupted by a series of spacious
squares, with a prospect of Etna in the
background. Immediately on the left we
come to the *Town Hall*. Beyond this, in
the Piazza dell'Università, is the **University** (founded 1444), in a handsome
building erected in 1818, and further on
the *Collegiate Church*, with a handsome
Baroque façade (1768). The next square
is the palm-shaded Piazza Stesícoro, with
a *monument to Bellini*. On the left side of
the square are the remains of a Roman

amphitheatre, partly demolished during
the reign of Theodoric in order to provide
material for building the town walls; only
the N end is visible. The amphitheatre
originally measured 126 by 106 m; its
unusually large arena (70 by 50 m) was
second only to the Colosseum in Rome
(86 by 54 m). A little way to the W is the
church of San Cárcere (13th c. doorway).
– Farther along Via Etnea, on the left, is the
main entrance to the **Villa Bellini**, an
attractive public garden (pleasant views
from terrace).

Along the N side of the Villa Bellini runs
the tree-lined Viale Regina Margherita,
which with its eastward continuation the
Viale XX Settembre and the wide Corso
Italia, beginning at the beautiful *Piazza
Verga* (with the modern Law Courts),
forms the main traffic artery of the
northern part of the city. At its eastern end
is the Piazza Europa, which looks down
on to the sea and from which a magnificent *coast road* (several outlook terraces) leads N to the suburban district of
OGNINA, with the little *Porto d'Ulisse* in a
sheltered bay.

SURROUNDINGS. – The most rewarding excursion
from Catania is the ascent of * *Etna or the subsidiary
craters of *Monti Rossi*, or alternatively the *trip round
the volcano*. See p. 109.

Cefalù

Region: Sicilia. – Province: Palermo (PA).
Altitude: 30 m. – Population: 13,000.
Post code: I-90015. – Dialling code: 0921.
ⓘ AA, Corso Ruggero 114;
tel. 2 10 50.

Hotels. – *Le Sabbie d'Oro*, II, 420 b., SP; *Kalura*, II,
115 b., SP; *La Calette*, 100 b., SP; *Santa Dominga*, II,
92 b.; *Tourist*, II, 92 b.; *Santa Lucia*, III, 85 b.; etc. –
Holiday village of Club Méditerranée, at Torre Santa
Lucia, to E. – CAMPING SITE.

EVENTS. – *Puppet Theatre*, Via Roma 72.

**The little port of Cefalù, pictur-
esquely situated under a bare limestone crag which falls sheer down
to the sea, has preserved much of
its character and charm in spite of
the thousands of visitors which it
attracts. It is the seat of a bishop.**

SIGHTS. – On the E side of the town's
principal street, the *Corso Ruggero*,
which runs N towards the sea, is the
spacious *Piazza del Duomo*, with the

Cefalù

are magnificent views. – 15 km S of Cefalù, in a situation offering panoramic views, is the *Santuario di Gibilmanna* (17th–18th c.), above which is an *observatory* (1005 m: *views). – Another attractive excursion from Cefalù is a hydrofoil trip to the **Lípari Islands** (see p. 141).

Cerveteri

Region: Lazio. – Province: Roma (ROMA).
Altitude: 81 m. – Population: 4000.
Post code: I-00052. – Dialling code: 06.
ⓘ **Pro Loco**, Piazza del Risorgimento;
     tel. 9 05 70 00.

HOTEL. – *El Paso*, IV, 17 b.

Town Hall and the *Cathedral, one of the finest buildings of the Norman period, which was begun by King Roger in 1131–32.

The INTERIOR (74 m long, 29 m wide) has 15 granite *columns* and one of cipollino, with beautiful capitals. The apse contains magnificent mosaics, including one of the *Saviour* (1148), as well as the "Virgin with four archangels", and the "Twelve Apostles". In the S aisle is a fine 12th c. font. The *cloister* (fine capitals) is entered from the N aisle.

W of the Piazza del Duomo is the little *Museo Mandralisca* (antiquities from the Lípari Islands, pictures). – There is a good beach at Cefalù.

SURROUNDINGS. – At the N end of the Corso Ruggero is the starting point of the climb ($\frac{3}{4}$–1 hour) of the crag known as the **Rocca** (269 m), which is composed almost entirely of fossils: remains of a medieval castle and of an ancient polygonal structure known as the Tempio di Diana. From the highest point, on which are remains of a Norman castle, there

The little country town of Cerveteri, now a place of no particular importance, occupies the site of the ancient Caere, once one of the leading Etruscan cities, on a tufa ridge 45 km NW of Rome.

SIGHTS. – In the Piazza Santa Maria is the medieval *Rocca*, a castle (12th c.) which is partly built on Etruscan walls of the 4th c. B.C. Opposite it is the **Museo Nazionale Cerite** (closed Mondays and public holidays), containing material from the Etruscan cemeteries round the town; the most important items, however, are in Rome (Etruscan Museum in the Vatican, Villa Giulia Museum).

SURROUNDINGS. – To the N of the town, extending along the edge of the tufa hill known as the *Banditaccia*, is a large *Etruscan cemetery (7th–1st c. B.C.), a city of the dead which bears impressive witness, in the scale of the necropolis and the richness of the buried goods, to the importance attached by the

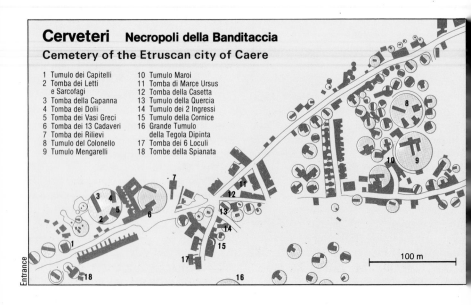

Cerveteri   Necropoli della Banditaccia
Cemetery of the Etruscan city of Caere

1 Tumulo dei Capitelli
2 Tomba dei Letti
   e Sarcofagi
3 Tomba della Capanna
4 Tomba dei Dolii
5 Tomba dei Vasi Greci
6 Tomba dei 13 Cadaveri
7 Tomba dei Rilievi
8 Tumulo del Colonello
9 Tumulo Mengarelli

10 Tumulo Maroi
11 Tomba di Marce Ursus
12 Tomba della Casetta
13 Tumulo della Quercia
14 Tumulo dei 2 Ingressi
15 Tumulo della Cornice
16 Grande Tumulo
   della Tegola Dipinta
17 Tomba dei 6 Loculi
18 Tombe della Spianata

100 m

Entrance

Etruscans to the cult of the dead. On either side of a "main street" some 2 km long, with a number of side streets, lie hundreds of tombs, including huge *tumuli up to 30 m in diameter and many tomb chambers hewn from the rock in the form of dwelling-houses, often with several rooms. Particularly fine is the *Tomba dei Rilievi, with painted bas-relief representations of everyday objects. Many tombs have holes showing the point of entry of early tomb-robbers. (A flashlight should be taken.)

Cinqueterre

Region: Liguria. – Province: La Spezia (SP).
ⓘ Pro Loco Monterosso al Mare, Via Fegina, I-19016 Monterosso al Mare; tel. (0187) 81 75 06.

HOTELS. – IN MONTEROSSO AL MARE: Porto Roca, in Corone, I, 84 b.; Cinque Terre, II, 102 b.; Palme, II, 88 b.; Degli Amici, III, 77 b.; Jolie, III, 56 b.; etc. – IN RIOMAGGIORE: Villa Argentina, III, 26 b.; etc.

The very picturesque coastal region known as the *Cinqueterre, fringed by tall and precipitous cliffs, lies between La Spezia and Levanto on the Riviera di Levante, with the five villages ("cinque terre") of Monterosso al Mare, Vernazza, Corniglia, Manarola and Riomaggiore.

These picturesque villages, linked with one another only by rough tracks but accessible individually by road, railway or boat, have in consequence of their remoteness preserved their old-world aspect. With their beautiful setting and their pleasant climate they have a charm and a character all their own. The population of some 7000 live by agriculture (vines grown on terraces, citrus fruit, olives) and fishing. This secluded area is only now being opened up to motorised tourism by the construction of a panoramic highway.

Vernazza, Cinqueterre

Città di Castello

Region: Umbria. – Province: Perugia (PU).
Altitude: 288 m. – Population: 16,000.
Post code: I-06012. – Dialling code: 075.
ⓘ AA, Piazza Garibaldi 2; tel. 85 34 17.

HOTELS. – Europa, III, 79 b.; Tiferno, III, 70 b.; etc.

Città di Castello, situated on the Tiber in northern Umbria, occupies the site of a Roman town, Tifernum Tiberinum, which was destroyed by the Ostrogothic king Totila. During the Renaissance period it was ruled by the Vitelli family, and later belonged to the Papal State.

SIGHTS. – The central feature of the town, which is still partly surrounded by its old walls, is the Piazza Matteotti, enclosed by fine old palaces. To the E is Piazza Gabriotti, in which is the fine rusticated Palazzo Comunale (Town Hall), built in the 14th c. Beyond this is the Cathedral (Santi Florido e Amanzio), originally 11th c. but remodelled in Renaissance style in the 15th and 16th c. The treasury contains an embossed silver antepedium with designs in silver-gilt (c. 1150). On the W side of the square is the little Giardino Pubblico (view).

SE of the cathedral is the Gothic church of San Domenico (1395), with old frescoes and a pretty monastic courtyard. Still farther S, by the town wall, stands the handsome Palazzo Vitelli della Cannoniera, which contains the municipal picture collection. – N of Piazza Matteotti the church of San Francesco contains a Vitelli Chapel built by Vasari.

Cividale del Friuli

Region: Friuli – Venezia Giulia.
Province: Udine (UD).
Altitude: 135 m. – Population: 11,000.
Post code: I-33043. – Dialling code: 0432.
ⓘ TCI, Piazza Duomo 2; tel. 7 10 63.

HOTELS. – Roma, III, 100 b.; Al Castello, III, 20 b.

Formerly capital of Friuli but now a quiet little country town, Cividale is picturesquely situated on the River Natisone below the Julian Alps (which have belonged to Yugoslavia since 1947), some 15 km E of Udine.

With its early medieval buildings, it has much of interest to offer the visitor. The town suffered some damage in an earthquake in May 1976.

HISTORY. – Cividale, the Roman *Forum Iulii* – which gave its name to the region of Friuli – was from 569 to 774 the seat of Lombard dukes, and from 730 the residence of the Patriarch of Aquileia. After his conquest of the Lombard kingdom in 774 Charlemagne made it the seat, under the name of *Civitas Austriae*, of a line of Frankish margraves (lords of the marches), the most important of whom, Berengarius I, ruled Italy as king from 888 to 924, with Cividale as his capital. Even after the seat of the Patriarchate was transferred to Udine in 1238 Cividale remained for centuries the most important place in Friuli by virtue of its command of major Alpine passes. In 1419 the town was occupied by the Venetians, who in 1439 compelled the Patriarch to renounce his secular authority. Thereafter the town fell into a steady decline. In 1752 the Patriarchate was replaced by the archbishoprics of Gorizia and Udine.

Cividale, on the river Natisone

SIGHTS. – In the Piazza del Duomo, in the centre of the town, stands the **Cathedral** (originally 8th c.; remodelled in Early Renaissance style by Pietro and Tullio Lombardi from 1502 onwards). It contains the remains of an octagonal *baptistery (8th c.) and a Romanesque silver-gilt antependium (*c.* 1200). Fine crypt; *treasury.

Also in the Piazza del Duomo are the *Palazzo del Comune* (Town Hall) and the *Palazzo del Provveditore*, built by Palladio. – Opposite the cathedral is the *Museo Archeologico Nazionale, with valuable Lombard antiquities (fine gold ornaments) and prehistoric, Roman and medieval material (including two *psalters which belonged to St Elizabeth of Thuringia, d. 1231). – S of the cathedral is the *Ponte del Diavolo*, which dates in part from the 14th c.

At *Porta Brossana* is the former Benedictine *convent of Santa Maria in Valle*, picturesquely situated on the banks of the Natisone, with the *Tempietto, the front part of a Lombard church destroyed by a spate of the river (stucco reliefs of the 8th–9th c.; 14th c. choir-stalls). – Lower down, on the river bank, is the *church of San Biagio*, with the remains of ancient frescoes.

SURROUNDINGS. – 10 km E, reached by steep and narrow roads, is the church of the Madonna del Monte (alt. 622 m: view), the most famous pilgrimage centre in Friuli.

Como

Region: Lombardia. – Province: Como (CO).
Altitude: 202 m. – Population: 100,000.
Post code: I-22100. – Dialling code: 031.
ⓘ **AA**, Piazza Cavour;
tel. 26 55 92.
EPT, Piazza Cavour;
tel. 26 20 91.
ACI, Viale Massenzio Masia 79;
tel. 55 67.
TCI, *Viaggi Ronchi*, Lungo Lario Trieste 12;
tel. 27 11 44.

HOTELS. – *Metropole e Suisse*, Piazza Cavour 19, I, 120 b.; *Villa Flori*, Via Provinciale per Cernobbio 12, I, 93 b.; *Barchetta*, Piazza Cavour 1, I, 92 b.; *Como*, Via Mentana 28, II, 132 b., SP; *Continental*, Via Innocenzo XI 15, II, 107 b.; *San Gottardo*, Piazza Volta 4, II, 92 b.; *Baradello*, Piazza Camerlata 9A, II, 78 b.; *Park*, Via Rosselli 20, 74 b.; *Terminus*, Lungo Lario Trieste 14, II, 47 b.; *Engadina*, Viale Rosselli 22, II, 39 b.; *Tre Re*, Via Boldoni 20, III, 54 b.; *Plinius*, Via Garibaldi 33, III, 50 b.; etc. – YOUTH HOSTEL, Via Bellinzona 6, 103 b. – Two CAMPING SITES.

The provincial capital of Como, an important centre of the silk industry, is magnificently situated at the S end of Lake Como, surrounded by rocky heights, partly forest-covered. The walled old town, with a rectangular layout derived from that of a Roman camp, is fringed by attractive suburbs.

HISTORY. – Como was founded by the Romans in 195 B.C., on the site of an earlier settlement, as the frontier fortress of *Comum*, directed against the Rhaetians. During the Middle Ages the town – which in 1058 had the status of an episcopal see independent of Milan – was the key to Lombardy and an important base of the German emperors. In 1447 it passed to the control of Milan.

SIGHTS. – The town's life centres on the *Piazza Cavour*, by the harbour, from which the short Via Plinio runs SE to the Piazza del Duomo. On the E side of this square is the *Broletto* (1215), formerly a lawcourt, now a banqueting hall. Adjoining it to the SE is the *Cathedral, built entirely of marble (originally erected 1396, remodelled in Renaissance style 1487–1596; dome over crossing 1730–70). On either side of the principal doorway, which has fine sculptured decoration, are statues (1498) of Pliny the Elder and Younger, natives of Como.

SE of the cathedral in Via Vittorio Emanuele II, Como's principal street, is the Romanesque *church of San Fedele* (12th c.). Opposite it is the Town Hall. – Farther S, in the *Palazzo Giovio*, is the **Museo Civico** (closed Sunday afternoons and Mondays).

Via Vittorio Emanuele II runs S to end at the **town walls**, which enclose Como on three sides. On the SE side of the old town are three well-preserved 12th c. towers. – 0·5 km from the SW corner of the town walls is the twin-towered church of *Sant'Abbondio, a basilica in Lombard Romanesque style (11th c., modernised in 1587). The choir contains 15th c. frescoes.

SW of Piazza Cavour is Piazzo Volta, with a statue of the physicist *Alessandro Volta* (1745–1827), a native of Como who was born in No. 50 Via Volta. – At the NE corner of the Giardino Pubblico, on the shores of the lake, stands the neoclassical *Tempio Voltiano*, with the Volta Museum, the exhibits in which include the first voltaic pile.

SURROUNDINGS. – From the Piazza Vittoria it is 5 km by road, or a shorter and more direct journey by funicular, to the villa suburb of **Brunate** (alt. 716 m; Hotel Milano, II, 143 b.; etc.), on a terrace on the hillside, with beautiful views of Como, the plain extending as far as Milan, the Pre-Alps and the mountains from Monte Rosa to Monviso. – There are even more extensive views from *San Maurizio* (alt. 871 m; Hotel Paradiso, III, 28 b.), 2·5 km above Brunate. – From Brunate there is a footpath (2 hours) to the top of *Monte Boletto* (1234 m: *views).

Lake Como

Region: Lombardia. – Province: Como (CO).
Altitude: 198 m.
ⓘ **EPT Como**, Piazza Cavour,
I-22100 Como (CO);
tel. (031) 26 20 91.

BOAT SERVICES (from Bellano throughout the year). – Up to three services daily between *Colico* and *Como*, with varying ports of call on both sides of the lake, several times daily between *Bellano* and *Como* and twice daily between *Varenna* and *Lecco*. In summer there are also hydrofoil services.

Lake Como (Lago di Como or Lario), the Roman Lacus Larius, lies 50 km N of Milan between the Lugano and the Bergamo Alps. Narrow and fjord-like, and divided into two arms half way along its length, the lake fills the glaciated valley of the Adda, which flows through it from end to end. From its northern end to its southern tip at Como the lake is 50 km long; at its half-way point, between Menaggio and Varenna, it is 4 km wide; it has an area of 146 sq. km; and its greatest depth is 410 m, making it the deepest of the lakes of northern Italy.

On the SW arm of the lake, with the town of Como at its southern end, are numerous villas surrounded by beautiful gardens and vineyards, which belong to the aristocracy of Milan. The rather more austere SE arm, the **Lago di Lecco**, with the outflow of the river Adda, is less crowded with visitors. On the steep hillsides bordering the lake, rising to 2610 m in *Monte Legnone*, are plantations of chestnuts and walnuts, the green of their foliage contrasting strongly with the greyish tints of the olives. The inhabitants live by fishing, the production of wine and oil, and by industry (ironworking, marble-quarrying, textiles).

ROUND THE LAKE (248 km). – Leave Como on the Lugano road, going NW. – 2 km: turn into S.S. 340, which runs up the W side of the lake. On the right of the road is the neo-classical *Villa Olmo* (1780–82), now an observatory and meteorological station; fine view from the park. – 3 km: **Cernobbio** (alt. 201 m; pop. 8000; hotels: *Villa d'Este, L, 257 b., SP; Regina Olga Reine du Lac, I, 125 b., SP; Miralago, II, 62 b.; etc.), with many villas set in beautiful gardens and the palatial Villa d'Este (1568), now a hotel. From here a narrow road winds its way up (16 km) to *Monte Bisbino* (1325 m: *views), on which there is a pilgrimage church. – 22 km: **Lenno** (alt. 200 m; Hotel Roma, III, 42 b.; etc.), the most southerly place in the district of *Tremezzina*, over which towers Monte Crocione (1636 m). From here an attractive visit can be made to the *Punta di Balbianello* or *Punta d'Avedo*, a

Lake Como, with Bellagio

long promontory projecting into the lake, with the *Villa Arconati* (1790: access only by boat), from the terrace of which there are beautiful views. – 3 km: **Tremezzo** (alt. 202 m; hotels: Grand Hotel Tremezzo, I, 180 b., SP; Bazzoni and du Lac, II, 230 b.; San Giorgio, II, 57 b.; etc.), a popular resort in a warm and sheltered situation on the lake, surrounded by beautiful gardens. – 0·5 km: *Villa Carlotta (formerly Sommariva, named after Charlotte, Duchess of Meiningen, mother of an earlier owner; now the property of the State). The palace (built 1747) contains Thorwaldsen's famous marble frieze of Alexander the Great's triumphal entry into Babylon. The *gardens are a riot of southern vegetation (azaleas in bloom in May). – 0·5 km: **Cadenabbia** (alt. 201 m; hotels: Bellevue, I, 188 b.; Britannia Excelsior, II, 265 b., SP; Belle Isole, III, 85 b.), with a Romanesque church, many villas and a beautiful lakeside promenade.

4 km: **Menaggio** (alt. 203 m; pop. 3000; hotels: Victoria, I, 148 b., SP; Menaggio, I, 110 b.; Bellavista, II, 69 b.; Corona, III, 40 b.; etc.), one of the most popular resorts on Lake Como. The road then passes the yellowish-brown *Sasso Rancio* ("Orange Rock"). –12 km: *Dongo* (alt. 208 m; Hotel Dongi, IV, 28 b.; etc.), outside which Mussolini and his mistress Clara Petacci

were caught by partisans while fleeing to Switzerland. They were shot on the following day at Mezzagra, near Lenno. – 10 km: *Gera* (alt. 208 m), the most northerly place on Lake Como.

4 km beyond Gera the road joins S.S. 36, coming from Chiavenna, which runs down the E side of the lake to Milan. – 19 km: *Dervio* (alt. 238 m; Hotel Stazione, IV, 28 b.), from which a detour can be made to *Monte Legnone* (2610 m: 18 km by road, then 4 hours' climb). – 8 km: **Varenna** (alt. 220 m; hotels: Royal, II, 51 b.; Victoria, II, 51 b.; Olivedo, III, 41 b.; etc.), situated on a promontory at the mouth of the *Valle d'Esino*, with beautiful gardens and quarries of black marble; magnificent *views of Bellagio on its promontory and of the three arms of the lake. The Villa Monasterio, occupied by the Italian Institute of Hydrobiology, has a beautiful *park. Romanesque frescoes in the parish church. – 11 km: *Mandello del Lario* (alt. 203 m; pop. 10,000; Hotel Giardinetto, III, 40 b.; etc.), on a delta running far out into the lake at the foot of the jagged Grigna Meridionale, with one of the largest motorcycle factories in Italy (Moto Guzzi). – 10 km: **Lecco** (alt. 214 m; pop. 55,000; hotels: Croce di Malta, III, 80 b.; Moderno, III, 61 b.; etc.), an industrial town magnificently situated at the SE tip of Lake Como, at the outflow of

the River Adda. In the Largo Manzoni is a monument to the novelist Alessandro Manzoni (1785–1873), author of "I Promessi Sposi", the scene of which is partly set in Lecco. E of Lecco are the *Piani d'Erna* (1329 m), reached by cableway or by road. To the N is the *Piano dei Resinelli* (1272 m: cableway), from which the *Grigna Meridionale* (2184 m) can be climbed ($2\frac{1}{2}$ hours).

At the far end of Lecco we leave S.S. 36 and turn right into a road which follows the W side of the Lago di Lecco below the precipitous slopes of Monte Moregallo (1276 m), passing through a number of tunnels. – 16 km: **Bellagio** (alt. 216 m; hotels: *Villa Serbelloni, L, 167 b., SP; Metropole, I, 90 b.; Du Lac, II, 88 b.; Florence, II, 80 b.; Excelsior Splendide, II, 69 b.; Belvedere, III, 90 b., SP; etc.), a very popular resort on the W side of the *Punta di Bellagio*, one of the great beauty spots of the N Italian lakes. On the promontory is the *Villa Serbelloni*, with a *park (conducted tours) from which there are views of the three arms of Lake Como. Farther along the road are the beautiful park of the *Villa Melzi* and the gardens of the *Villa Trotti*. – 14 km: **Nesso** (alt. 275 m), a picturesque old-world village at the mouth of the *Val di Nesso*, with a waterfall 20 m high. – 8 km: below the road on the right, in *Molina* bay, is the *Villa Pliniana* (1570), named after a spring mentioned by Pliny the Younger which daily changes its level. – 4 km: **Torno** (alt. 225 m; Hotel Vapore, III, 29 b.; etc.), finely situated on a rocky promontory, surrounded by villas. By the picturesque harbour is the church of Santa Tecla, with 15th c. frescoes. – 7 km: **Como**.

b.; *Corona*, II, 77 b.; *Franceschi*, II, 72 b.; *Majoni*, II, 69 b.; *Olimpia*, II, 64 b.; *Impero*, II, 56 b.; *Regina*, II, 50 b.; *Capannina*, II, 40 b.; *Corona*, II, 16 b.; *Tiziano*, III, 108 b.; *Italia*, III, 105 b.; *Aquila*, III, 78 b.; *Menardi*, III, 75 b.; *Des Alpes*, III, 65 b.; *Montana*, III, 54 b.; *Silvano*, III, 54 b.; *Trieste*, III, 54 b.; *Pontechiesa*, III, 52 b.; *Umbria*, III, 50 b.; etc. – Four CAMPING SITES.

RESTAURANTS. – *El Toulà* – *Da Alfredo*, Via Ronco 123 (view); *El Camineto*, Rumerlo; *El Camin*, Alverà; *Da Melon*, Sopiazes 1; *Piscina Cortina*, Guargnè; *Gambrinus*, Via C. Battisti 38.

EVENTS. – *International Sports Film Competition* (beginning of March); *Cortina-Ulisse European Literary Prize.*

WINTER SPORTS. – Numerous ski-lifts; ski school; ski trails; several ski jumps, including the Olympic Jump (54 m high) in Zuel; bobsleigh run; ice-rink; speed-skating rink.

The internationally renowned tourist centre of *Cortina d'Ampezzo, Italy's most popular winter sports resort (Winter Olympics 1956), lies at the E end of the **Strada delle Dolomiti in a wide valley enclosed by the high peaks of the Dolomites.

Cortina d'Ampezzo in winter

Cortina d'Ampezzo

Region: Veneto. – Province: Belluno (BL).
Altitude: 1224 m. – Population: 9000.
Post code: I-32043. – Dialling code: 0436.
(i) **AA**, Piazza Roma;
    tel. 27 11.
    CIT, Piazza Roma;
    tel. 20 01.

HOTELS. – *Miramonti-Majestic, L, 214 b., SP; Savoia, I, 210 b., SP; Alaska* (headquarters of Club Méditerranée), *I, 185 b.; Cristallo-Palace, I, 160 b., SP; De la Poste, I, 132 b.; Bellevue, I, 119 b.; Splendid Venezia*, II, 149 b.; *Ampezzo*, II, 134 b.; *Ancora*, II, 131 b.; *Concordia e Parco*, II, 105 b.; *Serena*, II, 104 b.; *Europa*, II, 88 b.; *Cortina*, II, 83 b.; *Parc Victoria*, II, 79

SIGHTS. – In the Corso Italia, the lively and fashionable main street of Cortina (pedestrian precinct), is the handsome *parish church (18th c.), with ceiling paintings and wall paintings in the choir by Franz Anton Zeiller (1774) and an altar dedicated to the Virgin by Andrea Brustolon (1703); panoramic *view from tower. – A short distance SE, in the **Ciasa de Ra Regoles**, are the *Mario Rimoldi Collection* (contemporary art) and the *Museum* (fossils; material of folk interest). Farther SE, by the cemetery, is the beautiful Baroque *church of the Madonna della Difesa*. – At the *Ice Stadium is a memorial to the French geologist *Déodat*

Dolomieu (1750–1801), after whom the Dolomites are named.

SURROUNDINGS. – Cableways E via the *Rifugio Mandres* (1480 m) and the Alpine meadows of *Faloria* (2120 m), to the **Tondi di Faloria** hut (2327 m: panoramic * view); SW to the * **Belvedere** on *Crepa* (1539 m), at the *Pocol* hotel village; and W by way of the *Col Druscié* (1770 m) and *Ra Valles* (2470 m) to the * **Tofana di Mezzo** (3243 m: 3 hours' climb from the upper station of the cableway).

Chair-lifts via the *Col Fiere* (1466 m) to the *Col Druscié* (1770 m); from the Alpine meadows of *Rumerlo* via the *Rifugio Duca d'Aosta* (2908 m) to the *Rifugio Pomedes* (2282 m); from *Ra Valles* W to *Bus Tofana* (2823 m) and N to *Pian Ra Valles* (2150 m). On the E side of the valley there are chair-lifts to *Piera* (1525 m: only in winter) and the *Rifugio Mietres* (1710 m).

Other very attractive trips are on the * * **Strada delle Dolomiti** to Bolzano; to the * *Lago di Misurina* and the * *Tre Cime*; to * *Nuvolau*; and to the *Ampezzo* and *Piave* valleys. See also the section on the Dolomites (p. 103) for other tours in the area.

Cortona

Region: Toscana. – Province: Arezzo (AR).
Altitude: 450–650 m. – Population: 12,000.
Post code: I-52044. – Dialling code: 0575.
(i) **AA**, Piazza Signorelli 10;
tel. 6 30 56.

HOTELS. – *San Luca*, II, 116 b.; *Oasi*, II, 69 b.; *Athens*, III, 46 b.; *Italia*, III, 45 b.; etc. – YOUTH HOSTEL, 80 b.

The little Tuscan town of Cortona is finely situated on a steep hill rising above the Chiana valley near Lake Trasimene.

HISTORY. – Cortona is one of the oldest towns in Italy. It was one of the 12 cities of the Etruscan League, and later became a Roman colony. During the Middle Ages it passed through various vicissitudes before coming under the control of Florence in 1411. The painter *Luca Signorelli* (d. 1523) was born in Cortona in the middle years of the 15th century.

SIGHTS. – The central feature of Cortona is the *Piazza della Repubblica*, on the W side of which stands the *Town Hall* (13th c., with later rebuilding and restoration), approached by a broad flight of steps. To the NW is the Piazza Signorelli, with the **Palazzo Pretorio**, the façade of which bears the coats of arms of former podestàs; it now houses the *Accademia Etrusca* (founded 1726) and the *Museum of Etruscan Antiquities* (bronze * candelabrum with 14 wick apertures, 5th c. B.C.).

NW of the Piazza Signorelli, in the *Piazza del Duomo* (wide views), is the **Cathedral** (originally Romanesque, remodelled in Renaissance style by Giuliano da Sangallo, 1456–1502). Opposite it, in the former *Baptistery* (or *Chiesa del Gesù*), is the * **Museo Diocesano**, which contains some fine pictures, including works by Fra Angelico, Luca Signorelli and Pietro Lorenzetti, and a Roman sarcophagus of the 2nd c. A.D.

To the E of the cathedral, from the *Porta Colonia*, there is an impressive view of the * **town walls** (2600 m long; lower parts Etruscan). – 1 km NE, below the Porta Colonia, is the *church of Santa Maria Nuova* (16th c.).

From the Piazza della Repubblica the Via Nazionale runs SE to the Piazza Garibaldi, outside the town walls. To the E of this square, on the N side of the *Giardino Pubblico* (view), is the 15th c. **church of San Domenico**, with pictures by Signorelli, Fra Angelico and others.

From Piazza Garibaldi a road descends 3 km, with a four sharp bends, to the *church of Santa Maria del Calcinaio*, a beautiful domed church on a cruciform plan by Francesco di Giorgio of Siena (15th c.; stained glass by Guillaume de Marcillat, 1518).

In the eastern part of the town, on top of the hill, is the modern *church of Santa Margherita*, with the tomb of St Margaret of Cortona (by A. and F. di Pietro, 1362). From the platform of the campanile there are magnificent views, as there are also from the 16th c. *Fortezza*, higher up the hill.

Cremona

Region: Lombardia. – Province: Cremona (CR).
Altitude: 45 m. – Population: 85,000.
Post code: I-26100. – Dialling code: 0372.
(i) **EPT**, Galleria del Corso 2;
tel. 2 32 33.
ACI, Via XX Settembre 19;
tel. 2 96 01.
TCI, *Viaggi Italbus*, Corso Campi 50;
tel. 2 15 78.

HOTELS. – *San Giorgio*, Via Dante 20, II, 87 b.; *Continental*, Piazza Libertà 27, II, 75 b.; *Impero*, Piazza della Pace 23, II 52 b.; *Astoria*, Via Bordigallo 19, II, 46 b.; *Este*, Viale Po 131, II, 44 b.; etc. – *Motel Agip*, 3 km E on S.S. 45, II, 147 b. – CAMPING SITE.

The provincial capital of Cremona, the centre of an active textile industry and an inland port on the Milan–Po Canal, lies in the fertile North Italian plain just N of the Po. It is world-famed for the violin-makers who worked here, particularly in the 16th–18th c. (Amati, Stradivari, Guarneri). The old town has fine churches and palaces, many of them with terracotta decoration.

HISTORY. – The Gallic settlement on this site became a Roman colony in 218 B.C., and in later centuries suffered destruction on many occasions – by Vespasian's army (in A.D. 70), by the Goths and the Lombards, and during the struggle between Guelfs and Ghibellines. It was an important base of the emperor Frederick II. In 1334 it passed to Milan. – Cremona was the birthplace of the composer *Claudio Monteverdi* (1567–1643).

SIGHTS. – In the *Piazza del Comune*, in the centre of the picturesque old town, stands the town's principal landmark, the imposing *Torrazzo* (1267), an octagonal tower 111 m high (view). E of the Torrazzo, linked with it by a Renaissance loggia (begun 1497, completed in the 18th c.), is the *Cathedral, in Lombard Gothic style (1107–90), which has a richly sculptured façade embellished with columns. It contains frescoes (1506–73) by Pordenone, Boccaccino and others and fine 15th c. choir-stalls. – Adjoining the cathedral are the octagonal *Baptistery* (1167) and the subterranean *Campo Santo*, with curious mosaic pavements. – On the W side of the square is the Gothic *Palazzo Comunale (Town Hall, 1206–45), which contains three violins by Stradivari and the Amati. To the left of the Town Hall is the Gothic *Palazzo dei Militi* (1292).

250 m SW of the cathedral, in the modern *Palazzo dell'Arte*, is the *Stradivarius Museum* (musical history). 250 m farther W the *church of San Pietro al Po* (1563–68) has rich stucco decoration and ceiling paintings by Antonio Campi (d. 1591).

A little way N of the cathedral is the Piazza Roma, laid out with gardens, on which the life of the town is centred. From here the Corso Mazzini (pedestrian precinct) leads to the *Palazzo Fodri* (15th–16th c.), formerly the Monte di Pietà, a handsome Renaissance mansion with a fine loggia-courtyard.

NW of the Piazza Roma, in Via Ugolani Dati, we find the imposing *Palazzo Affaitati* (1561), a massive Late Renaissance building with a Baroque courtyard and staircase which now houses the Museo Civico (closed Sunday afternoons and Mondays), with numerous works by the 16th c. Cremona school of painters founded by Boccaccio Boccaccino of Ferrara (c. 1467–1524).

SURROUNDINGS. – 2 km E of Cremona is the church of San Sigismondo, a superb Early Renaissance building by Bartolomeo Gadia (1463), with frescoes and pictures by Camillo Boccaccio, the younger Campi and others.

Dolomites

Regions: Trentino – Alto Adige and Veneto.
Provinces: Bolzano, Trento and Belluno.
ⓘ EPT Bolzano, Piazza Walther 22,
I-39100 Bolzano (BZ);
tel. (0471) 2 18 67.
EPT Belluno, Via R. Psaro 21,
I-32100 Belluno (BL);
tel. (0437) 2 20 43.

The magnificent range of mountains called the **Dolomites after the French geologist and mineralogist Déodat Dolomieu (1750–1801) is one of the most beautiful and most visited parts of the Alps. Taken in its widest sense, the range is bounded by the rivers Isarco, Adige, Brenta, Piave and Rienza. It offers endless scope for walkers, climbers and winter sports enthusiasts, and accordingly attracts visitors from far and wide at every time of the year.

The Dolomites are remarkably easy of access, thanks to the valleys which cut deeply into the mountains and to an excellent network of roads. In addition to large and widely famed winter sports and health resorts, such as Cortina d'Ampezzo and San Martino di Castrozza, there are numerous small and middle-sized resorts and a host of remote mountain hotels and inns, most of them reached by mountain roads. The military roads of the First World War, many of them still in good condition, make it possible even for non-climbers to reach the heights and enjoy the extensive views they offer. The summits are being brought within easier reach by the steadily increasing numbers of cableways and lifts of various kinds.

In the Ampezzo Dolomites

The undulating base of the Dolomites, covered with beautiful Alpine meadows and coniferous forests, is made up of the *Bolzano porphyries*, melaphyres (basalts) and sandstones of the late Permian, soft schists, clays and variegated marls of the Lower Trias and intrusive layers of dark-coloured lavas and volcanic tuffs. Rearing up from this foundation, in the western part of the range, are massive limestone crags of the Middle Tertiary (Middle Oligocene) or Lower and Middle Trias ("Silandro dolomites"), including *Sciliar, the *Catinaccio* group and the *Sassolungo* group, the *Odle* and the *Pala* group, and also much of the *Tre Scarperi* group to the E. In the Eastern Dolomites, particularly in the *Ampezzo Dolomites* (Antalao, Tofana, Monte Cristallo, Sorapis, all over 3200 m), these unstratified limestones are overlaid by clearly bedded limestones of the Upper Trias ("Dachstein dolomites"). The Silandro and Dachstein dolomites are separated by a band of soft rocks belonging to the Raibl sequence, seen very clearly in the *Sella group*.

While the groups just mentioned are built up of rock which contains magnesium as well as calcite, as Dolomieu discovered, ***Marmolada** (3342 m), the highest peak in the Dolomites, and the *Látemar* group

consist almost entirely of pure limestone. Particularly in the *Padon* ridge between Marmolada, the Sella group and the Sassolungo group, the hard dark-coloured lavas extruded while the mountains were being formed, build up into considerable heights (La Mesola, 2733 m). Between the Lago di Braies and the Sella group the Triassic dolomites are overlaid by clearly bedded Jurassic limestones, with no significant magnesium content, which tend to produce karstic formations, particularly in the *Fanes* group. To the S the granite mass of the *Cima d'Asta* (2847 m) breaks through the limestone.

The finest example of a typical Dolomite landscape is provided by the Alpine meadows of the ***Alpe di Siusi** (1826–2070 m), on a basis of fertile volcanic tuffs interspersed with limestone. Towering above this upland region, in fascinating contrast, are the white or yellowish walls of limestone, standing out against the blue southern sky in a constantly varying pattern of rock buttresses, towers, arêtes and pinnacles and forming one of the most distinctive and most beautiful landscapes in the Alps.

Scattered about among the mountains are beautiful little *lakes*, surrounded in summer by green Alpine meadows; these include the *Lago di Braies, Lago di Carezza, Lago di Misurina, Lago di Landrio* and *Lago d'Álleghe*.

The famous *"**Alpine glow**", bathing the Alps in the flaming red of the setting sun, is particularly beautiful in the Dolomites. The real Alpine glow, when the rock faces and snowfields are clad in brilliant hues of yellow, purple and red, occurs only very rarely, and then only for 5 to 10 minutes after sunset, when there is a light haze in the W and dusk has already fallen in the valleys.

FLORA. – The natural flora of the Dolomites is of Alpine character. The valley floors and gentler slopes are mostly covered with arable land and pasture, while the steeper slopes, up to 2200 m, are wooded – mostly with conifers but in the southern Dolomites also deciduous trees. Above the tree level are great expanses of upland meadows spangled with Alpine flowers.

POPULATION. – The Isarco valley and its side valleys and the Val Pustería were settled from the 6th c. onwards by German-speaking Bajuwari (Bavarians), while at the same time Italians advanced into the region from the S. The Rhaetians, speaking a Romance language and now known as Ladins, withdrew into the inner valleys of the Dolomites, and are now mainly found in the Val Gardena, Val Gádera and Val di Fassa, numbering altogether about 25,000. They are noted for their fine wood-carving, particularly in the Val Gardena. Their main source of income apart from stock-farming and forestry is tourism.

TOURS. – The most popular tourist route is the magnificent **Strada delle Dolomiti*, which runs through the northern Dolomites from Bolzano. After going over the *Passo di Costalunga*, the *Passo del Pordoi* and the *Passo di Falzárego* it comes to *Cortina d'Ampezzo* (109 km), and continues from there by way of the *Lago di Misurina* to *Carbonin* and *Dobbiaco* (34 km); then through the *Val Pusteria*, with a detour to the *Lago di Braies*, to *Brunico* and *Bressanone*, and from there back through the *Isarco* valley to Bolzano (102 km). – If time permits it is well worth making a detour from the W side of the Passo del Pordoi over the magnificent **Passo di Sella* and the *Passo di Gardena* into the picturesque *Corvara*

valley, and from there over the *Passo di Campolongo* to *Arabba* on the Strade delle Dolomiti (additional distance 21 km). – There is also a very attractive detour (26 km) from *Brunico* through the *Val Gadera* to *Corvara* (36 km), from there over the *Passo di Gardena* and through the **Val Gardena* to *Ponte Gardena* (42 km), and so back to Bolzano through the Isarco valley (23 km).

There is also a magnificent round trip from Bolzano through the southern Dolomites. The route goes through the *Isarco valley* and the **Val Gardena* and then over the **Passo di Sella* to join the ***Strada delle Dolomiti*, which it follows to *Cortina d'Ampezzo* (114 km); from there to *Venas*, over the *Cibiana* pass into the *Zoldo valley* and over the *Passo Duran* to *Ágordo* (70 km); then over the *Passo di Cereda* to *Fiera di Primiero* (32 km), on to *San Martino di Castrozza* and over the **Passo di Rolle* to *Predazzo*. From here there are alternative routes – either through the *Val di Fiemme* to *Ora* and from there up the *Adige valley* to Bolzano (99 km), or preferably via *Vigo di Fassa* and on the *Strada delle Dolomiti* over the *Passo di Costalunga* to Bolzano (97 km).

Elba

Region: Toscana. – Province: Livorno (LI).
Area: 223 sq. km. – Population: 30,000.
Post code: I-57030. – Dialling code: 0565.
ⓘ **Ente per la Valorizzazione dell'Isola d'Elba,**
Calata Italia 26, I-57037 Portoferraio;
tel. (0565) 9 26 71.

HOTELS. – IN PORTOFERRAIO: *Fabricia*, I, 119 b., SP; *Picchiaie Residence*, in Picchiaie, II, 183 b., SP; *Massimo*, II, 132 b.; *Garden*, in Schiopparello, II, 99 b.; *Adriana*, in Padulella, II, 60 b.; *Acquabona Golf*, in Acquabona, II, 45 b., SP; *Touring*, II, 41 b.; etc. – Several CAMPING SITES. – IN MARCIANA PROCCHIO: *Del Golfo*, I, 175 b., SP; *Désirée*, II, 133 b.; *Di Procchio*, II, 95 b.; *La Perla*, II, 94 b., SP; *Mona Lisa*, II, 65 b.; *Valle Verde*, II, 62 b.; *Fontalleccio*, II, 40 b.; *Brigantino*, III, 56 b.; etc. – IN MARCIANA MARINA: *La Primula*, I, 112 b., SP; *Gabbiano Azzurro*, II, 78 b., SP; *Marinella*, III, 112 b.; *La Conchiglia*, III, 82 b., SP; etc. – IN RIA MARINA: *Ortano Mare*, II, 319 b., SP; *Rio*, II, 63 b.; *Cristallo*, in Cavo, III, 90 b.; etc. – IN PORTO AZZURRO: *Cala di Mola*, II, 138 b., SP; *Plaza*, II, 46 b.; *Residence Reale*, III, 88 b.; etc. – Several CAMPING SITES. – IN MARINA DI CAMPO: *Iselba*, I, 90 b.; *Select*, II, 162 b.; *Marina Due*, II, 152 b., SP; *Dei Coralli*, II, 116 b., SP; *Riva*, II, 77 B.; *Santa Caterina*, II, 60 b.; *Acquarius*, II, 58 b.; *La Barcarola*, II, 56 b.; *Meridiana*, II, 54 b.; *Barracuda*, III, 70 b.; etc. – Several CAMPING SITES. – IN CAPOLIVERI-NARENGO: *Elba International*, I, 455 b., SP; etc.

BOAT SERVICES. – Regular service (car ferry) several times daily from *Piombino* to *Cavo* ($\frac{3}{4}$ hour) or *Portoferraio* (1–1$\frac{1}{2}$ hours); twice daily to *Rio Marina* and *Porto Azzurro*; daily from *Livorno* to *Portoferraio* (2$\frac{1}{2}$–5$\frac{1}{2}$ hours). In summer also hydrofoil services several times daily from *Piombino* and *Livorno* and daily from *Viareggio* to *Portoferraio*.

The island of Elba (Isola d'Elba), lying between the N Italian coast and the French island of Corsica, is the largest of the islands off Tuscany

Cableway up Lagazuoi

(27 km long, up to 18·5 km wide). It consists mainly of granite and porphyry, and has considerable deposits of high-quality iron ore, particularly in the eastern part of the island, with a metal content of 40–80%.

The possession of the iron-mines of Elba enabled the Etruscans to assert their dominance in Italy, and the mines were later worked by the Romans. Together with the tuna and anchovy fisheries and agriculture (fruit, wine) the working of iron is still one of the island's main sources of income. Elba's mild and equable climate, its great scenic beauty and the excellent conditions for scuba diving off its cliff-fringed coasts have drawn increasing numbers of visitors to the island in recent years.

HISTORY. – Elba belonged to Pisa from 962 onwards; then in 1290 it passed to Genoa, later to Lucca and in 1736 to Spain. After Napoleon's defeat in 1814 he was granted full sovereign rights over the island, and lived there from 4 May 1814 to 26 February 1815. Elba was returned to the Grand Duchy of Tuscany by the Congress of Vienna.

The chief place of the island, **Portoferraio** (alt. 10 m; pop. 2000), lies on a promontory on the W side of the entrance to a wide bay on the N coast. In the main street, Via Garibaldi, stands the Town Hall and a little way NE, in Via Napoleone, the Misericordia church, in which a mass is said for Napoleon's soul on 5 May every year; it contains a reproduction of his coffin and a bronze cast of his death-mask. On the highest point in the town is the Piazza Napoleone (view). To the W rises Forte Falcone (alt. 79 m), to the E, above the lighthouse, Forte Stella (48 m), both originally built in 1548 and completed by Napoleon. On the seaward side of the square the simple Villa dei Molini, Napoleon's official residence, contains his library and other relics.

6 km SW of Portoferraio, set amid luxuriant vegetation on the slopes of the wooded *Monte San Martino* (370 m), is situated the **Villa Napoleone**, the emperor's summer residence (fine views from terrace).

A road runs W from Portoferraio to the seaside resort of *Procchio*, in the bay of the same name, and the village of *Marciana Marina* (18 km), another popular resort. – 4 km inland is the fort

of *Poggio* (alt. 359 m), and 4 km W of this the village of *Marciana* (375 m), a summer resort surrounded by fine chestnut woods, has a ruined castle. – From here there is a cableway up **Monte Capanne** (1019 m), the island's highest peak (*view). – From Poggio there is an attractive walk up *Monte Perone* (630 m), to the SE (1 hour).

Marina di Campo. Elba

On the E coast are *Rio Marina* (pop. 2500), with large open-cast iron workings, and the little fishing port of **Porto Azzurro** (pop. 3000), picturesquely situated in a long inlet, which was fortified by the Spaniards in the 17th c. – On the lonely S coast is the popular seaside resort of **Marina di Campo**, finely situated in the Golfo di Campo.

Emilia-Romagna

EPT Bologna, Via Leopardi 1,
I-40100 Bologna (BO);
tel. (051) 23 74 14.
EPT Ferrara, Largo Castello 22,
I-44100 Ferrara (FE);
tel. (0532) 3 50 17.
EPT Forlì, Corso della Repubblica 23,
I-47100 Forlì (FO);
tel. (0543) 2 55 32.
EPT Modena, Corso Canalgrande 3,
I-41100 Modena (MO);
tel. (059) 22 24 82.
EPT Parma, Piazza Duomo,
I-43100 Parma (PR);
tel. (0521) 3 47 35.
EPT Piacenza, Via San Siro 17,
I-29100 Piacenza (PC);
tel. (0523) 2 73 98.
EPT Ravenna, Piazza San Francesco 7,
I-48100 Ravenna (RA);
tel. (0544) 2 51 11.
EPT Reggio nell'Emilia, Piazza C. Battisti 4,
I-42100 Reggio nell'Emilia (RE);
tel. (0522) 4 33 70.

Emilia-Romagna, the south-eastern part of the N Italian plain occupies an area of 22,122 sq. km extending from the River Po to the Apennines and then eastward to the Adriatic coast. It comprises the provinces of Bologna, Ferrara, Forlì, Modena, Parma, Piacenza, Ravenna and Reggio nell'Emilia, with a total population of some 4 million.

The high fertility of the soil and the advantages of its situation in an area of passage traversed by ancient traffic and trade routes between the Adriatic, northern Italy and the Gulf of Genoa enabled this region, and particularly the larger towns, to attain considerable prosperity from an early period, and Emilia-Romagna is still one of Italy's most highly developed regions. The main elements in its agriculture are meat and dairy farming, tomatoes and fruit, wine, sugar-beet, maize and rice. Its industries have an international reputation – petrochemicals, based on the recently developed resources of oil and natural gas in the Po plain, engineering, car manufacture, textiles, boots and shoes. On the Adriatic coast fisheries and the tourist trade also make important contributions to the economy of the region.

HISTORY. – **Emilia**, the western part of the region, derives its name from the Roman *Via Aemilia*, a military road running from Rimini along the S edge of the N Italian plain via Bologna, Parma and Piacenza to Tortona which was built by the consul Marcus Aemilius Lepidus in 187 B.C. to protect the Roman provinces N of the Apennines. After the Lombard conquest of northern Italy the SE part of the region, including Forlì and Ravenna, remained in Byzantine hands under the name of **Romagna**.

The modern **Via Emilia** is an attractive route, passing through a series of historic towns with much of interest to offer. – There are also a number of smaller places which are well worth a visit. Between Piacenza and Parma is **Fidenza** (alt. 72 m; pop. 25,000; Hotel Astoria, III, 57 b.; etc.), the ancient *Fidentia Iulia*, which was known between 387 and 1927 as Borgo San Donnino. *Cathedral in Lombard Romanesque style (12th c.), with lion doorways and *statues of prophets on the unfinished façade; Romanesque *holy-water stoup (to right of entrance). – 10 km SW of Fidenza is **Salsomaggiore Terme** (alt. 165 m; pop. 17,000; hotels: *Grand Hotel e Milano, L, 199 b., SP; Centrale Bagni, I, 182 b.; Porro, I, 153 b., SP; Regina, I, 147 b.; Bolognese-Cavour, I, 135 b.; Valentini, II, 215 b.; Europa, III, 125 b.; Casa Romagnosi, II, 85 b.; etc.), a spa attracting many visitors between April and November, with springs (high iodine, bromine and salt content) which are effective in the treatment of disorders of the joints, muscles, heart and nerves.

Within the triangle formed by Ravenna, Forlì and Rimini, also on the Via Emilia, is the walled town of **Cesena** (alt. 40 m; pop. 88,000; hotels: Casali's, II, 70 b.;

Landscape in Emilia

Barriera, II, 57 b.; Leon d'Oro, II, 49 b.; Savio, III, 52 b.; etc.), with the famous *Biblioteca Malatestiana (1452) and a Gothic cathedral (14th c.).

Between Chioggia and Ravenna, near the Adriatic coast, is the Benedictine *abbey of Santa Maria di Pomposa, which was abandoned in medieval times because of the prevalent malaria. It has a fine 11th c. church with an interesting atrium and a campanile 50 m high; fine mosaic pavement and mid 14th c. frescoes. Other remains of the abbey are the chapterhouse (frescoes), the refectory (c. 1320) and the Palazzo della Ragione (now a college of agriculture).

Castello di Lombardia, Enna

Enna

Region: Sicilia. – Province: Enna (EN).
Altitude: 948 m. – Population: 30,000.
Post code: I-94100. – Dialling code: 0935.
(i) **AA**, Piazza Calaianni;
    tel. 2 61 19.
    EPT, Piazza Garibaldi 1;
    tel. 2 11 84.
    ACI, Via Roma 429;
    tel. 2 18 23.

HOTELS. – *Grande Albergo Sicilia*, II, 102 b.; *Belvedere*, II, 97 b.; etc.

The town of Enna, previously known as Castrogiovanni, reverted to its classical name in 1926. It is picturesquely situated on a horseshoe-shaped plateau in the Monti Erei, in the centre of Sicily, and has been aptly called the belvedere and the navel of the island.

SIGHTS. – The main square, the *Piazza Vittorio Emanuele*, lies on the N side of the town, with the *church and convent of San Francesco* (15th c. campanile) and a terrace commanding fine views. From the smaller Piazza Crispi, to the W, there is a superb view of the little town of *Calascibetta*, 3 km NW. From the Piazza Vittorio Emanuele the SE section of the town's main shopping street, *Via Roma*, passes the *Theatre* and the *Town Hall* and reaches the Piazza Mazzini, on the N side of which stands the **Cathedral** or *Chiesa Madre* (begun in 1307): picturesque interior (14th c.), with four half-columns and eight full columns on bizarrely carved bases. Beyond the cathedral is the *Museo Alessi*, which contains the cathedral

treasury, Greco-Roman material and medieval paintings. The Via Roma ends at the **Castello di Lombardia**, a huge pile, with three courtyards, which still preserves six of its original 20 towers. From the platform of the *Torre Pisana* there are magnificent **views, particularly at sunset: to the E the towering mass of Etna, to the N the Monti Nébrodi and the Madonie range, to the S the Lago di Pergosa and, on clear days, the distant Mediterranean. – The SE section of the Via Roma runs from the Piazza Vittorio Emanuele past the churches of *San Cataldo* and *Santo Tommaso* to the *Giardino Pubblico*, in the centre of which, on a hill, is the octagonal *tower* of a castle built by Frederick II of Aragon (c. 1300: fine views).

SURROUNDINGS. – A fascinating excursion from Enna is via the *Lago di Pergusa* (Villaggio Turistico Garden, II, 72 b.) to **Piazza Armerina** (35 km; hotels: Jolly, I, 98 b.; Selene, II, 70 b.; etc.), a town of 25,000 inhabitants also known as *Chiazza*, with a handsome cathedral and the Norman church of Sant'Andrea (1096), 1 km N. 6 km S is the **Villa Romana del Casale*, a magnificent example of a Roman country house of the late Empire (3rd–4th c. A.D.; occupied until about 1200), with baths, a peristyle and a basilica. The villa is particularly notable for its splendid series of **mosaics, covering more than 3000 sq. m, which are among the largest and best of their kind.

From Piazza Armerina it is well worth while continuing SW (32 km) to *Caltagirone* (alt. 609 m; pop. 40,000), which is famous for its majolica and terracotta work. It has an interesting *Museum of Ceramics.

34 km SW of Enna is **Caltanisetta** (alt. 588 m; pop. 65,000; hotels: Concordia-Villa Mazzone, II, 130 b.; Di Prima, II, 127 b.; Europa, II, 41 b.), a provincial capital and the most important town in the interior of Sicily (sulphur mines). The main square of the town is the Piazza Garibaldi, in which are the cathedral (consecrated 1622; frescoes by Borreman, 1720; splendid Maundy Thursday procession) and the Town Hall (Museo Civico). Beyond the Town Hall are the Law Courts, in Baroque style. From the Piazza Garibaldi the Corso Umberto I runs S into the Viale Regina Margherita, in which are the Palazzo del

Governo and the Villa Amedeo gardens. In the E of the town are the disused church of Santa Maria degli Angeli (13th–14th c.) and the ruins of the Aragonese castle of Pietrarossa. On Monte San Giuliano (727 m: *view), to the N of the town, is a statue of Christ 18 m high.

Etna

Region: Sicilia. – Province: Catina (CT).
ⓘ **EPT Catania**, Largo Paisiello 5,
I-95100 Catania (CT);
tel. (095) 31 21 24.

**Etna (3326 m), in the Sicilian dialect called Mongibello, is Europe's largest active volcano and after the Alpine peaks the highest mountain in Italy.

It is one of the youngest geological features in Sicily, probably formed on land which in Tertiary times was an inlet of the sea. It has the form of a truncated cone with an almost circular base 40 km in diameter and 145 km in circumference. The upper slopes have only a meagre cover of vegetation, since the porous rock allows water to sink down rapidly to lower levels, where it meets an impervious bed of rock and emerges in many places as springs which water the fertile lower slopes. Oranges and lemons are grown up to about 500 m above sea level, olives and vines to 1300 m. Above this, reaching to about 2100 m, are forest trees and macchia, sometimes with recent lava flows cutting through them. The summit region, up to the snow-line, is a dull black wasteland which glistens in the sun. The volcanic vents, more than 260 in number, are mostly on the flanks of the mountain, in groups and rows. Major activity occurs at intervals of four to 12 years; the most recent occasion was in 1978.

ASCENT. – The little town of **Nicolosi** (alt. 698 m; pop. 3500; Hotel Biancaneve, II, 162 b., SP), on the S side of Etna, is the starting point for the ascent to the subsidiary craters of *Monti Rossi* (948 m; $\frac{3}{4}$–1 hour; view), the walls of which show clear volcanic stratification. At the foot of the Monti Rossi, to the NW, is a lava cave, the *Grotta delle Palombe*. – From Nicolosi the road runs first NW and then N between lava flows and comes in 17 km to the turning (1 km, left) to the *Grande Albergo Etna* (III, 50 b.) and in another 1 km to the *Casa Cantoniera* (roadman's house, 1881) which now houses the vulcanological and meteorological station of Catania University, near which is the *Rifugio-Albergo G. Sapienza* (IV, 110 b.), (with a restaurant). Opposite the rifugio is the lower station of the cableway

Etna in eruption

(5 km; 15 minutes) to the Observatory (2943 m), destroyed in 1971. From here it is a 45 minutes' climb (presenting no problems from mid June to mid October) to the **crater**, an abyss which is constantly changing its form and is almost always filled with gases. On a clear day the * *view can extend as far as Malta, 210 km away; the effect is particularly impressive at sunrise. – SE of the Observatory is the beginning of the **Valle del Bove** (Valley of the Ox), a black and desolate chasm 5 km wide surrounded on three sides by rock walls 600–1200 m high. Geologically it is a collapse valley enlarged by an explosive eruption into a gigantic gorge. The stratification of lava, tuffs and conglomerates is clearly visible. Experienced climbers (with a guide) can go down through the Valle del Bove to *Zafferana Etnea* (alt. 600 m; Albergio Primavera dell'Etna, II, 100 b.; Albergo del Bosco, III, 130 b.; etc.); the descent takes 5 hours.

ROUND ETNA. – An attractive drive of 144 km, starting from Catania (also possible by rail). The road runs via *Misterbianco* (alt. 213 m; pop. 15,000) and **Paternò** (280 m; pop. 43,000; Hotel Sicilia, II, 38 b.), with a castle built by Roger I in 1073 (rebuilt in 14th c.; well-preserved interior), to **Adrano** (564 m; pop. 32,000; Hotel Messina, IV, 26 b.), beautifully situated on a lava plateau, with an 11th c. Norman castle and the convent of Santa Lucia (founded 1157). – 9 km SW of Adrano, on a steep hill above the Simeto valley, with a magnificent view of Etna, is **Centuripe** (alt. 726 m; pop. 10,000), formerly *Centorbi*, with the so-called Castello di Corradino (1st c. B.C.). The Archaeological Museum contains material from the ancient Siculan town of *Centuripae*, which rose to importance in the late Hellenistic and Roman periods and was destroyed by Frederick II in 1233 (interesting Hellenistic and Roman house, Contrada Panneria, with paintings of the 2nd–1st c. B.C.). – From Adrano the road continues via **Bronte** (793 m; pop. 22,000), **Maletto** (940 m), with an old castle, **Randazzo** and *Linguaglossa* (525 m; pop. 8000) to *Fiumefreddo* (62 m). Then back to Catania on the motorway (A 18) or S.S. 114.

Faenza

Region: Emilia-Romagna. – Province: Ravenna (RA).
Altitude: 35 m. – Population: 55,000.
Post code: I-48018. – Dialling code: 0546.
ⓘ **Pro Faventia**, Piazza del Popolo 31;
tel. 2 23 08.

HOTELS. – *Vittoria*, II, 62 b.; *Cavallino*, II, 60 b.; *Da Pietro*, III, 28 b.; *Al Moro*, III, 27 b.; *Torricelli*, III, 26 b.

EVENTS. – Annual art pottery competition (end of July to end of Sept.).

Faenza, situated in the Po plain between Bologna and Rimini on the

The Palio Faenza

River Lamone, is famous for the faience (majolica) which is named after the town. The great age of this ware was in the 15th and 16th c., and it is only in recent years that the craft has again been practised and deliberately promoted.

SIGHTS. – The town, still surrounded by its old walls, suffered severe war damage, but this has been almost completely made good. The main street is the *Corso Giuseppe Mazzini*, at the E end of which are two elongated squares joining one another at right angles – the *Piazza della Libertà* to the N and the *Piazza del Popolo* to the S. In the Piazza della Libertà are the *Torre dell'Orologia* (Clock-Tower) and a beautiful fountain of 1621. At the far corner of the square stands the **Cathedral** (1474–1513), in early Renaissance style, with the tomb of St Savinus (by Benedetto da Maiano; after 1471) to the left of the high altar. In the Piazza del Popolo are the *Town Hall* (left) and the *Palazzo del Podestà* (right), both with high arcades.

In a palace in Via Santa Maria dell'Angelo are the *Pinacoteca*, with paintings by old masters of Emilia and Romagna, and the *Municipal Museum*. In Viale Baccarini we find the richly stocked **International Ceramic Museum** (*Museo Internazionale della Ceramiche*).

Fano

Region: Marche. – Province: Pesaro e Urbino (PS).
Altitude: 14 m. – Population: 50,000.
Post code: I-61032. – Dialling code: 0721.
ⓘ **AA**, Viale C. Battisti 43;
tel. 8 25 34.

HOTELS. – *Elisabeth*, I, 68 b.; *Continental*, II, 92 b.; *Beaurivage*, II, 90 b.; *Excelsior*, II, 60 b.; *Piccolo*, II, 48 b.; *Plaza*, II, 30 b.; *Astoria*, III, 77 b.; *Europa*, III, 60 b.; *King's Bay*, III, 51 b.; *Vittoria*, III, 50 b.; etc. – Several CAMPING SITES.

EVENTS. – Festival of Music and Drama (July–Aug.); *Carneval d'Estate* (Aug.).

Fano, the ancient Fanum Fortunae, named after a temple of Fortuna, and now a popular seaside resort, lies on the Adriatic SE of Pesaro.

SIGHTS. – The central feature of the town, which is still surrounded by its medieval walls and a deep moat, is the *Piazza XX Settembre*, in which are the *Palazzo della Ragione* (built 1299, used since 1862 as a theatre) and the *Torre Municipale* (1759). On the S side of the square is the beautiful *Fontana della Fortuna* (1593). The **Palazzo Malatestiano**, at the N end of the square, contains a *lapidarium* and a small *collection of pictures*.

To the S of the Piazza XX Settembre stands the **church of Santa Maria Nuova**, which contains a **"Madonna Enthroned with Six Saints"* by Perugino and a "Visitation" by Giovanni Santi.

Ferrara

Region: Emilia-Romagna. – Province: Ferrara (FE).
Altitude: 9 m. – Population: 155,000.
Post code: I-44100. – Dialling code: 0532.
(i) **EPT**, Largo Castello 22;
tel. 3 50 17.
ACI, Via Padova 17;
tel. 5 27 21.
TCI, *Centro Turismo Viaggi*, Via Borgo dei Leoni 33;
tel. 3 35 20.

HOTELS. – *De la Ville*, Piazzale Stazione 11, II, 135 b.; *Astra*, Viale Cavour 55, II, 123 b.; *Carlton*, Via Garibaldi 93, II, 115 b.; *Ferrara*, Piazza della Repubblica 4, II, 98 b.; *Europa*, Corso Giovecca 49, II, 59 b.; *Touring*, Viale Cavour 11, II, 57 b.; *Kennedy*, Via Piero Gobetti 11, III, 43 b.; etc. – *Motel Nord-Ovest*, Viale Po 52, III, 65 b. – YOUTH HOSTEL, Via Benvenuto Tisi da Garofalo 5, 64 b.

Ferrara, lying 5 km S of the River Po at the E end of the fertile N Italian plain, now the chief town of its province and the see of an archbishop, and with a small university, was once the splendid capital of the dukes of Este. Its wide streets,

frowning castle and sumptuous Renaissance palaces still bear witness to the great days of its past.

HISTORY. – The town first appears in the records at the time of the great migration. At the end of the 13th c. it fell into the hands of the **Este** family, one of the oldest noble houses in Italy (961–1598), which reached its period of greatest splendour in the 16th c. *Ariosto* (1474–1533), the greatest Italian poet of the day, and the poet *Torquato Tasso* (1544–95) lived at the brilliant Renaissance court of the dukes of Este, and *Girolamo Savonarola* was born in the town in 1452. In 1598 Ferrara was incorporated in the Papal State, and thereafter sank into insignificance, from which it has emerged only in quite recent times.

SIGHTS. – In the centre of the town is the picturesque ***Castello Estense**, the four-towered moated castle of the Este family, begun in 1385 and partly rebuilt after 1554. The castle (closed Mondays) contains frescoes by pupils of Dosso Dossi (1489/90–1542). – S of the Castello is the Piazza Savonarola, with a monument to Savonarola. Here too we find the *Palazzo Comunale*, once the palace of the dukes of Este (built 1243, rebuilt in the 18th c.).

Castello Estense, Ferrara

SE of the Castello rises the ***Cathedral** of San Giorgio, with a magnificent façade in Lombard Romanesque style (12th–13th c.); it contains pictures of the Ferrara school. At the SE corner is the unfinished *campanile* (15th–16th c.). Over the narthex is the *Cathedral Museum* (pictures, sculpture). – Facing the cathedral, to the S, is the Gothic *Palazzo della Ragione* (1321–26).

0·5 km SE of the cathedral stands the *church of San Francesco*, a brick-built Early Renaissance building (15th c.) roofed with a series of domes. Immediately E is the *University* (founded 1391), and farther SE the **Palazzo**

Schifanoia (1469), an Este palace incorporating the *Municipal Museum* (closed Sunday afternoons and Tuesdays), with fine *frescoes by Francesco del Cossa and his pupils (*c.* 1470). – 0·5 km S of the Palazzo Schifanoia is the **Palazzo di Ludovico il Moro** (16th c., unfinished), with a beautiful courtyard and fine frescoes, early examples of trompe-l'œil painting (*c.* 1500). It now houses the *Archaeological Museum* (closed Sunday afternoons and Mondays), which has a splendid collection of vases and other finds from the Greek and Etruscan necropolis of Spina, near Comacchio. – SW of San Francesco, in Via delle Scienze (No. 17), is the *Palazzo del Paradiso*, occupied from 1567 to 1963 by the university and now by the *Biblioteca Comunale Ariostea* (closed Sundays and 1–15 August), with Ariosto's tomb and some of his manuscripts. Here too can be seen the *Teatro Anatomico* (1731) of the university.

In the N of the town, at the intersection of Corso Ercole I d'Este with Corso Rosetti and Corso di Porta Mare, are two handsome palaces. On the NW corner is the *Palazzo Sacrati* or *Prosperi* (*c.* 1500), with a fine doorway. Opposite it, to the S, is the **Palazzo dei Diamanti**, a superb example of Early Renaissance architecture (1492–1567) which takes its name from the faceted stones of its façade. It now contains the *Municipal Collection of Contemporary Art* and the Boldini Museum (with works by the painter of that name, 1845–1931). – 0·5 km NW, at Via Ariosto 67, in the house in which Ariosto lived (closed Sundays), are various relics of the poet. – Farther NE is the *Certosa*, a former Carthusian house founded in 1452 and dissolved in 1796, now a cemetery.

Florence/Firenze

(Note that street numbers followed by the letter *r* (=red), differ from the black numbers.)

Region: Toscana. – Province: Firenze (FI). Altitude: 50 m. – Population: 470,000. Post code: I-50100. – Dialling code: 055.

ⓘ **EPT**, Via A. Manzoni 16; tel. 67 88 41.
ACI, Viale Amendola 36; tel. 2 78 41.
CIT, Via Cerretani 57–59; tel. 29 43 06.
Also Piazza Stazione 51*r*; tel. 28 41 45.
U.C.A., Viale Lavagnini 6*r*; tel. 47 41 92.

HOTELS. – *Excelsior Italia*, Piazza Ognissanti 3, L, 348 b.; *Villa Medici*, Via il Prato 42, L, 193 b., SP; *Savoy*, Piazza della Repubblica 7, L, 173 b.; *Aerhotel Baglioni*, Piazza Unità Italiana 6, I, 340 b.; *Michelangelo*, Viale Fratelli Rosselli 4, I, 253 b.; *Jolly Carlton*, Piazza Vittorio Veneto 4A, I, 249 b., SP; *Anglo-Americano*, Via Garibaldi 9, I, 202 b.; *Minerva*, Piazza Santa Maria Novella 16, I, 199 b., SP; *Plaza e Lucchesi*, Lungarno della Zecca Vecchia 38, I, 191 b.; *Croce di Malta*, Via della Scala 7, I, 188 b., SP; *Eurocrest*, Viale Europa 205, I, 184 b., SP; *Londra*, Via

Florence

Iacopo da Diacceto 16, I, 184 b.; *Grand Hotel Majestic*, Via del Melarancio 1, I, 183 b.; *Astoria*, Via del Giglio 9, I, 163 b.; *De la Ville*, Piazza Antinori 1, I, 128 b.; *Kraft*, Via Solferino 2, I, 124 b., SP; *Grand Hotel Villa Cora*, Viale Machiavelli 18, I, 97 b., SP; *Park Palace*, Piazzale Galileo 5, I, 52 b., SP; *Principe*, Lungarno Vespucci 34, I, 38 b.; *Mediterraneo*, Lungarno del Tempio 44, II, 668 b.; *Residence Firenze Nuova*, Via Pianchiatichi 51, II, 244 b.; *Monginervo*, Via di Novoli 59, II, 224 b.; *Adriatico*, Via Maso Finiguerra 9, II, 204 b.; *Ambasciatori*, Via Alamanni 3, II, 183 b.; *Cavour*, Via del Proconsolo 3, II, 171 b.; *Mirage*, Via Baracca 231, II, 164 b.; *Columbus*, Lungarno C. Colombo 22A, II, 156 b.; *Helvetia e Bristol*, Via de' Pescioni 2, II, 153 b.; *Concorde*, Viale L. Gori 10, II, 146 b.; *Milano Terminus*, Via Cerretani 10, II, 146 b.; *Corona d'Italia*, Via Nazionale 14, II, 149 b.; *Capitol*, Viale Amendola 34, II, 141 b.; *Lungarno*, Borgo San Jacopo 14, II, 138 b.; *Augustus e dei Congressi*, Vicolo dell'Oro 5, II, 134 b.; *Berchelli*, Lungarno Acciaiuoli 14, II, 134 b.; *Continental*, Lungarno Acciaiuoli 2, II, 124 b.; *Bonciani*, Via Panzani 17, II, 114 b.; *Auto Hotel Park*, Via Valdegola 1, III, 198 b.; *Nuovo Atlantico*, Via Nazionale 10, III, 174 b.; *Fleming*, Viale Guidoni 78, III, 172 b.; *Columbia-Parlamento*, Piazza S. Firenze 29, III, 162 b.; *Delle Nazioni*, Via L. Alamanni 15, III, 132 b.; *Porta Rossa*, Via Porta Rossa 19, III, 127 b.; etc. – YOUTH HOSTEL, Viale Augusto Righi 2–4, 400 b. – Two CAMPING SITES.

RESTAURANTS. – *Sabatini*, Via de' Panzani 9A; *Doney*, Via Tornabuoni 10; *Oliviero*, Via delle Terme 51r; *Paoli*, Via dei Tavolini 12r; *Al Campidoglio*, Via del Campidoglio 8r; *Otello*, Via Orti Oricellari 28r; *Giannino in San Lorenzo*, Via Borgo San Lorenzo 37r; *Buca Lapi*, Via del Trebbio 1r; *La Loggia*, Piazzale Michelangiolo 1; *Cammillo*, Borgo San Jacopo 57r; etc.

CAFÉS. – *Doney*, Via Tornabuoni 10: *Extrabar*, *Paszkowski*, *Moderno*, *Donnini*, *Gilli*, all in Piazza della Republica.

Florence (in Italian Firenze), the old capital of Tuscany, called "la Bella", and now a provincial capital, a university town and the see of an archbishop, is picturesquely situated on both sides of the River Arno, surrounded by foothills of the Apennines. While in ancient times the life of Italy was centred on Rome, from the Middle Ages to our own day Florence has been its intellectual centre. Here the Italian language and Italian literature were created (Dante, Boccaccio, Petrarch), and here Italian art attained its finest form.

With its astonishing abundance of art treasures concentrated in a relatively small area, its historical associations and its beautiful surroundings, Florence is one of the world's most fascinating cities and one of its greatest tourist centres.

Palazzo Vecchio, Florence

HISTORY. – The Roman town of *Florentia* played no great part in history. At the beginning of the 12th c. the fortunes of war and the industry of its people (wool, silk) made it the leading town in Central Italy, but the ruling noble families were weakened by continual internecine strife between Guelfs and Ghibellines. The town's craft guilds grew steadily in strength and in 1282 their leaders, the priori (convenors) gained control of the city's government. In 1434 power fell into the hands of the wealthy merchant family of the **Medici**, whose leading members *Cosimo* (1434–64), the "father of his country" (*pater patriae*), and *Lorenzo the Magnificent* (1469–92), brought the city to its greatest prosperity and made it a brilliant centre of art and learning. In 1494 the Medici were driven out, and four years later, in 1498, the great preacher and reformer *Girolamo Savonarola* was burned at the stake in the Piazza della Signoria. In 1512 the Medici returned to Florence under the protection of Spanish troops, but in 1527 they were again expelled. Only three years later, however, after the capture of the town by Charles V (1530), *Alessandro de' Medici* was installed as hereditary duke. After his murder in 1537 he was succeeded by *Cosimo I*, who became Grand Duke of Tuscany in 1569. – After the house of Medici became extinct in 1737 the Grand Duchy passed to the house of *Lorraine*, which held it, with an interruption during the Napoleonic period (1801–14), until 1860. Tuscany then became part of the kingdom of Italy, and Florence enjoyed a fresh period of prosperity as temporary capital of the new kingdom (1865–70).

ART. – From the end of the 13th c. Florence played a leading part in the development of art. *Arnolfo di Cambio* (d. 1302), the great forerunner of the architects of the Renaissance, worked on Santa Croce and the cathedral, and *Giotto* (1266–1337), father of modern painting, began his career here. Among his principal pupils were *Taddeo Gaddi* (d. 1366) and *Orcagna* (d. 1368), also noted as an architect and sculptor.

The year 1402 can be regarded as marking the beginning of the **Renaissance** (competition for the N door of the Baptistery), although in architecture the new spirit did not find full expression until 20 years later. *Filippo Brunelleschi* (1377–1446) applied his

Botticelli's "Birth of Venus" (Uffizi)

knowledge of ancient architecture to meet new requirements, and was followed by *Leon Battista Alberti* (1404–72).

The sculptors of the Florentine Renaissance included *Lorenzo Ghiberti* (1378–1455), *Luca della Robbia* (1400–82), noted for his glazed terracotta reliefs, and above all *Donatello* (1386–1466), the greatest master of the century. After Donatello's death the leading sculptor was *Andrea Verrocchio* (1436–88), also noted as a painter.

The pioneers of Renaissance painting were *Masaccio* (1401–28), *Andrea del Castagno* (1423–57) and *Paolo Uccello* (1397–1475). Outstanding in fervour of religious feeling was *Fra Angelico da Fiesole* (1387–1455), who influenced *Fra Filippo Lippi* (1406–69) and *Benozzo Gozzoli* (1420–97). The zenith of the Florentine Early Renaissance was reached in the work of *Andrea Verrocchio*, the brothers *Antonio* and *Piera del Pollaiuolo* (1429–98, 1443–c. 1495), *Sandro Botticelli* (1444–1510), Fra Filippo's son *Filippino Lippi* (c. 1459–1504) and *Domenico Ghirlandaio* (1449–94). Of the three great masters of Italian art the Tuscans *Leonardo da Vinci* and *Michelangelo* received their training in Florence, and here too *Raphael* shook off the trammels of his earlier years; from 1506 all three were working in Florence. About the same time *Lorenzo di Credi* (1459–1537), *Piero di Cosimo* (1462–1521), *Fra Bartolomeo* (1472–1517) and the talented colourist *Andrea del Sarto* (1486–1531) were also working in Florence, as were *Franciabigio* and *Pontormo*. Among painters of a slightly later period were *Agnolo Bronzino* (1503–72), *Alessandro Allori* (1535–1607) and *Giorgio Vasari* (1511–74), noted for his "Lives of the Artists". Leading sculptors of this period were *Benvenuto Cellini* (1500–71), also famous as a goldsmith, and *Giovanni Bologna* (c. 1524–1608): actually Jean Boulogne of Douai).

In LITERATURE Florence can claim **Dante** (1265–1321), author of the "Divine Comedy" and creator of the Italian literary language; **Boccaccio** (1313–75), Dante's first interpreter, whose "Decameron" provided the model for Italian prose; and **Petrarch** (1304–74), who played a major part in preparing the way for humanism.

SIGHTS. – The old centre of Florentine life is the picturesque *Piazza della Signoría*, on the E side of which stands the *Palazzo Vecchio* (Town Hall), built for the Signoria between 1298 and 1314 and extended to the rear in the 16th c. To the left of the entrance can be seen a modern copy of Michelangelo's "David".

In the outer courtyard (remodelled 1454) is a copy (original on first floor) of the charming *"Boy with a Fish" by Andrea Verrocchio. On the second floor the Salone dei Cinquecento (1495) houses Michelangelo's marble group "Triumph of Virtue over Vice" (c. 1520). The state apartments are on the first and second floors. From the wall-walk and the tower there are extensive *views. – At the NW corner of the palazzo in front of the *Neptune Fountain* (1575) is a stone slab marking the spot where Savonarola was burned at the stake.

Adjoining the Palazzo Vecchio is the *Loggia dei Lanzi** (1376–82), an open hall designed for addressing the people, named after Cosimo I's German pikemen (*Landsknechte*). In the loggia are a number of sculptures, including Giovanni

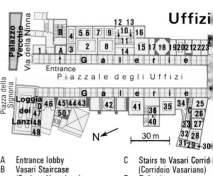

A	Entrance lobby	C	Stairs to Vasari Corridor
B	Vasari Staircase		(Corridoio Vasariano)
	(Scalone Vasariano)	D	Refreshments

UPPER FLOOR:
Galleria degli Uffizi (Picture Gallery)

1	Ancient sculpture (Rom. copy of Hellenistic Hermaphrodite)	19	Perugino, Francia
		20	Dürer, Cranach, Mantegna
2	13th c. Tuscan painters (Cimabue, Buoninsegna, Giotto)	21	Dürer, Bellini, Carpaccio, Giorgione
3	14th c. Sienese painters	22	Altdorfer, Holbein, David
4	14th c. Florentine painters	23	Correggio, Metsys
5–6	Early 15th c. Gothic painting	24	Miniatures (15th–18th c.)
7	Tuscan painters of the Early Renaissance	25	Raphael, Michelangelo, Bronzino
8	Lippi, Pollaiuolo	26	Sarto, Pontormo
9	Botticelli, Pollaiuolo	27	Pontormo
10	Botticelli	28	Titian
11	Botticelli, Lippi	29	Parmigianino
12	Memling; 15th c. Flemish painters	30	Parmigianino, Dossi
13	Lippi, Botticelli	31	Dossi
14	Lippi, Van der Goes, Ghirlandaio	32	Piombo, Bordone
15	Credi, Signorelli, Perugino, Verrocchio, Leonardo da Vinci	33	Various 16th c. painters
16	Maps of Tuscany; Leonardo da Vinci	34	Veronese
17	Umbrian painters	35	Tintoretto, Bassano, Baroccio
18	Tribuna: Medici Venus (4th c. B.C.) and other Greek sculpture. – Pictures by Bronzino, Vasari, Pontormo	36–40	In course of rearrangement
		41	Rubens, Van Dyck
		42	Niobe Room (Roman marble of a lost Greek original)
		43–50	In course of rearrangement

FIRST FLOOR:
**Gabinetto dei Disegni e delle Stampe
(Drawings and Prints)**

Bologna's marble group "Rape of the Sabine Women" (1583) and Benvenuto Cellini's bronze "Perseus with the Medusa's Head" (1553).

S of the Palazzo Vecchio, extending towards the Arno, stands the **Palazzo degli Uffizi** (closed Mondays), built 1560–74 as government offices and now occupied by the ****Galleria degli Uffizi**, one of the world's great art collections (some 4500 pictures, of which 700 are on display). They provide an almost complete survey of Florentine painting and also include major works by North Italian, particularly Venetian, painters, as well as outstanding pictures by Dutch and German masters.

From the Piazza della Signoria the busy *Via del Calzaiuoli* ("Street of the Hosiers") runs N to the Piazza del Duomo. At the end of Via Porta Rossa, on left, stands the ***church of Or San Michele**, built 1284–91 as a corn exchange, rebuilt 1337–1404. – Via Calzaiuoli ends in the Piazza del Duomo, in which, immediately on the right, is the *Oratory of the Misericordia*, a charitable fraternity which succoured the poor and the sick and buried the dead. To the left, at the corner of Piazza di San Giovanni, we find the Gothic *Loggia del Bigallo* (1352–58), in which foundlings were displayed. Opposite it is the ***Baptistery**, dedicated to San Giovanni Battista, an octagonal structure with a dome which was probably founded in the early Christian period on the remains of a Roman building and was rebuilt in the 11th–13th c., when it was clad externally and internally with variegated marble. It is famous for the three gilded bronze *doors with relief decoration, the S door by Andrea Pisano (1330–36), the N door (1403–24) and the principal door facing the cathedral (1425–52), the "Gate of Paradise", by Lorenzo Ghiberti. In the interior are 13th and 14th c. mosaics.

The ***Cathedral** (*Cattedrale di Santa Maria del Fiore*, so called after the lily which is the emblem of Florence), a mighty Gothic building, was begun by Arnolfo di Cambio in 1296, continued by Francesco Talenti from 1357 onwards and consecrated in 1436. The octagonal dome (1420–34) is Filippo Brunelleschi's master-work. The façade dates only from 1875 to 1887. The interior is bare and

dark. Steps lead down to the old cathedral of *Santa Reparata (4th–5th c.), which has been excavated since 1965. It is well worth the trouble of climbing up to the dome for the magnificent *view. – The Gothic ***campanile** (14th c.), faced with coloured marble, is one of the finest in Italy (extensive views from top). There is much sculpture by Donatello and his assistant Rosso (1420) and by Andrea Pisano and Luca della Robbia (1437).

SW of the cathedral lies the modern centre of the town, around the *Piazza della Repubblica*, which is the scene of lively activity, particularly in the evening. From the SE corner of the square Via Calimara runs S to the **Mercato Nuovo** (1547–51), where articles of woven straw and hand embroidery are now sold.

From the W side of the Piazza della Repubblica the Via degli Strozzi runs W into *Via de' Tornabuoni*, the most fashionable and busiest street in the old town, with handsome old palaces and elegant shops. Immediately on the left is the ***Palazzo Strozzi**, a magnificent example of Florentine palace architecture, built in 1489–1536 to the design of Benedetto da Maiano and Cronaca (in course of renovation). – In Via Tornabuoni to the S stands the **church of Santa Trinità**, originally one of the oldest Gothic churches in Italy, rebuilt in the 13th–15th c. Beyond it, to the W, the 17th c. **Palazzo Corsini** contains the most important privately owned collection of pictures in Florence (seen on application).

To the NW of the town centre, in the spacious Piazza Santa Maria Novella, stands the Dominican ***church of Santa Maria Novella**, a Gothic building (1278–1350) with an inlaid marble façade and a Renaissance doorway. In the choir are *frescoes which rank as Domenico Ghirlandaio's finest work. To the left of the church is the entrance to the *cloisters* (Chiostri monumentali); on the N side of the "Green Cloister" (Chiostro verde) we find the former chapterhouse, known as the **Cappellone degli Spágnoli* (1355). – To the N of the church is the **station**.

From the Piazza dell'Unità Italiana, on the E side of Santa Maria Novella, the short Via del Melarancio leads E to the **church**

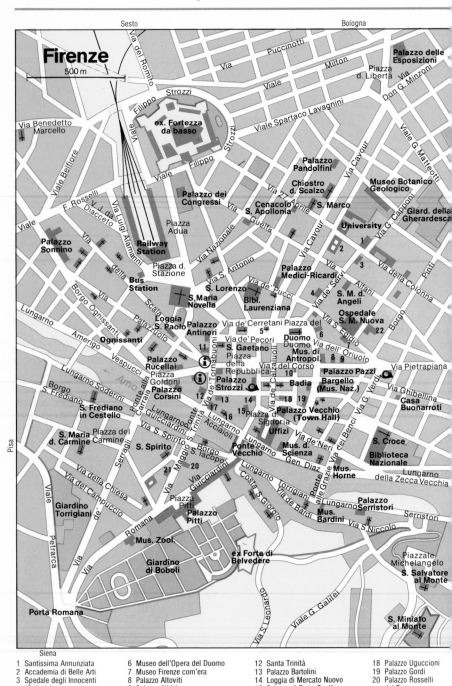

of San Lorenzo, originally consecrated by St Ambrose in 393 as Florence's first cathedral; the present building dates from 1421 onwards. The inside wall of the façade is by Michelangelo. In the N transept is the *Old Sacristy (by Brunelleschi, 1421–28), with sculpture by Donatello. From the cloister a staircase leads up to the *Biblioteca Laurenziana*, with 10,000 manuscripts of Greek and Latin classical authors collected by the Medici. – Behind the church, in the Piazza degli Aldobrandini, is the entrance to the **Medici Chapels**. From the crypt a staircase leads up to the *Chapel of the Princes*, decorated with fine stone mosaics, which was built in 1604–10 to house the sarcophagi of the Grand Dukes of Tuscany. To the left a passage leads to the **New Sacristy**, built by Michelangelo (1520–24) as the mausoleum of the Medici family. It contains the tombs of a son and grandson of Lorenzo the Magnificent, with statues of "Evening" and "Dawn". In two adjoining rooms are

...ture is the famous "David ("il Gigante"), carved from a single block of stone by the youthful Michelangelo (1501–03).

From the Piazza San Marco the Via Cesare Battisti runs past the former university to the magnificent *church of the Santissima Annunziata (1250, remodelled 1444–60). The forecourt contains *frescoes by Andrea del Sarto (1505–14) which rank among the finest achievements of the Florentine High Renaissance. – To the S of the church is the Foundling Hospital, begun in 1419 by Brunelleschi. Between the arches are coloured medallions with infants in swaddling clothes by Andrea della Robbia (c. 1463). – To the E of the church is the *Archaeological Museum, with a fine collection of Etruscan material and a notable Egyptian collection.

NE of the Piazza della Signoria in Piazza San Firenze stands the fortress-like *Palazzo del Podestà*, commonly known as the **Bargello**, begun in 1255. From 1574 it was the headquarters of the chief of

police and a prison, and since 1865 has housed the **National Museum**, devoted to the history of Italian culture and art in medieval and modern times. The *courtyard is a fine example of a medieval castle courtyard.

On the SE side of the old town, near the Arno, we find the *church of Santa Croce, a Franciscan church begun in 1295 but not completed until 1442, with a façade of 1857–63. It contains the tombs of many famous Italians, including Michelangelo, Dante, Alfieri, Machiavelli, Rossini, Cherubini and Galileo. Magnificent marble *pulpit by Benedetto da Maiano. On the far side of the *first cloister* is the *Pazzi Chapel* (by Brunelleschi, 1430). The *second cloister*, also by Brunelleschi, is one of the finest achievements of the Early Renaissance. – The **Biblioteca Nazionale Centrale**, Italy's largest library (3,500,000 volumes) adjoins the church to the S.

To the SE of the Piazza della Signoria the Arno is spanned by the *Ponte Vecchio, Florence's oldest bridge (rebuilt in 1345 after repeated destruction), which is lined with jewellers' shops.

SW of the Ponte Vecchio, at the foot of the Boboli hill, is the imposing *Palazzo Pitti, begun by Luca Pitti c. 1458 and extended in the 16th–18th c. In the left-hand half of the first floor the famous **Pitti Gallery* (Galleria Palatina), founded by the Medici in the 16th and 17th c., now contains over 600 pictures, including masterpieces by Raphael, Fra Bartolomeo, Andrea del Sarto and Titian. Adjoining the gallery are ten of the former *Royal Apartments* (18th–19th c.). On the ground floor is the *Silver Chamber*, with precious objects which belonged to the

Ponte Vecchio, Florence

Medici. On the second floor the *Gallery of Modern Art* houses 19th c. works, mostly by Tuscan artists. – To the S of the Palazzo Pitti extend the **Boboli Gardens**, laid out in 1560. From the terraces on the slopes of the hill there are attractive views of Florence. In a villa in the gardens is the *Porcelain Museum*. – Above the gardens to the E (entrance on S side) is the **Forte di Belvedere** (by Bernardo Buontalenti, 1590–96), with magnificent *views from the bastions.

NE of the Palazzo Pitti stands the *church of the Santo Spírito (by Brunelleschi, 1436–87), with a campanile of 1543. Notable features are the *Sacristy and numerous altarpieces. – Farther W is the **church of Santa Maria del Carmine**, almost completely rebuilt in 1782 after a fire. The **Brancacci Chapel** contains famous *frescoes on the lives of the Apostles (1424–27) which marked the beginning of Renaissance painting and served as a model for subsequent artists.

SURROUNDINGS. – The *Viale dei Colli, laid out from 1868 onwards, which runs along the S side of the town from the Porta Romana to the Piazza Francesco Ferrucci, a total distance of almost 6 km, is one of Italy's finest promenades. It winds its way up to the *Piazzale Michelangiolo*, with a spacious terrace from which there is a famous **view of the town and the Arno valley. – Above the square to the S is the monastic church of *San Miniato al Monte, conspicuous from afar with its inlaid marble façade, one of the finest examples of Tuscan Romanesque architecture of the 11th–12th c. Mosaics of 1297; crypt with graceful columns, some of them from Roman buildings. To the right of the church rises a fortress built by Michelangelo in 1529, now an Olivetan monastery.

8 km NE of Florence lies the little town of **Fiesole** (alt. 295 m; pop. 12,000; hotels: *Villa San Michele, L, 58 b.; Aurora, II, 43 b.; Villa Bonelli, III, 39 b.; etc.), originally an Etruscan town and later the Roman *Faesulae*, which still preserves parts of its massive walls. In the centre of the town is the cathedral (11th and 13th c.), in Tuscan Romanesque style, and behind it are the remains of a Roman theatre and an Etrusco-Roman temple (museum of antiquities). From the terrace of the church of Sant'Alessandro, a little way W of the cathedral, there is a very fine *view of the low-lying country around Florence.

5 km NW of Florence, near *Sesto Fiorentino* (*Porcelain Museum), is the **airport**.

Foggia

Region: Puglia. – Province: Foggia (FG).
Altitude: 74 m. – Population: 145,000.
Post code: I-71100. – Dialling code: 0881.

ⓘ **EPT**, Via Senatore Emilio Perrone 17;
    tel. 2 31 41.
    ACI, Via Monte Grappa 95;
    tel. 2 17 68.
    TCI, *Nuova Daunia Viaggi*, Via Lanza 5;
    tel. 7 40 10.

HOTELS. – *Cicolella*, Viale XXIV Maggio 60, I, 234 b.; *Palace Sarti*, Viale XXIV Maggio 48, I, 132 b.; *President*, Via Ascoli 80, II, 126 b., SP; *Asi*, Via Monfalcone 1, III, 168 b.; *Europa*, Via Monfalcone 52, III, 124 b.; etc.

Foggia, situated in the northern part of the Adriatic coastal region of Apulia, is both the geographical and the economic centre of the extensive Apulian plain, the Tavoliere di Puglia. Once a favourite residence of the Emperor Frederick II, it is the chief town of a province which was known until 1861 as the Capitanata.

Almost all the town's medieval buildings were destroyed in an earthquake in 1731. With its wide tree-lined streets and its many new buildings, including those erected after the Second World War to make good the severe destruction which the town had suffered, Foggia is now a town of very modern appearance.

SIGHTS. – The hub of the town's traffic is the *Piazza Cavour*, to the E of the centre. Adjoining the E side of the square, beyond a colonnade, is the *Giardino Pubblico*, extending eastwards in a long narrow swathe. From the Piazza Cavour Viale XXIV Maggio, lined by handsome buildings, runs NE to the station. – To the W of the Piazza Cavour is the Piazza Umberto Giordano, from the far end of which the busy *Corso Vittorio Emanuele*, Foggia's principal street, leads into the old town centre. 300 m W it is crossed by another busy street, the Corso Garibaldi, along which, to the SW, are the *Prefecture* and the *Town Hall*. A little way N is the **Cathedral**, built about 1179 in Pisan style but rebuilt in Baroque style after the 1731 earthquake. – Farther N, in Piazza Nigri, is the *Municipal Museum* (archaeology, folk traditions; collection of modern pictures).

SURROUNDINGS. – There is a very attractive trip of some 230 km around the *Monte Gargano promontory (1056 m), the "spur" on the Italian boot, a

The coast of Monte Gargano near Foggia

hilly tongue of land which extends 65 km into the Adriatic and, geologically, already belongs to the Dalmatian limestone formations. – Leave Foggia on S.S. 89 (the "Gargánica"), which runs NE through the extensive and well-cultivated Apulian plain. In 27 km, on the right, is *San Leonardo*, formerly a lodge of the Teutonic Order but now a farmhouse, with a square Romanesque *church (richly sculptured 13th c. doorway). Soon afterwards the road reaches the coast at **Siponto** (hotels: Apulia, II, 106 b., SP; Cicolella, II, 89 b.; Del Golfo, II, 69 b.; Sipontum, III, 28 b.; etc.), the Roman *Sipontum*, which was abandoned in the 13th c. Among the remains of the medieval town is the *Cathedral of Santa Maria Maggiore (consecrated 1117), on a square ground plan, with an interesting crypt.

43 km from Foggia the road comes to **Manfredonia** (alt. 5 m; pop. 40,000; hotels: Gargano, II, 92 b., SP; Svevo, II, 70 b.; Azzurro, III, 36 b.; etc.), a port founded in the 13th c. by King Manfred, son of Frederick II, in place of the abandoned town of Sipontum, and now the seat of an archbishop. After its destruction by the Turks in 1620 it was rebuilt on a regular plan with streets intersecting at right angles. Cathedral; church of San Domenico; castle (13th c.). There are boat services several times weekly to the Trémiti Islands (4¼–5¼ hours). – 7 km beyond Manfredonia the road forks: to the left is the shorter road through the hills, to the right the longer but scenically more attractive coast road.

9 km from the fork the hill road reaches **Monte Sant'Angelo** (alt. 843 m; pop. 22,000; Rifugio, III, 26 b.), a charmingly situated town with a handsome ruined castle (1491) and a pilgrimage church which is visited by something like a million pilgrims every year. The church of San Michele Arcángelo occupies a cave in the centre of the town which according to legend was chosen as a shrine by the Archangel Michael himself when he appeared to St Lawrence, archbishop of Sipontum, in 493. From the vestibule beside the campanile (1273) 86 steps lead down to the church, which has Biblical scenes on bronze doors and an inscription recording that they were cast in Constantinople. The church contains a fine 11th c. bishop's throne. Near the church is the so-called "tomb of Rothari" (a Lombard king), a curious domed

building (c. 1200) which was probably a baptistery. Nearby is the church of Santa Maria Maggiore (begun 1198), with a beautiful doorway. – 5 km beyond Monte Sant'Angelo a road goes off on the left to **San Giovanni Rotondo** (alt. 557 m; pop. 25,000; hotels: V.7, II, 96 b.; Casa Esercizi Spirituali Padre Pio, III, 121 b.; San Michele, III, 88 b.; etc.), situated below *Monte Calvo* (1056 m), the highest summit in the range. On the W side of the town is the modern church of Santa Maria delle Grazie, to the left of which is a Capuchin monastery famous as the home of Padre Pio da Pietrelcina (d. 1968), who bore the stigmata from 1918 until his death. The monastery is visited by large numbers of pilgrims seeking a cure for their ailments, and there is a modern hospital adjoining. – Beyond the turning for San Giovanni Rotondo the main road winds its way uphill and then crosses the karstic plateau of Monte Gargano and down through the magnificent beech forest of **Bosco d'Umbra** to the coast, joining the coast road from Manfredonia 43 km beyond San Giovanni.

The much more attractive *coast road (19 km longer), running partly inland and partly above the coast, through magnificent scenery, comes in 49 km to the picturesque little port of **Vieste** (alt. 50 m; pop. 13,000; hotels: Pizzomunno Vieste Palace, II, 341 b., SP; Degli Aranci, II, 135 b., SP; Mediterraneo, II, 100 b., SP; Falcone, II, 98 b.; Pizzomunno Residence, II, 68 b., SP; Porto Nuovo, III, 66 b.; Due Mari, III, 60 b.; etc.). From the castle there is a fine view of the coast. – Some 13 km beyond Vieste a road on the right leads to the hotel and villa colony of *Manacore* (hotels: Gusmay, I, 107 b.; Paglianza, II, 101 b., SP; Paradiso, II, 90 b.; etc.). – 5 km farther on is the old-world little town of **Peschici** (alt. 90 m; pop. 5000; hotels: Valle Clavia, II, 82 b.; Morcavallo, II, 52 b.; Peschici, III, 78 b.; etc.), picturesquely situated on a crag rising sheer from the sea. The road then continues, with many bends, to *Bellariva*, where it is joined by the road from Monte Sant'Angelo.

18 km beyond Bellariva is *San Menaio* (alt. 10 m; hotels: Nettuno, II, 51 b.; Pineta, III, 55 b.; La Playa, III, 32 b.; etc.; two camping sites), a seaside resort, with villas set amid pine-woods. – 7 km farther on is the port of **Rodi Gargánico** (alt. 46 m; pop. 5000; hotels: Helios, II, 63 b.; Della Fave, III, 68 b.; Miramare, III, 59 b.; etc.). From here there are boat services (several times weekly: 1½ hours) to the beautiful Trémiti Islands, 22 miles NW. – Soon afterwards the road skirts a coastal lagoon, the *Lago di Varano* (12 km long, 8 km across), which is separated from the sea by a long spit of sand and dunes known as the "Isola" ("Island"), and passes either to the S or to the N along the dunes. It then continues through barren hill country to join the motorway to Foggia either at *Poggio Imperiale* (45 km), at the W end of the *Lago di Lesina*, or at *San Severo* (65 km).

18 km W of Foggia, on a plateau above the wide Apulian plain, is **Lucera** (alt. 240 m; pop. 32,000; hotels: Stella Daunia, III, 33 b.; Al Passetto, III, 27 b.), the ancient *Luceria*. The town was developed into an important strong point, the key to Apulia, by the emperor Frederick II, and populated by 20,000 Saracens brought in from Sicily between 1233 and 1245. Most of the population was killed by Charles II of Anjou around 1300. Cathedral, built by Charles II after 1300 on the site of the old Saracen mosque; Museo Civico Giuseppe Fiorelli (coins, inscriptions, numerous terracottas, beautiful statue of Venus of the 1st c. A.D.). – 1 km W of the town, beyond the beautiful Giardino Pubblico, is a castle (alt. 251 m) built by Frederick II in 1233 and rebuilt by Charles I of Anjou, a

well-preserved example of medieval military architecture (far-ranging views). – 17 km S of Lucera is the little town of **Troia** (alt. 439 m; pop. 12,000), with a *cathedral (begun 1092) showing Pisan influence. The two bronze doors (by Oderisius of Benevento, 1119 and 1127) and the beautiful capitals of the columns inside the church and the pilasters outside offer fine examples of acanthus ornament in imitation of ancient models.

Foligno

Region: Umbria. – Province: Perugia (PU).
Altitude: 234 m. – Population: 25,000.
Post code: I-06034. – Dialling code: 0742.
ⓘ **AA**, Porta Romana;
    tel. 5 04 93.

HOTELS. – *Umbria*, II, 94 b.; *Nuovo Poledrini*, II, 90 b.; *Posta*, III, 73 b.; *Italia*, III, 50 b.; etc. – YOUTH HOSTEL, Piazza San Giacomo 11, 80 b.

The industrial town of Foligno lies between Assisi and Spoleto on the left bank of the River Topino, in the fertile Umbrian plain. The earliest printed book in Italy was published here in 1472 – the first edition of Dante's "Divine Comedy".

SIGHTS. – In the centre of the town is the spacious *Piazza della Repubblica*, on the E side of which is the **Cathedral** of San Feliciano, with a beautiful Romanesque façade (1133) and a neo-classical interior (1770); the crypt has columns dating from the 9th c. Facing the cathedral, to the SW, stands the *Town Hall* (17th c.). On the N side of the square is the *Palazzo Trinci* (14th–15th c.), in which are the Archaeological Museum, a library and an interesting collection of pictures. – From here Via A. Gramsci runs past the handsome *Palazzo Deli* (1510: on right) to the former church of *San Doménico* and the old church of *Santa Maria Infra Portas* (11th–12th c. porch). To the N is the *Scuola d'Arti e Mestieri* (School of Arts and Crafts), in the courtyard of which are casts of monuments of Umbrian art. Adjoining the school the *church of San Nicolò* houses some fine paintings. – In a narrow lane to the SE of the cathedral is the former *Oratorio della Nunziatella* (15th c.), with a fresco of the Baptism of Christ by Perugino.

SURROUNDINGS. – 10 km SW of Foligno, in the valley of the *Clitunno*, lies **Bevagna** (alt. 225 m; pop. 5500). In the picturesque main square are the churches of San Silvestro and San Michele, with façades dating respectively from 1195 and 1201. – From Bevagna it is 11 km up a winding road, with sharp bends, to the little walled hill town of **Montefalco** (alt. 473 m; pop. 7000), with churches which contain fine examples of Umbrian painting – outside the town gate the monastic church of Santa Chiara, inside the gate the church of Sant'Agostino, in the town the former church of *San Francesco (now a museum), with frescoes by Benozzo Gozzoli (1452). There are also frescoes by Gozzoli in the church of San Fortunato, 1·5 km S of the town.

5 km NW of Foligno, picturesquely situated on the lower slopes of *Monte Subasio*, is **Spello** (alt. 314 m; pop. 8000), the ancient *Hispellum*, which still preserves part of its walls and gates. Near the station is the Porta Consolare, with three portrait-statues, from which a street leads up to the church of Santa Maria Maggiore (12th c.), with a number of notable works of art – in the Cappella Baglioni *frescoes by Pinturicchio (1501), as well as majolica flooring from Deruta (1566); on the high altar a magnificent marble tabernacle by Rocco da Vicenza (1515); in the sacristy a Madonna by Pinturicchio. Above Santa Maria is the church of Sant'Andrea (13th c.), which has a "Madonna with Four Saints" by Pinturicchio and Eusebio da San Giorgio (1508). From the upper part of the town there are wide views of the plain, with Foligno and Assisi.

11 km S of Foligno, off S.S. 3 to the E, is **Trevi** (alt. 213 m; pop. 7000), the Roman *Trebiae*, magnificently situated on the slopes of a steep hill. Below the town, standing by itself, is the church of Santa Maria delle Lágrime (1487), with a beautiful doorway and fine pictures of the Umbrian school, including one by Perugino. The Town Hall, in Piazza Mazzini, contains a small picture gallery. The nearby church of Sant'Emiliano (12th c.) has a richly decorated altar by Rocco da Vicenza (16th c.). – 0·5 km N of the town is the church of San Martino, with fine frescoes (in the outer chapel a *Madonna by Lo Spagna).

Forlì

Region: Emilia-Romagna. – Province: Forlì (FO).
Altitude: 34 m. – Population: 105,000.
Post code: I-47100. – Dialling code: 0543.
ⓘ **EPT**, Corso della Repubblica 23;
    tel. 2 55 32.
    ACI, Corso Garibaldi 45;
    tel. 3 23 13.
    TCI, *Viaggi Ramilli*, Piazza Saffi 48;
    tel. 2 63 51.

HOTELS. – *Principe*, Viale Bologna 153, 72 b.; *Masini*, Corso Garibaldi 28, II, 56 b.; *Della Città*, Via A. Fortis 8, II, 39 b.; *Da Vittorino*, Via Baratti 4, II, 27 b.; *Astoria*, Piazza Ordelaffi 4, III, 47 b.; *Marta*, Via C. Cignani 11, III, 47 b.; *Moderno*, Via Roma 9, III, 35 b.; etc.

The industrial town and provincial capital of Forlì, situated on the Via Emilia between Bologna and Rimini, on the right bank of the River Montone, was the Roman city of Forum Livii and in the late medieval period an independent republic. It suffered heavy damage during the Second World War, but of this no trace now remains.

Rocca di Ravaldino, Forlì

SIGHTS. – In the centre of the town the large *Piazza Saffi* is surrounded by handsome palaces. On the W side of the square stands the *Palazzo del Municipio*, and opposite it, at the NE corner of the square, the Romanesque **church of San Mercuriale** (12th c.). To the right of the church is the cloister of the old Benedictine abbey (16th c.). – From Piazza Saffi the Corso Garibaldi runs NW to the *Cathedral* of Santa Croce (rebuilt 1844).

From Piazza Saffi the Corso della Repubblica runs SW to the municipal **Pinacoteca** and **Museum**, in a palace dating from 1172, with works by Guercino (*c.* 1590–1666), Melozzo da Forlì (1438–94), Dürer and Rembrandt. On the second floor are the *Romagna Folk Museum*, one of the finest of its kind, and a little *Museo del Risorgimento*.

At the end of the Corso della Repubblica is the spacious Piazzale della Vittoria, with a war memorial (1932) in the form of a tall marble column. – In the SW of the town is the Citadel, the *Rocca di Ravaldino* (1361).

Frascati

Region: Lazio. – Province: Roma (ROMA).
Altitude: 322 m. – Population: 18,000.
Post code: I-00044. – Dialling code: 06.
ⓘ **AA**, Piazza Marconi 1;
tel. 94 03 31.

HOTELS. – *Flora*, II, 59 b.; *Bellavista*, III, 44 b.; etc.

Frascati, situated on the NW slopes of the Alban Hills, with extensive views, is the chief of the so-called "Castelli Romani", a town famous for its wine and for its healthy climate, which makes it a favourite summer resort with the people of Rome. It is notable also for the many handsome villas belonging to old noble families, mostly dating from the 16th and 17th c., set in magnificent parks and gardens. Frascati now also has the Italian Euratom laboratories.

SIGHTS. – The focal point of the town is the *Piazza Roma*, with the adjoining *Piazza Marconi*. To the S is the beautiful park of the *Villa Torlonia* (destroyed). – Above the SE side of the Piazza Marconi rears the *****Villa Aldobrandini** or *Belvedere* (1598–1603), in a magnificent park (terrace with extensive views; grottoes, fountains, cascade).

N of the Piazza Roma is the *Piazza San Pietro*, the main square of the old town, with a beautiful fountain and the **Cathedral** of San Pietro (1700). To the SE we find the entrance to the picturesque park of the **Villa Falconieri** (1546), and 1·5 km farther E stands the *Villa Mondragone* (1573–75), since 1865 a Jesuit seminary, with magnificent cypresses. – Outside the town, to the SE, is the splendid *Villa Ruffinella* or *Tuscolana* (villa and park neglected and overgrown: no admission).

Villa Aldobrandini, Frascati

From Frascati a recently constructed *panoramic road* winds its way uphill through beautiful scenery and areas of forest to the remains of ancient **Tusculum**, 5 km SE. This was the birthplace of Cato the Elder and a favourite resort of Cicero. Held during the early Middle Ages by warlike counts, it was destroyed by Rome in 1191. There are remains, much overgrown, of an amphitheatre, a theatre, the forum, a well-house and a stretch of the old town walls. 15 minutes' walk up the hill above the site is a ruined *castle* (alt. 670 m), which commands extensive *views.

SURROUNDINGS. – There is a very attractive trip from Frascati to the little town of **Rocca di Papa** (alt. 620–760 m; pop. 7000; hotels: Villa Ortensie, II, 107 b.; Europa, II, 55 b.; Angeletto, II, 44 b.; La Locandina, III, 40 b.; etc.), picturesquely perched on a rock on the outer margin of a large extinct crater known as the *Campo di Annibale* and surrounded by beautiful woods. Like Frascati it is much favoured by the people of Rome as a summer resort, and there are numerous villas. From here it is possible either to walk (45 minutes) or drive (6·5 km) to the summit of *Monte Cavo** (949 m: television transmitter), the second highest of the Alban Hills, from which there are far-reaching views (particularly clear after rain) of most of Latium. Here there stood in antiquity a temple of Jupiter, the shrine of the Latin League.

Friuli

Region: Friuli – Venezia Giulia. – Provinces: Udine (UD), Pordenone (PN), Gorizia (GO), Trieste (TS).
(i) **EPT Udine**, Piazza Venerio 4,
    I-33100 Udine (UD);
    tel. (0432) 5 42 05.
    EPT Trieste, Via G. Rossini 6,
    I-04000 Trieste (TS);
    tel. (040) 3 55 52.

The old region of Friuli, in the basins of the Tagliamento and the lower Isonzo, extends from the Carnic and Julian Alps to the Adriatic. Together with the eastern part of the old province of Veneto it now forms the region of Friuli – Venezia Giulia, comprising the four provinces of Trieste, Gorizia, Pordenone and Udine.

HISTORY. – The region, originally occupied by an Illyrian tribe, the Carni, was conquered by Rome around 150 B.C. Its name comes from the Roman town of *Forum Iulii* (Cividale del Fruili). Later a Lombard duchy, in the time of Charlemagne it was held by a Frankish margrave, in 952 it passed to Bavaria, in 976 to Carinthia, and in 1077 to the Patriarchate of Aquileia. In the 15th c. the western (and larger) part was conquered by Venice, while the smaller eastern part was granted to the counts of Gorizia as a fief and in 1500 passed to Austria, which in 1797 also acquired the territory held by Venice. Italy secured the Ventian territory in 1866 and the county of Gorizia in 1919, but in 1947 was compelled to cede the eastern part, predominantly inhabited by Slovenes, to Yugoslavia.

FEATURES OF INTEREST. – Of the 1·2 million inhabitants of the region of Friuli – Venezia Giulia some 520,000 are **Friulians** (Italian *Friulani*, Friulian *Furlani*), the descendants of Rhaetians who were Romanised at an early date. They speak Friulian,

a Rhaeto-Romanic dialect. The economy is traditionally based on agriculture (including viticulture), but many Friulians now find employment in other parts of Italy in building or other trades. In the mountains the opening up of new skiing areas has made tourism an increasingly important element in the economy of the region.

Much of the region was ravaged by a series of earthquakes in 1976 in which more than 1000 people lost their lives and many valuable works of art and architecture were destroyed. The villages of *Gemona*, *Osoppo*, *San Daniele del Friuli* and *Venzone* were particularly hard hit. '

Aquileia, Cividale del Friuli, Gorizia and **Udine**: see separate entries.

Lake Garda

Regions: Lombardia, Veneto and Trentino – Alto Adige. – Provinces: Brescia, Verona and Trento. Altitude: 65 m.
(i) **AA Riva**, Giardini Spiaggia degli Olivi,
    I-38066 Riva;
    tel. (0464) 5 25 38.

An expanse of 370 sq. km of deep blue water, **Lake Garda (Lago di Garda), the Roman Lacus Benacus, is the largest of the N Italian lakes (52 km long, 5–16·5 km wide, up to 346 m deep), lying in a deeply slashed valley between Venetia and Lombardy. Its main feeder in the N is the River Sarca, and its outlet at the S end is the Mincio, which flows into the Po.

The northern part of the lake is narrow and fjord-like; towards the S end the shores slope down gradually to the extensive morainic cirque left by the old Garda glacier. The E side of the lake is separated from the Adige valley by the 80 km long limestone ridge of *Monte Baldo* (2218 m). The W side, hemmed in towards its northern end by sheer rock faces, opens out between Gargnano and Salò to form the beautiful and fertile coastal strip known as the *Riviera Bresciana*. – Until 1918 the northern tip of Lake Garda, with Riva and Torbole, belonged to Austria.

The climate in the area of Lake Garda is extraordinarily mild, and snow is rare. The

The Gardesana Occidentale road, Lake Garda

the road to Arco is the *church of the Inviolata*, with a Baroque interior (1603). – On the S side of the town stands the Ponale hydroelectric station (88,000 kW), fed by water brought from the Lago di Ledro, 585 m above Riva, in a pipeline 6 km long.

29 km from Riva on the road which follows the W side of Lake Garda, on the lower slopes of a precipitous hill, is the attractive village of *Gargnano* (alt. 98 m; hotels: Europa, IV, 39 b.; Riviera, IV, 36 b.; etc.), where the *Riviera Bresciana begins. The Villa Feltrinelli, a little way N of the lakeside promenade, was occupied by Mussolini from September 1943 to April 1945. – 2 km: *Bogliaco* (Hotel Roda, IV, 43 b.), with the large 18th c. country house of Count Bettoni (park). – 6 km: **Toscolano-Maderno** (alt. 70 m; hotels: Milano, II 68 b., Maderno, II, 51 b., Benaco, II, 48 b., SP, Rock, III, 64 b., Splendid, III, 63 b., all in Maderno; Adria, III, 61 b., SP, Adria, III, 44 b., SP, in Toscolano). In Maderno are the Romanesque church of Sant'Andrea (12th c.) and the Palazzo Gonzaga (17th c.). Beautiful views from the lakeside promenade. – 4 km: **Gardone Riviera** (alt. 70 m; hotels: Grand, I, 335 b., SP; Monte Baldo, II, 86 b., SP; Du Lac, II, 62 b.; Fiordaliso, II, 15 b.; Savoy, III, 145 b., SP; Bellevue, III, 62 b.; etc.), which attracts many visitors with its mild climate and luxuriant southern vegetation; magnificent *Hruska Botanic Garden. 1 km N is *Gardone di Sopra* (alt. 130 m), surrounded by beautiful gardens. Near the church (*view from terrace) is the Villa Vittoriale degli Italiani, the last home of Gabriele d'Annunzio (1863–1938), with mementoes of the poet. – 3 km: **Salò** (alt. 75 m; pop. 10,000; hotels: Duomo, II, 53 b.; Laurin, III, 70 b., SP; Metropole, III, 49 b.; etc.; *Whiskythek*, Lungolago 70, with 1000 brands of whisky), charmingly situated in a long narrow bay under *Monte San Bartolomeo* (568 m). This was the birthplace of Gasparo da Salò (1542–1609), inventor of the violin, and from 8 September 1943 the seat of the Fascist government of Italy (the "Republic of Salò"). Gothic parish church of Santa Maria Annunziata (1453). – 21 km: **Desenzano** (alt. 69 m; pop. 18,000; hotels: Park, II, 124 b.; Barchetta, II, 60 b.; Miralago, II, 48 b.; Ramazzotti, II, 42 b.; Tripoli, II, 42 b.; Mayer e Splendid, III, 93 b.; Nazionale, III, 59 b.; Astoria, III, 57 b.; City, III, 56 b.; etc.), at the SW tip of Lake Garda, has an old castle and remains of a Roman villa of the 3rd c. A.D. (mosaics).

lake is seldom entirely calm, and in a storm coming from the N can be quite rough. In fine weather a very cold wind known as the *ora* blows around midday in winter and spring.

The vegetation is luxuriant on the more sheltered stretches of the lakeside, in places almost Mediterranean. Olives grow up to 300 m, and palms, cedars, evergreen magnolias and agaves flourish in the gardens. – The lake fish are excellent.

ROUND THE LAKE (134 km). – The lake is surrounded by fine modern roads. Along the W side runs the famous *Gardesana Occidentale, a masterpiece of modern road engineering, with numerous galleries and tunnels hewn from the rock, and also a route of great scenic beauty, while on the E side there is the *Gardesana Orientale, a road of almost equal quality and beauty.

The tour of the lake begins at **Riva del Garda** (alt. 70 m; pop. 13,000: hotels: Du Lac et du Parc, I, 299 b., SP, with annexe, II, 122 b.; Lido Palace, I, 132 b., SP; Grand Hotel Riva, II, 186 b., SP; Astoria, II, 170 b., SP; Luise, II, 108 b., SP; Sole, II, 83 b.; Giardino Verdi, II, 78 b.; Liberty, II, 75 b.; Brione, III, 98 b.; Europa, III, 98 b.; Enrico, III, 84 b., SP; etc.; camping site), a summer and winter resort and congress centre at the NW tip of the lake. To the W of the town is the precipitous *Rocchetta* (1527 m), with a Venetian watch-tower.

The town's busiest traffic intersection is the square by the harbour, with arcades and a massive old *clock-tower*. To the E, by the lakeside, the little Piazza Carducci (views of lake) has an old moated castle of the Scaliger family, the *Rocca* (12th–15th c.), and on

From Desenzano S.S. 11 runs along the S end of the lake. – 4·5 km: road on right to the village of *San Martino della Battaglia* (alt. 110 m), 5 km SE, where a Piedmontese army, allied with the French, defeated the Austrians on 24 June 1859 (commemorative tower, museum). 11 km farther S is the village of *Solferino*; here a French army led by Napoleon III defeated the Austrians on the same day (museum, ossuary). From the Rocca, above the village, there are extensive views. The sufferings of the wounded in the battle of Solferino gave Henri Dunant the idea of founding the Red Cross.

2·5 km beyond Desenzano on S.S. 11 a road goes off on the left (3·5 km) to the picturesque little town of *Sirmione, on a long promontory reaching out into the lake (hotels: Terme, I, 118 b., SP; Villa Cortina Palace, I, 98 b., SP, *park; Sirmione, I, 91 b., SP, with annexe, I, 45 b.; Olivi, II, 103 b., SP; Continental, II, 95 b., SP; Giardino, II, 76 b.; Miramar, II, 64 b.; Broglia, II, 61 b., SP; Flaminia, II, 58 b.; Catullo, II, 50 b.; Ideal, II, 48 b.; Fonte Boiola, III, 106 b.; Mirabello, III, 80 b.; Serenella, III, 68 b.; Golf e Suisse, III, 62 b., etc.; motor cruisers for hire). The Roman poet Catullus (84–54 B.C.) had a villa here. There is a large and picturesque castle of the Scaligers (13th c., restored); *view from tower. 1 km N is the *Punta di Sirmione*, with a terrace (*views) built on late Roman substructures ("Grotte di Catullo"). Sirmione is also visited for its sulphur springs. – 7 km: **Peschiera del Garda** (alt. 68 m; pop. 8000; hotels: Milano, III, 100 b., SP; Rosetta, III, 70 b.; Johnson, III, 52 b.; etc.), a strongly fortified little town at the SE corner of Lake Garda, at the outflow of the River *Mincio*.

From Peschiera the road continues up the E side of the lake. – 9 km: *Lazise* (alt. 76 m; pop. 5000; hotels: Lazise, II, 85 b.; Casa Mia, II, 74 b., SP; Miralago, II, 41 b.; Giulietta e Romeo, III, 58 b., SP; etc.), with medieval town walls and a Scaliger castle (13th c.). – 5 km: *Bardolino* (alt. 68 m; hotels: Du Lac, in Santa Cristina, II, 152 b., SP; Nettuno, II, 127 b., SP; Villa Letizia, III, 99 b.; Cristina, III, 90 b.; Idania, III, 60 b., with annexe, III, 84 b., SP; etc.), famous for its wine. To the left of the road is the little Romanesque church of San Severo (8th and 12th c.). – 4 km: **Garda** (alt. 69 m; pop. 3500; hotels: Eurotel

Garda, I, 228 b., SP; Regina Adelaide, II, 97 b.; Garden, II, 74 b., SP; Flora, II, 66 b., with annexe, II, 28 b., SP; Gabbiano, II, 58 b.; Terminus e Garda, II, 52 b.; Palme, III, 296 b., SP; La Perla, III, 292 b., SP; Bisesti, III, 172 b., SP; Marco Polo, III, 138 b., with two annexes, III, together 80 b., SP; Continental, III, 107 b., SP; etc.; several camping sites on lake). A footpath leads up in 45 minutes to the *Rocca* (294 m), on the site of an earlier castle which gave its name to the lake.

3 km beyond Garda is the promontory of ***San Vigilio** (views), with the *Villa Guarienti*, set amid cypresses (1540: no admission). – 5 km: *Torri del Benaco* (alt. 68 m; hotels: Internazionale, in Fornare, III, 98 b.; Pace, III, 80 b.; Romeo, III, 68 b., SP; etc.), with an early medieval castle. From here an attractive excursion can be made to the summer holiday resort of **San Zeno di Montagna** (alt. 583 m; hotels: Diana, II, 76.; Bellavista, III, 74 b.), situated high above the lake (*views) on the SW slopes of the Monte Baldo range. – 11 km: **Malcésine** (alt. 90 m; hotels: Excelsior Bay, II, 110 b., SP; Italia, II, 80 b.; Malcesine, II, 76 b.; Du Lac, II, 67 b.; Lago di Garda, II, 67 b.; Paina, II, 52 b.; Vega, II, 35 b.; Lucia, III, 77 b.; Centrale, III, 65 b.; etc.), in a fine situation below the rugged cliffs of Monte Baldo (2218 m). At the N end of the town, almost sheer above the lake, is a Scaliger castle (13th–14th c.). Cableway (15 minutes) to the *Bocca Tratto Spin* (1720 m). – 14 km: **Tórbole** (alt. 70 m; hotels: Torbole, II, 87 b.; Piccolo Mondo, II, 41 b.; Lido Blu, III, 81 b.; Elisabetta, III, 54 b.; Pavesi, III, 52 b.; etc.), a picturesque little fishing village lying under bare crags at the NE corner of Lake Garda. – 4 km: **Riva**.

A BOAT TRIP on Lake Garda is an attractive way of seeing both sides of the lake. During the summer there is a boat twice daily (4½ hours) from *Riva* to *Desenzano*, calling in at various places on the E and W sides of the lake; also boats up to three times daily from *Toscolano–Maderno* to *Garda* and *Peschiera* or *Desenzano*. Hydrofoils three times daily (1½–2 hours) from *Riva* to *Desenzano*.

SURROUNDINGS. – From Riva there is a very rewarding trip up the *Ponale Road* to the **Lago di Ledro**, 10 km W. The road winds its way up above the W side of Lake Garda, with several sharp bends and magnificent views, skirts the cliffs of the Rocchetta and passes through a number of tunnels. At *Pieve di Ledro* (alt. 660 m; Garden Hotel, III, 73 b.; etc.), at the W end of the Lago di Ledro, are the remains of a Bronze Age settlement.

A road runs N from Riva through magnificent scenery to the hamlet of *Foci del Varone*, near which is the

*Cascata del Varone, a waterfall in a gloomy gorge, and **Ponte delle Arche** (26 km; alt. 401 m), an old road intersection where S.S. 237 runs E through the magnificent *Sarca gorge to Trento and W through the wild *Gola della Scaletta to Tione. 20 km farther N from Ponte delle Arche is the beautiful blue ***Lago di Molveno** (alt. 821 m; 4 km long, up to 119 m deep), below Monte Gazza (1990 m) to the E and the precipitous crags of the Brenta group to the W. At the N end of the lake is *Molveno*, a summer holiday resort, with a chair-lift to *Pradel* (1342 m) and the *Palòn di Torre* (1530 m), to the N. – 4 km N of Molveno is the holiday and winter sports resort of **Ándalo** (alt. 1042 m; hotels: La Baita, II, 114 b., SP; Stella Alpina, II, 112 b.; Maria, II, 91 b.; Splendid, II, 82 b.; Alpen, II, 43 b.; Ándalo, II, 76 b.; Sport, II, 70 b.; Garden, II, 55 b.; Piccolo, II, 51 b.; Corona, III, 84 b.; Eden, III, 81 b.; Paganella, III, 80 b.; etc.), with views of the Brenta group. Basket-lift to Malga Terlago (1772 m) and *Paganella (2125 m).

6 km NE of Riva, on the right bank of the Sarca, is the old town of **Arco** (alt. 91 m; pop. 11,000; hotels: Palace Città, II, 163 b., SP; Marchi, III, 39 b.; etc.), a resort set in luxuriant southern vegetation which attracts many visitors in winter as well as summer by reason of its mild climate. In the Kurpark is a monument to the painter Giovanni Segantini (1858–99), who was born in Arco. To the W are two beautiful promenades, one planted with magnolias and the other with palms. On a cypress-clad rock (284 m) are the ruins of a *castle* (view).

Genoa/Génova

(Note that street numbers followed by the letter *r* (=red), differ from the black numbers.)

Region: Liguria. – Province: (Génova (GE).
Altitude: 25 m. – Population: 820,000.
Post code: I-16100. – Dialling code: 010.
ⓘ **EPT**, Via Roma 11;
   tel. 58 14 07.
   ACI, Viale B. Partigiane 1;
   tel. 56 70 01.
   CIT, Via XXV Aprile 16;
   tel. 29 19 51.

HOTELS. – *Colombia-Excelsior*, Via Balbi 40, L, 288 b.; *Savoia-Majestic*, Via Arsenale di Terra 5, I, 195 b.; *Bristol-Palace*, Via XX Settembre 35, I, 175 b.; *Plaza*, Via M. Piaggio 11, I, 157 b.; *Aquila e Reale*, Piazza Acquaverde 1, II, 161 b.; *City*, Via San Sebastiano 6, II, 120 b.; *Astoria*, Piazza Brignole 4, II, 118 b.; *Londra e Continentale*, Via Arsenale di Terra 1, II, 91 b.; *Crespi*, Via Andrea Doria 10, II, 91 b.; *Metropoli*, Vico Migliorini 8, II, 86 b.; *Minerva-Italia*, Via XXV Aprile 14, II, 82 b.; *Moderno-Verdi*, Piazza Giuseppe Verdi 5, II, 77 b.; *Vittoria-Orlandini*, Via Balbi 45, II, 73 b.; *Tirreno*, Via dei Mille 17, II, 69 b.; *Milano Terminus*, Via Balbi 34, II, 64 b.; *Eliseo*, Via M. Piaggio 5, II, 65 b.; *Firenze e Zurigo*, Via Gramsci 199r, III, 150 b.; *Stella*, Via Andrea Doria 6r, III, 114 b.; *Torinese*, Via A. Gramsci 291r, III, 94 b.; *Rio*, Via Ponte Calvi 5, III, 84 b.; *Europa*, Vico Monachette 18, III, 80 b.; etc. – YOUTH HOSTEL in Genova-Quarto, Via Cinque Maggio 79, 180 b. – CAMPING SITES in Pegli and Voltri.

RESTAURANTS. – *Da Giacomo*, Corso Italia 1; *Cucciolo*, Viale Sauli 33; *Gino*, Via XX Settembre 190r, Piazza Acquaverde 14r and at Brignole Station; *Aladino*, Via Vernazza 8; *Bolognese*, Via Brera 5r; *Zeffirino*, Via XX Settembre 20; *Pichin*, Vico dei Parmigiana 6r; *Cardinali*, Via Assarotti 60r; *Gheise*, Via Boccadasse 29; *Italia*, in Quarto dei Mille.

Genoa (in Italian Génova), capital of the region of Liguria, a conurbation (Greater Genoa) extending from Nervi to Voltri for a distance of 35 km along the coast, is Italy's leading port and centre of maritime trade, ranking with Marseilles as one of the two principal Mediterranean ports. It is a university town and the see of an archbishop.

Genoa, known as "la Superba" on account of its splendid marble palaces, has a magnificent situation, particularly when seen from the sea, rising in a wide arc on the lower slopes of the Ligurian Apennines. The various parts of the town are linked by five road tunnels and high bridges, and two huge tower blocks form striking landmarks in the town centre.

The old town is a maze of narrow streets, many of them steep, which are filled with the colourful and noisy activity of a Mediterranean town. The newer parts of the town with their tall modern buildings, gardens and villas lie in the plain at the mouth of the River *Bisagno* and on the higher ground to the N and W. On the landward side Genoa has been protected since the 12th c. by a rampart 15 km long extending from the tall lighthouse on the W side of the town to the *Forte dello Sperone* (alt. 516 m) and then descending past *Forte Castellaccio* (382 m) into the Bisagno valley to the SE. – The districts of San Pier d'Arena and Cornigliano (with the Italsider works) are the main centre of Italian heavy industry. Other major industries are chemicals, foodstuffs, papermaking, textiles and transport.

HISTORY. – Genoa first appears in history in 218 B.C. as capital of the Ligurians. In the 10th c. A.D. it was an independent republic, which in 1284, after almost 200 years of war, finally defeated its most dangerous competitor, Pisa, in the naval battle of Melória. In the 14th c. the Genoese fought with Venice for control of the trade with the East, but were decisively defeated at Chioggia in 1380. During this period the town was torn by internal disputes and fell into the hands of foreign masters. The independence of the republic was restored by Admiral *Andrea Doria* (1466–1560) in 1528, but Genoa's power was now in decline. In 1684 the town was bombarded by a French fleet, and 1746 saw it occupied for some months by Imperial troops. In 1805 the "Ligurian Republic" was incorporated in the French Empire, and ten years later became part of the kingdom of Sardinia and

In Genoa harbour

Piedmont. – Famous natives of Genoa include the Italian freedom fighter and revolutionary *Giuseppe Mazzini* (1805–72), the national hero *Giuseppe Garibaldi* (1807–82), *Christopher Columbus* (Christóforo Colombo, 1446–1506), discoverer of America, and the great virtuoso of the violin *Niccolò Paganini* (1782–1840).

ART. – The old palaces of the nobility, more numerous and more splendid in Genoa than in any other Italian town, give some impression of the magnificent lifestyle of the 16th and 17th c. The pattern of the Genoese palace, with its grandiose distribution of architectural masses and its skilful use of rising ground, was set by the Perugian architect *Galeazzo Alessi* (1512–72) and his successors. – The churches of Genoa, many of them of very ancient origin, were mostly rebuilt during the Gothic period and adorned with Pisan and Lombard sculpture. – Outstanding Genoese painters were *Luca Cambiaso* (1527–85) in the 16th c. and *Bernardo Strozzi*, surnamed "*Il Prete Genovese*" (1581–1644), in the 17th.

SIGHTS. – The hub of the city is the *Piazza De Ferrari*, surrounded by public buildings, banks and the offices of the big shipping lines, and with the busiest streets in Genoa radiating from it in all directions. On the NE side of the square is the neo-classical *Teatro Comunale dell-'Opera* (1828), one of the largest opera-houses in Italy (burned down during the last war; restoration planned). To the right of the theatre stands the *Accademia Lingustica di Belle Arti* (picture gallery) and on the SE side of the square the *Exchange*, an imposing neo-Baroque building (19th c.). From here the city's

principal street, *Via XX Settembre*, runs SE, lined by handsome modern buildings and arcades containing numerous shops.

From the right-hand side of the Exchange a short street, Via Dante, leads S to *Piazza Dante*, surrounded by modern tower blocks. In the SE corner towers the **Grattacielo** ("Skyscraper", 108 m high; Martini Terraces), a building of 28 storeys (31 down to Via Fieschi, on a lower level). – On the W side of Piazza Dante is the Gothic *Porta Soprana* or *di Sant'Andrea*, the SE town gate (1155). The little house in front of it to the right is known as the *Casa di Colombo* (Columbus's House).

A short distance SW of the Piazza De Ferrari is *Piazza Matteotti*, in which stands the fine Jesuit *church of Sant'Ambrogio* (1589–1639: pictures by Rubens and Reni). On the N side of the square the old **Doge's Palace** (end of 13th c.; rebuilt in 16th c., restored in 1777 after a fire), has picturesque pillared courtyards; it is now occupied by the Law Courts. From here Via Tommaso Reggio (to the left of the Palace) and the Salita all'Arcivescovado lead to the little Gothic **church of San Matteo** (1278), with many relics of the noble Doria family (on the façade inscriptions in their honour, in the crypt the tomb of Andrea Doria). To the left of the church is a beautiful early Gothic cloister

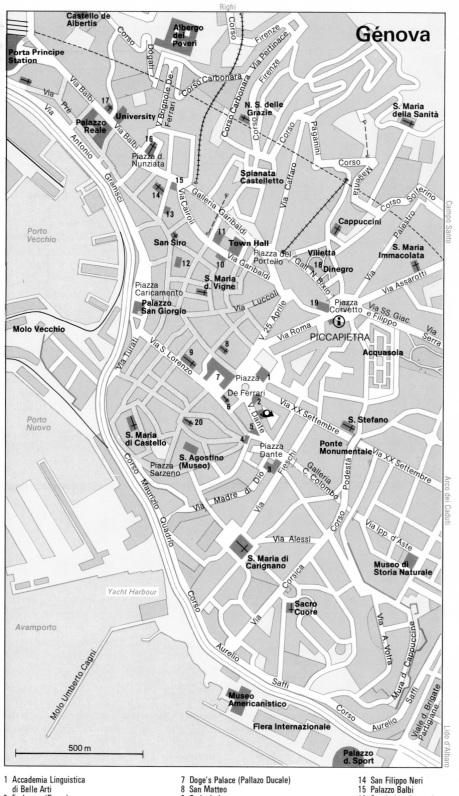

Génova

1 Accademia Linguistica
   di Belle Arti
2 Exchange (Borsa)
3 Grattacielo
4 Porta Soprana
5 Casa di Colombo
6 Sant'Ambrogio

7 Doge's Palace (Palazzo Ducale)
8 San Matteo
9 Cathedral
10 Palazzo Rosso
11 Palazzo Bianco
12 Palazzo Spinola
13 Casa di Mazzini

14 San Filippo Neri
15 Palazzo Balbi
16 Santissima Annunziata
17 San Carlo
18 Museo Chiossone
19 Prefecture
20 San Donato

(1308–10). In the square in front of the church are several *palaces of the Doria family*, some of them faced with black and yellow marble; and in the narrow surrounding streets, once the most aristocratic part of the town, are numerous other noble mansions.

From Piazza Matteotti the busy Via San Lorenzo runs NW to the harbour. Immediately on the right is the **Cathedral of San Lorenzo*, originally a Romanesque pillared basilica (consecrated 1118), remodelled in Gothic style in 1307–12 and crowned with a Renaissance dome by Galeazzo Alessi in 1567. It contains fine pictures and sculpture. In the N aisle is the large *Cappella San Giovanni Battista* (1448–96), the earliest example of Renaissance architecture in Genoa. In the S aisle can be seen an unexploded shell 1·40 m high which burst through the façade of the cathedral during a naval bombardment on 9 February 1941 without causing serious damage. Under the cathedral lies the **Treasury* (closed Sundays and Mondays).

From the Opera-House the busy *Via Roma*, in which are various entrances to the *Galleria Mazzini*, a shopping arcade, runs E to the Piazza Corvetto, where stands the *Palazzo Spinola* (Prefecture); from here the Via XXV Aprile runs N to the Piazza Fontane Marose. On higher ground to the NW of this square is the *Villetta di Negro park* (*view), with the *Museo Chiossone* (closed Sundays and Mondays), a collection of modern Japanese and Chinese art.

To the E of Via Roma, between the Piazza De Ferrari, the Piazza Corvetto and the Acquasola Park, is the PICCAPIETRA district, which suffered heavy bomb damage during the last war and was rebuilt in magnificent style from 1954 onwards, with modern office buildings and flats, including many tower blocks.

From Piazza Fontane Marose a major traffic artery formed by Via Garibaldi, Via Cairoli and Via Balbi runs NW to Piazza Acquaverde and the Porta Príncipe Station. Laid out in the 16th and 17th c., this area contains a number of churches and Genoa's finest palaces, approached by magnificent flights of steps which are one of the particular sights of Genoa. – In the narrow **Via Garibaldi*, designed by Galeazzo Alessi, are a succession of palaces,

with collections of pictures which are for the most part not open to the public. On the right (No. 9) is the former *Palazzo Doria Tursi*, now the **Palazzo Municipale** (Town Hall), begun in 1564. On the left (No. 18) is the **Palazzo Rosso**, a splendid 17th c. mansion which belonged to the Brígnole-Sale family, containing a picture gallery (on first and second floors: closed Sundays and Mondays) notable particularly for its fine family portraits (works by Van Dyck, Paris Bordone, Bernardo Strozzi, etc.). Almost opposite (No. 11) is the **Palazzo Bianco**, a Brignole palace (built 1565, altered 1711 onwards), which also houses a notable picture gallery (closed Sundays and Mondays), with works by Italian, Dutch and Flemish masters.

Crossing the Piazza della Meridiana, we enter the wide Via Cairoli. Off this street, to the left, is the **Old Cathedral** (*San Siro*: remodelled in Baroque style 1576 onwards). SW of the church is the *Galleria Nazionale di Palazzo Spínola* (closed Sundays and Mondays), notable particularly for its old masters. – Via Cairoli meets the Largo della Zecca, from which a road tunnel, the Gallerie Giuseppe Garibaldi, leads SE to Piazza del Portello (lower station of funicular to the **Righi*, 310 m); from here another tunnel, the Galleria Nino Bixio, continues to Piazza Corvetto. On the S side of the Largo della Zecca stands the *Palazzo Balbi*, with an unusual and distinctive staircase (1750). Beyond the palace is Via Lomellini, which runs S past the Baroque *church of San Filippo Neri* (1674) to the *Casa di Mazzini*, the birthplace of Giuseppe Mazzini (closed Sundays and Mondays), with a Museo del Risorgimento and a military museum. – The Largo della Zecca joins the Piazza della Nunziata, in which is the magnificent **church of the Santissima Annunziata**, originally belonging to the Capuchins (1587; neo-classical colonnade of 1843).

Beyond the church is the beginning of **Via Balbi*, laid out by Bartolommeo Bianco in the early 17th c. and lined with handsome palaces. Immediately on the right (No. 1) is the *Palazzo Durazzo-Pallavicini* (*c.* 1620), with a Rococo entrance hall and a fine staircase of 1780 and on the left (No. 4) the *Palazzo Balbi-Senárega* (1620 onwards); fine courtyard, with a glimpse of the orangery. No. 5 is the **Palazzo dell'Università**, begun

Palazzo Reale, Genoa

in 1634–40 as a Jesuit college, with the finest courtyard and gardens in Genoa. To the left of the university stands the *church of San Carlo* (sculpture of 1650). Opposite is the ***Palazzo Reale** (begun 1650), with handsome staircases, large balconies and a richly decorated interior (pictures).

Via Balbi joins the Piazza Acquaverde, a large square in front of the Porta Príncipe Station. To the W is the Piazza del Príncipe, in which is the *Palazzo Doria-Pamphili* or *Palazzo del Príncipe*, built in 1522–29 as a country house for Doge Andrea Doria, with frescoes by Perin del Vaga, a pupil of Raphael (1528–33). To the S of Piazza del Príncipe, beyond Via Adua and the railway line, is the **Stazione Maríttima** (Marine Station).

The **Harbour** (22 km of wharves, 128 km of railway lines; annual turnover 50 million tonnes) consists of the inner harbour or **Porto Vecchio**, constructed about 1250, the **Porto Nuovo** (1877 onwards) and the naval harbour or **Avamporto**, together with the recently constructed *Bacino della Lanterna* and *Bacino di San Pier d'Arena*. E of the Avamporto is the little *Porticciolo Duca degli Abruzzi*, used by yachts and sailing boats. The whole harbour is enclosed by two breakwaters, the *Diga Foranea* (over 5 km long) and the *Molo Duca di Galliera*. – At the W end of the harbour is the **Cristóforo Colombo Airport**. – There are very attractive boat trips round the harbour (about 2 hours).

From Piazza del Príncipe Via A. Gramsci runs alongside the high-level motorway which skirts the inner harbour to Piazza Caricamento, in which is the Gothic **Palazzo di San Giorgio** (*c.* 1260), occupied from 1408 to 1797 by the Banco di San Giorgio, an influential bank which financed the Genoese republic (beautiful courtyard). From here Via F. Turati runs S past the warehouses of the free port to the Piazza Cavour, the starting point of the *Circonvallazione a Mare*, a seafront highway (now flanked by a high-level motorway) laid out in 1893–95, which, under the names of Corso M. Quadrio and Corso Aurelio Saffi, passes the grounds of the *Fiera Internazionale* (International Trade Fair: main fair in October), on land recently reclaimed from the sea, to the Piazza della Vittoria.

A little way SE of Piazza Cavour is the Romanesque *church of Santa Maria di Castello*. In the adjoining Dominican monastery is the small *Museo di Santa Maria di Castello* (good pictures). – Farther E are the Romanesque *church of San Donato* (*triptych by Joos van Cleve, 1485) and the early Gothic *church of Sant'Agostino* (disused), both with fine companiles. From here Via Eugenio Ravasco and a viaduct 30 m high lead S to the conspicuous domed **church of Santa Maria di Carignano**, begun 1552 to the design of Galeazzo Alessi and completed about 1600, a smaller edition of the plan adopted by Bramante and Michelangelo for St Peter's in Rome. Under the dome are four large Baroque statues. From the dome there are magnificent *views of the city and the harbour.

From Piazza della Vittoria the Viale della Brigate Partigiane, built over the bed of the Bisagno and lined by tall modern blocks, leads S to join the *Passeggiata Lungomare, a handsome promenade which runs along the seafront under the names of Corso G. Marconi and Corso Italia. 2 km along this road, near its E end, is the **Lido d'Albaro**, a beautifully situated recreation park (bathing beach, restaurant, variety theatre).

From the Piazza Corvetto the Via Assarotti runs NE up to Piazza Manin, the starting point of the beautiful *Circonvallazione a Monte*, which runs W along the slopes of the hill to the *Spianata Castelletto* (alt. 79 m: two lifts down to the town), from which there are fine views, and then above the imposing buildings of the 17th c. *Albergo dei Poveri* (Poorhouse) to the

Corso Ugo Bassi, with the fortress-like *Villa Castello de Albertis* (Museum of America: closed Sundays and Mondays).

SURROUNDINGS. – From the Piazza della Vittoria it is 3 km N, up the Bisagno valley, to the beautifully situated **Campo Santo** or *Cimitero di Staglieno*, one of the most famous cemeteries in Italy. In the lower arcades are numerous monuments, richly decorated and often overloaded with ornament. Steps lead up to the upper arcades, the central feature of which is a domed rotunda. Above this is the tomb of Giuseppe Mazzini.

There are attractive trips from Genoa eastward along the *Riviera di Levante, particularly to the **Portofino promontory, and westward along the *Riviera di Ponente.

10 km N of Genoa, on a prominent conical hill, stands the 19th c. pilgrimage church of the *Madonna della Guardia* (alt. 804 m).

Gorizia

Region: Friuli – Venezia Giulia.
Province: Gorizia (GO).
Altitude: 84 m. – Population: 45,000.
Post code: I-34170. – Dialling code: 0481.
ⓘ **EPT**, Galleria del Corso 100E;
   tel. 38 70.
ACI, Via Trieste 171;
tel. 21 27.
TCI, *Viaggi Appiani*, Corso Italia 60;
tel. 22 66.

HOTELS. – *Palace*, II, 126 b.; *Internazionale*, II, 90 b.; *Posta*, III, 71 b.; etc. – *Motel Nanut*, on road to Trieste, III, 32 b.

The provincial capital of Gorizia (in German Görz), the see of an archbishop, lies just on the Yugoslav frontier at the W end of the karstic limestone country, where the fertile valley of the Isonzo emerges into the plain of Friuli.

The old town lies around the castle on its hill (148 m); the newer districts adjoin the station. – The town has some industry (cotton, silk, paper, furniture) and trade (wine, fruit).

HISTORY. – From 1500 until 1918 the county of Gorizia belonged to Austria. During the First World War, lying as it did on the road to Austria, it was almost continuously in the front line and was largely destroyed. In 1947 the eastern suburbs of the town, with the Montesanto station, were transferred to Yugoslavia.

SIGHTS. – At the foot of the NW side of the castle hill is the triangular *Piazza della Vittoria*, in which are the *Prefecture* and the Jesuit *church of Sant'Ignazio* (17th

c.). From here Via Rastello runs S to the **Cathedral** (14th c.; rebuilt 1918), with a treasury containing Romanesque items from Aquileia. – From the Piazza del Duomo a road climbs to the **Castello**, once the seat of the counts of Gorizia, which now houses the *Museo di Storia ed Arte* (local history, antiquities). From the vicinity of the *church of the Santo Spírito* (14th c.) there are magnificent views. – 0·5 km N of the Piazza della Vittoria is the *Museo della Guerra* (patriotic relics; small collection of pictures).

SURROUNDINGS. – From Gorizia the battlefields of the Isonzo, where 11 battles were fought in 1915–17, can be visited (though some of the battle area now lies within Yugoslavia). – 3·5 km N, on a hill (175 m) beyond the Isonzo, is the military cemetery of *Oslavia*, laid out in 1938, with an ossuary containing the remains of 57,000 Italians who fell in the First World War. – 11 km from Gorizia on the Trieste road a minor road branches off to *San Martino del Carso* (alt. 163 m) and *Monte San Michele* (277 m: far-ranging views), with old military positions and a small war museum.

Gubbio

Region: Umbria. – Province: Perugia (PU).
Altitude: 478–529 m. – Population: 30,000.
Post code: I-06024. – Dialling code: 075.
ⓘ **AA**, Piazza Oderisi 6;
   tel. 92 24 93.

HOTELS. – *Grand Hotel Ai Cappuccini*, I, 69 b.; *Bosone*, II, 60 b.; *San Marco*, III, 45 b.; etc.

The Umbrian town of Gubbio, the Roman Iguvium, is beautifully situated at the mouth of a gorge on the NE edge of a fertile basin, under Monte Calvo (983 m) and Monte Ingino (906 m).

Palazzo dei Consoli, Gubbio

SIGHTS. – The central feature of the town is the *Piazza della Signoria*, laid out on the slope of the hill. On the NW side of the square is the **Palazzo dei Consoli**, a massive Gothic battlemented structure of dressed stone (1332–46) which houses a *Museum* and the *Municipal Picture Gallery*. In the museum are the "Iguvine Tablets", found on the site of the ancient theatre in 1444 – seven (out of an original nine) bronze tablets with inscriptions partly in the Old Umbrian language and alphabet (2nd c. B.C.) and partly in Neo-Umbrian and the Latin alphabet, dating from a somewhat later period, which are the most important evidence we possess on the Umbrian language. – Opposite the Palazzo dei Consoli is the 14th c. *Palazzo Pretorio* (Town Hall).

To the N, above the Piazza della Signoria, stands the Gothic *Palazzo Ducale*, rebuilt 1476–80 on the model of the Ducal Palace in Urbino. Opposite, partly built into the hillside, is the **Cathedral** (12th and 13th c.), which contains some notable paintings.

The *church of Santa Maria Nuova*, with the "Madonna del Belvedere" (1403), one of the principal works of the Gubbio-born painter Ottaviano Nelli, is situated in the SE of the town, near the *Porta Romana*. Farther SE, outside the town gate, is the *church of Sant'Agostino*, with frescoes by Nelli in the choir.

NW of the Piazza della Signoria, in the medieval Via dei Consoli, are a number of old houses (see particularly No. 34) with "doors of the dead" set some distance above street level, said to have been used for the removal of the dead but probably in fact serving a defensive purpose.

In the lower SW part of the town is the Gothic *church of San Francesco*, and to the W of the church are the remains of an ancient *theatre* (dramatic performances in summer). – 0·5 km S we find the so-called *mausoleum of Pomponius Graecinus*.

SURROUNDINGS. – From the cathedral a steep road (2 km) ascends to the *monastery of Sant'Ubaldo* (820 m), on the slopes of **Monte Ingino** (906 m: chairlift; from the peak (20 minutes' walk) there are magnificent views.

Herculaneum/ Ercolano

Region: Campania. – Province: Napoli (NA).
Altitude: 44 m. – Population: 53,000.
Post code: I-80056. – Dialling code: 081.
(i) **EPT Napoli**, Via Partenope 10A, I-80100 Napoli (NA); tel. 40 62 89.

HOTEL. – *Ercolano*, III, 44 b.

The remains of Roman *Herculaneum lie within the area of modern Ercolano (until 1969 known as Resina), 8 km SE of Naples near the Tyrrhenian Sea. Although much of Herculaneum is still buried under the modern town, it offers a vivid impression of the aspect of an ancient city, comparable with the remains of Pompeii and Ostia.

HISTORY. – Probably founded by Greek settlers under the name of *Herakleion* and later occupied by Oscans, Etruscans and Samnites, **Herculaneum** fell into Roman hands in 89 B.C. In A.D. 63 it suffered severe damage in an earthquake, and in A.D. 79 it was buried under ashes and pumice during an eruption of Vesuvius. At that time the town, a favourite summer resort of the Romans, had a population of perhaps 6000. Subsequent eruptions increased the depth of ashes and lava to between 12 and 30 m. The hardness of this covering, in contrast to the situation at Pompeii, hindered the activity of plunderers in antiquity.

From 1719 onwards shafts were sunk into the site at random, yielding some splendid finds which now rank among the principal treasures of the National Museum in Naples, including papyrus rolls and bronze statues of superior quality to those found in Pompeii. Systematic excavations carried on since 1927 have brought to light the sumptuous villas of wealthy merchants, the furnishings of which have so far as possible been left in situ.

In contrast to the mostly single-storeyed buildings of Pompeii, the houses of Herculaneum are mostly of two or three storeys, with much use of wood in half-timbered construction, doors and staircases. Extensive excavations are still in progress.

SIGHTS. – From the main entrance (*general view) at the NE corner of the excavation site, the **Scavi d'Ercolano**, a road 400 m long leads to the S end of *Cardo III*, which runs through an area excavated in the 19th c. On the left is the *House of Aristides*, a sumptuous country villa, and beyond it the *House of Argus*, with wall paintings and a pillared garden. Opposite, on the right-hand side of Cardo III, the *Large Inn*, a patrician house converted into an inn, has a terrace overlooking the sea. Farther along, on the right, is the *House of the Skeleton* (wall

Herculaneum

Mosaic Atrium, a spacious and sumptuously furnished mansion and adjoining it on the E the *House of the Deer (frescoes of hunting scenes). – In the northern part of the street, on right, is the *House of the Charred Furniture*, and beyond it the **House of the Mosaic of Neptune and Amphitrite**.

To the SE, on the far side of *Cardo V*, the *House of the Gem* is beautifully painted in reddish-brown tones, and adjoining it on the SE are the *Suburban Baths. – To the NE of the House of the Gem, towards the sea, is the **House of the Relief of Telephus**, one of the most sumptuous mansions in the town, with a spacious colonnaded atrium containing a marble basin and a colonnade leading into the park. – On the E side of the town is the extensive complex of the *Palaestra.

paintings, mosaics), and on the left the *House of the Genius*, a handsome patrician mansion with a garden enclosed by colonnades.

Half way along its length Cardo III is crossed by the Decumanus Inferior, along which are the **recent excavations. Beyond the crossing, on the left of Cardo III, is the *House of Galba*, another handsome patrician mansion, with a cruciform water-basin. At the N end of Cardo III, on right, the *Sacello degli Augustali**, a square shrine lit by an opening in the roof, was originally dedicated to Hercules, patron of Herculaneum, but later consecrated to the Imperial cult (fine frescoes).

Along the *Decumanus Inferior* to the right is the *Cloth-Merchant's Shop*, with a wooden hand-press (restored). To the left are the *Baths, much of the structure well preserved, with separate sections for men and women. At the corner of the Decumanus Inferior and Cardo IV is the **Samnite House**, one of the oldest patrician mansions in the town, with regular paving and rich stucco and fresco decoration. Adjoining is the *House with the Large Doorway*.

On *Cardo IV*, immediately on the right, is the **House of the Wooden Partition**, a patrician house of Samnite type (without a peristyle or colonnaded court). The bedrooms still contain bedsteads and a wooden chest. The adjoining *Casa a Graticcio*, was a more modest house with interior walls of wattle. Immediately to the S is the *House of the Bronze Herm*, named after a bronze herm (head of Hermes) which is probably a portrait of the owner of the house. In the southern section of the street, on left, is the **House of the

On the *Decumanus Maximus*, parallel to the Decumanus Inferior on the N, the **House of the Bicentenary** contains on the first floor, the oldest known Christian cross.

Ischia

Region: Campania. – Province: Napoli (NA).
Area 46 sq. km. – Population: 40,000.
Post code: I-80070. – Dialling code: 081.
ⓘ **AA**, Piazzale Trieste;
tel. 99 11 46.

HOTELS. – IN ISCHIA PONTE: *Hermitage Park*, II, 114 b.; SP; *Miramare e Castello*, II, 82 b.; *Residence*, II, 35 b.; *Aragonese*, III, 41 b., SP; etc. – IN PORTO D'ISCHIA: *Jolly – Grande Albergo delle Terme*, I, 368 b., SP; *Punta Molino*, I, 156 b., SP; *Majestic*, I, 135 b.; *Excelsior Belvedere*, I, 126 b., SP; *Parco Aurora*, I, 100 b.; *Moresco*, I, 100 b., SP; *Aragona Palace*, I, 80 b., SP; *Bristol Palace*, I, 61 b.; *Continental Terme*, II, 357 b., SP; *Alexander*, II, 171 b., SP; *Flora*, II, 124 b.; *Royal Terme*, II, 116 b., SP; *Oriente*, II, 115 b.; *Solemar*, II, 104 b.; *Floridiana*, II, 83 b., SP; *Regina Palace*, II, 81 b., SP; *Felix Terme*, II, 77 b., SP; *Parco Verde Terme*, II, 77 b., SP; *Ambasciatori*, II, 73 b., SP; *Conte*, II, 72 b.; *Imperial*, II, 68 b.; *Nuovo Lido*, II, 68 b.; *Central Park*, II, 66 b., SP; etc. – IN CASAMICCIOLA: *Cristallo Palace*, I, 128 b., SP; *Manzi*, I, 119 b.; *La Madonnina*, I, 37 b.; *Elma*, II, 112 b., SP; *Gran Paradiso*, II, 85 b.; *L'Approdo*, II, 63 b., SP; *Stella Maris*, II, 58 b., SP; *Stefania*, II, 55 b.; *Ibsen*, II, 40 b.; *Candia*, III, 41 b.; etc. – IN LACCO AMENO: *Albergo della Regina Isabella e Royal Sporting*, L, 220 b., SP; *Augusto*, I, 185 b., SP; *San Montano*, I, 121 b., SP; *La Reginella*, I, 73 b., SP; *Grazia*, II, 90 b.; *Mediolanum*, II, 52 b.; *Antares*, II, 50 b.; *Il Fungo*, II, 45 b.; *Don Pepe*, II, 35 b., SP; *La Pace*, III, 143 b., SP; etc.; two camping sites. – IN FORIO: *Citara*, II, 97 b.; *Tritone*, II, 91 b., SP; *Green Flash*, II, 75 b.; *San Vito*, II, 68 b., SP; *Splendid*, II, 67 b., SP; *Punta del Sole*, II, 61 b., SP; *La Scogliera*, II, 60 b.; *Punta Imperatore*, II, 61 b., SP; *Santa Lucia*, II, 54 b.; etc. – IN SANT'ANGELO: *Cocumella*, I, 115 b.; *Parco del Sole*, II, 238 b., SP; *Majestic Palace*, II, 142 b.; *Caravel*, II, 141 b.; *Mediterraneo*, II, 108 b., SP; *Alpha*, II, 86 b.; *Milton*, II, 85 b.; *Cristina*, II, 73 b., SP; *Eliseo Parc's*, II, 59 b.; etc.

BOAT SERVICES (including car ferries). – Several times daily to and from *Naples, Capri, Procida* and *Pozzuoli*. – Hovercraft and hydrofoil services. – HELICOPTER SERVICES.

The volcanic island of *Ischia, lying at the entrance to the Bay of Naples, is the largest island in the vicinity of Naples. It was known to the Greeks as Pithekousa, to the Romans as Aenaria and from the 9th c. as Iscla.

An island of luxuriant vegetation (vineyards, fruit orchards, pinewoods), Ischia is of great scenic beauty, particularly on the N side. Its strongly radioactive hot springs attract many visitors seeking a cure for gout or rheumatism.

SIGHTS. – The chief place on the island is the little town of **Ischia Ponte** (pop. 4000), in a picturesque situation on the NE coast, with a strong *Castello (c. 1450) on a high craggy island (91 m) approached by a stone causeway. – 2 km W is the spa and seaside resort of **Porto d'Ischia**, with the island's only harbour, a former crater lake. During the summer there is a basket-lift to the top of the *Montagnone* (255 m; 4 minutes). – 4 km W of Porto d'Ischia, half way along the N coast of the island, **Casamicciola**, surrounded by gardens and vineyards, is situated on the lower slopes of Monte Ipomeo, with hot springs (65 °C – 149 °F) and a good bathing beach. From here it is 6 km SW, via the resort of **Lacco Ameno**

Castello, Ischia Ponte

(pop. 3000: photograph, p. 89), also with hot radioactive mineral springs (50 °C – 122 °F), to **Forio** (alt. 18 m; pop. 8000; thermal springs), on the W coast.

From Forio a beautiful *road (20 km) leads through the southern part of the island. It passes above the *Gardens of Poseidon* (magnificent bathing facilities, with thermal springs) and continues via *Panza* (alt. 155 m), where a road (3 km) goes off to the village of *Sant'Angelo* (hot springs), picturesquely situated on the slopes of a promontory; then on to *Serrara* (366 m), *Fontana* (452 m) and *Barano d'Ischia* (212 m: large beach of Maronti, with hot springs), past a Roman aqueduct and so back to Ischia Ponte. – From Fontana there is a rewarding climb (1 hour) up *Monte Epomeo (789 m), a massive volcano (extinct since 1302), with an almost vertical N face, in the centre of the island (panoramic *views). – Another very attractive excursion is a boat trip round the island.

Latium/Lazio

EPT Roma, Via Larigi 11, I-00100 Roma (ROMA); tel. (06) 46 18 51.
EPT Frosinone, Piazzale De Matthaeis, I-03100 Frosinone (FR); tel. (0775) 2 00 18.
EPT Latina, Via Duca del Mare 19, I-04100 Latina (LT); tel. (0773) 49 87 11.
EPT Rieti, Piazza Vittorio Emanuele 17, 1-02100 Rieti (RI); tel. (0746) 4 11 46.
EPT Viterbo, Piazza dei Caduti 16, I-01100 Viterbo (VT); tel. (0761) 3 00 92.

The present-day region of Lazio, the ancient Latium, takes in five provinces and has a population of 4·7 million, of whom half live in the capital, Rome. It occupies an area of 17,202 sq. km on the W side of the Central Apennines, extending SW from the Monti Sabini to the coast of the Tyrrhenian Sea between the mouths of the River Chiarone in the N and the Garigliano in the S.

Most of the region is occupied by four volcanic massifs of the Quaternary era, in the craters of which four large lakes and a number of smaller ones have been formed. To the NW are the **Monti Volsini** (highest point 639 m), with the *Lago di*

Bolsena; farther SE the **Monti Cimini** (1053), with the *Lago di Vico*, and the **Monti Sabatini** (612 m), with the *Lago di Bracciano*; and SE of Rome the **Monti Albani** or Alban Hills (948 m), with the *Lago Albano*.

Through the fertile volcanic soil of the region the Tiber has carved out its wide bed. Along the coast extends the *Maremma*, a broad strip of alluvial soil, once marshy and malaria-ridden, which has now been drained and brought under intensive cultivation. This varied geological and geographical pattern has made Latium a region of great scenic diversity.

The main elements in the economy of the region are still arable and sheep-farming. The lower-lying areas produce corn, vegetables and sugar-beet, while the volcanic soils of the uplands yield citrus fruits, olives and excellent wine. Along the coast (e.g. at Civitavecchia) fishing is of some economic importance.

In recent years there has been a rapid development of modern industry, particularly around Rome, in the Sacco and Liri valleys and in the catchment area of the Autostrada del Sole – chemicals and pharmaceuticals, metal-working, textiles, building materials, etc. There is a thermo-electric power station at Civitavecchia and an atomic power station at Borgo Sabatino. A considerable contribution is also made to the economy by tourism, particularly in and around Rome.

HISTORY. – Present-day Latium was occupied in early antiquity by *Etruscans* and, around the mouth of the Tiber, by the *Latin* peoples, who formed a league of 30 republics under the leadership of Alba Longa. During the 6th and 5th c. the rising city of Rome became a member of the Latin League and steadily increased in influence until, after the transfer of the federal sanctuary to the Temple of Diana on the Aventine, it became de facto the leading city of the League. The Latin towns sought to counter the predominance of Rome by force of arms (Latin War, 340–338 B.C.), but were defeated. Thereupon the League was dissolved and the various towns became subject to Rome, on varying terms, and thereafter shared the destinies of Rome.

The main centre of attraction in Latium is, of course, *Rome (see p. 217). – On the road *from Rome to Frosinone* and on to Naples there are numerous places of interest. 19 km SE of Rome on S.S. 6 (the Via Casilina), which runs parallel to the motorway, a minor road runs S via *Colleferro* (alt. 225 m; pop. 18,000; Hotel

Ponte dell'Abbadia, on the border with Tuscany

Astoria, III, 53 b.), with a castle on a hill and large chemical works, to (7 km) the little town of **Segni** (alt. 668 m; pop. 10,000; Hotel La Pace, III, 99 b.), situated on an outlier of the Monti Lepini, with extensive views. This was the very ancient city of *Signia*, and preserves most of its 2 km circuit of *town walls dating from the 6th c. B.C., with the remarkable Porta Saracinesca to the NW. On the acropolis stands the church of San Pietro, built on the central cella of an ancient temple. – 11 km farther along S.S. 6 a road goes off on the left to **Anagni** (alt. 460 m; pop. 15,000; hotels: Del Sole, in Sabatino, II, 84 b.; Della Fontana, III, 43 b.; Motel Parvesi, in La Macchia, II, 48 b.; etc.), on a hill 6 km NE, still partly surrounded by Roman walls. This was the ancient *Anagnia*, capital of the Hernici, and in the Middle Ages was frequently the residence of the Pope. The cathedral of Santa Maria (11th c., rebuilt 1350) contains a mosaic pavement by Magister Cosmas (1226), an Easter candlestick and a bishop's throne by Vasalletto (1263); in the crypt are old frescoes and an altar by Cosmas and his sons; to the right of the choir is the Diocesan Museum (papal vestments). Town Hall (13th c.).

13 km farther along S.S. 6 is the old town of **Ferentino** (alt. 393 m; pop. 9000; Hotel Bassetto, II, 144 b.; Motel Casilione, III, 26 b.; etc.), with an almost completely preserved circuit of town walls (on the S side the Porta Sanguinaria, on the E side the Porta Maggiore or Porta di Casamira). On the highest point in the town, the old acropolis, are the Bishop's Palace and the cathedral, which has a mosaic pavement by Magister Paulus, the earliest of the Cosmati (c.1116). To the NE, near the Porta Sanguinaria, stands the

beautiful church of Santa Maria Maggiore (13th c.), with a fine doorway.

12 km beyond Ferentino we reach the provincial capital, **Frosinone** (alt. 291 m; pop. 40,000; hotels: Cesari, II, 120 b.; Henry, II, 119 b.; Palace Hasser, II, 115 b.; Astor, II, 84 b.; Palombella, II, 66 b.; Progress, II, 48 b.; Sora Giulia, III, 137 b.; etc.), picturesquely situated on a hillside above the Cosa valley, with remains of ancient buildings. 16 km E is the Cistercian abbey of *Santi Giovanni e Paolo di Casamari* (1203–17), which ranks with Fossanova as one of the finest achievements of early Burgundian Gothic in Italy.

42 km beyond Frosinone on S.S. 6 a side road on the right branches off to the village of **Aquino** (alt. 102 m), the ancient *Aquinum*, home of the satirist Juvenal (*c.* A.D. 60–140) and of the scholastic philosopher Thomas Aquinas (1225–74), known as the "Doctor Angelicus" or "Doctor Ecclesiae", who was born in the castle of Roccasecca (10 km N) and trained in Montecassino abbey. On the Via Latina, which passed through the town, are remains of the Roman city. Near the river is the 11th c. church of Santa Maria della Libera, a Lombard foundation built on the ruins of a temple of Hercules, with a handsome doorway (friezes, mosaics, frescoes). – 12 km farther along S.S. 6 is the little town of Cassino (see p. 166).

40 km E of Rome on S.S. 155 (the Via Prenestina), which also leads to Frosinone, is **Palestrina** (alt. 465 m; pop. 10,000; Hotel Stelle, III, 56 b.), the ancient *Praeneste* and one of the oldest towns in Italy, birthplace of the greatest Italian composer of church music, Giovanni Pierluigi da Palestrina (1525–94: tomb in St Peter's, Rome). In 1630 the town fell into the hands of the noble Barberini family. Almost the whole area of the present-day town was occupied by the massive temple of Fortuna Primigenia, the seat of a frequently consulted oracle, which was built on four terraces on the slope of the hill. Its imposing remains were exposed by the bombing of the last war. On the second terrace, by the cathedral, are the well-preserved remains of the Antro delle Sorti ("Cave of Destiny") and the Aula dell'Oracolo, home of the oracle. On the fourth terrace, above the massive arches of the third, stands the Palazzo Baronale of the Barberini family

(15th and 17th c.: museum), on the site of the shrine of Fortuna, with magnificent views extending as far as Rome. – From here a road (3 km) winds its way up to the village of *Castel San Pietro Romano* (752 m), linked with Palestrina by ancient walls, with the massive ramparts of its acropolis and a ruined 15th c. castle. From the Spianata delle Torricelle there are panoramic views.

39 km E of Palestrina on S.S. 155, situated among beautiful forests of chestnut-trees, is **Fiuggi** (alt. 621–747 m; pop. 5000; hotels: *Palazzo della Fonte, I, 255 b., SP; Silva Splendid, I, 258 b., SP; Vallombrosa e Majestic, I, 145 b., SP; Villa Igea, I, 105 b.; Via del Parco, I, 27 b.; Bristol, II, 172 b.; Europa, II, 165 b.; San Marco, II, 162 b.; Ambasciatori, II, 159 b.; Tripoli, II, 157 b.; Imperiale, II, 148 b.; San Giorgio, II, 145 b.; Michelangelo, II, 134 b.; Cristallo, II, 120 b.; Boschetto, II, 108 b.; Italia, II, 107 b.; Fiuggi Terme, II, 105 b.; Ariston, II, 99 b.; Bonifacio, II, 96 b.; Astoria, II, 92 b.; Palace, II, 90 b.; Anemone, III, 58 b.; etc.). Fiuggi is the most popular spa in southern Italy, set in beautiful scenery, with radioactive thermal springs (120 °C – 248 °F) which are effective in the treatment of disorders of the urinary passages and kidneys and gout. – 3·5 km N is the medieval part of the town, *Fiuggi Città* (alt. 747 m). – 16 km beyond Fiuggi on S.S. 155 is **Alatri** (alt. 502 m; pop. 6000; Hotel Aletrium, II, 76 b.; etc.), the ancient *Aletrium*, which has the finest surviving circuit of ancient walls. Especially well preserved are the *walls (4th c. B.C.) of the acropolis, built of huge polygonal blocks: note in particular the SW gate, with a lintel slab 5 m long and 1·60 m thick. In this highest part of the town are the cathedral and the church of Santa Maria Maggiore. – 12 km beyond Alatri is Frosinone.

SE of Rome on S.S. 7 we reach **Cisterna di Latina** (alt. 81 m; pop. 17,000; Hotel Eden, III, 46 b.; etc.), 10 km NE of which, on an outlier of the Monti Lepini, is the little town of **Cori** (alt. 398 m; pop. 8000; Hotel del Colle, IV, 14 b.; etc.), the ancient *Cora*. The town, which claims to have been founded by the Trojan Dardanus, preserves considerable remains of its ancient polygonal walls. In the lower part of the upper town stands the church of Sant'Oliva, built on ancient foundations, with a two-storey cloister, ancient columns and unusual ceiling paintings (16th c.). Higher up, by the church of San

Pietro, is the antechamber of the so-called *Temple of Hercules (1st c. B.C.), probably in fact dedicated to the three Capitoline deities, Jupiter, Juno and Minerva. From here there are beautiful views over the town to the sea, the plain and Monte Circeo. Below the temple ($\frac{1}{2}$ hour's walk) are the remains of another temple dedicated to Castor and Pollux.

13 km E of Cisterna di Latina is *Ninfa, a ruined town still partly surrounded by its walls; Gregorovius called it the "Pompeii of the Middle Ages". The town, mostly dating from the 12th and 13th c. (castle of the Caetani family with an imposing tower, monastery, two small churches, etc.) was abandoned in the 17th c. on account of malaria. The enclosed area, with a garden of great botanic interest, is open only from April to October on the first Saturday in the month; it is private property, still belonging to the princely Caetani family.

8 km N of Ninfa, at *Norma* (alt. 417 m; pop. 4000), are the remains (15 minutes' walk on a hill track) of the old Volscian city of **Norba**, which became a Latin colony in 492 B.C. and was destroyed by supporters of Sulla during the Roman civil wars. The site, surrounded by a polygonal wall 2·5 km long dating from the 4th c. B.C., contains the remains of four temples; museum.

8 km NE of Ninfa is the little medieval town of **Sermoneta** (alt. 257 m; pop. 5000), dominated by a castle which belonged to the Caetani family from 1297 onwards, but which was taken over by Pope Alexander VI (Borgia) in 1500–03 for his daughter Lucrezia and was fortified by Cesare Borgia (14th–15th c. frescoes). The cathedral contains a Madonna ascribed to Benozzo Gozzoli.

In the extreme S of Latium, charmingly situated on a rocky promontory in the Golfo di Gaeta, the port of **Gaeta** (alt. 10 m; pop. 20,000; hotels: Mirasole, in Serapo, II, 234 b.; Summit, II, 138 b.; Serapo, in Serapo, II, 118 b.; Le Rocce, in San Vito, II, 106 b.; Il Ninfeo, in San Vito, II, 94 b.; Flamingo, II, 92 b.; etc.), was until 1861 the principal strong point of the kingdom of Naples and Sicily. The cathedral of Sant'Erasmo has a campanile in Sicilian Romanesque style (1180) and two ancient columns at the entrance. Modernised interior. Behind the high altar is a banner presented by Pope Pius V to Don John of Austria, the victor of Lepanto and opposite the principal doorway an Easter candlestick with late Romanesque reliefs (c. 1200), is borne on four lions. – A short distance W of the Piazza del Duomo stands the large church of San Francesco. The church of the Santissima Annunziata to the N was originally built 1320 (Baroque façade); to the S is the Citadel, with the Castello Angioino (Angevin Tower). – On the highest point

of the promontory (167 m) rises the conspicuous *Torre d'Orlando*, the imposing tomb of Lucius Munatius Plancus (d. after 22 B.C.), who worked successively for Caesar, Antony and Augustus. – At the SW tip of the promontory (2 km: extensive views) is the *Montagna Spaccata*, with a cleft in the rock which according to tradition was caused by the earthquake at the death of Christ. From the new pilgrimage church steps lead down to the beautiful *Grotta del Turco*, on the sea. – On the W side of the promontory is an excellent bathing beach, the *Spiaggia di Sérapo*. – 6 km N of Gaeta, the pretty little town of **Formia** is charmingly situated on the Golfa di Gaeta (alt. 10 m; pop. 25,000; hotels: Grande Albergo Miramare, I, 142 b., SP; Castello Miramare, in Pagnano, I, 20 b.; Fagiano Palace, II, 108 b.; Ariston, II, 101 b., SP; Caposele, II, 80 b.; Romantic, II, 74 b.; Marina di Castellone, II, 66 b., SP; Grand Hotel, II, 58 b.; Bajamar, in San Janni, II, 44 b.; Del Golfo, III, 57 b.; etc.); it is a resort much frequented by Italians in summer. At the W end of the town, near the sea, is the Villa Rubino or Villa di Cicerone, which once belonged to the kings of Naples.

On a promontory 15 km W of Gaeta lies the picturesque fishing village of **Sperlonga** (alt. 10 m; hotels: La Playa, II, 76 b., SP; Fiorelle, II, 49 b.; Miralonga Motel, II, 43 b.; Aurora, III, 92 b.; Amyclae, III, 69 b.; La Sirenella, III, 52 b.; etc.), still partly surrounded by walls, with a good bathing beach. Outside the town, in an olive-grove, the very interesting *Museo Archeologico Nazionale di Sperlonga* (closed Mondays) houses a large collection of original Greek sculpture in marble, most of the items now reduced to the condition of huge torsos. The finest piece is the "Ship of Odysseus", by the sculptor responsible for the famous Laocoön group now in Rome, which depicts Odysseus and his companions struggling with the marine monster Scylla. Between the museum and the sea are remains of the Emperor Tiberius's villa and of ancient basins hewn from the rock, which were used for the rearing of fish (*aquationes*). Close by is the entrance to the *Grotta di Tiberio*, in which the Emperor Tiberius is supposed to have caroused with his friends. It contains a large round basin of the Roman period, the marble cladding of which has disappeared. Since 1957 some 7000 fragments of Greek statues have been discovered here.

15 km N of Gaeta is the little town of **Itri** (alt. 170 m; pop. 8000), formerly notorious as a centre of brigandage. It was the birthplace of the bandit Fra Diavolo, the hero of Auber's opera. Some of the houses in the town are built into the substructures of the Via Appia; above it towers a massive ruined castle. – In the vineyards between Itri and Formia is a round tower known as the *Tomb of Cicero* (who was murdered in this area, near his country estate at Formia, in the year 43 B.C.). – 14 km NW of Itri is **Fondi** (alt. 8 m; pop. 15,000; Hotel Principe, III, 34 b.; etc.), still partly surrounded by ancient walls. In the Corso Appio Claudio, the main street which runs through the whole length of the town on the line of the old Via Appia, are the church of Santa Maria Assunta, with an early Renaissance doorway, and the Gothic church of San Pietro (pulpit and bishop's throne of the 12th–13th c.). On the SE side of the town is the Palazzo del Principe (15th c.), with the crenellated 13th c. Castello opposite it.

30 km *NE of Rome* is the provincial capital of **Rieti** (alt. 402 m; pop. 40,000; hotels: Quattro Stagioni, II, 70 b.; Miramonti, II, 52 b.; Cavour, II, 51 b.; Europa, III, 60 b.; Massimo d'Azeglio, III, 60 b.; Serena, III, 59 b.; etc.), situated on a fertile plateau, ringed by hills, on the right bank of the River Velino. Along the N side of the town stretch defensive walls and towers. In the central Piazza del Comune is the Palazzo Comunale, with the Museo Civico. To the SW stands the cathedral (completed 1456), with a 13th c. campanile and a fine 12th c. crypt; in the fourth chapel on the N side is a statue of St Barbara by Bernini. From the Piazza del Duomo there are fine views. Behind the cathedral lies the Bishop's Palace, with the beautiful Loggia Papale (13th c.). – From Rieti attractive trips can be made into the *Monti Reatini*, particularly to **Terminillo** (21 km NE: cableway, chair-lift, ski-lifts), a popular summer resort and winter sports centre, much favoured by the people of Rome (the "montagna di Roma"). From *Monte Terminillo* (2213 m), the highest peak in the Monti Reatini, there are panoramic views extending to the Gran Sasso and Maiella, and on clear days as far as the Adriatic and the Tyrrhenian Sea.

In northern *Latium*, situated at the W end of a tufa plateau surrounded by deep gorges, is the ancient town of **Civita Castellana** (alt. 145 m; pop. 15,000), capital of the Faliscan territory lying between Etruria and Latium. In 241 B.C. the Faliscan town, known to the Romans as *Falerii Veteres*, was destroyed by Roman forces and the inhabitants transferred to a new settlement at *Falerii Novi* (from which they later returned). The 12th c. cathedral of Santa Maria has a beautiful porch of 1210. In a commanding situation to the W of the town stands the Rocca or Citadel, built by Pope Alexander VI in 1494–1500 to the design of Antonio Sangallo the Elder; in the large arcaded courtyard are decorative paintings by the Zuccaro brothers (16th c.). – 6 km W are the remains of **Falerii Novi**, founded in 240 B.C. to rehouse the inhabitants of the older town of Falerii Veteres, which has preserved its complete circuit of walls (2108 m long, with nine gates and 50 towers). Within the walls, near the Porta di Giove on the W side, the ruined abbey of Santa Maria di Falleri has ancient columns in the nave. Near the Porta del Bove, to the SE, are the remains of a theatre, the forum and a swimming pool.

Another attractive spot in northern Latium is the *Lago di Bolsena* (alt. 305 m; area 114 sq. km; up to 146 m deep), known to the Romans as *Lacus Vulsiniensis*. The lake occupies the crater of a collapsed Tertiary volcano, which in a violent eruption spread ash over an area of 1300 sq. km extending from Orvieto almost to the sea. In the southern half of the lake are two little rocky islets, *Bisentina* (361 m) and *Martana* (377 m). On the island of Martana the Gothic queen Amalasuntha, only daughter of Theodoric the Great, was strangled in her bath in the year 535 on the orders of her co-Regent Theodahat. – At the NE corner of the lake the picturesquely situated little town of **Bolsena** (alt. 348 m; pop. 5000; hotels: Columbus del Lago, II, 80 b.; Le Naidi, II, 28 b.; Lido, II, 24 b.; Moderno, III, 35 b.; etc.), lies below the site of Etruscan *Volsinium*, political centre of the league of 12 Etruscan cities (remains of a wall of dressed stone), and the Roman *Volsinium Novum*, built after the destruction of the Etruscan town in 263 B.C. An ancient road paved with basalt blocks leads up ($\frac{1}{2}$ hour) to the scanty remains of the Roman town. Features of interest in Bolsena itself are the 13th c. Castello and the church of Santa Cristina (13th c.) to the S of the town. The church has a fine Renaissance façade (c. 1500) with two terracotta reliefs by Andrea della

Robbia above the doors. In the interior is the Grotta di Santa Cristina, with the saint's tomb, and, under the high altar, the stone with which she was drowned in the year 278. The altar is known as the Altare del Miracolo, following the *"miracle of Bolsena"* in 1263, when a Bohemian priest who had doubted the doctrine of transubstantiation (i.e. the transformation of bread and wine into the body and blood of Christ in the mass) was convinced of his error by the appearance of drops of blood on the consecrated Host. To commemorate the event Pope Urban IV made the feast of Corpus Christi (which had recently been initiated in Belgium) a universal festival of the Church (1264) and caused the splendid cathedral of Orvieto to be built. – SE of Bolsena, on a subsidiary crater just inland from the lake, is **Montefiascone** (alt. 633 m; pop. 12,000; hotels: Italia, III, 46 b.; Altavilla, III, 43 b.; etc.), noted for the famous sweet white wine Est Est Est. The cathedral of Santa Margherita (by Sanmicheli, 1519) has an octagonal dome. From the gardens round the ruined Rocca above the town there are extensive *views. To the NE, below the town on the Orvieto road, is the double church of San Flaviano (1030), with 14th c. frescoes.

Also in northern Latium is the beautiful **Lago di Bracciano** (alt. 164 m; area 57·5 sq. km; up to 160 m deep), the ancient *Lacus Sabatinus*, which, like Lake Bolsena, was created by the explosion and subsequent collapse of a volcanic cone which scattered tufa as far as Rome and the sea. Above the lake to the SW is the little town of **Bracciano** (alt. 279 m; Hotel Selene, III, 24 b.; etc.), with a massive five-towered *Castello (built 1470, in the possession of the princely Odescalchi family since 1696), a fine

example of a fortified medieval castle Notable interior and pillared courtyard (closed Monday afternoons and Fridays) from the wall-walk there are magnificent views of the lake.

****Cerveteri:** see p. 96.

Lecce

Region: Puglia. – Province: Lecce (LE).
Altitude: 51 m. – Population: 85,000.
Post code: I-73180. – Dialling code: 0832.
(i) **AA**, Via F. Filzi 28;
tel. 2 50 34.
   EPT, Via Monte San Michele 20;
   tel. 5 41 17.
   Via R. Visconto 14A;
   tel. 2 44 43.
   ACT, Via G. Candido 2;
   tel. 2 94 81.

HOTELS. – *President*, Via Salandra 6, I, 28 b.; *Astor* Via 140° Reggimento Fanteria 69, II, 117 b.; *Delle Palme*, Via Leuca 90, II, 192 b.; *Patria-Touring*, Piazza G. Riccardi 13, II, 92 b.; *Continental*, Via Vittorio Alfieri 11, III, 48 b.; etc.

The provincial capital of Lecce, successor to the ancient Messapian town of Lupiae, situated mid-way along the Salentine peninsula (the heel of the Italian boot), is one of the most interesting towns in southern Italy, notable for its magnificent Baroque buildings erected by local architects using the beautiful and easily worked yellow limestone of the area.

SIGHTS. – In the centre of the town is the Piazza Sant'Oronzo, with an ancient column bearing a statue of the saint. To the W of the column is the *Sedile*, a loggia built in 1592, and adjoining it the doorway of the little *church of San Marco* (founded 1543). On the S side of the square are the excavated remains of a Roman *amphitheatre*. – To the S, in Piazza Vittorio Emanuele, stands the *church of Santa Chiara* (18th c.), and farther S the *church of San Matteo* (*c.* 1700), with a remarkable Baroque façade.

From the Piazza Sant'Oronzo the Corso Vittorio Emanuele II runs W, past the Theatine *church of Sant'Irene* (1639) into the **Piazza del Duomo*, with the **Cathedral** of Sant'Oronzo (1658–70 tower 70 m high), the *Bishop's Palace* and the *Seminary*, which has a richly decorated façade and a courtyard containing a fountain. – 0·5 km S of the Piazza

Lago di Bracciano

Santa Croce, Lecce

Sirenuse, II, 233 b., SP; Jolly Park Hotel, II, 161 b.; Lido San Giovanni, II, 154 b.; Cristina, II, 51 b.; Rivabella, III, 66 b.; etc.), a little port beautifully situated on a rocky island in the Golfo di Taranto and linked by a bridge with its modern suburb on the mainland. At the E end of the bridge is a fountain of 1560, with ancient reliefs. Beyond the bridge, to the left, is the Castello (13th–17th c.), from which the main street, Via Antonietta de Pace, runs across the town. In this street, on the left, stands the cathedral (1629–96), with fine choir-stalls, and beyond it, on the right, the Municipal Museum. – There is an attractive road, the Riviera, running round the outside of the town. – A pleasant trip from Gallipoli is on a road, partly hewn from the rock, along the "Riviera Neretina" to the little bathing resort of *Santa Maria al Bagno*, 12 km N, and, 2 km farther on, the hamlet of *Santa Caterina Riviera*.

del Duomo is the large Dominican *church of Santa Maria del Rosario* (1691–1728).

N of Piazza Sant'Oronzo in the Piazza della Prefettura the magnificent *church of Santa Croce has an exuberantly decorated façade (begun 1549, completed 1697 onwards) and a fine interior. Adjoining it on the N the extensive and richly ornamented façade of the Celestine convent (13th c.) to which it belonged, is now occupied by the Prefecture, and behind this is the beautiful Giardino Pubblico. – E of Piazza Sant'Oronzo is the *Castello*, on a trapezoid ground-plan, built in the reign of Charles V (1539–48).

To the S of the town, in Piazza Argento, is the Palazzo Argento, which houses the *Provincial Museum* (ancient vases, terracottas, statues and coins; pictures).

From the Piazza della Prefettura we go N along Via Umberto I and in 100 m turn left into Via Principe di Savoia to reach the *Porta di Napoli*, a triumphal arch erected in 1548, on the W side of the old town. NW of this is the *Campo Santa*, with the **church of Santi Nicolò e Cataldo, built by the Norman Count Tancred in 1180, with a superb Romanesque doorway in the centre of the Baroque façade of 1716. The harmonious interior, showing strong influence of French Gothic, has beautiful capitals.

SURROUNDINGS. – There is an attractive drive (38 km SW) over the Apulian plain, passing through the little country town of *Galatone* (alt. 59 m; pop. 14,000), with a beautiful cathedral and the Baroque church of the Crocifisso, to **Gallipoli** (alt. 14 m; pop. 17,000; hotels: Grand Hotel Costa Brada, I, 122 b.; Le

Another attractive trip from Lecce is to Capo Santa Maria di Leuca, either on the direct road (65 km) via **Maglie** (alt. 81 m; pop. 13,000; Hotel Salento, III, 72 b.) or on the longer but scenically superior coast road (96 km). This road traverses the seaside resort of *San Cataldo* which has a good beach, a lighthouse and a camping site (shade), and comes to **Otranto** (alt. 15 m; pop. 4000; hotels: Miramare, II, 99 b.; Valtura Alimini, II, 610 b.), a little fishing town beautifully situated in a bay, the see of an archbishop. The Greek *Hydrus* and the Roman *Hydruntum*, often referred to in the ancient sources as a port of embarkation for Apollonia in Epirus, Otranto was destroyed by the Turks in 1480. From the Castello there is a view across the *Straits of Otranto* (75 km wide) to the mountains of Albania. The cathedral of the Santissima Annunziata (begun 1080) contains ancient columns with 12th c. capitals, a unique *mosaic pavement, completely preserved, with representations of the months and of heroic subjects (1163–66) and a five-aisled crypt. In a side street in the upper part of the town is the little church of San Pietro (9th c.), with a Byzantine dome and frescoes.

From Otranto there is a beautiful stretch of road, running inland for part of the way and then winding its way along the coast, to **Santa Cesarea Terme** (alt. 94 m; hotels: Palazzo, II, 81 b.; Oasi Beati Martiri Idruntini, III, 83 b.; etc.), charmingly situated above the sea. The town has recently developed into a popular resort. It has four springs of sulphureous water (36 °C – 97 °F) in large caves in the cliffs, recommended for the treatment of skin conditions and rheumatism (mud baths available). From here there is an interesting boat trip (4–5 km S) along the rocky coast with its numerous coves to two stalactitic caves which were inhabited in prehistoric times, the *Grotta Romanelli* and the *Grotta Zinzulusa*. – Beyond Santa Cesarea Terme the road continues along the rocky coast to the little fishing port of *Marina di Castro*, below the fortified village of *Castro*, and **Capo Santa Maria di Leuca** (alt. 59 m), the south-eastern tip of Italy, named after its white limestone cliffs (Greek *akra leuka*). On the cape is the *church of Santa Maria de Finibus Terrae* ("St Mary of the Ends of the Earth"), with an altar constructed of stone from the temple of Minerva which stood here, and an image of the Virgin which is revered as miraculous. From the lighthouse there are magnificent views, extending in clear weather as far as Albania. – W of the cape is the little seaside resort of *Leuca*; to the SW is *Punta Ristola*. – Attractive boat trips along the magnificent rocky coast, with numerous caves.

Leghorn (Livorno)

Region: Toscana. – Province: Livorno (LI).
Altitude: 3 m. – Population: 175,000.
Post code: I-57100. – Dialling code: 0586.

(i) **EPT**, Piazza Cavour 6;
   tel. 3 31 11.
   ACI, Via Giuseppe Verdi 32;
   tel. 3 46 51.
   TCI, *Viaggi Vietu*, Via Ricasoli 17–21;
   tel. 2 14 20.
   Via Maggi 2–4;
   tel. 2 35 63.

HOTELS. – *Palazzo*, Viale Italia 195, I, 227 b.; *Astoria*, Via Ricasoli 96, I, 170 b.; *Excelsior*, Via D. Cassuto 1, II, 105 b.; *Giappone*, Via Grande 65, II, 96 b.; *Granduca*, Piazza Micheli 16, II, 75 b.; *Touring*, Via Goldoni 61, II, 59 b.; *Boston*, Piazza Mazzini 40, II, 55 b.; *Genuario*, Viale Italia 301, II, 45 b.; *Corsica*, Corso G. Mazzini 148, III, 82 b.; etc.

Leghorn (in Italian Livorno), situated on the low-lying coast of the Tyrrhenian Sea to the S of the plain round the mouth of the Arno, is a busy port and commercial town, linked with the Arno by a canal 15 km long. It is capital of its province and the main centre for handling the produce of its Tuscan hinterland.

Leghorn owed its rise to the Medici, who during the 16th and 17th c. offered asylum to refugees from many lands – Catholics from Britain, Jews and Moors from Spain. The city, traversed by canals, is of modern aspect, and the heavy destruction of the Second World War has left it with no great monuments of the past. – It was the birthplace of the painter Amedeo Modigliani (1884–1920).

SIGHTS. – The central feature of the old town, which was completely destroyed during the last war, is the long *Piazza Grande*, now surrounded by modern buildings. At its S end stands the *Cathedral*, rebuilt according to the original plan; in the centre of the square is the *Palazzo Grande* (1951), at the NE corner the Town Hall. – From here Via Cairoli runs S to the Piazza Cavour, the new centre of the city's traffic, which is partly laid out over a canal, the *Fosso Reale*.

Leghorn's main street, the *Via Grande*, cuts across the Piazza Grande; at its E end is the *Piazza della Repubblica*, with statues of Ferdinand III (d. 1824) and Leopold II (d. 1870), the last Grand Dukes of Tuscany. Immediately N of the square is the *Fortezza Nuova*, surrounded by a canal.

At the W end of Via Grande, flanking the *Darsena* (Docks), is the Piazza Micheli, on the N side of which stands a **statue** of Grand Duke *Ferdinand I* (by Giovanni Bandini), with four *Moorish slaves* (by Pietro Tacca, 1624). At the N end of the Darsena is the *Fortezza Vecchia*, and to the W the large *Porto Mediceo*.

In Via del Tempio is the new Synagogue (1962), in contemporary style, replacing the previous one destroyed during the last war, the most splendid in Italy.

To the S of Piazza Micheli, reached by way of the Piazza Mazzini and the Piazza Orlando, the beautiful *Viale Italia* runs along the Tyrrhenian coast to the villa suburb of Ardenza (bathing beaches, *Aquarium, Stadium*).

Liguria

In Leghorn Harbour

(i) **EPT Genova**, Via Roma 11,
   I-16100 Genova (GE);
   tel. (010) 58 14 07.
   EPT Imperia, Viale Matteotti 54,
   I-18100 Imperia (IM);
   tel. (0183) 2 49 47.
   EPT Savona, Via Paleocapa 7,
   I-17100 Savona (SV);
   tel. (019) 2 05 22.
   EPT La Spezia, Viale Mazzini 45,
   I-19100 La Spezia (SP);
   tel. (0187) 3 60 00.

The historical Liguria, now an administrative region comprising the four provinces of Imperia, Savona, Genoa and La Spezia with Genoa as its capital, occupies an area of 5415

sq. km on the southern slopes of the arc of mountains which extends round the Gulf of Genoa (Ligurian Sea) from the Maritime Alps in the W by way of the Ligurian Alps to the Ligurian Apennines.

HISTORY. – The region, originally occupied by *Ligurians*, was Romanised in the 2nd c. B.C. Fragmented during the early medieval period into numerous Lombard and Frankish principalities, it fell from the 12th c. onwards under the control of *Genoa*, then growing in strength as a sea power. In 1805 Liguria was annexed by Napoleon, and in 1814 it was assigned by the Congress of Vienna to Piedmont, becoming part of the new united Italy in 1861.

The mountains which here fall steeply down to the sea provide almost complete protection against unfavourable weather from the N, and the region's southern exposure gives it a mild and sunny climate, particularly along the coastal strip known as the Riviera, which has long been a favourite winter resort and is now one of Italy's principal tourist regions.

The population of 1·9 million is mainly concentrated in the industrial areas round the ports of Genoa, La Spezia and Savona. In the country regions, with only moderately productive soil, vegetables and fruit are grown, as well as the flowers (also used in the manufacture of perfume) for which the region is renowned. Tourism is of great economic importance along the whole of the Riviera (see p. 214).

Lipari Islands (Aeolian Islands)

Region: Sicilia. – Province: Messina (ME).
Principal island: Lipari. – Population: 12,000.
Post code: I-98055. – Dialling code: 090.
ⓘ **EPT Lipari**, Corso Vittorio Emanuele 237; tel. 91 15 80.

HOTELS. – ON LIPARI: *Carasco*, II, 163 b., SP; *Gattopardo Park*, II, 78 b.; *Giardino sul Mare*, II, 60 b., SP; *Augustus*, III, 36 b.; etc. – ON VULCANO: *Eolian*, II, 162 b.; *Arcipelago*, II, 157 b., SP; *Garden Volcano*, II, 60 b.; *Les Sables Noirs*, II, 53 b.; *Mari del Sul*, III, 49 b.; etc. – ON FILICUDI: *Los Caracollos*, II. – ON ALICUDI: *Ericusa*, IV, 24 b. – ON PANAREA: *La Piazza*, III, 50 b.; *Lisca Bianca*, III, 44 b.; etc. – ON STROMBOLI: *La Sciara Residence*, II, 122 b., SP; *La Sirenetta*, III, 52 b.; etc. – YOUTH HOSTEL in Lipari, 120 b.

BOAT SERVICES. – Regular services several times daily from *Milazzo* and *Messina* and several times weekly from *Naples* to *Lipari*, *Vulcano*, *Salina* and *Panarea*, with connections three times weekly to

On the Lipari Islands

Filicudi and *Alicudi*. – Hydrofoil services in summer (once or twice daily) from *Milazzo*, *Messina* and *Palermo* (Cefalù, Capo d'Orlando).

The Lipari Islands (Isole Lípari), also known as the Aeolian Islands (Isole Eólie) after the Greek wind god Aeolus, lying between 30 and 80 km off the N coast of Sicily, are an archipelago of seven larger islands and ten uninhabited islets, the tips of mountains of volcanic origin rising from the sea-bed far below.

The islands, with a total area of 117 sq. km and a present-day population of 12,000, were long used as penal colonies and places of banishment. In more recent times their mild climate and unusual scenery have attracted increasing numbers of visitors. They offer excellent scuba diving.

The largest and most fertile of the islands is **Lipari** (area 38 sq. km, pop. 10,000). In the more southerly bay on the E coast lies the little town of **Lipari** (pop. 4500), the chief place of the island. To the S of the harbour, on a rocky promontory, is the Castello, within which are the cathedral (1654) and three other churches. Adjoining the cathedral, in the former Bishop's Palace, is a *museum (Antiquarium) containing the rich finds of the prehistoric period and historical times from recent excavations on the island (painted vases, a statuette of Isis, tombs, etc.). To the W of the cathedral, on an excavation site in front of the Immacolata church, can be seen a series of building levels ranging in date from the Early Bronze Age (17th c. B.C.) through the Iron Age (11th–9th c. B.C.) and the Hellenistic period to Roman times (2nd c. A.D.). N of the Castello is the fishermen's quarter; to the S the warehouses in which the island's exports (including pumice-stone, currants, Malvasia wine, capers and figs) are stored to await shipment.

3 km N of Lipari, beyond *Monte Rosa* (239 m), the village of **Canneto** (alt. 10 m) is the centre for the extraction, processing and export of pumice-stone. The pumice quarries in the valley of the *Fossa Bianca*, NW of the village (45 minutes) are an interesting sight. – W of Canneto (1½–2 hours), beyond the massive lava flows at *Forgia Vecchia*, rises **Monte Sant'Angelo** (594 m), the island's highest peak. From its summit, roughly in the centre of the archipelago, there is the best panoramic *view of the Lipari Islands. – At *Piano Conte*, in a valley near the W coast, are the *hot springs of San Calogero* (62 °C – 144 °F: steam baths). – From Lipari there is an attractive walk (1½ hours) to *San Salvatore* (3 km S), on the S tip of the island, and from there back to Lipari along the W side of *Monte Guardia* (369 m).

To the S of the island of Lipari, separated from it by the Bocche, a strait 1 km wide, on the W side of which is the basalt cliff of *Pietralunga* (60 m), the island of **Vulcano** (area 21 sq. km, pop. 400) offers excellent opportunities for studying volcanic phenomena. On the N side of the island is *Vulcanello* (123 m), with three craters, which rose out of the sea in 183 B.C. In the depression S of the hill are the harbours of *Porto di Ponente* (to the W) and *Porto di Levante* (to the E). On the shore beside Porto di Levante is a curiously shaped rock, the remnant of an old volcano, riddled with caves for the extraction of alum. The sea-water, here strongly radioactive, is warm and sometimes boiling as a result of under-water emissions of steam (recommended for the treatment of rheumatism and gout). – From the *Gran Cratere* (386 m: climbed from Porto di Levante in 1 hour) to the S of the depression, there are magnificent *views; half way up are numerous fumeroles. The crater, which since the eruptions of 1880–90 has the characteristics of a solfatara, measures 200 by 140 m

and is 80 m deep. – Farther S is the cone of *Monte Aria* (499 m), the island's highest peak.

4 km NE of Lipari lies the island of **Salina** (area 27 sq. km, pop. 2000), with two extinct volcanoes, *Monte de' Porri* (860 m) to the NW and *Monte Fossa delle Felci* (962 m) to the SE. – 20 km W of Salina is the well-cultivated island of **Filicudi** (775 m; area 9 sq. km, pop. 150). On its W coast a fine cave with basalt pillars can be visited. – 13 km farther W is the island of **Alicudi** (663 m; area 5 sq. km), with a population of some 130 shepherds and fishermen.

Panarea

The small group of islands between 14 and 21 km NE of the island of Lipari may have been a single island before the volcanic eruptions of 126 B.C. The largest of the group, **Panarea** (421 m; area 3·5 sq. km, pop. 250), has hot springs. At *Punta Milazzese*, the southernmost tip of the island, are the foundations (excavated 1948) of 23 huts belonging to a *Bronze Age village* (14th–13th c. B.C.), the best preserved in Italy. – 4 km NE of Panarea is a small uninhabited rocky island, **Basiluzzo** (capers).

14 km NE of Basiluzzo is the island of **Stromboli** (area 12·5 sq. km), reputed in ancient times to be the home of the wind god Aeolus. The population, which in 1935 was about 1800, has been reduced by emigration (particularly to Australia) to no more than 350. On the NE coast the chief place of the island, **Stromboli** (alt. 20 m), comprises the districts of *San Bartolomeo, San Vincenzo* and *Ficogrande*.

Like the Vulcano crater, *Stromboli (926 m), the red glow from which can be seen from a long way off, is one of the few European volcanoes that are still active. The ascent (3 hours), recommended to be undertaken from the N side, is a fascinating experience. The crater, to the N of the highest peak, emits at frequent intervals huge bubbles of lava which explode with a thunderous noise, throwing up showers of stones which fall back into the crater or roll harmlessly down the *Sciara*, a slope descending on the NW side at an angle of 35° to the sea and continuing for some distance below the surface. Only every few years are there more violent eruptions which cause damage to the cultivated parts of the island. When the vapour is not too thick it is possible to go down to the brink of the crater and look in. – 1·5 km NE of the village of Stromboli is the magnificent basalt cliff of *Strombolicchio*, rising 56 m sheer from the sea (steps cut in rock).

Lodi

Region: Lombardia. – Province: Milano (MI).
Altitude: 8 m. – Population: 45,000.
Post code: I-20075. – Dialling code: 0371.
(i) **TCI**, *Agenzia Minojetti*,
Piazza Vittoria 40;
tel. 5 24 41.

HOTELS. – *Europa*, II, 77 b.; *Anelli*, III, 33 b.; *Castello*, III, 21 b.; etc.

Lodi, situated on the right bank of the Adda in the fertile Po plain, is well worth visiting for the sake of its medieval churches. It is also a noted centre of cheese manufacture, particularly Parmesan.

HISTORY. – Lodi was founded by Frederick Barbarossa in 1160 after the destruction of the old town of Lodi Vecchio. Throughout the Middle Ages Lodi was one of Milan's bitterest opponents.

SIGHTS. – In the *Piazza della Vittoria*, in the centre of the town, rises the Romanesque *Cathedral (12th c.; restored 1961–64, when old frescoes were exposed; it has a beautiful pillared doorway, and Romanesque reliefs in the crypt. To the left of the cathedral is the *Broletto* (13th–14th c., with later rebuilding). – NW of the Piazza della Vittoria stands the *church of the Incoronata, a handsome building (1488–94) on a centralised plan, with an organ gallery of 1507

and richly carved choir-stalls (c. 1700). – N of the Piazza della Vittoria the *Museo Civico* houses a rich collection (archaeology, *pottery, pictures).

To the S of the Piazza della Vittoria, in Via Garibaldi, is the *church of San Lorenzo* (12th c.), with statues of about 1170 on the main doorway. – A short distance W of the cathedral, in Piazza Ospedale, we find the beautiful *church of San Francesco, in Lombard Gothic style (13th c.), with frescoes on the pillars in the interior. To the right of the church the *Ospedale Maggiore* has a fine pillared courtyard.

SURROUNDINGS. – 7 km W of Lodi is **Lodi Vecchio** (alt. 82 m; pop. 4000; Hotel Barbarossa, IV, 40 b.), the Roman *Laus Pompeia*, destroyed by the Milanese in 1111 and 1158, after which it declined into an unimportant little country town. There are two interesting churches – San Bassiano (11th c.), with 15th c. frescoes, and the Badia di San Pietro, also with frescoes.

16 km NE of Lodi is situated the busy little town of **Crema** (alt. 79 m; hotels: Palace, II, 66 b.; Al Platano, II, 41 b.; etc.), with a Romanesque cathedral (13th c.: beautiful brick façade), a 15th c. Town Hall and a 16th c. Palazzo Pretorio. – 1 km N of the town on the Bérgamo road is the *church of Santa Maria della Croce*, built 1490 onwards under the influence of Bramante.

Lombardy

(i) **EPT Bergamo**, Viale V. Emanuele 4,
I-24100 Bergamo (BG);
tel. (035) 24 22 26.
EPT Brescia, Corso Zanardelli 38,
I-25100 Brescia (BS);
tel. (030) 4 34 18.
EPT Como, Piazza Cavour 17,
I-22100 Como (CO);
tel. (031) 26 20 91.
EPT Cremona, Galleria del Corso 3,
I-26100 Cremona (CR);
tel. (0372) 2 17 22.
EPT Mantova, Piazza A. Mantegna 6,
I-46100 Mantova (MN);
tel. (0376) 2 16 01.
EPT Milano, Palazzo del Turismo,
Via Marconi 1,
I-20100 Milano (MI);
tel. (02) 87 00 16 and 87 04 16.
EPT Pavia, Corso Garibaldi 1,
I-27100 Pavia (PV);
tel. (0382) 2 77 06.
EPT Sondrio, Piazza Garibaldi,
I-23100 Sondrio (SO);
tel. (0342) 2 44 63.
EPT Varese, Piazza M. Grappa 5,
I-21100 Varese (VA);
tel. (0332) 28 36 04.

The historic old territory and modern administrative region of Lombardy, taking in nine provinces, with

Milan as its capital, occupies an area of 23,834 sq. km in northern Italy. It extends from the High Alps (Bernina massif, Ortles, Adamello group) in the N by way of the Bergamo and Brescia Alps to the Po plain, and includes the central part of that plain between the rivers Sesia and Mincio, bounded on the S by the Apennines.

Southern Lombardy, in the plain of the Po and the flat pre-Alpine uplands, is one of Italy's most highly developed industrial regions (chemicals and pharmaceuticals, metal-working, car manufacture, engineering and light engineering, textiles, leather goods) as well as one of its most productive agricultural regions (corn, rice, maize, market gardening, fodder crops). The hill regions are mostly devoted to dairy and pastoral farming, while the Valtellina is noted for its wine. Tourism makes a major contribution to the economy in the area around the beautiful Alpine lakes (lakes Maggiore, Como and Garda) and in the mountains (winter sports, climbing). The population of some 9 million is mainly concentrated in the densely settled conurbations centred on Milan, Brescia, Pavia and Varese.

HISTORY. – After the fall of the Western Roman Empire Lombardy (*Langobardia*) became in the 7th c. the heartland of the *Langobards* or *Lombards* and in 951 a kingdom, with its capital at Pavia. The conflict between the Lombard League and the *Hohenstaufen* rulers of Germany in the 12th and 13th c. led to the division of the Lombard towns between the Guelfs and Ghibellines, with a consequent internal decline and a splitting up of the kingdom. From the 14th c. *Milan* established its dominance in western Lombardy, while Venice gained control of the eastern part of the territory. In 1535 Milan passed to Charles V, in 1556 to the Spanish *Habsburgs* and in 1797, as the Cisalpine Republic, to *France*. The Congress of Vienna assigned Lombardy and Venetia to *Austria* as a Lombard-Venetian kingdom. Finally in 1859 Austria was compelled to cede Lombardy, and after 1866 Venetia as well, to the new kingdom of Italy.

FEATURES OF INTEREST. – The tourist attractions of northern Italy include not only towns such as Milan, Pavia, Bergamo, Brescia, Cremona and Mantua but also the Alpine lakes with their beautiful scenery and favoured climate. In addition to lakes Como, Garda and Maggiore there is also *Lake Lugano (Lago di Lugano* or *Lago Ceresio*: alt. 274 m., area 48 sq. km, greatest depth 279 m), most of which is in Switzerland. On the NE arm of this lake is the village of **Porlezza** (alt. 271 m: hotels: Regina, III, 62 b.; Europa, III, 55 b.; etc.),

from which an attractive road runs along the S side of the lake, via the little village of *Osteno*, to *Lanzo d'Intelvi* (alt. 907 m; Hotel Villa Annunziata, II, 57 b.; etc.), a summer resort in the upper reaches of the *Valle d'Intelvi*. A short distance NE is *Belvedere di Lanzo* (alt. 887 m; hotels: Villa Violet, I, 68 b.; Belvedere, III, 67 b.; etc.), commanding extensive views, from which a funicular runs down to Santa Margherita on the lake. 6 km from Lanzo is the * *Vedetta della Sighignola* (1302 m), from which there are magnificent views.

On the E side of Lake Lugano, within Swiss territory, is the Italian·enclave of **Campione d'Italia** (*Gran Hotel Campione d'Italia, L, 75 b.), with a popular casino. Church of the Madonna dei Ghirli (14th c.).

Another attractive lake is the *Lago d'Iseo (alt. 185 m; area 62 sq. km, greatest depth 251 m), known to the Romans as *Lacus Sebinus*. It is one of the most beautiful of the Italian Alpine lakes, dominated on the E by *Monte Guglielmo (1949 m: climbed from *Marone* in $4\frac{1}{2}$ hours), with charming scenery along its shores (though a broad band of vegetation interferes with bathing). The largest river flowing into the lake is the *Oglio*, which leaves it again at **Sárnico** (alt. 197 m; Hotel Cantiere, II, 38 b.; etc.). From the northern part of the lake, where the *ora*, a cold S wind, often blows about midday, there is a splendid view of the Adamello group. In the middle of the lake lies the steep-sided **Montisola** (559 m), the largest island in any Italian lake (3 km long), covered with dense chestnut forests. On its highest point is the pilgrimage church of the Madonna della Ceriola (*views). At the SE extremity of the island is the fishing village of *Peschiera Maraglio*, at its NW end the village of *Siviano*, at its SW tip *Sensole*.

At the N end of the lake, prettily situated on a sloping hillside, the little industrial town of **Lovere** (alt. 200 m; pop. 7000; hotels: Al Castello, III, 35 b.; Moderno, III, 34 b.; etc.) boasts the handsome Renaissance church of Santa Maria in Valvendra (16th c.: Baroque interior, pictures) and the Accademia Tadini, a picture gallery containing works by Bellini, Tintoretto and other artists. From the lakeside promenade there are beautiful views.

On the S side of the lake the little port of **Iseo** (alt. 198 m; Hotel Ambra, II, 61 b.; etc.) has a parish church and an old Scaliger castle.

13 km NE of Lovere, in the Val Camonica, is the spa of **Darfo Boario Terme** (alt. 225 m; hotels: Terme, II, 118 b.; Excelsior, II, 114 b.; Rizzi, II, 73 b.; Alpinist, II, 69 b.; Sorriso, III, 84 b.; Bossi, III, 76 b.; etc.), with chalybeate springs. From here there is an attractive excursion to the NW, through the 10 km long *Dezzo gorge*, known as the "Via Mala Lombarda", to Dezzo. – **Breno** (alt. 330 m; pop. 5000; hotels: Castello, III, 80 b.; Giardino, III, 66 b.) is situated 13 km NE of Darfo Boario Terme. It is the chief town of the Val Camonica, with a ruined castle and two interesting churches, San Salvatore and Sant'Antonio. To the N rises a fine dolomitic peak, the *Corna di Concarena* (2549 m), to the NE the *Pizzo Badile* (2435 m), the "Matterhorn of the Val Camonica". From Breno a beautiful road, narrow and sometimes steep, runs SE (49 km) via *Campolaro* (alt. 1442 m) to the **Passo di Croce Domini** (1895 m) and then continues through the *Valle Sanguinara* and the *Valle Cafforo* to the beautifully situated mountain village of **Bagolino** (alt. 730 m; Hotel Tre Valli, IV, 47 b.; etc.) and beyond this to the church of *Sant'Antonio* on the beautiful **Lago d'Idro** (alt. 368 m; 10 km long, $1\frac{1}{2}$–2 km wide, up to 122 m deep), known to the Romans as *Lacus Eridius*.

Loreto

Region: Marche. – Province: Ancona (AN).
Altitude: 127 m. – Population: 5000.
Post code: I-60025. – Dialling code: 071.
ⓘ **AA**, Via G. Solari 3;
tel. 97 71 39.

HOTELS. – *Bellevue e Marchigiano*, II, 140 b.; *Giardinetto*, II, 135 b.; *Casa San Gabriele*, III, 106 b.; *Santuario*, III, 88 b.; etc.

The little town of Loreto, situated on a hill near the Adriatic Sea S of Ancona, has been since the 14th c. Italy's second most important place of pilgrimage after Rome.

According to legend the Virgin's house in Nazareth, the Santa Casa, was transported by angels to Trsat near Rijeka in Yugoslavia in 1291, then in 1294 to a

Loreto

"laurel wood" (*lauretium*) at Recanati and in 1295 to its present site. In 1586 Pope Sixtus V gave the town a municipal charter and the right to build walls. Since 1920 the Madonna of Loreto has been the patroness of airmen.

SIGHTS. – In the *Piazza della Madonna*, with a beautiful 17th c. fountain, stands the ***Santuario della Santa Casa**, a Gothic hall-church with a fortress-like exterior begun in 1468 under Pope Paul II and continued in 1479–86 by the Florentine Giuliano da Maiano; the dome dates from 1500. The handsome façade was added in 1583–87 under Pope Sixtus V, a bronze statue of whom (1589) adorns the flight of steps leading to the entrance.

The INTERIOR of the church was altered from 1526 onwards. To the left of the entrance is a beautiful font (1607). – Adjoining the S transept are the two *sacristies*, with celebrated *wall paintings: on the right by Melozzo da Forlì (1438–94) and on the left much restored frescoes by Luca Signorelli and an assistant together with a marble fountain by Benedetto da Maiano. In the choir apse ("Cappella dei Tedeschi") are paintings by Ludwig Seitz (1893–1908).

In the centre of the church, under the dome, is the **Santa Casa**, a simple brick building (4·2 m high, 8·8 m long, 3·9 m wide) surrounded by a high marble *screen designed by Bramante (1510) and adorned with statues and high-reliefs by famous sculptors. – In the N transept is the entrance to the *Treasury*.

Opposite the Santuario in the Piazza della Madonna the *Palazzo Apostolico* (begun 1510) contains pictures, tapestries (from designs by Raphael) and majolica from Urbino.

Lucca

Region: Toscana. – Province: Lucca (LU).
Altitude: 17 m. – Population: 95,000.
Post code: I-55100. – Dialling code: 0583.
(i) **EPT**, Piazza Giudiccioni 2;
tel. 4 69 15.
Information office, Via Vittorio Veneto 40;
tel. 4 69 15.
ACI, Via Catalani 1;
tel. 5 25 26.
TCI, at EPT.

HOTELS. – *Universo*, Piazza Puccini 1, II, 122 b.;
Napoleon, Viale Europa 1, II, 98 b.; *Celide*, Viale G.
Giusti 27, III, 52 b.; *La Luna*, Corte Compagni 12, III,
46 b.; etc. – YOUTH HOSTEL, Via del Brennero, 90 b.

**The provincial capital of Lucca,
notable for its magnificent churches
and medieval fortifications, lies in a
fertile (and in summer very hot)
plain between the Monti Pisani and
the Alpi Apuane. It is the see of an
archbishop.**

The town has long been famous for its silk
factories; other products of economic
importance are woollen goods and olive
oil. Lucca was the home of the sculptor
Matteo Civitali (1436–1501) and the
composer Giacomo Puccini (1858–
1928).

HISTORY. – The ancient *Luca*, which became a
Roman colony in 177 B.C., belonged after the
fall of the Roman Empire to the Ostrogoths, the
Lombards and the Franks in turn. It later became
capital of the marquisate of Tuscia, and subsequently
fell into the hands of the Scaligers and Florence. In

1369 the town purchased its freedom from Charles IV
for 100,000 gold florins, and thereafter it remained
independent until the French invasion in 1799. In
1805 Napoleon gave Lucca together with Massa-
Carrara as a principality to his sister Elisa Baciocchi. In
1815 it passed to the house of Bourbon-Parma as a
duchy, and in 1847 was ceded to Tuscany. – Lucca
played a prominent part in the history of architecture
from the Lombard period onwards; but its early
medieval churches, partly built with ancient material,
were altered and restored in the 12th c. following
Pisan models, reflecting Lucca's rivalry with Pisa.

SIGHTS. – The central features of the
town are the *Piazza Napoleone*, the
largest square in Lucca, laid out under
Elisa Baciocchi, and the *Piazza Puccini*
which adjoins it to the SE. On the W side
of the Piazza Napoleone is the unfinished
Palazzo della Prefettura, the old ducal
palace (begun 1578, continued 1728), in
the S wing of which is the important
Pinacoteca Nazionale (closed Sunday
afternoons and Mondays), among whose
principal treasures are pictures by Fra
Bartolomeo.

A little way E of Piazza Puccini stands the
church of San Giovanni (12th c.), with a
fine relief of the Virgin (1187) above the
doorway. It has ten columns, mostly
ancient work, in the interior, and a
venerable baptistery at the end of the N
transept. – Beyond San Giovanni, in the
Piazza San Martino, is the *Cathedral of
San Martino, founded in the 6th c. and
mainly dating in its present form from the
12th c. (nave remodelled in Gothic style in
14th c.). On the richly decorated façade
(1204), to the right of the principal arch,
is St Martin with the beggar (copy:
the original is inside the church). In the
vestibule are *reliefs, probably early works
by Niccolò Pisano. The cathedral has
pictures and fine sculpture, including
work by Jacopo della Quercia (tomb of
Ilaria del Carretto, 1406) and Matteo
Civitali. The Tempietto, a small octagonal
chapel (by Civitali, 1482–84) in the N
aisle contains an ancient crucifix (8th c.?)
from the Holy Land known as the Volto
Santo, displayed only on certain feast
days in May and September. – Behind the
cathedral is the *Archbishop's Palace*
(Arcivescovado), rebuilt in the 18th c.,
with a fine library. Behind it is the graceful
Gothic *chapel of Santa Maria della Rosa*
(1309).

Abetone

Lucca

11
13
14
Via S. Giorgio
Via Fillungo
15
(i) **Town Hall**
7
8 ╬S. Cristoforo 6
Via
S. Paolino
9
Via S. Croce
Via Elisa
10 ╬S. Giusto
5
**Giardino
Botanico**
Pza.
Napo-
leone
2
3
1
Duomo
4
Mura
Corso
Garibaldi
delle
Baluardo
S. Regolo
Passeggiata
Baluardo
S. Colombano
Viale Giuseppe Giusti
Viale
Baluardo
S. Maria
Carducci
200 m
Glosue
Station
Viareggio
Siena
Autostrada

1 Palazzo della Prefettura	9 San Paolino
2 San Giovanni	10 Palazzo Pretorio
3 Arcivescovado	11 San Frediano
4 Santa Maria della Rosa	12 Anfiteatro
5 Santa Maria Forisportam	13 San Pietro Somaldi
6 Porta San Gervasio	14 San Francesco
7 Palazzo Guinigi	15 Museo Nazionale
8 San Michele in Foro	di Villa Guinigi

From the Piazza Napoleone the busy *Via
Vittorio Veneto* runs N to the Piazza San
Michele, on the site of the ancient forum.
On the right-hand side of this street is the

San Michele, Lucca

Palazzo Pretorio (begun 1492), in Early Renaissance style. On the N side of Piazza San Michele the **church of San Michele** (mid 12th c.) has a high Pisan-style façade and four arcaded galleries (much restored in 1866). – E of Piazza San Michele in Via Fillungo stands the Romanesque *church of San Cristoforo* (11th–12th c.). To the N is the *Chiesa del Salvatore* or *Misericordia*, also 11th–12th c.

Via Fillungo leads N past a number of old towers, belonging to noble families, to the Piazza San Frediano, on the W side of which is the *church of San Frediano, said to have been founded in the 6th c. by an Irish saint, Frigidianus. It was rebuilt in Romanesque style from 1112 onwards. On the façade is a 12th c. mosaic of Christ enthroned with Apostles. The church contains a 12th c. font with fine reliefs by Robertus (unusual inner basin) and a marble altar by Jacopo della Quercia (1422).

A short distance SE of Piazza San Frediano is the *Piazza del Mercato*, originally the arena (80 by 53·5 m) of the Roman **amphitheatre**, on the foundations of which the houses around the square have been built. Two series of 54 arches can still be seen on the NE side. – To the E of the amphitheatre stands the *church of San Pietro Somaldi*, a pillared basilica of the late 12th c. (façade 13th c.). – Farther E near the *church of San Francesco* (1228) is the *Villa Guinigi*, with the **Museo Nazionale** (closed Sunday afternoons and Mondays) containing ancient and medieval material and sculpture.

To the S of the amphitheatre, at Via Guinigi 29, is the *Palazzo Guinigi*, a brick-built Gothic palace (*c.* 1400) with a high tower. Opposite it (No. 20) is another palace of the same name. – A little way SE the *church of Santa Maria Forisportam* (12th c.), contains ancient columns. To the E of the church, at the end of Via Santa Croce, is the old *Porta San Gervasio*, a remnant of the town's second circuit of walls (13th c.), with two massive round towers.

The present *ramparts (4·2 km long), now shaded by fine old trees, were built between 1544 and 1645. There is an attractive walk around the whole circuit ("Passeggio delle Mura Urbane"), affording charming views, particularly on the W and N sides, of the town with its numerous towers and the beautiful surrounding hills.

SURROUNDINGS. – 13 km SW, prettily situated under the W side of the Monti Pisani, is the spa of **San Giuliano Terme** (alt. 10 m; pop. 24,000; hotels: California Park, in Madonna dell'Acqua, II, 141 b.; Terme, III, 36 b.), with radioactive sulphur springs. – 28 km N of Lucca, **Bagni di Lucca** (alt. 150 m; pop. 9000), comprises a number of separate villages, known as early as the 10th c. as the "Baths of Corsena", with springs containing salt and sulphur (37–54 °C – 99–129 °F: season May–September). The principal village is *Villa* (Hotel Roma, IV, 35 b.), once a residence of the dukes of Lucca, with its own thermal spring. – Higher up the hillside, 1 km away, are the villages of *Bagni Caldi* (Hotel Savoia, IV, 35 b.) and *Ponte a Serraglio* (Hotel Bridge, IV, 18 b.).

Lake Maggiore

Regions: Lombardia and Piemonte.
Provinces: Varese and Novara.
Altitude: 194 m.

(i) **AA Pallanza**, Corso Zannitello,
I-28048 Pallanza;
tel. (0323) 4 29 76.
AA Stresa, Piazzale Europa 1,
I-28094 Stresa;
tel. (0323) 3 01 50.

**Lake Maggiore (Lago Maggiore), known to the Romans as Lacus Verbanus, is the second largest of the N Italian lakes, with an area of 212 sq. km (length 60 km, breadth 3–5 km, greatest depth 372 m). Less intricately patterned than Lake Como and without the sheer rock faces of the northern part of Lake Garda, it nevertheless offers scenery of southern splendour which may lack the grandeur of the other lakes but is perhaps even more appealing.

Lake Maggiore – view over Stresa towards the Borromean Islands

The N part of the lake, with the town of Locarno, is in Switzerland, but the greater part of it is in Italy, the E side belonging to Lombardy and the W side to Piedmont. The lake's principal tributaries are the *Ticino* and the *Maggia* to the N and the *Toce* on the W side. The river which flows out of the S end, having carved a passage through massive morainic walls, preserves the name of Ticino. – The northern part of the lake is enclosed by mountains, for the most part wooded, while towards the S the shores slope down to the plain of Lombardy. In clear weather the water in the northern part of the lake is green, in the southern part deep blue.

The climate is mild. From midnight until the morning the *tramontana* blows, usually coming from the N; from midday until the evening the *inverna* blows from the S. The flora of Lake Maggiore, like that of lakes Garda and Como, includes numerous subtropical species: figs, olives and pomegranates flourish in the mild climate, and in August the myrtle blooms. On the Borromean Islands lemons, oranges, cork-oaks, sago-palms and carob-trees grow. The fisheries are very productive.

The most popular tourist areas are around Locarno and on the western arm of the lake between Pallanza and Stresa, where the **Borromean Islands** (Isole Borromee) are the main attraction.

Near the E side of the lake, at **Ispra** (Hotel Europa, II, 82 b.; etc.), is the first Italian atomic research centre, now a Euratom research centre, with an atomic reactor

(1959) and a tower 120 m high belonging to a meteorological station.

There is an attractive drive round the lake on an excellent road which keeps close to its shores.

Another very attractive excursion is a **boat trip** on the lake (services throughout the year). The boats ply between Locarno and Arona (twice daily in summer; also hydrofoil services), calling alternatively at places on the W and E sides; between Cannobio and Stresa (five times daily in summer); and between Verbania and Stresa (half-hourly or hourly). – Car ferry services.

On the W side of Lake Maggiore, beautifully situated near the Borromean Islands, lies **Verbania** (alt. 205 m; pop. 35,000; hotels: Maestoso, I, 187 b., SP, Astor, II, 129 b., Castagnola, II, 112 b., Belvedere, II, 97 b., Metropole, III, 82 b., and San Gottardo, III, 72 b., all in Pallanza; Miralago, II, 78 b., and Intra, III, 60 b., in Intra; etc.), a town formed by the amalgamation of *Pallanza* and *Intra* together with other adjoining villages. It attracts large numbers of visitors with its mild climate and beautiful scenery.

Pallanza lies on both sides of the *Punta della Castagnola* (magnificent *view from the park of the former Eden Palace Hotel). Just offshore, to the W, is the little island of *San Giovanni*. – On the lakeside road is the *Kursaal* with its park (fine views). Beyond this, by the lake, is the *mausoleum of General Cadorna* (1850–1928), commander-in-chief of the Italian army during the First World War. To the N of the mausoleum stands the *parish church of San Leonardo* (16th c., restored). Farther W are the *Palazzo di Città* (Town Hall) and the *landing-stage*, from which there are views of the Borromean Islands (with Isola Madre in the foreground) and Monte Mottarone. – 1·5 km N, at the foot of *Monte Rosso* (693 m), the domed *church of the Madonna di Campagna*, contains frescoes by Luini and the Procaccini. – On a hill 1 km N of the Punta della Castagnola is the park of the *Villa San Remigio* (no admission) and nearby is the little Romanesque *church of San Remigio* (11th c.). Immediately N is the magnificent * *park, laid out after the Second World War, of the **Villa Taranto** (open April–October; good guide, with plan; boat landing-stage), with botanical research laboratories and numerous rare and exotic plants.

NE of Pallanza, between the *Torrente San Bernardino* and the *Torrente San Giovanni*, is the industrial district of **Intra**, with the fine *church of San Vittore*. From here a car ferry plies to Laveno, on the E side of the lake. – From Intra a panoramic road runs 13 km N to the village of **Premeno** (alt. 808 m; hotels: Premeno, III, 98 b.; Moderno, III, 60 b.; etc.), a summer holiday resort much favoured by the people of Milan. – N of Intra rises *Monte Zeda (2157 m: extensive views), which can be climbed in 7 hours.

13 km NE of Intra **Cannero Riviera** (alt. 226 m; hotels: Cannero, III, 56 b.; Milano, III, 32 b.; etc.) is beautifully situated on the shores of the lake amid vineyards, orchards and olive-groves. The climate here is the mildest on the lake, and lemon- and orange-trees can survive the winter in the open. In the rock face under the parish church is the picturesque Chiesa della Grotta, facing E. Beautiful beach. – Farther N, on rocky islets in the lake, are the ruins of the two *Castelli di Cannero*, built by Lodovico Borromeo in 1519 in place of earlier castles which had been held by brigands. – 7 km N of Cannero, on a plateau at the mouth of the wide, cool *Valle Cannobina*, the old town of **Cannobio** (alt. 209 m; hotels: Villa Belvedere, II, 19 b.; Campagna, III, 36 b.; etc.), has picturesque narrow streets, a town hall of 1291 and near the landing-stage the Santuario della Pietà, a Renaissance church in the manner of Bramante (on the high altar "Christ bearing the Cross" by Gaudenzio Ferrari, *c.* 1525).

Also on the W side of Lake Maggiore, S of its western arm, the little town of **Stresa** (alt. 210 m; pop. 5000; hotels: *Grand Hôtel et des Iles Borromées, L, 267 b., SP; Bristol, I, 320 b., SP; Regina Palace, I, 208 b.; La Palma, I, 180 b., SP; Astoria, II, 171 b., SP; Milano au Lac, II, 132 b.; Speranza du Lac, II, 129 b.; Boston, II, 63 b.; Italia e Svizzera, II, 63 b.; Della Torre, II, 61 b.; Stresa e Croce Bianca, III, 92 b.; Moderno, III, 90 b.; etc.) looks on to the Borromean Islands. Stresa is the largest resort on Lake Maggiore after Locarno. Cooler and windier than other places on the lake, it is busiest during the warmer part of the year. The long lakeside road affords beautiful views of the lake and the Borromean Islands.

The life of Stresa centres on its lakeside promenade (fine views), on which are the *parish church* and most of the large hotels. – 1 km S, above the landing-place, is the *Collegio Rosmini* (alt. 267 m), an educational institution run by the Rosminians, a charitable order

founded by the priest and philosopher Antonio Rosmini (1797–1855), whose tomb is in the church. – 0·5 km farther on is the beautiful *park of the *Villa Pallavicino* (closed in winter), with luxuriant vegetation and an interesting menagerie.

From Stresa a toll road, the Via Borromea (21 or 30 km: also cableway), runs up via **Gignese** (alt. 707 m; Hotel Motta, IV, 16 b.; etc.), with an unusual Umbrella Museum, to the summit of *Monte Mottarone (1491 m), from which the view embraces the chain of the Alps from Monte Viso to Ortles, with Monte Rosa to the W (particularly fine in the morning). – Half way up, at the hamlet of *Alpino* (776 m), a road branches off to the *Giardino Alpinia* (807 m), 0·5 km N, with some 2000 species of plants (magnificent views).

From Stresa there is a very attractive boat trip to the * *Borromean Islands**. – The boat calls first at *Isola Bella (Hotel Elvezia, IV, 30 b.; etc.). The island owes its present appearance to Count Vitaliano Borromeo, who between 1650 and 1671 transformed what had been a barren rock, with a parish church and a few houses, by building up terraces of fertile soil brought from the mainland and creating a splendid summer residence. The *Palace*, left unfinished, contains magnificent state apartments, numerous pictures (including some good Lombard works of the 16th and 17th c.) and a gallery of 17th c. Flemish tapestries. The Italian-style *garden*, from which there are beautiful views, rises in ten terraces to a height of 32 m, and is covered with luxuriant southern vegetation – lemon- and orange-trees, cherry-laurels, cedars, magnolias, cork-oaks, sago-palms, carob-trees, camellias, oleanders, etc. – 0·5 km NW of Isola Bella is the **Isola dei Pescatori** or *Isola Superiore* (Hotel Verbano, II, 29 b.; etc.), with a picturesque fishing village. –

Waterfall in the upper Toce valley

Between the Isola dei Pescatori and Pallanza lies *Isola Madre, which, like Isola Bella, belongs to the Borromeo family. It has beautiful English-style grounds surpassing even Isola Bella in the variety and luxuriance of their vegetation. On the highest point is an uninhabited palace (*view).

4 km NW of Stresa is **Baveno** (alt. 210 m; hotels: Splendid, I, 172 b., SP; Simplon, II, 154 b., SP; Beau Rivage, II, 147 b.; Lido Palace, II, 138 b.; Ankara Touring, II, 123 b.; Alpi, II, 68 b.; etc.), a popular resort, with a fine parish church. From the lakeside promenade there is a picturesque though restricted view of the lake, with the *Borromean Islands. At the S end of the town stands the large Villa Branca, which belongs to the manufacturer of the well-known vermouth Fernet Branca (produced in Milan); beautiful park (no admission).

13 km S of Stresa is **Meina** (alt. 214 m; hotels: Victoria, II, 118 b.; Villa Paradiso, III, 78 b.; etc.), with the splendid Villa Farragiana (museum). An eminence S of the village is crowned by the "Carlone", a 23 m high statue of *St Charles Borromeo* (1538–84), Cardinal-Archbishop of Milan, who played an important part in the moral revival of Catholicism. – On the E side of the lake, opposite the statue, is *Angera*, with an old Visconti castle (view).

From Stresa or Verbania there is an attractive drive (42 or 45 km NW) to **Domodossola** (alt. 278 m; pop. 20,000; hotels: Europa, in Borgata Siberia, II, 38 b.; Milano Schweizerhof, III, 63 b.; Piccolo, III, 53 b.; etc.), a little hill town with a pretty market-place. The road skirts the *Lago di Mergozzo*, a former arm of Lake Maggiore which has been cut off by soil deposited by the River Toce, and then continues up the valley of the Toce. – Half way to Domodossola a road goes off on the left, passes through *Piedimulera* and continues up the *Anzasca* valley (gold-mines), the upper part of which has been occupied since the 13th c. by German-speaking settlers from the Valais, to **Macugnaga** (alt. 1195 m; hotels: Alpi, IV, 18 b., in the district of Borca; Edelweiss, III, 33 b., and Lagger, III, 29 b., in Pecetto; Monte Moro, III, 92 b., and Zumstein, III, 72 b., in Staffa; etc.), a holiday resort in a magnificent *situation below the E face of Monte Rosa.

Mantua/Mántova

Region: Lombardia. – Province: Mantova (MN).
Altitude: 19 m. – Population: 67,000.
Post code: I-46100. – Dialling code: 0376.
ⓘ **EPT**, Piazza Andrea Mantegna 6;
　　tel. 2 16 01.
　　ACI, Piazza 80° Fanteria 13;
　　tel. 2 56 91.

HOTELS. – *Rechigi*, I, 89 b., SP; *San Lorenzo*, I, 64 b.; *Italia*, II, 45 b.; *Dante*, II, 66 b.; *Apollo*, II, 61 b.; *Mantegna*, II, 54 b.; *Due Guerrieri*, III, 42 b.; etc. – YOUTH HOSTEL, Strada Legnaghese, 70 b.

The provincial capital of Mantua, in medieval times the seat of the Gonzaga family, lies between Lake Garda and the River Po on the lower course of the Mincino, which here forms a marshy lake divided into three parts (Lago Superiore, Lago di Mezzo and Lago Inferiore) by medieval embankments. The town, still surrounded by a ring of walls and bastions, has many fine old buildings, particularly of the 15th and 16th c.

HISTORY and ART. – Originally founded by the *Etruscans*, the town was noted in Roman times only as the home of the poet *Virgil* (70–19 B.C.). It rose to some importance in the 12th and 13th c. under the Hohenstaufen Emperors. – From 1328 the town was ruled by the Guelf house of **Gonzaga**, who acquired the title of marquis in 1433 and of duke in 1530 and made Mantua one of the most refined and cultivated of princely capitals, a great centre of art and learning. Marquis Lodovico II (1444–78) summoned the Florentine architect *Leon Battista Alberti* to Mantua, and in 1463 enrolled *Andrea Mantegna*, leader of the Padua school of painters, in his service; the beautiful and accomplished *Isabella d'Este* (1474–1539), wife of Giovanni Francesco III, carried on a lively correspondence with the great men of the day; and Raphael's greatest pupil, *Giulio Romano* (1492–1546), came to Mantua in 1524 and was active as an architect and painter. – After the Gonzaga line died out (1708) the town passed to Austria, which fortified it (as one corner of the defensive "quadrilateral" of Peschiera-Verona-Legnago-Mantua) and held it until 1866, with a brief interlude of French rule during the Napoleonic period. The Austrian patriot Andreas Hofer was shot in Mantua in 1810 on Napoleon's orders (memorial tablet on Citadel; permanent guard of honour).

SIGHTS. – In *Piazza Mantegna*, in the centre of the town, stands the *church of Sant'Andrea, a masterpiece of Early Renaissance architecture (by Leon Battista Alberti, 1472–94; transept and choir 1600, dome 1782). The white marble façade, in the style of a classical temple, has beside it the earlier Gothic tower of red brick (1414). The interior, with its massive barrel vault, is of imposing effect. In the first chapel on the left is the tomb of Andrea Mantegna, with a bronze bust; in the last chapel on the right are frescoes by Giulio Romano.

From Piazza Mantegna the arcaded *Corso Umberto I*, the town's principal shopping and business street, leads W to Piazza Cavallotti, from which the Corso della Libertà, a wide street built over an old canal, runs SE to Piazza Martiri di Belfiore.

Adjoining Piazza Mantegna on the E in the Piazza delle Erbe, are the *Torre dell'Orologio* (Clock-Tower), the *Palazzo della Ragione* (13th c., with much later alteration) and the little Romanesque

Castello San Giorgio, Mantua

church of San Lorenzo (12th c.), on a circular plan. – To the N, in Piazza Sordello (on left), are two crenellated Gothic palaces, the Palazzo Cadenazzi (12th–13th c.), with the 55 m high Torre della Gabbia, and the Palazzo Castiglioni (13th c.). Adjoining the Palazzo Castiglioni is the Baroque Bishop's Palace (18th c.). – On the NE side of Piazza Sordello stands the Cathedral of Santi Pietro e Paolo, originally built in Romanesque style as the burial church of the marquises of Canossa and the Gonzaga family, remodelled in Gothic style between 1393 and 1401 and reconstructed internally to the design of Giulio Romano after a fire in 1545; fine Baroque façade (1756). Behind the church rises a Romanesque campanile.

Opposite the cathedral the massive *Palazzo Ducale or Reggia (closed Mondays), the sumptuous residence of the Gonzagas and one of the most splendid palaces in Italy, now houses a number of important museums and collections – the Municipal Collection of Antiquities (Greek and Roman sculpture); the Museo Medievale e Moderno (mainly medieval sculpture); and the Galleria, a valuable collection of pictures displayed in a series of rooms richly decorated with frescoes and ceiling paintings. Outstanding among these rooms are the Appartamento degli Arazzi, with nine *tapestries made in Brussels about 1528 (scenes from the life of SS. Peter and Paul) after cartoons by Raphael which are now in the Victoria and Albert Museum in London; the Gallery of Mirrors (Galleria degli Specchi); the Appartamento del Paradiso, four rooms occupied by Isabella d'Este, have a beautiful view of the lakes; and, on the ground floor, the Gabinetti Isabelliani, with intarsia ceilings. – At the NE corner

of the Palazzo Ducale is the palace church, Santa Barbara, in High Renaissance style (1565). – Immediately N is the older castle, the massive Castello San Giorgio (1395–1406). On the first floor the Camera degli Sposi contains magnificent *frescoes by Mantegna (1474), depicting the brilliant life of the court of Lodovico III and his wife Barbara of Hohenzollern. On the ceiling are trompe-l'œil paintings, the earliest of their kind.

NW of Piazza Sordello is the Piazza Virgiliana, with a monument to Virgil (1927). – In the S of the town, at Via Carlo Poma 11, is the Palazzo di Giustizia (late 16th c.), with colossal hermae (heads of the god Hermes). – S of the Palazzo di Giustizia the church of San Sebastiano was the first Renaissance church built on a Greek cross plan (1460–1529); the crypt serves as a war memorial chapel. – Farther S still, beyond the Porta Pusterla, is the single-storey *Palazzo del Té (closed on Mondays), built 1525–35 by Giulio Romano as a country house for the Gonzagas and decorated with frescoes and stucco work under his direction.

SURROUNDINGS. – 3 km W on the Cremona road, lying off the road on the right, on the Lago Superiore, the church of Santa Maria degli Angeli (1429) is in Lombard Gothic style, with a beautiful altarpiece by Mantegna. – 4 km farther on, near the W end of the Lago Superiore, stands the Gothic pilgrimage church of Santa Maria delle Grazie (1399). The over-furnished interior contains 44 figures in wood and wax of notable visitors to the shrine (including Charles V) and a fine altarpiece ("St Sebastian") by F. Bonsignori.

20 km SE of Mantua is the little town of San Benedetto Po (alt. 18 m; pop. 12,000), with a former Benedictine monastery founded in 984 by Marquis Tedaldo of Canossa and dissolved in 1789. The *church, originally built in Gothic style in 1246, was remodelled by Giulio Romano (1539 onwards) as a splendid Renaissance building with an octagonal dome over the crossing and a fine portico.

Marches/Marche

ⓘ **EPT Ancona**, Via Marcello Marini 14, I-60100 Ancona (AN);
tel. (071) 2 36 39.
EPT Ascoli Piceno, Corso Mazzini 229, I-63100 Ascoli Piceno (AP);
tel. (0736) 5 11 15.
EPT Macerata, Piazza della Libertà 12, I-62100 Macerata (MC);
tel. (0733) 4 58 07.
EPT Pesaro-Urbino, Via Mazzolari 4, I-61100 Pesaro (PS);
tel. (0721) 3 14 33.

The region of Marche (the Marches) in Central Italy, with the four provinces of Ancona, Ascoli Piceno, Macerata and Pesaro-Urbino and its capital at Ancona, covers an area of 9692 sq. km of mountainous country, consisting partly of inhospitable terrain (Monte Vettore, 2476 m) but mostly of very fertile uplands, which extends between the rivers Foglia and Tronto down the eastern slopes of the Appennino Umbro-Marchigiano to the Adriatic coast.

FEATURES OF INTEREST. – Apart from the towns along the Adriatic coast and Ascoli Piceno it is well worth visiting the provincial capital of **Macerata** (alt. 311 m; pop. 28,000; hotels: Della Piaggia, II, 41 b.; Centrale, II, 32 b.; Motel Agip, II, 102 b.; etc.), which occupies a commanding situation on high ground between the rivers Chiento and Potenza. The central feature of the town is the Piazza della Libertà, in which are the Palazzo Communale (statues of toga-clad figures and inscriptions from Helvia Ricina in courtyard), the Prefecture (in a 16th c. Gonzaga palace), the beautiful Loggia dei Mercanti (16th c.) and the Theatre. From the Piazza della Libertà the Corso della Repubblica leads to the Piazza Vittorio Véneto, with the Biblioteca Comunale, which contains the municipal collection of pictures (including works by the local painter Paganini, Carlo Crivelli, Allegretto Nuzi da Fabriano and Lanfranco). Also of interest are the cathedral and the Sferisterio (1829), a stadium for ball games. There is a small university.

Another town worth a brief visit is **Fermo** (alt. 319 m; pop. 35,000; hotels: Astoria, II, 114 b.; Casina delle Rose, II, 42 b.; etc.), the see of an archbishop, with churches containing a number of fine pictures. At Porta San Francesco are remains of the town's ancient cyclopean walls. In the Piazza del Popolo, reached by steep lanes running up from the Porta San Francesco, are the Town Hall and the Palazzo degli Studi (library, museum, picture gallery). On the commanding Rocca is the 13th c. cathedral, in the porch of which is the Gothic tomb of Giovanni Visconti (d. 1366) by Tura da Imola. Nearby are remains of the ancient theatre. Under the church of San Domenico, below the Piazza del Popolo, is an ancient cistern (1st c. A.D.).

In the N of the region, 30 km SW of Ancona, is **Iesi** (alt. 96 m; pop. 35,000; hotels: Mariani, III, 98 b.; Motel dei Nani, III, 76 b.; etc.), birthplace of the German Emperor Frederick II of Hohenstaufen (1194–1250) and Giovanni Battista Pergolesi (1710–36), composer of the "Stabat Mater". The main features of interest in the town, which is still surrounded by picturesque and well-preserved medieval walls, are the handsome Palazzo della Signoria, in Early Renaissance style (1487–1503: fine pillared courtyard), and the Pinacoteca, which contains pictures by Lorenzo Lotto.

Marsala

Region: Sicilia. – Province: Trapani (TP).
Altitude: 12 m. – Population: 85,000.
Post code: I-91025. – Dialling code: 0923.

HOTELS. – *Stella d'Italia*, II, 70 b.; *Motel Agip*, II, 62 b. – CAMPING SITE.

The port and commercial town of Marsala, situated at the western tip of Sicily, is best known for its rich golden-yellow dessert wine.

The principal wine-making establishments (*stabilimenti* or *bagli*: visitors admitted) lie along the shore to the S of the town. The *Woodhouse* establishment near the station was named after its English founder, who introduced wine-making to Marsala about 1773. 0·5 km farther S is *Florio*, the town's most famous

On the Costa di Conero, Marche

establishment, and another 0·5 km beyond this *Ingham-Whitaker*. Other leading firms are *Rallo* and *Pellegrino*.

SIGHTS. – The hub of the town's traffic is the *Piazza della Repubblica*, with the beautiful 18th c. *Old Town Hall*, built in the form of a loggia, and the **Cathedral**, dedicated to St Thomas of Canterbury, which contains fine sculpture by Antonello Gagini and eight magnificent 16th c. Flemish tapestries, displayed only on certain feast days.

From the Piazza della Repubblica the town's main street, *Via XI Maggio*, runs NW past the *monastery* and *church of San Pietro* (16th c.) to the *Porta Nuova*. On a house on the left is a plaque commemorating a visit in 1862 by Garibaldi, whose victorious campaign against the Bourbons had begun two years earlier, on 11 May 1860, with his landing in Marsala harbour. Beyond the Porta Nuova, to the right, are the *Villa Cavallotti gardens*, at the N end of which is a belvedere affording wide views.

Below the belvedere and along the Viale Vittorio Veneto, which continues the line of Via XI Maggio, are remains of the ancient *Lilybaeum*, including fragments of the town walls. Off the road to the right are the ruins of the **Insula Romana**, living quarters of the 3rd c. A.D., with a fine animal mosaic in the associated *baths*. From the end of the avenue there is a beautiful view of the sea and the coast; and from **Capo Boeo** or Capo *Lilibeo*, a little way SW, there are more extensive views NE over the old harbour to Monte Erice and NW of the Isole Égadi. – Half way between the cape and the Porta Nuova, off the road to the right, is the *church of San Giovanni Battista*, from which steps lead down to the "Grotta della Sibilla" (Roman mosaic).

Merano

Region: Trentino – Alto Adige.
Province: Bolzano (BZ).
Altitude: 324 m. – Population: 35,000.
Post code: I-39012. – Dialling code: 0473.

(i) **AA di Soggiorno e Cura**, Corso Libertà 45;
   tel. 2 63 93–4.
   CIT, Corso Libertà 1–3;
   tel. 2 24 60.

HOTELS. – *Bristol*, I, 270 b.; SP; *Palace*, I, 166 b., SP (indoor and outdoor), thermal baths; *Meranerhof*, I, 118 b., SP; *Riz-Stefanie*, I, 105 b., SP;

Schloss Rundegg, Via Scena 2, I, 60 b., SP, sauna, sunbathing lawn; *Eurotel Astoria* (no rest.), Via Winkel 21, I, 162 b., SP; *Emma*, I, 250 b., SP; *Bellevue*, II, 113 b.; *Eurotel* (no rest.), Via Garibaldi 5, II, 226 b.; *Regina*, II, 129 b.; *Castel Labers* (no rest.), II, 55 b., SP; *Esplanade* (no rest.), III, 190 b.; *Duomo Raffl*, III, 100 b.; *Siegler im Turm*, III, 120 b., SP; *Posta-Maiserhof*, III, 114 b.; *Einsiedler*, IV, 26 b. – Quiet accommodation available in the surrounding hill villages. – CAMPING SITE at racecourse.

RESTAURANTS. – In hotels; also *Andrea*, Via Galilei 8; *Meraner Weinkost*, Corso della Libertà 37; *Wienerwald-Rafflkeller*, Piazza del Duomo 23; *Cacciatora*, Via Petrarca 31; *Birreria Forst*, Corso della Libertà 90; *Kavalier* (diet), Via Carducci 29; *Sigmund*, Piazza della Rena 3; *Merano*, Piazza del Duomo 4; *Verona*, Via dei Portici 119; *Terlaner Weinstube*, Via dei Portici 231; *Golden Rose*, Via dei Portici 272; *Hairainer Weinstube*, Via dei Portici 102.

DANCING. – *Burgtaverne*, Via dei Portici 242; *Ca' de' Bezzi*, Via dei Portici 84; *Sphinx*, Via delle Corse 6.

SPORT and RECREATION. – Salvar thermal baths, Lido open-air pool (near station), sauna, tennis courts, bowling alleys, mini-golf, *bocce*, children's playground, coach-rides, riding school, canoeing on River Passirio, climbing school.

WINTER SPORTS at *Merano 2000*, on the *Punta Cervina* and on the Giogo di San Vigilio. Ice rink near Merano station.

Canoe race on the Passirio

EVENTS. – Theatre, concerts, five cinemas; racecourse in Maia Bassa (flat racing and steeplechasing, particularly at Easter, August and end of September; Merano Grand Prix and international riding tournament; "Countrymen's Gallop" on Haflinger horses in spring and autumn; *international canoe race* on the Passirio in June; *torchlight procession* to the village of Tirolo in mid September; *vintage festival* and wine-tasting excursions in autumn, with processions of decorated floats and traditional costumes; cultural and sporting events; congresses.

The old town of *Merano (in German Meran) in the largely German-speaking Alto Adige (Südtirol) is the largest health resort on the S side of the Eastern Alps, with its main

season in spring and autumn for the grape cure and with radioactive thermal springs recommended for the treatment of rheumatism. It is also a popular congress centre. It is magnificently situated amid luxuriant orchards and vineyards at the outflow of the River Passirio into the broad valley of the Adige which emerges from the Val Venosta; the town is surrounded by mountains with many old castles.

HISTORY. – Merano came into the hands of the counts of Tirol in 1233, and in 1310, together with the Passirio and Ultimo valleys, was formed into a separate burgraviate. From 1317 to 1420 it was capital of Tirol. – From the middle of the 19th c., thanks to its sheltered situation under the S side of Monte Benedetto and the low humidity of the air, Merano developed into a popular health resort.

SIGHTS. – At the SW corner of the old town, near the right bank of the Passirio, is the *Piazza del Teatro*, Merano's busiest square, with the **Municipal Theatre** (by Martin Dülfer, 1899–1900). – From here the *Corso della Libertà* runs W to the *station* and E, past the Kursaal, to the Piazza della Rena. The busy Via delle Corso, which bounds the old town on the W, runs N from the Piazza del Teatro to the Piazza del Grano and beyond this the *Porta Venosta*. – From the Piazza del Grano the old-world **Via dei Portici** (Laubengasse), a busy shopping street, runs E through the old town, lined with arcades (the Portici di sinistra or Berglauben to the left and the Portici di destra or Wasserlauben to the right). Half way along the Portici di sinistra is the *Town Hall* (1928–32), behind which stands the *Castello Principesco* (*c.* 1450), still with its original furnishings (open to visitors). A little way NW of the castle, at Via Galilei 5, is the rich *Municipal Museum* (prehistoric material, local history, medieval sculpture, modern pictures: closed Saturday afternoons and Sundays). – At the E end of the Via dei Portici is the *Piazza del Duomo*, with the Gothic *parish church of San Nicolò* (14th–15th c.), whose characteristic campanile dominates the town. – From here the old *Porta Bolzano* leads into the Piazza della Rena.

Along the broad embankment on the right bank of the Passirio runs the **Passeggiata Lungo Passirio**, in which is the **Kursaal** (1907). Farther W is the Protestant *Church of Christ* (1885). The Passeggiata Lungo Passirio is continued eastward by the sheltered *Passeggiata d'Inverno*.

On the left bank of the Passirio the district of MAIA BASSA (Untermais) is reached from the Piazza della Rena by way of the *Ponte Nazionale*. Immediately beyond the bridge is the late Gothic *church of the Santo Spirito* (15th c.). A little way W are the **Salvar Baths** (1971), with an indoor bath (radioactive water, 30–33 °C – 86–91 °F), an outdoor pool, sauna facilities, a treatment centre, a restaurant and a *Congress Centre*. – From the Santo Spirito church Via Cavour climbs E to the select villa suburb of MAIA ALTA (obermais), in which are many old aristocratic residences such as *Castello di Nova* (Trautmannsdort), *Castello Rametz*, *Castello Labers* (hotels), *Castello Rundegg* (hotel), *Castello Planta* (pensione) and *Castello Gaiano* (Schloss Goyen).

From the Ponte Nazionale the *Passeggiata d'Estate* follows the left bank of the Passirio and is linked by a bridge with the Passeggiata d'Inverno on the right bank. The two promenades run upstream to the *Ponte Romano* (1616), from which the *Passeggiata Gilf* continues along the right bank to the gorge under Castello San Zeno. – From the Ponte Romano and the Passeggiata Gilf we can continue on the famous [*]**Passeggiata Tappeiner**, a beautiful high-level promenade which begins at the medieval *Torre della Polvere* and runs for 4 km at a height of some 150 m above Merano (magnificent views, particularly from the Torre della Polvere) along the slopes of **Monte Benedetto** (Küchelberg, 531 m; Panorama café-restaurant). There is a chair-lift up the hill from near the Castello Principesco, and it makes an attractive trip to take the lift up and walk down. From Monte Benedetto there is a footpath ($\frac{1}{2}$ hour) to the village of Tirolo.

SURROUNDINGS. – From the *Porta Passiria* a good road (4 km) runs NE alongside the Passeggiata Gilf and past *Castello San Zeno* (12th and 13th c.: private property), and then turns NW up the slopes of Monte Benedetto to the village of *Tirolo* (alt. 596 m: cableway up La Mutta, 1350 m). – From here it is a 25 minutes' walk, passing above Castel Fontana and through a narrow gorge 52 m long, to the 12th c. [*]**Castel Tirolo** (Schloss Tirol, alt. 639 m), the residence in the 12th and 13th c. of the counts of Tirol (who died out in 1253), which has given its name to the whole region of Tirol. The castle is now the property of the regional authorities. – 0·5 km W of Castel Tirolo (reached by way of the Val Venosta road and Via Laurino, then a narrow access road: 5 km) is *Castello Torre* (Schloss Thurnstein, alt. 551 m: good wine restaurant with beautiful view). Lower down is *Castello Fontana* (Brunnenburg), which was restored in 1904. – From *Plars di Mezzo* (Mittelplars), 5 km W of the town centre, there is a chair-lift to *Velloi* (908 m: inn), and from there a basket-lift to the *Leiter-Alm* (1528 m). – On the opposite side of the valley there is a chair-lift from *Foresta* up *Monte San Giuseppe*.

3·5 km N of Maia Alta, above the village of *Scena* (alt. 587 m), at the mouth of the Passirio valley, the *Castello di Scena (Schloss Schenna, 14th–16th c.: alt. 596 m) commands magnificent views. The castle (admission charge) contains a collection of arms and armour, Renaissance furniture, portraits of members of princely families and Andreas Hofer's cradle. – 2 km NE of Scena is a cableway up Monte Scena (*Taser*, 1460 m: inn).

The *cableway from Maia Alta to Avelengo*, SE of Merano (15 minutes: no road), is the starting point of a very rewarding excursion. From the upper station (1235 m), below the conspicuous *chapel of Santa Caterina* (1246 m), a path to the left leads in 5–10 minutes to the Belvedere and Miramonti hotels, from which a road climbs 3 km to the little village of **Avelengo** (Hafling, 1298 m), famous for the Haflinger or Avelignese horses which are bred here. – NE of Avelengo, now easily accessible by various cableways and lifts, is the extensive skiing area of **Merano 2000**. From the outlying district of *Falzében* (alt. 1610 m), to the NE, reached by a road (6 km, dusty: bus service) from Avelengo or the upper station of the cableway, a chair-lift (lower station at Rosa Alpina inn) runs up to the *Malga Pivigna* (Pifinger Köpfl, 1905 m), which can also be reached by a cableway from the *Val di Nova* (Naiftal: lower station 4 km E of Merano). From here there is a cableway to *Sant'Osvaldo* (Kirchsteiger Alm, 1938 m), from which there are chair-lifts NE to the *Kesselwand-Joch* (2265 m: ski-lift in winter) and SE to *Monte Catino* (Mittager, 2234 m).

From Merano to the Giogo di San Vigilio (8 km by road, then cableway). – The road runs W from Maia Bassa past the sports ground, crosses the Adige and continues S along the W side of the broad Adige valley. On the hillside to the right is the prettily situated village of **Marlengo** (Marling, alt. 370 m), from which the *Waalweg (good views), a footpath following the line of an irrigation canal half way up the slope, runs N to Tel (Töll) or S below *Castello Monteleone* (open Sat.–Thurs.) to Lana di Sopra. – 8 km: *Lana di Sopra* (Oberlana), the most northerly part of the large village of **Lana** (pop. 7000), at the mouth of the **Val d'Último** (Ultental), which attracts visitors who want a quiet holiday either in summer or in winter (reservoirs; facilities for winter sports). – From Lana di Sopra a *cableway runs up in 7 minutes to the Hotel Monte San Vigilio (Vigiljoch, 1486 m), from which there are magnificent *views of the Adige valley and the Dolomites. – From the upper station of the cableway there are two possibilities – either by chair-lift (15 minutes) to the *Dosso dei Lárici* (Larchbühel, 1824 m: restaurant), 10 minutes NE of the Albergo al Giogo; or on an easy winding footpath (1 hour) which runs close to the Albergo Gampl before reaching the Albergo al Giogo. From the Albergo al Giogo it is only a few minutes' climb to the old chapel of San Vigilio on the *Giogo di San Vigilio* (Vigiljoch, 1795 m), from which there are magnificent views of the Val Venosta, the Ötztal Alps and the Texel group.

2 km S of Lana di Sopra by way of *Lana di Mezzo* is *Lana di Sotto*, the parish church of which has a richly gilded Gothic *altar of carved wood, the largest in Tirol, by the Merano sculptor Hans Schnatterpeck (1503–11) (conducted visits from 10 onwards). The Romanesque church of Santa Margherita is also of interest.

From Lana di Sopra a good *road (S.S. 238, 31 km), affording far-ranging views, ascends the side of the valley, passing above the *Castello Leone* (Leonburg), with a view ahead of the chapel of San Cristoforo on its hill and beyond it Monte Macaion (Gantkofel); then on to the village of *Tésimo* (Tisens, 631 m). From here a rewarding detour (1·5 km) can be made to *Prissiano* (617 m) and from there on foot (40 minutes) to the hamlet of *Grissiano* (922 m), with the chapel of San Giácomo, which contains 13th c. *frescoes (earliest representation of the Dolomite peaks). – Beyond Tésimo the road continues past the little spa of *Caprile* (Bad Gfrill, 1183 m) and through a tunnel to the **Passo delle Palade** (Gampenjoch, 1520 m: inn). – Then on past the villages, still predominantly German-speaking, of *Senale* (1342 m) and *San Felice* (1255 m) in the Val di Non, lying below the road, through a tunnel and down to **Fondo** (987 m).

Messina

Region: Sicilia. – Province: Messina (ME).
Altitude: 5 m. – Population: 250,000.
Post code: I-98100. – Dialling code: 090.
(i) **AAS**, Via G. Bruno 121;
tel. 3 64 94.
EPT, Via Calabria;
tel. 77 53 56.
Information office in station;
tel. 77 53 35.
ACI, Via L. Manara 125;
tel. 3 30 31.

HOTELS. – *Riviera Grand*, Via della Libertà, Isolato 516, I, 265 b.; *Jolly Hotel dello Stretto*, Via Garibaldi 126, I, 150 b.; *Royal*, Via Tommaso Cannizzaro, II, 166 b.; *Venezia*, Piazza Cairoli 4, II, 136 b.; *Excelsior*, Via Maddalena 32, LL, 71 b.; *Monza*, Viale San Martino 63, III, 93 b.; *Commercio*, Via I Settembre 73, III, 90 b.; etc. – *Europa*, in Pistunina, 6 km S, II, 186 b.

EVENTS. – *Fiera di Messina* (industrial, agricultural and craft fair), August.

The active port of Messina, a university town and the see of an archbishop, lies near the NE tip of Sicily on the busy Strait of Messina (the bridging of which is planned), with its western districts extending picturesquely along the foothills of the Monti Peloritani.

After the great earthquake in 1908 which killed some 60,000 people – half the population – and destroyed 91% of its houses Messina was rebuilt with wide streets intersecting at right angles, and

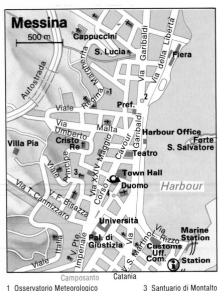

1 Osservatorio Meteorologico   3 Santuario di Montalto
2 Fontana di Nettuno   4 Fontana di Orione

Piazza del Duomo, the centre of the old town, with the richly decorated *Orion Fountain* (1547–51) by Angelo Montorsoli, a pupil of Michelangelo. On the E side of the square, dominating the town, is the **Cathedral**, originally built by Roger II in the 12th c., destroyed in 1908 and rebuilt in its original form in 1919–29, incorporating architectural fragments from the ruins, and again rebuilt after being damaged by fire in 1943. The interior is 93 m long. In the apse is a beautiful mosaic, a reproduction of the 13th c. original which was destroyed in 1943. Adjoining the church rises the 50 m high *campanile* (1933), on the main front of which is an elaborate astronomical clock, with seven tiers and numerous moving figures. The lion, above, roars at 12 noon; the cock, below, crows. The clock was the work of the Strasbourg clock-maker Ungerer.

A short distance SE of the cathedral, in Corso Garibaldi, a beautiful Norman church, the **Santissima Annunziata dei Catalani** (12th c.; restored) is to be found. Beside the church is a bronze *statue of Don John of Austria*, hero of the battle of Lepanto (1571), by Andrea Calamech (1572).

NW of the cathedral is the circular **Piazza Antonello**, with the *Palazzo della Provincia*, the *Town Hall* and the *Head Post Office*. – From here Corso Cavour runs N, passing the *Teatro Vittorio Emanuele*, to the **Villa Mazzini** public gardens on the N side of which stands the Prefecture. W of the gardens is the *Franciscan church* (1254; rebuilt).

From the NE corner of the gardens the Viale della Libertà runs N past the buildings of the Fiera di Messina and along the seafront (bathing stations) to the **Museo Nazionale** (closed Sunday afternoons and Mondays), which contains material salvaged from the Municipal Museum after the 1908 earthquake, together with sculpture and pictures from the hundred or so churches which were also devastated at the same time. A particularly notable item is a *polyptych by Antonello da Messina (1479), the central panel of which depicts a charming Madonna and Child.

now presents the aspect of an entirely modern city.

HISTORY. – Messina was founded by Greek settlers about 730 B.C. on the site of an earlier Siculan settlement and named *Zankle* ("sickle") after the shape of the harbour. It was renamed *Messana* about 493 B.C., when it was occupied by Greek refugees from Samos and Miletus. – It was destroyed by the Carthaginians in 396 B.C. and subsequently rebuilt, and became a Roman town in 264 B.C. It was captured by the Saracens in A.D. 843 and by the Normans in 1061. Under the Normans the town enjoyed a long period of prosperity, which continued into the 17th c. under Spanish rule. – Thereafter Messina suffered a rapid decline, due partly to internal conflicts but mainly to the town's bitter rivalry with Palermo, the process being hastened by a plague in 1740 and severe earthquakes, particularly in 1783. Its subsequent recovery was promoted by its favourable situation on one of the most important traffic routes in the Mediterranèan.

SIGHTS. – From the *Marine Station* on the S side of the **Harbour** it is a short distance W to the N end of the town's main street, Viale San Martino, which cuts through the southern part of the city. In 400 m it crosses the tree-shaded **Piazza Cairoli**, Messina's busiest traffic intersection, and in another 1·5 km joins the spacious Piazza Dante, on the W side of which is the **Camposanto** (or *Cimitero*), one of Italy's most beautiful cemeteries. On top of the hill is an Ionic colonnade, the Pantheon of the town's leading citizens, from which there are fine *views of the city and the straits.

From Piazza Cairoli the broad Corso Garibaldi runs N. 1·5 km along this street Via I Settembre leads left into the large

SURROUNDINGS. – There is a pleasant drive round Messina on the **Via della Circonvallazione**, which, under various names, describes a circuit above the W side of the town, passing the *Santuario di Montalto*, a pilgrimage centre, and the modern *church of Cristo Re.*

There is also a very attractive trip (57 km) along the coast road, which runs NE, between villas and gardens (views), passes two salt-water lagoons, the *Pantano Grande* and *Pantano Piccolo* (also known as the *Laghi di Ganzirri*), and comes to the village of **Torre di Faro**, on the *Punta del Faro*, Sicily's north-eastern tip (fine *view from the lighthouse). – From Torre di Faro the coast road continues round the most northerly cape in Sicily; then the return to Messina is over the *Colle San Rizzo* (465 m).

Milan/Milano

Region: Lombardia. – Province: Milano (MI).
Altitude: 122 m. – Population: 1,700,000.
Post code: I-20100. – Dialling code: 02.
ⓘ **EPT**, Via Marconi 1;
tel. 80 88 13.
Information offices in Central Station (tel. 20 60 30) and in Galleria Vittorio Emanuele (tel. 87 05 45).
ACI, Corso Venezia 43;
tel. 77 45.
TCI, Corso Italia 10;
tel. 80 87 51.
Viaggi Ferrovie Nord Milano, Piazzale Cadorna 14;
tel. 89 63 31.
S.E.L.I., Piazza Liberty 4;
tel. 79 00 02.
Galassia Viaggi, Via Taramelli 20;
tel. 68 87 010.
Viaggi Duse, Piazza Firenze 14;
tel. 32 38 41.

HOTELS. – *Principe e Savoia*, Piazza della Repubblica 17, L, 494 b.; *Milano Hilton*, Via Galvani 12, L, 461 b.; *Excelsior Gallia*, Piazza Duca d'Aosta, L, 427 b.; *Palace*, Piazza della Repubblica 20, L, 329 b.; *Grand Hôtel et de Milan*, Via Manzoni 29, L, 133 b.; *Aerhotel Executive*, Via Don Luigi Sturzo 45, I, 840 b.; *Leonardo da Vinci*, Via Senigallia 2, I, 590 b.; *Touring e Gran Turismo*, Via Ugo Tarchetti 2, I, 518 b.; *Michelangelo*, Via Scarlatti 33, I, 452 b.; *Jolly President*, Largo Augusto 10, I, 378 b.; *Aerhotel Fiera Milano*, Viale Boezio 20, I, 357 b.; *Cavalieri*, Piazza Missori 1, I, 291 b.; *Duomo*, Via S. Raffaele 1, I, 278 b.; *Rosa*, Via Pattari 5, I, 250 b.; *Francia Europa*, Corso Vittorio Emanuele 9, I, 239 b.; *Plaza*, Piazza Diaz 3, I, 224 b.; *Select*, Via Baracchini 12, I, 209 b.; *Splendido*, Via Andrea Doria 4, I, 207 b.; *Nasco*, Via Spallanzani 40, I, 198 b.; *De la Ville*, Via Hoepli 6, I, 198 b.; *Cavour*, Via Fatebenefratelli 21, I, 192 b.; *Windsor*, Via Galileo Galilei 2, I, 183 b.; *Royal*, Via Cardano 1, I, 196 b.; *Diana Majestic*, Viale Piave 42, L, 156 b.; *Manin*, Via Manin 7, I, 150 b.; *Marino alla Scala*, Piazza della Scala 5, I, 141 b.; *Carlton Senato*, Via Senato 5, I, 127 b.; *Berna*, Via N. Torriani 18, I, 127 b.; *Anderson*, Piazza Luigi di Savoia 20, I, 118 b.; *Bristol*, Via Scarlatti 32, I, 111 b.; *Amedei*, Via Amedei 2, I, 98 b.; *Crivi's*, Via Crivelli 27, I, 91 b.; *Atlantic*, Via N. Torriani 24, I, 91 b.; *Auriga*, Via Pirelli 7, I, 90 b.; *Lloyd*, Corso Porta Romana 48, I, 80 b.; *Ascot*, Via Lentasio 3–5, I, 66 b.; *American*, Via Finocchiaro Aprile 2, II, 413 b.; *Capitol*, Via Cimarosa 6, II, 168 b.; *Cristallo*, Via Scarlatti 22, II, 167 b.; *Ambasciatori*, Galleria del Corso 3, II, 160 b.; *Raffaello*, Viale Certosa 108, 160 b.; *Ritter*, Corso Garibaldi 68, II, 155 b.; *Mediterraneo*, Via Ludovico Muratori 14, II, 141 b.; *Andreola*, Via Scarlatti 24, II, 136 b.; *Monopole de la Gare*, Via F. Filzi 43, II, 132 b.; *Adriatico*, Via Conca del Naviglio 20, II, 126 b.; II, 118 b.; *Rubens*, Via Rubens 21, II, 116 b.; *Mennini*, Via Boscovich 22, II, 111 b.; *Ambrosiano*, Via Santa Sofia 9, II, 111 b.; *Domus*, Piazza Gerusalemme 6, II, 109 b.; *Lombardia*, Viale Lombardia 74, II, 108 b.; *Terminus*, Viale Vittorio Veneto 32, II, 103 b.; *Madison*, Via Gasparotto 8, II, 102 b.; *Aosta*, Piazza Duca d'Aosta 14, II, 80 b.; *Piccadilly*, Via Ugo Bassi 1A, III, 111 b.; *Argentina*, Via F. Filzi 3, III, 107 b.; *Rex*, Via Marco Agrate 34, III, 104 b.; *Cervo*, Piazza Principessa Clotilde 10, III, 101 b.; etc. – YOUTH HOSTEL, Via Martino Bassi 2, 400 b. – CAMPING SITES: at the Idroscalo (Hydrofoil Station), to the E; in Metanopoli, to the SE.

RESTAURANTS. – *Savini* and *Biffi*, both in the Galleria Vittorio Emanuele; *Giannino*, Via A. Sciesa 8; *Alfio-Cavour*, Via Senato 31; *Marchesi*, Via Bonvesin de la Riva 9; *St Andrews*, Via Sant'Andrea 23; *Da Romani*, Via Trabazio 3; *El Toula*, Piazza Ferrari 6; *Cavallini*, Via Macchia 2; *Barbarossa*, Via Cerva 10; *Prospero*, Via Corridoni 10; *La Pesada Rino*, Via Morsini 12; *Grattacielo*, Piazza della Repubblica (in tower block); *Don Lisander*, Via Manzoni 12A; *Bagutta*, Via Bagutta 14; *Crispi*, Corso Venezia 3; *Pam-Pam*, Via S. Paolo 15; etc.

SHOPPING. – The centre of the city's pulsating activity is the *Piazza del Duomo*, the chief attraction of tourists throughout the year. On the N side of the square is the imposing *Galleria Vittorio Emanuele*, with good restaurants, cafés and elegant shops. The city's principal shopping street, the *Corso Vittorio Emanuele*, leaves the NE corner of the square and is continued by the *Corso Venezia*. – Fashion articles, shoes and handbags, which are reasonable in price and of recognised elegance, are all worth buying in Milan. Books, particularly art books with coloured illustrations, are also good value.

EVENTS. – *Fiera Campionaria* (Trade Fair) in the second half of April.

Milan (Milano), capital of Lombardy and Italy's second largest city, lies in the fertile Lombard plain near the southern end of important passes through the Alps and is linked by shipping canals with the Ticino, the Po, Lake Maggiore and Lake Como. It is Italy's principal industrial centre, its most important railway junction and its leading banking and commercial city, one of the largest silk markets in Europe, the see of an archbishop and a university town, with a State and a Catholic university.

The main industries are textiles, the manufacture of cars, machinery and rolling-stock, chemicals (the Montecatini group) and papermaking. – Milan has an underground railway system, the Metropolitana, opened in 1964. – Airports at *Forlanini*, 6 km E, and *Malpensa*, 45 km NW.

Milan – panorama at sunset

Milan is a city of predominantly modern aspect. Even the old town centre around the Piazza del Duomo, though it still has many narrow old streets, is traversed by wide arteries radiating in all directions. Between the old town and the outer ring of *bastioni*, on the line of the Spanish ramparts built in 1549, is a zone of more modern streets, and farther out are the city's steadily expanding suburbs. Since the last war large modern buildings, including tower blocks of 30 storeys or more, have been erected in every part of the city. Nevertheless Milan is still full of art treasures and fine old buildings which have survivied war damage, which was particularly severe in the town centre, or have been rebuilt in the original style.

HISTORY. – Milan, founded by Celts about 400 B.C., was conquered by Rome in 222 B.C. and thereafter, as *Mediolanum*, became the second most important town in northern Italy (after Verona) and a frequent residence of the emperor in the 4th c. Later it became one of the capitals of the *Lombard* and *Frankish* kingdoms. As capital of the *Lombard League* it led the opposition to the Hohenstaufens. In consequence it was destroyed by Frederick Barbarossa in 1162, but was rebuilt five years later. Internal feuds between the nobility and the people led to the dominance of the *Visconti* family, who won control of much of northern Italy; and in 1395 Gian Galeazzo (d. 1402) gained the ducal title. In 1450 the Viscontis were succeeded by the dynasty founded by the mercenary leader Francesco *Sforza*, but the Sforza line died out in 1535, and the duchy then passed to *Spain* under Charles V. In 1714, after the War of the Spanish Succession, it was assigned to *Austria*, which apart from an interlude of French occupation in Napoleonic times (1797–1814) held on to it until 1859, inspite of repeated popular risings. In 1919 Mussolini founded the Fascist party in Milan; and in April 1945 the body of the fallen dictator was put on show in Piazzale Loreto.

ART. – Remains of early Christian architecture have been preserved in one or two churches, notably San Lorenzo and Sant'Ambrogio. 13th c. buildings are to be found mainly in the Piazza dei Mercanti. The Gothic period is represented almost exclusively by the cathedral. – Around 1450 the Florentines *Filarete* and *Michelozzo* brought the Tuscan Early Renaissance to Milan (Ospedale Maggiore). The heyday of Milanese art began with the coming of *Bramante* and *Leonardo da Vinci*, who produced his major works here between 1485 and 1500; and these two masters influenced the work of subsequent generations of painters, including *Andrea Solario, Bramantino, Luini, Sodoma* and *Gaudenzio Ferrari*. The present aspect of central Milan is due to the architects of the Late Renaissance and Baroque periods, particularly *Galeazzo Alessi* and *Pellegrino Tibaldi*, the neo-classical architect *Giuseppe Piermarini* and two practitioners of the Empire style, *Luigi Canonica* and *Luigi Cagnola*. A competent neo-classical painter was *Andrea Appiani*.

SIGHTS. – The life of Milan centres on the *Piazza del Duomo*, flanked on the N and S sides by palatial buildings designed by Mengoni and erected from 1876 onwards. Near the W end is an *Equestrian statue of Victor Emmanuel II* (1896). Under the square are the foundations of the *Basilica di Santa Tecla* (4th–5th and 7th c.) and the 4th c. *baptistery of San Giovanni*, which were discovered during the construction of the Metropolitana (access from the cathedral).

The ****Cathedral**, a cruciform basilica faced with white marble, is one of the world's largest and most magnificent churches. With a length of 148 m and a breadth across the façade of 61·5 m, it covers an area of 11,700 sq. m and can accommodate a congregation of 40,000. The dome rises to 68 m, and its total height including the statue of the Virgin known as the "Madonnina" is 108 m. The roof is adorned with 135 pinnacles, the exterior with some 2300 marble statues. Building, in Gothic style, began in 1386 but made slow progress (dome completed c. 1500, spire 1765–69, façade 1805–09). The imposing bronze doors are modern (the large central door 1908, the reliefs on three others 1948–51, the last one 1965).

The rather dark INTERIOR, in striking contrast to the brilliant and richly patterned exterior, nevertheless makes a powerful impression with its 52 gigantic pillars. The stained-glass windows in the nave (mostly 15th–16th c.) are the largest in the world; the eight windows in the dome date from 1968. – In the N transept is a fine seven-branched bronze candelabrum by Nicholas of Verdun (c. 1200), and on the E wall of the S transept is a statue, by Marco Agrate (1562), of St Bartholomew, flayed. – In the crypt is the Cappella San Carlo Borromeo, containing the saint's reliquary, richly adorned with gold and jewels. – In the S sacristy is the valuable Treasury.

A walk on the ROOF of the cathedral is an impressive experience, offering magnificent *views in all directions, which extend on clear days to the mountains flanking the W side of the Po plain. (Access outside the cathedral, on the W side of the N transept: 158 steps, or lifts on E side of transept; then 73 steps to the platform of the dome, and another 139 steps to the highest gallery of the tower.)

On the S side of the cathedral is the Palazzo Reale, the former Royal Palace, built in 1788 on the site of an earlier palace which had belonged to the Visconti and Sforza families. The Cathedral Museum (closed Mondays) occupies 12 rooms on the ground floor. – To the rear of the palace stands the old palace church, San Gottardo, with a fine tower (c. 1330). To the E the Archbishop's Palace (by Pellegrino Tibaldi, 1570) has a handsome colonnaded courtyard. – Adjoining the palace on the W is the Palazzo del Turismo, to the S of which is the Piazza Diaz, surrounded by modern buildings, including a 16-storey office block.

SE of Piazza Diaz, in an area rebuilt since the last war (with the Torre Velasca, a 99 m high office block erected in 1958), is the old Ospedale Maggiore, a brick building 285 m long, the town's first hospital, begun in 1457 by Antonio Filarete and continued from 1465 onwards in Gothic and Renaissance style. It

now houses the Rector's Office and two faculties of the State university. – 0·5 km E of the Ospedale Maggiore, between the broad Corso di Porta Vittoria and Via San Barnaba, rises the massive Palazzo di Giustizia (Law Courts), completed in 1940.

Adjoining the Piazza del Duomo to the NW is the Piazza dei Mercanti, beyond which are the Piazza Cordusio and the Castello Sforzesco. From the cathedral to the Piazza Cordusio extends an underground passage, with numerous shops and the Terraquarium. – On the N side of the Piazza del Duomo, giving access to the Piazza della Scala, is the *Galleria Vittorio Emanuele, designed by Giuseppe Mengoni and built 1865–67. It was then the largest shopping arcade in Europe (195 m long, dome 48 m high).

In Piazza della Scala, to the N, is a monument to Leonardo da Vinci (1872). On the NW side of the square stands the *Teatro alla Scala (1776–78), one of the largest and most important operahouses in the world. To the left of the main building is the Museo Teatrale, with material on the history of the theatre; it incorporates a Verdi Museum with numerous mementos of the composer (d. in Milan 1901). – On the SE side of the square the Palazzo Marino (by Galeazzo Alessi, 1558–60) is now the headquarters of the municipal administration. – Behind the Palazzo Marino, in Piazza San Fedele, stands the fine Jesuit church of San Fedele (by Tibaldi, 1569). – Beyond San Fedele, in the beautiful Piazza Belgioioso, is the handsome Palazzo Belgioioso (by Piermarini, 1777). At the corner of Via Morone (No. 1) is Manzoni's House (museum: closed Sundays and Mondays), with the room in

La Scala, Milan

which the novelist Alessandro Manzoni (1785–1873) worked and in which he died. Almost opposite (Via Manzoni 12), in an elegant old patrician house, the **Museo Poldi-Pezzoli** (closed Mondays), contains pictures of the Lombard, Venetian and Florentine schools, Flemish and Persian carpets, tapestries, jewellery, silver, bronzes and weapons.

From Piazza Belgioioso the Corso Matteotti, recently rebuilt with handsome modern buildings, runs E to the Piazza San Babila, which has been considerably enlarged since the last war, with large modern blocks and the little Romanesque *church of San Babila*. – From the SW corner of the square the *Corso Vittorio Emanuele*, the city's busiest street, lined with elegant shops, leads towards the cathedral. On the right-hand side of this street is the *church of San Carlo*, a circular building modelled on the Pantheon (by Carlo Amati, 1836–47).

From Piazza San Babila the line of Corso Vittorio Emanuele is continued NE by the broad *Corso Venezia*. On the right-hand side of this street, at the corner of Via San Damiano, is the *Palazzo Serbelloni-Busca* (1794), and beyond it the *Palazzo Rocca-Saporiti* (1812), both in neo-classical style. Almost opposite the Palazzo Rocca-Saporiti is the **Museum of Natural History** (closed Mondays), notable in particular for its large collection of birds (25,000 specimens). – The Corso Venezia joins the Piazzale Oberdan, in which are two little gatehouses of the *Porta Venezia*. From here the busy Corso Buenos Aires continues the line of Corso Venezia NE to the circular Piazzale Loreto. – 1 km W, at the end of the broad Via Andrea Doria, is the **Central Station**, an imposing building richly clad in marble (by Ulisse Stacchini, 1925–31), and one of the largest stations in Europe (main front 210 m long). In the station is a *Wax Museum*. Facing the station, to the SW, is the 32-storey **Pirelli Building** (1955–59), 127 m high (conducted tours).

From the station Via Pisani runs SW to the spacious *Piazza della Repubblica*, laid out from 1931 onwards on the site of the old railway station and now surrounded by huge modern buildings, including the 31-storey Grattacielo (Skyscraper), 114 m high, built in 1955. From the NW corner of the square the wide Viale della Liberazione leads to the *Porta Garibaldi*

Station, 1 km away, which relieves pressure on the Central Station. The area W of the Piazza della Repubblica is being rebuilt under an ambitious redevelopment plan as the administrative quarter ("Centro Direzionale") of Milan.

From the Piazza della Repubblica the Via Turati runs S to the Piazza Cavour, a busy traffic intersection at the SW corner of the beautiful **Giardini Pubblici**, laid out in 1782–85, with a small zoo in the western part of the gardens. On the SE side of Piazza Cavour are three tower blocks, including the 22-storey *Centro Svizzero* (1952). – A little way E of the square, to the W of the Natural History Museum, stands the neo-classical *Villa Reale* (1790), which houses the large **Galleria d'Arte Moderna** (closed Tuesdays: 19th and 20th c. painting and sculpture); behind the villa is a beautiful public garden. – From Piazza Cavour the Via Alessandro Manzoni runs S to the Piazza della Scala.

W of Piazza Cavour and NW of Piazza della Scala, in Via Brera, is the Renaissance **Palazzo di Brera** (1651–86), originally a Jesuit college, which has been occupied since 1776 by the *Accademia di Belle Arti*. In the courtyard can be seen a *monument to Napoleon I* by Canova (1809). The palace contains a *Library* (800,000 volumes) founded in 1770 and an *Observatory*. On the first floor is the ****Pinacoteca di Brera**, one of Italy's finest picture galleries, now only partly open to the public following the execution of urgent renovation work on the palace.

The chief strength of the PINACOTECA DI BRERA lies in the works of the N Italian masters. Notable among 15th c. pictures are works by *Mantegna* (*"Madonna in a Ring of Angels' Heads", "Lamentation"), *Carlo Crivelli* (*Madonna della Candeletta", etc.), *Gentile* ("Preaching of St Mark in Alexandria"), *Giovanni Bellini* (*"Lamentation" and two Madonnas) and *Cima da Conegliano*. – Pictures of later periods include works by *Paolo Veronese*, *Titian* (*"Count Antonio Porcia" and "St Jerome") and *Tintoretto* (**"Finding of St Mark's Body" and "Descent from the Cross"), and portraits by *Lorenzo Lotto* and *Giovanni Battista Moroni*. – The Lombard masters, disciples of Leonardo da Vinci, are well represented, with works by *Boltraffio* and

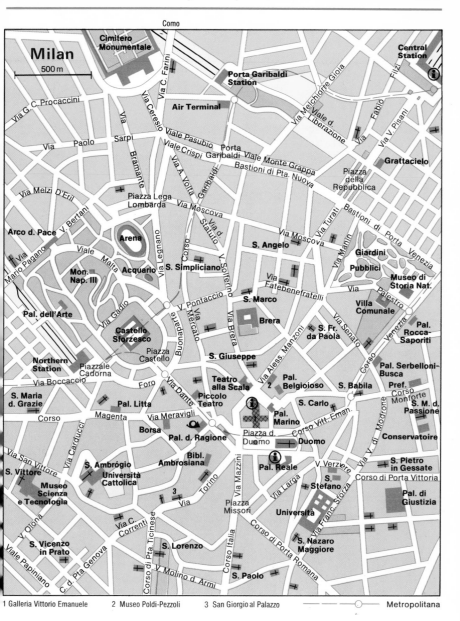

Milan

500 m

Como

Cimitero Monumentale

Central Station

Porta Garibaldi Station

Air Terminal

Via G. C. Procaccini

Via C. Farini

Via Ceresio

Via Melchiorre Gioia

Viale della Liberazione

Fabio

Filzi

V. Pisani

Via Paolo

Sarpi

Bramante

Viale Pasubio

Viale Crispi

Porta Garibaldi

Viale Monte Grappa

Bastioni di Pta. Nuova

Via A. Volta

Via Garibaldi

Piazza della Repubblica

Grattacielo

Via Melzi D'Eril

Piazza Lega Lombarda

Via Moscova

Via d. Statuto

Via Moscova

Arco d. Pace

V. Bertani

Arena

Via Legnano

Corso Garibaldi

V. Solferino

S. Angelo

Via Turati

Bastioni di Porta Venezia

Giardini Pubblici

Museo di Storia Nat.

Via

Mario Pagano

Viale

Malta

Mon. Nap. III

Acquario

S. Simpliciano

Via Fatebenefratelli

Via Manin

Via Palestro

Pal. dell'Arte

Via Gadio

Via Pontaccio

Via Mercato

S. Marco

Villa Comunale

Venezia

Pal. Rocca-Saporiti

Castello Sforzesco

Bonaparte

Via Brera

Brera

Via Aless. Manzoni

S. Fr. da Paola

Via Senato

Piazza Castello

S. Giuseppe

Pal. Serbelloni-Busca

Northern Station

Piazzale Cadorna

Foro

Via Dante

Teatro alla Scala

Pal. Belgioioso

S. Babila

Pref.

Corso Monforte

S. M. d. Passione

Via Boccaccio

Piccolo Teatro

S. Carlo

S. Maria d. Grazie

Pal. Litta

Via Meravigli

Pal. Marino

Conservatoire

Corso

Magenta

Borsa

Pal. d. Ragione

Piazza d. Duomo

Corso Vitt. Eman.

Via Carducci

Via San Vittore

Bibl. Ambrosiana

Duomo

V. di Modrone

S. Pietro in Gessate

S. Ambrógio

Università Cattolica

Pal. Reale

V. Verziere

Corso di Porta Vittoria

S. Vittore

Via Torino

Via Mazzini

S.

Stefano

Pal. di Giustizia

Museo Scienza e Tecnologia

3

Via

Piazza Missori

Via Larga

Via Franc. Sforza

Università

Via C. Correnti

Corso Italia

Corso di Porta Romana

Via Olona

S. Vicenzo in Prato

Via Papiniano

C. d. Pta Genova

Corso di Pta. Ticinese

S. Lorenzo

V. Molino d. Armi

Piazza

S. Nazaro Maggiore

S. Paolo

1 Galleria Vittorio Emanuele   2 Museo Poldi-Pezzoli   3 San Giorgio al Palazzo   ——————○——— Metropolitana

Andrea Solario among others. – Outstanding among the frescoes by *Bernardino Luini* is the *"Burial of St Catherine", among his easel paintings the "Madonna of the Rose-Garden". – Artists of the Ferrarese school include *Ercole de' Roberti* ("Madonna with Saints") and *Dosso Dossi*. – *Correggio* is represented by a *"Nativity" and an "Adoration of the Kings". – There is an excellent representation of the Umbrian school, including works by *Gentile da Fabriano* ("Coronation of the Virgin, with Saints"), *Piero della Francesca* (*"Madonna with Saints and Duke Federico da Montefeltro") and *Bramante* (eight *frescoes, "Christ of the column"). – The most famous picture in the gallery is *Raphael*'s **"Marriage of the Virgin" ("Lo Sposalizio"), the finest work of his first period. – There are also important works by 17th and 18th c. artists. – Outstanding among foreign masters are *Rembrandt* (portraits of women, including "The Artist's Sister"), *Van Dyck* (*"Princess Amalie of Solms"), *Rubens* ("Last Supper") and *El Greco* ("St Francis").

From the Piazza della Scala the Via Santa Margherita runs SW into the *Piazza dei Mercanti*, centre of the old town of Milàn, which adjoins the Piazza del Duomo on the W. In the centre of the square is the single-storey *Palazzo della Ragione* (1228–33), originally a law court, with an equestrian statue of the builder on the S side. The *Palazzo dei Giureconsulti* (1564), on the N side of the square, has a tower dating from 1272. On the S side is the Gothic *Loggia degli Osii* (1316).

NW of the Piazza dei Mercanti the oval Piazza Cordusio is the meeting-place of important streets. To the SE the Via Orefici, lined with shops, leads to the Piazza del Duomo; to the W the Via Meravigli goes past the *Exchange* to the church of Santa Maria delle Grazie; to the NW the Via Dante leading to the Castello Sforzesco. From here, too, an underground shopping arcade extends to the Piazza del Duomo. – A little way S of Piazza Cordusio is the **Palazzo dell'Ambrosiana** (1603–09), with a famous *Library* (750,000 printed volumes, 35,000 manuscripts, 2500 incunabula) and an important *Picture Gallery* founded in 1618 by Cardinal-Archbishop Federico Borromeo (works by Leonardo da Vinci, including the "Codex Atlanticus", and by Botticelli, Ambrogio de Predis, Raphael and Titian).

The Largo Cairoli at the NW end of Via Dante is crossed by the broad Foro Buonaparte which has a bronze equestrian statue of Garibaldi. From here the short Via Cairoli continues into the beautiful *Piazza Castello*.

The *__Castello Sforzesco__, held successively by the Viscontis and the Sforzas, was built in 1368, demolished by the people of Milan in 1447 and rebuilt from 1450 onwards. The Torre Umberto I, on the nearside (70 m high), is a reproduction (1905) of the original gatetower. The Castello houses the *Museo d'Arte Antica* (closed Mondays), with a collection of sculpture which consists mainly of medieval and modern works together with some Early Christian material and graves. Its greatest treasure is the **"Pietà Rondanini"**, Michelangelo's last masterpiece, brought here in 1953 from the Palazzo Rondanini in Rome. Other important items are the unfinished tomb of Gaston de Foix and the large tomb, with an equestrian statue, of Bernabò Visconti (d. 1385) by Bonino da Campione. There is also a collection of decorative art, as well as pictures by old masters (including Bellini, Correggio, Mantegna, Bergognone, Foppa, Lotto and Antonello da Messina), prehistoric and Egyptian antiquities, a collection on musical history and an armoury.

Between the two rear courtyards of the Castello is a passage leading to the **park**, laid out in 1893–97, once the pleasure garden of the dukes of Milan and later a military training ground. In the NE of the park is the *Arena*, an amphitheatre constructed in 1907 for sporting and other events. To the SE is an interesting *Aquarium* (closed Wednesdays, Friday afternoons and Mondays). On the W side of the park stands the *Palazzo dell'Arte*, used for exhibitions of modern art (the 'Triennale"). An *outlook tower* to the N of this, 109 m high, was built in 1933 (lift; bar). On the NW side of the park are the *Porta del Sempione* and the *Arco della Pace*, a triumphal arch of white marble (1806–38). 1 km W of the Porta Sempione are the grounds of the *Milan Trade Fair*.

SW of the Castello, past the *Northern Station* and along Via Boccaccio and Via Caradosso, can be found the **church of Santa Maria delle Grazie**, in the Corso Magenta. This is a brick-built Gothic structure (begun about 1465) with a choir and a massive 16-sided dome in the finest Early Renaissance style designed by Bramante (1492 onwards). During the repair of war damage in the dome old sgraffito paintings were brought to light. At the end of the N aisle is the Baroque chapel of the Madonna delle Grazie, with an altarpiece of the Madonna. In the refectory of the former Dominican monastery adjoining the chuch is **Leonardo da Vinci's **"Last Supper"** (the *Cenácolo Vinciano*: closed Mondays), his most famous work, painted on the wall in tempera between 1495 and 1497: a dramatic presentation of the scene which was quite novel and marked an important new stage in the development of art. The painting is much damaged from the flaking off of the paint; the most recent restoration was in 1952.

Leonardo da Vinci's "Last Supper"

To the S of Santa Maria delle Grazie, in Via San Vittore, stands the beautiful *church of San Vittore*, a very early foundation which was remodelled by Galeazzo Alessi in Late Renaissance style in 1560, with a sumptuous Baroque interior. Adjoining it on the E is the **Leonardo da Vinci National Museum of Science and Technology** (closed Mondays), housed in a former Olivetan monastery. The museum, opened in 1953, illustrates the history of science and technology down to modern times. Of particular interest are the Leonard da Vinci Gallery; the department of physics, with apparatus used by Galileo, Newton, Volta and other scientists, and experiments which visitors can carry out for themselves; and the departments of optics, acoustics, telegraphy, transport, shipping, railways, flying, metallurgy, motor vehicles, clocks and watches, and timber. There are also a library, a reading room and a cinema for film presentations.

The *church of Sant'Ambrogio* E of the National Museum was founded in 386 by St Ambrose. The present church is a masterpiece of Romanesque architecture (12th c.; choir 10th c.). The atrium and façade have preserved the form of the original Early Christian building. Notable features of the interior are the pulpit, restored about 1200, with late Romanesque carving and, below it, an Early Christian sarcophagus of the 5th c.; the casing (*paliotto*) of the high altar, a masterpiece of Carolingian art (made in 835 at either Milan or Rheims); and the ciborium (11th c.), with gilded stucco reliefs. – On the NW side of the church are the *Museo di Sant'Ambrogio* (closed Tuesdays) and a monumental *war memorial* (1928). The *Catholic University of the Sacred Heart*, adjoining the church on the SE, was founded in 1921 and has two cloisters by Bramante.

SE of Sant'Ambrogio, in the Corso di Porta Ticinese, another important church, *San Lorenzo*, a fine building on a centralised plan, dates from the Early Christian period; it has a Renaissance dome (1574) and the chapel of St Aquilinus (4th c. mosaics). In front of the church a *portico* of 16 Corinthian columns, the largest surviving monument of Roman *Mediolanum* has been re-erected. – 0·5 km farther S the **church of Sant'Eustorgio**, a Gothic basilica

(12th–13th c.) has a fine campanile (1297–1309) and a façade which was added in 1863. Beyond the choir is the *Cappella Portinari* (by Michelozzo, 1462–68), the earliest example of Renaissance architecture, with frescoes by Vincenzo Foppa and the marble tomb (1339) of St Peter Martyr, a Dominican monk murdered in 1252. – Just N of the church of San Lorenzo the Corso di Porta Ticinese runs into the Piazza Carrobbio. In Via Torino, which runs NE from this square to the Piazza del Duomo, stands the *church of San Giorgio al Palazzo*, with paintings by Bernardino Luini. Farther along the street on the right, just before it reaches the Piazza del Duomo, is the little **church of San Satiro** (by Bramante, 1479–1514), with a campanile dating from 876 (?) and a modern façade. The interior has what appears to be a choir but is in fact an ingenious piece of trompe-l'œil painting. The *baptistery, in the S aisle is a gem of Lombard Early Renaissance architecture by Bramante (1480–88). At the end of the N transept is the curious little domed Cappella della Pietà (9th c.).

In north-western Milan, at the Porta Volta, lies the *Cimitero Monumentale** (opened 1866), Italy's most splendid cemetery, with numerous highly elaborate marble tombs.

SURROUNDINGS. – 7 km SE of Milan is *Chiaravalle Milanese*, noted for its Cistercian *abbey church, a fine brick edifice with a tall tower; it was founded by St Bernard of Clairvaux in 1135 and remodelled between 1170 and 1221 and has magnificent Baroque choir-stalls of 1640, an elegant little cloister and a cemetery.

8 km SE of Milan, in the commune of *San Donato Milanese*, is **Metanópoli** (alt. 188 m; Motel Agip, II, 525 b.; Hotel Santa Barbara, III, 175 b.), a satellite town which has grown up since 1940, with the headquarters or branch establishments of the leading Italian oil companies, such as *ENI* (*E*nte *N*azionale *I*drocarburi), *SNAM* (*S*ocietà *N*azionale Metano-dotti), *AGIP* (*A*zienda *G*enerale *I*taliana *P*etroli, with departments of mining and atomic research) and *ANIC* (*A*zienda *N*azionale *I*drocarburi).

An excursion well worth making from Milan is to **Lake Maggiore** (see p. 147). The road passes through **Rho** (alt. 158 m; pop. 50,000; Hotel Speria, II, 74 b.; etc.), **Legnano** (alt. 190 m; pop. 50,000; hotels: Pagoda, II, 100 b.; Europa, II, 87 b.; etc.), with a monument (erected 1900) to the Lombard League's victory over Frederick Barbarossa in 1176, **Busto Arsizio** (alt. 225 m; pop. 80,000) and **Gallarate** (alt. 238 m; pop. 45,000), which has cotton-spinning mills. – Another very attractive trip is to **Lake Como** (see p. 99).

15 km NE of Milan, on the River *Lambro*, is the industrial town of **Monza** (alt. 162 m; pop. 118,000;

hotels: Della Regione, II, 138 b.; De la Ville, II, 73 b.; Castello e Falcone, III, 46 b.; etc.), which together with Padua was the place of coronation of the Lombard kings from the 11th c. In the Piazza Roma stands the old Town Hall ("Arengario") of 1293, and close by the *cathedral, founded in 590 and rebuilt at the end of the 14th c. in Lombard Gothic style, with a beautiful façade and a harmonious interior. In the Cappella di Teodolinda are frescoes and the famous "Iron Crown" (reproduction under the baldacchino), said to be the royal crown of the Lombards, with which the German emperors were crowned as kings of Italy. Under the little cloister on the left side of the cathedral the Museo Serpero (closed Mondays) contains the rich *Cathedral Treasury. The neo-classical *Villa Reale* (by G. Piermarini, 1777–80) in the N of the town has a small picture gallery. Close by is the main entrance to the large park, through which the River Lambro flows. In the park are the Mirabello racecourse and the famous *Monza car racing circuit* (18 km), now closed after a number of fatal accidents (the most recent, in 1978, involving the Swedish driver Ronnie Peterson). The races which formerly took place here are now run on the Dino Ferrari circuit at Imola (Bologna).

Modena

Region: Emilia-Romagna. – Province: Modena (MO).
Altitude: 34 m. – Population: 175,000.
Post code: I-41100. – Dialling code: 059.
ⓘ EPT, Corso Canalgrande 3;
tel. 22 24 82.
ACI, Via Emilia Est;
tel. 23 90 22.
TCI, *Viaggi ITER*, Via San Carlo 5;
21 92 31.
Viaggi Domus, Largo Garibaldi 6;
tel. 22 34 96.

HOTELS. – *Canalgrande*, Corso Canalgrande 6, I, 139 b.; *Fini*, Via Emilia Est 441, I, 123 b.; *Palace*, Via Emilia Est 27, I, 95 b.; *Europa*, Corso Vittorio Emanuele II 52, II, 164 b.; *Donatello*, Via Giardini 402, II, 138 b.; *Milano*, Corso Vittorio Emanuele II 68, II, 96 b.; *Estense*, Via Berengario 11, II, 87 b.; *Roma*, Via Farini 44, II, 60 b.; *Libertà*, Via Blasia 10, II, 41 b.; *Castello*, Via Pica 321, III, 45 b.; etc. – *Motel Agip*, 6 km W, on A 1, II, 366 b. – CAMPING SITE.

The provincial capital of Modena, situated between the rivers Secchia and Panaro near the southern edge of the N Italian plain, offers visitors the attractions of its fine cathedral and rich art collections. It is a university town and the see of an archbishop.

The town centre has wide arcaded streets and large squares, and the old forti-fications have given place to beautiful avenues and gardens. Modena is an important marketing centre for the pro-duce of the fertile surrounding area; the local sausages (Coteghino, Zampone) are renowned.

HISTORY. – Originally a Celtic settlement of the Boii, the town, lying astride the ancient Via Aemilia, became a Roman colony in 183 B.C. under the name of *Mutina*. In 984 it came into the hands of the house of Este, acquiring some 500 years, acquiring the ducal title in 1452. In 1814 the territory passed into the possession of Archduke Francis of Austria and his son Francis V. After several attempted risings against Francis V's reactionary rule, which were ruthlessly repressed, Modena at last broke free in 1859 and was united with the new Italian kingdom in the following year. The private possessions of the Este family and their name were inherited by the heir to the Austrian throne, Francis Ferdinand, who was assassinated in 1914.

In the history of ART Modena is noted for its fine 14th c. school of painters and for its terracottas – dramatic groups conceived for pictorial rather than plastic effect, a genre developed by the strongly realistic *Guido Mazzoni* (1450–1518) and perfected by *Antonio Begarelli* (1498–1565).

SIGHTS. – The main traffic artery of the town is the *Via Emilia*, on the line of the old Roman road. Just off the S side of this street, in the central *Piazza Grande*, stands the handsome *Cathedral, begun in 1099 in Romanesque style, consecrated in 1184 and completed in the 13th c., with beautiful sculpture on the exterior walls and in the interior. On the façade are scenes from the Creation by Willigelmus (*c.* 1100), and the doorways are also very fine. The interior is notable for some good pictures and for *sculptures of the Passion (12th c.) on the choir screen and the pulpit. In the crypt, its roof supported by 30 slender columns, is a realistic group representing the *"Adoration of the Infant Christ" by Guido Mazzoni (after 1480). – On the N side of the cathedral, in the Piazza della Torre, rises the 87 m high *Torre Ghirlandina* (slightly off the per-pendicular), one of the finest campaniles in northern Italy and a distinctive city landmark. Also on the N side of the cathedral stands the *Museo Lapidario del Duomo*, which has Romanesque *metopes from the cathedral roof.

NW of the cathedral is the recently replanned *Piazza Matteotti*, a large square on the W side of which, at the corner of Via Emilia, stands the *church of San Giovanni Battista*, a plain domed building (17th c.) containing, to the left of the high altar, a beautifully painted terracotta of the "Lamentation" by Mazzoni (1477–80). – The **Palazzo dei Musei**, farther W along Via Emilia, houses the municipal col-lections – in the courtyard the *Museo Lapidario*; on the ground floor the *Museo*

Civico del Risorgimento (closed Mondays); on the first floor the *Biblioteca Estense* (700,000 printed volumes and 15,000 manuscripts: particularly notable is a Bible which belonged to Borso d'Este); on the second floor the *Museo Civico* (archaeology and ethnology), the *Museo Estense* (sculpture, objets d'art) and the *Este Picture Gallery*, with works by Correggio, Dosso Dossi, Titian, Tintoretto, Guercino, Veronese, Velázquez and many other artists.

Adjacent to the museums is the 17th c. **church of Sant'Agostino**, the "Pantheon" of the house of Este, "one of the most imaginative flat-roofed creations of the Baroque" (Burckhardt). To the right of the entrance is a "Lamentation", an early work by Antonio Begarelli. – Other terracottas by Bergarelli can be seen in the *church of San Francesco*, near the SW corner of the old town, and the *church of San Pietro* (1476), in the SE of the old town.

In the N of the old town, in the *Piazza Roma* (0·5 km NE of the cathedral), rises the massive **Palazzo Ducale** (17th c.), now a military academy, with an imposing courtyard. – Farther NE is the beautiful *Giardino Pubblico*, with the *Botanic Garden* adjoining it on the SE.

SURROUNDINGS. – 18 km N of Modena is the interesting town of **Carpi** (alt. 28 m; pop. 59,000; hotels: Touring, I, 100 b.; Molly, II, 44 b.; Tre Corone, III, 38 b.; etc.). In the centre of the town is the large Piazza dei Martiri, in which stands the new cathedral (begun 1514; façade 1667), the Loggia, the 15th c. Colonnades (52 arches) and the old Castello (now partly occupied by a museum) of the Pio family, who reigned here from 1327 to 1525; in the second courtyard is a memorial to the victims of the concentration camps. Behind the Castello is the old cathedral, founded in 751, La Sagra (Romanesque interior, with a 12th c. pulpit), adjoining which is a campanile of 1221. Near the Loggia is the Franciscan church of San Nicolò (1493–1522).

Palazzo Ducale, Modena

Molise

Provinces: Campobasso and Isernia.
ⓘ **EPT Campobasso**, Piazza della Vittoria 14,
I-86100 Campobasso (CB);
tel. (0874) 9 56 62.
   EPT Isernia, Via Kennedy 80,
I-86170 Isernia (IS);
tel. (0865) 39 92.

The region of Molise, one of the poorest and remotest in Italy, consisting of the two provinces of Campobasso and Isernia, covers an area of 4438 sq. km in the Neapolitan Apennines (Appennino Napolitano) in eastern Central Italy.

Ancient theatre, Pietrabbondante

Bounded on the N by the region of Abruzzi, with which it is linked by historical and cultural tradition and with which it was combined until 1963 to form the region of *Abruzzi e Molise*, Molise extends from the karstic hills of the *Monti del Matese* (*view from Monte Miletto, 2050 m) in the SW to the edge of the wide Apulian plain in the E and the Adriatic to the NE. The 320,000 inhabitants gain a modest subsistence from arable and pastoral farming.

SIGHTS. – The principal town in the region is **Campobasso** (alt. 686 m; pop. 42,000; hotels: Roxy, I, 56 b.; Skanderbeg, II, 121 b.; Eden, II, 63 b.; etc.), capital of the province of the same name and the see of a bishop. Above the town are the ruins of the Castello di Monforte (16th c.: view). Other features of interest are the Romanesque church of San Bartolomeo and the Museo Provincale Sannítico (Samnite Museum).

The capital of Molise's other province is **Isernia** (alt. 457 m; pop. 15,000; hotels: La Tequila, II, 140 b.; Europa, II, 55 b.;

etc.), also the see of a bishop. – 20 km NW in the Volturno valley are the ruins of the *Abbazia di San Vincenzo*, founded about 700 and destroyed by the Saracens in 880. The crypt, with fine *frescoes (9th c.), has been preserved. – 30 km NE of Isernia, at *Pietrabbondante*, are the excavated remains of a Samnite town (*theatre, temple, etc.).

Montecassino/ Cassino

Region: Lazio. – Province: Frosinone (FR).
Altitude: 45 m. – Population: 25,000.
Post code: I-03043. – Dialling code: 0776.
ⓘ **AA**, Via Verdi;
    tel. 2 12 92.

HOTELS in Cassino. – *Silvia Park*, II, 84 b., SP; *La Pace*, II, 70 b.; *Alba*, II, 52 b.; *Excelsior*, II, 43 b.; *La Campagnola*, III, 37 b.; etc.

The town of Cassino, the ancient Casinum, lies on the Via Casilina between Rome and Naples, in southern Latium, and is noted chiefly for the great abbey of Montecassino which towers above it on a hill. During the Second World War there was bitter fighting around Cassino, and the town was completely destroyed and rebuilt on a new site slightly farther S.

The Benedictine mother house of Montecassino

SIGHTS. – The road to the abbey of Montecassino (9 km) winds steeply up the hill in hairpin bends from the W side of the town. Just outside the town, on the left of the road, are the remains of the Roman *Casinum*, including the massive ruins of an amphitheatre, a mausoleum and a theatre. At the next bend, on the right, are the ruins of the *Rocca Ianula* (alt. 193 m), built 949–86. – Just before the monastery, on the right, is a road

leading to the *Polish military cemetery*, with over 1000 graves. Beyond this are pre-Roman polygonal walls (5th c. B.C.).

On the summit .of the hill (519 m) is the *abbey of Montecassino, founded by St Benedict in 529, and acknowledged as the cradle of the Benedictine order, which became a great centre of learning and art. During the Second World War the hill of Montecassino was a cornerstone of the German defensive line from October 1943 to May 1944, and on 15 February 1944 the abbey was almost completely destroyed by an Allied air attack, although the Germans had declared that it was clear of troops. The abbey has since been rebuilt in its original form, the only surviving features of the old buildings being the crypt, with paintings by Benedictines from Beuron in Württemberg (1898–1913) and the tombs of St Benedict and his twin sister St Scholastica (both *c.* 1480–1543). The contents of the valuable library (80,000 volumes), the abbey's archives and many pictures were removed to safety in the Vatican during the fighting. – Above the abbey is *Monte Calvario* (593 m), crowned by a Polish war memorial, from which there are magnificent views.

Montecatini Terme

Region: Toscana. – Province: Pistoia (PT).
Altitude: 27 m. – Population: 21,000.
Post code: I-51016. – Dialling code: 0572.
ⓘ **AA**, Viale Verdi 66;
    tel. 7 01 09.
    TCI and **CIT**, Viale Verdi 47.

HOTELS. – *Tamerici e Principe*, I, 250 b., SP; *Grand Hotel e la Pace*, I, 230 b., SP; *Croce di Malta*, I, 186 b., SP; *Nizza et Suisse*, I, 180 b.; *Panoramic*, I, 142 b., SP; *Vittoria*, I, 132 b., SP; *Ambasciatori e Cristallo*, I, 126 b., SP; *Cristallino*, I, 89 b., SP; *Du Park e Regina*, I, 84 b., SP; *Bellavista Palace e Golf*, I, 83 b.; *Tettuccio*, I, 80 b.; *Francia Quirinale*, II, 189 b., SP: *De la Ville*, II, 176 b.; *Belvedere*, II, 176 b.; *Ercolini e Savi*, II, 154 b.; *Imperial Garden*, II, 149 b., SP; *Terme Pellegrini*, II, 143 b.; *Biondini*, II, 140 b.; *Minerva*, II, 128 b.; *Settentrionale Esplanade*, II, 112 b.; *Adua*, II, 112 b., SP; *Columbia*, II, 102 b., SP; *Astoria*, II, 98 b., SP; *Corallo*, II, 93 b., SP; *Cappelli – Croce di Savoia*, II, 91 b., SP; *San Marco*, II, 91 b.; *Manzoni*, II, 91 b.; *Ariston*, II, 90 b.; *Augustus*, II, 87 b.; *Centrale*, II, 82 b.; *Torretta*, II, 80 b., SP; *Select Petrolini*, II, 71 b.; *President*, II, 68 b.; *Michelangelo*, II, 68 b.; *Salus*, II, 64 b.; *Santa Barbara*, II, 63 b.; *Mediterraneo*, II, 54 b.; *Ambrosiano*, III, 108 b., SP; *Lido Palace*, III, 90 b.; *Valtorta*, III, 86 b.; *Reale*, III, 86 b.; *Universo*, III, 85 b., SP; *Massimo d'Azeglio*, III, 85 b.; etc.

Montecatini Terme, lying between Pisa and Florence on the southern edge of the Apennines, in the fertile but in summer very hot Niévole valley, is Italy's leading spa, attracting large numbers of visitors, mainly Italians, between April and November (high season July–August). The baths and mineral springs (temperature 19–25 °C – 66–77 °F; water containing sulphur and sodium carbonate), which have been used for treatment since the 14th c., are recommended for metabolic disorders.

SIGHTS. – The central feature of the town is the *Piazza del Popolo*, with the neoclassical *parish church* (1833). A little way NW is the **Kursaal**. The main centre of activity in the morning is the *Viale Verdi*, which runs NE from the Piazza del Popolo, while in the afternoon the beautiful gardens around the *Torretta* bathing establishment, to the N of the spa park, are a favourite place of resort. The large *Stabilimento del Tettuccio* and *Terme Leopoldine*, like the park, date from the time of Grand Duke Leopold I of Tuscany (1784), the *Terme Excelsior* from 1968.

From near the Stabilimento del Tettuccio a funicular ascends in 10 minutes to the outlying district of VAL DI NIEVOLE (alt. 290 m), NE of the town centre (also accessible by road, 4·5 km). This was formerly the headquarters of the Società di Montecatini, Italy's largest chemical firm, now based in Milan.

SURROUNDINGS. – 14 km NW of Montecatini Terme is the picturesque village of *Collodi* (alt. 125 m; Hotel Collodi, IV, 14 b.), with the magnificent* park of the Villa Garzoni, in which are a children's playground, a "Fairytale Park" and a monument to Pinocchio (1955), the famous character created by Carlo Lorenzini, a native of Collodi.

Montepulciano

Region: Toscana. – Province: Siena (SI).
Altitude: 605 m. – Population: 4000.
Post code: I-53045. – Dialling code: 0578.
ⓘ **Pro Loco**, Via Cavour 11;
   tel. 7 71 88.

HOTEL. – *Il Marzocco*, III, 29 b.

*Montepulciano, situated on a hill in SE Tuscany near Lake Trasimene, is one of the most attractive little towns in Central Italy, with its medieval walls and its beautiful Gothic and Renaissance buildings.

Montepulciano was the birthplace of the poet A. Ambrogini (1454–94), who took the name Poliziano (Politian) after his native town, and of Cardinal Roberto Bellarmino (1542–1621), a protagonist of the Counter-Reformation.

Palazzo Comunale, Montepulciano

SIGHTS. – The life of the town centres on the *Piazza Vittorio Emanuele* or Piazza Grande, on the S side of which is the **Cathedral**, begun in 1570 by Bartolomeo Ammannati and completed by Ippolito Scalza, with the exception of the façade, in 1630. Inside, to the left of the main doorway, is a recumbent figure of Bartolomeo Aragazzi from the magnificent tomb by Michelozzo (1427–36) which was taken down in the 18th c., parts of it being dispersed about the cathedral and some parts being lost. – To the right of the cathedral stands the **Palazzo Comunale** (14th c.: view from tower), to the left the *Palazzo Contucci*, begun in 1519 by Antonio da Sangallo the Elder and completed by Peruzzi. Opposite the cathedral is the *Palazzo Tarugi*, the town's finest Renaissance palace, and to the left of it a fountain of 1520.

N of the Piazza Vittorio Emanuele, in Via Ricci (on right), is the *Palazzo Neri-Orselli* (14th c.), with the *Museo Civico* (collection of pictures). – To the E of the square Via Garibaldi with its northward continuation, Via Cavour, is the main street of the town and is lined with handsome palaces and churches. At the N end of Via Cavour, on the right, is the *Palazzo Cervini*, by Antonio da Sangallo the Elder. Farther N, in Via Roma (on left), the *church of Sant'Agostino* has a Renaissance façade by Michelozzo which still shows reminiscences of Gothic.

The *church of the Madonna di San Biagio, 0·5 km SW, below the town, was built in 1518–37 by Sangallo the Elder on the site of an earlier church: it is a centralised structure showing the influence of Bramante. To the left of the church stands the *Casa di Sangallo* (1518), with a beautiful loggia.

SURROUNDINGS. – 14 km W of Montepulciano is **Pienza** (alt. 491 m; pop. 4000), named after Pope Pius II (b. here in 1405), who adorned the town with splendid buildings, mainly designed by Bernardo Rossellino, the leading Florentine architect of the day. *Piazza Pio II, surrounded by buildings erected between 1459 and 1462, offers a compact survey of Early Renaissance architecture. On the N side of the square is the cathedral, which contains a number of fine pictures, including works by the Sienese painter Matteo di Giovanni and by Lorenzo Vecchietta, and beautiful Gothic choir-stalls. The Bishop's Palace to the left of the cathedral adjoins the Cathedral Museum (with a cope which once belonged to Pius II). On the S side of the square are the Palazzo Comunale and the Palazzo Ammannati. To the right of the cathedral is the Palazzo Piccolomini, from the roof-garden of which there are magnificent *views of the Val d'Orcia and Monte Amiata. In front of the palace is a fountain of 1462.

23 km SE of Montepulciano, above the Chiana valley, lies the little walled town of **Chiusi** (alt. 398 m; pop. 9000), the Etruscan *Chamars* or *Clevsin* (Roman *Clusium*), one of the 12 towns of the Etruscan League and a bitter opponent of Rome about 500 B.C. During the Middle Ages the population was devastated by malaria. In the Piazza del Duomo is the Museo Etrusco, with a rich collection of material from the Etruscan tombs of the area. The cathedral (10th c.) is built almost entirely with stone from Roman buildings (11 antique columns). A walk round the town affords attractive views of the surrounding countryside. – Scattered round the outskirts of the town, in separate mounds, are a number of interesting *Etruscan tombs, the finest of which (3 km N) is the *Tomba della Scimmia*, with wall paintings. To the E of the town is the *Tomba Bonci Casuccini*.

Naples/Nápoli

Region: Campania. – Province: Napoli (NA).
Altitude: 10 m. – Population: 1,255,000.
Post code: I-08100. – Dialling code: 081.
ⓘ **EPT**, Via Partenope 101;
　tel. 40 62 89.
　ACI, Piazzale Tecchio 49D;
　tel. 61 11 04.
　CIT, Piazza Municipio 72;
　tel. 32 54 26.
　Viaggi S.I.T.I., Piazza Amedeo 18;
　tel. 39 08 51.

HOTELS. – *Vesuvio*, Via Partenope 45, L, 291 b.; *Excelsior*, Via Partenope 48, L, 259 b.; *Royal*, Via Partenope 38, I, 508 b., SP; *Ambassadors Palace*, Via Medina 40, I, 460 b.; *Terminus*, Piazza Garibaldi 91, I, 441 b.; *Mediterraneo*, Via Nuovo Ponte di Tappia 25, I, 388 b.; *Oriente*, Via A. Diaz 44, I, 277 b.; *Santa Lucia*, Via Partenope 46, I, 220 b.; *Majestic*, Largo Vasto a Chiaia 68, I, 213 b.; *Parker's*, Corso Vittorio Emanuele 135, I, 155 b.; *Universo*, Piazza Carità 13, II, 317 b.; *Grilli*, Via Galileo Ferraris 40, II, 306 b.; *Stadio*, Via Tansillo 28, II, 196 b.; *San Gennaro*, Via Domiziana, II, 183 b., SP; *Britannique*, Corso Vittorio Emanuele 133, II, 157 b.; *Sant'Elmo*, Via G. Bonito 21, II, 152 b.; *Cavour*, Piazza Garibaldi 32, II, 151 b.; *Palace*, Piazza Garibaldi 9, II, 141 b.; *Paradiso*, Via Catullo 11, II, 139 b.; *Serius*, Viale Augusto 74, II, 128 b.; *Torino*, Via Depretis 123, II, 91 b.; *Domitiana*, Viale Kennedy 143, II, 64 b.; *Toledo e Regina*, Via Roma 352, III, 105 b.; *Bologna*, Via Depretis 72, III, 96 b.; *San Giorgio*, Vico III Duchessa 27, III, 95 b.; *San Pietro*, Via San Pietro ad Aram 18, III, 92 b.; *Washington*, Corso Umberto I 311, III, 90 b.; etc. – *Motel Agip*, on S.S. 7b (Via Appia), III, 111 b. – YOUTH HOSTEL, Salita della Grotta a Piedigrotta 23, 200 b. – CAMPING SITE.

RESTAURANTS. – *Il Cantinone*, Via San Pasquale a Chiaia 56; *Il Galeone*, Via Posillipo 16; *Le Arcate*, Via Aniello Falcone 249; *Starita*, Borgo Marinaro 4; *La Bersagliera*, Banchina Santa Lucia; *Birreria Bavarese*, Piazza Municipio 66; *Belvedere*, Via Tito Angellini 13 and 51–55; *Al Paradiso*, Via A. Manzoni; *Da Ciro a Santa Brigida*, Via Santa Brigida 71; *Da Ciro*, Borgo Marinaro; *Giuseppone*, Via F. Russo 13; *Da Umberto*, Via Alabardieri 30; *Da Giovanni*, Via D. Morelli 14; *Pizzeria Ragno d'Oro*, Via Ugo Niutta 6 (Vomera); *Pizzeria Santa Chiara*, Via Benedetto Croce 59.

The S Italian port town of Naples (Nápoli), once capital of the kingdom of Naples and now a provincial capital, a university town and the see of an archbishop, is Italy's third largest city, coming after Rome and Milan. It is magnificently situated on the N side of the *Bay of Naples, on the Tyrrhenian Sea, extending along the lower slopes of attractive hills.

The old town with its narrow streets and stepped lanes and its tall balconied houses is ringed on the W and N by extensive villa suburbs and on the E by an industrial zone. In recent years, particularly since the destructions of the Second World War, much of the city has been redeveloped with new buildings and realigned streets, particularly in the area round the harbour, the Rione Santa Lucia.

– Naples possesses many historical monuments going back almost 3000 years, particularly the treasures, to be seen in the National Museum, garnered from the cities engulfed by Vesuvius; the port of Naples is of major importance, serving the whole of southern Italy; and the surroundings of Naples contain some of the most beautiful scenery in the world.

HISTORY. – Naples was originally a Greek foundation. As early as the 8th c. B.C. the site was occupied by the Rhodian settlement of *Parthenope*, near which settlers from *Kyme* (Latin *Cumae*), itself a colony established by Ionians from Euboea, founded the "old town", *Palaiopolis*, in the 7th c. In the 5th c. the "new town", **Neapolis**, was founded, mainly by incomers from Chalcis on Euboea. In 326 B.C. the three settlements became allies of Rome and were amalgamated. Although favoured by Rome for its faithfulness to the alliance, Neapolis preserved its independence and its distinctive Greek characteristics until late in the Imperial period. The town became a favourite residence of the Roman magnates, and Virgil composed some of his finest poetry here. – During the period of the great migrations, in 543, the town fell into the hands of the Goths, but returned to Byzantine rule in 553 and thereafter succeeded in asserting its independence until conquered by the Normans in 1139 and incorporated by *Roger II* in his kingdom of Sicily. Roger's grandson *Frederick II* of Hohenstaufen founded the university in 1224. In the reign of *Charles of Anjou* (1266–85) Naples became capital of the kingdom. In 1442 *Alfonso I of Aragon* reunited the kingdoms of Sicily and Naples. From 1503 to 1707 Naples was the residence of *Spanish viceroys*. Following the War of the Spanish Succession the territory passed in 1713 to the *Habsburgs*, and after the War of the Austrian Succession (1748) to the *Bourbons*, with whom it remained until its incorporation in the new united Italy in 1860.

SIGHTS. – The city's busiest traffic intersection is the *Piazza Trieste e Trento*, on the E side of which stands the **Teatro San Carlo** (1737), one of the largest theatres in Europe (2900 seats). Immediately N is the *Galleria Umberto I* (1887–90), a shopping arcade which rivals Milan's Galleria Vittorio Emanuele in size. – Adjoining the Piazza Trieste e Trento on the S is the large *Piazza del Plebiscito*, occupied on the W side by the **church of San Francesco di Paola** (1817–31), an imitation of the Pantheon in Rome. Along the E side of the square is the **Palazzo Reale**, the former Royal Palace (begun 1600, by Domenico Fontana; restored 1837–41). On the façade (169 m long) are eight marble statues of the various kings who ruled Naples. The palace (closed Sunday afternoons and Tuesdays) contains a grand staircase of white marble (1651), a theatre, 17 richly appointed state apartments and the valuable *Biblioteca Nazionale* (1,500,000 volumes, 12,000 manuscripts, 5000 incunabula).

Behind the palace to the NE, on the S side of the Piazza del Municipio, is the five-towered **Castel Nuovo**, also known as the *Maschio Angioino*, once the residence of kings and viceroys of Naples. Originally built by Charles I of Anjou in 1279–83, it was enlarged at various times

Naples – view over the bay to Vesuvius

between the 15th and 18th c. and has recently been restored. The entrance is formed by a splendid Early Renaissance *triumphal arch, with rich sculptured decoration, erected between 1453 and 1467 in honour of the entry of Alfonso I of Aragon. In the courtyard is the Gothic *church of Santa Barbara*, and to the left of this the large and beautifully vaulted *Barons' Hall*.

In the centre of the *Piazza del Municipio*, which is laid out in gardens, stands an *equestrian statue of Victor Emmanuel II* (1897). On the W side of the square is the handsome **Town Hall** (1819–25), originally built to house government departments. Adjoining it the *church of San Giacomo degli Spagnoli* (1540) has behind the high altar, the sumptuous tomb of Viceroy Don Pedro de Toledo, founder of the church.

To the E of the Palazzo Reale and the Castel Nuovo extends the **Harbour**, divided up into separate docks and basins by a series of piers and breakwaters, which is always a bustle of activity. Extending E from the Piazza del Municipio is the *Molo Angioino*, on which is the *Marine Station*. To the W of this is situated the *Eliporto* (Heliport), from which there are regular helicopter services to Capri, Ischia, Capodichino Airport (7 km N), etc. Farther S, from the quay on the Calata di Beverello, boats sail to Sorrento, Capri and Ischia.

To the W of the Piazza del Plebiscito, on the slopes of Pizzofalcone and extending down to the sea, lies the district of SANTA LUCIA. S of the wide Via Santa Lucia this is an area of modern streets laid out on a regular plan, but to the N of that street it is a picturesque huddle of narrow stepped lanes in which the traditional Neapolitan way of life can be observed at any time of day but particularly in the evening. – From the SE corner of the Piazza del Plebiscito a succession of streets runs round the E and S sides of the Santa Lucia district – first Via Cesario Console, which passes the *Giardini Pubblici*; then Via Nazario Sauro and Via Partenope, in which there are several large luxury hotels; and finally, beyond the Piazza della Vittoria, *Via Caracciolo*, which affords magnificent views of the Bay of Naples. From Via Partenope a causeway and a bridge lead to a little rocky islet on which stands the

Castel dell'Ovo, begun in the 12th c., completed by Frederick II and rebuilt in the 16th c.

Between Via Caracciolo and the fine *Riviera di Chiaia* to the N extends the *Villa Nazionale, a park laid out in 1780, almost 1·5 km long, which is the city's most popular promenade. Half way along we find the *Zoological Station*, an important biological research institution founded by a German scientist, Anton Dohrn, in 1872–74. In the central block is an **Aquarium**, with 31 tanks which give an excellent survey of the fauna of the Bay of Naples. – NW of the Aquarium, in a park just N of the Riviera di Chiaia, is the *Villa Pignatelli*, once the residence of Prince Diego Aragona Pignatelli Cortes, with a richly appointed interior in the styles of the 18th and 19th c. which is well worth a visit.

From the Piazza Trieste e Trento **Via Roma** (also called Via Toledo after Don Pedro de Toledo, who built it), the city's principal traffic artery, a scene of constant bustle and activity, runs N for a distance of 2 km, rising gently uphill. It is crossed by numerous streets and lanes, many of those on the left being stepped lanes climbing up to the *Corso Vittorio Emanuele* (4 km long: beautiful views). The streets on the right, descending to the harbour and the Marine Station, are the centre of the city's business and commercial life. – At the N end of Via Roma is the spacious Piazza Dante.

From the Piazza del Municipio the Via Medina runs N past the 14th c. *church of the Incoronata* into a part of the city which has recently been transformed by the construction of new streets. Near the end of Via Medina, on the left, is the 32-storey *Grattacielo della Cattolica* (1958), and a little way farther N the Piazza Matteotti, with the *Post and Telegraph Office* (by Vaccaro, 1936), one of the finest achievements of modern Italian architecture. In a little square just E of this building stands the *church of Santa Maria la Nuova* (16th c.: beautiful interior), with two Renaissance cloisters of the monastery to which it belonged. – The line of Via Medina is continued NW by Via Monteoliveto, which runs into the Piazza Monteoliveto, with the *church of Monteoliveto* or *Sant'Anna dei Lombardi*, begun in 1411 and later continued in Early Renaissance style; it contains eight good

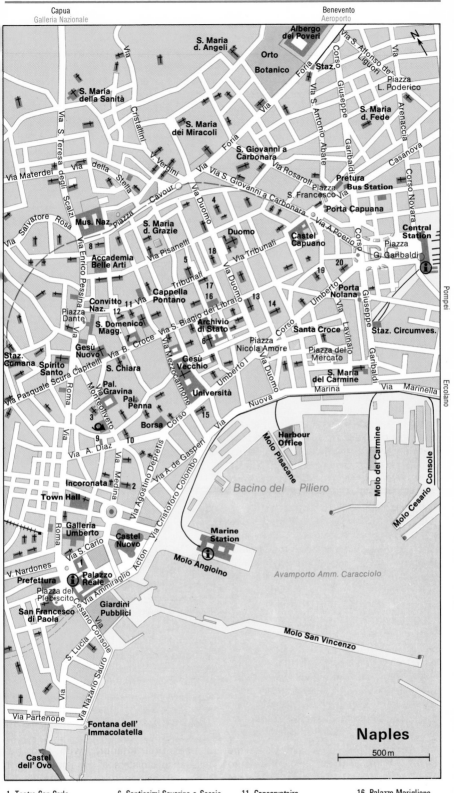

Capua
Galleria Nazionale

Benevento
Aeroporto

Naples

500 m

1 Teatro San Carlo
2 La Pietà dei Turchini
3 Sant'Anna dei Lombardi
4 Donnaregina
5 San Paolo Maggiore

6 Santissimi Severino e Sossio
7 Palazzo Filomirino
8 Galleria Principe di Napoli
9 Palazzo della Provincia
10 Santa Maria la Nova

11 Conservatoire
12 San Pietro a Maiella
13 San Giorgio Maggiore
14 Sant'Agostino della Zecca
15 San Pietro Martire

16 Palazzo Marigliano
17 San Lorenzo Maggiore
18 Gerolomini
19 SS. Annunziata
20 San Pietro ad Aram

terracottas (15th–16th c.) and beautiful 16th c. choir-stalls. – From the Piazza Monteoliveto the Calata Trinità Maggiore leads to the Piazza Gesù Nuovo, with a gilded statue of the Virgin (1748). On the N side of the square is the Jesuit *church of Gesù Nuovo* (1584), and to the SE the **church of Santa Chiara** (founded 1310), which contains the *tomb (1343–45) of Robert the Wise (1309–43) and other fine Gothic tombs belonging to members of the house of Anjou. The Nuns' Choir, behind the high altar, was used by the Poor Clares until 1925. In the adjoining Franciscan monastery is a beautiful cloister decorated with Capodimonte majolica.

To the E of the Gesù Nuovo, in Piazza San Domenico Maggiore, is the **church of San Domenico Maggiore** (c. 1300), which in spite of much later alteration is still one of the most interesting churches in Naples, with much Early Renaissance work. The sacristy contains 45 sarcophagi belonging to members of the house of Anjou. – The *Cappella Sansevero* (museum), a little way E, was built in 1590 as the burial chapel of the Sangro family and elaborately embellished in Baroque style in the 18th c.; it contains some fine sculpture, including a *Christ in a winding-sheet by Sammartino (1753). – From Piazza San Domenico Maggiore the Via San Biagio dei Librai runs E: 300 m along this street, on the left, is Via San Gregorio Armeno, in which stands the little *church of San Gregorio Armeno* (1580), one of the most richly decorated Baroque churches in Naples, with a cloister. – Via Biagio continues E and leads into Via del Duomo. 100 m along this street to the right the **Palazzo Cuomo**, a handsome Early Renaissance building (1464–88), now houses the *Museo Filangieri* (closed on Sunday afternoons and Mondays), with arms, majolica, porcelain, enamel-work and pictures. On the opposite side of the street, a little farther N, is the *church of San Giorgio Maggiore*, founded in the 5th c. and rebuilt in the 17th.

400 m N, on the right-hand side of Via del Duomo, stands the **Cathedral**, dedicated to St Januarius (San Gennaro), patron saint of Naples. Originally built between 1294 and 1323 in French Gothic style, it was considerably restored and altered after an earthquake in 1456. In the centre of the W front, which dates from 1877 to 1905, is an older doorway (1407). In the S aisle is the sumptuously appointed *chapel of St Januarius* (1608–37), on the principal altar of which is a silver bust containing the skull of St Januarius, bishop of Beneventum, who was martyred in 305, in the time of Diocletian. In the tabernacle are two vessels containing the saint's blood, which is believed to have the power of liquefaction. The liquefaction, which, according to the legend, occurred for the first time when the saint's remains were transferred to Naples in the time of Constantine, takes place three times a year on several successive days celebrated as special festivals (particularly on the first Saturday in May in the church of Santa Chiara and on 19 September in the cathedral), as well as for a few minutes every morning. The saint's tomb can be seen in the richly decorated *confessio or crypt (1497–1508) under the high altar. – Adjoining the cathedral on the N is the little church of *Santa Restituta*, a remnant of Naples' first cathedral, built in the time of Constantine (remodelled in the 18th c.). – Opposite the cathedral is the *Pinacoteca Girolamini*.

To the left of the cathedral stands the *Archbishop's Palace*, and to the N of this, in Largo Donnaregina, is the Baroque *church of Santa Maria Donnaregina* (1649: no admission). Adjoining this church on the N is the older Gothic *church of the same name (deconsecrated: entrance at Vico Donnaregina 25), restored 1928–34, with the *tomb of Queen Mary of Hungary (d. 1323) and fine *frescoes by Giotto's contemporary Pietro Cavallini and his school (c. 1308) in the raised nuns' choir. – W of the cathedral, in Via dei Tribunali, are two fine Baroque churches – the *church of the Gerolomini* (Hieronymites) or of *San Filippo Neri* (1592–1619), with a collection of pictures, and *San Paolo Maggiore* (1590–1603), built on the ruins of a temple of the early Empire (remains on façade). To the S of San Paolo Maggiore, in Via San Gregorio Armeno, is the recently restored Gothic *church of San Lorenzo Maggiore* (1266–1324), with fine tombs and frescoes. The adjoining Franciscan monastery, in which Petrarch stayed in 1345, has a notable cloister and a frescoed chapterhouse. – The *Castel Capuano*, usually known as the *Vicaria*, at the E end of Via dei Tribunali was a

Hohenstaufen and later an Angevin stronghold which has been occupied since 1540 by law courts. – Opposite the NE corner of the Castello is the domed church of Santa Caterina a Formello (1523) and farther E the *Porta Capuana, a beautiful Renaissance gateway (1485; further work 1535).

0·5 km NW of the Castel Capuano, in Via Carbonara, the former *church of San Giovanni a Carbonara (begun 1344, enlarged in the 15th c., recently restored) contains the Gothic tomb of King Ladislaus (d. 1414).

A short distance SE of the Porta Capuana in the spacious Piazza Garibaldi is the Central Station, built in 1960–64 some 250 m E of the old station. – From here the Corso Garibaldi runs S to Piazza G. Pepe, to the right of which stands the church of Santa Maria del Carmine, containing the tomb of Conradin of Hohenstaufen, Frederick II's grandson, who was beheaded at the age of 16. Above the tomb is a statue of Conradin from a design by Thorwaldsen (1847). – NW of Santa Maria del Carmine, in the Piazza del Mercato, is the church of Santa Croce al Mercato, on the spot on which Conradin was executed on 29 October 1268 on the orders of Charles I of Anjou. Inside the church, to the left of the entrance, a commemorative porphyry column can be seen.

From Piazza Garibaldi the broad Corso Umberto I runs SW to the University, with its massive main building (1909) facing the street and behind it the former Jesuit college (1605) which was the only university building from 1780 to 1908. To the E is the church of Santi Severino e Sossio (1494; rebuilt 1731 onwards). – Corso Umberto I runs into the Piazza Giovanni Bovio, with the new Exchange (Borsa) and an old Fountain of Neptune.

From Piazza Dante the Via Enrico Pessina, the continuation of Via Roma, leads to the **National Museum (closed Sunday afternoons and Mondays), with one of the world's finest collections of antiquities. The building, originally erected in 1586 as a barracks and from 1616 the home of the university, was converted in 1790 to house the royal collections. It contains the art treasures of the kings of Naples, the Farnese collections from Rome and Parma, the collections from the palaces of Portici and Capodimonte and material from Pompeii, Herculaneum and Cumae which is of unrivalled importance and interest.

The GROUND FLOOR is devoted mainly to the **collection of sculpture in marble. Items of particular importance are the figures of *Harmodius and Aristogeiton, a marble copy of a bronze group by Critius and Nesiotes (477 B.C.) which stood in the Agora in Athens; the so-called *Hera Farnese, the head of a statue of Artemis in the earlier severe style; *Orpheus and Eurydice with Hermes, a copy of a famous relief by Phidias; and Pallas Athene, a copy of an original of the time of Phidias. – In the Galleria degli Imperatori are the *Farnese Hercules, a colossal statue 3·17 m high (after a 4th c. original) found in the Baths of Caracalla in Rome, and the *Farnese Bull, the largest marble group which has come down to us from antiquity, a copy of a Rhodian work by Apollonius and Tauriscus (3rd–2nd c. B.C.).

On the MEZZANINE FLOOR is the *collection of ancient mosaics, mainly from Pompeii. Among the most notable items is the famous *Alexander's Battle, a mosaic 6·20 m long (copied from an important painting of the 4th c. B.C.) which was found in Pompeii in 1831. It shows Alexander, with his horsemen, charging the Persian king Darius at the battle of Issus (333 B.C.) and transfixing a Persian general who has been thrown from his horse, while Darius in his chariot prepares for flight.

On the FIRST FLOOR, in the central Salone dell'Atlante, is the *Farnese Atlas. Here too is the collection of **bronze sculpture, mostly from Herculaneum (recognisable by the dark patina) but also from Pompeii (with green oxidation). Particularly notable are the *Apollo playing a lyre (a 5th c. original from the Peloponnese, found in the Casa del Citarista in Pompeii), a *Dancing Faun from the Casa del Fauno in Pompeii and the so-called *Narcissus. actually the youthful Dionysus, a masterpiece of the school of Praxiteles. – Also on the first floor are the **collection of ancient wall paintings, mainly from Herculaneum, Pompeii and Stabiae, and· the *small bronzes (household utensils, etc.), together with terracottas and a large model of Pompeii (1879) on the scale of 1:1100. – The famous collection of erotic art from Pompeii is shortly to be opened to the public.

On the second floor is the *collection of ancient vases, one of the largest of its kind.

From the National Museum the Corso Amedeo di Savoia runs N, slightly uphill, to the park of Capodimonte, 2 km away. In 750 m it comes to the Ponte della Sanità, a viaduct (lift) which carries the road over the low-lying Sanità district. Below, to the right, is the large domed church of Santa Maria della Sanità (1602–13), with the Catacombs of San Gaudioso (4th c.).

The Corso Amedeo di Savoia ends at a roundabout, the Tondo di Capodimonte, on the W side of which is the entrance to the 2nd c. *Catacombs of San Gennaro (open Saturdays and Sunday mornings). Like the Roman catacombs, these consist of a maze of passages and tomb chambers, but are more ambitious architecturally and have finer paintings than their Roman counterparts. The *church of San Gennaro extra Moenia* dates from the 5th c. (restored). – From the Tondo di Capodimonte the Via Capodimonte, to the left, leads in 200 m to the imposing *pilgrimage church* (on left) of the *Madre del Buon Consiglio* (1920–60). Beyond this the road curves up to the *Porta Grande*, the main entrance to the magnificent *Capodimonte Park (297 acres). In the park is the *Palazzo Reale di Capodimonte* (1738–1839), situated on high ground (149 m) and commanding panoramic views. With over a hundred rooms, the palace houses the *Capodimonte Museum (19th c. pictures, arms and armour, porcelain, furniture, ivories and bronzes) and the **National Gallery, one of the finest collections in Italy, with more than 500 pictures, including works by Titian (portraits of members of ruling families from the Farnese collection), Mantegna and Neapolitan artists of the 17th and 18th c.

To the W of the old town, on a plateau above the Corso Vittorio Emanuele, the district of VOMERO, built from 1885 onwards, can be reached from the lower part of the city by a number of streets and three funiculars. In the southern part of this district is the *Villa Floridiana* public park, with the *Museo Duca di Martina* (closed Sunday afternoons and Mondays), which contains enamels, ivories, pottery and porcelain from many different countries. – On the eastern edge of the Vomero plateau is the Castel Sant'Elmo (alt. 224 m), built in 1329 and extended between the 15th and 17th c., with massive walls and underground passages hewn from the rock; it is now a military prison. – To the E of the castle is the former Carthusian *monastery of San Martino (1325; rebuilt in the 17th c.), with the *Museo Nazionale di San Martino* (closed Saturday afternoons and Mondays). Notable features of the monastery are the church, richly decorated with marble and pictures of the 17th and 18th c., the sacristy, the treasury, the Chiostro dei Procuratori and the main cloisters, with 60 columns of white marble. The museum contains porcelain, *presepi* (cribs: i.e. Nativity scenes), including the

famous Presepe del Cuciniello, a state coach of Charles III's reign (18th c.) and relics of the history of Naples and southern Italy in the 18th and 19th c. From the room known as the Belvedere there are superb *views of Naples, its bay and Vesuvius, extending to the Apennines.

SURROUNDINGS. – The best view of Naples and its beautiful surroundings is to be had from the Camaldulensian monastery of *Camaldoli, 11 km NW of the city on the highest point in the Phlegraean Fields (458 m). The monastery (no admission for women, or for men in summer) was founded in 1585. The **prospect from the terrace on a clear day is one of the finest in Italy. – The same view can be enjoyed from the *Belvedere della Pagliarella (open without restriction), 0·5 km S, reached in 15 minutes by a footpath through the scrub.

12 km SW of Naples is Posillipo, a ridge of hills 6 km long, covered with villas and gardens, between the Bay of Naples and the Bay of Pozzuoli, with magnificent views. The name comes from a villa called Pausilypon ("Sans-Souci") which belonged to the notorious epicure Vedius Pollio and later to Augustus. – From Via Caracciolo, which ends in Mergellina, the *Via di Posillipo runs SW above the sea. Climbing slightly, it comes in 4 km, after passing the end of Via Boccaccio, to the Parco Virgiliano (alt. 153 m), lying at the SW end of the ridge almost vertically above the sea and the rocky volcanic island of *Nisida*. From the road encircling the park there are beautiful *views. – Via Boccaccio runs uphill into Via Manzoni, from which *Via Petrarca continues gently downhill, affording extensive views, to Via Orazio. On the upper part of this road to the left is the *pilgrimage church of Sant'Antonio*, from which there is a famous *view of Naples. Beyond this the road runs down to the suburb of *Mergellina*, with a picturesque harbour, Porto Sannazzaro (hydrofoil services to Capri and Ischia). A little way N, at the exits of two tunnels through the hill of Posillipo, are the Piazza Sannazzaro and the Piazza di Piedigrotta, where stands the *church of Santa Maria di Piedigrotta* (13th c.), with a Renaissance cloister (famous traditional *festa* from 5 to 13 September: principal celebrations on 7 September). To the W of the church, immediately beyond the railway underpass, is the entrance (on left) to the *Park of Virgil*, in which are the tomb of the poet Giacomo Leopardi (1798–1837) and a Roman structure (actually the columbarium of an unknown family) known as the Tomb of Virgil (70–19 B.C.), who had a villa on Posillipo and desired to be buried there. – From the entrance to the park the Galleria delle Quattro Giornate leads W to the suburb of Fuorigrotta, which has grown enormously since the last war, with huge blocks of apartments, a stadium (1959) seating 100,000 spectators, the new buildings of the Technical University (1965) and the Mostra d'Oltremare complex, originally built in 1939–40 to display the achievements of the Italian overseas possessions and rebuilt after war damage in 1952 as a large exhibition centre, with two theatres, a swimming pool, an illuminated fountain, a zoo and a large amusement park, Edenlandia.

15 km W of Posillipo or Fuorigrotta is Pozzuoli (alt. 39 m; pop. 60,000; hotels: Terme Puteolane, III, 132 b.; Terme La Salute, III, 114 b.; American, III, 76 b.; Hideaway, III, 70 b.; etc.), a port situated on the slopes of a tufa ridge projecting into the sea, on the edge of

the area of volcanic hills known as the *Phlegraean Fields* (Campi Flegrei). Founded in the 6th c. B.C. by Greeks from Samos under the name of *Dikaiarcheia*, it passed into the hands of the Romans in 318 B.C., and as *Puteoli* developed into the principal Italian port for trade with Egypt and the East. In the old town, which is situated on a peninsula, is the cathedral of San Procolo (destroyed by fire in 1964), which was built on the site of a temple of the 3rd–2nd c. B.C. and has six ancient columns on the NE side. It contains the tomb of the composer Pergolesi (1710–36). – 0·5 km N, on the sea, is the so-called Serapeum, an ancient market (*macellum*), which preserves some columns of its colonnade. SW of the Serapeum are baths. In the harbour to the NW remains of a temple with 14 columns and a sculptor's workshop were discovered on the sea-bottom. Above the old town, on the left of the road to Naples, is the Roman *Amphitheatre, the third largest in Italy after the Colosseum in Rome and the amphitheatre of Santa Maria Capua Vetere (147 m long, 117 m across; seating for 40,000). Particularly impressive are the underground passages which housed the machinery and the wild beasts' dens. The arena (72 m long, 42 m across) could be filled with water for naval battles.

1·5 km E, near the road from Naples, is the entrance to the *Solfatara*, a semi-extinct volcano (only recorded eruption 1198). This is a circular area enclosed by tufa hills, with numerous fissures (fumaroles) which emit steam and sulphurous gases. The ground sounds hollow. The temperature of the largest fumarole is 162 °C (324 °F), of the smaller ones around 100 °C (212 °F). The volume of vapour is considerably increased if a piece of burning paper or a torch is held at the mouth of one of the vents.

6 km W of Pozzuoli is **Baia** (pop. 6000), prettily situated on the W side of the Bay of Pozzuoli. As *Baiae* this was the most fashionable watering-place of Imperial Rome, and impressive *Baths dating from this period have been excavated (closed Thursdays). At the near end of the town, amid vineyards to the right of the road, is the so-called Temple of Mercury, a large circular building with a vaulted roof open in the centre, adjoining which are the Baths of Mercury. Farther on, to the right, are the Baths of Sosandra, with the semicircular Theatre of the Nymphs and a statue of Sosandra. Immediately W are the Baths of Venus, opposite the so-called Temple of Venus.

2 km SE of Baia along the W side of the Bay of Pozzuoli (on the left the 16th c. Castello di Baia) we come to **Bacoli** (pop. 21,000; Hotel Misano, III, 30 b.; etc.). On a tongue of land 0·5 km E is a two-storey Roman structure known as the *Cento Camerelle*, the upper storey of which was a cistern. 0·5 km S of Bacoli, above the *Mare Morto*, is the *Piscina Mirabilis*, an excellently preserved Roman reservoir 71 m long by 25 m wide, with a vaulted roof borne on 48 massive pillars. – From the nearby village of *Miseno* it is a half hour's climb to the top of **Monte Miseno** (167 m), a curiously shaped crater rising out of the sea (described by Virgil as the tomb of Aeneas's trumpeter Misenus), from which there is one of the finest *views of the Bay of Naples and Gaeta. – There are also very fine views from *Capo Miseno* (79 m), half an hour S. Near here was Lucullus's villa, in which the Emperor Tiberius died.

10 km N of Bacoli (7 km NW of Pozzuoli) are the remains of *Cumae (Italian *Cuma*, Greek *Kyme*), the oldest Greek settlement in Italy, founded in the 8th c. B.C. and destroyed by the Saracens in the 9th c. A.D. The site has been excavated since 1926. Beyond a short tunnel, to the right, is the so-called Roman Crypt, a tunnel of Augustan date, 180 m long, which runs under the acropolis to the sea. Opposite this, to the left, is the entrance to the Cave of the Sibyl (Antro della Sibilla), described by Virgil (*Aeneid* VI, 43 ff.) as having a hundred entrances and a hundred issues, "from which resound as many voices, the oracles of the prophetess". This is a passage hewn from the rock, 131 m long, 2·5 m wide and 5 m high, with numerous side passages opening on to the sea which provide light and air. At the far end is the actual cave of the oracle, a square chamber with three vaulted recesses. From the Cave of the Sibyl a ramp leads up to the acropolis. The road leads past an outlook terrace to the remains of the Temple of Apollo and beyond this, on the summit of the hill, the ruins of a Temple of Jupiter which was used as a church in early Christian times. From the top of the hill there are magnificent *views of the sea, extending as far as Gaeta and the Isole Ponziane, and of the Phlegraean Fields to the E. – On the S side of the excavated area is the *Amphitheatre* (129 m long, 104 m across, 21 rows of seats). – To the SE is the *Lago del Fusaro*, linked with the sea by two canals, a shallow lake (8 m deep) which is used for oyster-culture.

One excursion which no visitor to Naples should miss is the beautiful run on S.S. 18 to Amalfi and Salerno (the motorway is shorter but less attractive). – 10 km E of Naples is **Portici** (alt. 26 m; pop. 70,000; Hotel Poli Bellavista, IV, 30 b.), with a former royal palace which now houses the Faculty of Agriculture of Naples University. – 1 km: main entrance to the excavations of **Herculaneum** (see p. 131). – 3 km: **Torre del Greco** (alt. 51 m; pop. 93,000; hotels: Scobel, II, 132 b.; Sakura, II, 96 b.; etc.), which has in the course of its history been repeatedly covered with lava and destroyed by earthquakes. – 8 km: **Torre Annunziata** (alt. 14 m; pop. 57,000; Motel Pavesi, III, 82 b.), with a villa painted in Pompeian style, a relic of the Roman town of *Oplontis*. This is the starting point for the ascent of **Vesuvius** (see p. 319). – 9 km: **Castellammare di Stabia** (alt. 5 m; pop. 70,000; hotels: Delle Terme, II, 190 b.; SP; Miramare, II, 134 b.; Dei Congressi, II, 132 b.; Stabia, II, 109 b.; Villa Serena, II, 91 b.; Virginia, III, 86 b.; Orazzo, III, 82 b.; etc.), a port built at the foot and on the lower slopes of an outlier of Monte Sant'Angelo, occupying the site of the Roman *Stabiae*, which was destroyed along with Pompeii in A.D. 79 (recent excavations; museum). The town is a favourite resort of the Neapolitans on account of its mineral springs, impregnated with sulphur and carbonic acid gas. In the Piazza del Municipio is the 16th c. cathedral. In the SW of the town are the harbour, with a long breakwater, and the spa establishments, with a ruined castle (13th c.) on the hill above. In the Scanzano district, above the cathedral to the E, are the new Baths. – Above Castellammare to the SE ($\frac{1}{2}$ hour) is the beautiful park of the *Villa Quisisana* ("Here you recover your health"); the house is at the SE end of the park. From here there is an attractive drive (12 km: also cableway) up **Monte Faito** (1131 m: *view), to the S.

Beyond Castellammare the Amalfi road runs close to the coast again, affording magnificent *views of the Bay of Naples, Vesuvius and the steep rock coast of the Sorrento peninsula. – 15 km: **Meta** (alt. 111 m; pop. 7000; Hotel Giosuè a Mare, III, 50 b.). The road then goes over a pass (310 m) in the Monti Lattari to reach the S side of the Sorrento peninsula, looking on to the Bay of Salerno. The following stretch of ** road as far as Salerno, blasted out of the rocky coast high above the sea, is one of the most beautiful roads in the world, its charm enhanced by the many little towns and villages in a rather Oriental style of architecture which cling to the precipitous slopes. Out to sea, as the road reaches the coast, can be seen the little "Isles of the Sirens", usually known as *Li Galli*. – 13 km: **Positano** (alt. 20 m; pop. 3000), a very picturesque little town extending up the steep rocky slopes above the sea, with square flat-roofed houses reminiscent of the Saracen period. From here the road continues along the wild and rugged coast, passing several old watch-towers on the coast below. – 15 km: **Amalfi** (see p. 55).

Beyond Amalfi the road runs round the *Capo d'Amalfi* and along a stretch which is almost entirely blasted out of the cliffs or carried over gorges on viaducts, affording splendid views. – 4 km: **Minori** (alt. 40 m; pop. 3000; hotels: Bristol, II, 70 b.; Villa Romana, III, 101 b.; etc.), once the arsenal of Amalfi. Roman villa (1st c. A.D.) with well-preserved wall paintings. – 1 km: **Maiori** (alt. 15 m; pop. 6000; hotels: Regina Palace, I, 107 b., SP; Pietra di Luna, II, 160 b., SP; Panorama, II, 152 b.; Garden, II, 147 b.; Sole Splendid, II, 122 b.; San Francesco, II, 84 b.; Due Torri, II, 69 b.; Mare, II, 58 b.; San Pietro, II, 56 b.; Sole, II, 49 b.; Panoramic Residence, III, 61 b.; etc.), a popular resort at the mouth of the *Tramonti* valley. On the coast near the town are a sulphur spring and a number of stalactitic caves, including the *Grotta Pandona*, which resembles the Blue Grotto on Capri. – 10 km: *Cetara* (alt. 15 m; Hotel Cetara, II, 36 b.), a fishing village picturesquely situated in a deep ravine which was the first settlement established by the Saracens. – 8 km: **Salerno** (see p. 254).

There is also a very attractive trip (28 km E) from Naples to **Nola** (alt. 40 m; pop. 25,000; Hotel Scala, III, 66 b.), where St Paulinus (354–431), a native of Bordeaux and an accomplished poet, is said to have invented the church-bell (hence the Italian word for a bell, *campana*, Nola being in Campania); his feast, the Festa dei Gigli ("Feast of Lilies"), is celebrated with great pomp on the last Sunday in June. In the Piazza del Duomo is a bronze statue of Augustus, who died here in A.D. 14. The cathedral, built over the remains of an ancient temple and rebuilt in 1870 after a fire, has a fine crypt. In the Piazza Giordano Bruno is a monument to the philosopher Giordano Bruno, born in Nola in 1548, who was burned at the stake in 1600 in Rome as a heretic. – 20 km E of Nola on the road to Avellino is a side road leading N (5 km) to the pilgrimage centre of *Montevergine* (alt. 1270 m; cableway from Mercogliano; Hotel Romito, II, 71 b.). In the church of the monastery founded by St William of Vercelli in 1119 on the ruins of a Temple of Cybele are a number of fine tombs and, in the S aisle, a chapel with a figure of the Virgin venerated as miraculous; the head of the figure is Byzantine. Pilgrimages at Easter and on 7–8 September. – It is a 45 minutes' climb from the monastery to the top of *Montevergine* (1480 m), crowned by a large cross, from which there are magnificent views of the Bay of Naples and Salerno and the mountains of the interior.

Novara

Region: Piemonte. – Province: Novara (NO).
Altitude: 159 m. – Population: 100,000.
Post code: I-28100. – Dialling code: 0321.
ⓘ **EPT**, Corso Cavour 2;
    tel. 2 33 98.
   ACI, Via Rosmini 36;
    tel. 3 03 21.

Novara – a bird's eye view

HOTELS. – *Europa*, Corso Cavallotti 38, II, 106 b.; *Il Girarrosto*, Corso della Vittoria 101, III, 71 b.; *D'Italia*, Via Cairoli 3–5, III, 69 b.; *Cristallo*, Corso Vercelli 7, III, 41 b.; etc.

The provincial capital of Novara, the Roman Novaria, situated in the Piedmontese plain between the rivers Ticino and Sesia, is an industrial town with a varied range of industry (Montecatini, Pavesi) and a large map-making institute (De Agostini), and the centre of a large rice-growing area. The town is surrounded by a ring of attractive boulevards on the line of the old fortifications.

SIGHTS. – In the centre of the town, in the arcaded *Via Fratelli Rosselli*, stands the **Cathedral**, built between 1831 and 1865 in place of an earlier church. It has an attractive cloister, entered from the S aisle. There are important cathedral archives. Opposite the imposing entrance court is a 5th c. *baptistery* (10th c. frescoes). – N of the cathedral, reached by way of the beautiful courtyard of the *Broletto*, is the *Corso Italia*, one of the town's two main traffic arteries (the other being the *Corso Cavour*, which crosses it at right angles).

A little way N of the Broletto, at the end of Via Gaudenzio Ferrari, the **church of San Gaudenzio** (by Pellegrino Tibaldi, 1577) has an 18th c. campanile and a prominent dome (1875–78). – W of the cathedral is the large Piazza Martiri della Libertà, with the *Teatro Coccia* and the *Palazzo del Mercato* (1840). On the S side are the remains of the *Castello Sforzesco*, with the Giardino Pubblico behind it.

SURROUNDINGS. – There is a very attractive drive (56 km NW) up the Sesia valley to **Varallo Sesia** (alt. 453 m; pop. 8000), charmingly situated in the Pre-

Alps at the mouth of the narrow valley of the Mastallone, with the collegiate church of San Gaudenzio, picturesquely perched on a crag, and the church of Santa Maria delle Grazie (*frescoes by Gaudenzio Ferrari, 1507–13). At Santa Maria begins the ascent, with Stations of the Cross (also cableway), to the *Sacro Monte (608 m), a much visited shrine founded in 1486 by the Franciscan friar Bernardo Caimi. On the summit of the hill are 43 chapels with painted terracotta groups and frescoes depicting scenes from the scriptural story; in the 38th chapel is a *Crucifixion by Gaudenzio Ferrari. There are fine frescoes in the dome of the imposing church (1614–49; the façade is modern). – 36 km beyond Varallo, beautifully situated at the head of the Sesia valley, is **Alagna Valsesia** (alt. 1191 m; hotels: Delle Alpi, II, 85 b.; Alagnese, IV, 23 b.; etc.), from which a cableway (20 minutes) runs up via *Zaroltu* (1825 m) and the *Bocchetta della Pisse* (2406 m) to the *Punta Indren* (3260 m), a southern outlier of Monte Rosa.

45 km N of Novara to **Lake Orta**, the Roman *Lacus Cucius* (area 18 sq. km, greatest depth 143 m), the S end of which is particularly beautiful. In a picturesque setting at the foot of the *Monte d'Orta* or *Sacro Monte di San Francesco* (410 m; 20 pilgrimage chapels; *view of Monte Rosa) is the little town of *Orta San Giulio** (alt. 293 m; pop. 1000; hotels: San Rocco, I, 81 b.; Orta, III, 53 b.; etc.). In the main square is the Town Hall (1592). From the W end of the square there is a beautiful view of the *Isola San Giulio*, with a church traditionally said to have been founded by St Julius in 390 and a large seminary. There is a pleasant drive up *Monte Mottarone* (1491 m), from which there are panoramic views.

23 km S of Novara is the old provincial capital of **Vercelli** (alt. 131 m; pop. 56,000; hotels: Viotti, II, 84 b.; Savoia, II, 55 b.; Europa, II, 36 b.; Brusasca, III, 45 b.; Riz, III, 45 b.; etc.) the Roman *Vercellae*; it is the see of an archbishop, the centre of the largest rice-growing area in Europe and has many fine old churches. In the N of the town, near the station, stands the cathedral, remodelled in Baroque style, with the exception of the tower, from the 16th c. onwards; the cathedral library contains valuable manuscripts. A short distance SW is the imposing four-towered church of Sant'Andrea (1219–24), with a Romanesque façade and a notable interior. The adjoining Cistercian abbey has a beautiful cloister. In the southern part of the town is the Dominican church of San Cristoforo, with frescoes by Gaudenzio Ferrari. – S of Vercelli, on the road to Casale, were the Campi Raudii, where the Roman consul Marius defeated the Cimbri in 101 B.C.

31 km E of Novara is **Magenta** (alt. 138 m; pop. 24,000; Hotel Excelsior, III, 69 b.; etc.), scene of the famous battle on 4 June 1859 in which the French and Piedmontese defeated the Austrians, who thereupon withdrew from Lombardy (church of San Martino, built in 1903 to commemorate the victory; charnel-house). – 9 km S of Magenta **Abbiategrasso** (alt. 120 m; pop. 23,000; hotels: Italia, II, 65 b.; Moretto, III, 28 b.) boasts the fine parish church of Santa Maria (*façade by Bramante, 1497). – 12 km SW of Abbiategrasso is **Vigevano** (alt. 116 m; pop. 70,000; hotels: Internazionale, II, 50 b.; Europa, II, 42 b.; etc.), an important centre of shoe manufacture. In the market square (by Bramante, 1493) are arcades which still preserve remains of their Early Renaissance decoration. Other features of interest are the cathedral (16th c.) and the Visconti castle, rebuilt by Bramante and Leonardo da Vinci in 1492 (fine courtyard).

Orvieto

Region: Umbria. – Province: Terni (TR).
Altitude: 325 m. – Population: 10,000.
Post code: I-05018. – Dialling code: 0763.
ⓘ AA, Piazza del Duomo 24;
tel. 51 72.
TCI, *Fabbri Viaggi*, Via del Duomo 58;
tel. 3 34 48.

HOTELS. – *Maitani*, I, 75 b.; *Italia*, I, 69 b.; *La Badia*, I, 41 b.; *Grand Hotel Reale*, II, 57 b.; *Virgilio*, II, 27 b.; *Aquila Bianca*, III, 40 b.; etc.

The Umbrian town of Orvieto is magnificently situated on a tufa crag which rears up out of the Paglia valley. Founded by the Etruscans, it was known in late antiquity as Urbibentum or Urbs Vetus (the "old town"), and later became a stronghold of the Guelf party, in which the Popes frequently sought refuge. – The white wine of Orvieto is renowned.

SIGHTS. – The ****Cathedral**, in the SE of the town, in the *Piazza del Duomo*, one of the most splendid examples of Italian Gothic architecture, was built in alternating courses of black basalt and greyish-yellow limestone and decorated by the finest artists of the day. It was founded before 1285 in honour of the "miracle of Bolsena" (see p. 138) and consecrated in 1309. The *façade, begun in 1310 but not completed until the 16th c., is decorated with scenes from the Old and New Testaments by Sienese artists (14th c.) and mosaics of overwhelming richness (mostly restored). The intricately carved

Orvieto Cathedral

modern bronze doors are by Emilio Greco (1969).

In the INTERIOR, richly decorated with frescoes, is the **Cappella Nuova* or *Cappella della Madonna di San Brizio*, with frescoes (Apocalyptic visions), begun by Fra Angelico da Fiesole in 1447 but mainly painted by Luca Signorelli from 1499 onwards, which are among the supreme achievements of 15th c. painting. – Behind the altar of the *Cappella del Corporale* is a *reliquary (1338) containing the bloodstained chalice-cloth of the "miracle of Bolsena", which is displayed only on Easter Day and Corpus Christi.

To the right of the cathedral is the 13th c. **Palazzo dei Papi**, with the *Museo dell'Opera del Duomo* (pictures and sculpture from the cathedral), and facing the cathedral the *Palazzo Faina*, with a collection of Etruscan and Greek vases; the archaeological section of this museum is in the adjoining *Palazzo dell'Opera del Duomo*.

From the cathedral the Via del Duomo runs NW into the *Corso Cavour*, the main street of the town, which traverses it from E to W. At the junction of the two streets rises the *Torre del Moro*, and a short distance N of this point is the Piazza del Popolo, with the 12th c. *Palazzo del Popolo*. – At the W end of Corso Cavour is the busy Piazza della Repubblica, with the *church of Sant'Andrea* (12-sided 11th c. tower) and the massive **Palazzo Comunale** (12th c.; façade rebuilt in 16th c.).

At the E end of the town, to the N of the *Fortezza* (now public gardens), can be seen the *Pozzo di San Patrizio* (1527–40), a well 61 m deep with two separate spiral staircases winding round the shaft, one for the descent and the other for the ascent of the donkeys which brought up water from the well. Nearby are remains of an *Etruscan temple*.

Below the N side of the town, to the left of the road to the station, is an interesting *Etruscan necropolis*, with tombs mostly dating from the 5th c. B.C.

Ostia

Region: Lazio. – Province: Roma (ROMA).
Altitude: 3 m.
Post code: I-00050. – Dialling code: 06.

Ostia, the port of ancient Rome, now lying 5 km inland, is the largest excavation site in Italy after Pompeii. The remains give a vivid picture of life in the Roman town.

HISTORY. – Ancient Ostia was founded about the 4th c. B.C. in an area of salt-pans at the mouth (*ostia*) of the Tiber. From about 300 B.C. it was the principal Roman naval base, and under the Empire developed into a considerable town of 70,000–80,000 inhabitants, Rome's largest suburb and commercial port, through which the city's supplies of corn were brought in. After the fall of the Roman Empire Ostia was left without protection from the raids of Berber pirates from North Africa and fell a victim to decay and the ravages of malaria. The harbour silted up, and in 1558 the Tiber changed its course. – The excavated remains date mainly from the 2nd–4th c. A.D., i.e. the period following the destruction of Pompeii. In contrast to Pompeii with its single-storey houses occupied by separate families Ostia's swarming population was housed in blocks of apartments (*insulae*) several storeys high, with numerous windows opening on to the street and on to the interior garden and often with loggias and balconies facing the street – typical examples of the architecture of Imperial Rome. – Recent excavations have brought to light a 4th c. Christian basilica measuring 43 by 16 m, similar in style to the basilicas erected in Rome in the reign of Constantine.

Thefts of cars and attacks on visitors, in public places and in broad daylight, are a frequent occurrence in Ostia. You have been warned!

TOUR OF THE EXCAVATIONS (*Ostia Scavi: closed Mondays). – Just beyond the main entrance, along the ancient *Via Ostiensis* and in the parallel street to the S, the *Via delle Tombe* (even more impressive), are *rows of tombs*, both individual tombs, sometimes of considerable size, and columbaria with niches for large numbers of urns. The Via Ostiensis leads to the remains of the *Porta Romana*, the most important of the town's three gates. From here the *Decumanus Maximus*, the main street of ancient Ostia, runs SW for more than a kilometre. Beyond the gate, on the left, is the *Piazzale della Vittoria*, named after the statue of *Minerva Victoria* (1st c. A.D.) which was found here. – Farther along, at the corner of *Via dei Vigili* (on right), are the *Baths of Neptune*, with heating arrangements at the NE corner (good general view from a terrace on the first floor). – At the end of Via dei Vigili, on the left, are the *Watchmen's Barracks* (2nd c. A.D.), with an imposing central courtyard. Continuing along the Decumanus past the Baths, we come to the **Theatre**, originally built in the time of Augustus and enlarged under Septimius Severus,

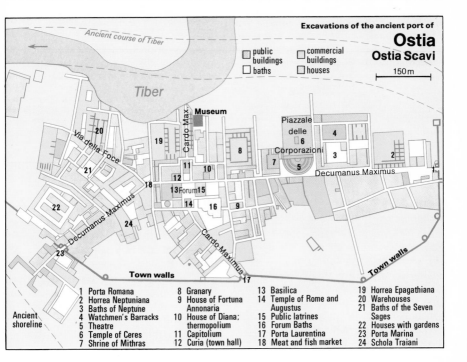

Excavations of the ancient port of
Ostia
Ostia Scavi

□ public buildings   □ commercial buildings   □ baths   □ houses

150 m

1	Porta Romana	8	Granary
2	Horrea Neptuniana	9	House of Fortuna Annonaria
3	Baths of Neptune	10	House of Diana; thermopolium
4	Watchmen's Barracks	11	Capitolium
5	Theatre	12	Curia (town hall)
6	Temple of Ceres	13	Basilica
7	Shrine of Mithras	14	Temple of Rome and Augustus

15	Public latrines
16	Forum Baths
17	Porta Laurentina
18	Meat and fish market
19	Horrea Epagathiana
20	Warehouses
21	Baths of the Seven Sages
22	Houses with gardens
23	Porta Marina
24	Schola Traiani

which was adapted in 1927 to accommodate theatrical performances in the summer. From the highest tier of seating there is a good view of the excavations, particularly of the *Piazzale delle Corporazioni* immediately N of the theatre, with the columns of the *Temple of Ceres*. Along the E side of this square are the offices (*scholae*) of the various *shipping corporations* trading with overseas ports, mainly in Africa. – To the W of the theatre is the House of *Marcus Apuleius Marcellus* (2nd–3rd c. A.D.), with a peristyle and atrium of Pompeian type. Adjoining it on the N is a shrine of Mithras.

Farther along the Decumanus, on the right, are four small *temples* built on an older substructure, with a large *granary* (*horreum*) to the W. Beyond this, also on the right-hand side of the Decumanus, is a well-preserved *thermopolium*, a bar with a stone counter containing basins for cooling the drinks and tiers of shelves for drinking vessels. Beyond this, to the right, the imposing **Capitolium** (2nd c. A.D.) the temple of the Capitoline triad (Jupiter, Juno and Minerva), was the religious centre of the town. Standing on a high brick base, this was the only building of ancient Ostia which remained above ground throughout the Middle Ages. To the S of the Capitolium is the **Forum**, in the centre of the town at the intersection

of the Decumanus with the *Cardo Maximus*, the principal transverse street. On the S side of the Forum are the remains of the *Temple of Rome and Augustus* (1st c. A.D.). To the W, beyond a *basilica*, is a *rotunda* (3rd c. A.D.) in the style of the Pantheon. SE of the Forum are large 2nd c. *Baths*.

At the N end of the Cardo Maximus is the interesting **Museo Ostiense** (closed Mondays), with a rich collection of material recovered during the excavations. – At the SE end of the Cardo is the triangular *Campo della Magna Mater*, with a temple of the Great Mother (2nd–3rd c. A.D.). A short distance SE is

The Capitolium, Ostia

the well-preserved *Porta Laurentina* and 150 m N the *House of Fortuna Annonaria* (3rd–4th c. A.D.). – On the right of the Decumanus, W of the Capitolium, is a *bazaar*, a courtyard surrounded by 18 shops. To the N of this lay the *Small Market*. – 100 m W of the Capitolium is the ancient *W gate*, and close by, towards the Tiber, are the *Horrea Epagathiana*, privately owned warehouses with a handsome gateway and a two-storey arcaded courtyard.

Beyond the W gate is an area excavated between 1938 and 1942. Notable features here are the *House of Serapis* (2nd c. A.D.), with upper storeys, in Via della Foce, off the Decumanus to the right; the *Baths of the Seven Sages* (large circular mosaic), the *Terme della Trinacria* (mosaics) and the *House of the Charioteer*. – The Decumanus Maximus ends some 300 m SW of the W gate at the *Porta Marina* (car park). Beyond this excavation has brought to light remains of the harbour.

To the E of the excavations, on the line of the ancient Via Ostiensis, is the modern town of **Ostia Antica** (pop. 3000), dominated by a castle built in 1483–86 to protect the harbour, a fine example of medieval Italian military architecture (Museo della Rocca). Adjacent to the castle is the 15th c. church of Santa Aurea. – 4 km SW of Ostia Antica, on the Tyrrhenian Sea, the seaside resort of **Lido di Ostia** (hotels: Satellite Palace, I, 460 b., SP; Airport Hotel Palace, I, 453 b., SP; Ping Pong, II, 38 b.; Belvedere, III, 95 b.; etc.) has a beach 7 km long. From here a road runs SE past the beautiful Parco di Castel Fusano to the resort of *Lido di Castel Fusano*, 4 km from Lido di Ostia, at the end of the expressway from Rome, the Via Cristoforo Colombo.

Padua/Pádova

Region: Veneto. – Province: Padova (PD).
Altitude: 12 m. – Population: 240,000.
Post code: I-31500. – Dialling code: 049.
(i) **EPT**, Riviera Mugnai 8;
    tel. 65 18 56.
    ACI, Via Enrico degli Scrovegni 19;
    tel. 65 47 33.
    CIT, Via Matteotti 12;
    tel. 2 53 49.
    Mondadori per Voi, Via E. Filiberto 1;
    tel. 3 83 56.

HOTELS. – *Plaza*, Corso Milano 40, I, 261 b.; *Le Padovanelle*, in Ponte di Brenta, Via Chilesotti, 80 b., SP; *Villa Altichiero*, in Altichiero, II, 122 b., SP; *Grande Italia*, Piazzale Stazione, II, 109 b.; *Biri*, Via Grassi 2, II, 105 b.; *Corso*, Corso del Popolo 2, II, 95 b.; *Milano*, Via Vicenza 2, II, 93 b.; *Europa*, Largo Europa 9, II, 81 b.; *Monaco*, Piazzale Stazione 3, II, 79 b.; *Majestic Toscanelli*, Via dell'Arco 2, II, 70 b.; *Leon Bianco*, Piazzetta Pedrocchi 12, II, 45 b.; *Casa del Pellegrino*, Via M. Cesarotti 21, III, 203 b.; *Al Cason*, Via ˙Fra Paolo Sarpi 40, III, 84 b.; *Igea*, Via Ospedale Civile 87, III, 71 b.; etc.

EVENT. – *Trade Fair* (Fiera del Santo) in June.

The provincial capital of Padua (Pádova), 30 km W of Venice on the edge of the Euganean Hills, is noted mainly for its old university and for its associations with St Antony of Padua. It also possesses in Giotto's and Mantegna's frescoes and Donatello's equestrian statue of Gattamelata works of art of the very first rank.

The older part of the town has a medieval aspect with its narrow arcaded streets, the ancient bridges over the many arms of the River Bacchiglione and the Byzantine domes of its churches.

HISTORY and ART. – Under the early Empire the Roman *Patavium* was one of the wealthiest cities in Italy. It was destroyed by the Huns in 452, but thereafter enjoyed a further period of prosperity. In 1164 it became the first town in northern Italy to free itself from Hohenstaufen rule. During the subsequent conflicts it usually supported the Guelfs. In 1318 it passed into the hands of the house of Carrara, and in 1405 was annexed by Venice. – The Roman historian *Livy* lived in Padua and died there in A.D. 17. In the early 13th c. the eloquent preacher *St Antony* (b. Lisbon 1195, d. 1231 at Arcella, 2·5 km N of Padua) lived and worked in Padua. Padua's importance during the medieval period and at the Renaissance rested mainly on its university, founded in 1222 and extended by Frederick II in 1238, which became the first centre of humanism and also exerted a great attraction on artists. – During the 14th c. the finest works of art produced in Padua were by incomers like *Giotto, Giovanni Pisano* and *Altichiero*; and the great flowering of art in the 15th c. was due to Florentine artists, among them *Donatello, Paolo Uccello* and *Andrea del Castagno*, who influenced sculptors such as *Bartolomeo Bellano* and *Andrea Riccio* as well as the great painter *Andrea Mantegna* (1431–1506).

SIGHTS. – In the centre of the old town is the *Piazza Cavour*, from which the busy *Via VIII Febbraio* and *Via Roma* run S. On the right of Via VIII Febbraio is the neoclassical *Caffè Pedrocchi* (rebuilt after the Second World War), which when it was first opened in 1831 was the largest café in Europe. It played an important part in the history of the Risorgimento, and is still the resort of professors and students of the university. Beyond this stands the *Palazzo Municipale* (Town Hall), with a façade of 1930 and an older building to the rear (16th c.). – Opposite the Town Hall is the **University**, built in the 16th c. In the colonnaded courtyard (1552) and inside the building are numerous names and coats of arms of distinguished graduates. Handsome Great Hall; chairs of Galileo and other famous professors; Anatomy Theatre (1594), the oldest of its kind. – From the university two streets run W, leading respectively to the Piazza delle Frutta and the Piazza delle Erbe. Between the two squares we find the **Salone** or *Palazzo della Ragione*, built 1172–1219 as a law court, now an exhibition and conference hall (entrance from the Piazza delle Erbe, on right). The huge*hall (81 m long, 27 m wide, 27 m high), rebuilt in 1420, contains a large wooden horse (1466), a copy of Gattamelata's horse in Donatello's famous statue, and astrological frescoes (15th c., restored) on the walls.

Farther W is the *Piazza dei Signori*, in which can be seen the *Loggia del Consiglio* or *Loggia della Gran Guardia*, an elegant Early Renaissance building

Basilica of St Antony, Padua

with an open loggia below and a closed upper storey (1496–1526). On the W side of the square, on the site of an earlier Carrara palace, is the *Palazzo del Capitanio* (1532), formerly the seat of the Venetian governor, with a handsome clock-tower and remains of a late Gothic loggia which belonged to the earlier palace. – To the SW stands the **Cathedral**, a High Renaissance building (1551–77) with an unfinished façade. To the right of the cathedral the elegant brick-built *Baptistery* (13th c.) has interesting *frescoes by Giusto de' Menabuoi (*c.* 1380).

SW of the university, beyond the wide modern streets (Riviera Vittorio Livio and Riviera dei Ponti Romani) built over an arm of the Bacchiglione, is the *Prefecture*. In front of this is a medieval sarcophagus, popularly called the Tomb of Antenor, the mythical founder of Padua. To the E is the Via del Santo, which runs S to the *Piazza del Santo*, with the *church of Sant'Antonio, known as "il Santo" for short, containing the Tomb of St Antony of Padua, a shrine visited by countless pilgrims. The massive structure (1232–1307), a pillared basilica which shows a fantastic mingling of Romanesque, Gothic and Byzantine features, is highly picturesque, with its two slender towers, the conical dome over the crossing and seven other round domes (heightened in 1424).

INTERIOR. – In the N aisle is the *Cappella del Santo* (1500–46), with nine 16th c. high reliefs (scenes from the life of St Antony, by Jacopo Sansovino, Antonio and Tullio Lombardi and others); within the altar, hung with numerous ex-votos, are the saint's remains. The high altar, originally by Donatello (1446–50), was subsequently removed but restored in 1895 with

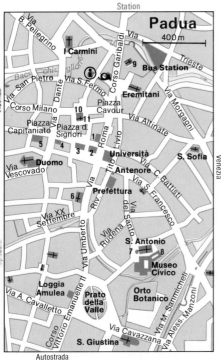

Station

Padua

400 m

I Carmini

9 Bus Station

Eremitani

Piazza Cavour

Piazza d. Signori

Università

S. Sofia

Duomo

Antenore

Prefettura

S. Antonio

Museo Civico

Orto Botanico

Loggia Amulea

Prato della Valle

S. Giustina

Autostrada

the original *sculpture (angel musicians, entombment, etc.). On the left of the altar is a magnificent bronze candelabrum by Riccio. Beyond the ambulatory in the *Cappella del Tesoro* or *delle Reliquie* (1690) are fine examples of goldsmith's work. – On the S side of the church are four beautiful *cloisters* (13th–16th c.), the first of which in particular contains many old gravestones.

In front of the church is Donatello's ****equestrian statue** (1447) of **Gattamelata** (Erasmo da Narni, commander of the Venetian army in 1438–41, whose diplomatic skill earned him the name of Gattamelata, the "spotted cat"), the first large bronze statue made in Italy since ancient times.

On the S side of the Piazza del Santo is the *Scuola del Santo*, on the first floor of which are 17 frescoes (mostly repainted) depicting the saint's miracles. In the adjoining *Cappella San Giorgio* are frescoes by Altichieri and Avanzi. – To the right of the Sculoa del Santo is the **Museo Civico** (closed Mondays), with a library, a collection of antiquities and a picture gallery. It is planned to move the museum to a new building. – To the S of the museum is the beautiful *Botanic Garden*, the oldest in Europe (founded 1545). – A short distance W in the centre of a spacious square, the Prato della Valle, is an oval area planted with trees which contains 82 statues of distinguished citizens of Padua and students of the university. In the SE corner of the square stands the imposing **church of Santa Giustina** (1501–32), in High Renaissance style. Behind the high altar is a fine painting by Paolo Veronese ("Martyrdom of St Justina", *c.* 1568); fine carved stalls (1560) in the choir.

Just N of Piazza Cavour is the busy *Piazza Garibaldi*, from which a short street, Via Emanuele Filiberto, runs W to the Piazza dell'Insurrezione, now the city's busiest traffic intersection; this was laid out since the last war and is surrounded by tall modern buildings. To the S are the *church of Santa Lucia* and the *oratory of San Rocco* (frescoes).

NE of Piazza Garibaldi is the former Augustinian **church of the Eremitani** (13th c., restored after war damage), with famous *frescoes by Mantegna in the *Cappella Ovetari*. – Immediately N of the church is the **chapel of the Madonna dell'Arena**, built in 1303–05 as the chapel of a palace which was demolished around 1820; the chapel is also known as the *Cappella degli Scrovegni* or as the *Chiesa di Giotto*, after Giotto's splendid **frescoes (scenes from the life of the Virgin and the life of Christ: 1303–06), his earliest, largest and best preserved, a landmark in the history of painting. Particularly fine are the "Kiss of Judas" and the "Lamentation" in the third row, depicting the Passion with great dramatic force.

Villa Nazionale, Strà

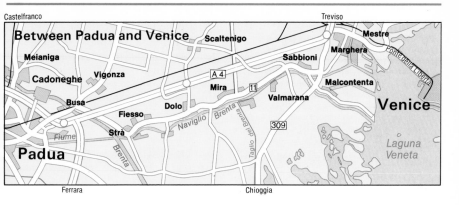

SURROUNDINGS. – SW of Padua rise the beautiful **Euganean Hills** (Colli Euganei), a volcanic range rising abruptly out of the plain and reaching a height of 577 m in Monte Venta. There are numerous hot springs and a number of popular spas in the hills, among them the world-famous thermal resort of **Abano Terme** (alt. 14 m; hotels: *Royal Orologio, L, 220 b., Savoia Todeschini, I, 240 b., Bristol Buja, I, 231 b., La Résidence, I, 177 b., Trieste e Victoria, I, 152 b., Terme Grand Torino, II, 270 b., Ariston Molino Antiche Terme, II, 247 b., Terme Mioni Pezzato, II, 234 b., Ritz, II, 218 b., Terme Internazionale, II, 207 b., Centrale, II, 200 b., Europa Terme, II, 186 b., President, II, 186 b., Columbia, II, 181 b., Terme Excelsior, II, 170 b., Terme Astoria, II, 157 b., Terme Helvetia, II, 156 b., Plaza, II, 145 b., Park, II, 144 b., Due Torri Morosini, II, 141 b., Ambassador Terme, III, 399 b., Terme Italia, III, 240 b., Sanat, III, 223 b., all with their own bathing facilities; many other hotels and *pensioni*), the Roman *Aquae Patavinae* or *Fons Aponi*, with hot radioactive springs (up to 87 °C – 187 °F) which are cooled in large basins, depositing the mud (*fango*) which is effective in the treatment of gout and rheumatism. From here wine-lovers can take an attractive trip on the "Wine Road" (*Strada dei Vini*: white, red and muscatel wine) through the Euganean Hills. – 4 km W of Abano Terme is the **Convento di Praglia** (alt. 21 m), a Benedictine abbey founded in 1080 (present buildings 17th and 18th c.).

Another popular spa is **Montegrotto Terme** (alt. 10 m; hotels: International Bertha, I, 200 b., Esplanade Tergesteo, I, 179 b., Caesar, II, 235 b., Augustus Terme, II, 180 b., Garden Terme, II, 175 b., Terme Sollievo, II, 172 b., Terme, II, 165 b., Des Bains, II, 151 b., Montecarlo, II, 145 b., Terme Neroniane, II, 144 b., Continental, II, 140 b., Terme Olimpia, II, 133 b., Terme Miramonti, II, 127 b., Terme Antoniano, III, 232 b., Mondial, III, 168 b., Marconi Terme, III, 162 b., all with their own bathing facilities; and many others), where the remains of Roman baths and a theatre have recently been brought to light. Slightly farther S is **Battaglia Terme** (hotels: Terme Euganee, III, 66 b.; Nuovo Regina, III, 40 b.).

There is a very attractive run from Padua along the canalised River *Brenta* (also "Burchiello" boat service in summer). 11 km: **Strà**, a favourite resort of the Venetians in summer. At the far end of the village, in a park to the left of the road between the Brenta canal and its tributary the *Veraro*, is the 18th c. *Palazzo Pisani or Villa Nazionale, with a splendid ballroom containing a large *ceiling painting by Tiepolo (1762). – The road then continues E alongside the navigable Brenta canal (*Naviglio di Brenta*), past a series of country houses and villas surrounded by parks. – 10 km beyond Strà, at the straggling village of **Mira**, the road crosses a broad lateral canal, the *Taglio Nuovissimo di Brenta*, and in another 19 km reaches the Piazzale Roma in **Venice** (see p. 305).

30 km SW of Padua, under *Monte Calaone* (415 m), is the little town of **Este** (alt. 15 m; pop. 17,000; hotels: Centrale, III, 36 b.; Beatrice d'Este, III, 34 b.; etc.), the Roman *Ateste*, which was held from 961 to 1288 by the princely family of Este. The *Museo Nazionale Atestino, in the former Palazzo del Castello or Palazzo Mocenigo (16th c.), has rich prehistoric and Roman collections. Adjacent is the 14th c. Castello Carrarese, surrounded, particularly on the E side, by massive walls. Also of interest is the 18th c. Basilica di Santa Tecla, which has a picture of the saint by Tiepolo in the choir. – 15 km farther W is **Montagnana** (alt. 16 m; pop. 10,000; Hotel Moro, IV, 22 b.; etc.), with medieval *town walls and 24 battlemented towers, best seen from the ring road which makes a circuit of the town. Outside the Porta Padova, on the E side of the town, is the Villa Pisani (by Palladio, 1565). In the town centre are the Gothic cathedral (15th c.) and the Palazzo Pretorio (16th c.), now the Town Hall.

Paestum

Region: Campania. – Province: Salerno (SA).
Altitude: 18 m.
Post code: I-84063. – Dialling code: 0828.
(i) **AA**, at the Annunziata church;
    tel. 84 30 56.

HOTELS. – *Poseidon*, II, 100 b.; *Cerere*, II, 80 b., SP; *Ariston*, II, 74 b., SP; *Mec*, II, 68 b.; *Calypso*, II, 60 b.; *Esplanade*, II, 58 b.; *Autostello ACI*, II, 26 b.; *Sogaris*, III, 48 b., SP; etc. – YOUTH HOSTEL, 60 b. – Numerous CAMPING SITES.

With its ruined *temples and its cemeteries Paestum, situated in a plain near the sea in southern Campania, possesses the finest remains of Greek architecture on the mainland of Italy.

HISTORY. – Paestum was founded by Greeks from Sybaris about 600 B.C., under the name of *Poseidonia*. In the 4th c. B.C. it passed in to the hands of the Lucanians, and in 273 it became a Roman colony. In the time of Augustus it already had a bad name for the malaria-ridden marshland which surrounded it, and after the devastation of the region by the Saracens in the 9th c. its inhabitants abandoned the town, taking with them a relic of St Matthew which had according to tradition been preserved in Paestum since the 4th c., and founded a new settlement on the neighbouring hills at Capaccio, of which Paestum with its few modern houses is now a part. In the 11th c. the deserted town was despoiled of its columns and sculpture by the Norman leader Robert Guiscard, and thereafter was forgotten until the 18th c., when there was a revival of interest in classical Greek art.

SIGHTS. – The site of the ancient city is enclosed by a magnificent circuit of **town walls** 4·75 m long, with four gates and a number of towers (*walk round the walls recommended). – In the centre of the area, on the E side of the modern road (S.S. 18), is the ***Museum**, with pre-historic material, painted pottery and fine metopes from the Temple of Hera on the Sele, N of Paestum, and the archaic Treasury.

Immediately S of the museum S.S. 18 cuts across the *Amphitheatre* of the Roman period, the rounded end of which can still be distinguished. Some 300 m farther S, on the right, is the entrance to the site, near the S side of the ancient city.

Temple of Hera, Paestum

Opposite the entrance is the magnificent **Temple of Hera**, a consummate ex-ample of the mature, strictly disciplined architecture of the 5th c. B.C., reflecting the Greek ideal of harmony and pro-portion. The stone is a porous limestone to which the passage of time has given a beautiful yellow tone. At the E end of the temple the tip of an earlier oval structure emerges frpm the ground. 10 m E are the remains of the sacrificial altar associated with the temple.

To the S of the Temple of Hera can be seen the misnamed *Basilica, the oldest temple on the site, dated by the marked swelling of the columns and the form of

the capitals to the second half of the 6th c. B.C. As with the Temple of Hera, there are remains of an earlier oval temple at the E end and, 27 m farther E, a sacrificial altar 21 m wide. – Just beyond the W end of the basilica is a section of the ancient Via Sacra (Sacred Way) which ran across the city from N to S.

200 m N of the Temple of Hera is the **Forum** (150 m long, 57 m across), which was surrounded by a colonnade of late Doric columns. N of the Forum are the massive substructures of the *Tempio Italico* (273 B.C.), with one re-erected column. – Still farther N the so-called *Temple of Ceres has traces of stucco and painting on the gable, which shows Ionic influences.

Outside the town walls three large **cemeteries**, with **tomb paintings** of the highest quality, have been discovered since 1968. – On the S side are tombs of the 5th c. B.C., the heyday of Magna Graecia, with frescoes in the style of the classical vase-painters ("Tomb of the Diver"). – To the N are 70 tombs dating from the 4th c. (the period of Lucanian predominance) painted in vivid colours, with scenes from everyday life which throw fresh light on the discovery of colour, of light and shade and of spatial representation in Western art. – On the W side was found a cemetery covering an area of 25,000 sq. m with thousands of 3rd c. tombs painted in a style which demonstrates that even during the Roman period southern Italy still belonged to the Greek (Hellenistic) cultural sphere. – Altogether more than 500 tomb paintings have been discovered so far. It is planned to establish a special gallery to display them.

Palermo

Region: Sicilia. – Province: Palermo (PA).
Altitude: 19 m. – Population: 650,000.
Post code: I-90100. – Dialling code: 091.
ⓘ **AA**, Salita Belmonte 1;
   tel. 54 01 41.
   Information office in Harbour;
   tel. 24 23 43.
   EPT, Piazza Castelnuovo 35;
   tel. 58 38 47.
   Information office at Cinisi – Punta Raisi Airport, 31 km W;
   tel. 23 59 13.
   CIT, Via Roma 320;
   tel. 21 57 40.

HOTELS. – *Villa Igiea Grand Hotel*, Salita Belmonte 1, L, 171 b., SP; *Jolly Hotel del Foro Italico*, Foro Italico 32, I, 468 b., SP; *Grande Albergo e delle Palme*, Via Rome 398, I, 282 b.; *Politeama Palace*, Piazza Ruggero Settimo 15, I, 177 b.; *Ponte*, Via Francesco Crispi 99, II, 270 b.; *Motel Agip*, Viale della Regione Siciliana 2620, II, 200 b.; *Centrale*, Corso Vittorio Emanuele 327, II, 164 b.; *Europa*, Via Agrigento 3, 143 b.; *Mediterraneo*, Via Cerda 44, II, 99 b.; *Terminus*, Piazza G. Cesare 37, III, 135 b.; *Elena*, Piazza G. Cesare 14, III, 88 b.; *Sausele*, Via Vincenzo Errante 12, III, 68 b.; *Regina*, Corso Vittorio Emanuele 316, III, 65 b.; etc. – CAMPING SITE. – IN MONDELLO LIDO: *Mondello Palace*, I, 124 b., SP; *Splendid Hotel La Torre*, II, 266 b., SP; *Conchiglia d'Oro*, III, 69 b.; etc.

EVENT. – *Trade Fair* (May–June).

Palermo, magnificently situated in a beautiful bay on the N coast of Sicily, is the capital of the island and its principal port, a university town and the see of an archbishop. It is bounded on the S and W by the artificially irrigated and fertile fruit-growing plain known as the Conca d'Oro ("Golden Shell"), with a wide arc of imposing mountains forming the background.

Although Palermo now has the aspect of an entirely modern city, it preserves a distinctive character, thanks to its Norman buildings with their rather Oriental style of architecture, the Baroque architecture it has inherited from the period of Spanish rule and the urgent tempo of its traffic; and the old town with its narrow and twisting side streets is still the scene of a vigorous popular life. Its numerous gardens and palm-shaded promenades give it a particular charm.

HISTORY. – Palermo, founded by the Phoenicians and known to the Greeks as *Panormos*, became the principal Carthaginian base in Sicily until its capture by the Romans in 254 B.C. In A.D. 353 the Byzantine general Belisarius recovered it from the Ostrogoths, and thereafter it remained in Byzantine hands until its capture by the Saracens in 830. The Saracens were followed in 1072 by the Normans, who were in turn succeeded in 1194 by the Hohenstaufens and in 1266 by the house of Anjou, whose brief period of rule was ended by the popular rising known as the Sicilian Vespers in 1282. Palermo then came under Aragonese and Spanish rule, passed to the Bourbons in the 18th c. and was finally liberated by Garibaldi on 27 May 1860.

SIGHTS. – The busiest traffic intersection in the old town is the square, laid out in 1609, known as the *Quattro Canti ("Four Corners")* or *Piazza Vigliena*, at the crossing of the Corso Vittorio Emanuele, which runs across the city from NE to SW for a distance of 2 km, and the Via Maqueda, which runs NW from the

station to the newer part of the city, offering views of the Baroque townscape of Palermo with the long rows of uniform buildings and glimpses of attractive side streets, all set against a background of great scenic beauty. – At the S corner of the Quattro Canti is the **church of San Giuseppe dei Teatini** (1612–45), a massive pillared basilica with a sumptuous Baroque interior. Adjoining it on the S is the *University*, and beyond this to the S the imposing Baroque *church of the Gesù* (1564–1636).

From the Quattro Canti the Corso Vittorio Emanuele runs SW past the handsome Baroque *church of San Salvatore* (on left) to the Piazza della Cattedrale. On the NW side of this square, which is surrounded by a stone balustrade erected in 1761, with 16 large statues of saints, stands the *Cathedral*, originally Romanesque but frequently altered and enlarged, with a beautiful S front (1300–59) but disfigured by a dome added between 1781 and 1801. In the S aisle are six *royal tombs* – the majestic porphyry sarcophagi, surmounted by temple-like canopies, of the Emperor Frederick II (d. 1250: on left), his father Henry VI (d. 1197: on right), Roger II (d. 1154: behind, on left), his daughter the Empress Constance (behind, on right), William, son of Frederick II of Aragon (in niche on left) and Constance of Aragon, wife of the Emperor Frederick II (by the wall, to right). In the chapel to the right of the choir a silver sarcophagus contains the remains of St Rosalia, the city's patron saint. The sacristy, at the end of the S aisle, houses the rich cathedral Treasury. In the crypt are antique and early Christian sarcophagi containing the remains of early archbishops.

Palermo

Immediately SW of the cathedral is the **Archbishop's Palace** (Palazzo Arcivescovile, 16th c.), with the *Diocesan Museum* (entrance in courtyard to right). On the opposite side of the Corso Vittorio Emanuele is the *Piazza della Vittoria*, with the palm-shaded park of the *Villa Bonanno* (remains of Roman houses). At the SE corner of the square is the *Palazzo Sclafani* (1330), at the SW corner a *monument to Philip V* (1856). The W side of the square is occupied by the **Palazzo dei Normanni**, the former royal palace, a fortress-like building originally dating from the Saracen period which was remodelled by the Norman kings. The last gateway on the left gives access to the palace courtyard (Renaissance arcades) and to the famous***Cappella Palatina* (on

first floor), dedicated to St Peter, which was built by Roger II in 1132–40. This is surely the most beautiful palace chapel in the world with its splendid mosaic decoration and its mingling of Western and Oriental elements. The glass mosaics on a gold ground (some of them restored) which cover the walls depict scenes from the Old Testament, the life of Christ and the lives of the apostles Peter and Paul. Near the chapel rises the *Torre di Santa Ninfa*, with a 15 m high room on the ground floor which was probably the strong-room of the Norman kings. On the second floor is an *observatory*, from the roof of which there is a fine *view of Palermo. There are also good views from the balconies of various rooms in the palace (conducted tour).

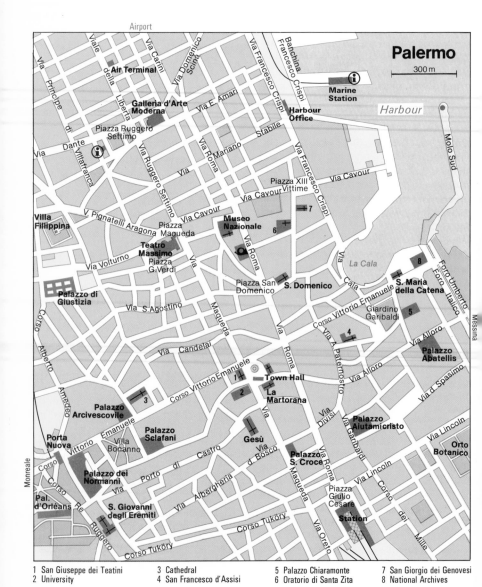

1 San Giuseppe dei Teatini
2 University
3 Cathedral
4 San Francesco d'Assisi
5 Palazzo Chiaramonte
6 Oratorio di Santa Zita
7 San Giorgio dei Genovesi
8 National Archives

Just beyond the Palazzo dei Normanni the Corso Vittorio Emanuele is spanned by the **Porta Nuova** (1535), the upper storey of which (accessible from the palace) affords another magnificent view. – 1·5 km W of the Porta Nuova, on the edge of the town, is the **Convento dei Cappuccini** (1621), with underground passages which, in spite of fire in 1966, still contain the mummies or skeletons of ecclesiastics or well-to-do citizens in the clothes they wore during life (and which are sometimes renewed by their descendants). No further burials of this kind have been permitted since 1881. – 0·5 km N of the convent is a former Norman palace known as **La Zisa**, a plain building based on Arab models which was erected by William I between 1154 and 1166. On the ground floor is a square garden room with a fountain, Byzantine mosaics and a high stalactitic ceiling.

Just S of the Palazzo dei Normanni is Palermo's most unusual ruined church, *San Giovanni degli Eremiti (1132), a building of decidedly Oriental aspect with its fine tall red domes. Adjoining the church are the remains of a small mosque. On its N side is a picturesque cloister (tropical plants). – W of the church, in the Piazza dell'Indipendenza, the *Villa d'Aumale* or *Villa d'Orléans*, now the offices of the autonomous region of Sicily, has a beautiful public park (closed Sundays).

On the E side of San Giuseppe dei Teatini is the *Piazza Pretoria*, with a Florentine fountain (1550) in the centre. On the S side of the square stands the **Palazzo del Municipio** (Town Hall). At the E corner is the side entrance to the *church of Santa Caterina* (Baroque interior), with its main front on Piazza Bellini. In this square also, a flight of steps leads up to the little *church of San Cataldo* (1161), in Byzantine style, with a dome. On its E side is the fine *church of La Mortorana (1143), also known as *Santa Maria dell'Ammiraglio* after its founder Georgios Antiochenos, grand admiral of the Norman king Roger I (excellent Byzantine mosaics, fine painting in the vaulting).

The eastern section of the Corso Vittorio Emanuele cuts across the busy Via Roma (200 m E of the Quattro Canti), a modern street driven through the old town from N to S, passes near the Gothic *church of San Francesco d'Assisi* (1277), off to the right, and comes to the *church of Santa Maria della Catena* (c. 1500: beautiful portico), on the left. It then runs into the Piazza Santo Spirito, closed on the seaward side by the ruins of the *Porta Felice. – W of Santa Maria della Catena lies the picturesque boating harbour, *La Cala*, and to the S is the Piazza Marina, almost entirely occupied by the tropical *Giardino Garibaldi. The *Palazzo Chiaramonte*, usually known as *Lo Steri*, on the E side of this square, was built between 1307 and 1380 and later became the residence of the viceroy. – To the SE, in Via Alloro, which leads to the Foro Umberto I, is the *Palazzo Abatellis* (1495), with a crenellated tower and an unusual Gothic doorway. The palace now houses the *Galleria Nazionale Siciliana**, which gives a comprehensive view of Sicilian painting from the Middle Ages to modern times. Particularly notable is a magnificent *wall painting, the "Triumph of Death", by an unknown 15th c. master (in Room II, the former chapel).

Along the seafront to the E and SE of the Porta Felice extends the *Foro Italico, a broad boulevard which affords magnificent views of the Bay of Palermo and is a popular resort of the citizens on summer evenings. At the S end of the Foro Italico is the beautiful **Villa Giulia** park, also known as *La Flora* (laid out in 1777). On the W side of this the **Botanic Garden** has a magnificent variety of plants including date and coconut palms, banana-trees and fine stands of bamboos and papyrus.

From the Quattro Canti Via Maqueda runs NW to the busy *Piazza Giuseppe Verdi*, lying between the old and the new town, with the *Teatro Massimo** or *Teatro Vittorio Emanuele* (1875–97), one of the largest theatres in Italy (3200 seats). – From the Piazza Verdi Via Ruggiero Settimo continues the line of Via Maqueda through the new town to Piazza Ruggiero Settimo, with monuments to Sicilian patriots. On the NE side of the square, in the *Politeama Garibaldi*, is the **Galleria d'Arte Moderna** (works by Sicilian artists). From here the broad Via della Libertà continues NE for 2·5 km to the *Giardino Inglese*, a public garden. On the left is an *equestrian statue of Garibaldi* (1892).

From the Teatro Massimo Via della Bara runs E to the Piazza dell'Olivella, in which are the *Olivella church* (1598) and the

*Archaeological Museum (Museo Archeologico: closed Sunday afternoons and Mondays), one of Italy's finest museums, housed in a former monastery of the Compagnia di San Filippo Neri. In addition to prehistoric material and an Etruscan collection the museum contains many important classical antiquities, among them the famous *metopes from Selinunte (c. 550–450 B.C.), 56 waterspouts in the form of lions' heads from Himera (5th c. B.C.) and fine Greek bronzes (including Heracles and the Cerynaean hind, a fountain group from Pompeii excavated in 1805, and a large ram from Syracuse).

From the E side of the Archaeological Museum Via Roma runs S past the *Head Post Office* (on right) to the Piazza San Domenico, in which is a 30 m high marble column bearing a *statue of the Virgin* (1726). On the E side of the square stands the **church of San Domenico** (14th c., rebuilt 1636–40), which can accommodate a congregation of 8000. It contains a number of good pictures and many monuments to prominent Sicilians. In the chapel to the right of the choir is a charming relief of the Virgin with angels by Antonio Gagini. Adjoining the church is a picturesque *cloister* (14th and 16th c.). – Behind San Domenico, in Via Bambinai, the *Oratorio della Compagnia del Rosario di San Domenico* (entrance at No. 16, to right), has stucco decoration by Giacomo Serpotta (1656–1732). On the high altar is the *Madonna del Rosario (1624–25), by Van Dyck. – To the N of the Oratorio in the *church of Santa Zita* can be seen a triptych (1517) by Antonio Gagini. Behind the church, in Via Valverde, is the *Oratorio della Compagnia del Rosario di Santa Zita*, with stucco-work by Serpotta. – NE of Santa Zita is the *church of San Giorgio dei Genovesi* (1591). From here Via Francesco Crispi runs N to the busy **Harbour.**

SURROUNDINGS. – 13 km SW of Palermo is the former Benedictine monastery of **San Martino delle Scale** (alt. 507 m; Hotel Messina, III, 248 b.; etc.). The present buildings date from 1778 (church 1590). – From the former Minorite house of **Santa Maria di Gesù** (alt. 50 m), 4 km S of Palermo, on the lower slopes of *Monte Grifone* (832 m) one can enjoy perhaps the finest**view of Palermo and the Conca d'Oro, particularly in morning light.

13 km N of Palermo on the *Spianata della Sacra Grotta,* is the **Grotta di Santa Rosalia** (alt. 429 m), a cave converted into a church in 1625. According to the legend St Rosalia, daughter of Duke Sinibaldo and niece of King William II, withdrew to this remote hermitage at the age of only 14. In front of the church is a tablet commemorating Goethe's visit in 1787. From here a steep path runs SE (½ hour) to the summit of *Monte Pellegrino (606 m: two television towers), from which there are panoramic views. – From the Spianata della Sacra Grotta a good road descends, with many bends and fine views, to *Mondello* (8 km).

There is also a very attractive tour **round Monte Pellegrino** (27 km). The road runs N from Palermo past the former royal country house of **La Favorita** (park, orangery; camping site), near which is the little *Palazzina Cinese*, with the *Museo Etnografico Siciliano Pitrè* (folk traditions; puppet theatre). From here it continues along the foot of Monte Pellegrino and through the northern suburbs of *Pallavicino* and *Partanna*, on the southern slopes of *Monte Gallo* (527 m), to **Mondello** (or *Mondello Lido*), Palermo's seaside resort (good sandy beach), lying on the Bay of Mondello between Monte Gallo and Monte Pellegrino. From here the return route runs along the coast, round the *Punta di Priola*, past the *Cimitero Monumentale* (or *Cimitero dei Rótoli*), Palermo's largest cemetery, and through the coastal suburbs of *Arenella* (with the magnificent *Villa Belmonte*) and *Acquasanta* to Palermo.

Another excursion, through country of particular scenic beauty, is to **Piana degli Albanesi** (alt. 725 m; pop. 8000), 24 km S via *Altofonte* (12 km; 354 m; pop. 5500), known until 1930 as *Parco*, after a hunting park of William II's. Piana degli Albanesi, formerly called *Piana dei Greci*, was founded by Albanian settlers in 1488, and the people still preserve their distinctive dialect and the Eastern rite of the Catholic Church. The town is the seat of a bishop whose diocese extends to all the Albanians in Italy. Picturesque Albanian costumes are worn on feast-days.

There is an attractive trip by boat (3 hours; 4–6 times weekly) or hydrofoil (1¼ hours; several times daily) to the volcanic island of **Ústica** (area 9 sq. km; pop. 1100; wine, fruit, arable farming), 67 km N. The highest point on the island is the *Punta Maggiore* (244 m), a remnant of the old crater rim. Formerly a place of banishment and a penal colony, the island is now attracting increasing numbers of visitors with its beautiful scenery. On its eastern tip is the only settlement, *Ustica* (alt. 54 m; hotels: Punta Spalmatore, II, 200 b.; Grotta Azzurra, II, 90 b., SP; Diana, II, 64 b.; Patrice, III, 74 b.; etc.), with the harbour. To the S accessible only by boat, are a number of caves – the *Grotta Azzurra*, the particularly beautiful *Grotta dell'Acqua* and the *Grotta Pastizza*. There is also a very pleasant walk round the island, which is 4·5 km long and almost 3 km wide.

Parma

Region: Emilia-Romagna. – Province: Parma (PR).
Altitude: 57 m. – Population: 180,000.
Post code: I-43100. – Dialling code: 0521.

ⓘ **EPT**, Piazza Duomo 5;
tel. 3 47 35.
ACI, Via Cantelli 15;
tel. 3 34 54.
CIT, Via Mameli 9;
tel. 2 41 30.
TCI, *Viaggi Donzelli*, Via Albertelli 12;
tel. 7 29 41.
Mondadori per Voi, Via Mazzini 50.

HOTELS. – *Palace Hotel Maria Luigia*, Viale Mentana 140, I, 129 b.; *Park Hotel Toscanini*, Viale A. Toscanini 4, I, 72 b.; *Park Hotel Stendhal*, Via Bodoni 3, I, 67 b.; *Terminus*, Via Trento 9, II, 113 b.; *Milano*, Viale Bottego 9, II, 71 b.; *Button*, Via San Vitale 7, II, 62 b.; *Bristol*, Via Garibaldi 73, II, 57 b.; *Daniel*, Via Gramsci 16, II, 56 b.; *Torino*, Via A. Mazza 7, II, 39 b.; *Moderno*, Via A. Cecchi 4, III, 76 b.; *Principe*, Via Emilia Est 46, III, 63 b.; etc. – YOUTH HOSTEL, Via Passo Buole 7, 48 b. – CAMPING SITE.

The former capital of the duchy of Parma, now a provincial capital and a university town, lies at the foot of the Apennines in the N Italian plain on the banks of the River Parma, a tributary of the Po.

In spite of its long history the town, situated on the old Roman main road, the Via Aemilia, is a city of modern aspect, with straight streets on a regular plan. In the crowded housing areas destroyed during the Second World War fine new squares have been laid out.

HISTORY. – Parma became a Roman colony in 183 B.C. During the Middle Ages it became a place of some consequence through its woollen mills and its university, founded in the 11th c. The town, always on the Guelf side, belonged to Milan from 1346 to 1512, when it was annexed to the States of the Church. In 1545 Pope Paul III granted the duchies of Parma and Piacenza to his natural son *Pier Luigi Farnese*. When the Farnese male line died out in 1731 the duchies passed to a collateral line of the Bourbons. They came under French rule in 1807, and in 1815 were granted to Napoleon's wife Marie Louise for life, reverting to the Bourbons on her death. After the expulsion of the Bourbons in 1859 the territory was incorporated in the new kingdom of Italy. – The painter *Antonio Allegri*, known as *Correggio* (1489–1534), the great master of chiaroscuro, lived and worked in Parma.

SIGHTS. – The central feature of the town is the *Piazza Garibaldi*, on the line of the old Via Aemilia, with the *Palazzo del Governatore* (13th c.: astronomical clock) and the *Palazzo del Municipio* (1627–73). – The **University**, in a former Jesuit college (16th c.) a short distance SW, has various natural history collections. Opposite, to the SE, is the *Pinacoteca Stuard* (closed Saturdays and Sundays), the finest private collection in Parma.

From Piazza Garibaldi the busy Via Cavour runs N. On the right the short Via al Duomo leads to the *Piazza del Duomo*. On the left of this square is the *Bishop's Palace*, on the right the *Baptistery, a massive octagonal marble building begun in Romanesque style by Benedetto Antélami in 1196–1214 (the doorways, with reliefs of scriptural subjects, are his work)

Cathedral and Baptistery, Parma

and completed in Gothic style in 1256–70; it contains 13th c. reliefs and frescoes. – On the E side of the square is the *Cathedral, a Romanesque pillared basilica dating from the second third of the 12th c., whose wide façade forms an impressive group with the adjoining *campanile* (63 m high) of 1284–94. In the dome is a huge *fresco of the Assumption of the Virgin by Correggio (1526–30). In the S transept is a relief by Benedetto Antelami of the *Descent from the Cross (1178), originally on a pulpit. In the crypt are two fine Roman mosaics. – Behind the cathedral stands the *convent church of San Giovanni Evangelista*, a Renaissance building (1510) with a Baroque façade of 1607 and a slender tower of 1614. It contains fine frescoes by Correggio (in the dome: 1521–23) and his pupil Parmigianino.

From the Piazza del Duomo the Via al Duomo and Via Pisacane lead W to the *Piazza della Pace*, which was much enlarged after the Second World War. On the W side of this square is the **Palazzo della Pilotta**, a hugh brick building begun in 1583 but left unfinished, which has a handsome courtyard. In the palace are the *Museum of Antiquities* (closed Mondays), the *Biblioteca Palatina*, the *Bodoni Museum* (printing) and a rich *Picture Gallery* (closed Mondays), with important works by Correggio (*Madonna di San Girolamo", *"Madonna della Scodella"), Parmigianino, Fra Angelico, Giulio Romano, Cima da Conegliano, Tiepolo, Canaletto, Carracci, El Greco, Holbein the Younger and many other artists. On the same floor is the **Teatro Farnese**, built entirely in wood by G. B. Aleotti, a pupil of Palladio, in 1618–28; it was then the largest theatre in the world (4500 seats). – On the E side of the Piazza della Pace is the *Museo G. Lombardi*.

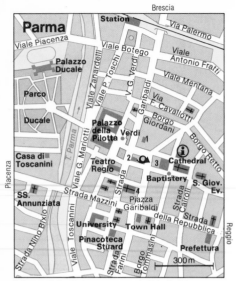

1 Camera di San Paolo
2 Museo Lombardi

3 Bishop's Palace
4 Madonna della Steccata

A short distance E of the Piazza della Pace, in a former Benedictine nunnery, is the *Camera di San Paolo*, with well-preserved *frescoes by the young Correggio (1518–19: Diana; the Goddess of Love, with the famous "putti del Correggio"). – S of the Piazza della Pace, on the right-hand side of Via Garibaldi, is the *Teatro Regio* (1821–29), one of Italy's finest theatres. Beyond it, on the left, is the handsome domed **church of the Madonna della Steccata** (1521–39), modelled on St Peter's in Rome (Greek-cross plan), with a very fine *interior.

From Piazza Garibaldi Via Mazzini runs W over the *Ponte di Mezzo* (fragments of the old Roman bridge, rebuilt, in underpass) spanning the River Parma into the Oltre Torrente district, the oldest part of the town. At the near end of *Via Massimo d'Azeglio*, on left, is the **church of the Santissima Annunziata**, a Baroque building (1566) with an unusual ground-plan and a boldly designed dome (1626–32). At the end of the street, also on the left, the Romanesque *church of Santa Croce* contains good 17th c. frescoes. – A short distance N of the church, the birthplace of the conductor *Arturo Toscanini* (1867–1957), at Borgo Rodolfo Tanzi 13, is opened for a brief period on Wednesdays, Saturdays and Sundays. Farther N, extending to the banks of the Parma, is the large **Parco Ducale**, in the NE corner of which is the *Palazzo Ducale* (1564), now a military academy.

SURROUNDINGS. – 18 km S is the Apennine village of **Torrechiara** (alt. 220 m), with a 15th c. castle of the Sforza-Cesarini family, magnificently situated above the valley of the Parma (Camera d'Oro, with beautiful painted wall tiles and frescoes by Benedetto Bembo). – 35 km SE is the ruined castle of **Canossa** (alt. 576 m), to which the Emperor Henry IV came in 1070 to seek absolution from Pope Gregory VII (small museum; *view).

30 km NE of Parma is the interesting little town of **Sabbioneta** (alt. 18 m), which Vespasiano Gonzaga (1531–91) made the very model of a small princely residence of the Renaissance period (fortifications, Palazzo Ducale, Palazzo del Giardino, Galleria Ducale, Chiesa dell'Incoronata; theatre in which performances are given in summer).

Pavia

Region: Lombardia. – Province: Pavia (PV).
Altitude: 77 m. – Population: 90,000.
Post code: I-27100. – Dialling code: 0382.

(i) **EPT**, Corso Garibaldi 1;
tel. 2 77 06.
ACI, Piazza Guiccardi 6;
tel. 2 67 88.
TCI, *Viaggi Ticinum*, Corso Cavour 41;
tel. 2 61 53.

HOTELS. – *Rosengarten*, Piazzale Policlinico 19, II, 96 b.; *Ariston*, Via A. Scopoli 10D, II, 75 b.; *Palace Pavia*, Viale della Libertà 89, II, 62 b.; *Moderno*, Viale Vittorio Emanuele 11, III, 62 b.; etc.

The old Lombard town of Pavía, now a provincial capital and the seat of a famous university, lies on the River Ticino near its junction with the Po, in the western part of the N Italian plain. It is linked with Milan by a shipping canal, the Naviglio di Pavia. With its old brick buildings it has preserved much of its medieval aspect and is notable particularly for its beautiful churches in Lombard Romanesque style. Of its once numerous towers, the fortified residences of noble families, few now remain, but it still has remains of the ramparts and bastions of the Spanish period.

HISTORY. – Pavia, the Roman *Ticinum*, was a favourite residence of Theodoric the Great, and after the fall of Ravenna became for a short time the Ostrogothic capital. From 572 to 774 it was capital of the Lombard kingdom. From the 7th c. the town was known as *Papia*. During the Middle Ages many kings of Italy were crowned in the church of San Michele, as were the emperors Henry II and Frederick Barbarossa. The town remained for the most part faithful to the emperor, until it was handed over to the Visconti family by Charles IV in 1359. Francis I of France was defeated and taken prisoner at Pavia in 1525.

SIGHTS. – In the centre of the town, in the *Strada Nuova*, Pavia's main street, is the **University**, founded in 1361 on the basis of an earlier law school established in the 11th c. The present building was begun in 1490 and enlarged in the 18th c. In the five courtyards are monuments and memorials to famous professors and students; in the second courtyard are a statue of Volta (1878) and reliefs from the tombs of professors. The library, founded about 1770, contains some 370,000 volumes. Beyond the first courtyard there is a picturesque view of three old brick *towers*, formerly belonging to noble families.

SW of the university is the long *Piazza della Vittoria*, in which is the *Broletto*, the old Town Hall. – Farther SW stands the **Cathedral**, a building in Early Renaissance style on a centralised plan, begun by Cristoforo Rocchi in 1487 and continued with the collaboration of Amadeo and Bramante, with a dome over the crossing added in 1884–85 and a façade of 1898. To the left of the cathedral rises the *Torre Maggiore* (78 m high), which is first mentioned in the records in 1330.

From the cathedral we go S along Via dei Liguri and then turn right into Via Pietro Maffi to reach the Romanesque *church of San Teodoro*, which has frescoes (including a view of Pavia, 1522, immediately left) and a fine crypt (12th c.). – 0·5 km E of San Teodoro, on the far side of the Strada Nuova, is the old *coronation church of San Michele* (1155), in Lombard Romanesque style, with a beautiful façade (rich ornament and figural reliefs in a series of bands, surmounted by a gabled gallery) and fine interior.

At the S end of the Strada Nuova, on the banks of the Ticino, is the Piazzale Ponte Ticino, from which the *Ponte Coperto* (built 1353, restored after war damage) leads into the suburban district of *Borgo Ticino*. To the right, upstream, the *Ponte della Libertà* crosses the river.

N of the cathedral and W of the university is the large *church of Santa Maria del Carmine*, a beautiful early Gothic church built in brick, with a ring of chapels (1390). A little way N of the church in Piazza Petrarca stands the *Palazzo Malaspina*, with a fine *Picture Gallery* (some 500 pictures, including works by Bellini, Bergognone, Crivelli and Correggio); there are plans to transfer the pictures to the Castello Visconteo. – In the N of the town is the old *convent church of San Pietro in Ciel d'Oro* (1132; restored 1875–99), in Lombard Romanesque style. In the choir is the splendid marble *tomb (1362) of St Augustine (354–430). – The **Castello Visconteo** (1360–65) to the E, on the NE side of the town, houses the *Municipal Museums*.

SURROUNDINGS. – 10 km N, on the road to Milan, is the **Certosa di Pavia**, the most famous Carthusian house after the Grande Chartreuse near Grenoble, founded by Gian Galeazzo Visconti in 1396, suppressed in 1782 but reoccupied between 1843 and 1881 and again since 1929. A tour of the monastery (national monument: closed Mondays) takes 1–1½ hours. At the entrance is a good restaurant.

On the W side of the outer courtyard the old *Pharmacy* now produces a liqueur (tasting room). To the N is the pilgrims' hospice, to the S the *Palazzo Ducale*, built about 1625 to accommodate distinguished visitors (museum, with pictures, etc.).

Building of the **church**, on the E side of the courtyard was started in 1396 in Gothic style and continued by Guiniforte (d. 1481) from 1453 onwards. The famous marble façade, a masterpiece of North Italian Early Renaissance architecture, was begun in 1491 in the design of Giovanni Antonio Amadeo (1447–1522) and carried on by Benedetto Briosco in 1500–07; the upper part, however, was left unfinished about 1540. The plinth is adorned with medallions of Roman emperors and other decoration. Above the windows are niches with numerous statues.

INTERIOR. – The nave, flanked by aisles, is still entirely Gothic in character, but the transepts, choir and dome show Renaissance features. The altarpieces and decoration of the side chapels are mainly 17th c.; the splendid choir screen dates from around 1600. Outstanding among the many works of art in the church are the marble recumbent figures of Lodovico Sforza, il Moro (d. 1508) and his wife Beatrice d'Este (d. 1496) by Cristoforo Solari (in N transept); the richly decorated altar (1568) and stalls (1486–98) designed by Bergognone in the choir; an elaborate Renaissance fountain (1490) in the lavatorium, to the right of the choir; the magnificent tomb of Gian Galeazzo Visconti (d. 1402), begun in 1494 by Gian Cristoforo Romano and Benedetto Briosco but not completed until 1560 (by Galeazzo Alessi and others), in the S transept; and an Assumption by Andrea Solario in the New Sacristy.

An elegant Early Renaissance doorway (1466) leads from the S aisle into the *Front Cloister (Chiostro della Fontana)*, with marble colonnettes and charming terracotta decoration (1463–78). From the W side there is a fine view of the nave and S transept of the church. – Around the *Great Cloister*, to the rear, are 24 small apartments for monks.

Perugia

Region: Umbria. – Province: Perugia (PU).
Altitude: 493 m. – Population: 130,000.
Post code: I-06100. – Dialling code: 075.
ⓘ EPT, Corso Vannucci 30;
tel. 2 48 41.
AA, Via Mazzini 21;
tel. 2 36 15.
Information office, Piazza IV Novembre;
tel. 2 33 27.
ACI, Via M. Angeloni 1;
tel. 7 19 41.
CIT, Corso Vannucci 2 ;
tel. 2 60 61.

Perugia – the upper town

HOTELS. – *Brufani*, Piazza Italia 12, L, 44 b.; *Excelsior Lilli*, Via L. Masi, I, 177 b.; *Brufani Palace*, Piazza Italia 12, I, 131 b.; *La Rosetta*, Piazza Italia 19, II, 166 b.; *Posta*, Corso Vannucci 97, II, 86 b.; *Astor*, Piazza Vittorio Veneto 1, II, 80 b.; *Grifone*, Via S. Pellico 1, II, 80 b.; *Italia*, Via Boncambi 8, III, 68 b.; *Priori*, Via dei Priori 40, III, 55 b.; etc.

EVENTS. – *Musical Festival* in September; *Jazz Festival* in summer.

Perugia, capital of its province and of the region of Umbria, situated on a hill some 300 m above the Tiber valley which commands far-ranging views, is worth visiting not only for the beauty of its setting but also for its fine old 14th and 15th c. buildings. It is the see of an archbishop and a university town, with an ancient university founded in 1276 and a University for Foreigners.

HISTORY. – The ancient *Perusia*, one of the 12 cities of the Etruscan federation, came under Roman rule in 310 B.C., and in the middle of the 3rd c. A.D. was raised to the status of a military colony under the name of *Colonia Vibia Augusta Perusia*. Considerable sections of the Etruscan walls, which extended for 2800 m round the town, have been preserved. In 547 Perusia was captured by the Ostrogothic king Totila. In the 14th and 15th c. it was the most powerful city in Umbria. From 1534 until the unification of Italy in the 19th c. it belonged to the States of the Church. – Perugia is renowned as the principal centre of the Umbrian school of painting, the leading members of which, *Pietro Vannucci*, called *Perugino* (1446–1524), and *Bernardino Betti*, called *Pinturicchio* (1455–1513), both worked here. The young Raphael worked in Perugino's studio until 1504.

SIGHTS. – The town centre is closed to cars. – The main square of Perugia is the picturesque *Piazza IV Novembre*, in the centre of which is the *Fontana Maggiore* (1277–80), one of the most beautiful fountains of the period, with reliefs by Niccolò and Giovanni Pisano. On the W side of the square is the *Archbishop's Palace*, and beyond it the vaulting of the so-called *Maestà delle Volte*, a relic of the

Palazzo del Podestà which was burned down in 1534. – On the N side of the square stands the **Cathedral** of San Lorenzo, a 15th c. Gothic hall-church (unfinished). On the steps leading up to the entrance, to the left, is a bronze statue of Pope Julius III (1555). Fine choir-stalls (1486–91). The *Museo dell'Opera del Duomo* to the left of the cathedral houses sculpture, valuable missals and pictures.

On the S side of the square is the *Palazzo Comunale* (Town Hall), also known as the *Palazzo dei Priori*, a massive building in Italian Gothic style (1281 and 1333), with its main front on the Corso Vannucci. On the side facing the Piazza IV Novembre are a griffin (the heraldic emblem of Perugia), a 14th c. bronze lion and chains which commemorate a victory over the Sienese in 1358. On the first floor of the palace, which is entered through the richly decorated main doorway in the Corso, is the splendid Sala dei Notari, on the second floor the Municipal Library (150,000 volumes), and on the third floor the *Galleria Nazionale dell'Umbria* (closed Sunday afternoons and Mondays), with an important collection of Umbrian painting, including works by Perugino and Pinturicchio, Benedetto Bonfiglio (d. 1496), Bartolomeo Caporali (d. about 1509), Fiorenzo di Lorenzo (d. 1525) and other artists. The *Sala del Collegio della Mercanzia* also repays a visit.

From the Town Hall the *Corso Vannucci*, Perugia's principal street, runs S to the *Piazza Italia*. Immediately after the Via dei Priori, on the right, is the *Collegio del Cambio*, the old Exchange.

In the Piazza d'Italia, which occupies the site of the Papal citadel, demolished in 1860, stands the **Prefecture**. From the terrace on the S side there are magnificent *views of the Umbrian plain, with Assisi, Spello, Foligno, Trevi and numerous villages, and of the Tiber valley. – From the Piazza Italia Via Baglioni, running parallel to Corso Vannucci, leads to the Piazza Matteotti, built on massive substructures, some of which date from the Etruscan period. On the E side of the square are the *Palazzo del Capitano del Popolo* (1473) and the *Old University* (1467).

A short distance N of the cathedral the *Arco d'Augusto, one of the Etruscan town gates, bears an inscription, "Augusta Perusia", dating from the Roman period. In Piazza Fortebraccio, the small square outside the gate, the *Palazzo Gallenga* (18th c.) now houses the University for Foreigners (language courses: actually only a faculty of the State University, a short distance NW). – From Piazza Fortebraccio the Corso Garibaldi runs NW, passing the *church of Sant'Agostino*, to the *Porta Sant'Angelo*. To the N of this gate is the **church of Sant'Angelo**, a round church (5th–6th c.) of great architectural interest, with 16 ancient columns in the nave.

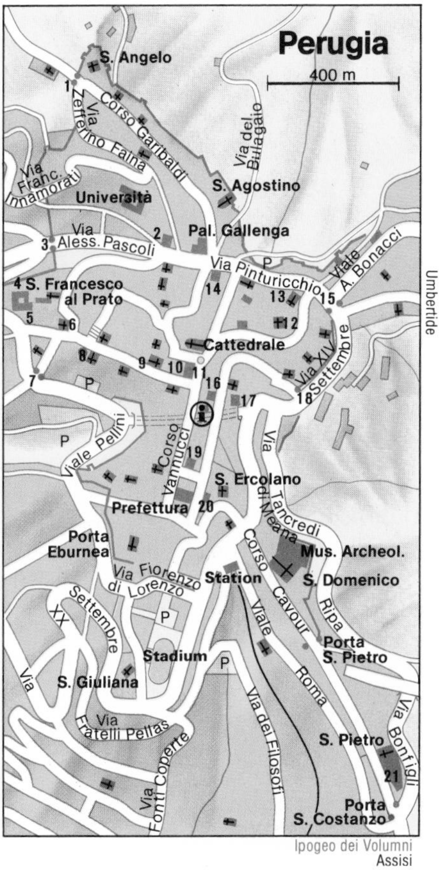

E of the cathedral in the former *monastery of San Severo*, is a chapel containing Raphael's first independent fresco (the Trinity, 1505).

From the Corso Vannucci Via dei Priori, entered through an archway under the Palazzo Comunale, runs W ‚past the medieval *Torre degli Sciri* and the little Renaissance *church of the Madonna della Luce* to the Piazza di San Francesco, in which, straight ahead, is the *Oratorio di San Bernardino**, with a magnificent façade of coloured marble and terracotta (by Agostino di Duccio, 1457–61).

From the Piazza Italia Via Marzia leads SE past the substructures of the former citadel to the *Porta Marzia*, at the beginning of the lower town, a remnant of one of the Etruscan town gates. Here is the entrance to what is left of the old 16th c. fortress, the **Rocca Paolina** (escalator from the lower town under construction). Beyond this in Viale dell'Indipendenza, is the little Gothic *church of Sant'Ercolano* (1297–1326). – Then along Corso Cavour to the **church of San Domenico**, a brick structure begun in 1304 and altered in 1621–34, with a huge Gothic window (23 by 9 m) and the tomb of Pope Benedict XI (1304). In the adjoining monastery is the **Museo Archeologico Nazionale dell'Umbria**, with Roman and Etruscan antiquities (including the Tabulae Perusianae, one of the longest known Etruscan inscriptions).

Corso Cavour ends at the finely decorated *Porta San Pietro* (1475). Outside the gate, in Borgo XX Giugno (on left), we find the fine *church of San Pietro dei Cassiensi**, an early Christian structure rebuilt in the 12th c., containing 18 ancient columns, beautiful choir-stalls (1535) and many pictures of the early Umbrian school and the 17th c. – To the SW of the church, extending to the Porta

Perugia
400 m

1 Porta Sant'Angelo
2 Mosaico Romano
3 Porta Conca
4 Accademia di Belle Arti
5 San Bernardino
6 Madonna della Luce
7 Porta
   Santa Susanna
8 Torre degli Sciri
9 San Filippo Neri
10 Palazzo dei Priori
   (Comunale)
11 Fontana Maggiore
12 San Severo
13 Santa Maria Nuova
14 Arco Etrusco (Arco d'
   Augusto)
15 Porta Pesa
16 Head Post Office
17 Palazzo del Capitano del
   Popolo
18 Porta Santa Margherita
19 Palazzo della Ragione
20 Porta Marzia
21 Facoltà Agraria

San Constanzo, lies the *Giardino del Frontone* (views).

SURROUNDINGS. – 5 km E of Perugia, 1 km before *Ponte San Giovanni* (alt. 189 m), is a modern building which houses the entrance to the underground *Tomb of the Volumnii (Ipogeo dei Volumni:* closed Mondays), one of the finest tombs in Etruria, dating from the 2nd c. B.C. It imitates the plan of an ancient house, with nine chambers grouped round a central space, containing tomb chests with extraordinarily expressive carvings. Photograph, p. 29.

Pesaro

Ducal Palace, Pesaro

Region: Marche. – Province: Pesaro e Urbino (PS).
Altitude: 11 m. – Population: 85,000.
Post code: I-61100. – Dialling code: 0721.
ⓘ **EPT**, Via Mazzolari 4;
    tel. 3 14 33.
    AA, Via Rossini 41;
    tel. 6 93 41.
    ACI, Via San Francesco 44;
    tel. 3 33 68.
    TCI, *Vittorcucchi T. e C.,*
    Viale della Repubblica 32;
    tel. 6 75 51.

HOTELS. – *Vittoria,* Piazzale della Libertà 2, I, 49 b.; *Cruiser,* Viale Trieste 281, II, 280 b., SP; *Perticari,* Viale Zara 67, II, 176 b., SP; *Astoria,* Viale Trieste 81, II, 161 b.; *Flaminio,* Via Parigi, II, 160 b., SP; *Continental,* Viale Trieste 70, II, 156 b.; *Majestic,* Viale Trieste 80, II, 140 b., SP; *Excelsior,* Lungomare N. Sauro, II, 132 b., SP; *International,* Viale Leonardo da Vinci 140, II, 130 b., SP; *Spiaggia,* Viale Trieste 76, II, 116 b.; *Caravelle,* Viale Trieste 269, II, 115 b., SP; *Brig,* Viale Marconi 44, II, 112 b.; *Garden,* Viale Trieste 351, II, 99 b.; *Beaurivage,* Viale Trieste 30, II, 98 b., SP; *Napoleon,* Viale Trieste 118, II, 98 b.; *Principe,* Viale Trieste 180, II, 98 b.; *Delle Nazioni,* Viale Trieste 60, II, 95 b.; *Royal,* Viale C. Battisti 144, II, 83 b.; *San Marco,* Viale XI Febbraio 32, II, 92 b.; *Rex,* Viale Trieste 98, II, 90 b., SP; *Baltic,* Viale Trieste 36, II, 88 b.; *Clipper,* Viale Marconi 54, II, 87 b.; *Nautilus,* Viale Trieste 26, II, 85 b., SP; *Nettuno,* Viale Trieste 367, II, 85 b., SP; *Sporting,* Lungomare N. Sauro 23, II, 84 b., SP; *Due Pavoni,* Viale Fiume 79, II, 84 b.; *Diplomatic,* Via Parigi 2, II, 84 b.; *Figaro,* Viale Trieste 71, II, 84 b.; *Palace,* Lungomare N. Sauro 5, II, 83 b.; *Ambassador,* Viale Trieste 291, II, 80 b.; *Leonardo da Vinci,* Viale Trieste 54, III, 80 b.; *Capitol,* Viale Rovereto 19, III, 77 b.; *Losanna,* Viale Dante 39, III, 72 b.; etc. – YOUTH HOSTEL, Strada Panoramica dell'Ardizio, 88 b. – Two CAMPING SITES.

Pesaro, situated at the mouth of the River Foglia, on the NW Adriatic coast of Italy between Rimini and Ancona, is capital of the province of Pesaro e Urbino and a very popular seaside resort.

In the 16th and 17th c. Pesaro was the residence of the Della Rovere family, dukes of Urbino, and a centre of art and literature, famous for its majolica manufactories. The composer *Gioacchino Rossini* (1792–1868) was born here.

SIGHTS. – The life of the town centres on the *Piazza del Popolo,* in which are the *Town Hall* and the old **Ducal Palace** (begun about 1461 for the Sforzas, completed in the 16th c. for the Della Rovere), now occupied by the *Prefecture.* A little way SE is the *church of San Francesco,* with a beautiful Gothic doorway. Farther SE are the spacious Piazza Matteotti and the adjoining *Giardino Cialdini,* with a 15th c. fortress, the **Rocca Constanza,** now used as a prison.

In Via Rossini, which runs from the Piazza del Popolo to the seafront, is Rossini's birthplace (No. 34, on right), containing a number of pictures and caricatures. Farther along, on the right, is the 13th c. **Old Cathedral** (Duomo Vecchio). – To the W of the Old Cathedral, in the *Palazzo Toschi-Mosca,* are the *Musei Civici,* with a notable collection of pictures (works by Bellini, *"Coronation of the Virgin",* and Marco Zoppo) and an outstanding *collection of majolica,* the finest in Italy.

Piacenza

Region: Emilia-Romagna. – Province: Piacenza (PC).
Altitude: 61 m. – Population: 107,000.
Post code: I-29100. – Dialling code: 0523.
ⓘ **EPT**, Via San Siro 17;
    tel. 2 73 98.
    ACI, Via Chiapponi 37;
    tel. 2 29 59.
    TCI, *Viaggi Laneri,* Piazza dei Cavalli 31;
    tel. 2 29 69.
    Piazzale Marconi 5/4;
    tel. 2 16 70.

HOTELS. – *Grande Albergo Roma*, Via Cittadella 14, I, 172 b.; *Nazionale*, Via Genova 35, II, 129 b.; *Croce Bianca*, Largo Matteotti 16, II, 122 b.; *Del Cappello*, Via Mentana 6, II, 96 b.; *Milano*, Viale Risorgimento 47, II, 75 b.; *Florida*, Via C. Colombo 29, II, 62 b.; *Piacenza*, Via Buffalari 4, III, 35 b.; etc. – *Motel K 2*, Via Emilia Parmense 133, III, 73 b.

The provincial capital of Piacenza, situated in the N Italian plain near the right bank of the Po and just N of the Apennines, has fine churches and Renaissance palaces, mostly of brick, and a well-preserved circuit of mid 16th c. walls 6·5 km long.

HISTORY. – Piacenza was founded by the Romans in 219 B.C., under the name of *Colonia Placentia*, to defend the Po crossing against the Gauls. During the Middle Ages it was a member of the Lombard League, and thereafter belonged to the Viscontis, the Sforzas and (from 1512) the States of the Church. From 1545 onwards the Farnese duchy of Piacenza together with the duchy of Parma formed an independent principality, which was incorporated in the kingdom of Italy in 1860.

SIGHTS. – The life of Piacenza centres on the picturesque *Piazza dei Cavalli*, named after the prancing Baroque equestrian statues of dukes Alessandro and Ranuccio Farnese (1587–92, 1592–1622), by the Tuscan sculptor Francesco Mocchi (1612–29). – On the SW side of the square is the **Palazzo Gotico** (Town Hall), built from 1281 onwards, the model for many other Italian town halls. On the ground floor is an arcade with five pointed arches; above this is a large hall with round-arched windows richly decorated with terracotta; the attic is crowned with battlements. – On the SE side of the square, set a little back, is the large brick Gothic *church of San Francesco* (1278).

From the Piazza dei Cavalli Via XX Settembre (closed to cars) leads SE to the *Cathedral*, begun in 1122 in Lombard Romanesque style and completed in the mid 13th c. under Gothic influence, with three beautiful doorways. The dome has *frescoes (prophets and sibyls) by Guercino. The crypt has 100 columns. – A short way E of the cathedral is the *church of San Savino* (1107), with early ribbed vaulting. The choir and crypt have mosaic pavements (12th c.). – SW of the Piazza del Duomo, at the end of Via Chiapponi, is the **church of Sant'Antonino** (11th–12th c., with much later alteration), the former cathedral, with a large Gothic porch of 1350. 300 m farther SW is the *Galleria d'Arte Moderna Ricci Oddi*.

From the Piazza dei Cavalli the busy *Corso Cavour*, Piacenza's main street, runs NE to the massive **Palazzo Farnese**, begun by Vignola in 1558 for Duke Ottavio Farnese and left unfinished in 1590 with only about a third of the projected building completed. After restoration the municipal collections will be displayed here. – To the NW, near the N edge of the town, is the **church of San Sisto** (1499–1511), in Early Renaissance style, with a Baroque façade and a fine Ionic colonnade. It was for this church that Raphael painted the "Sistine Madonna" (*c.* 1515), now in Dresden, which was sold to the king of Poland in 1754 and replaced by a copy (*c.* 1725). – Near the NW edge of the town is the **church of Santa Maria di Campagna**, an Early Renaissance church on a centralised plan (by Alessio Taramello, 1522–28) containing *frescoes by Pordenone (1529–31).

SURROUNDINGS. – 3 km SE, on the road to Parma, the **Collegio Alberoni** has an interesting picture gallery, library (100,000 volumes) and observatory.

Piedmont/
Piemonte

(i) **EPT Alessandria**, Via Savona 26,
I-15100 Alessandria (AL);
tel. (0131) 5 10 21.
EPT Asti, Piazza Alfieri 34,
I-14100 Asti (AT);
tel. (0141) 5 03 57.
EPT Cuneo, Corso Nizza 17,
I-12100 Cuneo (CU);
tel. (0171) 6 80 15.
EPT Novara, Corso Cavour 2,
I-28100 Novara (NO);
tel. (0321) 2 33 98.
EPT Torino, Via Roma 222,
I-10100 Torino (TO);
tel. (011) 53 51 81.
EPT Vercelli, Viale Garibaldi 90,
I-13100 Vercelli (VC);
tel. (0161) 6 46 31.

Town Hall, Piacenza

Piedmont, in northern Italy, is the most westerly of the Italian regions, taking in six provinces with a population of 4·6 million, with Turin as its capital. It covers an area of 25,399 sq. km in the fertile upper Po basin and the adjoining pre-Alpine moraine and hill region, bounded on the S, W and N by the mighty mountain arc of the Apennines and the Alps, which here reach their highest points in Mont Blanc, Monte Rosa, the Gran Paradiso and the Matterhorn.

The geographical diversity of the region is reflected in different economic patterns. The upland area round Turin, Ivrea and Biella, with good communications and adequate energy supplies (hydroelectric power from the mountains, natural gas in the Po plain, oil from Genoa), is one of the most progressive industrial areas in Italy. The main elements in a very varied range of industries are metal-working, the manufacture of machinery and cars, an old-established textile industry which developed out of the famous silk-manufacturing industry of earlier days, leather goods and foodstuffs. Agriculture is still predominant on the fertile alluvial soil of the Po valley, where fruit-growing, arable farming (wheat, maize, rice, fodder crops) and cattle-farming achieve high yields through the application of modern methods. White truffles – the finest and most expensive form of this delicacy – are found in the Alba area. In the hill regions tourism has developed rapidly in recent years, supplementing the traditional pastoral farming and the relatively unproductive mining (lead, zinc, copper, coal).

HISTORY. – Originally occupied by a number of different peoples, Piedmont was Romanised in the time of Augustus. After the fall of the Roman Empire it was held successively by the *Lombards* (Langobardi) and the *Franks*. It was devastated by the Magyars in 899 (massacre of Vercelli) and later by the Saracens. Thereafter it split up into a patchwork of counties, duchies and marquisates, the most important of which in the 10th c. were *Ivrea* and *Turin*, joined by *Saluzzo* and *Monferrato* in the 12th. In the 11th c. most of present-day Piedmont passed to the house of *Savoy* as a result of a dynastic marriage; and the territory became in the 13th c. the county, and in 1416 the duchy, of Piedmont. Thereafter it was disputed between the Habsburgs and France, owing its importance and the vicissitudes of its subsequent history largely to its control of the western Alpine passes (the Great and Little St Bernard). In 1720 Piedmont acquired Sardinia in exchange for Sicily, and as the *kingdom of Sardinia* played a leading part in the unification of Italy. In 1861 Victor Emmanuel II (1849–78), son of the last king of Sardinia, became king of Italy, with Turin, the old Piedmontese capital, as temporary capital of the new kingdom until 1865.

FEATURES OF INTEREST. – The most attractive tourist areas in Piedmont are to be found in the mountains – the Graian,

The source of the Po on the Piano del Re (Piedmont)

Cottian and Ligurian Alps – and around Lake Maggiore (see p. 147).

The principal towns of interest to visitors are **Turin**, **Novara** and **Asti** (see the entries for these places), but there are many others. In eastern Piedmont, between Vercelli (see p. 177) and Alessandria, is the old town of **Casale Monferrato** (alt. 116 m; pop. 45,000; hotels: Garden, II, 95 b.; Principe, III, 53 b.; Leon d'Oro, III, 52 b.; Milano, III, 50 b.; etc.), from the 14th to the early 18th c. the residence of the marquises and later dukes of Monferrato. In the centre of the town is the imposing Town Hall (1778), and to the N of this the Romanesque cathedral of Sant-Evasio, with a beautiful porch (12th c.) and a number of fine works by Lombard sculptors in the interior. Between the cathedral and the bridge over the Po stands the church of San Domenico, with remains of frescoes and a fine cloister. To the W, near the river, is the old Castello (1590).

In southern Piedmont is the provincial capital of **Cuneo** (alt. 535 m; pop. 55,000; hotels: Augustus Minerva, I, 80 b.; Royal Superga, II, 92 b.; Fiamma, II, 85 b.; Principe, II, 61 b.; Cervino, II, 24 b.; Torrismondi, III, 36 b.; etc.), beautifully situated on a wedge-shaped plateau above the junction of the rivers Gesso and Stura di Demonte. In the centre of the town is a large arcaded square, the *Piazza D. Galimbarti*, lying on the town's main traffic artery, formed by Via Roma to the NE and Corso Nizza in the newer SW part of the town. The cathedral, in Via Roma, has a neo-classical façade. Farther N, in Piazza Virginio, are the Loggia dei Mercanti (14th c., restored) and the former Franciscan church (now a warehouse), in late Romanesque transitional style (1227) with a Gothic tower (1399) and a doorway of 1481. Nearby is the church of Santa Croce, on an elliptical ground-plan (1712). From the promenades on the line of the old fortifications there are fine views of the Alps. – 27 km E of Cuneo is **Mondovì** (pop. 22,000), which had a university from 1560 to 1719. From the industrial lower town, *Mondovì-Breo* (alt. 395 m; hotels: Park, II, 85 b.; Nuovo Torrismonti, III, 71 b.; Genova, III, 57 b.; etc.), a road and a funicular lead to the upper town, *Mondovì-Piazza* (alt. 550 m; Pensione La Madonnina, III, 30 b.), with an 18th c. cathedral (sumptuous interior)

and the fine Baroque church of the Gesù, also 18th c. From the Belvedere (571 m), with a 14th c. Gothic tower, one can enjoy impressive Alpine views. 13 km S is the winter sports area of **Frabosa Soprana** (800–2382 m; cableways and lifts; hotels: Excelsior, I, 114 b.; Miramonti, III, 94 b.; Bossea, III, 87 b.; etc.). – 6 km SE of Mondovì is the *Santuario di Vicoforte* (alt. 512 m; Hotels Edelweiss, IV, 28 b.; etc.), a magnificent pilgrimage church (1596–1733; façade and towers 19th c.). 1 km away is a small spa (sulphur and chalybeate springs).

The old town of **Saluzzo** (alt. 342 m; pop. 19,000; hotels: Astor, II, 46 b.; Persico, III, 32 b.; etc.), 35 km N of Cuneo, on an outlier of Monte Viso, was from the 12th to the 16th c. the chief place in the county of Saluzzo. In the lower town is the cathedral of San Chiaffredo (1491–1501), with a large crucifix of 1500 in the choir. In the upper town are the Palazzo del Comune (1462); the Casa del Cavazza, a Renaissance mansion which now houses the Municipal Museum; and the church of San Giovanni, in French Gothic style, with a *choir on a high substructure, containing many works of sculpture of the Lombard school (tomb of Lodovico II, d. 1504). From the old Castello Via Griselda leads to the *Belvedere, a terrace from which there are splendid views of the Alps. – 4 km S is the village of *Manta* (alt. 464 m), with a castle containing fine 15th c. frescoes.

Pisa

Region: Toscana. – Province: Pisa (PI).
Altitude: 4 m. – Population: 102,000.
Post code: I-56100. – Dialling code: 050.
(i) **EPT**, Lungarno Mediceo 24;
tel. 2 03 51.
ACI, Via San Martino 1;
tel. 4 73 33.
TCI, *Viaggi ASTI*, Lungarno Pacinotti 4;
tel. 2 22 84.
Mondadori per Voi, Viale A. Gramsci 21–23;
tel. 2 47 47.

HOTELS. – *Grand Hotel Duomo*, Via Santa Maria 94, I, 167 b.; *Dei Cavalieri*, Piazza della Stazione 2, I, 144 b.; *Royal Victoria*, Lungarno Pacinotti 12, II, 139 b.; *Terminus e Plaza*, Via Colombo 45, II, 103 b.; *La Pace*, Via Gramsci 14, II, 99 b.; *Villa Kinzica*, Piazza Arcivescovado 4, II, 63 b.; *Touring*, Via G. Puccini 24, II, 59 b.; *Ariston*, Via Cardinale Maffi 42, II, 52 b.; *Arno*, Piazza della Repubblica, II, 51 b.; *Roma*, Via Bonanno 111, 50 b.; *Capitol*, Via E. Fermi 13, II, 30 b.; *Bologna*, Via Mazzini 57, III, 87 b.; *La Torre*, Via C. Battisti 15, III, 54 b.; *Fenice*, Via Catalani 8, III, 51 b.; etc. – CAMPING SITES at Marina di Pisa.

Piazza del Duomo, Pisa – a bird's eye view

The provincial capital of *Pisa, second only to Florence among the tourist attractions of Tuscany, mainly by virtue of the superb group of buildings in the Piazza del Duomo, lies astride the Arno 10 km from the Ligurian Sea, which has retreated 7 km since ancient times as a result of the deposition of soil by the river. Pisa has a university, which is mentioned in the records as early as the 12th c., and is the see of an archbishop.

HISTORY and ART. – Pisa, the Roman *Pisae*, originally an Etruscan trading station, became a Roman colony in 180 B.C. From the 11th c. onwards it developed into one of the leading maritime and commercial powers in the Mediterranean, rivalling Genoa and Venice. It took the lead in the struggle against Islam, defeating the Muslims in Sardinia, Sicily and Tunis and playing a prominent part in the Crusades. The town celebrated its victories by the erection of splendid buildings, and the building of its cathedral in the 11th c. marked a new epoch in Tuscan art and architecture. Pisa also took a leading place in sculpture, with Niccolò Pisano (c. 1220 – after 1278), the great forerunner of the Renaissance; and Niccolò's son *Giovanni* (1265–1314), his pupil *Arnolfo di Cambio* (d. about 1302) and Giovanni's pupil *Andrea Pisano* (1273–1348) formed links with the art of Florence. The fall of the Hohenstaufens was a heavy blow for the town, which supported the Ghibelline cause. In the long-continued conflict with Genoa the Pisan fleet suffered a decisive defeat off the island of Meloria in 1284. Internal partisan struggles led to the occupation of the town by the Florentines in 1406; and Pisa finally lost its earlier importance at the end of the 17th c. when Livorno became the leading port in Tuscany.

SIGHTS. – In the NW of the old town, enclosed on two sides by the old battlemented town walls, is the **Piazza del Duomo** or "Piazza dei Miracoli", with the cathedral, the Leaning Tower, the Baptistery and the Campo Santo – a harmoniously composed group of unrivalled beauty. The *Cathedral, a Romanesque basilica of white marble with transepts and an elliptical dome over the crossing, was built after a Pisan naval victory over the Saracens at Palermo (1063–1118) and restored in 1597–1604 after a fire. The most magnificent part is the façade (second half of 12th c.), the upper part of which has four pillared galleries. The bronze doors of the main entrance (usually closed) date from 1606, the door of the S transept, decorated with reliefs from scriptural history, from 1180.

INTERIOR. – There are 68 ancient columns, trophies of the Pisans' military campaigns. The nave has a richly gilded Renaissance coffered ceiling. The *pulpit (by Giovanni Pisano, 1302–11) is decorated with nine vigorous reliefs (New Testament scenes, Last Judgment). The beautiful bronze lamp (1587) is said to have given Galileo the idea of the pendulum as it swung to and fro. – In the S transept is the splendid *Cappella di San Ranieri*, with the sarcophagus of the town's patron saint. To the left is the *tomb of the Emperor Henry VII*, by Tino da Camaino (1315). – The choir contains fine Renaissance *choir-stalls* and pictures by Andrea del Sarto and Sodoma. In the semi-dome are fine *mosaics* by Cimabue (1302).

At the W end of the cathedral is the almost entirely marble-clad *Baptistery, a circular structure built between 1153 and

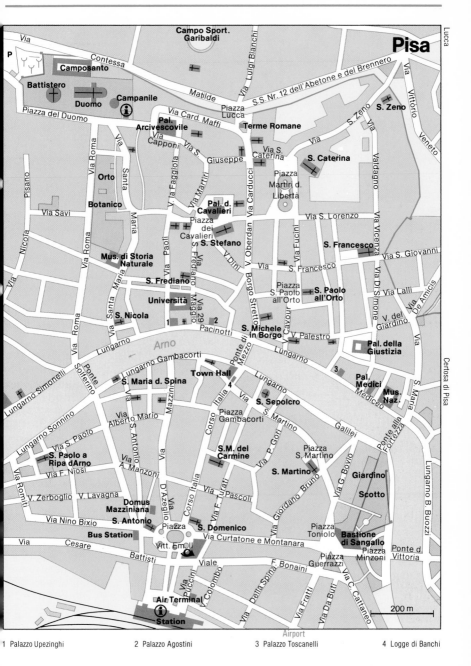

1 Palazzo Upezinghi   2 Palazzo Agostini   3 Palazzo Toscanelli   4 Logge di Banchi

1278, with 14th c. Gothic additions. In the interior, under the conical dome, are a marble font by Guido Begarelli and the famous *pulpit by Niccolò Pisano (1260), with reliefs of Biblical scenes. – Near the E end of the cathedral stands the celebrated **Leaning Tower (*Torre Pendente*), a campanile built between 1173 and 1350, 55 m high, with a series of six superimposed pillared galleries. The tower leans to the SE and is at present 5°30' off the vertical, with its highest point 2·25 m beyond the base. When the foundations were found to be sinking during the construction of the tower the upper section, from the 3rd floor upwards, was given a tilt towards the N. Galileo, born in Pisa in 1564, made use of the inclination of the tower in his experiments on the law of gravity. From the platform (294 steps) there are magnificent *views of the whole town.

Along the N side of the Piazza del Duomo is the *Campo Santo, the most famous cemetery of its kind, a colonnaded quadrangle (126 m long by 52 m across) in Tuscan Gothic style, built by Giovanni di Simone in 1278–83 and completed in 1462. Earth for the cemetery had been brought from Jerusalem in 1203.

The INTERIOR, in the form of a cloister, has tall round-arched windows filled with beautiful tracery opening on the central courtyard. The world-famous *frescoes on the walls (notably by Benozzo Gozzoli) were mostly destroyed by melted lead from the roof during a fire caused by Allied bombing on 27 July 1944, but some have been restored and are displayed in the cloister and in two adjoining rooms. Some of the Etruscan, Roman and medieval **sculpture** disposed round the cloister is of high artistic value. The pavement is composed of gravestones.

In the *Piazza dei Cavalieri* in the centre of the old town are the *church of Santo Stefano dei Cavalieri* (1565–96), the *Palazzo Conventuale dei Cavalieri* and a marble statue of Grand Duke Cosimo I (1596). – NE is the tree-shaded Piazza Santa Caterina, at the NE corner of which is the **church of Santa Caterina** (1253), with a façade in Pisan Gothic style. – A little way SE the Gothic *convent church of San Francesco* (13th c.) has a handsome campanile and 14th c. frescoes. – Along each bank of the Arno extends a riverside street (Lungarno), under various names. In the Lungarno Mediceo, on the right bank, stands the 13th c. *Palazzo dei Medici*, now the Prefecture. Immediately E of this is the *church of San Matteo*, with the former Benedictine nunnery of San Matteo, now housing the **Museo Nazionale** (closed Mondays). – At the W end of the Lungarno Mediceo is the Piazza Garibaldi, from which the Borgo Stretto, a busy street flanked by arcades, runs N. At the near end of this street, on the right, we find the *church of San Michele in Borgo*, with a beautiful façade in Pisan Gothic style. – In Lungarno Pacinotti is the Gothic **Palazzo Agostini** (14th c.), built in brick. A short distance NW is the *University* (1493), with an Early Renaissance courtyard. To the N the Romanesque *church of San Frediano* (12th c.) contains a number of ancient columns. To the W of the university is the *church of San Nicola*, with a leaning tower.

On the left bank of the Arno, at the W end of the Lungarno Sonnino, is the **church of San Paolo a Ripa d'Arno**, a basilica built about 1200 with a very fine façade. – 0·5 km E stands the **church of Santa Maria della Spina**, in French Gothic style, built in 1239 and enlarged in 1323, an elegant little church with external sculpture by pupils of Giovanni Pisano. – Still farther E, at the Ponte di Mezzo, are the Gothic *Palazzo Gambacorti* (Town Hall) and the *Logge di Banchi* (1605). – A little way E of this is the octagonal *church of San Sepolcro* (12th c.). – The *San Giusto* airport is situated 3 km S of Pisa.

Pistoia

Region: Toscana. – Province: Pistoia (PT).
Altitude: 65 m. – Population: 95,000.
Post code: I-51100. – Dialling code: 0573.
ⓘ **EPT**, Corso Gramsci 110;
   tel. 3 43 26.
   ACI, Via Ricciardetto 2;
   tel. 3 21 01.
   TCI, *Viaggi AVIP*, Piazza Gavinana 12;
   tel. 2 13 59.

HOTELS. – *Milano*, II, 102 b.; *Residence il Convento*, II, 42 b.; *Leon Bianco*, III, 50 b.; *Patria*, III, 49 b.; etc.

The provincial capital of Pistoia lies at the NW end of the Florentine basin between the Apennines and the Tuscan hills, not far from the River Ombrone. It has an old-established hardware industry, and the pistol is said to have been invented here.

HISTORY. – Pistoia was the Roman *Pistoria*. During the Middle Ages it was the scene of bitter conflicts between Ghibellines and Guelfs, and in 1295 it came under Florentine rule – a subjection confirmed in 1530. The town's surviving medieval buildings demonstrate the vigorous spirit of enterprise of even the smaller Tuscan towns. In the older churches the influence of the Pisan style, widely diffused in the 12th c., is still predominant, but from the 14th c. the artists working here came almost exclusively from Florence.

SIGHTS. – In the centre of the rectangular area occupied by the old town is the *Piazza del Duomo*, on the S side of which stands the **Cathedral** of San Zenone, a

Pistoia Cathedral

12th c. Romanesque building (apse rebuilt in Baroque style in 1601). The campanile was originally a fortified tower (1200), to which three orders of columns, Pisan-style, were later added. In the porch, added in 1311, is a terracotta medallion of the Madonna with Angels by Andrea della Robbia. The interior has been much marred by alterations. To the left of the entrance is the fine tomb of Cardinal Niccolò Forteguerri (d. 1473), designed by Andrea Verrocchio. In the Capella del Sacramento, to the left of the choir, is a *Madonna by Verrocchio (1485). To the right of the choir is the *Dossale di San Iacopo, a rich silver altar (13th–14th c.). – The Gothic *Baptistery (14th c.) opposite the cathedral has an external pulpit and a fine Early Renaissance wooden door. On the font are richly decorated panels from the old pulpit (1199).

Adjoining the baptistery is the 14th c. *Palazzo Pretorio*, with a picturesque arcaded courtyard; in the arcades and on the façade are the coats of arms of podestàs of the past. – On the N side of the square stands the Gothic **Palazzo del Comune** (1295–1385), also with a beautiful courtyard. The *Museo Civico* on the top floor contains pictures, sculpture and material recovered by excavation.

NE of the Piazza del Duomo stands the *church of San Bartolomeo in Pantano*, a pillared basilica in Tuscan Romanesque style. Fine interior; *pulpit (1250) with eight reliefs from the life of Christ. – In the nearby Piazza dello Spedale, to the NW, is the **Ospedale del Ceppo** (1277; later rebuilt). In the porch is a *frieze of terracotta reliefs, coloured and glazed (the Seven Works of Mercy), by Giovanni della Robbia and his school (1514–25).

W of the hospital is the **church of Sant'Andrea**, a 12th c. pillared basilica in Pisan style. It has a richly decorated *pulpit, with numerous figures (1298–1301), one of Giovanni Pisano's principal works, copied from the pulpit by his father Niccolò in Pisa. – A short distance W of Sant'Andrea, in the spacious Piazza San Francesco d'Assisi, the *Church of San Francesco al Prato*, a Gothic convent church built in 1294, has frescoes in the chapterhouse modelled on Giotto's frescoes at Assisi (14th c.). – From here we go S on Via Bozzi and Via Curtatone e Montanara and then turn right along Via della Madonna to reach the *church of the Madonna dell'Umiltà (1494–1509), with a beautiful porch and an octagonal dome added by Vasari in 1576 on the model of the dome of Florence Cathedral.

To the E of the *Piazza Gavinana*, the town's busiest traffic intersection, is the church of San Giovanni Fuorcivitas (1160–70), in Tuscan Romanesque style. It contains a *pulpit (c. 1270) by Fra Guglielmo, a pupil of Niccolò Pisano, and a *terracotta group (the Visitation) by Luca della Robbia (c. 1445). – From here Via Cavallotti leads S to the *convent church of San Domenico* (1380), with remains of frescoes and fine monuments. – A little way E, in the broad Corso Silvano Fedi, is the *church of San Paolo (c. 1302)*, with a fine Pisan-style façade.

Pompeii/Pompei

Region: Campania. – Province: Napoli (NA). Altitude: 16 m. – Population: 12,000. Post code: I-80045. – Dialling code: 081.
(i) **AA**, Via Sacra 1; tel. 8 63 10 41.
Information office in Auditorium, on S side of site.

HOTELS. – *Rosario*, II, 170 b.; *Bristol*, II, 62 b.; *Del Sole*, II, 58 b.; *Diomede*, III, 39 b.; etc. – CAMPING SITE.

EVENTS. – Performances of classical plays in the ancient *Theatre* (July and August).

The ruined city of **Pompeii (Italian Pompei), 20 km SE of Naples at the foot of Vesuvius, is the finest example of a Roman town and its way of life, presented to modern eyes by excavation.

To the E of the ancient site is the newer settlement, known until 1929 as *Valle di Pompei*, with a conspicuous domed church, Santa Maria del Rosario, which is visited by countless pilgrims (particularly on 8 May and on the first Sunday in October).

HISTORY. – Pompeii, probably founded by the Oscans, an Italic people, became Roman after the Samnite wars (290 B.C.), and by the 1st c. A.D. was a prosperous provincial capital with a population estimated at 20,000. In A.D. 63 much of the town was destroyed by a severe earthquake, and rebuilding had not been completed when an eruption of Vesuvius in

Amid the ruins of Pompeii

A.D. 79 covered the whole town, as well as Herculaneum, with a layer of ashes and pumice-stone 6–7 m deep – though a proportion of the population were able to escape in time. The town was now abandoned, after some at least of the survivors had recovered objects of value from the loose covering of ash. – Since the 18th c. something like three-fifths of the total area of the town (the walls of which had a perimeter of 3100 m) have been recovered by large-scale excavation, carried out systematically from 1869 onwards. Although the buildings are in a ruinous state and it is only in the more recently excavated areas (since 1911) that the internal arrangements and domestic equipment have, so far as possible, been left as they were found, visitors to Pompeii get a more immediate and more vivid impression of ancient life – in luxurious mansions and more modest houses, in the markets and the streets, in baths, theatres and temples – than on any other ancient site; and much of what they see will strike them as astonishingly modern.

In modern times the site has been divided into nine *regiones* (I–IX) separated by the principal streets. The blocks (*insulae*) within the *regiones* are, like them, numbered with Roman numerals; individual houses are numbered with Arabic numerals.

The streets are paved with polygonal slabs of lava, with raised pavements on either side. At intersections and at other places along the streets are stepping-stones designed to help pedestrians to cross. Deep ruts in the paving bear witness to heavy traffic. At many street corners are fountains for public use. The inscriptions on the outside walls of houses, in the manner of modern posters, mostly relate to municipal elections; but then, as now, there was also much casual scribbling on walls.

The **Roman house** was entered from the street by a narrow passage (*fauces, ostium*), often flanked by shops and workshops (*tabernae*), leading into a large court or *atrium* with a roof which sloped inwards. In the centre of the roof was a square opening (*compluvium*), below which, sunk into the ground, was a basin for catching rain-water (*impluvium*). On each side, and sometimes in front, were bedrooms (*cubicula*); and on each side too were *alae*, open spaces originally designed for the statues of ancestors. The fourth side of the atrium was entirely occupied by a large open apartment, the *tablinum*. Beyond this front portion of the house, in which visitors were received, lay the private apartments used by the family; these were built round a garden-like courtyard, known as the *peristylium* from the columns which enclosed it. Beyond this there was sometimes a

flower-garden (*xystus*). Opening off the peristylium were the *triclinium* (dining-room) and sitting-room (*oecus*). The position of the kitchen (*culina*) and cellars varied. Many houses also had an upper floor with balconies.

It is interesting to compare the Pompeian single-storey house occupied by one family with the blocks of apartments built round a large central courtyard which became general under the Empire and are found as Ostia but not at Pompeii.

TOUR OF THE SITE. – The **main entrance** to the site (open daily) is near the *Pompei – Villa dei Misteri* railway station. 300 m from the entrance is the *Porta Marina*, the ancient gate at the SW corner of the town. Immediately beyond this, on the right, is the **Antiquarium**, containing excavated material from Pompeii dating from the pre-Samnite period to Roman times. Particularly impressive are the casts of human bodies and of a dog found buried under the ashes.

Beyond the Antiquarium, also on the right, is the *Basilica*, used as a market and a law-court. To the left is the *Temple of Apollo*, surrounded by 48 Ionic columns. Beyond these two buildings is the *Forum, the principal square of the Roman town, which was enclosed by colonnades. At the N end of the forum is the *Temple of Jupiter*, on a base 3 m high. At the NE corner is the *Macellum*, a hall for the sale of foodstuffs. Down the E side are the *Shrine of the Lares*, the *Temple of Vespasian* (probably dedicated originally to Augustus) and the *Building of Eumachia*, probably a hall for the sale of wool. On the S side of the forum is the *Curia*, the meeting-place of the town council, flanked by three other rooms.

Beyond the forum the *Via dell'Abbondanza*, one of the principal streets of the ancient town, continues E, to the right of the Building of Eumachia, towards the new excavations. The second street on the right (Via dei Teatri) leads to the tree-shaded **Triangular Forum** (Foro Triangolare), intended mainly for theatre-goers, which is entered through a fine arcade. On the S side of this little square are the remains of a *Greek temple*, facing this, to the E, are *barracks for gladiators*. Adjoining the northern half of the Triangular Forum, built into the sloping ground, is the *Large Theatre (Teatro Grande or Teatro Scoperto), which could seat some 5000 spectators and is now used for "son et lumière" shows in summer. From the top rows there are fine views. Adjoining this the better preserved *Little Theatre (Teatro Coperto), the earliest example of a roofed Roman theatre (c. 75 B.C.); with seating for 1500, was used mainly for musical performances.

On the E side of the Little Theatre is the *Via Stabiana*, which runs NW. Immediately on the left is the little "Temple of Aesculapius". To the W of this, in the Via del Tempio d'Iside, the *Temple of Isis*, has an inscription scratched on its wall by the French novelist Stendhal (Henri Beyle) during a visit in 1817. Beyond this, on the E side of the Via Stabiana, is the *Casa del Citarista*, one of the largest houses in Pompeii. Just beyond this the Via Stabiana joins the Via dell'Abbondanza. – 100 m along the Via dell'Abbondanza to the right is the beginning of the New Excavations (Nuovi Scavi), in which wall paintings and furniture have been left in place and in many cases the upper storey with its balconies and loggias has been preserved through the insertion of girders. In this area there are many election "posters" and other casual inscriptions painted on the walls, with the help of which the former director of excavations, Della Corte, was able to compile a "directory" containing 550 names. This part of the town dates from Pompeii's final period and was mostly occupied by tradesmen. Among the establishments to be seen here are an *ironmonger's shop*; beyond this to the right a *fuller's and dyer's workshop* (fullonica), with two restored pressing machines; and beyond this, to the S, the *House with the Cryptoporticus*, with a magnificent painted *frieze (in a passage leading to the cellar) depicting 20 episodes from the "Iliad" and other Homeric poems.

Still farther S is the large and well-preserved *House of Menander (Casa del Menandro) which belonged to a wealthy merchant; it was named after a likeness of the Greek comic playwright Menander in a niche in the magnificent peristylium. Adjoining this is the charming little *House of the Lovers*. – Farther along the Via dell'Abbondanza, on the left, is the *Thermopolium*, a tavern fully equipped with drinking vessels, a kettle, a stove and a lamp, with the last customer's money still on the counter. Beyond this, on the left, is the interesting *House of Trebius*

Valens, the front wall of which is covered with inscriptions; and beyond this again, on the right, is the rich *House of Marcus Loreius Tiburtinus*, with a restored double door and an interesting interior.

Farther E, to the S of the Via della Abbondanza, are the most recent excavations (1951–59). Of particular interest in this area are the *House of Venus*, with a fine *painting of Venus; the *House of the Orchard* (Casa del Frutteto); and the *Villa di Giulia Felice*. – Farther S, outside the *Porta di Nocera*, is a **necropolis**, such as lay outside the walls of all ancient towns.

S of the House of Marcus Loreius Tiburtinus is the **Palaestra**, with colonnades round three sides (each 140 m long) and a swimming pool in the centre. Immediately E of this is the massive **Amphitheatre** (136 m long, 104 m across, seating for 20,000 spectators), the oldest surviving Roman amphitheatre (80 B.C.).

At the corner of the Via dell'Abbondanza and the Via Stabiana are the *Stabian Baths, the largest and best-preserved baths in Pompeii (entrance from Via dell'Abbondanza). The entrance leads into the colonnaded palaestra, with a swimming pool on the left; on the right are the male and female baths, separated by the stoves for heating the water. Each establishment has a circular cold bath (frigidarium), a changing room (apodyterium) with racks for clothing, a warm bath (tepidarium) and a hot (Turkish) bath (caldarium) heated by air-ducts in the floor and walls. – Immediately N of the baths is the *House of Siricus* (entrance from Vico del Lupanare), the occupant of which also owned the bakery next door. On the threshold is the inscription "Salve lucrum" ("Long live profit!"); fine paintings in the interior. – Farther along the Via Stabiana, on the right, is the *House of Marcus Lucretius*, also with well-preserved paintings. – In another 100 m the Via Stabiana crosses the *Via di Nola*, one of the principal streets of the town, and 100 m farther on again comes to an intersection at which the Vico delle Nozze d'Argento (on right) leads to the House of the Silver Wedding (fine atrium and peristylium) and the Vicolo di Mercurio (on left) leads past the House of the Vettii to the House of Sallust. Farther along the Via Stabiana, also called the Via del Vesuvio in this northern section, is the

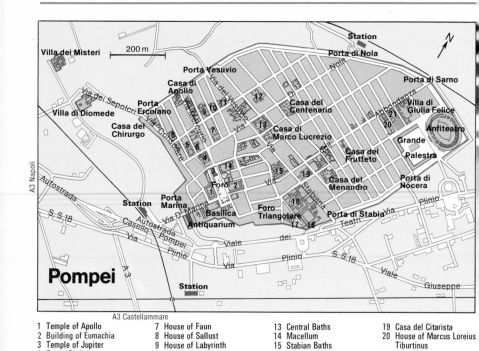

1 Temple of Apollo
2 Building of Eumachia
3 Temple of Jupiter
4 Forum Baths
5 House of Pansa
6 House of Tragic Poet

7 House of Faun
8 House of Sallust
9 House of Labyrinth
10 House of Vettii
11 House of Gilded Cupids
12 House of Silver Wedding

13 Central Baths
14 Macellum
15 Stabian Baths
16 Large Theatre
17 Doric Temple
18 Gladiators' Barracks

19 Casa del Citarista
20 House of Marcus Loreius
     Tiburtinus
21 House of Venus

elegant **House of the Gilded Cupids** (Casa degli Amorini Dorati), with a garden which still preserves its original marble decoration. The Via Stabiana ends at the *Porta del Vesuvio*; from the hill outside the gate there is a fine view.

The very interesting *House of the Vettii** in the Vicolo di Mercurio has well-preserved ornamental paintings. The peristylium (partly rebuilt) still has its original marble decoration and has been replanted with the plants which originally grew here. The kitchen still contains its cooking utensils. – SW of the House of the Vettii is the *House of the Labyrinth*, with two atria, and opposite this, to the S, is the *House of the Faun** (entrance from the Via di Nola), the most palatial mansion in Pompeii, taking up a whole *insula* (80 by 35 m). By the impluvium is a copy of the statuette of a faun which was found here. The famous mosaic of "Alexander's Battle" was found in the room with red columns.

In the *Via delle Terme*, the westerly continuation of the Via di Nola (the W part of which is also called the Via di Fortuna), are the *Forum Baths**, smaller and more modest than the Stabian Baths but also occupying a whole *insula*. On the S side of the Baths is a modern bar. – To the N of

the Baths is the elegant and richly appointed *House of the Tragic Poet*, on the threshold of which is a mosaic of a chained dog with the inscription "Cave canem" ("Beware of the dog"). Adjoining it on the W is the **House of Pansa** (98 by 38 m), one of the largest and most regularly planned houses in Pompeii. – On the N side of the House of the Tragic Poet is a *fuller's workshop*, to the left of which are the *House of the Large Fountain* and the *House of the Small Fountain*, with the beautiful fountains after which they are named. From the latter house the Vicolo di Mercurio runs W to the *House of Sallust*, with good paintings. From here the *Via Consolare* runs NW to the *Porta Ercolano*, which probably dates from the Augustan period.

Outside the gate is a suburban district of which only the main street has been excavated. This *Street of Tombs** is, from the scenic point of view, the most attractive part of Pompeii. Lined with handsome monuments, it ranks with the Via Appia outside Rome as the most impressive surviving example of the Roman practice of erecting tombs along public roads. At the NW end of the street is the large *Villa of Diomedes**, with an extensive garden enclosed by a portico 33 m long each way. In the centre of the garden is a basin and six columns which belonged to a pavilion. In an underground passage (cryptoporticus) were found the bodies of 18 women and children. Near the garden door (now walled up) was the body of a man, presumably the owner of the house, with a key in his hand, with a slave beside him carrying money and valuables.

200 m NW of the Villa of Diomedes, outside the main excavation area, is the magnificent *Villa of the Mysteries (Villa dei Misteri: reached from the main entrance to the excavations on a road which runs past the station (500 m) and continues for another 700 m), with the finest surviving ancient wall paintings, preserved in all the brilliance of their original colouring. The most remarkable of these is a frieze 17 m long in the large triclinium with almost life-size figures, dating from the pre-Augustan period (probably based on models of the 3rd c. B.C.), which depicts scenes from the Dionysiac mysteries.

Pontine Islands/ Isole Ponziane

Region: Latium. – Province: Latina (LT).
Population: 5000.
Post code: I-04027. – Dialling code: 0773.
(i) EPT Latina, Via Duca del Mare 19,
    I-04100 Latina (LT);
    tel. 49 87 11.

BOAT SERVICES. – Six times weekly from *Formia*, three times weekly from *Anzio*, once weekly from Naples via Prócida, Ischia, Santo Stéfano and Ventotene to *Ponza*; also hydrofoils from *Anzio*.

The Pontine Islands, lying off the coast of southern Latium, are of volcanic origin and are frequently shaken by minor earth tremors. The 5000 inhabitants live mainly from wine-growing and fishing; in recent years there has also been a developing tourist trade.

The north-western group of islands consists of the almost uninhabited islands of *Palmarola* and *Zanone* (known to the Romans as *Palmaria* and *Sinonia*) and the well-cultivated main island of **Ponza**, a crater ridge 7·5 m long, rising to a height of 283 m at the S end in *Monte della Guardia* and fringed by picturesque coves

and cliffs. Under the N side of the hill is a bay forming a sheltered harbour, with the villages of *Ponza* (alt. 19 m; hotels: Chiaia di Luna, I, 109 b.; Baia, II, 54 b.; Cernia, II, 52 b.; etc.) and *Santa Maria*. – The south-eastern group consists of the islands of *Ventotene*, part of a former crater (3 km long by 1 km across), with a village of the same name and a castle (conversion to a hotel planned), and *Santo Stéfano*, a granite island with a former prison which it is also planned to convert into a hotel.

Portofino

Region: Liguria. – Province: Genova (GE).
Altitude: 3 m. – Population: 800.
Post code: I-16034. – Dialling code: 0185.
(i) AA, Via Roma, 35–37;
    tel. 6 90 24.

HOTELS. – *Splendido*, L, 123 b., SP; *Nazionale*, II, 100 b.; *Piccolo*, II, 45 b.; *San Giorgio*, II, 36 b.

The former fishing village of *Portofino*, picturesquely situated in a narrow cove at the SE tip of the Portofino promontory, owes its popularity with visitors to its beautiful setting, its agreeable climate and its luxuriant Mediterranean vegetation.

SIGHTS. – To the S, above the harbour, is the *church of San Giorgio*, from which there is a beautiful view of Portofino. There are still more extensive *views from the platform beside *Castel San Giorgio*, to the E, extending NW to Capo Mele and the Maritime Alps.

SURROUNDINGS. – There is a very attractive *boat trip* (1¼ hours) under the precipitous S side of the promontory to *San Fruttuoso*, a former abbey which appears in the records as early as 986, with an early

Portofino harbour

Gothic church and a cloister, picturesquely situated in a small rocky cove. Offshore, 17 m below sea level, is a bronze figure of Christ 2·5 m high (1954) on a concrete base weighing 80 tons. – From San Fruttuoso there is a pleasant walk (2 hours), steep in the first section, to the Semáforo Vecchio (610 m), the highest point on the *Portofino promontory, which thrusts out squarely into the sea for 4–5 km, affording wide views which extend in clear weather as far as Corsica. From here it is half an hour's walk to the Portofino Vetta promontory (450 m), the** view from which is famous. To the NW can be seen the coastline from Camogli to Genoa and beyond this Capo Berta, above which, best seen in the morning light, are the snow-covered Cottian Alps; to the SE are Rapallo, Chiávari and Sestri, the islands off Portovénere and the Apuan Alps. Here too is the aerial tower, 117 m high, of the Genoa television transmitter. – On the W side of the Portofino promontory the picturesquely situated little port of *Camogli (alt. 11 m; pop. 7000) has a beautiful parish church and the ruined Castello Dragone.

Prato

Region: Toscana. – Province: Firenze (FI).
Altitude: 61 m. – Population: 150,000.
Post code: I-50047. – Dialling code: 0574.
(i) AA, Via Cairoli 48;
tel. 2 41 12.

HOTELS. – Palace, II, 170 b., SP; President, II, 143 b.; Milano, II, 102 b.; Flora, II, 57 b.; Villa Cristina, II, 46 b.; Moderno, II, 24 b.; San Marco, III, 98 b.; etc. – CAMPING SITE.

EVENTS. – Philatelists' and Numismatists' Exchange (Mar.); International Organ Festival (Mar.); Trade Fair (Sept.).

The old Tuscan town of Prato, known as the "Italian Manchester" on account of its important wool industry, lies on the River Bisenzio, on the S side of the Apennines. The town, which belonged to Florence from 1350 onwards, is still surrounded by its medieval walls and contains many fine works of Early Renaissance art and architecture by Florentine artists.

SIGHTS. – The town centre is closed to cars. – In the Piazza del Duomo, in the northern part of the town, stands the **Cathedral**, begun in the 12th c. in Tuscan Romanesque style and remodelled in Gothic style in 1317–20, with a Lombard tower (1340). On the façade (1413 onwards) is a *pulpit by Donatello and Michelozzo with reliefs of dancing children (1434–38). Above the main entrance is a terracotta relief by Andrea della Robbia of the Madonna with SS. Stephen and Lawrence (1489). The

interior is dark. The Cappella del Sacro Cingolo has wall paintings by Agnolo Gaddi (scenes from the life of the Virgin, 1392) and a statuette of the Virgin by Giovanni Pisano. In the choir are *frescoes by Fra Filippo Lippi (St John the Baptist and St Stephen) which rank among his finest work. In the S transept is a rich marble pulpit with reliefs by Mino da Fiesole and Antonio Rossellino (1473). – N of the cathedral is the Bishop's Palace, with the Diocesan Museum (cloister).

From the Piazza del Duomo Via Mazzoni runs S to the Piazza del Comune, in the centre of the town. At the SW corner of the square stands the 13th c. **Palazzo Pretorio**, on the first floor of which is the Galleria Comunale, with pictures by Florentine masters, including Filippino Lippi and Fra Filippo Lippi. Opposite is the Palazzo Comunale.

From the Piazza del Comune Via Ricasoli runs S to the Piazza San Francesco, on the left side of which is the 13th c. church of San Francesco. In the beautiful cloister to the right of the church we find the entrance to the chapterhouse, which has fine wall paintings of the school of Giotto (N. Gerini, 14th c.). – In the adjoining square to the E, on left, is the *church of the Madonna delle Cárceri, a good example of a church on a Greek cross plan with a dome – a technical problem which exercised architects of the transitional period between the Early and the High Renaissance. It contains a fine high altar by Sangallo (1512) and medallions of the Evangelists and a beautiful terracotta frieze by Andrea della Robbia.

To the S of the Madonna della Carceri the Castello dell'Imperatore, a castle (well restored), was built in the reign of the Emperor Frederick II (c. 1250). – In the Viale della Repubblica is a Textile Museum.

Prócida

Region: Campania. – Province: Napoli (NA).
Altitude: 0–91 m. – Population: 10,000.
Post code: I-80079. – Dialling code: 081.
(i) AA, in the harbour.

The volcanic island of Prócida, with a length of 3·5 km and an area of 3·75 sq. km, lies on the W side of the Bay

Prócida

of Naples between Capo Miseno and the island of Ischia. It is formed of two adjoining craters, the southern rims of which have been invaded and eroded by the sea, leaving two bays on the SE coast of the island. The Bay of Chiaiolella to the SW may have been formed by another smaller crater, while a fourth gave rise to the neighbouring islet of Vivara.

SIGHTS. – On the N side of the island, extending inland from the coast on to a hill, is the little town of **Prócida** (alt. 32 m; hotels: Arcate, III, 72 b.; Riviera, III, 42 b.; L'Oasi, III, 28 b.), whose gleaming white houses have a rather Oriental air. Particularly picturesque are the *fishing harbour with its brightly coloured boats and the district of *Corricella*. On a precipitous crag above the town towers a massive castle (now a prison), commanding extensive views of the neighbouring islands and peninsulas. – From the town a narrow road runs 3 km S to *Chiaiolella Bay*. To the E, higher up, is the old *church of Santa Margherita*; offshore to the W is the little islet, planted with olives, of *Vivara* (alt. 109 m: private property, no visitors), which is connected to Prócida by a bridge.

40 b.; *Miramare*, II, 39 b.; *Rosa Bianca*, II, 33 b.; *De la Promenade*, II, 28 b.; *Vittorio*, III, 67 b.; *Giulio Cesare*, III, 53 b.; etc. – CAMPING SITE.

The little port town of Rapallo, a popular resort both in summer and in winter, lies on the Riviera di Levante, tucked away in the Bay of Rapallo, which has recently been given the name of Golfo Tigullio, after its ancient inhabitants.

SIGHTS. – The town's busiest square is the *Piazza Cavour*, in which is the old *parish church* (façade 1857; leaning tower 1753). To the SW, near the mouth of the little River Boato, is the small *Giardino Pubblico*, from which there is a charming view of Sestri. – 1 km S of Piazza Cavour, on the road to Santa Margherita, is the *Kursaal*. – On the SE side of the fishing harbour (now silted up), beyond the mouth of the *Torrente San Francesco*, is a medieval *Castello*, now a prison.

Rapallo

SURROUNDINGS. – 11 km N, up the valley of the *Rio di Monte*, is the **pilgrimage church of the Madonna di Montallegro**, high up on the hillside (612 m; also reached by cableway, 10 minutes). – From Rapallo there is a magnificent *coast road (S.S. 227: crowded during the summer) running 8 km S to **Portofino** (see p. 205).

Rapallo

Region: Liguria. – Province: Genova (GE).
Altitude: 2 m. – Population: 28,000.
Post code: I-16035. – Dialling code: 0185.
ⓘ TCI, *Polly Viaggi*, Piazza delle Nazioni 1;
tel. 5 51 75.

HOTELS. – *Bristol*, I, 146 b., SP; *Grand Hotel e Europa*, I, 121 b.; *Eurotel Rapallo*, I, 99 b., SP; *Grand Italia e Lido*, II, 100 b.; *Moderno e Reale*, II, 86 b.; *Savoia Grand*, II, 84 b.; *Marsala*, II, 51 b.; *Riviera*, II, 45 b.; *Cavour*, II, 44 b.; *Astoria*, II, 42 b.; *Bel Soggiorno*, II,

Ravenna

Region: Emilia-Romagna. – Province: Ravenna (RA).
Altitude: 3 m. – Population: 136,000.
Post code: I-48100. – Dialling code: 0544.
ⓘ EPT, Piazza San Francesco 7;
tel. 2 51 11.
AA, Via San Vitale 2;
tel. 2 52 80.
ACI, Piazza Mameli 4;
tel. 2 25 67.
TCI, *Viaggi Classense*, Via Diaz 13;
tel. 3 33 47.

HOTELS. – *Jolly Mameli*, I, 114 b.; *Bisanzio*, I, 58 b.; *Trieste*, II, 96 b.; *Centrale Byron*, II, 61 b.; *Argentario*, II, 57 b.; *Astoria*, II, 34 b.; *Roma*, III, 69 b.; *Italia*, III, 62 b.; etc. – YOUTH HOSTEL, Via Aurelio Nicolodi, 120 b. – CAMPING SITE.

Ravenna, a provincial capital and the see of an archbishop, situated in the SE corner of the N Italian plain, here traversed by numerous drainage canals, is one of the most fascinating towns in Italy, offering a magnificent conspectus of early medieval art with its fine old *buildings and its splendid **mosaics. Originally a seaport, it is now connected with the sea by a canal 10 km long linking it with Porto Corsini (established 1736).

Mosaic in San Vitale, Ravenna

Ravenna has a large oil refinery, and other major elements in its economy are the natural gas found in the area and wine-growing (Wine-Growing Museum).

HISTORY. – In the time of the Etruscans and Romans Ravenna was a lagoon town like Venice. Augustus made the port of *Portus Classis*, 5 km from the town, the base of the Roman Adriatic fleet. Ravenna's heyday began, however, when the Western Roman Emperor *Honorius* moved his court from Milan to the natural fortress of Ravenna, protected by the surrounding marches, in 404. While the rest of Italy was being devastated during the great migrations, an active programme of building was carried out here under Honorius and his sister *Galla Placidia* (Regent 425–450), and the art of mosaic-working flourished. After the fall of the Western Roman Empire the Herulian *Odoacer* was proclaimed king by the Germanic mercenary troops and ruled the whole of Italy from Ravenna (476–493). After his murder the Ostrogothic king Theodoric the Great, who had been brought up in Constantinople (493–526), brought further splendour to the town, building several churches for the Arian Church, to which the Ostrogoths belonged, as well as a royal palace. In 539, under *Justinian* (527–565), the Byzantine general Belisarius drove out the Ostrogoths. Thereafter Ravenna became the seat of a Byzantine governor (Exarch), and, favoured by the emperor, enjoyed a third period of prosperity, which introduced Byzantine art to the West. In 751, however, the Lombards put an end to the Exarchate. From 1297 to 1441 Ravenna was ruled by the Ghibelline *Polenta* family, for a period thereafter belonged to the Venetians and from 1509 to 1860 was incorporated in the States of the Church.

SIGHTS. – In the centre of the town is the *Piazza del Popolo*, with the *Palazzo Municipale* (Town Hall, 1681) and a *portico* of eight granite columns (with Theodoric's monogram on four of the capitals). In front of the Town Hall are two granite columns erected by the Venetians in 1483.

0·5 km NW of the Piazza del Popolo is the ****church of San Vitale**, an externally unadorned octagonal structure on a centralised plan (diameter 35 m) with an octagonal dome, begun in 526 during the reign of Theodoric and consecrated in 547. Apart from its architecture its principal interest lies in its magnificent brilliantly coloured mosaics. The interior, which has been freed from later additions with the exception of the Baroque frescoes in the dome, is divided by eight piers into a central space and a surrounding ambulatory. In the choir apse are mosaics (below, left and right) glorifying Justinian and his wife Theodora, who are accompanied by their suite (next to the emperor is Archbishop Maximian); above is Christ on a sphere symbolising the world, flanked by archangels and by St Vitalis (on left) and St Ecclesius (on right). The altar is of translucent alabaster. At the entrance to the apse are two Roman reliefs from a Temple of Neptune.

Beyond San Vitale is the ***mausoleum of Galla Placidia** (*c.* 440), in the form of a Latin cross, with a barrel-vaulted roof and a dome over the crossing. The interior is decorated with beautiful *mosaics on a dark blue ground – a cross, the symbols of the Evangelists, Apostles, above the door Christ as the Good Shepherd. To the rear and in the two lateral arms of the cross are marble sarcophagi, said to be those of Gallia Placidia, her second husband Constantius III (d. 421) and her son Valentinian III (d. 455). – To the W, adjoining San Vitale, is the interesting **Museo**

Nazionale d'Antichità (closed Mondays), with inscriptions, architectural elements, sculpture, carved ivories, etc.

A short distance SW of the Piazza del Popolo is the **Cathedral** of Sant'Orso, built 1734–44 on the site of the oldest church in Ravenna, founded by St Ursus (d. 396); the campanile and crypt date from this earlier church. In the nave, on the right, the 6th c. pulpit was reconstructed from the separate marble slabs, decorated with animal figures, of which it was originally composed. In the second chapel on the right and in the S transept are Early Christian marble sarcophagi. – Immediately N of the cathedral is the *Baptistery of the Orthodox or *San Giovanni in Fonte*, an octagonal brick structure (5th c.). The mosaics in the dome (some of which have been restored) are among the oldest in Ravenna. The font is 16th c., but the parapet is ancient.

Dante's Tomb, Ravenna

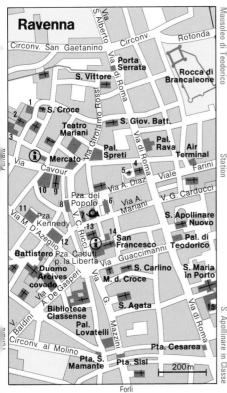

Ravenna

1 Mausoleum of Galla Placidia
2 San Vitale
3 Museo Nazionale d'Antichità
4 Spirito Santo
5 Battistero of Arians
6 Teatro Alighieri
7 Prefettura
8 Palazzo Municipale
9 San Domenico
10 Istituto Musicale Giuseppe Verdi
11 Palazzo Rasponi dalle Teste
12 Palazzo Rasponi Murat
13 Santa Maria Maddalena
14 Cassa di Risparmio
15 Gall. di Belle Arti

Behind the cathedral, to the SE, stands the **Archbishop's Palace**, on the first floor of which, to the left, are the *Cappella di San Pier Crisólogo*, with mosaics of the 6th–7th c., and the so-called throne of Archbishop Maximian, actually 6th c. Egyptian work, with ivory reliefs. – To the E is the modern Piazza dei Caduti per la Libertà, from which Via Ricci runs N to the Piazza del Popolo. On the W side of the square the *Accademia di Belle Arti* (16th c.) has a *picture gallery in the Loggetta Lombardesca and a Renaissance cloister. Farther E is the Franciscan *church of San Francesco*, founded in the 5th c., with a Romanesque tower (10th c.). – To the N of the church **Dante's Tomb** can be seen. The exterior is neo-classical (1780); in the interior is a sarcophagus containing the remains of the poet, who died in exile in Ravenna in 1321 at the age of 56.

In the busy Via di Roma, on the E side of the town, is the *church of Sant'Apollinare Nuovo*, a basilica built by Theodoric after 500 as an Arian cathedral and converted into a Roman Catholic church in 560. The porch and the apse date from the 16th and 18th c. The interior of the church, with 24 marble columns from Constantinople, is a rare example of a well-preserved Early Christian interior, with the exception of the ceiling, which was modernised in 1611. The walls of the nave have interesting 6th c. *mosaics: on the left-hand wall the Roman port of Classis, with ships; on the right-hand wall the town of Ravenna, with its churches and Theodoric's palace, and saints in Byzantine costume; above this prophets; and above the windows interesting compositions from the New Testament, 13 on each side – on the left the sayings and miracles of Christ (who is shown beardless), on the right scenes from the Passion (with a bearded Christ).

A little way S of Sant'Apollinare, at the corner of Via Alberoni, are remains of the *Palace of the Exarch* (richly articulated façade, with a central projection). – Farther S stands the large Baroque **church of Santa Maria in Porto** (1533 onwards; façade 1784). The adjoining *Monastero di Porto* has a two-storey cloister and a beautiful loggia on the E front. – NE of Sant'Apollinare, in the area round the station, which suffered heavy damage during the Second World War and has been completely redeveloped since then, is the *church of San Giovanni Evangelista*, founded by Gallia Placidia in 424 and rebuilt in its original form after severe war damage. – A short distance W (entered from Via Paolo Costa) are the *Basilica of the Santo Spirito*, built in the reign of Theodoric, and the former **Baptistery of the Arians** (later *Santa Maria in Cosmedin*), with 6th c. mosaics (Baptism of Christ), heavily restored, in the dome.

750 m E of the *Porta Serrata* (at the N end of the Via di Roma) is the *Tomb of Theodoric, built about 520, probably on the orders of Theodoric himself. This is a monumental two-storey rotunda built in square blocks of Istrian limestone and roofed with a single huge block 11 m in diameter. The tomb is reminiscent of Syrian rather than Roman models. The ornamentation shows clear Germanic influence. The lower floor is a barrel-vaulted chamber in the form of a Greek cross, on the upper floor is an antique porphyry sarcophagus.

SURROUNDINGS. – 5 km S, on the road to Rimini, stands the fine *church of Sant'Apollinare in Classe Fuori, the largest and best preserved basilica in Ravenna, with a porch and a round campanile. The church, begun about 535 on a site just outside the port of Classis, was consecrated in 549; it was restored in 1779 and freed from encroaching buildings in 1904. The spacious interior contains 24 Byzantine columns. On the walls are medallions with portraits of bishops and archbishops of Ravenna (18th c.). In the aisles are marble sarcophagi of archbishops of the 5th–8th c. The 12th c. crypt has an ancient bronze window-grating. The mosaics in the apse and on the triumphal arch date from the 6th–7th c. (restored). – 5 km SE of Sant'Apollinare are the remains of the *Pineta di Classe*, a once famous pinewood which has been much reduced by felling and fire.

11 km NE of Ravenna, on the Adriatic coast, is the seaside resort of **Marina di Ravenna** (alt. 3 m; hotels: Park, I, 156 b., SP; Marepinta, II, 81 b., annexe, II, 36 b.; Belvedere, III, 70 b.; Internazionale, III, 50 b.; etc.). Beyond the *Naviglio Candiano* (ferry) is *Porto Corsini*, the port of Ravenna.

Reggio di Calabria

Region: Calabria. – Province: Reggio di Calabria (RC).
Altitude: 29 m. – Population: 165,000.
Post code: I-89100. – Dialling code: 0965.

ⓘ **EPT**, Via C. Colombo 9;
tel. 9 84 96.
AA, Via Roma 3;
tel. 2 11 71.
Information office, Corso Garibaldi 329;
tel. 9 20 12.
ACI, Via de Nava 43;
tel. 9 79 01.
TCI, *Azienda Soggiorni*, Via Osanna 6;
tel. 9 20 12.

HOTELS. – *Excelsior*, Piazza Indipendenza, I, 195 b.; *Grande Albergo Miramare*, Via Fata Morgana 1, II, 145 b.; *Palace Hotel Masoanri*, Via Veneto 95, II, 123 b.; *Primavera*, Via Nazionale 177, II, 196 b.; *Delfino*, Via Gebbione a Mare, II, 70 b.; *Continental*, Via Florio 10, II, 59 b.; *Lido*, Via 3c Settembre 6, II, 50 b.; *Moderno*, Via Torrione 67, III, 45 b.; *Eremo*, Via Eremo Botte, III, 44 b.; etc. – CAMPING SITE.

EVENTS. – Annual *International Agricultural Show*.

The port of Reggio, with the affix "di Calabria" to distinguish it from the other town of the same name in Emilia, is the largest town in Calabria, the capital of a province and the see of an archbishop. It was the Greek Rhegion and the Roman Rhegium.

Reggio lies on the E side of the Strait of Messina. It was destroyed by an earthquake in 1783, and again suffered heavy damage in 1908, when some 20,000 people lost their lives. Thereafter it was rebuilt and recovered all its former economic importance. – Reggio is the world's principal centre for the production of oil of bergamot.

SIGHTS. – The town's busiest square is the Piazza Italia, near the sea, in which are the *Prefecture*, the *Palazzo Provinciale*, and the *Town Hall*. – Along the SE side of the square runs the *Corso Garibaldi*, the busy main street of the town, 2 km long. To the SW along this street is the Piazza

Castello Aragonese, Reggio di Calabria

del Duomo, with the imposing cathedral, in Romanesque-Byzantine style, rebuilt in 1908. – Farther SW are the gardens of the *Villa Comunale* (view). – From the 15th c. *Castello Aragonese*, to the E of the cathedral, there are magnificent views. There are also fine views from Via Reggio Campi, 500 m farther E.

From the Piazza Italia the Corso Garibaldi runs NE past the *Tempio della Vittoria*, a war memorial (1933), to the **National Museum** (closed Mondays), with pre-historic, medieval and modern sculpture and early Italic and Greek archaeological material.

From the National Museum the Viale Domenico Genoese Zerbi runs N, passing close to a large bathing station, and crosses the *Torrente Annunziata* to reach the harbour (ferry services to Messina).

Running SW from the National Museum the **Lungomare Giacomo Matteotti*, a beautiful seafront promenade some 3 km long, affords fine views of the coast of Sicily.

SURROUNDINGS. – An interesting trip can be made to the forest-clad **Aspromonte**, which in ancient times was counted as part of the Sila range. The best point of approach is **Gambarie di Aspromonte** (alt. 1270 m), a holiday resort (also popular with winter sports enthusiasts) 24 km NE of Reggio (chair-lift to the *Puntone di Scirocco*, 1660 m, to the SE). – From Gambarie 3·5 km S on S.S. 183, then 15 km E on a moderately good mountain road (open in summer), through pine and beech forests, to **Montalto** (*Monte Cocuzza*, 1958 m), the highest point in the Aspromonte. On the summit is a statue of Christ; magnificent **views of the sea and of Calabria and Sicily.

Reggio nell'Emilia

Region: Emilia-Romagna.
Province:Reggio nell'Emilia (RE).
Altitude: 58 m. – Population: 130,000.
Post code: I-42100. – Dialling code: 0522.
ⓘ **EPT**, Piazza C. Battisti 4;
tel. 4 33 70.
ACI, Via Secchi 4;
tel. 3 57 45.

HOTELS. – *Astoria*, Viale S. Nobili 2, I, 158 b.; *Europa*, Viale Olimpia 2, II, 98 b.; *Posta*, Piazza C. Battisti 4, II, 85 b.; *San Marco*, Piazzale Marconi 1, II, 74 b.; *Scudo d'Italia*, Via Vescovado 5, III, 54 b.; etc.

The old provincial capital of Reggio nell'Emilia lies on the Via Emilia near the southern edge of the N Italian plain. Known in Roman times as Regium Lepidi, it was the scene of bitter party strife during the Middle Ages. The poet Lodovico Ariosto (1474–1533) was born in the town.

SIGHTS. The town centre is closed to cars. – In the centre is the *Piazza Cesare Battisti*, with the 13th c. *Palazzo del Capitano del Popolo*. The square lies on the line of the ancient Via Aemilia, which traverses the town under the name of *Via Emilia a San Pietro* (to the E) and *Via Emilia a Santo Stefano* (to the W). – A little way S is the large *Piazza Prampolini*, on the E side of which stands the **Cathedral** (13th c., rebuilt in 15th–16th c.). Behind the unfinished Renaissance façade is the original Romanesque structure, with remains of frescoes and sculpture (on the façade and in the interior) by Prospero Clemente (d. 1584), a pupil of Michelangelo's, and Bartolomeo Spani, both natives of Reggio. – To the SE is the 16th c. **church of San Próspero**, on the site of an earlier Romanesque church. On the façade (rebuilt 1748) are six marble lions from the original building. The church has frescoes by Camillo Procaccini (1585–89).

To the N of Piazza Cesare Battisti in the Piazza Cavour are the large *Municipal Theatre* and the **Municipal Museum** (an 18th c. natural history collection, works of art, local archaeology). To the W is the *Galleria Parmeggiani* (pictures).

In the western part of the town, in the broad Corso Garibaldi, is the ***church of the Madonna della Chiaira**, a Baroque church built 1597–1619, on a Greek cross plan with a dome over the crossing.

The interior, notable for the beauty of its proportions, has charming stucco decoration and frescoes.

SURROUNDINGS. – SW of Reggio on S.S. 63 is *Felina* (alt. 645 m), where a road branches off on the left to the little hill town of *Carpineti* (7 km: alt. 556 m), with a castle in which the quarrelsome monk Hildebrand, later Pope Gregory VII (1073–85), once found refuge. – 7 km beyond Felina is **Castelnovo ne' Monti** (alt. 700 m; hotels: Pineta del Sole, IV, 60 b.; Miramonti, IV, 42 b.; etc.), a popular summer holiday resort on the NW slopes of the conspicuous rocky peak, mentioned by Dante in the "Divine Comedy", of the *Pietra di Bismantova* (alt. 1047 m), from the top of which there are magnificent *views of the Apennines. A road (5 km) ascends the hill; then 15 minutes' walk to the top.

Rimini

Region: Emilia-Romagna. – Province: Forlì (FO).
Altitude: 7 m. – Population: 120,000.
Post code: I-47037. – Dialling code: 0541.
ⓘ **EPT** and **TCI**, Piazzale C. Battisti;
    tel. 2 79 27.
    ACI, Via Roma 66;
    tel. 2 42 75.

HOTELS. – *Grand*, Piazzale Indipendenza, I, 186 b., SP; *Savoia-Excelsior*, Viale A. Vespucci 44, I, 156 b.; *Ambasciatori*, Viale A. Vespucci 22, I, 120 b., SP; *Bellevue*, Piazza Kennedy 12, I, 118 b., SP; *Imperiale*, Viale A. Vespucci 15, I, 112 b., SP; *Residenza*, Piazzale Indipendenza, I, 88 b., SP; *Waldorf*, Viale A. Vespucci 28, I, 82 b.; *Abarth*, Viale Mantegazza 12, II, 156 b.; *Continental*, Viale A. Vespucci 40, II, 148 b.; *Sporting*, Viale A. Vespucci 20, II, 138 b., SP; *Admiral*, Via Regina Elena 37, II, 136 b.; *Diplomat*, Viale Regina Elena 70, II, 131 b.; *Corallo*, Viale A. Vespucci 46, 128 b.; *Biancamano*, Via Cappellini 2, II, 124 b.; *Amati*, Viale Regina Elena 6, II, 123 b., SP; *National*, Viale A. Vespucci 42, II, 122 b.; *Atlantico*, Viale Trieste 3, II, 120 b., SP; *Villa Bianca*, Viale Regina Elena 24, II, 118 b.; *Palace*, Viale Dante 46, II, 117 b.; *Farioli*, Viale Vittorio Veneto 14, II, 114 b.; *Villa Adriatica*, Viale A. Vespucci 3, II, 114 b.; *Comfort*, Viale Boccaccio 7, II, 112 b.; *Londres*, Viale A. Vespucci 24, II, 107 b.; *Mariani*, Viale A. Vespucci 23, II, 102 b.; *Milton*, Viale Cappellini 16, III, 138 b.; *Atlas*, Viale Regina Elena 74, III, 122 b.; *Romagna*, Viale Tripoli 11, III, 108 b.; *Astoria*, Viale A. Vespucci 27, III, 105 b.; *Galles*, Viale Regina Elena 179, III, 95 b.; etc. – YOUTH HOSTEL in Miramare, Via Flaminia 300, 89 b.

IN RIVABELLA: *Cia*, III, 106 b.; *Prinz*, III, 89 b.; *Neframa*, III, 77 b.; *Gaston*, III, 75 b.; *Euromar*, III, 67 b.; *Alexander*, III, 66 b.; *Driade*, III, 62 b.; *Della Valle*, III, 60 b.; *Iones*, III, 60 b.; etc. – IN VISERBA: *Blumen*, III, 156 b.; *Crown*, III, 110 b.; *Terminus*, III, 102 b.; *Panoramic*, III, 78 b.; *Stella d'Italia*, III, 73 b.; etc. – IN VISERBELLA: *Helvetia*, II, 117 b., SP; *Life*, II, 72 b., SP; *Baia*, III, 70 b.; *Anglia*, III, 69 b.; *Gallia*, III, 69 b.; *Serena*, III, 69 b.; etc. – IN TORRE PEDRERA: *Punta Nord*, I, 270 b., SP; *Mose*, II, 104 b.; *El Cid*, II, 77 b.; *Graziella*, III, 126 b.; *Montmartre*, III, 104 b., SP; *Avila*, III, 98 b.; *Doge*, III, 85 b.; *Du Lac*, III, 80 b.; *Ciondola d'Oro*, III, 75 b.; *Bolognese*, III, 71 b.; etc. – IN MIRAMARE: *Terminal*, II, 140 b., SP; *Roma*, II, 124 b.; *La Fiorita*, II, 115 b.; *Mulazzani*, II, 115 b.; *Touring*, II,

108 b.; *Miramare e de la Ville*, II, 102 b.; *Due Mari*, II, 100 b.; *Astor*, II, 95 b.; *Regina*, II, 90 b.; *Ascot*, II, 79 b.; *Coronado Airport*, II, 44 b.; *Concordia*, III, 120 b.; *Centrale*, III, 111 b.; *Pecci*, III, 88 b.; *Nettunia*, III, 82 b.; *San Giorgio*, III, 80 b.; etc.

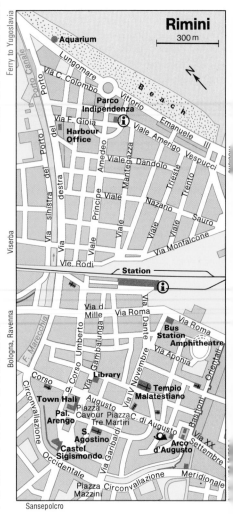

Sansepolcro

The well-known seaside resort of Rimini lies on the Adriatic in the SE corner of the N Italian plain, at the meeting-place of two important ancient roads, the Via Aemilia and the Via Flaminia. Apart from a beach 20 km long, the Riviera del Sole, which makes it one of the most popular resorts in Italy, Rimini offers the attractions of important Roman remains and medieval buildings.

HISTORY. – The ancient *Ariminum* became a Roman colony in 268 B.C., commanding the road into northern Italy. In the 13th c. it fell into the hands of the *Malatesta* family, and in 1528 was incorporated in the States of the Church.

SIGHTS. – In the centre of the old town is *Piazza Cavour*, in which are the *Palazzo Comunale* (1562), the *Palazzo dell'Arengo* (begun 1204), in Romanesque and Gothic style, and the *Theatre*, destroyed during the Second World War (rebuilding planned). – From Piazza Cavour the broad Corso di Augusto runs NW to the **Ponte di Tiberio**, a Roman bridge over the *Mareccia*, begun in the reign of Augustus and completed in A.D. 20, during the reign of Tiberius.

SE of Piazza Cavour stands the *church of San Francesco (Tempio Malatestiano)*, a 13th c. Gothic structure remodelled in Renaissance style in 1447–56. The façade was designed by Leon Battista Alberti, who drew his inspiration from the Arch of Augustus, and it was the first structure to be based on ancient models at the very beginning of the Renaissance. The interior is finely decorated. – At the SE end of the Corso di Augusto rises the **Arch of Augustus** (Arco d'Augusto), a triumphal arch built in 27 B.C. to commemorate the construction of the Via Flaminia. – To the NE of the old town, beyond the railway, extends the resort of Rjmini, with numerous villas, hotels and *pensioni*. Its principal street is the *Lungomare Vittorio Emanuele III* along the seafront. – To the NW are the outlying districts of *Rivabella*, *Viserba* (miniature town, "Italia in Miniatura"), *Viserbella* and *Torre Pedrera*, all with excellent facilities for visitors. – 3 km SE, on the road to Riccione, is *Miramare*, also a popular resort, with a large airport.

SURROUNDINGS. – 8 km SE of Rimini is another very popular resort, **Riccione** (alt. 12 m; hotels: Grand, I, 244 b., SP; Lido Mediterraneo, I, 180 b., SP; Corallo, I, 151 b.; Spiaggia Savioli, I, 127 b., SP; Atlantic, I, 124 b., SP; Beaurivage, I, 96 b.; Abner's, I, 88 b.; A.B.C., I, 68 b.; Augustus, I, 64 b., SP; Vienna e Touring, II, 144 b.; Vittoria, II, 138 b.; Croce del Sud, II, 127 b.; Des Bains, II, 126 b.; Nautico, II, 120 b.; Club, II, 110 b.; Lungomare Laeta Domus, II, 108 b.;

Arizona, II, 106 b.; Cristallo, II, 102 b.; Ca' Bianca, II, 102 b.; Sarti, II, 100 b.; Stella, III, 120 b.; Kursaal, III, 106 b.; Mauritius, III, 103 b.; Gran Bretagna, III, 102 b.; Sirius, III, 100 b.; etc. – 5 camping sites), with thermal springs. – 3 km beyond this is the little health resort of *Misano Adriatico* (alt. 3 m; hotels: Nettuno, II, 72 b.; Gala, II, 41 b.; Savoia, III, 149 b.; Ghirlandia, III, 104 b.; Blumen, III, 85 b.; etc.), and another 4 km down the coast is **Cattolica** (alt. 10 m; hotels: Victoria Palace, I, 160 b.; Caravelle, I, 70 b., SP; Cormoran, II, 295 b., SP; Piccadilly, II, 216 b., SP; Kursaal, II, 147 b.; Linda, II, 145 b.; Negresco, II, 135 b.; Doge Mare, II, 134 b.; Baltic, II, 131 b.; Nord-Est, II, 129 b.; Leon d'Oro, II, 125 b.; Diplomat, II, 122 b.; Spiaggia, II, 121 b.; Acropolis, II, 120 b.; Savoia, II, 119 b.; Imperiale, II, 112 b.; Europa Monetti, II, 105 b., SP; London, II, 102 b.; Royal, II, 102 b., SP; Murex, II, 101 b., SP; Alexander, II, 100 b.; International, III, 120 b.; Universal, III, 100 b.; Gabbiano, III, 90 b.; Luxor, III, 90 b.; etc.). – On a hill 8 km S of Cattolica the little town of *Gradara* (alt. 142 m), has a completely preserved circuit of walls and towers and a very interesting castle.

20 km NW of Rimini is the popular seaside resort of **Cesenatico** (alt. 4 m; pop. 18,000; hotels: Esplanade, I, 96 b.; Grande Albergo Cesenatico, II, 164 b.; Palace, II, 150 b.; San Pietro, II, 121 b.; Genny, II, 113 b.; Eritrea, II, 96 b.; Da Pino, II, 95 b.; Internazionale, II, 93 b.; Sabrina, II, 92 b.; Torino, II, 89 b.; Britannia, II, 82 b.; Riz, II, 80 b.; Lido, III, 99 b.; Favorita, III, 96 b.; Delle Nazioni, III, 96 b.; etc.), with a picturesque old town, modern buildings on the seafront and a small canal harbour. – 8 km beyond Cesenatico is the rising resort of **Cervia** (alt. 3 m; pop. 25,000; hotels: Buenos Aires, II, 94 b.; Conchiglia, II, 77 b.; Nettuno, II, 77 b.; Athena, II, 74 b.; Excelsior, II, 74 b., SP; Beaurivage, II, 68 b.; K2, II, 66 b.; Ducale, II, 66 b.; Prater, II, 61 b.; Astoria, II, 60 b.; Lungomare, III, 100 b.; Trevi, III, 89 b.; Bristol, III, 84 b.; Odeon, III, 82 b.; Al Faro, III, 81 b.; etc.), with thermal and mud baths and a broad beach of fine sand. Beyond the canal harbour is the suburb of *Milano Marittima* (hotels: Aurelia, I, 189 b., SP; Gallia, I, 185 b.; Miami, I, 150 b., SP; Le Palme – Spiaggia, I, 142 b.; Rouge, I, 140 b.; Doge, I, 139 b., SP; Mare e Pineta – Villa Regina, I, 137 b., SP; Bellevue Beach, I, 124 b.; Imperiale, I, 121 b.; San Giorgio, I, 112 b.; Mare e Pineta, I, 105 b., SP; Michelangelo, I, 91 b.; Mare e Pineta – Pavillon, I, 63 b., SP; Adria, II, 200 b.; Rio, II, 154 b.; Internazionale, II, 142 b.; Metropolitan, II, 135 b.; Lido, II, 130 b.; Deanna, II, 126 b.; Savini, II, 120 b.; Sahara, II, 112 b.; Ariston, II, 112 b.; Embassy, II, 112 b.; Terminus, II, 109 b.; Promenade, II, 108 b.; Ambasciatori, II, 104 b.; Corona, II, 100 b.; Villa Fiorita, II, 100 b.; Crystal, III, 92 b.; Riviera, III, 88 b.; Vela, III, 83 b.; Michaela, III, 77 b.; Gianlore, III, 74 b.; Silvana, III, 73 b.; Franca, III, 72 b.; etc.), beautifully situated on the edge of a pinewood, with an excellent beach.

To San Leo (32 km). – Leave Rimini on S.S. 258 (the Arezzo road), which runs up the wide valley of the *Mareccia* and in 16 km passes below the little town of *Verucchio* (alt. 333 m; pop. 5000), with a Malatesta castle (magnificent *views*), lying off the road to the left. In another 3 km a road goes off on the left to **San Marino** (see p. 256), from which it is possible to return direct to Rimini, making an attractive **round trip of 82 km. – The main road continues up the valley to (4 km) the little village of *Villa Nuova*, where a road branches off on the left up a side valley, climbs steeply and comes in another 9 km to**San Leo (alt. 583 m; pop. 3000), picturesquely situated on a conical hill, with a massive castle, a Romanesque cathedral and the 9th c. church of La Pieve.

Cattolica

Riviera

ⓘ **EPT Genova**, Via Roma 11,
I-16100 Genova (GE);
tel. (010) 58 14 07.
EPT Imperia, Viale Matteotti 54,
I-18100 Imperia (IM);
tel. (0183) 2 49 47.
EPT La Spezia, Viale Mazzini 45,
I-19100 La Spezia (SP);
tel. (0187) 3 60 00.
EPT Savona, Via Paleocapa 7,
I-17100 Savona (SV);
tel. (019) 2 05 22.

The ** Riviera ("coast") is the narrow coastal strip which extends
along the Mediterranean from Marseilles to La Spezia. The Italian
Riviera, between Ventimiglia and La
Spezia, is one of the most beautiful
scenic stretches in Italy, with its
precipitous cliffs, its old-world little
port towns and its ruined watch-
towers standing above the brilliant
blue sea. The hills shelter it from the
rough north winds, and with its
southern exposure it benefits to the
full from the power of the sun and
the warmth of the sea. Mild winters
and warm summers promote the
growth of luxuriant southern vegetation. During winter and spring
many visitors seek relaxation in
the resorts, to which even larger
numbers come in summer for the
bathing.

The Italian Riviera is divided by the Gulf of
Genoa into two parts. To the E is the
*Riviera di Levante, with a mild but
somewhat variable climate and large areas
of forest, the south-eastern part of which,
beyond Sestri, still preserves its original
character. The towns and villages have
narrow streets and tall houses huddled on
the narrow coastal plains and side valleys.
In this section there are relatively few
comfortable hotels outside the main
centres. To the W of the Gulf of Genoa is
the *Riviera di Ponente, with a more
equable climate than the Riviera di
Levante. The coastal plain is wider,
accommodating many large resorts with
numerous first-class hotels and (for the
most part) excellent beaches. The western
part of the Riviera di Ponente, between
Alassio and the French frontier, is known
as the *Riviera dei Fiori on account of its
large-scale flower-growing industry.

**Along the Riviera di Ponente from Genoa to
Ventimiglia** (163 km). – The road runs W from the
station, past the Old Harbour, and comes in 6 km to
Cornigliano Ligure (alt. 10 m; Hotel Serafino, IV, 30
b.), a busy suburb of Genoa, with a new industrial area
extending some 800 m into the sea on reclaimed land.
Beyond the town a road goes off on the left to Genoa's
Cristoforo Colombo Airport. To the right, on a high
conical hill, is the *church of the Madonna del Gazzo*
(421 m). – 5 km: **Pegli** (alt. 6 m; hotels: Méditerranée,
II, 111 b.; Puppo, III, 29 b.; etc.), a popular resort for
holidays and weekends throughout the year, with
beautiful parks and villas. Near the station is the * **Villa
Pallavicini**, with an archaeological museum and a
park (closed Sundays and Mondays) extending up
the hillside, with a profusion of almost tropical
vegetation, fountains and other water-works, grottoes, an underground lake and a medieval-style castle.
In the Villa Doria, also near the station, is the Genoa
Naval and Maritime Museum (closed Sundays and
Mondays), with mementoes of Columbus. – 5 km:
Voltri (alt. 5 m), Genoa's last industrial suburb, with
the attractive large park (open to cars) of the *Villa
Galliera*. At the upper end of the park is the *pilgrimage
church of the Madonna delle Grazie* (fine views).

Beyond Voltri the road leaves the extensive built-up
area of Genoa. – 7 km: **Arenzano** (alt. 6 m; hotels:
Grand, I, 112 b., SP; Punta San Martino, I, 32 b., SP;
Miramare, II, 77 b.; Roma, III, 76 b.; etc.), a charmingly
situated resort (good beach) with an old castle and a
beautiful park round the Villa Sauli-Pallavicini. The
road then runs inland past the promontory of *Bric
Torretta*, covered with woodland and macchia, and

Varazze

returns to the coast. – 12 km: **Varazze** (alt. 5 m; pop.
15,000; hotels: Le Palme, II, 111 b.; Eden, II, 97 b.;
Savoya, II, 92 b.; Cristallo, II, 91 b.; Terminus, II, 67 b.;
Palace, II, 67 b.; Torretti, II, 64 b.; El Chico, II, 63 b.;
Coccodrillo, II, 63 b.; Piccolo, II, 62 b.; Royal, II, 62 b.;
Ariston, II, 53 b.; Delfino, II, 48 b.; Gran Colombo, III,
87 b.; Buccitti, III, 85 b.; Europa, III, 70 b.; Genovese,
III, 70 b.; etc.), a summer and winter resort, prettily
situated amidst orange-groves, with a beach 2 km
long. – 4 km: *Celle Ligure* (alt. 44 m; hotels: Riviera, II,
104 b.; San Michele, II, 104 b.; Aloha, II, 77 b.; Villa
Adele, III, 72 b.; Colombo, III, 55 b.; etc.), an attractive
resort above which is a fine old pinewood. – 4 km:
Albisola Marina (alt. 19 m; hotels: Astoria, II, 56 b.;
Corallo, II, 48 b.; Villa Verde, II, 48 b.; Villa Chiara, III,
47 b.; Europa, III, 36 b.; etc.), a popular resort with a
beach of fine sand. 1 km N is the little town of *Albisola*

Superiore, with the Villa Gavotti, formerly called the Villa delle Rovere, in which Pope Julius II (1503–13) was born.

Beyond Albisola Marina the road runs past the port of Savona and comes in another 3 km to the town of **Savona** (alt. 10 m; pop. 80,000; hotels: Riviera-Suisse, II, 95 b.; Astoria, II, 66 b.; Miramare la Terrasse, II, 31 b.; Pessano, III, 78 b.; Italia, III, 75 b.; Motel Agip, II, 120 b.; etc.), a provincial capital situated on the River *Letimbro*, with an important harbour in a long inlet and a variety of industry (large steel rolling-mill). On the harbour quay stands the Torre Pancaldo, named after the navigator of that name. In Via Paleocapa, which runs from here to the station, is the church of San Giovanni Battista (16th and 18th c.), with a fine painting (at the end of the N aisle) by Samuel van Hoogstraeten (1627–78), a pupil of Rembrandt. A little way S the Museo Civico houses pictures, sculpture and majolica. Close by is the cathedral (1604; façade 1886). – 6 km: *Vado Ligure* (alt. 12 m; pop. 10,000; Hotel Cicciun, IV, 28 b.), an industrial town at the end of the Roman Via Aurelia and the beginning of the Via Iulia Augusta. The Via Iulia Augusta runs round *Capo Vado* (lighthouse: fine view back towards Savona), an attractive stretch of road which for part of the way has been hewn out of the rock. Beyond the cape the rocky islet of *Bergeggi*, crowned by a Roman tower, can be seen on the left. – 7 km: **Spotorno** (alt. 10 m; hotels: Royal, I, 161 b.; Esperia, II, 98 b.; Park, II, 75 b.; Ligure, II, 74 b.; Tirreno, II, 74 b.; Delle Palme, II, 64 b.; La Pineta, II, 55 b.; Corallo, II, 54 b.; Miramare, II, 52 b.; Clio, II, 50 b.; Vallega, II, 48 b.; Helvetia, III, 78 b.; Villa Rina, III, 64 b.; etc.), a bathing resort with a beautiful beach. Beyond the town there is a fine view, ahead, of Capo Noli. – 3 km: **Noli** (alt. 4 m; hotels: Capo Noli, II, 105 b.; Tripodoro, II, 27 b.; Miramare, II, 52 b.; Diana, II, 50 b.; etc.), a charmingly situated little fishing town and seaside resort with a picturesque old town, remains of town walls, old towers, a castle and the late Romanesque church of San Paragorio (13th c.). Pleasant walk (1 hour) to *Capo Noli* (276 m), with a signal station and the church of Santa Margherita (*view).

Beyond Noli the road runs through a tunnel (114 m long) under Capo Noli and continues along the high overhanging cliffs of the *Malpasso* to (9 km) **Finale Ligure** (alt. 3 m; pop. 14,000; hotels: Moroni, I, 193 b.; Residenza Punta Est, I, 28 b.; Astoria, II, 112 b.; Boncardo, II, 94 b.; Orizzonte, II, 84 b.; La Pergola, II, 82 b.; Colibri, II, 77 b.; Miramare, II, 61 b.; Europa, II, 60 b.; etc.), a prettily situated resort, with the 14th c. Castelfranco above the town, the fine Baroque church of San Giovanni Battista (by Bernini) and a small museum containing local archaeological finds. Near the station is a small Capuchin church. 2 km NW, amid orange-groves, is the walled village of *Finalborgo*, with a beautiful parish church. Still farther NW, at *Perti*, are limestone caves, some of them containing Stone Age graves. – Beyond Finale the road cuts across the precipitous *Caprazoppa* promontory and comes in another 6 km to *Pietra Ligure* (alt. 3 m; hotels: Royal, I, 174 b.; Paco, I, 68 b., SP; Minerva, II, 164 b., SP; Sartore, II, 135 b.; Méditerranée, II, 135 b.; Bristol, II, 102 b.; Cristal, II, 58 b.; Azucena, II, 45 b.; Stella Maris, III, 181 b.; Lido, III, 92 b.; Geppi, II, 78 b.; etc.), a resort (sandy beach) with an interesting church and a ruined castle on an isolated crag. On the hillside is the *Pietranuova* sanatorium (sun and sea-air cures). – 4 km: **Loano** (alt. 4 m; pop. 13,000; hotels: Garden Lido, I, 166 b., SP; Moderno, II, 150 b.; Continental, II, 120 b.; Perelli, II, 64 b.; Excelsior, III, 67 b.; Motel Residence Casarino, III, 60 b., SP; etc.), a

popular resort with a former Doria palace (1578), now the Town Hall. On the hillside to the right is the former *monastery of Monte Carmelo*.

Beyond Loana there is an attractive view, to the right, of the Ligurian Alps, with *Monte Carmo* (1389 m). – 10 km: **Albenga** (alt. 5 m; pop. 20,000; hotels: Italia, III, 23 b.; Giardino, III, 23 b.; etc.), with a picturesque old town centre, old town walls and many towers which belonged to noble families. Other features of interest are the cathedral, partly Gothic, partly rebuilt in Baroque style (baptistery and lower part of façade 5th c.); the early Romanesque chapel of Santa Maria in Fontibus (10th c.); and museums of antiquities and of Roman shipping. Near the Via Aurelia is the Ponte Lungo, a medieval bridge 147 m long over the former course of the River Centa. Beyond Albenga the rocky islet of *Gallinara* (90 m), with the ruins of a 13th c. Benedictine abbey, can be seen on the left. – 7 km: **Alassio** (alt. 5 m; pop. 14,000; hotels: Méditerranée, I, 148 b.; Spiaggia, I, 145 b.; Diana, I, 119 b., SP; Europa e Concordia, I, 102 b.; Ambassador, I, 94 b.; Park, I, 87 b., SP; La Puerta del Sol, I, 43 b., SP; Méditerranée, I, 43 b.; Majestic, II, 126 b.; Toscana, II, 123 b.; Ideale, II, 120 b.; La Balnearia, II, 102 b.; New West End, II, 102 b.; Corso, II, 92 b.; Ritz, II, 92 b.; Tirreno, II, 91 b.; Beau Séjour, II, 90 b.; Ligure, II, 90 b.; Lido, II, 80 b.; Holiday, II, 79 b.; Nuovo Suisse, II, 77 b.; Aida, II, 76 b.; Regina, II, 76 b.; Rosa, II, 74 b.; Savoia, II, 72 b.; Bristol, III, 94 b.; Rio, III, 87 b.; Curtis Hotel Centrale, III, 84 b.; Tirrenia, III, 74 b.; Alfieri, III, 71 b.; etc.), a large and very popular resort with a beach of fine sand more than 3 km long. On the seafront promenade stands an old watch-tower. – 3 km: *Laigueglia* (alt. 11 m; hotels: Laigueglia, I, 90 b.; Splendid, I, 74 b.; Windsor, II, 76 b.; Le Palme, II, 75 b.; Del Sole, II, 73 b.; Atlantic, II, 56 b.; Beau Séjour, II, 63 b.; Residence Paradiso, II, 62 b.; Aquilia, II, 60 b.; Mediterraneo, II, 57 b.; Royal, II, 55 b.; Bristol, II, 51 b.; Ambassador, II, 50 b.; Savoia, III, 66 b.; Villa delle Viole, III, 62 b.; Villa Ida, III, 58 b.; La Giacomella, III, 58 b.; Tritone, III, 55 b.; Continental, III, 52 b.; etc.), a closely built little town with a beautiful 18th c. parish church and a good beach.

The road continues along the precipitous coast, high above the sea. – 3 km: *Capo Mele* (lighthouse), with a fine view of Alassio to the rear. Then on through *Marina di Andora* and round *Capo Cervo*. – 7 km: *Cervo* (alt. 66 m; Hotel Columbia, II, 39 b.; etc.), a picturesquely situated hillside village. The road then continues through the resort of *San Bartolomeo al Mare* (alt. 26 m; hotels: Mayola, III, 156 b.; San Giacomo, III, 83 b.; Stella Maris, III, 81 b.; Europa, III, 72 b.; etc.). – 3 km: **Diano Marina** (alt. 4 m; hotels: Diana Majestic, I, 160 b., SP; Teresa, II, 173 b.; Torino, II, 149 b.; Bellevue-Méditerranée, II, 144 b., SP; Villa Igea, II, 124 b., SP; Royal-Esplanade, II, 119 b., SP; Caravelle, II, 96 b., SP; Kristall, II, 93 b.; Olimpic, II, 90 b.; Tiziana, II, 87 b.; Sasso, II, 85 b.; Palace, II, 85 b.; Raffy, II, 80 b.; Golfo e Palme, II, 77 b.; Metropol, II, 72 b.; Marinella, III, 99 b.; Gabriella, III, 98 b.; Paradiso, III, 91 b.; Silvano, III, 87 b.; etc.). 2 km NW is the walled village of *Diano Castello* (alt. 135 m).

Beyond Diano Marina the road winds its way gently uphill to *Capo Berta*, from which there is a magnificent *view to the rear, extending as far as Capo Mele. – 6 km: **Imperia** (alt. 10 m; pop. 42,000; hotels: Robinia, II, 103 b.; Croce di Malta, II, 72 b.; Corallo, II, 68 b.; Kristina, II, 40 b.; Ariston, III, 75 b.; etc.), a provincial capital, comprising the districts of *Oneglia* (to E) and *Porto Maurizio* (to W), separated by the broad stony bed of the River *Impero*. Porto Maurizio (alt. 47 m) is picturesquely situated on the slopes of a promontory;

it has an imposing domed church (1780). – 18 km: *Arma di Taggia* (alt. 10 m; hotels: Vittoria-Grattacielo, I, 147 b., SP; Miramare, II, 94 b.; Arma, II, 68 b.; etc.), a resort with a beautiful beach, situated at the mouth of the River *Argentina*, or *Fiumare di Taggia*. 3 km up the valley is the picturesque little town of **Taggia** (alt. 39 m), with old patrician houses. In the church of the Dominican convent are pictures of the early Ligurian school. – 8 km: **San Remo** (see p. 257). – 6 km: **Ospedaletti** (alt. 30 m; hotels: Le Rocce del Capo, I, 45 b., SP; Petit Royal, II, 56 b.; Firenze, III, 53 b.; etc.), a popular resort, with an attractive Casino and a beautiful palm-shaded avenue, the Corso Regina Margherita. Above the town is the "Pépinière", with luxuriant southern vegetation.

Beyond Ospedaletti the road continues along the steep and rocky coast, through beautiful scenery. To the left, by the shore, is a fine park planted with palms (no admission); on the right, at the mouth of the *Val del Sasso*, are the *Vallone Gardens*, laid out by a German gardener named Ludwig Winter (d. 1912), also private property and not open to the public. – 6 km: **Bordighera** (see p. 81). Farther on, shortly before Ventimiglia, is the entrance (on left) to the remains of the Roman town of *Albintimilium* (closed mornings and Sundays), with a theatre (2nd c. A.D.). – 5 km: **Ventimiglia** (alt. 9 m; pop. 27,000; hotels: Francia, II, 104 b.; Bel Soggiorno, II, 100 b.; Splendid, II, 50 b.; La Riserva, II, 44 b., SP; Calipso, III, 52 b.; Sea Gull, II, 52 b.; Sole e Mare, II, 52 b.; etc.), the frontier town, situated at the mouth of the River *Roia*, with an important flower market. In the new town, to the E of the river, are the Town Hall and the palm-shaded Giardino Pubblico; in the picturesque walled old town, on the hill W of the river, are the Romanesque cathedral, with an adjoining baptistery, and the 11th c. church of San Michele (columns with Roman inscriptions). From the Piazzale del Capo, a little way S of the cathedral, there are magnificent *views, extending westward as far as Cap Ferrat. – From Ventimiglia an attractive excursion may be made up the beautiful *Nervia valley* to the little town of **Dolceacqua** (alt. 50 m), picturesquely situated on a hillside, with an old bridge 10 m high borne on pointed arches and a ruined castle which was the ancestral home of the famous Doria family of Genoa. – 4 km farther on is the village of *Isolabona* (ruined castle), and 2 km beyond this in a side valley is the hill village of *Apricale*, clinging picturesquely to a steep hillside. From here it is another 8 km to *Baiardo* (900 m).

Inland from the coastal resorts, with their crowds of summer visitors, are many quiet little villages, well off the beaten tourist track, which are well worth visiting not only for the beauty of their setting, on hilltops or precipitous slopes, but also for the picture they give of typical Italian hill settlements. Characteristic examples of such villages can be seen on the road from *San Remo* via *Ceriana* to *Baiardo* (25 km) or on the road from *Ventimiglia* via *Dolceacqua* to *Apricale* (13 km). It is also possible to take in these places on the way from San Remo to Ventimiglia (additional distance 29 km).

Along the Riviera di Levante from Genoa to La Spezia (113 km). – Leave Genoa by way of Corso G. Marconi; then E along Corso Italia. – 5 km: *Sturla* (alt. 18 m), a suburb of Genoa, with bathing stations (views of the olive-clad slopes of the Apennines, with houses scattered about among the plantations). To the left is the entrance to the large *Giannina Gaslini Children's Hospital*, built by the Italian "oil king" Count Gerolamo Gaslini in memory of his daughter Giannina. – 3 km: *Quinto al Mare* (alt. 20 m), another

The Portofino promontory

Genoa suburb, surrounded by orange-groves and palms, with handsome villas. – 2 km: **Nervi** (alt. 27 m; hotels: Savoia-Beeler, I, 74 b.; Astor Residence, I, 59 b.; Nervi, II, 61 b.; Giardino Riviera, II, 48 b.; Mondial, II, 45 b.; Villa Bonera, III, 42 b.; etc.), the oldest winter resort (rocky beach) on the Riviera di Levante, in a sheltered situation amid olive-, orange- and lemon-groves, with a *seafront promenade 1·8 km long hewn from the rock. On the E side of the Viale delle Palme lies the *Parco Municipale, with many exotic plants and the Galleria d'Arte Moderna (closed Sundays and Mondays). To the E, in a beautiful park in *Sant'Ilario*, is the Museo Luxoro (closed Sundays and Mondays), with applied art, pictures and furniture.

11 km beyond Nervi is **Recco** (alt. 5 m; pop. 10,000; hotels: Elena, III, 52 b.; Villa Trieste, III, 37 b.; etc.), from which there is an attractive detour to *Uscio* (alt. 370 m), 11 km N. From Uscio it is possible to return to Genoa via *Apparizione* on a beautiful *panoramic road (20 km). – 4 km: *Ruta* (alt. 290 m), a straggling villa suburb on the saddle between the coastal hills and the *Portofino promontory, projecting squarely into the sea for some 4–5 km, with scenery which is among the finest on the Riviera. – 7 km: **Rapallo** (see p. 207). – 6 km: *Zoagli* (alt. 30 m; hotels: Le Terrazze and Zoagli, II, 90 b.; Paradiso, III, 40 b.; etc.), with many villas on the slopes of the hillside; *panoramic road to Sant'Ambrogio (3 km). – 6 km: **Chiávari** (alt. 3 m; pop. 32,000; hotels: Giardini, II, 59 b.; Monterosa, III, 127 b.; Castagnola, III, 115 b.; Stella del Mare, III, 86 b.; Moderno, III, 72 b.; Santa Maria, III, 64 b.; Europa Tours, III, 62 b.; etc.), a seaside resort situated in a fertile plain at the mouth of the *Entella*, with a ruined castle (11th c.). Near the station, at the end of a beautiful avenue of palms, stands the cathedral (1613; pillared portico added 1841). – 2 km: **Lavagna** (alt. 5 m; pop. 15,000; hotels: Sud Est, III, 110 b.; Eden, III, 68 b.; Tigullio, III, 66 b.; Ancora, III, 56 b.; Elena, III, 54 b.; etc.), a resort with a large yacht harbour (1976).

Beyond Lavagna the road runs close to the shore. – 6 km: **Sestri Levante** (alt. 4 m; pop. 20,000; hotels: Villa Balbi, I, 190 b., SP; Dei Castelli, I, 82 b.; Grande Albergo, II, 152 b.; Victor, II, 120 b.; Metropole, II, 90 b.; Vis à Vis, II, 76 b.; Miramare e Europa, II, 70 b.; Mimosa, II, 44 b.; Elisabetta, III, 60 b.; Helvetia, III, 56 b.; etc.), a seaside and winter resort in a picturesque setting on the saddle of the Isola promontory (70 m), between two small bays. From the beautiful seafront promenade in the flat bay to the W there are extensive views of the Golfo Tigullio. From the square beside the harbour, at the S end of the bay, there is a road (fine views) to the tip of the promontory, which is crowned by the *Castello Gualino*. There is also a pleasant walk

(1 hour) SE to the *Telegrafo*, a signal station on the southern spur of the pine-clad *Monte Castello* (265 m: *views).

Beyond Sestri Levante the Via Aurelia runs inland, bypassing a stretch of rocky coast more than 60 km long, some of the places on which – such as the picturesque fishing villages of the *Cinqueterre (see p. 97) – can be reached only by the railway, running through tunnels for much of its course. – 18 km: **Passo del Bracco** (615 m). On an isolated crag by the roadside is the small aerial of the Savona television station (view). – 2 km: *La Baracca* (alt. 589 m). From here a scenic road (S.S. 332) winds its way down (15 km S), mostly through pine forests, to the little town, frequented by visitors both in summer and in winter, of **Lévanto** (alt. 11 m; hotels: Stella d'Italia, II, 65 b.; Crystal, II, 35 b.; Primavera, II, 35 b.; Palace, III, 76 b.; etc.), with remains of its medieval town walls and castle. From here the view by morning light can sometimes extend as far as Monte Viso, 210 km W. – 35 km: **Passo della Foce** (241 m), with *views of the bay of La Spezia and the Apuan Alps. – 6 km: **La Spezia** (see p. 273).

Rome/Roma

Region: Lazio. – Province: Roma (ROMA).
Altitude: 11–139 m. – Population: 3,000,000.
Post code: I-00100. – Dialling code: 066.

(i) **EPT di Roma**, Via Parigi 11;
tel. 46 18 51.
Information office in Stazione Termini.
ACI: *Head office*, Via Marsala 8;
tel. 49 98.
Rome office, Via Cristoforo Colombo 261;
tel. 51 06.
Breakdown service, Via Solferino 32;
tel. 4 75 52 51.
TCI. Via Oviedo 7A;
tel. 38 86 58.
Vatican Information Bureau
(*Ufficio Informazioni Pellegrini e Turisti*),
on S side of St Peter's Square.

EMBASSIES. – *United Kingdom*: Via XX Settembre 80A, I-00187 (tel. 4 75 54 41, 4 75 55 51). – *United States of America*: Via Veneto 119A, I-00187 (tel. 46 74). – *Canada*: Via Zara 30, I-00198 (tel. 8 44 18 41–45).

AIRPORTS. – All scheduled international services: **Aeroporto Intercontinentale Leonardo da Vinci**, *Fiumicino* (25 km SW of city centre: motorway). Airport buses to and from Air Terminal, Via Giovanni Giolitti 36 (on SW side of Stazione Termini). – Charter flights: *Aeroporto Ciampino* (15 km SE of city centre). Air Terminal at Via Sicilia 52–56. – Sightseeing flights (light aircraft and helicopters) and private flying: *Aeroporto dell'Urbe*, Via Salaria 825.

RAILWAY STATIONS. – The main station (for the principal Italian main-line services and international services) is the **Stazione Centrale Roma Termini** (Termini Station for short), Piazza dei Cinquecento. There are a number of subsidiary stations for various domestic services.

CITY TOURS, run by many travel agencies, allow first-time visitors to get a general impression of the main sights and thus to plan their further sightseeing more effectively. A tour lasting 3 hours, with a competent

guide, costs about 5000 lire. The usual starting point is the Piazza della Repubblica (CIT office, No. 64); for ATAC tours the bus station at Stazione Termini.

HORSE-CARRIAGES (*carrozzelle*). – A drive in one of these old-fashioned vehicles, popularly called *botticelle* ("little barrels") is to be recommended particularly for a ride through the parks, for example to the Villa Borghese or the Janiculum.

HOTELS. – NEAR THE TERMINI STATION: *Mediterraneo*, Via Cavour 15, L, 452 b.; *Grand Hôtel et de Rome*, Via V. Emanuele Orlando 3, L, 328 b.; *Metropole*, Via P. Amedeo 3, I, 450 b.; *Universo*, Via P. Amedeo 5B, I, 381 b.; *Palatino*, Via Cavour 213, I, 380 b.; *San Giorgio*, Via G. Amendola 61, I, 340 b.; *Quirinale*, Via Nazionale 7, I, 318 b.; *Massimo d'Azeglio*, Via Cavour 18, I, 302 b.; *President*, Via E. Filiberto 173, I, 249 b.; *Royal Santina*, Via Marsala 22, I, 208 b.; *Londra e Cargill*, Piazza Sallustio 18, I, 193 b.; *Anglo-Americano*, Via 4 Fontaine 12, I, 165 b.; *Mondial*, Via Torino 127, I, 138 b.; *Atlantico*, Via Cavour 23, I, 129 b.; *Napoleon*, Piazza Vittorio Emanuele 105, I, 141 b.; *Commodore*, Via Torino 1, I, 97 b.; *Diana*, Via P. Amedeo 4, II, 293 b.; *Nord – Nuova Roma*, Via G. Amendola 3, II, 250 b.; *Lux Messe*, Via Volturno 32, II, 189 b.; *Genova*, Via Cavour 33, II, 181 b.; *Madison*, Via Marsala 60, II, 179 b.; *Globus*, Viale Ippocrate 119, II, 174 b.; *Torino*, Via P. Amedeo 8, II, 165 b.; *Touring*, Via P. Amedeo 34, II, 165 b.; *Y.M.C.A.*, Piazza Indipendenza 23C, II, 162 b.; *Milani*, Via Magenta 12, II, 150 b.; *Sorrento e Patrizia*, Via Nazionale 251, II, 150 b.; *Esperia*, Via Nazionale 22, II, 147 b.; *Siracusa*, Via Marsala 50, II, 142 b.; *La Capitale e Santa Maria Maggiore*, Via C. Alberto 3, II, 137 b.; *Medici*, Via Flavia 96, II, 125 b.; *San Remo*, Via M. d'Azelgio 36, II, 120 b.; *San Marco*, Via Villafranca 1, II, 118 b.; *Archimede*, Via dei Mille 19, II, 117 b.; *Nizza*, Via M. d'Azeglio 16, II, 100 b.; *Rex*, Via Torino 149, II, 95 b.; *Tirreno*, Via S. Martino ai Monti 17, II, 77 b.; *Impero*, Via Viminale 19, II, 70 b.; *Marconi*, Via G. Amendola 97, III, 124 b.; *Ariston*, Via F. Turati 16, III, 124 b.; *Venezia*, Via Varese 18, III, 106 b.; *Stazione*, Via Gioberti 36, III, 102 b.; *Igea*, Via P. Amedeo 97, III, 63 b.; *Del Popolo*, Via d. Apuli 41, IV, 184 b.; etc.

BETWEEN THE QUIRINAL AND THE VILLA BORGHESE: *Excelsior*, Via V. Veneto 125, L, 671 b.; *Parco dei Principi*, Via G. Frescobaldi 5, L, 366 b.; SP; *Flora*, Via V. Veneto 125, L, 275 b.; *Ambasciatori Palace*, Via V. Veneto 70, L, 240 b.; *Bernini Bristol*, Piazza Barberini 23, L, 216 b.; *Eden*, Via Ludovisi 49, L, 190 b.; *Hassler – Villa Medici*, Piazza Trinità de'Monti 6, L, 170 b.; *Jolly*, Corso d'Italia 1, I, 346 b.; *Boston*, Via Lombardia 47, I, 231 b.; *Regina Carlton*, Via V. Veneto 72, I, 229 b.; *Savoia*, Via Ludovisi 15, I, 203 b.; *Majestic*, Via V. Veneto 50, I, 172 b.; *Victoria*, Via Campania 41, I, 160 b.; *Imperiale*, Via V. Veneto 24, I, 137 b.; *Eliseo*, Via di Porta Pinciana 30, I, 110 b.; *King*, Via Sistina 131, II, 122 b.; *Alexandra*, Via V. Veneto, II, 72 b.; etc.

IN THE OLD TOWN: *De la Ville*, Via Sistina 69, I, 348 b.; *Plaza*, Via del Corso 126, I, 311 b.; *Minerva*, Piazza della Minerva 69, I, 292 b.; *Delta*, Via Labicana 144, I, 279 b.; SP; *Marini Strand*, Via del Tritone 17, I, 212 b.; *Forum*, Via Tor de' Conti 25, I, 153 b.; *Moderno*, Via M. Minghetti 30, I, 141 b.; *Milano*, Piazza Montecitorio 12, I, 140 b.; *Delle Nazioni*, Via Poli 7, I, 139 b.; *Raphael*, Largo Febo 2, I, 135 b.; *Nazionale*, Piazza Montecitorio 131, I, 142 b.; *Cardinal*, Via Giulia 62, I, 114 b.; *Valadier*, Via d. Fontanella 15, I, 67 b.; *Bologna*, Via Santa Chiara 4A, II, 194 b.; *Casa Pollotti* (pensione), Via dei Pettinari 64, II, 192 b.; *Inghilterra*, Via Bocca di Leone 14, II, 174 b.; *Adriano*, Via di

Pallacorda 2, II, 116 b.; *Pace-Elvezia*, Via IV Novembre 104, II, 110 b.; *Santa Chiara*, Via Santa Chiara 21, II, 110 b.; *Cesare*, Via di Pietra 89A, II, 95 b.; *Genio*, Via G. Zanardelli 28, II, 86 b.; *Lugano*, Via Tritone 132, II, 53 b.; *Sole al Pantheon*, Via del Pantheon 63, II, 48 b.; *Regno*, Via del Corso 331, II, 41 b.; *Paradiso*, Largo dei Chiavari 79, III, 77 b.; *Sole*, Via del Biscione 76, IV, 89 b.; etc.

IN THE NORTHERN DISTRICTS: *Sporting*, Via Civinini 46, I, 378 b.; *Residence Palace*, Via Archimede 69, I, 323 b.; *Beverly Hills*, Largo B, Marcello 220, I, 315 b.; *Ritz*, Piazza Euclide 43, I, 234 b.; *Hermitage*, Via E. Vajna 12, I, 170 b.; *Claridge*, Viale Liegi 62, I, 156 b.; *Fleming*, Piazza Monteleone di Spoleto 20, II, 489 b.; *Borromini*, Via Lisbona 7, I, 147 b.; *Parioli*, Viale B. Buozzi 54, II, 147 b.; *Garden Roxy*, Piazza B. Gastaldi 4, II, 105 b.; *Rivoli*, Via Taramelli 7, II, 86 b.; *Park*, Via A. Morelli 5, II, 50 b.; etc.

IN THE EASTERN DISTRICTS: *Nuova Italia*, Via Como 1, II, 113 b.; *San Giusto*, Piazza Bologna 58, II, 98 b.; *Porta Maggiore*, Piazza Porta Maggiore 25, III, 202 b.; etc.

IN THE SOUTHERN DISTRICTS: *American Palace EUR*, Via Laurentina 554, II, 160 b., SP; *Dei Congressi*, Viale Shakespeare 29 (EUR), II, 152 b.; *Autostello ACI*, km 13 on Via C. Colombo, II, 141 b., SP; *Piccadilly*, Via Magna Grecia 122 (at Porta San Giovanni), II, 101 b.; *EUR Motel*, Via Pontina 416, II, 41 b.; etc.

ON THE RIGHT BANK OF THE TIBER: **Cavalieri Hilton*, Via Cadlolo 101 (at foot of Monte Mario), L, 758 b., SP; *Holiday Inn*, Via Aurelia Antica 415, I, 670 b., SP; *Villa Pamphili*, Via della Nocetta 105, I, 513 b., SP; *Ville Radieuse*, Via Aurelia 641, I, 500 b.; *Visconti Palace*, Via F. Cesi 37, I, 475 b.; *Leonardo da Vinci*, Via dei Gracchi 324, I, 415 b.; *Cicerone*, Via Cicerone 55, I, 445 b.; *Michelangelo*, Via Stazione di S. Petro 14, I, 264 b.; *Marc'Aurelio*, Via Gregorio XI 135, I, 220 b., SP; *Giulio Cesare*, Via d. Scipione 287, I, 145 b.; *Motel Agip*, 8·4 km on Via Aurelia, II, 250 b.; *Clodio*, Via S. Lucia 10, II, 224 b.; *Columbus*, Via d. Conciliazione 33, II, 190 b.; *Nova Domus*, Via G. Savonarola 38, II, 149 b.; *Motel Cristoforo Colombo*, Via C. Colombo 710, II, 141 b.; *Rest*, Via Aurelia 325, II, 135 b.; *Fiamma*, Via Gaeta 61, II, 127 b.; *Pacific*, Viale Medaglie d'Oro 51, II, 120 b.; *Olympic*, Via Properzio 2A, II, 117 b.; *Imperator*, Via Aurelia 619, II, 79 b.; *Nordland*, Via A. Alciato 14, III, 198 b.; *Giotto*, Via Cardinal Passionei 35, III, 133 b.; *Motel Boomerang*, km 10·5 on Via Aurelia, III, 84 b., SP; *Alicorni*, Via Scossacavalli 11, III, 75 b.; etc. – *Holiday Inn Parco dei Medici*, Via della Magliana 821 (in SW of city), I, 335 r. – *Midas Palace*, Via Aurelia 800 (in W of city), I, 720 b., SP.

AT FIUMICINO AIRPORT: *Airport*, Viale dei Romagnoli 165, I, 453 b., SP.

Many PENSIONI and HOSTELS FOR PILGRIMS.

YOUTH HOSTEL: *Albergo per la Gioventù*, Foro Italico, Viale delle Olimpiadi 61, 600 b. (about 100 lire per night).

CAMPING SITES. – *Flaminio* (to N), 8·2 km on Via Flaminia Nuova (5 km from centre); *Seven Hills* (to N), Via Cassia 1216 (13 km from centre); *Tiber* (to N), 1·4 km on Via Tiberina (14 km from centre); *Roma* (to NW), 8·2 km on Via Aurelia (6 km from centre); *Pineta Fabulous* (to SW), 18 km on Via C. Colombo (17 km from centre). – *Capitol Camping Club*, Ostia Antica. – *ENAL Camping*, Lido di Ostia.

RESTAURANTS. – In most hotels. – BETWEEN PIAZZA NAVONA, PIAZZA COLONNA AND THE MAUSOLEO D'AUGUSTO: *Hostaria dell'Orso*, Via Monte Brianzo 93 (on the Tiber); *El Toulà*, Via della Lupa 29B; *31 Al Vicario*, Via degli Uffici del Vicario 31; *Alfredo all'Augusteo*, Piazza Augusto Imperatore 31; *Alfredo alla Scrofa*, Via della Scrofa 104; *Passetto*, Via Zanardelli 14; *La Capricciosa*, Largo dei Lombardi 8; *Valle-Biblioteca*, Largo del Teatro Valle 7–9; *Fontanella*, Largo Fontanella Borghese 86; *La Maiella*, Piazza S. Apollinare 45; *Tre Scalini*, Piazza Navona 30; *Berardo*, Galleria Colonna 200; etc. – W OF PIAZZA VENEZIA: *Da Pancrazio*, Piazza del Biscione 92; *Piperno*, Via Monte dei Cenci 9; *Da Gigetto al Portico d'Ottavia*, Via Portico d'Ottavia 21; *Angelino a Tomargana*, Piazza Margana 37. – E OF PIAZZA VENEZIA: *Taberna Ulpia*, Piazza Foro Traiano 2. – ROUND FONTANA DI TREVI: *Tullio*, Via S. Nicola da Tolentino 26; *Gino*, Via Rasella 52; *Sergio e Ada*, Via del Boccaccio 1; *Necci*, Piazza dell'Oratorio 50; etc. – BETWEEN PIAZZA DI SPAGNA AND PIAZZA DEL POPOLO: *Ranieri*, Via Mario de' Fiori 26; *Dal Bolognese*, Piazza del Popolo 1–2; *Nino a Via Borgognona*, Via Borgognona 11; etc. – NEAR VIA VENETO: *George's*, Via Marche 7; *Cesarina*, Via Piemonte 109; *Capriccio*, Via Liguria 38; *Il Caminetto*, Viale Pariole 89; etc. – N OF TERMINI STATION: *Coriolano*, via Ancona 14; *Taverna Flavia*, Via Flavia 9; *Berardino*, Via Quintino Sella 1; etc. – IN TRASTEVERE: *Sabatini*, Via Arco di S. Callisto 45 (near Santa Maria); *Vincenzo alla Lungaretta* (fish a speciality), Via della Lungaretta 173; *Galeassi*, Via S. Maria in Trastevere 3; *Gino in Trastevere* (seafood a specialty), Via della Lungaretta 85; *Corsetti*, Piazza S. Cosimato 27; *La Cisterna*, Via della Cisterna 13; *Da Meo Patacca*, Piazza de' Mercanti 30 (with music); etc.

CAFÉS. – *Alemagna*, Via del Corso 181; *De Paris*, V. Veneto 90; *Doney*, Via V. Veneto 145; *Harry's Bar*, Via V. Veneto 150; *Grande Italia*, Piazza d. Repubblica 40; *Greco*, Via Condotti 86; etc.

EVENTS. – The *Opera House* (Teatro dell'Opera) is in Via Viminale (Piazza Beniamino Gigli, near the Termini Station); during July and August *open-air performances* of opera are given in the Baths of Caracalla. During these months the Accademia di Santa Cecilia gives *concerts* in the Basilica of Maxentius; apart from this concerts are given in the Auditorium in Via della Conciliazione and the hall in Via dei Greci 7. *Classical plays* are performed during the summer months in the Roman theatre at Ostia Antica. – Rome has a large number of other concert halls and over 20 theatres. – It is difficult to make advance bookings for the theatre and the opera: the easiest way to get tickets is to go direct to the box-office.

SHOPPING. – Popular shopping streets are Via Vittorio Veneto, Via Barberini, Via XX Settembre, Via Nazionale, Via del Tritone and Via del Corso. The more exclusive shops are to be found in the streets and lanes (mostly closed to traffic) around the Piazza di Spagna, including the Via dei Babuino, Via dei Condotti and Via Margutta.

**Rome is capital of the Republic of Italy, the region of Latium and the province of Rome, as well as Italy's largest city. Within its precincts is the Vatican City, residence of the Pope and seat of the Papal Curia. Rome lies in latitude 41°52′ N (about the same as Istanbul, Chicago and

Roman cuisine does not go in for elaboration and refinement: it is good honest country cooking which achieves its results by the use of good-quality ingredients and careful preparation, using simple traditional recipes.

Some typical Roman dishes ("alla romana")

Abbacchio: sucking lamb in white wine, flavoured with rosemary.
Anguilla: eel steamed in white wine.
Anitra: stuffed duck with calves' feet.
Broccoli romani: broccoli in white wine.
Calzone: a kind of pizza with ham, mozzarella cheese and salami, covered with dough.
Cannelloni: pasta stuffed with meat, calf's brains, spinach, egg and cheese.
Cappone: capon with bread stuffing, flavoured with cheese.
Carciofi alla giudià: artichokes cooked in oil.
Carciofi alla romana: artichokes spiced with leaves of peppermint, sometimes stuffed with anchovies.
Fettuccine: flat pasta, served with a sauce of butter, eggs, anchovies and cheese.
Gnocchi di polenta: little cakes of maize flour baked in fat.
Gnocchi alla romana: semolina dumplings.
Lumache: snails in tomato sauce, spiced with ginger.
Panzarottini: small pouches of pasta stuffed with cheese and butter and sometimes with egg, anchovies, etc.
Polenta: slices of baked maize flour with mutton stew.
Pollo: chicken in tomato sauce with white wine.
Salsa romana: a sweet-sour brown sauce (with game), with raisins and chestnut and lentil puree.
Saltimbocca: slices of veal and ham, with a leaf of sage, rolled together and cooked in butter, with a glass of Marsala added while cooking.
Suppli di riso: boiled rice and egg balls, eaten with a meat stew.
Testarelle di abbacchio: sucking lambs' heads roasted in oil, with rosemary.
Trippa: tripe in tomato sauce, with white wine.
Zuppa: chicken consommé with vegetables, meat balls, rice or pasta.

Tashkent) and longitude 12°30' E, some 20 km from the Tyrrhenian Sea in the middle of the hilly Campagna di Roma, on the River Tiber (Tévere), the third longest river in Italy (after the Po and the Adige). The city itself covers an area some 9 km in diameter; the commune of Rome has an area of more than 1500 sq. km.

Rome is an important centre of air, rail and road communications, a major financial and commercial city (port at Civitavecchia, 75 km NW) and an international centre of fashion and the film industry (Cinecittà). The city's industries, established mainly to the E and S, provide

employment for more than 200,000 workers principally in engineering, printing and publishing, chemicals, the manufacture of telephones, textiles and foodstuffs.

The city's numerous cultural institutions enjoy an international reputation. Among the many educational and research establishments run by the Italian state, the Roman Catholic Church and a number of foreign countries are Rome University (founded 1303), the Pontifical Universitas Gregoriana, the Università Urbaniana for the propagation of the Catholic faith, the Free International University of Social Studies, the Technical University, the Commercial College, the Academy of Music, the Accademia Nazionale dei Lincei (founded in 1603 for the advancement of science and letters), the Academy of Fine Arts, the Pontifical Academy of Sciences and the Pontifical Ecclesiastical Academy; large libraries and collections of archives including the National Library, the University Library, the FAO Library and the Vatican Library and Archives; and a variety of learned societies and foreign cultural and research institutes. Rome is also the headquarters of the Food and Agriculture Organisation of the United Nations. The numbers of its churches and the art treasures in its museums are too numerous to count.

TOPOGRAPHY. – The Tiber flows through the city from N to S, with three fairly sharp bends; it is spanned by some 25 bridges. On the left bank are the famous seven hills of Rome – the Capitoline (50 m), Quirinal (52 m), Viminal (56 m), Esquiline (53 m), Palatine (51 m), Aventine (46 m) and Caelian (50 m). The ancient city was built on these hills, but thereafter, until recent times, they remained for the most part undeveloped. Between the hills and the river is a level area, the Campus Martius, which was until recent times the main urban area. Three other hills, the Pincian (50 m) to the N of the Quirinal and the Vatican (60 m) and Janiculum (84 m) on the right bank of the river, were for long outside the city, but from the time of Augustus there was a densely populated suburb on the right bank, Trans Tiberim (now Trastevere). Imperial Rome was enclosed by the Aurelian Walls, but in modern times the city has been constantly expanding outside these bounds, with whole new suburban districts springing up on the outskirts. Meanwhile many areas in the inner city have decayed and are in much need of modernisation and improvement.

HISTORICAL SIGNIFICANCE. – Already known in ancient times as the Eternal City (Roma aeterna), Rome was for a millennium and a half the cultural centre of Europe and the scene of great historical events. It was the first city of world stature, capital of an empire which extended from Scotland to the Sahara, from the Straits of Gibraltar to the Persian Gulf, and thereafter the home of the Popes with their world-wide spiritual authority. In the heyday of the Roman Empire, at the beginning of the 2nd c. A.D., the city had a population of over a million. All the cultures of the ancient world came together here and were welded into a unity which was transmitted to later centuries. Rome was the birthplace of the Roman Catholic Church, the most powerful single religious community in the history of the world, and it was here that about A.D. 1200 Innocent II established a secular Papal state which subsisted until 1870 and was succeeded in 1929 by the new sovereign state of Vatican City. The name of Rome acquired a significance which remained with the city through all the vicissitudes of its history, and was perpetuated in the Holy Roman Empire which played such a central role in European history for many centuries. Present-day Rome is a creation of its long past, and its attraction and interest to visitors are enhanced by an awareness of that past.

After the devastation suffered by Rome during the period of the great migrations and its vicissitudes in subsequent centuries the population in the 14th c. was barely 20,000 and at the beginning of the 16th c. only 55,000. In 1832 it was 148,000 and in 1870 221,000. By 1921 it had risen to 660,000. After the First World War, and still more after the Second, the population began to grow on a massive scale, bringing it to its present figure of 3 million.

History and Art

The **ancient city** was founded, according to the Roman tradition, in 753 B.C.; but there must have been a Latin settlement of some consequence before then on this convenient site near the mouth of the Tiber. The oldest part of the town consisted of the Palatine and Quirinal hills and between them the Forum, at the foot of the Capitol.

After the destruction of the town by the Gauls (c. 387 B.C.) the development which was to make Rome capital of the Empire began – a development reflected in its architecture. In 312 the first aqueduct and the first paved road, the Via Appia, were constructed, and the characteristic Roman technique of building vaulted structures of rubble bound with mortar was evolved. The city developed still farther in the time of Augustus (27 B.C.–A.D. 14), who "found Rome of brick and left it of marble" and extended the built-up area on to the Campus Martius, and again after the great fire in the time of Nero (54–68) which destroyed most of Rome. The high point of its development was reached in the 2nd c. A.D.

The development of **medieval Rome** was shaped by **Christianity**, which came to Rome in the mid 1st c. and thereafter, in spite of successive persecutions, particularly during the 3rd c. and in 303 during the reign of Diocletian (the final wave of persecution), demonstrated its ability to withstand the declining authority of paganism. In 313 Constantine the Great granted freedom of religious exercise. Although some of the great families still held fast to the pagan faith, the old religion received a final blow in 408, when the Emperor Honorius decreed the confiscation of all its property. The old temples were destroyed and their columns and other materials used in the building of Christian churches (basilicas); later whole temples were converted for use as churches. The number of churches increased rapidly. There were 25 parish churches (titoli) and five patriarchal churches. The patriarchal churches – of which the Pope himself was priest and to which all the faithful belonged – were San Giovanni in Laterano, San Pietro in Vaticano, San Paolo fuori le Mura, San Lorenzo fuori le Mura and Santa Maria Maggiore. In addition to these five churches there were two others which enjoyed particular veneration, Santa Croce in Gerusalemme and San Sebastiano, above the catacombs on the Via Appia. These were the Seven Churches of Rome, visited by pilgrims from all over the Western world down to the present day.

In political terms, however, Rome's importance declined. Constantine's decision in 330 to transfer the Imperial residence to Byzantium and Milan reduced Rome to the status of a provincial town. The Campagna reverted to wasteland, and malaria spread inland from the coastal regions. The stormy years of the great migrations, in particular the sack of Rome by Alaric's Goths and again in 455 by Gaiseric's Vandals, brought a further decline. Only the tradition of the great battles and victories of the Christian faith, which were indissolubly linked with Rome, preserved the city from total extinction.

The conversion of ancient Rome into Christian Rome made the **Papacy** the supreme spiritual power in the West. Particularly powerful representatives of Papal authority were popes Leo the Great (440–461) and Gregory the Great (590–604). The secular power of the popes and their authority over Rome began to develop in the 8th c., when the foundations of the States of the Church were laid by the grant of territory to the Pope by the Lombard king Luitprand (727) and the Frankish king Pepin (755). On Christmas Day 800 Leo III (795–816) crowned Charlemagne Emperor and thus re-established the secular empire which was to preserve for a millennium at least the name of the old Roman Empire.

In subsequent centuries Rome was ravaged by enemy attacks, the struggle between the Empire and the Papacy and strife between the great noble families. It suffered a further blow with the exile of the popes to Avignon (1309–77), during which Cola di Rienzo tried to establish a republic on the ancient Roman model (1347). The population now fell to barely 20,000.

The Renaissance, breathing fresh life into learning and art throughout Italy, established itself at the Papal court and brought a new flowering to Rome. Tuscan architects, sculptors and painters had already been summoned to Rome in considerable numbers during the 15th c., but it was in the following century that the great Renaissance popes Julius II (1503–13) and Leo X (1513–21) made the city the real centre of the High Renaissance. From here Bramante (1444–1514), Michelangelo (1474–1564) and Raphael (1483–1520) set the artistic pattern of the whole 16th c. (Cinquecento). Leonardo da Vinci (1452–1519) also worked in Rome in 1513–15. Among noted architects of this period were Baldassare Peruzzi (1481–1536) and Antonio da Sangallo the Younger (1483–1546).

After the occupation and sacking of Rome by Charles V's forces in 1527, which drove away almost all the city's artists, recovery was slow. In 1546 Michelangelo built the Palazzo Farnese, the plan of which was to have enormous influence on the palaces of the Baroque period. The reign of Pope Sixtus V (1585–90), for whom Domenico Fontana designed a whole series of fine buildings, saw the beginnings of the vigorous and powerful Baroque style of the 17th c. The architects of this period – in particular the Neapolitan Lorenzo Bernini (1598–1680), his like-

Castel Sant'Angelo, Rome

minded contemporary *Francesco Borromini* (1599–1667), *Carlo Maderna* (1556–1629) and *Carlo Rainaldi* (1611–91) – created the magnificent churches and palaces, with their impressive command of space and picturesque effect, which still largely determine the architectural character of the older parts of Rome. In the field of painting *Caravaggio* (*c.* 1573–1610), the most gifted artist of the Early Baroque, was the leader of the naturalistic school; the chief representatives of the opposite trend, the "Eclectics" of Bologna, were *Annibale Carracci* (1560–1609) and his pupils *Guido Reni* (1575–1642), *Domenichino* (1581–1641) and *Guercino* (1591–1666). In the following century *Antonio Canova* (1757–1822) produced the first works of monumental sculpture in neo-classical style.

In the **18th and 19th centuries** the economic importance and artistic achievement of Rome both declined. Nevertheless the city continued to attract increasing numbers of artists and connoisseurs from many lands in quest of the classical art of antiquity, particularly after the publication of *Johann Joachim Winckelmann*'s history of Greek art, written in Rome about 1760. A revival of the city's life and art came only with its incorporation in the new kingdom of Italy in 1870, which gave Rome the status of a national capital and royal residence. This was the period of the "Third Rome" ("Terza Roma"). New and imposing public buildings were erected, usually aiming at a kind of ancient Roman monumentality (Banca d'Italia, Ministry of Finance, Palace of Justice, National Monument) but employing overcharged Renaissance and Baroque forms. It was only in the 20th c. that this style gave place to simpler and more straightforward structures.

The **20th century** created the "Fourth Rome" ("Quarta Roma"). A development plan initiated in 1931 provided for the opening up of overcrowded slum areas, the disengagement and restoration of ancient

buildings (the Theatre of Marcellus, Trajan's Market and Trajan's Column, the Imperial Fora and the Arch of Constantine, the Mausoleum of Augustus, Castle Sant'Angelo, etc.), the construction of large new avenues (Via dei Fori Imperiali, Corso del Rinascimento, Via Regina Elena, the Via della Conciliazione between the Ponte Sant'Angelo and St Peter's Square, etc.) and the creation of public parks and gardens and well-planned modern suburbs. Notable among recent developmnts are the University City, the Air Ministry building, the Via del Mare to Lido di Ostia, the new ring road (the Grande Raccordo Anulare), the EUR exhibition area, the Termini Station and the new underground railway system (Metropolitana). In 1960 Rome was host to the 17th Olympic Games, for which the Olympic Village, a number of major sporting facilities and new link roads (including the Strada Olimpia from the EUR to the Foro Italico) were constructed. In consequence of chronic financial difficulties the 1965 development plan has been only very partially carried out, and many buildings are still awaiting the urgent renovation they require.

In March 1957 the treaties establishing the European Economic Community and the European Coal and Steel Community (the *Rome treaties*) were signed in Rome. In 1968 economic leaders and experts from more than 30 countries formed the "*Club of Rome*".

Museums, Galleries, etc.

The following list gives the addresses, opening times and other practical details about Rome's museums and similar institutions. It includes a number of museums omitted on grounds of space from the subsequent itineraries.

The *opening times* are subject to frequent change. The public **museums** (most of them inadequately heated in winter) are usually open from 9 or 10 to 1 or 2, and again from 2 or 3 to 5 or 6, rarely to 7; exceptionally, some of them remain open throughout the day, without a lunchtime break. In winter the opening times are shorter, but frequently without a lunchtime break. All museums are closed on Sunday afternoons and most of them on Mondays; some are closed on Fridays. They are all closed on statutory public holidays. On certain other days the non-State-owned museums are closed, while the State museums are open only in the mornings. In addition there may frequently be unplanned closings on account of shortage of staff, strikes or restoration work. Before visiting a museum it is advisable to check that it will be open: a useful publication for this purpose is the weekly ''La Settimana a Roma'' (also published in an English edition – available at any news-stand) which regularly lists opening times.

The larger **churches** are mostly open until midday, and usually also from 4 or 5 until dusk; some of the principal churches are open throughout the day. It is possible to see the interior of a church even during a service, provided due discretion is observed. Care should be taken to be appropriately dressed: sleeveless or décolleté dresses or blouses and miniskirts should be avoided by women, short-sleeved shirts by men, shorts by both women and men. Visitors who are unsuitably dressed may be denied admittance; at the entrance to St Peter's suitable coverings can be hired. During Lent almost all altarpieces are covered and not shown to visitors.

Ara Pacis Augustae,
Via Ripetta (Ponte Cavour);
Tues.–Sat. 10–5 or 9–1 and 3–6; Sun. 9–1.

Biblioteca Nazionale Centrale Vittorio Emanuele II,
Viale Castro Pretorio;
Mon., Wed., Fri. 9–6.30; Tues., Thurs., Sat. 9–1.30.

Capitoline Museum: see Musei Capitolini.

Casa di Keats e Shelley,
Piazza di Spagna 26;
Mon.–Fri. 9–12.30 and 2.30–4 or 9–12 and 4–6.

Casino Borghese: see Galleria Borghese.

Castel Sant'Angelo or **Mausoleo di Adriano,**
Lungotevere Castello;
Tues.–Sat. 8.30–1; Sun. 8.30–12.

Catacombe;
Tues.–Sun. 8–12 and 2.30 to 5.30 or 6.

Città del Vaticano: see Vaticano.

Colosseo,
Piazza del Colosseo;
Mon.–Sat. 9 a.m. to dusk; admission free.

Domus Aurea,
Via Labicana;
Mon.–Sat. 9 a.m. to sunset.

Folk Museum: see Museo del Folklore.

Fori Imperiali (*Foro di Augusto, di Cesare, di Nerva, Traiano*),
Via dei Fori Imperiali;
Tues.–Sat. 10–4 or 9–1 and 3–5; Sun. 10–1.

Foro Romano – Palatino,
Via dei Fori Imperiali;
Mon., Wed.–Sat. 9–4 or 9–1 and 3–6; Sun. 10–1.

Gabinetto Nazionale delle Stampe,
Via della Lungara 230 (Villa Farnesina);
Mon.–Sat. 9–1.

Galleria Borghese,
Via del Museo 3;
Tues.–Sat. 9–2; Sun. 9–1 (closed alternate Sundays).

Galleria Colonna,
Via della Pilotta 17;
Sat. 9–1.

Galleria Comunale d'Arte Moderna,
Piazza S. Pantaleo 1;
Tues.–Sun. 10–1; Tues. and Thurs. also 5–8.

Galleria Doria Pamphili,
Piazza del Collegio Romano 1A;
Tues., Fri., Sat., Sun. 10–1.

Galleria Nazionale d'Arte Antica
(*Palazzo Barberini*),
Via Quattro Fontane;
Tues.–Sat. 9–2; Sun. 9–1 (closed alternate Sundays).

Galleria Nazionale d'Arte Moderna,
Viale delle Belle Arti 131;
Tues.–Sat. 9–2, Sun. 9–1.

Galleria Spada,
Piazza Capo di Ferro 3;
Tues.–Sat. 9–2, Sun. 9–1.

Goethe Museum,
Via del Corso 18;
Tues.–Sat. 10–1 and 4–7; Sun. 10–1.

Golden House: see Domus Aurea.

Imperial Fora: see Fori Imperiali.

Keats and Shelley House: see Casa di Keats e Shelley.

Musei Capitolini e Pinacoteca
(*Museo Capitolino* and *Palazza dei Conservatori*),
Piazza del Campidoglio 1;
Tues.–Sat. 9–2, Sun. 9–1; Tues. and Thurs. also 5–8; Sat. also 10.30–11.30.

Museo Africano,
Via Ulisse Aldrovandi 16A;
temporarily closed.

Museo dell'Alto Medievo,
Viale Lincoln 1 (EUR);
Tues.–Sat. 9.30–2, Sun. and pub. holidays 9.30–1.30.

Museo Antico e Militare di Castle Sant'Angelo,
Lungotevere Castello 1;
Tues.–Sat. 9–2, Sun. 9–1.

Museo Antiquarium Forense e Palatino,
Piazza Santa Maria Nuova 53;
Mon. and Wed.–Sat. 9–2, Sun. 9–1.

Museo Archeologico Sacro e Profano,
Via Appia Antica 136;
Mon.–Wed. and Fri–Sun. 9–12 and 2–5.

Museo Astronomico e Copernicano,
Via Trionfale 204;
only by special arrangement (tel. 34 70 56).

Museo Barracco,
Corso Vittorio Emanuele 168;
Tues.–Sat. 9–2, Sun. 9–1; Tues. and Thurs. also 5–8.

Museo delle Celebrità
(*Wax Museum*),
Piazza G. Agnelli (EUR);
Tues.–Sat. 9–2, Sun. 9–1; Tues. and Thurs. also 5–8.

Museo Centrale del Risorgimento,
Via di San Pietro in Carcere (in National Monument to Victor Emmanuel II);
Wed., Fri. and Sun. 9–1.

Museo della Civiltà Romana,
Piazza G. Agnelli (EUR);
Tues.–Sat. 9–2, Sun. 9–1; Tues. and Thurs. also 5–8.

Museo del Folklore e dei Poeti Romaneschi,
Piazza S. Egidio 1B;
Tues.–Sat. 9–2, Sun. and pub. holidays 5–8; Tues.
and Thurs. also 5–8.

Museo Francescano dei Cappuccini,
Via V. Veneto 27;
Mon.–Sat. 9–1.

Museo Israelita,
Lungotevere Cenci;
Mon.–Fri. and Sun. 10–4.

Museo Napoleonico,
Via Zanardelli 1;
at present closed.

Museo Nazionale d'Arte Orientale,
Via Merulana 248;
Tues.–Sat. 9–2, Sun. 9–1.

Museo Nazionale delle Arti e delle Tradizioni Populari,
Piazza Marconi 8 (EUR);
Tues.–Sat. 9–1.30, Sun. 9–1; closed in August.

Museo Nazionale Romano delle Terme Diocleziane.
Via delle Terme di Diocleziano;
closed until further notice.

Museo Nazionale di Villa Giulia,
Piazzale di Villa Giulia 9;
Tues.–Sat. 9–2, Sun. 9–1.

Museo Numismatico della Zecca,
Via XX Settembre 97;
Mon.–Sat. 9–12.

Museo di Palazzo Venezia,
Via del Plebiscito;
Tues.–Sun. 9–2.

Museo della Preistoria e Protostoria del Lazio,
Viale Lincoln 1 (EUR);
Tues.–Sun. 9–1.

Museo del Presepio Tipologico Internazionale
(*Museum of Cribs*, i.e. Nativity scenes),
Via Tor de' Conti 31A;
Sat. 5–8 p.m.

Museo di Roma,
Piazza S. Pantaleo 10;
Tues.–Sat. 9–2, Sun. 9–1; Tues. and Thurs. also 5–8.

Museo Storico della Lotta di Liberazione,
Via Tasso 145;
Sat. 5–8, Sun. 10–1.

Museo Storico delle Poste e Telecomunicazioni,
Via Andreoli 11;
Tues.–Sun. 9–1.

Museo di Strumenti Musicali,
Piazza Santa Croce in Gerusalemme 9A;
by special arrangement (tel. 7 57 59 36).

Museo Tassiano,
Salita di Sant'Onofrio 5C;
apply to priest of Sant'Onofrio.

Musical Instruments, Museum of: see Museo di Strumenti Musicali.

National Library: see Biblioteca Nazionale.

Palazzo Barberini: see Galleria Nazionale d'Arte Antica.

Palazzo Colonna: see Galleria Colonna.

Palazzo dei Conservatori: see Musei Capitolini.

Palazzo Doria: see Galleria Doria-Pamphili.

Palazzo Farnese,
Piazza Farnese 67;
closed (admission to courtyard Sun. 11–12).

Palazzo del Quirinale,
Piazza del Quirinale;
Thurs. afternoons only (on presentation of identity document).

Palazzo Spada: see Galleria Spada.

Pantheon,
Piazza della Rotonda;
daily 9–5.

Papal Audiences: see Vaticano.

Santa Maria della Concezione: see Museo Francescano dei Cappuccini.

St Peter's: see Vaticano.

Sepolcro degli Scipioni,
Via di Porta San Sebastiano 9;
Tues.–Sat. 10–1 or 9–1 and 3–5; Sun. 9–1.

Terme Diocleziane: see Museo Nazionale Romano delle Terme Diocleziane.

Tomb of Scipios: see Sepolcro degli Scipioni.

Vaticano (Vatican)

Basilica di San Pietro (*St Peter's*),
daily 7 a.m. to an hour before sunset.
Dome 8–4.45 or 6.30 (visitors admitted to 4.15 or 6).
Museo Storico-Artistico and Tesoro 9–12 and 3–5 (no tickets issued after 4.30).
Sacre Grotte Vaticane 7 a.m. to about ½ hour before closing of St Peter's; admission free.
Necropoli Precostantiniana (excavations under St Peter's, with the tomb of St Peter): group conducted visits only, under arrangements made by Ufficio Informazioni Pellegrini e Turisti (information bureau on S side of St Peter's Square, Mon.–Sat. 8 to 6.30 or 7, Sun. 8–1).

Giardini (*Vatican Gardens*): conducted visits and bus tours only; tickets from information bureau in St Peter's Square 2 days in advance.

Musei Vaticani (*Vatican Museum*): Mon.–Sat. 9–2 or 9–5 (no tickets issued after 1 or 4); admission free on last Sun. in month 9–1.

Papal audiences: every Wed. at 11 in Audience Hall. Tickets issued only Tue. and Wed. 9–12 (travel agencies Mon. 9–12) in Vatican Secretariat (entrance through Portone di Bronzo).

Villa Farnesina,
Via della Lungara 230;
Mon.–Sat. 10–1.

Villa Giulia: see Museo Nazionale di Villa Giulia.

Sightseeing in Rome

From the Piazza Venezia to the Colosseum and the Baths of Caracalla (Ancient Rome)

The busiest traffic intersection in Rome is the **Piazza Venezia**, at the S end of the Via del Corso. On the W side of the square is the **Palazzo Venezia**, originally a fortress-like building erected about 1455,

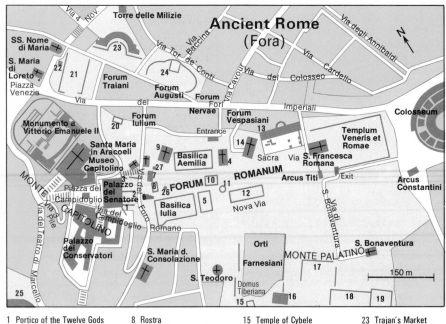

1   Portico of the Twelve Gods
2   Temple of Vespasian
3   Temple of Concordia
4   Temple of Faustina
5   Temple of Castor and
     Pollux
6   Temple of Saturn
7   Arch of Septimius Severus

8   Rostra
9   Curia Iulia (church of
     Sant'Adriano)
10   Temple of Caesar
11   Temple of Vesta
12   House of Vestal Virgins
13   Basilica of Maxentius
14   Church of Santi Cosma e
     Damiano

15   Temple of Cybele
16   House of Livia
17   Palace of Flavians
18   Palace of Augustus
19   Stadium
20   Temple of Venus Genetrix
21   Basilica Ulpia
22   Trajan's Column

23   Trajan's Market
24   Temple of Mars Ultor
25   Theatre of Marcellus
26   Column of Phocas
27   Lapis Niger

from 1564 the Venetian and from 1797 the Austro-Hungarian embassy to the Vatican, from 1926 to 1943 Mussolini's official residence and now a museum. It has a fine arcade (unfinished) in the *inner courtyard. In the E wing the *Museo di Palazzo Venezia*, houses pictures, carving, furniture and other decorative and applied art of the medieval and Renaissance periods.

On the S side of the Piazza Venezia stands the huge *National Monument to Victor Emmanuel II*, in white Brescia marble, begun in 1885 to the design of Count Giuseppe Sacconi as a symbol of the newly united Italy and inaugurated in 1911. This is the largest and most magnificent monument in Italy, 135 by 130 m and 70 m high. At the top of several flights of steps is the *Altare della Patria*, the Tomb of the Unknown Soldier, and above this are an equestrian statue of Victor Emmanuel II in gilded bronze, 12 m high, and a massive colonnade (*view from top) which dominates the city's skyline. At the E end of the monument is the *Museo Centrale del Risorgimento*.

Behind the National Monument, to the S, rises the **Capitol** (Italian **Campidoglio** or *Monte Capitolino*), the smallest but historically the most important of Rome's hills. On the N side of the hill (alt. 50 m), approached by a long flight of steps, is the **church of Santa Maria in Aracoeli** ("on the Altar of Heaven"), on the site of the Capitoline Temple of Juno. It contains 22 ancient columns and has a gilded 16th c. ceiling; in the N aisle is a carved wooden image of the Infant Christ (the "Santo Bambino"), which is the subject of particular veneration at Christmas. It was in this church that Gibbon conceived the idea of writing his "Decline and Fall". The *Capitoline Museum* (Museo Capitolino), adjoining the church on the S, contains the municipal collection of ancient sculpture. Particularly notable items are the *"Dying Gaul" (in the Sala del Galata Morente on the upper floor), a copy of a Greek bronze statue which was formerly thought to represent a dying gladiator, and (in a side room of the Galleria) the *Capitoline Venus, a variant of the Cnidian Aphrodite of Praxiteles.

The Capitoline Museum forms the N side of the **Piazza del Campidoglio**, which is approached from the W by a staircase of shallow steps designed by Michelangelo and by the winding Via delle Tre Pile. The square itself, also designed by Michelangelo and constructed from 1547 onwards, is one of the most finely conceived of Renaissance squares. In the centre is an ancient *equestrian statue of the Emperor Marcus Aurelius (bronze, originally gilded) which was preserved from destruction throughout the Middle Ages by the popular belief that it represented the Christian Emperor Constantine. On the SE side of the square is the **Palazzo Senatorio**, the official residence of the Mayor of Rome, with a façade of 1598 (damaged by a bomb in 1979). On the SW side of the square, partly built on the substructures (of dressed tufa blocks) of the Temple of Jupiter, is the **Palazzo dei Conservatori** (1568), originally the seat of the city council, which houses a collection of major importance. Notable items are the *"Boy with a Thorn" ("Il Spinario", 1st c. B.C.), a work of great truth to nature (in the Sala dei Trionfi di Mario), and the *Capitoline She-Wolf, an Etruscan work of the 5th c. B.C. (in the adjoining Sala della Lupa). On the 2nd floor the Pinacoteca Capitolina has a fine collection of pictures, including works by Titian, Tintoretto, Velázquez and Rubens. The adjoining Palazzo Caffarelli houses the *Museo Nuovo* (sculpture of the 5th c. B.C., sarcophagi, urns, etc.). At the SW corner of the Palazzo dei Conservatori is the *Tarpeian Rock* (Rupe Tarpea), from which in Roman times condemned prisoners were hurled to their death.

From the Via del Campidoglio, between the Palazzo dei Conservatori and the Palazzo Senatorio, there is a magnificent *view of the remains of the **Forum Romanum** and the massive brick walls of the Palatine, crowned by pines and holm-oaks, with the Arch of Titus and the Colosseum to the rear.

The area of low ground SE of the Capitol, between the Palatine and the Esquiline, was drained in the 6th c. B.C. by the construction of the Cloaca Maxima, with its outlet into the Tiber, and thereafter was occupied by markets and other trading activities and became the meeting-place of popular assemblies and courts of law. Caesar set in train a large-scale extension of the Forum, and his plans were carried through by Augustus. Under Augustus and his successors the old buildings of the Republican period were restored and rebuilt and the Forum was embellished with the splendid new buildings, triumphal arches, columns and statues, resplendent in rare marbles and gilded bronze, which gave visible expression to Rome's status as capital of the known world.

The destruction of the Forum began in the 6th c. Columns and other architectural elements were torn out of the ancient buildings and used in the construction of churches or other new buildings, and the marble that still remained was burned to produce lime. An accumulation of rubbish covered the ancient pavements to a depth of up to 13 m. It was only at the beginning of the 19th c. that some individual buildings began to be disinterred; and the systematic clearance of the Forum and Palatine began only in 1871.

The Palazzo Senatorio is built over the remains of the *Tabularium*, constructed in 78 B.C. to house the State archives of Rome (*tabula*="document") in the form of an open two-storey hall facing on to the Forum.

Below the Tabularium, separated from the rest of the Forum excavations by the modern Via del Foro, are the remains of three ancient shrines – the *Portico of the Twelve Gods*, dating from the last days of the pagan faith (restored as late as A.D. 367); the *Temple of Vespasian* (A.D. 81), of which three columns and a fine entablature survive; and the *Temple of Concordia*, originally built in 366 B.C. and splendidly restored by Tiberius.

Beyond the Via del Foro is the enclosed area containing the main part of the Forum (entrance from the Via del Fori Imperiali, on the N side). Immediately left of the entrance is the *Temple of Faustina (A.D. 141), of which the portico and part of the cella survive; it is now the *church of San Lorenzo in Miranda*. To the right of the entrance are the remains of the *Basilica Aemilia*, a portico built in 179 B.C. to provide additional accommodation for traders.

Opposite the Basilica Aemilia, on the far side of the *Sacra Via*, the oldest street in Rome, which climbed up to the Capitol as the Clivus Capitolinus, stands the *Basilica Iulia*, and to the E of this the *Temple of Castor and Pollux*, originally built by Julius Caesar in 46 B.C., with three handsome Corinthian columns of Greek marble dating from the Augustan period which are one of the most characteristic landmarks of Rome. NW of the Basilica Iulia are the eight granite columns of the portico of the *Temple of Saturn*, which contained the city treasury (*Aerarium publicum*), and the imposing marble *Arch of Septimius Severus (23 m high, 25 m wide), erected in A.D. 203 in honour of the victories over the Parthians won by the emperor and his sons Caracalla and Geta.

To the left of the Arch of Septimius Severus are the *Rostra*, the orators' tribune erected in the time of Augustus and named after the ships' prows (*rostra*) which stood here and bounded the Forum proper, paved with limestone slabs. In front of the Rostra, on a high brick pedestal, we find the Column of Phocas, commemorating the emperor of that name, a centurion who had himself crowned emperor in Constantinople about 600. To the right of the Rostra, under a protective roof, is the *Lapis Niger* ("Black Stone"), a piece of black marble on a square pillar bearing a mutilated inscription in an early form of Latin (4th c. B.C.), which was believed in Cicero's time to be the tomb of Romulus. Beyond it, to the N, is the **Curia Iulia** or Senate House, originally built by Julius Caesar and restored about A.D. 303. In this are temporarily displayed two marble slabs, the *Anaglypha Traiani*, with fine reliefs relating to benefactions of the Emperor Trajan, showing in the background the Forum as it was at that period.

At the NE corner of the Temple of Castor and Pollux is the substructure of the *Temple of Caesar*, erected by

Augustus in 29 B.C. on the spot on which Caesar's body was burned in 44 B.C. after his murder. To the S of this can be seen one of the most sacred shrines of ancient Rome, the **Temple of Vesta**, dedicated to the virgin goddess of the domestic hearth. Beyond it is the *Atrium Vestae*, the house of the vestal virgins, with a rectangular courtyard containing statues of the head vestals and three cisterns for storing rain-water (since the vestal virgins were forbidden to use water from the ordinary piped supply). To the E of the vestals' house are the three massive arches of the **Basilica of Maxentius** (access from the Via dei Fori Imperiali: see below), with the *church of Santi Cosma e Damiano* to the left.

Adjoining the Basilica of Maxentius to the SE is the site of the *Temple of Venus and Rome*, erected by the Emperor Hadrian in A.D. 135, which is now occupied by the *church of Santa Francesca Romana*. A little way S rises the * **Arch of Titus**, erected to commemorate the capture of Jerusalem (A.D. 70), with fine reliefs under the arch (triumphal procession with Jewish prisoners, the table with the show-bread, the seven-branched candlestick).

Above the S side of the Forum rises the **Palatine Hill** (Monte Palatino, 51 m), the site of the earliest settlement ("Roma Quadrata"). In late antiquity visitors to the Palatine were shown the hut occupied by Romulus and the cave of the she-wolf which suckled Romulus and Remus. Augustus, who was born on the Palatine, built on the hill the great imperial palace, the Palatium, which gave its name to all later palaces, and later emperors enlarged and embellished the structures on the hill. From the 4th c. the Palatine decayed along with the rest of Rome, and by the 10th c. the ruins of the imperial palaces gave place to gardens, convents and defensive towers. Systematic excavation began in 1871 and was extended in subsequent years.

Under the *Farnese Gardens*, which occupy the highest part of the Palatine, to the NW, are the remains of the *Palace of Tiberius*. The terraces on the NW side afford magnificent *views of the Forum, the Colosseum, the Capitol and the city from the Lateran to the Janiculum. At the other end of the gardens a flight of steps leads down to the brick substructures of the *Temple of Cybele* (191 B.C.) and the *House of Livia* (mother of Tiberius and later wife of Augustus), which contains fine but poorly preserved wall paintings. To the E of the Farnese Gardens is the site of the **Palace of the Flavians**, which dates from the time of Domitian, the greatest builder on the Palatine (c. A.D. 92), with the throne room in which the emperor gave audiences, the basilica in which he dispensed justice and (beyond a square garden) a large dining-room. To the S are the substructures of the *Palace of Augustus* and the *Stadium*, a garden in the shape of a racecourse.

From the NE corner of the Stadium steps lead up to the ruins of the *Palace of Severus* and the *Belvedere*, a terrace laid out over three storeys of substructures which affords magnificent views. From here can be seen the whole area of the **Circus Maximus**, Rome's

"largest circus", with seating for 185,000 spectators and thus exceeding in size the largest sports arenas of the present day. Along its S side runs the Via del Circo Massimo.

From the Piazza Venezia the * **Via dei Fori Imperiali**, flanked by gardens, runs past the *Imperial Fora* to the Colosseum. The massive growth of the city in late Republican and Imperial times made it necessary to erect new buildings to house markets and courts, and the first of a series of new forums was built by Julius Caesar. He was followed by Augustus and his successors Trajan, Nero and Vespasian, each of whom created a new forum in an area previously occupied by a maze of narrow streets and embellished it with a temple as the central feature, colonnades, law courts and a profusion of monuments and works of art. From 1925 onwards the remains were systematically cleared of later buildings (good views from outside).

At the near end of the Via dei Fori Imperiali, on the right, is the **Forum Iulium** (Caesar's Forum), with its colonnade and the high substructure of the *Temple of Venus Genetrix* (the mythical mother of the gens Iulia), completed only in A.D. 113 by Trajan, of which three columns and part of the fine entablature (re-erected) have survived. To the N is the * **Forum Traiani** (entrance from Trajan's Market: see below), built A.D. 107–118, the largest and most magnificent of the Imperial Fora, made up of four elements – the unexcavated Forum proper, in front of the massive semicircle of Trajan's Market, the partly excavated *Basilica Ulpia*, an unexcavated temple and two libraries of which nothing is now left. Here too stands the 27 m high * **Trajan's Column**, which originally held, concealed in the base, a golden urn containing the emperor's ashes. Round the column runs a spiral band of carvings 200 m long with scenes from Trajan's Dacian wars (A.D. 101–106) which give a mass of detailed evidence on the Roman army and Roman military operations. The column, formerly crowned by a statue of Trajan, now bears a figure of the Apostle Peter set up in 1587.

On the NE side of Trajan's Forum is * **Trajan's Market** (excavated 1626–30), a two-storeyed semicircular structure in brick, 60 m long, which acted as a retaining wall on the slopes of the Quirinal. Between this and an inner semicircle faced with marble lay a paved street flanked by shops, and above this, to the rear, rose a range of multi-storeyed buildings.

Immediately SE of Trajan's Forum is the **Forum Augusti** (Forum of Augustus), with the *Temple of Mars Ultor* (Avenging Mars), built by Augustus in fulfilment of a vow made at the battle of Philippi (42 B.C.) in which he defeated the army of Caesar's murderers.

Farther SE is the **Forum Nervae** (Nerva's Forum), which preserves two fine Corinthian columns and a section of the entablature on its SE side. Adjoining Nerva's Forum is the unexcavated **Forum Vespasiani** (Vespasian's Forum), which had a Temple of Peace erected after the destruction of Jerusalem. Here too, on the S side of the Via dei Fori Imperiali, is the entrance to the *church of Santi Cosma e Damiano*, founded in the 6th c. on a site in the Forum Romanum. On the triumphal arch in the upper church and in the apse are 6th c. *mosaics which are perhaps the finest in Rome. In a room to the right of the entrance is a gigantic Neapolitan *presepio* (crib, Nativity scene), an 18th c. work 15 m long by 7 m deep and 9 m high, containing 1000 figures, 500 animals and 50 buildings.

Farther along the Via dei Fori Imperiali, on the right, we come to the entrance to the massive * **Basilica of Maxentius**, which was enlarged by his conqueror Constantine and is therefore also known as the *Basilica of Constantine*. Its massive barrel vaulting served as a model to many later architects, including Bramante and Raphael, in the building of St Peter's. In July and August concerts are given in the basilica. At the SE corner, built partly on the site of the Temple of Venus and Rome, is the *church of Santa Francesca Romana* (patron saint of motorists) or *S. Maria Nova*, originally built in the 10th c. but subsequently much altered, with a handsome Baroque façade (1615) and a richly appointed interior.

Near the SE end of the Via dei Fori Imperiali and the Forum Romanum stands the ** **Colosseum** or *Flavian Amphitheatre*, one of the world's most celebrated buildings.

Colosseum, Rome

With its monumental proportions and severely disciplined structure the Colosseum has long been the symbol of the greatness of Rome. Originally built by Vespasian (A.D. 75 onwards) with three storeys, it was heightened to four storeys by Titus and inaugurated in A.D. 80 with gladiatorial contests and other shows lasting 100 days and involving 1000 gladiators and 5000 animals. It is elliptical in plan, measuring 188 by 156 m and standing 48·5 m high. The exterior is constructed of travertine blocks; the interior also incorporates tufa and brick. The NE part still preserves its original four storeys, the three lower storeys being in the form of arcades, the pillars of which have semi-columns of the Doric, Ionic and Corinthian orders, while the solid wall of the fourth storey has windows set between Corinthian pilasters. On the projecting brackets round the top were sockets for the masts supporting the awnings which were stretched over the spectators.

There are four main entrances, each with a triple opening; those at the ends were reserved for the emperor, while those on the sides were used for the processional entry of the gladiators and other participants. The spectators (some 40,000–50,000) entered through the lower arcades, which were numbered, and found their way to their seats by the appropriate staircases. The seats in the lowest row (*podium*) were occupied by the emperor, senators and vestal virgins. The arena, measuring 85 by 55 m, had extensive substructures accommodating hoists and other stage machinery, cages for wild beasts, etc. The bloody gladiatorial contests were abolished by the Emperor Honorius in A.D. 404; the fights with wild beasts continued until the time of the Gothic ruler Theodoric the Great. – During the Middle Ages some sections of the walls collapsed during earthquakes, and further damage was caused by the use of parts of the structure by Roman nobles as fortresses and by its later use as a quarry of building materials. Finally Pope Benedict XIV (1740–58) consecrated the remains to the Passion of Christ, in commemoration of the blood of the martyrs which had flowed in the Colosseum, and set up a bronze cross (re-erected in 1926). Although two-thirds of the structure has disappeared the part that remains is still of overwhelming effect, particularly on moonlit nights. On account of the danger of collapse only the lower part is at present open to visitors (restoration in progress).

SW of the Colosseum stands the * **Arch of Constantine**, a triumphal arch of white marble with a triple opening, erected by the Senate to commemorate Constantine's victory over Maxentius in the battle of the Milvian Bridge (A.D. 312). Rome's best preserved triumphal arch, it incorporates architectural elements and sculpture (now exposed to damage from air pollution) from earlier monuments of the time of Trajan, Hadrian and Marcus Aurelius.

From the Arch of Constantine a handsome avenue, the **Via di San Gregorio** (the ancient *Via Triumphalis*), runs S between the Caelian Hill and the Palatine. 350 m along this street a side street branches off on the left to the *church of Santi Giovanni e Paolo* (originally founded *c.* 400 but several times rebuilt or altered), with very early frescoes.

Farther along Via di San Gregorio, also on the left, is the *church of San Gregorio Magno*, founded by Pope Gregory I in 575 in his family palace and completely rebuilt in the 17th and 18th c.

Via di San Gregorio runs into the *Piazza di Porta Capena*, at the E end of the Circus Maximus. On the S side of the square stands the *Axum Obelisk* (3rd–4th c.),

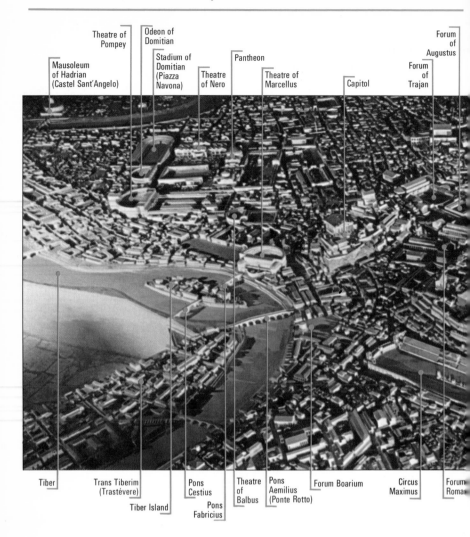

Theatre of Pompey · Odeon of Domitian · Forum of Augustus · Mausoleum of Hadrian (Castel Sant'Angelo) · Stadium of Domitian (Piazza Navona) · Pantheon · Forum of Trajan · Theatre of Nero · Theatre of Marcellus · Capitol · Theatre of Balbus

Tiber · Trans Tiberim (Trastévere) · Pons Cestius · Theatre of Balbus · Pons Aemilius (Ponte Rotto) · Forum Boarium · Circus Maximus · Forum Roma· Tiber Island · Pons Fabricius

brought here from Ethiopia in 1937. Beyond it, extending along Viale Aventino rises the massive **FAO Building**, erected in 1948 to house the Food and Agriculture Organisation, with the *Lubin Memorial Library* (founded 1946: 600,000 volumes). In the SW wing is part of the Ministry of Posts.

From the E corner of the FAO Building the Viale Guido Baccelli runs through the *Parco di Porta Capena*, which contains some ancient remains, to the *Baths of Caracalla (Terme di Caracalla;* Latin *Thermae Antonianae),* a gigantic bathing establishment (330 m square, with an area of 109,000 sq. m) built by Caracalla in A.D. 216. The baths proper, in the centre of the courtyard, include a hot bath (*caldarium*), a pool for cold dips (*frigidarium*), facilities for gymnastics, etc. In spite of the loss of their rich marble decoration and their columns and the collapse of the roof, the Baths still display

the architectural skill of their builders and give some impression of what they were like in their heyday, when thousands of Romans could enjoy all this splendour for a very modest admission charge. – During the summer, performances of opera are given in the Baths.

From Piazza di Porta Capena the Via delle Terme di Caracalla runs SE to the *Piazzale di Numa Pompilio* and then S into the *Via Cristoforo Colombo,* a fine modern highway built for the 1960 Olympic Games which continues SW into the EUR district. Alternatively it is possible to bear SE along *Via di Porta San Sebastiano* to the **Tomb of the Scipios** (Sepolcro degli Scipioni), built in 312 B.C. (still preserving the original sarcophagi), which lies under a Roman house of the Imperial period. Close by is the *Columbarium of Pomponius Hylas* or *of the Freedmen of Octavia* (Nero's wife), a subterranean

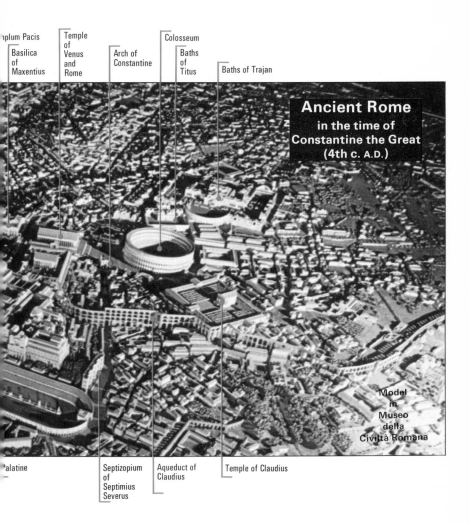

Temple Pacis | Basilica of Maxentius | Temple of Venus and Rome | Arch of Constantine | Colosseum | Baths of Titus | Baths of Trajan

Ancient Rome
in the time of
Constantine the Great
(4th c. A.D.)

Model in Museo della Civiltà Romana

Palatine | Septizopium of Septimius Severus | Aqueduct of Claudius | Temple of Claudius

tomb with good stucco decoration and painting.

Via di Porta San Sebastiano ends at the so-called **Arch of Drusus** (probably in fact dating from the time of Trajan). Immediately beyond it, in the Aurelian Walls, is the crenellated *Porta San Sebastiano*, the ancient *Porta Appia*, from which the Via Appia Antica runs S to the Catacombs (see below, p. 251).

The **Aurelian Walls** (Mura Aureliane), a circuit of massive brick walls 19 km long, with gates and towers, were built by the Emperor Aurelian in A.D. 272–278, after a period of some 500 years during which no enemy had approached the city. Long stretches of the walls are still preserved, though frequently restored since the 5th c.; it is possible to walk along some sections. It is only in modern times that Rome has grown out beyond the Aurelian Walls. – The principal gates are the *Porta del Popolo*, the *Porta Pinciana*, the *Porta Salaria* and the *Porta Pia* on the N; the *Porta San Lorenzo* and the *Porta Maggiore* on the E; the *Porta San Giovanni*, the *Porta San Sebastiano* and the *Porta San Paolo* on the S; and the *Porta San Pancrazio* on the W.

From the Colosseum to the Lateran and San Lorenzo

The Lateran is reached from the Colosseum either by going SE along Via di San Giovanni in Laterano or by going S along Via Claudia and then turning NE past Santo Stefano Rotondo along Via di Santo Stefano Rotondo.

On the left-hand side of *Via di San Giovanni in Laterano*, built over an ancient temple of Mithras, is the *church of San Clemente** (1108), a good example of an early Christian basilica. The nave is flanked by aisles, but there is no transept; fine marble choir screens, with two ambos; atrium, with fountain for ablutions; wall paintings (8th–11th c.) in the old lower church. To the S of Via di Santo Stefano Rotondo, on the Caelian, stands the **church of Santo Stefano Rotondo** (460–480), an imposing round church, also built over a temple of Mithras, with 56 columns in the interior and a timber roof structure. Excavations under the church brought to light remains of a Roman barracks (*Castra Peregrinorum*) and a mithraeum of the 3rd c. A.D. (frescoes, sculpture).

Via di San Giovanni joins the *Piazza di San Giovanni in Laterano*, in the centre of which rises a red granite Egyptian **obelisk** (15th c. B.C.), set up in the Circus Maximus in A.D. 357 and re-erected here in 1588; it is the largest of its kind, standing 32 m high (not counting the base). In the SW corner of the square is the *baptistery of San Giovanni in Fonte*, the oldest baptistery in Rome (432–440) and the model for all later buildings of the same kind.

On the S side of the square, behind the Lateran Palace, stands the *church of **San Giovanni in Laterano**, built by Constantine the Great in a palace belonging to the Laterani, one of the five patriarchal churches of Rome, "mother and head of all churches". It was much altered between the 10th and 15th c., and its present Baroque form dates from the mid 16th c.; the massive Late Baroque façade, with its conspicuous attic storey and its crown of statues, dates from 1735; the new choir was added in 1885. Of the five doorways the central one has ancient bronze doors from the Curia Iulia.

The present *INTERIOR, with double lateral aisles, was designed by Francesco Borromini (16th–17th c.); the magnificent timber *ceiling* is by Daniele da Volterra (1564–72); the richly inlaid pavement is 15th c. – The ancient columns in the nave were joined in pairs by Borromini to form piers; the large statues of the Apostles in niches were added after 1700. – Four steps lead up into the transept, in the centre of which is the **Altare Papale**, at which only the Pope or his representative can celebrate mass. The tabernacle dates from 1369. The relics preserved here are the heads of the Apostles Peter and Paul. – The choir is richly decorated with marble. In the apse are mosaics (much restored) dating from 1290. – In the S aisle, on the first pier of the nave, is a fresco (Pope Boniface VIII proclaiming the first jubilee year, 1300) attributed to Giotto but much retouched. – Numerous monuments.

A door beside the last chapel in the N aisle leads into the early 13th c. * **Cloister**, which has numerous twisted colonnettes with mosaic decoration.

Adjoining the N side of the church is the **Lateran Palace**, built in 1586 on the site of an earlier palace, occupied by the popes from the time of Constantine onwards, which was burned down in 1308, and left in the possession of the Pope in 1871. It formerly housed the Lateran Museums, now in a new building in the Vatican Gardens, and is at present occupied by the Vicariate of the city of Rome.

Opposite the Lateran Palace to the NE, in a 16th c. building, is the *Scala Santa*, a flight of 28 marble steps (now covered with wood for protection) which is believed to be the staircase ascended by Christ in Pilate's palace in Jerusalem and which the faithful climb only on their knees. At the top, beyond a grille, is the chapel known as the *Sancta Sanctorum*, with 13th c. mosaics.

Close by, on the S side of Piazza di Porta San Giovanni, stands the 16th c. *Porta San Giovanni*, from which the Via Appia Nuova runs SE.

From Piazza di Porta San Giovanni the Viale Carlo Felice runs E to the **church of Santa Croce in Gerusalemme**, one of the seven pilgrimage churches of Rome (rebuilt 1743), which may have been founded by St Helena.

To the N of the church the *Museum of Musical Instruments* (Museo degli Strumenti Musicali) houses a collection dating from ancient times to 1800.

Farther N towers the massive **Porta Maggiore**, originally an arch carrying the *Aqua Claudia* (Aqueduct of Claudius) over the Roman road, later a gate in the Aurelian Walls.

From here we go along Viale Giovanni Giolitti, which leads to the Termini Station, as far as the *church of Santa Bibiana* (rebuilt by Bernini, 1627), where we turn right under the railway to reach the new gate 100 m S of the old **Porta San Lorenzo**, the Roman *Porta Tiburtina*.

From the new Porta San Lorenzo the Via Tiburtina runs NE (1 km) to the *Basilica **San Lorenzo fuori le Mura**, one of the five patriarchal churches of Rome, originally founded by Constantine the Great, entirely remodelled in the 6th and again in the 13th c., partly destroyed during the Second World War – the only bomb damage in Rome – but restored after the war. The floor of the nave and choir dates from the 12th–13th c., the baldacchino over the high altar from 1148. The triumphal arch has 6th c. mosaics. Adjoining the church is a picturesque Romanesque *cloister*.

Beside the church, on gently rising ground, is a large cemetery, the *Campo Verano*.

To the W of Piazza San Lorenzo is the **University City** (Città Universitaria) of Rome University (founded by Pope Boniface VIII in 1303; 90,000 students), a large complex of buildings set amid gardens established here in the 1930s. The Biblioteca Alessandrina, the University Library, founded in 1661, contains more than 800,000 volumes. Still farther W is the massive *Air Ministry* (Ministero della Difesa Aeronautica, 1931). To the N of the University City are the extensive grounds of the *Policlinico Umberto I*, to the W of which, in the Castro Pretorio, is the **National Library** (Biblioteca Nazionale Centrale Vittorio Emanuele II), built 1971–75. This contains some 3 million volumes, 1883 incunabula, 6169 manuscripts and 30,000 autographs, and consists of a long ten-storey book-stack, an office block, a building housing the catalogue rooms and eight reading rooms, and a low conference building.

From the Colosseum to the Termini Station and the North-Eastern Districts

NE of the Colosseum, in the *Parco Traianeo* on the Esquiline Hill, are the remains of *Nero's Golden House* or *Domus Aurea*, a palace complex planned with a lavish disregard of expense and containing numerous magnificent State apartments which was left unfinished after leading to the bankruptcy of the State. Trajan later used it as the substructure of his Baths. The palace contained much fine painting, which Raphael took as his model for the Loggias in the Vatican. – Some 500 m NE, in the Palazzo Brancaccio, is the *Museo Nazionale d'Arte Orientale*.

N of the Parco Traianeo stands the *church of San Pietro in Vincoli, an aisled basilica with 20 ancient columns, originally built in 442 to house the chains (*vincula*) of St Peter and completely rebuilt in the 15th c. In the S transept is the powerful figure of *Moses by Michelangelo (1513–16), one of his finest and most impressive works, created for the unfinished tomb of Pope Julius II, a symbol of strength controlled by superhuman will-power. The second altar in the N aisle has 7th c. mosaic decoration; adjoining it is the tomb of Cardinal Nicolaus Cusanus (d. 1464). A shrine under the high altar, with bronze doors (1477), contains the chains of St Peter, which are displayed annually on 1 August.

A little way N of San Pietro is Via Cavour, which branches off the Via dei Fori Imperiali and runs NE to the *Piazza dell'Esquilino*. On the SE side of this square is the imposing *church of Santa Maria Maggiore, one of Rome's five patriarchal churches and the largest of its 80 or so churches dedicated to the Virgin. Founded in the 5th c., it was rebuilt in the 16th and 17th c.; the main front with its loggia dates from 1743. The tower (1377) is the highest in Rome (75 m). From the porch (13th c. mosaics), with its five doorways, four entrances lead into the church; the fifth, the Porta Santa (to the left), is opened only in Holy Years.

The aisled *INTERIOR is splendidly decorated. The pavement of the nave dates from the 12th c., the magnificent *ceiling*, richly gilded with the first gold brought from America, from 1493 to 1498. Above the architrave, borne on 40 Ionic columns, as well as on the triumphal arch, are 5th c. *mosaics* (best seen in the early morning light). In the apse are mosaics by J. Torriti (1295).

In the S transept the magnificent *Sistine Chapel*, or Chapel of the Holy Sacrament, has a domed roof; the chapel was built in 1585 in the reign of Sixtus V. In the N aisle is the *Borghese Chapel* (1611), also domed, with an image of the Virgin, believed to be miraculous, on the high altar.

300 m NW of Santa Maria Maggiore stands the *church of Santa Pudenziana*, with a 12th c. tower, which legend claims to be the oldest church in Rome. The apse contains *mosaics (Christ with Apostles, 401–417) which are among the finest in Rome.

Just S of Santa Maria Maggiore, concealed among buildings, is the *church of Santa Prassede*, built in 822 and several times restored, most recently in 1869. Beautiful interior, with fine 9th c. *mosaics on the triumphal arch, in the apse and in the chapel of San Zeno (S aisle).

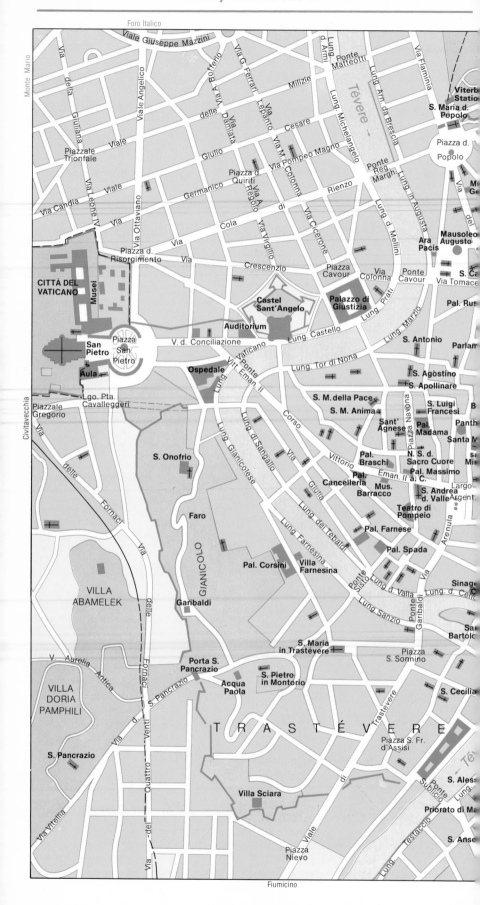

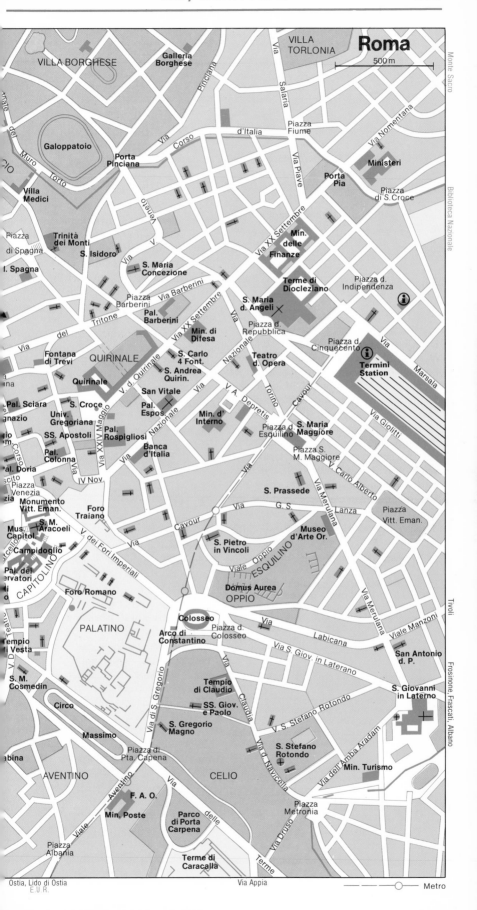

Roma

500 m

VILLA BORGHESE
Galleria Borghese
VILLA TORLONIA

Via Pinciana
Via Corso d'Italia
Via Salaria
Piazza Fiume
Via Plave
Via Nomentana

Galoppatoio
Porta Pinciana
Ministeri
Porta Pia
Piazza di S.Croce

Villa Medici
Piazza di Spagna
Trinità dei Monti
S. Isidoro
I. Spagna
S. Maria Concezione
Via Veneto
Via XX Settembre
Min. delle Finanze

Piazza Barberini
Via Barberini
Pal. Barberini
Via Tritone
Via del Tritone
Terme di Diocleziano
Piazza d. Indipendenza
Piazza d. Repubblica

Fontana di Trevi
QUIRINALE
Min. di Difesa
S. Carlo 4 Font.
S. Andrea Quirin.
S. Maria d. Angeli
Piazza d. Cinquecento
Termini Station
Via Marsala

Quirinale
San Vitale
Via Nazionale
Teatro d. Opera
Via Torino
Via Cavour
Via Giolitti

Pal. Sciara
S. Croce
Univ. Gregoriana
Pal. Espos.
Min. d' Interno
Piazza d. Esquilino
S. Maria Maggiore

SS. Apostoli
Pal. Rospigliosi
Banca d'Italia
Via A. Depretis
Piazza S. M. Maggiore
V. Carlo Alberto

Pal. Colonna
Pal. Doria
IV Nov.
S. Prassede
G. S. Lanza
Via Merulana
Piazza Vitt. Eman.

Piazza Venezia
Monumento Vitt. Eman.
Foro Traiano
Via Cavour
Museo d'Arte Or.

S. M. Aracoeli
Mus. Capitol.
Campidoglio
S. Pietro in Vincoli
ESQUILINO
Via Oppio

Pal. dei servatori
CAPITOLINO
V dei Fori Imperiali
Foro Romano
Domus Aurea
OPPIO

Tempio di Vesta
PALATINO
Colosseo
Arco di Constantino
Piazza d. Colosseo
Via Labicana
Viale Manzoni
San Antonio d. P.

S. M. Cosmedin
Via di S. Gregorio
Tempio di Claudio
Via S. Giov. in Laterano
S. Giovanni in Laterno

Circo
SS. Giov. e Paolo
S. Gregorio Magno
Via Claudia
V. S. Stefano Rotondo
Via d. Navicella

Massimo
Piazza di Pta. Capena
S. Stefano Rotondo
Via dell'Amba Aradam
Min. Turismo

AVENTINO
CELIO
Piazza Metronia

abina
F. A. O.
Min. Poste
Parco di Porta Carpena
Via Druso
Via delle Terme

Piazza Albania
Terme di Caracalla

Monte Sacro
Biblioteca Nazionale
Tivoli
Frosinone, Frascati, Albano

At the NE end of Via Cavour we come to the large **Piazza dei Cinquecento**. On the SE side of this square is the *Termini **Station** (*Stazione Centrale Roma-Termini*), completed in 1950, an imposing structure of distinctive design, making much use of glass and steel, which was a landmark in the development of modern railway architecture. In the concourse is the entrance to the *Metropolitana* line (partly underground, partly above ground) which runs by way of the Porta San Paolo to the EUR district. (Further lines are under construction, running SE to Cinecittà and W to the Piazza del Risorgimento, near the Vatican.) Here too is a small *Aquarium* (open 8 a.m. to 9 p.m.). – Outside the Termini Station is a large *bus station*.

The N side of the Piazza dei Cinquecento and the area to the N are occupied by the **Baths of Diocletian** (Terme di Diocleziano), built A.D. 298–305, which were no less magnificent than the Baths of Caracalla and measure 350 m each way. Michelangelo was commissioned by Pope Pius IV to convert the Baths into a Carthusian monastery, and transformed the large vaulted *tepidarium* (warm bath) into the *church of Santa Maria degli Angeli* (1563–66). Since 1886 the monastic buildings have housed a museum. The great semicircle described by the outer wall now forms the *Piazza della Repubblica* (fountain). In a rotunda at the W end is the round *church of San Bernardo*, consecrated 1600.

The **Museo Nazionale Romano o delle Terme** (Roman National Museum or Baths Museum), founded 1886, contains material discovered on state property in and around Rome and has developed into the most interesting museum of antiquities in the city. The museum was closed in March 1979 following the collapse of part of the roof.

The *old rooms* around the S transept of Santa Maria degli Angeli contain the largest collection in Italy of Roman sarcophagi and mosaics. Particularly notable items in the *new rooms* are the marble *Ludovisi Throne (or Throne of Aphrodite), the upper part of the altar, a marvellous example of mature archaic art (5th c. B.C.: Room II); ** "Niobe Wounded", a Greek original of the 5th c. B.C. (Room III, Sala dei Capolavori); the ** "Maiden of Anzio", an original work of the early Hellenistic period; the headless and armless * Venus of Cyrene (4th c. B.C.); a * "Kneeling Youth" from Subiaco (3rd c. B.C.); a bronze * "Defeated Pugilist" (3rd c. B.C.); and a copy of Myron's "Discobolus" (5th c. B.C.).

In the *Small Cloister* (Piccolo Chiostro) is the *Ludovisi Collection* (temporarily closed). Notable items here are the * "Galatian and his Wife" (a Roman copy), "Ares Resting", the *Ludovisi Juno and the *head of a sleeping Fury, the so-called Ludovisi Medusa.

The *Large Cloister* (Grande Chiostro), completed in 1565, with a fountain in the centre, contains marble sculpture, architectural elements, sarcophagi, mosaics and inscriptions.

Some 200 m S of the Piazza della Repubblica, in Via Torino, stands the **Opera House** (Teatro dell'Opera), built in 1880 and later reconstructed.

A little way N of the Museo delle Terme is the **Via XX Settembre** commemorating 20 September 1870, when Italian troops marched into Rome after the withdrawal of the French. In this street which leads to the north-eastern districts of the city, to the N of San Bernardo, is the *church of Santa Maria della Vittoria*, a sumptuous Baroque church designed by Carlo Maderna (1608–20), which contains (fourth chapel on left) one of the great masterpieces of the High Baroque style, Bernini's *"Ecstasy of St Teresa" (1647). Opposite the church is the imposing *Acqua Felice Fountain* (by Domenico Fontana, 1585–87), with marble sculpture. Farther along, on the right, the *Ministry of Finance* (1870–77) can be seen.

Via XX Settembre ends at the **Porta Pia** in the old town walls (designed by Michelangelo, 1561–65).

Immediately outside the Porta Pia, on the right-hand side of *Via Nomentana*, which continues the line of Via XX Settembre to the NE, is the *Ministry of Public Works*. – A kilometre farther on, also on the right, lies the beautiful **park of the Villa Torlonia** (32 acres), a good example of Romantic landscape gardening. Under the ground are Jewish catacombs. In the park is the early 19th c. *Palazzo Torlonia* (Mussolini's residence from 1925 to 1944), the cellars of which (no admission) contain one of Italy's largest private collections of antiquities (over 600 works of art: establishment of a museum under consideration).

Another 2 km out on Via Nomentana, on the left, is the **church of Sant'Agnese fuori le Mura**, founded by Constantine the Great to house the tomb of St Agnes and rebuilt in the 7th and 15th c. and again in 1856. The *apse contains mosaics dating from the first half of the 7th c.

Under the church are catacombs, some still in their original state (before A.D. 300). Adjoining Sant'Agnese is the round *church of Santa Costanza*, built as a mausoleum for Constantine's daughter, with fine 4th c. mosaics.

Via Nomentana then continues NE to the **Quartiere Monte Sacro**, a large suburban area which has grown up since the last war on and around the gently rising *Mons Sacer*, rendered famous by the secession of the Roman plebs in 494 B.C.

From the Piazza Venezia to the Quirinal and the Villa Borghese

From the N side of the Piazza Venezia it is a short distance E along Via Cesare Battisti to the elongated *Piazza Santi Apostoli*, with the **Palazzo Colonna**, begun about 1417 by Pope Martin V (Colonna), in the heyday of the Colonna family – whose power, like that of the Orsini family, was predominant in Rome until the 16th c. – and much altered in the 17th and 18th c. The richly decorated rooms on the 1st floor contain a fine collection of pictures, the *Galleria Colonna* (entrance in Via della Pilotta).

On the N side of the Palazzo Colonna is the *church of the Santi Apostoli* (1702), with a porch dating from 1475. At the end of the N aisle is the *tomb of Pope Clement XIV (by Canova, 1789). NE of the church, in Piazza Pilotta, stands the **Universitas Gregoriana** or Pontifical University, founded in 1553; the present buildings date from 1930.

From the Palazzo Colonna Via IV Novembre runs S to the medieval *Torre delle Milizie* or *Torre di Nerone* and the Largo Magnanapoli. By the Torre delle Milizie is the entrance to Trajan's Market and Forum. From here **Via Nazionale**, one of Rome's main traffic arteries, runs NE, past the *Banca d'Italia* (on right), the *Palazzo Rospigliosi* (1603: *ceiling paintings by Guido Reni) and the *Palazzo delle Esposizioni* (1880–83), to the Piazza della Repubblica. Beside the Palazzo delle Esposizioni is the mouth of the *tunnel* (348 m long) driven under the Quirinal in 1902, providing a link with the Piazza di Spagna.

From the Largo Magnanapoli Via XXIV Maggio runs N past the *church of San Silvestro al Quirinale* (1524: on left) and the W wing of the Palazzo Rospigliosi to the *Piazza del Quirinale*, on the **Quirinal Hill**. In the centre of the square are the two famous marble statues of the *"Horse-Tamers"* (*Dioscuri*), fine examples of the classical style of sculpture of the Imperial period, based on Greek models of the 5th c. B.C. On the E side of the square are the *Palazzo della Consulta* (built 1732–34, with a beautiful staircase: no admission) and the **Palazzo del Quirinale**, an imposing pile built on the summit of the Quirinal Hill. Begun in 1574 as a summer residence for the Pope, it was enlarged and altered in later centuries. From 1870 to 1946 it was a royal palace, and it is now the official residence of the President of Italy (though he does not in fact live here). It is set in a beautiful park.

To the E of the Quirinal Palace stands the *church of Sant'Andrea al Quirinale* (by Bernini, 1658–70), one of the most harmonious creations of Roman Baroque architecture, on an oval ground-plan. Still farther E, at the junction of Via del Quirinale with Via Quattro Fontane, are the *Quattro Fontane* (Four Fountains). To the right is the little *church of San Carlo alle Quattro Fontane* or *San Carlino*, a spirited Baroque building by Borromini.

In the northern part of Via Quattro Fontane, on the right, is the **Palazzo Barberini**, an imposing Baroque structure begun in 1626 by Carlo Maderna and completed in 1633 by Borromini and Bernini. It now houses the *Galleria Nazionale d'Arte Antica*, with works by Italian and foreign artists of the 13th–16th c. (including a number of fine works by Dutch masters, Germans, including Hans Holbein the Younger's* "Portrait of Henry VIII", French and Spanish artists, such as El Greco's *"Baptism of Christ" and *"Nativity", and Raphael's *"La Fornarina"); a fine *ceiling painting in the principal room depicting the "Triumph of the Barberini Family", by Pietro da Cortona, a masterpiece of Baroque monumental painting (1633–39); and 17th and 18th c. pictures from the Palazzo Corsini.

Adjoining the Palazzo Barberini to the NW in the centre of the **Piazza Barberini**, an elongated square which is a busy traffic intersection can be seen the beautiful *Fontana del Tritone* (by Bernini, 1640), with a figure of a triton blowing a conch.

From the N end of the Piazza Barberini the famous **Via Vittorio Veneto** (Via Veneto for short), a wide tree-lined avenue, climbs in an S-shaped curve to the *Porta Pinciana*, a distance of almost a kilometre. A little way along the lower part, on the right, underneath the Capuchin *church of Santa Maria della Concezione* (1626) are five mortuary chapels, the walls of which are covered with the remains of more than 4000 Capuchins. Beyond this are various large buildings occupied by government offices and banks. The upper section of the street, beyond the intersection with Via Ludovisi and Via Boncompagni (on the right the *Palazzo Margherita*, with the U.S. Embassy), is the territory of the "dolce vita", the rendezvous of the famous and fashionable, with elegant luxury shops, hotels and cafés (the best known of which is the Café de Paris).

Beyond the Porta Pinciana is the large and beautiful park of the *Villa Borghese, laid out by Cardinal Scipio Borghese in the 17th c., which was purchased by the State in 1902 and thrown open to the public under the name of *Villa Umberto I*. At the S end of the park is a large underground car park. Scattered about in the shady grounds, planted with chestnut-trees, holm-oaks and beautiful umbrella pines, are a variety of ornamental buildings, fountains and monuments. In the southern section of the park is a *galoppatoio* (race-track). To the E is the **Casino Borghese**, built about 1615 and richly decorated with marble and frescoes at the end of the 18th c. The ground floor houses a figure of *Pauline Borghese, Napoleon's sister, as Venus (1807), the most famous idealised portrait of the Empire period, and several youthful works by Bernini, including "David with his Sling" and "Apollo and Daphne". On the upper floor the **Galleria Borghese, one of Rome's finest picture galleries, has masterpieces by Raphael (*"Entombment"), Titian (**"Sacred and Profane Love"), Caravaggio (*"David", *"Madonna dei Palafrenieri"), Correggio (*"Danaë"), works by painters of the Roman Baroque school, as well as by Rubens, Lucas Cranach, Domenichino and Andrea del Sarto.

In the northern part of the park is a *Zoo*, established by Karl Hagenbeck in 1911. To the W of this the **Galleria Nazionale d'Arte Moderna** contains the largest collection of modern art in Italy, covering the period from the beginning of the 19th c. to the present day (Italian neo-classical artists and Neo-Impressionists, other European Impressionists and Expressionists, contemporary painting and sculpture).

Still farther W is the *Villa Giulia, built for Pope Julius III by Vignola (1550–55), with beautiful stucco-work and painting by Taddeo Zuccaro. The villa now houses the large State collection of Etruscan antiquities from the province of Rome, outstanding among which are the *Cista Ficoroni (3rd c. B.C.: a cylindrical toilet casket with finely engraved scenes from the story of the Argonauts), the Apollo of Veii (a painted terracotta statue dating from about 500 B.C.) and a terracotta sarcophagus from Cerveteri with the reclining figures of a man and his wife (6th c. B.C.).

From the Piazza Barberini the busy *Via del Tritone* runs W to join the Via del Corso. Going along this street and in 200 m turning right along Via Due Macelli, we come to the **Piazza di Spagna**, under the S side of the Pincio. It is named after the large *Palazzo di Spagna*, which has been the residence of the Spanish ambassador to the Holy See since the 17th c. In front of the palace rises the *Column of the Immacolata*, erected to commemorate the proclamation of the dogma of the Immaculate Conception by Pope Pius IX in 1854. On the S side of the square is the *Palazzo di Propaganda Fide*, a centre and college for the propagation of the Roman Catholic faith (missionary archives). In the centre of the square is the *Barcaccia, a low fountain in the shape of a boat (by Bernini, 1629). At the foot of the Spanish Steps is the *Keats-Shelley Memorial House*, in which Keats died in 1821.

From the Piazza di Spagna the famous *Spanish Steps (*Scalinata della Trinità dei Monti*), a magnificent Baroque staircase (137 steps, alternating with ramps) designed by Francesco de Sanctis (1723–26), gay with flowers in summer, climb up to the twin-towered French **church of the Santissima Trinità dei Monti**, founded in 1495, on the Pincio (*view). A little way N of the church is the 16th c. *Villa Medici*, which came into the hands of the Medici family in the 17th c. and has been occupied since 1803 by the French Academy of Art; beautiful gardens.

To the W and NW of the Piazza di Spagna are a number of busy streets, including *Via dei Condotti*, *Via del Babuino* and *Via Margutta*, with elegant shops and boutiques, jewellers, antique-dealers, arts and crafts shops and galleries.

Farther N, above the E side of the Piazza del Popolo, is the **Pincio**, a beautiful park laid out in 1908–14 on the hill of that name (alt. 50 m), the most northerly of Rome's hills, with numerous busts and monuments commemorating famous Italians and a monumental piece of sculpture, 11 m high, by Giacomo Manzù (1975). From the terrace on the W side of the park there is a famous *prospect of Rome, with an impressive view of St Peter's. – At the E end of the park is a bridge linking it with the Villa Borghese park.

Along the Via del Corso from the Piazza Venezia to the Piazza del Popolo

The **Via del Corso**, which runs NW from the Piazza di Spagna to the Piazza del Popolo on the line of the ancient *Via Flaminia*, flanked by numerous Baroque palaces, has long been Rome's principal street (1·5 km long but only 12 m wide).

The first building on the left-hand side is the 17th c. *Palazzo Bonaparte*, and just beyond this another 17th c. mansion, the **Palazzo Doria**, has a handsome pillared courtyard. On the upper floor of this palace is the *Galleria Doria-Pamphili*, which contains Velázquez's famous **portrait of Pope Innocent X (Pamphili), a masterpiece notable equally for its sharp delineation of character and its brilliance of colour (1650). The gallery has also fine works by Raphael, Titian, Tintoretto, Correggio, Caravaggio (*"Rest on the Flight into Egypt") and Claude Lorrain.

Beyond the Palazzo Doria a short and narrow street, Via Lata, runs W into the Piazza del Collegio Romano, on the right-hand side of which we come to the *Collegio Romano* (by Bartolomeo Ammannati and Giuseppe Valeriani,

1583–85), a Jesuit college until 1870 and now a State school.

In a small square to the W of the Collegio Romano stands the *church of Santa Maria sopra Minerva, built before 800 on the site of Domitian's temple of Minerva and rebuilt in 1280. It is Rome's only medieval church in the Gothic style, which never flourished in Italy to the same extent as in northern Europe. In front of the high altar, to the left, is Michelangelo's *statue of the Risen Christ with the Cross (1521). The altar itself contains the relics of St Catherine of Siena (1347–80). The Cappella Caraffa, in the S transept, has frescoes by Filippino Lippi (1489). There are numerous fine monuments; to the left of the choir is the tombstone of the Dominican Fra Giovanni Angelico (1387–1455).

NW of Santa Maria sopra Minerva, in the *Piazza della Rotonda*, is the *Pantheon, the only ancient building in Rome which still preserves its walls and vaulting.

The Pantheon was built in 27 B.C. by Marcus Vipsanius Agrippa, Augustus's friend and general, and several times rebuilt or restored, notably by Hadrian in 120–126. After the extinction of paganism the Eastern Emperor Phocas presented it to Pope Boniface IV, who consecrated it in 609 as the *church of Santa Maria ad Martyres*, popularly called *Santa Maria Rotonda*. The portico has 16 ancient granite columns 12·5 m high, and the entrance still preserves its massive ancient bronze-clad doors. The huge dome of the Pantheon, lit only by a round aperture 9 m in diameter (the "Eye"), ranks as the supreme achievement of Roman interior architecture. The overwhelming effect of the building depends on the consummate harmony of its proportions no less than on its huge dimensions: its height (43·2 m) is the same as its diameter, and the hemisphere of the dome is the same height as its vertical walls. The figures of the gods which once stood in the seven principal niches and the rest of the valuable furnishings of the Pantheon have been removed in the course of the centuries. In the second niche on the right is the tomb of King Victor Emmanuel II (d. 1878); opposite this is the tomb of Umberto I (assassinated 1900); and to the right is the tomb of Raphael (1483–1520).

From the Pantheon Via del Seminario runs E, past the *Ministry of Posts*, to the Baroque **church of Sant'Ignazio** (by O. Grassi, 1626–50), built on the model of the Gesù (below, p. 239) in honour of the founder of the Jesuit order, Ignatius of Loyola (1491–1556), who was canonised in 1622. It has a famous ceiling painting by Andrea Pozzo, a masterpiece of perspective (best seen from the middle of the nave).

Facing the church, to the N, is the **Exchange** (Borsa). The N front, on Piazza di Pietra, has 11 Corinthian *columns, 12·9 m high, probably from a temple built in honour of the Emperor Hadrian (A.D. 76–138).

To the E of Sant'Ignazio, on the E side of the Via del Corso, is the 17th c. *Palazzo Sciarra-Colonna*. A little way N, off the W side of the Corso, the busy *Piazza Colonna* was named after the *Column of Marcus Aurelius** (29·5 m high) which stands in the centre of the square. Like Trajan's column, it is covered with reliefs (originally painted) depicting Marcus Aurelius's campaigns against the Marcomanni and other Germanic tribes on the Danube. The column is topped by a bronze statue of the Apostle Paul which was erected by Pope Sixtus V.

On the E side of the Piazza Colonna (and of the Corso) is the *Galleria Colonna*, with a Y-shaped arcade. The *Palazzo Wedekind*, on the W side of the square, has a portico of 16 Ionic columns from the Etruscan city of Veii. On the N side is the **Palazzo Chigi** (begun 1562, completed by Carlo Maderna), which now houses the Italian Cabinet offices.

Adjoining the Piazza Colonna on the W is the *Piazza di Montecitorio*, on an eminence formed by an accumulation of rubble from ancient buildings. In the centre of

this square rises a 26 m high Egyptian **obelisk** (6th c. B.C.). The N side of the square is occupied by the Italian **Parliament Building** (*Camera dei Deputati* or *Parlamento*), also known as the *Palazzo di Montecitorio*. Originally built by Bernini in 1650 for the Ludovisi family, it was converted for the use of the Papal courts in 1694 by Carlo Fontana and again altered in 1871 to house the new Italian Parliament.

Some 250 m E of the Piazza Colonna is the popular *Fontana di Trevi**, built against the S end of the Palazzo Poli. The most monumental of Rome's Baroque fountains, it was the work of Niccolò Salvi, based on designs by Bernini (1735–62). In the central niche is a figure of Neptune, flanked by figures of Health and Fertility; in front is a large stone basin, some 20 m across. It is an old custom when leaving Rome to throw a coin backwards over your head into the basin in order to ensure that you will return.

Facing the Trevi Fountain, to the SE, is the *church of Santi Vincenzo ed Anastasio*, with a Baroque façade of 1650.

350 m N of the Piazza Colonna, on the left-hand side of the Via del Corso, is the *Palazzo Rúspoli* (begun 1556), with a fine staircase of about 1650. Beyond this, to the right, there is a charming glimpse along Via dei Condotti of the Spanish

The Pantheon after dark

Steps. Farther N again, on the left, stands the **church of San Carlo al Corso**, a handsome Baroque structure (17th c.).

A little way NW of San Carlo is the **Mausoleum of Augustus** (Mausoleo di Augusto: at present closed), a monumental rotunda, 89 m in diameter at the base and originally 44 m high, built by Augustus in 28 B.C. as a burial-place for himself and his family, which also contained the remains of some of his successors down to Nerva (96–98). From the 11th c. it was a fortress of the Colonna family, in the 19th c. it was used as a circus and from 1908 as a concert-hall, and in 1936 it was restored to its original condition.

Between the Mausoleum and the Tiber, in a glass hall in Via di Ripetta, is the *Ara Pacis Augusta, an altar dedicated to the goddess of peace, re-erected here in 1938. Built on the Campus Martius in 13–9 B.C., after Augustus's return from Spain and Gaul, it is decorated with fine plant ornament and noble carved friezes (a ceremonial procession led by Augustus and his family).

At Via del Corso 18 is the **Goethe Museum** (pictures, books, manuscripts, sketches, etc.), in a house where Goethe lived during his stay in Rome (1786–88).

The Via del Corso runs into the oval **Piazza del Popolo**, laid out in its present form in 1816–20. On the N side stands the **Porta del Popolo** (1565 and 1655), the old N gate of Rome. In the centre of the square, at the point of intersection of three streets from the S (Via di Pipetta, Via del Corso, Via del Babuino), rises an Egyptian **obelisk** (24 m high; including base and cross 36 m) erected by Pope Sixtus V in 1589.

On the S side of the square are two domed churches, *Santa Maria in Monte Santo* to the E and *Santa Maria dei Miracoli* to the W, both begun by Rainaldi in 1662 and completed by Bernini and Carlo Fontana in 1675 and 1679 respectively.

Adjoining the Porta del Popolo is the *church of **Santa Maria del Popolo**, built in 1472–77, with a new choir by Bramante (1505–09) and a Baroque interior (remodelled 1655). It contains numerous works of art, in particular 15th

c. monuments. In the chapel to the left of the choir are two magnificent *pictures by Caravaggio ("Conversion of Paul", "Crucifixion of Peter"). In the Augustinian convent which formerly stood here Luther stayed during his visit to Rome in 1510–11.

On the E side of the church is an entrance to the Pincio park (see above). Beyond the Porta del Popolo, in Piazzale Flaminio, is an entrance to the Villa Borghese park.

2 km farther N are the *Stadio Flaminio* (1959: seats for 50,000 spectators), the circular *Palazzetto dello Sport* (1957: 3000 seats) and the *Olympic Village*, built in 1960 to house 8000 athletes and now occupied by government employees and their families. Through the village runs a viaduct 1 km long carrying the Corso di Francia to the *Ponte Flaminio* over the Tiber.

350 m W of the Ponte Flaminio the *Ponte Milvio** or *Ponte Molle*, the Roman *Pons Milvius*, originally built to carry the Via Flaminia (constructed in 220 B.C.) over the Tiber, was rebuilt in stone in 109 B.C. and restored and improved in the 15th and 19th c. Over this bridge many visitors to Rome, including Charlemagne, Luther and Goethe, made their entry into the city.

Along the Corso Vittorio Emanuele from the Piazza Venezia to the Castel Sant'Angelo

From the Piazza Venezia it is a short distance W along Via del Plebiscito to the *Piazza del Gesù*, where stands the *Gesù church** (1568–75), the principal church of the Jesuit order and one of the richest and most sumptuous churches in Rome, the model for all the other splendid Jesuit churches and a magnificent example of Baroque architecture. It has a wide, high nave, with the aisles converted into chapels. In the N transept is the splendid Altar of St Ignatius (1696–1700), under which is a gilded bronze sarcophagus containing the remains of St Ignatius of Loyola (1491–1556).

From the far side of the Piazza del Gesù the busy **Corso Vittorio Emanuele II**, driven through the medieval town from

1870 onwards to provide a link between the Piazza Venezia and Vatican City, continues W. A short distance along this street, on the left, is the *Largo di Torre Argentina*. In this low-lying square, in front of the *Teatro Argentina*, are the remains (excavated 1927–30) of *four temples* of the Republican period (3rd c. B.C.), which – unlike those in the Forum – have preserved much of their original form. A short distance S of the Largo di Torre Argentina, in the little Piazza Mattei, is the *Tortoise Fountain* (Fontana delle Tartarughe), a charming bronze group by Taddeo Landini (1585).

Piazza Navona, Rome

Farther along the Corso Vittorio Emanuele, on the left, stands the domed **church of Sant'Andrea della Valle**, begun by F. Grimaldi and G. della Porta in 1591, completed by Carlo Maderna in 1625. with a richly decorated façade of 1665 and a sumptuous interior. Particularly notable are the fine frescoes by Domenichino (1624–28) in the pendentives under the dome and on the vaulting of the apse.

Farther along the Corso, on the right, is the *Palazzo Mássimo alle Colonne*, one of the handsomest Renaissance buildings in Rome (by Baldassare Peruzzi, 1532–36), with a curved façade adapted to a bend in the old street and a picturesque double courtyard. Beyond this, on the left (Piazza di San Pantaleo), we find the *Piccola Farnesina* (1523), a Renaissance palace which houses the **Museo Barracco**, with a fine collection of ancient sculpture (Greek, Assyrian, Egyptian) and Etruscan tombstones. On the opposite side of the Corso, in the *Palazzo Braschi* (1792), is the interesting **Museo di Roma**, illustrating the history of Rome in recent centuries (three railway coaches which belonged to Pope Pius IX, two State carriages, etc.); on the top floor pictures by modern Roman artists; special exhibitions from time to time.

N of the Palazzo Braschi we come to an elongated square, the busy *Piazza Navona* (pedestrians only), the most characteristic of Rome's 17th c. squares. Its shape (240 by 65 m) and rounded ends reflect the fact that it occupies the site of the Circus or Stadium of Domitian, as its official name of *Circo Agonale* (Greek *agon* = contest, fight) also indicates. It is embellished with three

*fountains, the one at the N end erected in 1878, the other two by Bernini c. 1650; the finest is the centre one, with magnificently vigorous figures representing the rivers Danube, Ganges, Nile and Plate and an ancient obelisk. Opposite this fountain, on the W side of the square, is the *church of Sant'Agnese* (by Borromini and Rainaldi, 1652–73), an imposing Baroque church on a centralised plan, with a sumptuous *interior (7th c. mosaics in apse).

NW of the Piazza Navona is the *church of Santa Maria dell'Anima* (1500–14), the old church of the German-speaking Catholics, with a beautiful interior (entered only through a rear courtyard). Immediately NW of this church the *church of Santa Maria della Pace* (1480 has a beautiful semicircular porch added in 1657). Above the first chapel on the right are figures of *Sibyls painted by Raphael, grouped with consummate spatial sense round the arch (1514), and in the octagonal dome are other fine 16th c. frescoes. The cloister is by Bramante (1504).

To the E of Piazza Navona, in the *Corso del Rinascimento*, stands the **Palazzo Madama** (1642), the seat of the Italian Senate since 1871. On its N side is the French national church, *San Luigi dei Francesi* (consecrated 1589), with a fine interior containing three notable *pictures by Caravaggio (scenes from the life of St Matthew). In a little square just N of San Luigi the *church of Sant'Agostino* (by Giacomo da Pietrasanta, 1469–83), one of the first domed churches to be built in Rome, has a notable interior; on the third pillar on the left is a *fresco by Raphael of the prophet Isaiah (1512), in the first chapel on the left Caravaggio's "Madonna dei Pellegrini" (1605).

Just beyond the Piazza di San Pantaleo, on the left of the Corso Vittorio Emanuele, in the elongated *Piazza della Cancelleria*, is the *Palazzo della Cancelleria, the Papal Chancery, one of the noblest Renaissance buildings in Rome (1486–1511), in a style suggesting Florentine influence; particularly notable is the handsome arcaded courtyard.

From the Piazza della Cancelleria a street runs S by way of the spacious *Campo dei Fiori* to the *Piazza Farnese*, in which are two fountains with ancient basins. On the SW side of the square we come to the *Palazzo Farnese, one of the most typical of Rome's old palaces, now occupied by the French embassy. Built for Cardinal Alexander Farnese (later Pope Paul III), it was begun in 1514 by Antonio da Sangallo the Younger and continued from 1546 onwards by Michelangelo (who was responsible for the much admired cornice and the top storey in the courtyard). On the vaulting of the long gallery on the 1st floor are mythological paintings by Annibale Carracci and others (1597–1604) which served as models for the monumental painting of the Baroque period.

SE of the Palazzo Farnese is the **Palazzo Spada** (*c.* 1540) with a handsome façade, the seat of the Italian Council of State. At the end of the second courtyard is a colonnade by Borromini which achieves an effect of depth by a skilful and typically Baroque use of perspective. On the 1st floor (entrance in the inner courtyard) is the *Galleria Spada*, a picture gallery notable particularly for works of the 17th c. Bologna school (Guercino, Reni, etc.).

Farther along the Corso Vittorio Emanuele, on the right, stands the **Chiesa Nuova** or *Santa Maria in Vallicella*, built between 1575 and 1605 for the Oratorian order founded by St Philip Neri in 1575. To the left of the church is the *Oratorio dei Filippini*, with a curved façade, one of Borromini's finest buildings (1637–50); it has been restored and is now used for concerts and lectures. The name of the order and the word "oratorio" are both derived from the spiritual exercises and musical performances instituted by St Philip Neri in oratories. – The Corso Vittorio Emanuele II ends at the *Ponte Vittorio Emanuele* (1911). On the far side of the Tiber, to the right, is the **Castel Sant'Angelo** (see below, p. 244).

From the Piazza Venezia to the Aventine and San Paolo

From the Piazza Venezia we go S, to the right of the National Monument, into *Via del Teatro di Marcello*, which skirts the W side of the Capitol, passing the two flights of steps leading up to Santa Maria in Aracoeli and the Campidoglio. Beyond this, on the right, is the *Theatre of Marcellus (Teatro di Marcello), built by Augustus in 17–13 B.C. and named after his nephew Marcellus, who had died young in 23 B.C. The curved outer wall of the auditorium, which could seat an audience of 13,000–14,000, originally had three storeys, but the top storey was destroyed during the Middle Ages, when the theatre was converted into a fortress and residence for the Orsini family. In front of the theatre, to the right, stand three re-erected columns from a temple of Apollo. – Farther along the street, on the right, is the *church of San Nicola in Cárcere*, with fragments of three ancient temples.

Via del Teatro di Marcello joins the spacious and picturesque **Piazza Bocca della Verità**, at the E end of the *Ponte Palatino*. On the N side of the square is the well-preserved *Temple of Fortuna Virilis* or Tempio di Portuno, a graceful Ionic temple of the late Republican period (1st c. B.C.), to the S of which another smaller circular temple has been known since medieval times as the *Temple of Vesta*, with 19 (formerly 20) Corinthian columns and a medieval roof.

At the E end of the square rises the so-called *Ianus Quadrifrons* ("four-sided Janus") or Arco di Giano, a triumphal arch with four façades which probably dates from the time of Constantine. Here too is the ancient *church of San Giorgio in Velabro*, well restored, which contains 16 Roman columns. Adjoining the church is the richly decorated *Arco degli Argentari* or Arch of the Money-Changers (A.D. 204).

On the S side of the Piazza Bocca della Verità we find the **church of Santa Maria in Cosmedin,** originally built at some time before the 6th c. on the foundations of a temple of Hercules (within which the crypt was hollowed out) and of a market hall (to which the marble columns on the entrance wall belonged) and rebuilt in the 11th–12th c. In the porch is the Bocca della Verità ("Mouth of Truth"), a large antique marble disc with the mask of a Triton, into whose mouth, according to the medieval belief, the Romans used to insert their right hands when taking an oath. The church has a fine interior (aisled), with ancient columns and a 12th c. mosaic pavement, one of the finest of its kind in Rome.

On the N side of the Ponte Palatino, in the middle of the Tiber, is a pier belonging to the old *Pons Aemilius,* originally built in 181 B.C. but frequently damaged by spates of the Tiber and finally abandoned after its destruction by flood-water in 1598: hence its Italian name of *Ponte Rotto,* the "Broken Bridge". On the S side of the Ponte Palatino, in a niche in the embankment wall, can be seen (provided the water level is not too high) the threefold arch at the mouth of the ancient *Cloaca Maxima,* the drain from the Forum area, which continued in use until the 20th c.

Immediately S of the Piazza Bocca della Verità is the **Aventine** (Monte Aventino, 46 m), on which the plebeians lived in the earliest days of Rome. Later the hill was occupied by convents and vineyards, and it is only in quite recent times that it has been more intensively built up and has developed into a pleasant residential area. On the W side of the Aventine, in Via di Santa Sabina, which runs parallel with the Tiber above the *Lungotevere Aventino* on the embankment, is the *****church of Santa Sabina,** originally built between 423 and 435 and subsequently much altered and rebuilt. This was the place of origin of the Dominican order (1215), and since its restoration in 1914–19 and 1936–38 it presents an excellent example of an Early Christian basilica. The cypress-wood door of the principal doorway is decorated with fine 5th c. *reliefs, including (above, left) one of the earliest known representations of the Crucifixion. Fine interior, with 24 ancient marble columns. In the nave is the *schola cantorum* (choir),

rebuilt during the last restoration. The cloister dates from the 13th c. – SW of Santa Sabina the *church of Sant'Alessio,* which is referred to in the 7th c. with a dedication to St Boniface, was completely rebuilt in the 13th and 18th c.

Farther SW, in a little square, is the entrance to the **Villa del Priorato di Malta,** residence of the Grand Master of the order of the Knights of Malta, founded in 1070. The round aperture above the keyhole of the park gate affords a famous *view of the dome of St Peter's, glimpsed at the end of the main avenue. There is also a beautiful view from the gardens (admission only by special arrangement). In the *church of Santa Maria Aventina* (reached from the gardens) are the tombs of knights of the order. – Immediately S of the priory is the *International Benedictine Seminary,* with the *church of Sant'Anselmo* (consecrated 1900).

From here Via di Porta Lavernale and its continuation lead S into the broad Via della Marmorata, at the S end of which, in the Aurelian Walls, is the **Porta San Paolo,** the ancient *Porta Ostiensis.* To the right of the gate rises the **Pyramid of Cestius,** 37 m high, a brick structure faced with marble blocks, built about 12 B.C. as the tomb of Gaius Cestius, a member of the priestly college of the Epulones. Immediately SW, inside the Aurelian Walls, lies the *Protestant Cemetery,* or more precisely the Cimitero degli Stranieri Acattolici (entrance on the N side), the cemetery for non-Catholic foreigners, in which Keats is buried.

To the W of the cemetery is **Monte Testaccio** (from *testa,* "potsherd"), an isolated mound rising to a height of 35 m above the Tiber and about 850 m in circumference, composed entirely of fragments of the large earthenware jars in which wine and oil were shipped to Rome and discharged at a nearby quay on the banks of the Tiber. The hill is honeycombed with cellars, some of them belonging to wine-shops and taverns.

Some 500 m NE of the Porta San Paolo is the *church of San Saba* (12th–15th c.).

2 km S of the Porta San Paolo, on the *Via Ostiense,* the road to ancient Ostia and Lido di Ostia, stands the *****church of San Paolo fuori le Mura,** one of Rome's five

patriarchal churches, founded by Constantine the Great in 324 over the tomb of the Apostle Paul, rebuilt in 386 as an aisled basilica, destroyed by fire in 1823 with the exception of the choir and thereafter rebuilt on the original plan (1854). The bronze door of the main entrance is by A. Maraini (1930–31).

The *INTERIOR is imposing (120 m long, 60 m wide, 23 m high). There are double aisles on each side, separated by 80 granite columns. Rich coffered stucco ceiling, partly gilded; sumptuous marble decoration. Above the columns are portraits of all the popes from Peter to Paul VI. Beautiful mosaics (440–461, restored) on the triumphal arch and in the apse (originally 1218). Above the high altar is a Gothic *tabernacle* (1285); to the right a fine paschal candlestick (c. 1180). In the S aisle, near the entrance, is a *bronze door* of 1070, damaged in the fire but later restored.

On the S side of the church is a *cloister (probably first half of 13th c.) which belonged to a Benedictine monastery (museum); it ranks with that of the Lateran as one of the most beautiful cloisters in Rome.

Trastevere and the Janiculum

To the rear of the Theatre of Marcellus the *Ponte Fabricio*, the oldest of Rome's present-day bridges, built in 62 B.C., by which one reaches the **Tiber Island** (Isola Tiberina), with the *church of San Bartolomeo*, perhaps occupying the site of a temple of Aesculapius.

From the Tiber Island the *Ponte Cestio* leads into the densely populated district of **Trastevere**, on the right bank of the Tiber. In the time of Augustus it was a suburb of Rome (*Regio Transtiberina*), with numerous villas; later, when the Aurelian Walls were built, it was incorporated in the city proper. Later still it became the haunt of freed slaves and prostitutes. In the 19th and 20th c. it was a working-class district with a vigorous and down-to-earth character of its own; then from about 1970 a programme of slum clearance and redevelopment was begun, unfit houses being pulled down and replaced by new blocks of apartments. It is now noted for its many little restaurants; but visitors should be on their guard (pickpockets, beggars), particularly after dark.

Some 300 m S of the Ponte Cestio is the *church of Santa Cecilia in Trastevere*, which is supposed to occupy the site of a house in which the patron saint of music (martyred c. 230) lived. The church founded before 500 but much rebuilt and restored in later centuries, is preceded by a spacious court and has a 12th c. campanile. On the high altar is a beautiful tabernacle of 1283; the apse has 9th c. mosaics. In the crypt is the saint's sepulchral chapel, well restored.

Some 500 m SW of Santa Cecilia, near the Ponte Sublicio, is the *Porta Portese*, where a flea-market is held on Sunday mornings.

500 m NW of Santa Cecilia stands the **church of Santa Maria in Trastevere**, one of the oldest churches in Rome, founded in the 3rd c. and rebuilt in the 12th c., with a porch added in 1702. It has a picturesque interior, with 22 ancient columns, a richly decorated ceiling (1617) and fine 12th and 13th c. *mosaics. Close by, in Piazza Sant'Egidio, is a *Folk Museum* (Museo del Folclore Romano).

500 m N of Santa Maria, on the banks of the Tiber beyond the *Porta Settimiana*, we come to the *Villa Farnesina, a Renaissance palace surrounded by gardens which was built by B. Peruzzi in 1509–11 for the Pope's banker Agostino Chigi and decorated with * *frescoes by Raphael and other artists – scenes from the story of Amor and Psyche (1515–18) designed by Raphael and executed by his pupils, and Galatea borne over the sea in a shell, by Raphael himself (1514). From 1580 to 1731 the villa belonged to the Farnese family; it is now State-owned, and also houses the *Gabinetto Nazionale delle Stampe* (prints and engravings).

Immediately W of the villa is the **Palazzo Corsini**, occupied from 1668 to 1689 by Queen Christina of Sweden (daughter of Gustavus Adolphus, who became a Catholic) and rebuilt in 1729–32 for Cardinal Neri Corsini, with pillared courtyards and a beautiful view of the gardens. It now houses the *Biblioteca Corsiniana* and the *Accademia Nazionale dei Lincei*, which has a large library. The 17th and 18th c. pictures belonging to the Galleria Nazionale d'Arte Antica, formerly housed here, are now in the Palazzo Barberini.

From the S side of the Porta Settimiana the *Via Garibaldi* runs SW and then winds its way up the long ridge of the **Janiculum** (Monte Gianícolo), with wide views. At the foot of the ascent is the **church of San Pietro in Montorio**, an

Early Renaissance church (15th c.) founded on the spot on which, according to a medieval legend, the Apostle Peter was crucified; fine interior. In the adjoining cloister is the *Tempietto*, a small round pillared temple by Bramante (1502). From the square in front of the church a magnificent *view can be enjoyed.

Via Garibaldi then continues uphill to the *Fontana Paola*, an elaborate fountain built for Pope Paul V in 1612 by Giovanni Fontana and Carlo Maderna as the terminal point of the restored *Aqua Traiana* (aqueduct), and ends at the *Porta San Pancrazio*, on the summit of the Janiculum (84 m). To the W is the entrance to the *Villa Doria Pamphili, a large park laid out by Algardi after 1644 for Prince Camillo Pamphili; it is now municipal property and open to the public.

To the N of the Fontana Paola is a gate which marks the S entrance to the *Passeggiata del Gianicolo, a broad avenue which runs along the ridge of the Janiculum through an attractive park. In the Piazzale Garibaldi is an *equestrian statue* (by Gallori, 1895) of *Giuseppe Garibaldi* (1807–82). Beyond this, on the left, is a *monument* (1912) to his first wife *Anita Garibaldi*. Nearby is a *cannon*, usually fired at noon. Farther on, to the right, stands a marble *beacon* (erected 1911) which at night flashes its green, white and red lights over Rome. The *views of Rome and the Campagna from the Passeggiata del Gianicolo, which are particularly fine towards sunset, have a variety and beauty almost surpassing those from San Pietro in Montorio.

At the northern end of the Janiculum is the **church of Sant'Onofrio** (begun 1439), with 15th–16th c. frescoes; view. In the adjoining convent is the small *Museo Tassiano*, with relics and mementoes of the poet Torquato Tasso (1544–95), who died here.

Some 500 m S of the Porta San Pancrazio is the *Villa Sciarra*, a public park with a luxuriant growth of southern vegetation and an outlook pavilion.

Castel Sant'Angelo and the Vatican

At the end of the Corso Vittorio Emanuele II the *Ponte Vittorio Emanuele* crosses to the right bank of the Tiber a little way downstream from the Castel Sant'Angelo. Just above it the imposing *Ponte Sant'Angelo makes straight for the Castel Sant'Angelo. This bridge, for long the only road access to the Vatican from

St Peter's and the Vatican Gardens

the left bank, was originally built in A.D. 136 by the Emperor Hadrian and called the *Pons Aelius* after his family name; the three central arches are still Roman work. The ten colossal figures of angels which now adorn it were designed by Bernini and set up on the bridge in 1668.

At the end of the Ponte Sant'Angelo, rising above the right bank of the Tiber, is the *Castel Sant'Angelo or **Mausoleo di Adriano**, built by Hadrian in A.D. 130 as a mausoleum for himself and his successors and completed by Antoninus Pius in 139. From the 6th c. onwards it was used by the rulers of Rome as a fortress, and in 1379 passed into the hands of the popes. During the Middle Ages it was transformed into a defensive bridgehead, with outer works and a covered passage leading to the Vatican. Between 1870 and 1901 the building was used as a barracks and a prison; thereafter it was restored and fitted out as a *museum*.

On a square substructure measuring 84 m each way rises a huge cylinder 64 m in diameter, originally faced with marble. Visitors are shown the *tomb chambers* in which the Roman emperors down to Caracalla (d. A.D. 217) were buried, a *collection of weapons, models* illustrating the history of the structure, historical apartments, several chapels, the *treasury* and the library. From the upper terrace there is a magnificent *view. On the highest point is a *bronze statue of the Archangel Michael* (1752), recalling a vision of Pope Gregory the Great (590) to which the Castel Sant'Angelo owes its name.

To the E of the Castel Sant'Angelo is the massive **Palazzo di Giustizia** (Law Courts: by Calderini, 1910), at present in course of renovation.

From the Castel Sant'Angelo the **Via della Conciliazione**, a wide avenue laid

VATICAN CITY (*Stato della Città del Vaticano*) is the sovereign state under the Pope's authority which was established by the Lateran treaties of 11 February 1929 as a substitute for the Papal States or States of the Church which had been abolished in 1870. Under the treaties the Italian government recognised the sovereignty of the Pope in international relations and his jurisdiction over the territory of Vatican City, comprising St Peter's Church, St Peter's Square, the Vatican and the Vatican gardens, with a total area of 0·44 sq. km. The thousand or so inhabitants of Vatican City include 525 Vatican nationals, five cardinals and numerous diplomats and representatives of international organisations.

The **Pope** (at present *John Paul II*, elected 1978), supreme head of the Roman Catholic Church (over 700 million adherents), has legislative, executive and judicial powers. In external affairs he is represented by the *Cardinal Secretary of State*, while the administration (*Curia*) is headed by a *Governor* responsible only to the Pope.

The Pope's bodyguard consists only, since the abolition of the *guardia nobile*, the *guardia palatina* and the *gendarmeria* in 1970, of the

Swiss Guards (Roman Catholic citizens of Switzerland aged between 19 and 25, unmarried; minimum height 1·74 m; period of service 2–20 years), with a present strength of 90 including officers. They wear Renaissance-style uniforms in the colours of the Medici popes (yellow, red and blue).

The Vatican City has its own currency (1 Vatican lira=1 Italian lira), postal service (issuing stamps which are valid throughout Rome), telephone and telegraph services, newspapers and journals (in particular the "Osservatore Romano", with a circulation of 60,000–70,000), radio station (Radio Vaticana: transmissions on medium and short waves in some 35 languages), a fleet of 100 vehicles (registration letters SCV) and its own railway station and helicopter pad.

The Vatican flag has vertical stripes of yellow and white, with two crossed keys under the Papal tiara (triple crown) on a white ground.

Papal possessions outside Vatican City – the three basilicas of San Giovanni in Laterano, San Paolo fuori le Mura and Santa Maria Maggiore, the Papal administrative offices and the Pope's summer residence at Castel Gandolfo (see below, p. 252) – enjoy extra-territorial status and are not subject to Italian law.

The territory of Vatican City, with the exception of certain permitted areas (St Peter's, the museums, the Camposanto Teutonico, etc.), can be entered only with special permission. Vehicles are subject to a speed limit of 30 km/h. within Vatican City.

out between 1937 and 1950 and lined with large modern buildings, leads to the Vatican. Its name commemorates the reconciliation between the Italian government and the Vatican enshrined in the Lateran treaties of 1929.

HISTORY OF THE PAPAL STATES. – 4th–6th c. *The authority of the Church* is established: Pope Leo I, the Great (440–461); Pope Gregory I, the Great (590–604). – 8th c. *The Patrimonium Petri becomes the embryo of the Papal states*: efforts by the popes to make the Church's possessions independent of the Eastern Empire.

754–867 Emergence and development of the Papal states: The Frankish king Pepin, answering the Pope's appeal for help, repels the Lombards, confirms the Pope in his possession of the whole of the former Duchy of Rome, makes over to him the Exarchate of Ravenna and the territories of Rimini, Ancona and Perugia, and becomes the Protector of Rome. In 774 Charlemagne confirms the independence of the Papal states. Separation of the Greek Orthodox Church in Constantinople. – End of 9th c. to middle of 11th c. *Powerlessness of the Popes*, dependent on aristocratic factions. – About 1050 to 1200 *Efforts at reform*: Pope Leo IX (1049–54) seeks to repress simony (the buying and selling of ecclesiastical preferment); Nicholas II (1058–61) establishes the principle of the election of popes by the cardinals; Gregory VII (1073–85) sets the Church

above secular states, introduces priestly celibacy and establishes that secular rulers may not hold high ecclesiastical office. – 1076–1122 the *Investiture Conflict*: The emperor refuses to give up the right of investing ecclesiastical dignitaries with temporal authority, Henry IV persuades the German bishops to declare Pope Gregory deposed, the Pope excommunicates him and Henry is compelled to do penance at Canossa; Henry besieges the Pope in Castel Sant'Angelo (1084); the Concordat of Worms (1122) ends the conflict (German bishops to be invested with temporal authority before their ecclesiastical consecration).

1198–1216 Papal power at its peak under Pope Innocent III: recovery of lost territories, recognition of Papal possession of Spoleto.

1309–1377–1417 Schism: Pope Clement V (1305–14) is compelled by King Philip of France to move to Avignon in 1309; Gregory IX returns to Rome in 1377; Urban VI (elected 1378) remains in Rome, while 13 cardinals appoint Clement VII Pope, with his residence in Avignon (where subsequent anti-popes also reside); the Schism is ended by the Council of Constance in 1417. – 15th c. *Renaissance*: The popes consolidate their temporal authority by wars and live in great splendour (patronage of art, much building activity). Pope Nicholas V (1447–55) founds the Vatican Library. Sixtus IV (1471–84) builds the Sistine Chapel. Alexander VI Borgia reigns with a total lack of scruple. Leo IX establishes the trade in indulgences as a source of income (1514–16). Charles V's troops occupy and plunder Rome. – 16th

Swiss Guards in St Peter's Square

surmounted by balustrades with 140 colossal *statues of saints*. In the centre of the square is an Egyptian *obelisk* 25·5 m high hewn in the reign of Caligula (A.D. 37–41) and set up here in 1586; it had previously stood in Nero's Circus, where many Christians suffered martyrdom during the persecutions of A.D. 65. On either side of the obelisk are two handsome *fountains* 14 m high (1613, 1675).

On the W side of the central oval is a narrower forecourt, with a fine *staircase* leading up to the portico of St Peter's. On the S side of this forecourt are the *Vatican Information Office* (Ufficio Informazioni Pellegrini e Turisti: bus tours of Vatican museums) and a *post office* (Ufficio Postale: sale of Vatican City stamps). To the rear, farther S, is the large **Audience Hall** (*Aula*: entrance beside Palazzo del Santo Uffizio), built by P. L. Nervi (1964–71), with seating for 6300 or standing room for up to 12,000 (for admission to Papal audiences see above, p. 223). – To the left of St Peter's Church is the *Arco delle Campane*, the entrance to Vatican City (Swiss guards).

The W side of St Peter's Square is occupied by * *St Peter's Church (*San Pietro in Vaticano*), on the site of an Early Christian basilica.

and 17th c. *Counter-Reformation*; *the Baroque period*: Internal renewal of the Church; Theatine order founded 1524; Council of Trent (1545–63); the Jesuits (approved by the Pope in 1540) increase their activity; Pope Gregory XIII reforms the calendar; magnificent Baroque buildings in Rome; Ferrara and Urbino are incorporated in the Papal states. – 18th c. *Political impotence of the Popes*. Rome attracts large numbers of artists and art-lovers. – 1796–1815 *Napoleonic period*: The Papal State is compelled to cede some of its territory; Napoleon annexes the rest (1809) and holds Pope Pius VII prisoner. The Congress of Vienna (1814–15) re-establishes the Papal States.

1815–70 Dissolution of the Papal States: A rising in the N is repressed (1831); the Pope refuses to take part in the war against Austria (1848), whereupon French troops occupy Rome, remaining there until 1870. After 1859 the northern parts of the Papal States join the new kingdom of Italy, only the area round Rome remaining under the Pope's authority. – 1870–1929 *The Pope possesses no territory of his own*: Italian troops occupy Rome in 1870, and the rest of the Papal state is incorporated in the kingdom of Italy; the Pope becomes a prisoner in the Vatican.

1929 Establishment of the state of Vatican City: The Lateran Treaties (11 February 1929) regulate relationships between the Holy See and the Italian state. Italy recognises the sovereignty of the Pope in international relations and the Vatican City as his exclusive territory; Papal possesions outside the Vatican are granted extra-territorial status.

The Via della Conciliazione runs W from the Castel Sant'Angelo to end in * *St Peter's Square (*Piazza di San Pietro*: closed to vehicles), a magnificent creation by Bernini (1656–67), 340 m long, up to 250 m wide, which enhances the effect of the most imposing church in Christendom. On either side are semicircular *colonnades*, formed by 284 columns and 88 pillars of the Doric order in four rows,

The original church was built by Constantine the Great at the request of Pope Sylvester I (314–336) over the tomb of the Apostle Peter, beside Nero's Circus, and consecrated in 326. It was a basilica with double aisles and a pillared forecourt, later enlarged and surrounded by chapels and convents. At Christmas in the year 800 Charlemagne received the Roman imperial crown from the hands of Pope Leo III in front of the high altar, and many emperors were subsequently crowned here. In the course of time the church fell into a state of dilapidation and was demolished and replaced by the present building, begun by Bramante in 1506 in the reign of Pope Julius II. The new church was conceived by Bramante in the form of a Greek cross (i.e. with arms of equal length) with a central dome. After his death in 1514 the work was directed by Raphael (1515–20), Antonio da Sangallo (1520–46) and other masters, and finally (1547) by Michelangelo, who designed the mighty **dome**, 132 m high (1586–93). In 1605 the centralised plan favoured by Bramante and Michelangelo was replaced by a Latin-cross plan with a nave. The nave and the **Baroque façade** (completed 1614: 112 m wide, 44 m high) were the work of Carlo Maderna. The effect of the dome as conceived by Michelangelo is thus entirely lost except from a distance. From the loggia above the central doorway the Pope gives his benediction "urbi et orbi" (to the city and the world) on solemn occasions (Easter, Christmas); in addition he usually gives a benediction on Sundays at 12 noon, often with a short address, from a window in the Papal residence (to the right).

The **portico** of St Peter's is 71 m long, 13·5 m deep and 20 m high. The bronze doors of the large **central doorway** were the work of Antonio Filarete (1433–45). The door on the left (1964) has bronze reliefs by Manzù (life of John XXIII, etc.). The door on the right (the Seven Sacraments) is by Messina (1965). To the right of this is the *Porta Santa*, which is opened in Holy Years (first proclaimed by Pope Boniface VIII in 1300; every 25 years, most recently 1975; plenary indulgence for all pilgrims to Rome).

The ****INTERIOR** (approriate dress required) is of overwhelming effect, with its huge dimensions (186 m long, with space for a congregation of 60,000). The effect is increased as the visitor realises the beauty of the individual features and the symmetry and harmony of the proportions. In the pavement, beginning at the central doorway, are marked the lengths of other great cathedrals: St Paul's, London, 158·1 m, Florence 149·28 m, Rheims 138·69 m, Milan and Cologne 134·94 (Milan actually 148 m), San Petronio, Bologna, 132·54 m, Seville and Notre-Dame, Paris, 130 m, etc. The total length of St Peter's including the portico, is 211·5 m, its width 114·7 m (across the transepts 152 m), its area 15,160 sq. m (Milan 11,700, St Paul's 7875, St Sophia in Istanbul 6890, Berlin Cathedral 6270, Cologne 6166 sq. m).

In the **nave** (in which the 2nd Vatican Council met in 1962–65) is a seated *figure of St Peter* in bronze (4th pillar on right), probably dating from the 13th c., whose right foot has been worn smooth by the kisses of the faithful. The huge *dome* which soars above the Papal altar and the crypt containing the tomb of St Peter has a diameter of 42 m and an internal height of 123·4 m (external height including cross 132·5 m). It is borne on four huge piers, each with a circumference of 71 m.

St Peter's Church
San Pietro in Vaticano

75 m

St Peter's Square

1 Principal entrance
2 Porta Santa
3 Michelangelo's Pietà
4 Monument to Christina of Sweden
5 St Sebastian's Chapel
6 Chapel of the Sacrament
7 Gregorian Chapel
8 Altar of St Jerome
9 Statue of St Peter
10 Altar of the Archangel Michael
11. Altar of St Peter (restoring Tabitha to life)
12 Tomb of Pope Urban VIII
13 Throne of St Peter (by Bernini)
14 Tomb of Pope Paul III
15 Chapel of the Column
16 Altar of St Peter (healing the lame man)
17 Altar of the Crucifixion of St Peter
18 Statue of St Andrew; entrance to Sacre Grotte Vaticane
19 Tomb of Pope Pius VII; entrance to Sacristy and Museum
20 Clementine Chapel
21 Altar of St Gregory
22 Choir Chapel
23 Tomb of Pope Pius X
24 Tomb of Pope Innocent VII
25 Monument to Maria Clementina Sobieska; entrance to dome
26 Baptistery
27 Sacristy
28 Museo Storico-Artistico (Tesoro)
29 Canons' Sacristy

Above the **Papal altar** is a bronze *canopy or *baldacchino*, 29 m high, with four richly gilded spiral columns and a fantastic superstructure (by Bernini, 1633). In front of the altar, enclosed by a balustrade with 95 sanctuary lamps which are always lit, is the *confessio*, a devotional area over St Peter's tomb, to which a double marble staircase leads down (at the foot a statue of Pope Pius VI in prayer, by Canova, 1822). The nave ends beyond the central domed area in the apse.

In the first chapel in the S aisle, protected by a glass screen, is Michelangelo's *Pietà (photograph, p. 36), a profoundly sensitive work created by the young Michelangelo at the age of 25 (1499; damaged by a vandal in 1972, skilfully restored 1973). Throughout the church are numerous *Papal tombs, some of them of great magnificence; particularly impressive are those of Urban VIII and Paul III (both in the apse) and Innocent VIII (2nd pillar on left).

From the N aisle we enter the *Sacristy* (1776–84) and the interesting **Museo Storico-Artistico** or *Tesoro di San Pietro* (Treasury of St Peter): a cross which belonged to Emperor Justin II (d. 578), sarcophagi of the consul Iunius Bassus (d. 359) and Pope Sixtus IV (d. 1484).

Also in the N aisle (ticket office beyond the first chapel) is the entrance to the *dome (steps or lift to roof), then easy steps to the galleries round the dome (at heights of 53 m and 73 m), from which there are astonishing views of the interior of the church. On the inner wall of the dome is a frieze 2 m high with the inscription, in blue mosaic letters on a gold ground, "Tu es Petrus et super hanc petram aedidicabo ecclesiam meam et tibi dabo claves regni caelorum" ("Thou art Peter, and upon this rock I will build my church . . . . And I will give unto thee the keys of the kingdom of heaven": Matt. 16, 18–19). From the colonnade on the lantern of the dome (123·5 m above floor level) there are far-ranging views and glimpses of the Vatican Gardens.

From the space under the dome (SE pier) a staircase leads down to the interesting **Sacre Grotte Vaticane** or *Crypt*, lying between the floor of the present church and that of the original basilica, 3·5 m below. The 16th c. chambers, beneath the dome, contain numerous *monuments* from the old basilica, together with the plain stone sarcophagi of Pius XII (d. 1958), John XXIII (d. 1963), Paul VI (d. 1978) and John Paul I (d. 1978). In the older parts, under the nave, are numerous *Papal tombs* and Early Christian *sarcophagi*.

Under the Sacre Grotte Vaticane are the new excavations (mostly carried out since the end of the last war) of the *Necropoli Precostantiniana*, which led to the discovery, under the *confessio*, of the **tomb of St Peter**, as indicated by inscriptions found nearby.

To the right of St Peter's, occupying an area of some 55,000 sq. m, stands the ***Vatican Palace**, originally begun in the 6th c. but the Pope's permanent residence only since the 14th c., when it replaced the Lateran, and much enlarged and altered since then. The rooms in which the Pope lives and works are on the upper floors of the square building on the right-hand side of St Peter's Square. Among the principal features of the palace are the Stanze, the Sistine Chapel, the Logge di Raffaello, the former Garden-House or Belvedere, the Vatican Library and the Vatican collections, with major works of ancient art and valuable pictures. Altogether there are some 1400 rooms, chapels and other apartments.

The *Portone di Bronzo* (Swiss guard: access only to office which issues tickets for Papal audiences, see p. 223), at the end of the right-hand colonnade in St Peter's Square, is the entrance to the Papal apartments, which form only a small part of the whole palace. The corridor straight ahead leads to the *Scala Regia*, remodelled by Bernini in 1663–66. In spite of the limited space, which contracts towards the top, an imposing effect was achieved by the skilful arrangement of the columns and decoration. To the right is the *Scala di Pio IX* (19th c.), leading to the Cortile di San Dámaso.

The *entrance to the State apartments* – i.e. to the museums, the Library, the Borgia apartments, the Stanze, the Sistine Chapel, etc. – is on the N side of the palace, 800 m from St Peter's Square. There are regular bus services from spring to autumn to and from the Information Office, going through the Vatican Gardens (recommended; departure from upper entrance to museums). Pedestrians should go N along Via di Porta Angelica to the Piazza del Risorgimento, then W along the Vatican walls and round the bastion on Via Leone IV into Viale Vaticano.

From the entrance to the ****Vatican Museums**, with statues of Raphael and Michelangelo, visitors make their way up on a curving staircase or by lift to the *vestibule* (ticket-offices, information, sales counters, cloakroom, lavatories, etc.). The tour is for the most part a one-way route marked by coloured arrows, with video-electronic surveillance (total length 7 km). Half way round there is an exit at the Sistine Chapel (no admission).

From the vestibule we go E (left) through the *Atrio dei Quattro Cancelli* (before which, downstairs, is a self-service restaurant) and up the Scala Simonetti to reach the Vatican ****collection of antiquities**, the largest in the world, with several thousand pieces of sculpture. The origins of the collection go back to the Renaissance period, when it was housed in the Belvedere (built 1486–92); the collection as we see it today, however, really began in the time of Clement

XIV (1769–74). The main part of the collection, the Museo Pio-Clementino, is named after him and his successor Pius VI, who continued to extend it. Pius VII added the Museo Chiaramonti and the Braccio Nuovo, Gregory XVI (1831–46) the Egyptian and Etruscan museums. Most of the items were found in and around Rome, and the enormous quantity of sculpture to be seen here and in the other museums in Rome gives some idea of the extraordinary wealth of art in the public buildings and private houses of ancient Rome and bears witness to the Roman interest in the culture of Greece. There are very few Greek originals, but numerous copies of famous works of art, made by either Greek or Roman sculptors, as well as specifically Roman works of art, have survived into modern times, often little the worse for their burial under the accumulated rubbish of the centuries. Although the restorations and retouching practised in the past may sometimes give an erroneous impression, here as nowhere else we can get a general impression of the whole range of ancient creative art.

We come first to the **Museo Pio-Clementino**. – In the first room, the *Sala a Croce Greca*, are the porphyry sarcophagi of St Helena and Constantia, mother and daughter of Constantine the Great (4th c. A.D.). – Beyond this is the *Sala Rotonda*, with a fine bust of Zeus from Otrícoli (4th c. B.C.). – Then comes the *Sala delle Muse*, which in addition to statues of the Muses contains the famous *Belvedere Torso, a seated figure of a powerfully muscled man (by Apollonius of Athens, 1st c. B.C.), and a series of portrait herms. – The next room is the *Sala degli Animali*, with many figures of animals in white and coloured marble, many of them much restored. – To the left is the *Galleria delle Statue*, with the Apollo Sauroctonus (the Lizard-Killer), a copy of the 4th c. B.C. Beyond this is the *Sala dei Busti*, and to the left the little *Gabinetto delle Maschere*, with the famous *Venus of Cnidos, an imitation of the Cnidian Aphrodite of Praxiteles. We now return into the Sala degli Animali and turn left into the *Cortile Ottagono*, originally the courtyard of the Belvedere. In the first little room on the right is the famous group of **Laocoön and his two sons being killed by two snakes, a late Hellenistic work (1st c. B.C.–1st c. A.D.) by Agesandrus, Polydorus and Athenodorus of Rhodes (restored 1957–60). In the second little corner room is the **Apollo Belvedere, after a bronze original of the 4th c. B.C. – In the vestibule of the Belvedere, on the E side of the Cortile Ottagono, is the **Apoxyomenus, a youth scraping the oil and dust of the palaestra from his arm with a strigil, a Roman copy of the original by Lysippus (4th c. B.C.). – Beyond this is the **Museo Chiaramonti**, a corridor some 100 m long, mostly containing Roman copies of Greek sculpture. In the adjoining *Galleria Lapidaria* (shut off by a grating: admission by special arrangement) are some 5000 inscriptions.

Adjoining the S side of the Museo Pio-Clementino the **Egyptian Museum** (*Museo Gregoriano Egizio*) consists of ten rooms containing Egyptian sculpture, mostly found in and around Rome (principally booty brought back from Egypt in the Imperial period), mummies, papyri, etc.

On the floor above (reached by way of the "Staircase of the Assyrian Reliefs" from the Sale a Croce Greca) we come to the very interesting **Etruscan Museum** (*Museo Gregoriano Etrusco*), with 18 rooms containing Etruscan antiquities recovered by excavation or received by gift (sarcophagi, ornaments and other small items) and a collection of Greek vases.

In the W wing of the upper floor (to the right of the Assyrian Staircase) is the Sala della Biga, a circular domed hall with a view of the Vatican Gardens, with the two-horse chariot (biga) from which the room takes its name (only the body of the chariot and part of the right-hand horse are ancient) and two *Discus-Throwers, one of them after an original by Myron (5th c. B.C.: head modern).

In the corridor to the S are the Galleria dei Candelabri, the Galleria degli Arazzi (tapestries of the 16th–18th c.) and the Galleria delle Carte Geografiche, with maps and views of towns painted on the walls (1580–83). At the end of the corridor is the Chapel of Pius V (tapestries, fine decoration).

In the S wing of the upper floor, above the Appartamento Borgia, are the **Stanze di Raffaello** (tape-recorded guide), a suite of three rooms and a larger hall, the private apartments of Pope Julius II, with paintings by the 25-year-old Raphael, his teacher Perugino and his pupils (1509–20). The finest paintings are, in the *Stanza dell'Incendio del Borgo, the "Fire in the Borgo" (showing the original St Peter's Church); in the **Stanza della Segnatura, the most famous of the rooms, named after the Papal court (the Segnatura di Grazia) which met here weekly, the "Disputa" (the glorification of the Christian faith) and "The School of Athens" (an assembly of scholars, with Plato and Aristotle in the middle); in the *Stanza d'Eliodoro "Heliodorus driven out of the Temple in Jerusalem by a Heavenly Horseman" and "The Mass of Bolsena" (see p. 138); and in the Sala di Costantino frescoes by Giulio Romano and others, some of them based on sketches by Raphael.

From the Sala di Costantino we go diagonally across the Sala dei Palafrenieri which adjoins it on the S into the *Chapel of Nicholas V, with frescoes by Fra Angelico (scenes from the lives of SS. Lawrence and Stephen, 1447–50).

Returning across the Sala dei Palafrenieri, we enter the *Loggias around the Cortile di San Damaso, traditionally known as the Logge di Raffaello, the W wing of which has stucco decoration and ceiling paintings of Biblical scenes ("Raphael's Bible") by pupils of Raphael, including Giovanni da Udine (1517–19).

From the Loggias we go down the staircase in the Borgia Tower to the *Appartamento Borgia at the S end of the ground floor: six rooms occupied by Pope Alexander VI Borgia with brilliantly coloured wall paintings executed under the direction of Pinturicchio (1492–95). Particularly fine is the fourth room, the Sala della Vita dei Santi. Here is housed part of the *Museum of Modern Religious Art (Collezione d'Arte Religiosa Moderna, established 1973), most of which is accommodated in 55 rooms under the Sistine Chapel (works by Barlach, Rodin, Klee, Dix, Picasso, Chagall, Dalí, Moore, de Pisis, etc.).

We now come to the **Sistine Chapel (Cappella Sistina), the Papal domestic chapel, built in 1474–81, in the reign of Sixtus IV, and the meeting-place of the Conclave which elects a new Pope. The chapel (40·5 by 13·2 m and over 20 m high: tape-recorded guide) owes its fame to the magnificent frescoes which cover its walls and ceiling. The *paintings on the upper part of the side walls (Old Testament scenes on one side, New Testament scenes on the other) were the work of the best Florentine and Umbrian painters of the day –

Perugino, Pinturicchio, Botticelli, Ghirlandaio, Roselli, Signorelli (1481–83, restored 1965–74). The *ceiling paintings by Michelangelo (1508–12), ranking among the most powerful master-works of world art, depict the story of the Creation, the Fall and its consequences, with the superhuman figures of seven prophets and five sibyls at the foot of the vaulting. Almost 30 years later (1534–41) Michelangelo painted the huge fresco of the *Last Judgment on the altar wall, with more than a hundred figures depicted with lively vigour.

At the Sistine Chapel there is an exit from the Vatican (no readmission).

From the Sistine Chapel we continue N into the *Vatican Library (Biblioteca Apostólica Vaticana), founded by Pope Nicholas V about 1450, which now contains some 800,000 books, 80,000 manuscripts, 10,000 incunabula and over 100,000 engravings and woodcuts. At the S end of the Library is the Museo Sacro, with material excavated in the catacombs, reliquaries, carved ivories, glass, enamel-work and textiles.

In the Sala delle Nozze Aldobrandine are ancient paintings, including scenes from the "Odyssey" and the *Aldobrandini Marriage, one of the finest surviving ancient pictures, probably an Augustan copy of a Greek original of the 4th c. B.C. – From the Museo Sacro we continue through the Library's exhibition rooms (frescoes, decorative art).

We then come to the more southerly of the two cross-wings, in which is the *Salone Sistino, originally the main library hall, with items of particular importance in glass cases. Beyond this is the N cross-wing, the Braccio Nuovo ("new arm"), a hall 70 m long containing numerous statues. Notable among them are a statue of *Augustus found at Prima Porta, the finest figure of Augustus we have; a colossal group representing the Nile surrounded by 16 playing children (symbolising the 16 cubits which the river rises when in flood); and a *Doryphorus (Spear-Bearer) after Polycletus. – From here we continue through a series of frescoed rooms belonging to the Library to the Museo Profano (ancient small sculpture, etc.), which we leave at the Atrio dei Quattro Cancelli.

Associated with the Library are the famous **Secret Archives of the Vatican**, with a school of palaeography and diplomatics.

Near the entrance to the museums, under the Cortile della Pinacoteca (to the left), is a self-service restaurant and snack bar (posto di ristoro).

From the Cortile della Pinacoteca we reach the **Picture Gallery (Pinacoteca Vaticana), in a building erected in 1927–32, with 15 rooms which give an excellent survey of Italian painting from the 13th to the 17th c. Room I: Byzantine and early Italian paintings. Room II: Giotto and his school. Room III: Fra Filippo Lippi, Fra Angelico, Benozzo Gozzoli, etc. Room IV: frescoes by Melozzo da Forlì (heads of Apostles, angel musicians, the foundation of the Vatican Library), etc. Rooms V and VI: Francesco del Cossa, Lucas Cranach the Elder, Crivelli, Giotto. Room VII: Perugino and Umbrian painters of the 15th c. Room VIII: Raphael, with the chief treasures of the collection – his "Madonna of Foligno" (1512: in the background the town of Foligno), "Transfiguration" (1517–20, his last great work; restored 1972–76) and ten tapestries (arazzi) of scenes from the lives of the

Apostles (woven in Brussels 1516–19 from cartoons by Raphael). Room IX: pictures by various 16th c. masters including Leonardo da Vinci. Room X: Titian ("Madonna in Glory"), Caravaggio, Guido Reni, Fra Bartolomeo and Veronese. Room XI: Renaissance and Baroque masters. Room XII: 17th c. (Baroque). Rooms XIII and XIV: 17th and 18th c. pictures. Room XV: portraits. Rooms XVI–XVIII: contemporary painting.

A new building (1970) parallel to the Pinacoteca on the N houses the former Lateran museums. The *Museo Gregoriano Profano contains some outstanding Greek and Roman sculpture, either in the original or in copies, and ancient sarcophagi. In the second side room on the right is a figure of *Niobe which may be an original from a group by the school of Scopas (4th c. B.C.). The Museo Pio Cristiano has Early Christian sarcophagi (mostly 4th–5th c.), sculpture and inscriptions. The Museo Missionario Etnologico (on the lower floor) gives an excellent survey of the missionary activities of the Roman Catholic church and the ethnology, prehistory and natural history of the mission lands.

From here a passage leads to the Museo Storico (Historical Museum, opened 1973), situated underground to the S of the Pinacoteca, which contains vehicles and relics of the military forces of the former Papal States.

To the S of the Arco delle Campane (the main visitors' entrance to Vatican City, to the left of St Peter's) is the Camposanto Teutonico, the old German cemetery. The church, originally 15th c., was restored in 1973. To the rear is the large new Audience Hall.

Another gateway, between St Peter's and the Sacristy, leads into the Piazza di Santa Maria. Here, straight ahead, is the Tribunale, the Vatican law court, with the School of Mosaic Art beyond it. To the right is the Governor's Palace. S of the Mosaic School is the Vatican railway station; W of the Governor's Palace is the Ethiopian College, and to the NW the Papal radio station, Radio Vaticana.

On higher ground to the N of St Peter's is the elegant Casina Pio IV, built by Pius IV in 1558–62, which now houses the Pontifical Academy of Sciences.

The beautiful *Vatican Gardens, laid out in the 16th c., can be seen only in certain particular circumstances (for example on bus trips to the Vatican museums). At the W end of the gardens is a helicopter pad (eliporto).

On the N side of St Peter's Square, between Via di Porta Angelica (from which there is an entrance to Vatican City, at the church of Sant'Anna; Swiss guard; on left, barracks of the Swiss Guards), the Piazza del Risorgimento and the Vatican museums are the Vatican Bank, a post office (open to the public), the Head Post Office (admission only for despatching telegrams), a medical centre, a shopping centre, the Vatican printing works, the offices of the "Osservatore Romano", a central heating station and a vehicle depot – all within Vatican City.

From the Vatican to the Foro Italico

From the Piazza del Risorgimento a broad traffic artery, beginning with Via Ottaviano, runs N to the Piazza Maresciallo Giardino, from which Via di Villa Madama continues NW to Villa Madama, on the eastern slopes of Monte Mario. The villa (admission only with the permission of the Foreign Ministry) was built by Giulio Romano in 1516–27 from designs by Raphael, but only a small part was completed; it has a loggia with charming stucco and fresco decoration by Giovanni da Udine.

On Monte Mario (139 m), the Italian zero meridian (marked by the Torre del Primo Meridiano), are a public park (view) and an observatory. On the SE slopes are the headquarters of the Italian radio and television corporation RAI (Radiotelevisione Italiana). Higher up, to the W, is the church of the Madonna del Rosario, with a fine viewpoint. Farther S is the large Hotel Cavalieri Hilton.

From the Piazza Maresciallo Giardino the Lungotévere Maresciallo Cadorna runs alongside the Tiber to the Piazza De Bosis, where the Ponte Duca d'Aosta (1939) provides a link with the Via Flaminia. On the W side of the square, marked by a monolith 17 m high, is the entrance to the *Foro Italico or Campo della Farnesina, a sports centre built shortly before and after the Second World War in which the principal events in the 1960 Summer Olympic Games were held. Notable features of the centre are the Stadio dei Marmi, surrounded by 60 statues of athletes in Carrara marble, the Stadio Olimpico (1953), with seating for 100,000 spectators, the Piscina Coperta (an enclosed swimming pool) and the Stadio del Nuoto (Swimming Stadium). On the N side of the complex is the Ministry of Foreign Affairs (Ministero degli Affari Esteri). Higher up, on the slopes of the Monti della Farnesina, is the French Military Cemetery (*view).

Esposizione Universale di Roma (EUR)

On the southern outskirts of the city, some 7 km from the Piazza Venezia on the road to Lido di Ostia and Anzio, straddling the Via Cristoforo Colombo, is the extensive area (1038 acres, well provided with open spaces) of the *Esposizione Universale di Roma, or EUR for short (Metropolitana from Termini Station). This was the site selected for a great international exhibition to be held in 1942, and numbers of grandiose buildings were erected, most of them completed only after the war and now occupied by government departments, offices of various kinds and museums; there is also a residential area. The sports facilities in this area were provided for the 1960 Olympics (see above, Foro Italico).

At the NW corner of the area, near the Magliana Metro station, is the striking Palazzo della Civiltà del Lavoro, 68 m high. Some distance SW is the large domed church of Santi Pietro e Paolo.

From the Palazzo della Civiltà the broad Viale della Civiltà del Lavoro runs E to the Palazzo dei Congressi, to the NE of which is a large amusement park (giant wheel, etc.).

100 m W of the Palazzo dei Congressi, in Piazza Marconi, we find the *Museo Nazionale delle Arti e Tradizioni Populari, with departments of folk art and folk traditions. – 200 m S is the Museo Preistorico ed Etnografico Luigi Pigorini, with material illustrating the prehistory of Latium and ethnographical collections from Ethiopia, Oceania, South America and other countries. To the E of this museum is the Museo dell'Alto Medioevo (Museum of the Early Medieval Period). Farther E again is the *Museo della Civiltà Romana, an impressive collection of material illustrating the development and the greatness of the Roman Empire; a particularly notable feature is the model of Rome as it was in the 4th c. A.D. (Room 37). – Some 5000 m NE, on the spot where St Peter is supposed to have been beheaded, is

the Trappist Abbazia delle Tre Fontane (Abbey of the Three Fountains), with three churches (13th and 16th c.).

On the N side of the EUR is situated the large Centro Sportivo delle Tre Fontane; to the S, on higher ground beyond an ornamental lake, the circular Palazzo dello Sport (1960), with seating for 15,000 spectators, and 750 m W of this is the Velodromo Olimpico (1960), a cycle-racing track.

8 km S of the EUR, on S.S. 148 near Castel de Décima, a large Latin cemetery of the 9th–7th c. B.C. was discovered in 1974 (princely graves with rich burial goods).

SURROUNDINGS OF ROME
The Via Appia Antica and the Catacombs. – A trip along the *Via Appia Antica, starting from the Porta San Sebastiano, offers both archaeological interest and beautiful scenery. It is planned to establish an "archaeological park" here. The road, constructed by the censor Appius Claudius Caecus about 312 B.C., originally ran from Rome via Terracina to Capua and was later extended to Benevento and Brindisi. Alongside the road can be seen the remains of the rows of tombs which in accordance with Roman custom lined the roads outside the city, together with the well-preserved or restored individual tombs of wealthy Romans, which combine with the huge arches of Roman aqueducts such as the Aqua Marcia and the Aqua Claudia, at varying distances from the road, to make up the particular charm of the Roman Campagna. – At Via Appia Antica 136 is the Museo Archeologico Sacro e Profano.

Some 800 m from the Porta San Sebastiano, on the left of the road at the point where the Via Ardeatina branches off on the right, is the little church of Domine Quo Vadis, so named from the legend that Peter, fleeing from Rome to escape martyrdom, met Christ here and asked "Domine, quo vadis?" ("Master, where are you going?") and received the answer "Venio iterum crucifigi" ("I come to be crucified a second time"); whereupon Peter, ashamed of his weakness, returned to Rome. In the church is a copy of Christ's footprint. – 1 km farther on, at a clump of cypresses on the right (Via Appia Antica 110), is the entrance to the *Catacombs of St Calixtus (Catacombe di San Callisto), the most interesting of these Early Christian underground burial-places which encircle Rome.

The *catacombs were originally the officially recognised burial-places of both Christians and pagans, known by the Greek name of coemeteria ("places of rest"). Until the early 9th c. the cemeteries containing the remains of martyrs were much venerated, and many relics were removed and deposited in churches. Thereafter the cemeteries were abandoned and neglected, and even their old name was forgotten. The present name is derived from a burial-place of this kind at a spot called Catacumba, near San Sebastiano. The scientific exploration of the catacombs began at the end of the 16th c. Recent research has shown that the catacombs were used only for burial and for Masses for the dead, not as places of refuge for persecuted Christians or for ordinary religious services. The arrangement of the catacombs is very simple – narrow passages with long recesses, hewn from the walls in several tiers, for the reception of bodies, the individual recesses being closed by tablets of marble or terracotta. Non-Christian burials had smaller niches for the reception of ash-urns. The style of decoration (painting, more rarely sculpture) reflects that of the pagan art of the period. The decorative themes are mainly symbolic – the sacrificial lamb, the fish (Greek *ichthys*, which consists of the initial letters of the Greek phrase "Jesus Christ, Son of God, Saviour"). There are also early representations of the Last Supper and the Virgin Mary. The older inscriptions give only the name of the dead person.

Notable features of the Catacombs of St Calixtus, which extend over a considerable area on several levels, are the *Cubiculum Pontificium*, containing the tombs of a number of 3rd c. popes (Urban I, Pontianus, Anterus, Fabianus, Lucius, Eutychianus); the empty *tomb of St Cecilia*; the *tomb chamber of Pope Eusebius* (309–311); and the *tomb of Pope Cornelius* (251–253), in what was originally the separate *Cemetery of Lucina*.

A short distance beyond the Catacombs of St Calixtus, near the point where the Via Appia Pignatelli branches off the Via Appia Antica on the left, is the *Catacomb of St Praetextatus* (martyred in the time of Diocletian), with the tomb chamber of the 2nd c. martyr Januarius. (Admission only by special arrangement.)

500 m from the Catacombs of St Calixtus, on the right of the Via Appia Antica, is the **church of San Sebastiano**, one of Rome's seven pilgrimage churches, built in the 4th c. on a spot thought to have been the temporary resting-place ("Ad Catacumbas") of the bodies of the Apostles Peter and Paul. The church was rebuilt in the 17th c. with a portico of ancient columns. In the first chapel on the right is a stone with what is believed to be the footprint of Christ. On the left are St Sebastian's Chapel, the sacristy and the entrance to the impressive **Catacombs of St Sebastian**. Under the centre of the church is an assembly room (*triclia*) for memorial services, with numerous inscriptions dating from the turn of the 2nd–3rd c. scratched on the walls. The invocations to the Apostles Peter and Paul seem to confirm the tradition that during the Valerian persecution in the year 258 the remains of the two Apostles were brought here or hereabouts from the Vatican and the Via Ostiense for safety. There are also tomb chambers on several levels dating from the 1st c., with good paintings, stucco decoration and inscriptions. Behind the apse of the church steps lead down to the Platonia, with the tomb of the martyr Quirinus. To the left of this is a cell with the inscription "Domus Petri" and 4th c. wall paintings.

Just before San Sebastiano the Vicolo delle Sette Chiese branches off the Via Appia Antica on the right. 650 m along this are the **Fosse Ardeatine**, with a mausoleum commemorating the 335 Italians who were shot here by the Germans in March 1944 in reprisal for a bomb attack. – 300 m farther on are the extensive *Catacombs of Domitilla*, with Early Christian inscriptions and wall paintings, and the 4th c. *Basilica of St Petronilla* (restored in the 19th c.).

Continuing along the Via Appia, we come to a large gateway on the left, near which is the *Circus of Maxentius*, constructed in A.D. 311, which was used for chariot races (482 m long, 79 m across). – Just beyond this, also on the left, is the *Tomb of Caecilia Metella, the best-known ruin in the Campagna, a circular structure 20 m in diameter faced with travertine, with a marble frieze adorned with wreaths of flowers and ox-skulls. In the 13th c. it was

used as a fortified tower by the Caetani family and equipped with battlements. – Beyond this point the original paving of the Via Appia is visible in several places. The road runs SE, with beautiful views of the Alban Hills straight ahead and the arches of the Aqua Marcia and Aqua Claudia on the left. On both sides are the remains of numerous tombs, including two tumuli from which there are extensive views of the Campagna. – Some 2·5 km beyond the Tomb of Caecilia Metella, near the farm of Santa Maria Nuova, are the extensive remains of a large villa of the time of Hadrian, the *Villa dei Quintili* or *Roma Vecchia*. – 1·25 km farther on, at *Casale Rotondo*, is a large tomb of the 1st c. A.D.

To Frascati and through the Alban Hills to Albano (33 km). – Leave Rome by way of Porta San Giovanni and the Via Appia Nuova, and very shortly turn left into the Via Tuscolana (S.S. 215). – 10 km: **Cinecittà**, a large complex of film studios which produces most Italian films. – 1 km: road on right (10 km) to **Grottaferrata** (alt. 329 m; pop. 12,000; hotels: Villa Fiorio, I, 37 b., SP; Villa Ferrata, II, 100 b., SP; Imperatore Traiano, II, 58 b., SP, with annexe, III, 153 b.; etc.), a little town in the Alban Hills, with a fortress-like monastery of Greek Basilian monks and an old church, almost entirely rebuilt in 1754; in the chapel of St Nilus in the S aisle are fine frescoes by Domenichino (1609–10). – 10 km: **Frascati** (see p. 121).

3 km beyond Frascati on the road to Albano one reaches the *Ponte Squarciarelli*, where roads go off on the right to Grottaferrata (2 km) and on the left to Rocca di Papa and Monte Cavo (11 km). – 3 km: **Marino** (alt. 355 m; pop. 20,000), picturesquely situated on a spur of the Alban Hills. – 1 km farther on an attractive scenic road, the *Via dei Laghi* (17 km), branches off on the left, runs high above the Lago Albano and comes in 9 km to a side road (on right, 2 km) to the village of *Nemi* (alt. 521 m; hotels: Al Rifugio, III, 57 b.; Al Bosco, III, 37 b.; etc.), above the *Lago di Nemi* (alt. 318 m; area 1·7 sq. km, perimeter 5·5 km, greatest depth 34 m), a crater lake surrounded by tufa cliffs 200 m high. In the village is the Museo delle Navi Romane, with reduced scale models of the two State galleys of the Emperor Caligula which were discovered during drainage of the lake in 1928–31 and were burned by German forces in 1944. The road then continues through wooded country to *Velletri*. – The *Lago Albano* (alt. 293 m; perimeter 10 km, greatest depth 170 m), above which lay the Latin federal capital of *Alba Longa*, destroyed at an early stage by the Romans, is, like Lake Nemi, of volcanic origin, and is drained by an ancient tunnel (*emissario*: guided visit) said to have been constructed by the Romans in 396 B.C. – The road to Albano continues beyond the turn-off of the Via dei Laghi, running high above the W side of the Lago Albano. – 3 km: **Castel Gandolfo** (alt. 426 m; pop. 5000; Hotel Mirador, IV, 18 b.; etc), the summer residence of the Pope, beautifully situated above the Lago Albano. In the centre of the little town is the Piazza del Plebiscito, with the parish church of San Tommaso (by Bernini, 1661), built on a centralised plan, and the Pope's Summer Palace (by Carlo Maderna, 1629), which along with the adjacent Villa Barberini was made part of the Vatican City State in 1929. Here too is the Papal observatory (established 1578; in the Vatican until 1935). In the grounds of the palace is an audience hall, with one wall entirely of glass, which can accommodate 8000 people. From Castel Gandolfo there is a funicular down to the lake. – From here Albano can be reached either on foot along the scenically attractive Galleria di Sopra, flanked by

evergreen oaks (3·5 km: not recommended for cars), or by car on the *Galleria di Sotto*, which is 1 km shorter but relatively featureless. – 2 km: **Albano Laziale** (alt. 384 m; pop. 25,000; hotels: Miralago, III, 62 b.; Nuova Albano, III, 45 b.; Motel del Mare, III, 48 b.; etc.), on the high W side of Lago Albano, the see of a bishop since 460 and a resort much favoured by the people of Rome in summer for its beautiful setting. In the south-eastern outskirts of the town, on the right-hand side of the Via Appia, is a cube-shaped tomb of the late Republican period known (without any justification) as the Tomb of the Horatii and Curiatii. On the NW side of the town, in the garden of a house at Via Saffi 86, are the remains of a large underground cistern known as II Cisternone, dating from the time of Septimius Severus. Farther NW, between the convent of San Paolo and a Capuchin convent, the remains of an amphitheatre (seating 15,000 spectators), also dating from the reign of Septimius Severus (3rd c. A.D.) can be seen through a gate.

Over the Agro Pontino to Terracina (115 or 122 km). – Leave Rome by the Porta San Paolo or by the Porta Ardeatina and then on the *Via Pontina* (S.S. 148), which gives a good impression of the land reclaimed from the former Pontine Marshes. – After passing through the *EUR* the road runs through the **Roman Campagna**. – 31 km: road on right (1 km) to the little town of **Pomezia** (alt. 89 m; pop. 2000), founded in 1939. 2 km SE is the largest German military cemetery in Italy. – 15 km: the Via Pontina enters the **Agro Pontino**, an area of some 800 sq. km criss-crossed by countless canals and water channels. This low-lying area between the Monti Lepini and the sea, fringed by lines of dunes, degenerated after the abandonment of the Roman drainage system into marshland (the Pontine Marshes). From 1928 onwards the land was drained and brought into cultivation, and is now occupied by the families of more than 4000 settlers, mostly ex-soldiers. – 26 km: **Latina** (alt. 21 m; pop. 28,000; hotels: Europa, I, 120 b.; Garden, I, 105 b.; SP; De la Ville, II, 125 b.; Park, II, 96 b.; etc.), founded in 1932 and known until the Second World War as *Littoria*, with concentric rings of streets round a large central square, the Piazza del Popolo; it is the provincial capital. – From Latina to Terracina there are alternative routes – either 6 km N to the Via Appia and then 37 km SE, or (preferably) 23 km SE to *Sabaudia* (alt. 12 m; pop. 4000) and then 27 km on the coast road.

Via Lido di Ostia and Anzio to Terracina (143 km). – Leave Rome by the Porta San Paolo and the Via Ostiense, and shortly before the church of San Paolo fuori le Mura bear right into S.S. 8 (the "Via del Mare", of motorway standard), which runs close to the Tiber for most of the way. – 8 km: road on right (motorway standard) over the Tiber to the *Leonardo da Vinci Airport*, Fiumicino (20 km). – 16 km: road to the *excavations of ancient **Ostia** (see p. 178). – 4 km: **Lido di Ostia** (see p. 180).

The road to Anzio runs along the SE side of Lido di Ostia, past the end of a road from Rome running through the area once occupied by an international exhibition, and then skirts the beautiful *Pineta di Castel Fusano*, 4 km long, in which the paving of the ancient Via Severiana has been brought to light. It then follows the coast, passing close to the excavations of ancient *Lavinium*. – 20 km: *Tor Vaiánica* (alt. 3 m; hotels: California Beach, III, 90 b.; Sayonara, III, 80 b.; etc.), a small bathing resort. – 11 km: road (sharp left) to *Ardea* (8 km), with the Museo Manzù, devoted to the work of the famous sculptor. – 6 km: *Lavinio Lido di Enea* (alt. 20 m; Hotel Belvedere, III,

70 b., SP; etc.), a seaside resort on the territory of Anzio. – 8 km: **Anzio** (alt. 10 m; pop. 24,000; hotels: Dei Cesari, II, 144 b., SP, with annexe, II, 72 b.; Banzai, II, 96 b.; Esperia e Parco, II, 60 b.; Lido Garda, II, 60 b.; La Bussola, III, 51 b.; etc.), situated at the end of a small promontory. Known in Roman times as *Antium*, and then as now a popular resort, it was the birthplace of the emperors Caligula and Nero and a favourite resort of Cicero. On the E side of the town is the new harbour built by Pope Innocent XII in 1698. To the W of the pier (view extending to Capo Circeo and the Pontine Islands) is Nero's harbour, now silted up, with remains of the old breakwater. Attractive boat trips along the coast, which is littered with ancient remains. Below the lighthouse the promontory is riddled with ancient passages, the "Grotte di Nerone", which led to a large imperial villa. To the NW is the Arco Muto, an artificial archway in the rock.

The road to Terracina continues past villas and bathing beaches. – 3 km: **Nettuno** (alt. 11 m; pop. 26,000; hotels: Scacciapensieri, II, 110 b.; Astura, II, 96 b.), which had developed in recent years into an increasingly popular seaside resort. It was the scene of heavy fighting in January 1944, when American forces landed here. In the northern outskirts of the town is the largest *American military cemetery* in Italy (7500 graves). Also in Nettuno is the tomb of Maria Goretti (1890–1902), who was canonised in 1950. – 12 km: narrow side road on right to the *Torre d'Astura*, 2 km S on an islet linked to the mainland by a bridge. The tower is the only remnant of a castle of the Frangipani family in which Conradin of Swabia vainly sought shelter after the battle of Tagliacozzo in 1268. – Shortly after this the main road returns to the coast and then runs inland in a wide bend between the *Lago di Fogliano* on the left and the little *Lago dei Mónaci* on the right. Beyond this it skirts the *Lago di Caprolace* (4 km long). – 28 km: road on left to Sabaudia (3 km), along the N side of the *Lago di Sabaudia*, a much indented lake 7 km long.

Beyond the turning for Sabaudia the coast road runs between the W side of the Lago di Sabaudia and the sea. – 7 km: the road crosses the *Emissario Romano*, an ancient channel from the Lago di Sabaudia, which was used as a harbour in Roman times. Beyond this is **Monte Circeo**, the Roman *Promontorium Circaeum*, the traditional site of the palace of the Homeric enchantress Circe. The promontory is an isolated outlier of the Apennines which has been joined to the mainland by alluvial deposits (rich flora: national park). – Beyond the bridge over the Emissario, on the hillside to the right, is the massive *Torre Paola*, from which a footpath (sometimes closed) ascends to *Circe's Cave* (no entry); the walk takes half an hour. – The road continues along the N side of the promontory. 5 km: road on right (2 km) to the village of *San Felice* (alt. 89 m; pop. 7000; hotels: Maga Circe, I, 81 b., SP; Neanderthal, II, 97 b.; Carillon, II, 96 b.; Punta Rossa, in Quarto Caldo, II, 75 b., SP; Pleiadi, II, 54 b.; etc.), in a commanding situation on the NE slope of Monte Circeo, with an old castle which belonged to the Caetani family (beautiful view from tower). Above the village is a wall of polygonal cyclopean masonry known as the *Cittadella Vecchia*, a relic of the town of *Cercei* or *Circei* which was still in existence in the time of Cicero. From here a narrow and winding hill road climbs (3·5 km W) to the *Semáforo* (448 m: military area, permit required), from which there are superb *views SW as far as Ischia, Capri and Vesuvius, S to the Pontine Islands. From the Semáforo there is a rewarding climb (1 hour) to the summit of the hill (541 m), from which the dome of St Peter's can be seen in clear weather. – Beyond the turn-off for San Felice the main road continues to Terracina (15 km), keeping close to the coast all the way.

Terracina (alt. 16 m; pop. 35,000; hotels: L'Approdo Grand Hotel, I, 97 b.; Torre del Sole, II, 234 b.; River, II, 186 b.; Palace, II, 135 b.; Riva Gaia, II, 108 b.; Il Guscio, II, 51 b.; Rotino, III, 41 b.; Piccolo, III, 21 b.; etc.) is magnificently situated on the Golfo di Gaeta at the foot of high limestone crags, on the boundary between central and southern Italy. In the upper town which rises above the main road to the N, the Volscian town of *Anxur* which the Romans renamed *Terracina*, stands the 12th c. cathedral of San Cesareo, incorporating a temple of Rome and Augustus, with a portico borne on 11 ancient columns and a handsome campanile (view); fine interior, with remains of a mosaic pavement, a magnificent pulpit and a richly ornamented Easter candlestick, all 13th c. Cosmatesque work. – From the cathedral a *strada panoramica* leads (3 km) to the summit of *Monte Sant'Angelo* or *Monte Teodorico* (228 m), from which there are splendid *views, extending in fine weather as far as Vesuvius. On a projecting spur of rock is a terrace, partly supported on arcades with the remains of an imposing temple of Jupiter Anxur (1st c. B.C.). – On the eastern outskirts of the town is the *Taglio di Pisco Montano*, a notable example of Roman road-building, where the rock face was cut away to lower the course of the Via Appia by some 40 m.

32 km SW of Rome, on the coast, is the little town and resort of **Fiumicino** (pop. 15,000), founded only in 1825. (Take the Via Ostiense: the old road, the Via Portuense, is 4 km shorter, but hilly and winding.) Near the town are the excavations of the old port of Rome; it is planned to establish a museum for the Roman ships which were found here. Just before the town, to the right, is the large **Leonardo da Vinci Airport**, opened in 1961. – From Fiumicino a road runs SE past the *necropolis of Porto*, off the road to the left, crosses the Tiber (the estuarial plain of which is advancing into the sea at the rate of 4 m a year) and joins the "Via del Mare", coming from Rome. From here it is 2 km to *Lido di Ostia* (see p. 180). – The place of the ancient port of Rome, now entirely silted up, has been taken by **Civitavecchia** (alt. 11 m; pop. 45,000; hotels: Sunbay Park, I, 130 b., SP; Mediterraneo-Suisse, II, 119 b.; Miramare, III, 42 b.; etc.), 85 km NW of Rome. The only feature of interest in the town, which was almost completely destroyed during the last war and was rebuilt after the war in modern style, is the Forte Michelangelo, begun by Bramante and completed by Michelangelo.

Salerno

Region: Campania. – Province: Salerno (SA).
Altitude: 4 m. – Population: 155,000.
Post code: I-84100. – Dialling code: 089.
(i) **EPT**, Via Velia 15;
    tel. 23 14 32.
    AA, Piazza Amendola 8;
    tel. 22 47 44.
    ACI, Via Giacinto Vicinanza 11;
    tel. 22 67 66.
    CIT, Corso Garibaldi 144;
    tel. 32 17 03.
    TCI, *Viaggi Transcontinental*,
    Corso Garibaldi 243;
    tel. 2 25 49.

Salerno

HOTELS. – *Lloyd's Baia*, 3·5 km W, I, 250 b.; *Jolly Hotel delle Palme*, Lungomare Trieste 1, I, 140 b.; *Campania*, Via Generale Clark 45, I, 99 b.; *Diana*, Via Roma 16, II, 195 b.; *Montestella*, Corso Vittorio Emanuele 156, II, 85 b.; *Plaza*, Piazza Ferrovia, II, 75 b.; *Fiorenza*, Via Trento 145, II, 55 b.; *Elea*, Via Trento 98, II, 55 b.; etc. – YOUTH HOSTEL, Lungomare Marconi 34, 48 b.

The industrial town and provincial capital of Salerno, the see of an archbishop, lies 50 km SE of Naples at the N end of the beautiful Gulf of Salerno, where the hills of the Sorrento peninsula fall steeply down to the sea and the fertile Salerno plain begins.

The old town, rising up the slopes of the hill on the site of the ancient *Salernum*, still preserves many memories of its great days during the medieval period. It had the oldest medical school in Europe, which flourished from the 11th c. until it was closed down by Murat in 1812.

SIGHTS. – Along the seafront to the E of the *harbour*, now used only by local shipping, extends the *Lungomare Trieste*, a handsome promenade lined by fine modern buildings and affording extensive views. Parallel to this street is the modern *Via Roma*, which with its continuation to the SE, the Corso Giuseppe Garibaldi, is the town's principal traffic artery. At the W end of Via Roma we come to the Piazza Améndola, bounded on the E by the *Palazzo di Città* (Town Hall) and on the SW by the *Prefecture*. Behind the Prefecture are the beautiful *Public Gardens*, on the W side of which is the *Teatro Verdi*. Half way along Via Roma stands the

Palazzo di Provincia. From here Via del Duomo runs N, crossing the picturesque Via dei Mercanti, to the *Cathedral of San Matteo, built about 1080 in the time of Robert Guiscard and restored in 1768 and after 1945. A flight of steps leads up to an atrium with 28 ancient columns from Paestum and 14 ancient sarcophagi. The magnificent bronze doors were made in Constantinople in 1099.

INTERIOR. – Above the doorway is a large *mosaic figure of St Matthew,* of the Norman period. In the nave are two *ambos* (1175) with rich Cosmatesque mosaic decoration, and near the right-hand one is an *Easter candlestick* decorated in similar style. At the end of the N aisle is the splendid tomb of Margaret of Anjou (d. 1412). – The pavement of the choir and the choir screens are decorated with mosaics of the Norman period. Under the altar of the chapel to the right of the high altar is the tomb of Pope Gregory VII (Hildebrand), who died in Salerno in 1085; in the apse of the chapel is a mosaic figure of the Archangel Michael (1260). – In the **Cathedral Museum** is a 9th c. *altar frontal, locally made, with ivory reliefs of Biblical scenes. – In the richly decorated *crypt* under the altar lie the remains of the Evangelist Matthew, brought here from Paestum.

A little way E of the cathedral, in Via Benedetto, is the interesting *Provincial Museum* (antiquities, including an over-life-size bronze head of Apollo of the 1st c. B.C., and pictures).

On the hill NW of the town (45 minutes' walk) is an old Lombard **castle** (alt. 275 m) which was captured and strengthened by Robert Guiscard in the 11th c. (wide views).

San Gimignano

Region: Toscana. – Province: Siena (SI).
Altitude: 324 m. – Population: 4000.
Post code: I-53037. – Dialling code: 0577.
ⓘ **Pro Loco,** Piazza del Duomo;
    tel. 9 53 21.

HOTELS. – *La Cisterna,* II, 85 b.; *Bel Soggiorno,* III, 60 b.; *Leon Bianco,* III, 40 b.; *Pescille,* III, 26 b.

San Gimignano, situated on a hill between Florence and Siena, visible from afar and itself commanding far-ranging views, lies rather off the beaten tourist track and may therefore be missed by many visitors; yet it is one of the most attractive little towns in Tuscany, still preserving a **picturesque medieval aspect with its circuit of walls and its 13 (originally 56) towers, once the strongholds of noble families.

HISTORY. – In the 13th and 14th c. San Gimignano was an independent city, but in 1353 it became subject to Florence and thereafter fell into an economic decline. In consequence it remained almost untouched by subsequent centuries, so that it is still much as it was in the time of Dante. The old palaces are mainly Gothic in style.

SIGHTS. – The central feature of San Gimignano is the *Piazza Cisterna,* surrounded by tall towers; in the centre of the square is a beautiful fountain. Adjoining this square on the NW is another, the *Piazza del Duomo,* on the S side of which is the *Palazzo Comunale (formerly known as the Palazzo del Popolo), built in 1288–1323 as the *Nuovo Palazzo del Podestà,* with the tallest tower in the town, the *Torre del Comune* (53 m high, 140 steps: view). The palace houses the *Municipal Museum,* with a large collection of pictures; particularly notable is a large fresco, "Maestà", by Lippo Memmi (14th c.). – Adjoining the Palazzo Comunale is the *Cathedral,* usually called the *Collegiata, dating from the 12th c. and enlarged after 1466. It has fine 14th and 15th c. frescoes, particularly those on the side walls by Domenico Ghirlandaio (painted before 1475) depicting the vision and the burial of St Fina. The saint's remains are preserved in the beautifully decorated Capella di Santa Fina (last chapel on right). – Facing the cathedral is the *Palazzo Antico del Podestà* (13th–14th c.). The taller of its two towers, the *Torre dell'Orologio* (51 m), marks the height which privately built towers were not allowed to exceed.

To the left of the cathedral an archway leads to the *Palazzo della Prepositura* (12th–13th c.), with the *Museum of Religious Art.* – To the right of the

The towers of San Gimignano

cathedral a street leads up to the ruined *Rocca*, from which there is a fine view of the town's many towers.

At the NW end of the town the **church of Sant'Agostino** (1280–98), has *frescoes by Benozzo Gozzoli depicting scenes from the life of St Augustine (1463–67).

San Marino

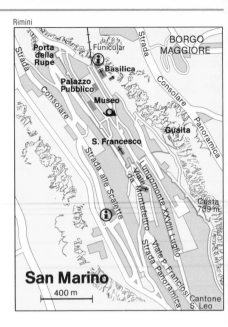

Repubblica di San Marino.
Altitude: 643 m.
Population: 19,000 (country); 4500 (town).
Post code: I-47031. – Dialling code: 0541.
(i) **EGT** (Ente Governativo per il Turismo),
Palazzo del Turismo;
tel. 99 21 02.

HOTELS. – *Grand Hotel San Marino*, L, 106 b.; *Titano*, I, 109 b.; *Joli San Marino*, I, 45 b.; *Quercia Antica*, II, 53 b.; *Tre Penne*, II, 35 b.; *Diamond*, II, 12 b.; *Excelsior*, III, 54 b.; etc. – CAMPING SITE.

San Marino, capital of the little republic of the same name, lies 23 km SW of Rimini on the eastern fringe of the Apennines. With its magnificent *situation on Monte Titano (745 m), its three castles crowning the triple peaks of the hill and its picturesque old houses and streets, it attracts large numbers of summer visitors, particularly from the seaside resorts round Rimini.

HISTORY. – Legend has it that San Marino was founded in A.D. 301 by *St Marinus*, a stone-mason from the Dalmatian town of Rab who fled here during the Diocletianic persecutions. The present republic developed out of a settlement which grew up around a convent mentioned in the records in 885. It received the constitution which is still in force in 1263, was recognised by Pope Urban IV in 1631 and has since maintained its independence, from 1862 under the protection of Italy. Its stamps and coins are much sought after. – With an area of 61 sq. km and a population of 19,000, San Marino is one of the smallest states in Europe (Vatican City 0·5 sq. km, pop. 1000; Andorra 462 sq. km, pop. 25,000; Liechtenstein 160 sq. km, pop. 24,000; Monaco 2 sq. km, pop. 24,000). – Legislative power rests with the 60 members of the *Consiglio Grande e Generale*, executive power with the ten deputies of the *Congresso di Stato* and the two *Capitani reggenti*, who change every six months. Old medieval costumes are worn at the ceremonial change-over on 1 April and 1 October and on San Marino's National Day (3 September).

SIGHTS. – On the SW side of the town is the 14th c. *Porta San Francesco*. Just inside the town walls, on the right, stands the *church of San Francesco* (14th c.),

with old pictures. – NW of the church is the *Museum* (pictures, coins, stamps, etc.).

In the centre of the old town is the *Piazza della Libertà*, the town's attractive main square, with fine views from the SW side. On the NW side of the square is the neo-Gothic **Palazzo del Governo** or *Palazzo Pubblico* (1894), with a sumptuously appointed interior, particularly notable features being the Hall of the Grand Council, the Audience Chamber and the Voting Chamber (which contains a painting of St Marinus by Guernico). From the roof of the palace there are magnificent views. – A little way N of the main square

Rock fortress, San Marino

s the neo-classical *Basilica di San Marino*
1836), with a richly decorated interior;
the remains of the saint are preserved in
the high altar. To the right of the basilica is
the *chapel of San Pietro*, which claims to
possess the stone beds of St Marinus and
his companion St Leo. – Just above the
basilica is the Nido del Falco restaurant,
with a terrace from which there are
extensive views. – NW of the main square
is a lookout terrace, with the upper station
of a funicular whose lower station is on
the *Strada Panoramica* which runs round
the town and Monte Titano. To the right is
the *State Tourist Office.*

From the Basilica di San Marino a road
runs SE to the three peaks of Monte
Titano, with their three *castles*: first the
11th c. *Rocca* or *Guaita*; then the 13th c.
Cesta or *Fratta*, on the highest peak (745
m), commanding wide views, with a
museum of arms and armour; and finally
the 13th c. *Montale*, at the foot of which is
the Kursaal.

San Remo

Region: Liguria. – Province: Imperia (IM).
Altitude: 11 m. – Population: 65,000.
Post code: I-18038. – Dialling code: 0184.
ⓘ **AA**, Largo Nuvoloni;
  tel. 8 56 15.
  ACI, Corso O. Raimondo 47;
  tel. 8 56 28.
  TCI, *Riviera Tours*, Corso Imperatrice 31;
  tel. 8 88 64.
  Albatros, Piazza Eroi Sanremesi 71–72.

HOTELS. – *Royal*, L, 255 b., SP; *Londra*, I, 250 b., SP;
Des Etrangers, I, 199 b.; *Grand Hotel & des Anglais*, I,
61 b.; *Astoria West End*, I, 152 b.; *Méditerranée*, I,
29 b., SP; *Miramare*, I, 108 b., SP; *Résidence
Principe*, I, 86 b.; *Colombia Majestic*, I, 83 b.; *Nike*, I,
82 b.; *Europa & della Pace*, II, 137 b.; *Nazionale*, II,
37 b.; *De la Ville & Tivoli*, II, 92 b.; *Plaza*, II, 88 b.;
Ariston Montecarlo, II, 78 b.; *Bel
Soggiorno*, II, 75 b.; *Globo*, II, 74 b.; *Belvedere*, III, 97
b.; *Eden*, III, 93 b.; *Centrale*, III, 90 b.; *Bobby Motel*, III,
89 b., SP; *Paradiso*, III, 72 b.; etc. – CAMPING SITE.

EVENT. – *Italian Popular Song Festival* (Feb.).

**San Remo, Italy's largest and oldest
(since 1861) winter health resort,
lies on the "Riviera dei Fiori", in a
bay 9 km long enclosed by a semicircle of hills.**

Here olive-groves have given place to
glasshouses in which carnations, roses
and other flowers are grown for export.
Thanks to its sheltered situation San

Remo has a mild and equable climate in
winter, and in summer it is a lively and
popular resort (with a beach which is
partly artificial).

SIGHTS. – On a steep hill between the
short valleys of the *Torrente San Francesco* and *Torrente di San Romolo* is the
OLD TOWN (*Città Vecchia* or *La Pigna*), a
huddle of narrow lanes, flights of steps
and tall sombre houses, linked by arches
as a protection against earthquakes.

The NEW TOWN occupies the low-lying
alluvial land at the foot of the hill. Its main
traffic artery is *Via Matteotti*, a long street
lined with shops. At its W end is the
Casino Municipale, with gaming rooms, a

The Casino, San Remo

theatre and other facilities. A short
distance NE stands the *Cathedral* of San
Siro, founded in the 12th c. Via Matteotti
is continued westward by the *Corso
dell'Imperatrice*, a promenade shaded by
Canary palms (*Phoenix canariensis*)
which skirts the W bay, with the beautiful
Giardino dell'Imperatrice at its far end.
The main traffic artery of the E bay is the
Corso Garibaldi, the eastward continuation of Via Matteotti, with the Flower
Market near its W end. The main seafront
promenade in this part of the town is the
Corso Trento e Trieste. – Between the E
and W bays lies the *Harbour*, with the
old Genoese *Forte Santa Tecla* (now a
prison).

SURROUNDINGS. – There is an attractive trip (45
minutes) by cableway or by road via the *golf-course*
(18 holes) and the summer holiday resort of *San
Rómolo* (alt. 786 m) to the summit of *Monte
Bignone* (1299 m: restaurant), with far-ranging
views in clear weather of the Riviera and the Maritime
Alps, extending S to Corsica.

Another rewarding excursion (25 km N) is to **Baiardo** (alt. 900 m; Hotel Bellavista, III, 30 b.; etc.), situated on a hill commanding extensive views, with a beautiful parish church and the ruins of another church (16th c.) destroyed by an earthquake in 1887. From a nearby terrace there are magnificent *views of the mountains. From Baiardo the trip can be continued on an attractive road via Apricale to Ventimiglia.

Sardinia / Sardegna

San Maria Navarrese, Sardinia

ⓘ **Assessorato al Turismo della Regione Sarda**,
ESIT, Via Mameli 95,
I-09100 Cagliari (CA);
tel. (070) 66 85 22.
EPT Cagliari, Piazza Deffenu 9,
I-09100 Cagliari (CA);
tel. (070) 65 19 46.
EPT Nuoro, Piazza d'Italia 19,
I-08100 Nuoro (NU);
tel. (0784) 3 00 83.
Pro Loco Oristano, Vico Umberto I 15,
I-09025 Oristano (OR);
tel. (0783) 7 06 21.
EPT Sassari, Piazza d'Italia 19,
I-07100 Sassari (SS);
tel. (079) 3 01 29.

BOAT SERVICES. – Regular services (carrying cars) several times daily from *Civitavecchia* to *Golfo Aranci* (8–9 hours) and daily from *Genoa* to *Porto Torres* (13 hours), *Genoa* or *Civitavecchia* to *Olbia* (14 hours or 7 hours) and *Civitavecchia* to *Cagliari* (12 hours); also five times weekly from *Genoa* via *Porto Torres* (13 hours) to *Cagliari* (20 hours).

AIR SERVICES. – *Cagliari International Airport*, 4 km W of town; airports for domestic services at *Olbia* and *Alghero*.

Sardinia, the second largest island in the Mediterranean (area 24,000 sq. km, population 1·5 million), separated from the neighbouring French island of Corsica by the narrow Strait of Bonifacio, is an autonomous region of Italy, made up of the four provinces of Cagliari, Nuoro, Oristano and Sassari. The population, which from the late Middle Ages until the beginning of this century was decimated by malaria, is concentrated in the fertile and well-cultivated coastal areas.

Geologically the island is a remnant of a rump mountain range composed of gneisses, granites and schists, overlaid by a band of limestones running from N to S and partly covered with recent volcanic deposits. The only plain of any size, the Campidano, lies between the Iglesiente uplands with their rich mineral resources to the SW and the rest of the island, a hilly region with gentler slopes in the W and more rugged country in the E, rising in Gennargentu to a height of 1834 m and falling steeply down to the sea in the sheer cliffs on the E coast. The summers are hot and dry; the winters bring heavy rain.

More than half the population obtain their subsistence from agriculture. Corn, wine olives, citrus fruits, vegetables and tobacco are grown in the Campidano plain, in the coastal areas and in the fertile valleys of the numerous rivers. The upland regions are mainly devoted to pastoral farming (sheep and goats, and in recent years some cattle). The produce of Sardinian agriculture is just sufficient to meet local needs. In the coastal region fishing (tunny, anchovies, spiny lobsters) also makes a contribution to the economy.

Mining, already an important activity in ancient times, has made considerable strides in recent years as a result of measures designed to promote the industrialisation of economically under-developed regions. The main mining area is Iglesiente, where zinc, lead, manganese and barytes are worked. The recent development of opencast coal-mining round Carbonia has led to the establishment of a coal-burning power station at Portovesme; and this station, together with the hydroelectric stations supplied by dams on some of the island's many rivers, produces enough power to meet Sardinian needs and leave some over for export to the Italian mainland. Another recent development has been the construction of an oil terminal at Cagliari, followed by the establishment of petrochemical industries in the area. The extraction of magnesium and cooking salt from sea-water is also an industry of some significance.

In recent years tourism has developed into an important element in the island's economy. In addition to the established tourist areas round Alghero and Santa Teresa a very modern and progressive holiday region has been developed on the Costa Smeralda.

HISTORY. – Evidence of the earliest inhabitants of Sardinia is provided by the remains of numerous prehistoric settlements, in particular the **nuraghi** (singular *nuraghe*), massive towers characteristic of the island culture of the Bronze and Iron Ages which show a striking similarity to the *talayots* of the Balearics. Like the talayots, they no doubt served as fortresses, watch-towers and burial-places, and can be dated to the period between 1500 and 500 B.C.

From the 9th c. onwards Phoenicians and later Carthaginians settled on the coasts. In 238 B.C. the island was occupied by the Romans, attracted by its rich deposits of minerals. About A.D. 455 it fell into the hands of the Vandals and later became subject to Byzantium. Between the 8th and 11th c. it was frequently ravaged by Saracen raids; but these piratical activities were repressed by Pisa and Genoa following an appeal by the Pope, who rewarded them with the grant of the territory. The traditional system of rule by four *giudici* (judges) in the districts of Torres, Gallura, Cagliari and Arborea was, however, maintained. In 1297 Sardinia was granted by the Pope to the crown of Aragon. Under the treaty of Utrecht in 1713 it was assigned to Austria, and in 1720 was exchanged with Sicily and passed to the dukes of Savoy as the kingdom of Sardinia. In 1948 it was given the status of an autonomous region within the Republic of Italy.

Thanks to the ruggedness and remoteness of much of the island its old customs and traditions are still vigorously alive. The Sardinian language is a Romance tongue which has developed independently of mainland Italian and preserves certain archaic features.

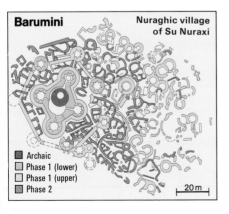

Barumini   Nuraghic village of Su Nuraxi

■ Archaic
□ Phase 1 (lower)
□ Phase 1 (upper)
■ Phase 2   20 m

TOUR OF THE ISLAND (*c.* 720 km). – Leave Cagliari on S.S. 131 (the Sassari road), which runs NW and comes in 20 km to *Monastir* (alt. 83 m), a village of Oriental aspect on the slopes of a volcanic hill (rock-cut tombs). 5·5 km SW at *San Sperate* is an open-air museum of modern sculpture. Beyond Monastir the road follows the E edge of the Campidano plain. – 23 km; **Sanluri** (alt. 135 m; pop. 8000; Motel Ichnusa, III, 22 b.; etc.), with a 14th c. castle containing a small military museum.

24 km NE of Sanluri is the village of **Barumini**, near which (1 km W, to the left of the road to Tuili) is the largest nuraghic village in Sardinia,**Su Nuraxi, with 396 houses and a massive central structure with several towers.

Su Nuraxi, near Barumini, Sardinia

From Sanluri S.S. 197 runs W to the wooded *Costa Verde*, a coastal region now being developed as a popular holiday area, with new roads, villas, hotels and sports facilities.

9 km beyond Sanluri on the main road is *Sárdara* (alt. 163 m). By the little church of Santa Anastasia is an underground spring sanctuary of nuraghic type. 3 km W is a small spa with thermal springs (50 and 68 °C – 122 and 154 °F). – 36 km: *Santa Giusta* (alt. 10 m), on the N side of a marshy lake, the Stagno di Santa Giusta, with a beautiful 12th c. church in Pisan style (ancient columns). – 3 km: **Oristano** (alt. 9 m; pop. 27,000; hotels: I.S.A., II, 71 b.; Piccolo, III, 18 b.; etc.), which is noted for its pottery. It still preserves a number of towers belonging to its medieval defences; cathedral (18th c.), on the site of an earlier building of the 13th–14th c.; Archaeological Museum, with finds from the ancient city of Tharros, which lay to the NW of the Gulf of Oristano. Beautiful traditional costumes

can often be seen here on market days. –
16 km: *Bauladu* (alt. 29 m), on the N edge
of the Campidano plain. The road then
continues up the Bobólica valley.

5 km farther on S.S. 131d branches off on
the right. Running diagonally across the
island, this is the quickest and shortest
route from Cagliari or Oristano to Olbia
(309 km and 182 km respectively). In 58
km it bypasses the provincial capital of
Nuoro (alt. 553 m; pop. 30,000; hotels:
Grazia Deledda, I, 108 b.; Paradiso, II, 148
b.; Moderno, II, 102 b.; Motel Agip, II, 102
b.; etc.), charmingly situated on a hillside,
between limestone hills of Alpine type to
the S and the peak of *Ortobene* (995 m:
*view) to the E. Beautiful local costumes
are worn on the feast of the Saviour
(29–31 August). Nuoro was the birthplace of the writer Grazia Deledda
(1893–1936; Nobel prize 1926).

On the SE side of the town stands the neo-classical
Cathedral (19th c.). The most conspicuous building is
the prison, a reminder of the days when brigands were
active in the area. – 1·5 km NE are the pilgrimage
church of *Nostra Signora della Solitudine* (*view)
and, beyond the *Colle di San Onofrio* (594 m: view),
the *Sardinian Museum of Costume*, housed in over 20
buildings in the style of Sardinian peasants' houses.
Around the town are several *nuraghi*.

From Nuoro there is a beautiful drive S to
the village of **Mamoiada** (alt. 644 m:
costumes) and **Fonni** (alt. 1000 m; pop.
6000), the highest village on the island.
In the surrounding area are numerous
nuraghi and "fairies' houses" (*domus
de janas*, rock-cut tombs). Fonni is the
starting point for the ascent (4 hours, with
guide) of **Bruncu Spina** (1829 m:
panoramic views), the northern peak of
the *Gennargentu massif, from which

Sardinian costume, Fonni

the southern peak, **Punta la Mármora**
(1834 m), can be climbed (¾ hour).

Continuing on S.S. 131, we see on the
left, shortly after the turning for Nuoro, the
well-preserved nuraghe of *Losa*, with a
number of subsidiary structures. – 2 km:
Abbasanta (alt. 313 m), the largest
livestock market in Sardinia, on the
southern edge of the Abbasanta plain, an
area of black basaltic rock. 10 km SE is the
Tirso Dam, once Europe's largest dam,
which has impounded the water of the
island's principal river to form the *Lago
Omodeo*, 22 km long and up to 5 km wide.
– 16 km: **Macomer** (alt. 563 m; pop.
10,000; hotels: Motel Agip, II, 192 b.;
Marghine, III, 31 b.; Nuraghe, III, 31 b.;
etc.), situated on a bleak plateau of
basalts and trachytes on the slopes of the
Catena del Marghine, with beautiful far-
ranging views.

In front of the church are three Roman milestones
found in the area. Some of the best-preserved nuraghi
in Sardinia can be seen in the immediate surroundings
of the town. Particularly fine is the nuraghe of *Santa
Barbara* (alt. 648 m), a conical structure on a high
square base (a torch should be taken).

3 km beyond Macomer S.S. 129 bis goes
off on the left to the village of *Suni* (23 km:
wide views) and, 6 km beyond this, the
little port of **Bosa** (alt. 10 m; pop. 8000),
with the ruined castle of Serravalle (*c.*
1100). 16 km S of Suni lies **Cuglieri** (alt.
479 m; pop. 5000), on the lower slopes of
Monte Ferru (1050 m), an extinct volcano. – 2 km: on the left of the road, the
almost completely preserved nuraghe of
Succoronis (*Muradu*). – 27 km: road on
right (1 km) to the three-storey nuraghe
of *Sant'Antine*, 16 m high. – 5 km:
Bonnanaro (alt. 405 m), where a road
goes off on the left (4 km SW) to the richly
ornamented *church of San Pietro di
Sorres* (Pisan period, 12th c.). Beyond
Bonnanaro the road runs through the
beautiful wooded uplands of **Logudoro**.
– 21 km: S.S. 597, the direct road from
Sassari to Olbia, goes off on the right.
2 km along this road is the former abbey
church of *Santissima Trinità di Sac-
cargia*, the finest example of Pisan
architecture in Sardinia (13th c. frescoes).
– 15 km: **Sassari** (see p. 262).

For the next section of the tour, from
Sassari to Olbia, there are alternative
routes – either the direct road on S.S. 597
(101 km) or the more interesting S.S. 127.
– 14 km: **Ósilo** (alt. 600 m; pop. 6000),

renowned for the beautiful costumes of its women. From the ruined Malaspina castle and the nearby Cappella di Bonaria there are beautiful views. The road continues through the wooded *Angola* district. – 39 km: road on left, through beautiful scenery, via the village of *Sédini* (16th c. church), picturesquely situated above gorges, to the little walled port town of **Castelsardo** (alt. 114 m; pop. 5000; hotels: Peddra Ladda, II, 144 b., SP; Riviera, III, 55 b.; Castello, III, 40 b.; etc.), in a magnificent *situation on a promontory which falls sheer down to the Golfo dell'Asinara. This is the principal basketwork centre in Sardinia. In the parish church is a beautiful 15th c. Madonna, a masterpiece of the Sardinian-Spanish school of painting. From the ruined castle there are fine *views.

Some 4 km beyond the turning for Castelsardo, at *Pérfugas* (just off S.S. 127), a fortified village of the nuraghic period and a spring sanctuary have been excavated. – 26 km: **Tempio Pausania** (alt. 566 m; pop. 9000; hotels: Petit, II, 82 b.; San Carlo, III, 89 b.; Delle Sorgenti, III, 35 b.; etc.), formerly chief town of the district of Gallura, situated below the N face of the jagged *Monti di Limbara* (cork industry). – 10 km: *Calangiánus* (alt. 518 m; pop. 6000), an old town surrounded by forest, with a pretty parish church. – 35 km: **Olbia** (alt. 15 m; pop. 26,000; hotels: President, I, 60 b.; Mediterraneo, II, 133 b.; Royal, II, 129 b., SP; Motel Olbia, II, 40 b.; Minerva, III, 59 b.; Mastino, III, 58 b.; etc.), formerly known as *Terranova Pausania*, lying at the W end of the deeply indented *Gulf of Olbia*. A causeway carrying the road and the railway links the town with the little *Ísola Bianca*, where the ships from Civitavecchia come in.

Beside the town railway station is the 11th c. **church of San Simplicio**, in Pisan style, with a collection of Roman inscriptions (particularly milestones) and a sarcophagus with a decoration of garlands. From the church and from the harbour there are fine views of the bay and the massive offshore island of **Tavolara** (555 m; area 6 sq. km).

To the N of Olbia, extending along the shores of a large peninsula, is the beautiful *Costa Smeralda* (Emerald Coast), whose beaches of fine sand are being developed as a holiday area by the construction of new roads and the provision of tourist facilities. The roads to the various resorts branch off S.S. 125, which runs N from Olbia to Palau. – 6 km: road

(8 km) to the *Golfo di Marinella* (Hotel Abi d'Ori, I, 102 b.). – 1 km: coast road via *Cala di Volpe* (15 km; hotels: Cala di Volpe, I, 246 b., SP; Nibaru, II, 60 b., SP; etc.) and *Romazzino* (17 km; Hotel Romazzino, I, 200 b., SP; etc.) to **Porto Cervo** (30 km; hotels: Cervo, I, 176 b., SP; Luci di la Muntagna, II, 136 b., SP; Le Ginestre, II, 102 b., SP; etc.), the chief place on the Costa Smeralda. 3 km N, beyond *Capo Ferro*, is the bay of *Liscia di Vacca* (hotels: Pitrizza, I, 52 b., SP; Liscia di Vacca, II, 80 b., SP; Balocco, II, 56 b., SP; etc.), and 5 km farther on *Baia Sardinia* (hotels: Ringo, II, 261 b., SP; Smeraldo Beach, II, 248 b., SP; Delle Vigne, II, 158 b.; Cormorano, II, 112 b., SP; La Biscaccia, II, 110 b., SP; Punta Est, II, 98 b., SP; Club, II, 97 b.; Residence Park, II, 90 b., SP; Mon Repos Hermitage, II, 86 b., SP; Villaggio Forte Cappellini, II, 64 b., SP; etc.). – At the S end of the Costa Smeralda the holiday centre of *Portisco* is in course of development.

17 km farther N on S.S. 125 is *Arzachena*, and in another 12 km *Palau* (alt. 5 m; hotels: Excelsior Vanna, II, 60 b.; La Roccia, II, 42 b.; etc.).

From Palau there is a boat service several times daily (15 minutes) to **La Maddalena** (alt. 29 m; pop. 11,000; hotels: Cala Lunga, II, 139 b., SP; Excelsior, II, 54 b.; Il Gabbiano, III, 57 b.; etc.), a port on the island of the same name (157 m; area 20 sq. km), which until the Second World War was strongly fortified, commanding the Strait of Bonifacio between Sardinia and Corsica. – The island is traversed by a *panoramic road* 7 km long which is carried by a swing bridge over the *Passo della Moneta*, a strait fully 500 m wide, on to the neighbouring island of **Caprera** ("Goat Island", 212 m; area 15·75 sq. km). 1·5 km E of the bridge is a house once occupied by Garibaldi, who died here on 2 June 1882 (collection of mementoes). In front of the house stands a monument to Garibaldi, behind it an olive-grove containing his tomb, which attracts visitors from all over Italy, particularly on the anniversary of his death.

The return trip from Olbia to Cagliari is on S.S. 125, which runs SE past a number of salt-water lagoons, with the rocky island of *Tavolara* lying offshore on the left. Thereafter the road continues at varying distances from the coast. – 57 km: **Siniscola** (alt. 42 m; pop. 6000; Hotel Montalbo, III, 36 b.), at the W end of a large coastal plain, from which a *panoramic road (edges not guarded) runs along the rocky ridge of *Monte Albo* (1127 m), through a region well stocked with wildlife, to *Bitti* (alt. 549 m; pop. 6000). 6 km NE of Siniscola is the developing resort of *La Caletta* (hotels:

La Caletta, II, 127 b., SP, with annexe, II, 81 b., SP; Villa Pozzi, III, 74 b.; etc.).

From Siniscola it is possible to return to Cagliari either by taking the shorter but less interesting road via Nuoro and Oristano or by continuing on the coast road. – 36 km: **Orosei** (alt. 19 m; pop. 4000), on the right bank of the River *Cedrino*, with a ruined castle. – 21 km: **Dorgali** (alt. 387 m; pop. 7000; Hotel Quercetto, III, 40 b.; etc.), a little town famous for its wine, situated on the slopes of *Monte Bardia* (882 m); local costumes. In the surrounding area are a number of beautiful stalactitic caves (*Grotta Toddeittu, Grotta del Bue Marino*) and some of the rock-cut tombs known as "fairies' houses" (*domus de janas*). 11 km NW of Dorgali is the nuraghic village of *Serra Orrios*. – 2 km: side road (7 km) which winds its way down to the little port of *Cala Gonone* (alt. 25 m; hotels: Villaggio Palmasera, II, 650 b., SP; Mastino delle Grazie, III, 88 b.; Cala Luna, III, 52 b.; etc.).

Beyond Dorgali the road passes through beautiful mountainous country. – 61 km: **Tortolì** (alt. 15 m; pop. 5000; hotels: Victoria, III, 61 b.; Il Giardino, II, 54 b.), at the beginning of an extensive plain. 5 km E is the attractively situated little port of **Arbatax** (pop. 500; hotels: Telis, III, 326 b.; La Bitta, III, 25 b.; etc.), formerly also known as *Tortolì Marina*, which ships the agricultural produce and minerals of the Ogliastra region. Nearby are picturesque red porphyry cliffs. – From Tortolì there is a very attractive alternative route to Cagliari, first of S.S. 198 through the Ogliastra uplands, with hills of crystalline limestone, sometimes in curiously contorted shapes, to **Lanusei** (alt. 595 m; pop. 5000), prettily situated amid vineyards, **Seui** (alt. 800 m) and the *Cantoniera de Santa Lucia*; then on S.S. 128 and S.S. 131 to Cagliari.

Beyond Tortolì S.S. 125 follows a winding course through the south-eastern part of the Ogliastra region. – 10 km: *Barì Sardo* (alt. 50), from which there is a view of the Gennargentu massif. The road continues, with many bends, through lonely hill country. – 121 km: **Quartu Sant'Elena** (alt. 6 m; pop. 23,000), a thriving town, in an area which produces the famous white wine, Malvasia. On the feast of St Helena (21 May) there is a picturesque procession of richly decked teams of oxen. – 8 km: **Cagliari** (see p. 84).

Sassari

Region: Sardegna. – Province: Sassari (SS).
Altitude: 225 m. – Population: 110,000.
Post code: I-07100. – Dialling code: 079.

(i) **EPT**, Piazza d'Italia 19;
tel. 3 01 29.
ACI, Viale Adua 22b;
tel. 27 14 62.
TCI, *Sardaviaggi*, Via Cagliari 44;
tel. 2 34 31.

HOTELS. – *Jolly Grazia Deledda*, I, 228 b., SP; *Jolly Standard*, II, 79 b.; *Turritania*, III, 133 b.; *Castello*, III, 46 b.; etc.

EVENTS. – *Cavalcata Sarda* (picturesque traditional costumes) on Assumption; *Processione dei Candelieri* on 14 August.

Sassari, Sardinia's second largest town, the capital of a province, an archiepiscopal see and a university town, lies on a limestone plateau, falling steeply down on the E side, in the NW of the island. It is a town of predominantly modern aspect.

SIGHTS. – The hub of the town's traffic is the palm-shaded *Piazza Cavallino de Honestis*, immediately SE of which is the large *Piazza d'Italia*, with a *monument to Victor Emmanuel II* and a modern *Prefecture*. – From the Piazza d'Italia the tree-lined Via Roma runs SE to the **Museo Nazionale G.A. Sanna** (closed Mondays), with the collections assembled by Giovanni Antonio Sanna, a member of the Italian Parliament (prehistoric, Punic and Roman antiquities; over 350 pictures of the 16th–19th c.).

NW of the Piazza Cavallino de Honestis, reached by way of Piazza Azuni, is the Corso Vittorio Emanuele, Sassari's principal street. From this we turn left along Via del Duomo to reach the **Cathedral** of San Nicola, with a Baroque façade (interior restored). E of this in Via Santa Catarina is the handsome *Palazzo del Duca*, now the Town Hall. – To the W of the cathedral, in the spacious Piazza Santa Maria, stands the church of *Santa Maria di Betlem*, rebuilt in modern style but still preserving its severe Gothic façade of the Pisan period. – On the N side of the town is the pretty *Fonte del Rosello*, with a Baroque well-house of 1605.

SURROUNDINGS. – A pleasant drive through the coastal district of *Nura* leads (19 km NW) to the little industrial town of **Porto Torres** (alt. 10 m; pop. 17,000; hotels: Torres, II, 112 b.; La Casa, III, 99 b.; Motel Lybissonis, III, 81 b., SP; etc.), the port of Sassari, situated in the *Golfo dell'Asinara*. On the E side of the town is the church of San Gavino (11th–13th c.; fortified in the 8th c.); in the interior are 22 ancient columns and six pillars, and in the crypt the tomb of San Gavino. To the W of the harbour a seven-arched Roman bridge spans the little Rio Turritano, and near this are the remains of a large Temple of Fortuna, popularly known as the "Palazzo del Re Barbaro" (Palace of the Barbarian King). – 29 km NW of Porto Torres we come to the charmingly situated fishing village of **Stintino** (alt. 9 m), and 5 km beyond this, on a road offering extensive views, is the *Punta del Falcone*, the NW tip of Sardinia. Lying off the promontory to the N is the little *Isola Piana* (24 m), and beyond this the long *Isola Asinara* (17·5 km long; up to 408 m high; area 52 sq. km), with numerous bays and inlets.

Another very attractive trip is to the charmingly situated town and seaside resort of **Alghero**, 37 km SW, whose inhabitants still speak a Catalan dialect (alt. 7 m; pop. 33,000; hotels: Villa las Tronas, I, 56 b., SP; Gran Catalunya, II, 313 b.; Calabona, II, 226 b., SP; Solemar e Quattro Mori, II, 220 b., SP; Oasis, II, 195 b., SP; San Marco, II, 157 b.; Eleonora, II, 134 b.; La Margherita, II, 118 b.; etc.). Features of interest are the cathedral (1510: Spanish Gothic doorway), the church of San Francesco (cloister), the picturesque Spanish bastions and towers and many old houses. – 14 km W of Alghero (also by motorboat, 3 hours), on the W side of the precipitous *Capo Caccia*, is a beautiful stalactitic cave, the *Grotta di Nettuno*.

Selinunte

Region: Sicilia. – Province: Trapani (TP).
Altitude: 74 m.
ⓘ **EPT Trapani**, Corso Italia 10,
I-91100 Trapani (TP);
tel. (0923) 2 72 73.

The ruins of *Selinunte*, lying on both banks of the little rivers Modione (ancient Greek Selinon) and Gorgo di Cotone, near the SW coast of Sicily, are one of the most striking and interesting sites on the island.

HISTORY. – *Selinus*, the most westerly Greek colony in Sicily, was founded about 628 B.C. on a hill near the sea, and later extended on to the Plateau to the N. A sacred precinct was established on the hill to the E during the 6th c. B.C. In 409 B.C. the flourishing city was conquered and destroyed by the Carthaginians, and a new fortified town built on the western hill from 407 onwards was in turn destroyed by the Carthaginians in 250 B.C., during the first Punic War.

The size and importance of the ancient city is attested by the extent and scale of the ruins, in particular the massive remains of eight Doric temples (6th–5th c. B.C.), which probably collapsed as a result of earthquakes between the 5th and 8th c. A.D. and were then gradually covered with blown sand. Since 1925 restoration and further excavation has been carried on steadily: two temples have been re-erected, and others are to follow.

SIGHTS. – On the western hill are the remains of the *Acropolis (450 m long and up to 350 m across), formerly surrounded by walls and traversed by two principal streets, one running N–S, the other E–W. In the SE sector are the remains of the small *Temple A* and the foundations of the very similar *Temple O*. Immediately N of the E–W street is the tiny *Temple B*, of which no columns remain erect, and to the N of this, on top of the hill, is *Temple C* (columns re-erected in 1925 and 1929), the oldest on the Acropolis and one of the two most striking features of the site (the other being Temple E, referred to below). Farther N

Temple E, Selinunte

again is the rather later *Temple D*. – On the northern edge of the Acropolis are the excavated remains of the Greek **defensive walls** (restored in 407 B.C.), an excellent example of the highly developed Greek art of fortification. Beyond this point, on the *Manuzza* plateau to the N of the Acropolis, extends the town proper, of which only a few remains have been preserved.

Following the E–W street westward from the Acropolis, we cross the River Modione (at the mouth of which the W harbour was situated) and come to the hill of *Manicalunga*, on the slopes of which in the sacred precinct lie the remains of the **Temple of Demeter**, dedicated to *Demeter Malophoros* (the "Fruit-Bringer"). At the N corner of the precinct is the little shrine of *Zeus Meilichios* ("the Forgiving"). – To the W of the Temple of Demeter is a necropolis extending for some 2 km.

From the Acropolis a road 1·5 km long runs E over the River Gorgo di Cotone (at the mouth of which was the eastern harbour) to the eastern hill, with the remains of three large temples which even in their present state of ruin are overwhelmingly impressive. To the S is *Temple E, dedicated to Hera, which was re-erected in 1959, with 38 columns. To the N are *Temple F* and *Temple G* (111 m long), probably dedicated to Apollo, which with the Temple of Zeus at Agrigento and the Artemision at Ephesus ranks as the largest of all Greek temples.

Distant view of Etna

Sicily/Sicilia

(i) **EPT Palermo**, Piazza Castelnuovo 35,
I-90100 Palermo (PA);
tel. (091) 21 68 47.
EPT Agrigento, Via C. Battisti,
I-92100 Agrigento (AG);
tel. (0922) 2 67 23.
EPT Caltanissetta, Corso Vittorio Emanuele 109,
I-93100 Caltanissetta (CL);
tel. (0934) 2 17 31.
EPT Catania, Largo Paisiello 5,
I-95100 Catania (CT);
tel. (095) 31 21 24.
EPT Enna, Piazza Garibaldi,
I-94100 Enna (EN);
tel. (0935) 2 11 84.
EPT Messina, Via Calabria,
I-98100 Messina (ME);
tel. (090) 77 53 56.
EPT Ragusa, Via Natalelli,
I-97100 Ragusa (RG);
tel. (0932) 2 14 21.
EPT Siracusa, Corso Gelone 92,
I-96100 Siracusa (SR);
tel. (0931) 2 76 07.
EPT Trapani, Corso Italia 10,
I-91100 Trapani (TP);
tel. (0923) 2 72 73.

Sicily, the largest and most populous island in the Mediterranean (area 25,708 sq. km, population 4·8 million), is a largely autonomous region with its capital at Palermo and nine provinces. It is an almost entirely mountainous island, bearing the marks of vigorous volcanic activity. Its most notable landmark is the massive snow-covered cone of Etna (3326 m), Europe's largest active volcano, which rises above the E coast, visible from afar. The main concentrations of populations are on the fertile and well-watered coastal plains.

Sicily's productive and rapidly developing agriculture gives it a leading place among the farming regions of Italy. Intensive vegetable growing (tomatoes, cucumbers, early potatoes, etc.), fruit orchards (citrus fruits, almonds, olives) and wine production, particularly at the western tip of the island round Marsala, predominate in the fertile coastal areas; the dry and hilly interior is suitable only for extensive arable cultivation (wheat alternating with beans) and some pastoral farming (sheep, goats). The traditional feudal system and the (often inefficient) working of the land by small tenant farmers, which is its legacy, stand in the way of the more rapid development which the potential of the land would permit. – Significant contributions to the economy are also made by the coastal fisheries (tuna, anchovies, cuttlefish, swordfish) and the extraction of salt in the Trapani area.

Sicily has little industry. The only industrial activities of any consequence are petrochemicals (around Syracuse and Gela), the mining of potash (which has superseded the once considerable sulphur-workings), and the working of asphalt (around Ragusa) and marble. In recent years, however, there has been a significant development of industry which has helped to reduce the drift of population to the highly industrialised states of northern Europe.

Sicily's magnificent scenery and its beautiful beaches, particularly on the N and E coasts, its great range of ancient remains, including the best preserved Greek temples to be found anywhere, and the very remarkable art and architecture of its Norman rulers have long made the island one of the great Meccas of travellers and tourists; and the development of a modern tourist industry is now making rapid progress.

CIRCUIT OF SICILY (930 km). – The first part of the circuit, *from Messina to Palermo*, is partly on the A 20 motorway and partly on S.S. 113 (the "Settentrionale Sicula"), following the coast of the Tyrrhenian Sea through scenery of great beauty and variety. – The road runs NW from Messina through garden suburbs, crosses the *Colle San Rizzo* pass (465 m: motorway tunnel) in the wooded **Monti Peloritani** (1374 m) and descends to the sea. – 37 km: *Milazzo/Isole Eolie* motorway exit. 6 km N is **Milazzo** (alt. 20 m; pop. 25,000; hotels: Silvanetta Palace, II, 245 b., SP; Residenzial, II, 124 b.; Riviera Lido, II, 67 b.; Saverly, II, 64 b.; etc.); good beaches, boat services to Lipari Islands). The town, founded by the Greeks in 716 B.C., has a Norman castle. 7 km farther N we come to the *Capo di Milazzo*. – 12 km along S.S. 113 lies the spa (sulphureous water) of *Castroreale Terme* (Grand Hotel Terme, I, 122 b.; La Giara, III, 180 b.; etc.). The S.S. 185 goes off on the left 3 km farther on and follows a winding course to the little town of *Novara di Sicilia* (alt. 675 m), 20 km inland; then over the *Portella Mandrazzi* (1125 m) to the ridge of the Monti Peloritani; on, with a magnificent * view of Etna, to *Francavilla di Sicilia* (alt. 675 m); and from there another 22 km, passing close to the * Gola dell'Alcantara, to Giardini, below Taormina.

Farther along S.S. 113 a road branches off on the right, passes the *monastery of the Madonna del Tíndari*, traverses the village of Tíndari and comes in 2 km to the remains of **Tyndaris**, the last Greek colony in Sicily, founded by Dionysius I in 396 B.C. and probably destroyed by the Saracens (remains of town walls, a theatre and a Roman basilica; mosaic pavements; museum).

29 km beyond Milazzo/Isole Eolie on the motorway is the exit for **Patti** (alt. 153 m; pop. 12,000; hotels: Santa Febronia, II, 88 b.; La Plaja, II, 82 b.), with large monasteries and a *Cathedral* which occupies the site of an earlier castle and contains the tomb of Adelasia of Montferrat (d. 1118), mother of King Roger of Sicily. – 9 km: tunnel through the precipitous **Capo Calavà**, and beyond this a fine view of the fertile coastal area, with *Capo Orlando* (93 m) reaching far out to sea. – 24 km: exit for **Capo d'Orlando** (alt. 12 m; pop. 9000; hotels: La Tartaruga, II, 70 b., SP; Villaggio Testa di Monaco, II, 82 b.; Bristol, III, 100 b.; Villaggio Nettuno, III, 99 b.; etc.), a little town which is also a seaside resort. From here S.S. 116 runs S via *Naso* (alt. 497 m) and over the *Portella del Zoppo* (1264 m), a pass on the ridge of the *Monti Nébrodi* (1847 m), to **Randazzo** (alt. 754 m; pop. 15,000; Motel Agip, III, 30 b.), which, with its old houses built of dark-coloured lava blocks, still preserves much of its medieval character.

At the E end of the main street, Via Umberto I, stands the *church of Santa Maria* (1217–39); Baroque interior, with columns which are each hewn from a single block of black lava. From here Via degli Archi runs W to the *church of San Nicolà* (originally Norman, remodelled in the 16th c., badly damaged during the Second World War), which contains a statue of St Nicholas by Antonio Gagini (1523). Beyond the church, to the NW, is the *Palazzo Finocchiaro* (1509), and at the W end of Via Umberto I the *church of San Martino*, has a 14th c. campanile; nearly opposite is a tower of the old ducal palace.

From Capo d'Orlando we continue on S.S. 113 over the fertile coastal plain, the *Piana del Capo*, and then through the *Bosco di Caronia*, the largest forest in Sicily (mainly scrub). – 49 km: S.S. 117 branches off and runs S via *Mistretta* (alt. 950 m; pop. 11,000) and over the *Portella del Contrasto* (1120 m), a pass on the ridge of the Monti Nebrodi, to **Nicosia** (46 km; alt. 720 m; pop. 20,000; Hotel Patria, IV, 15 b.), with the 14th c. cathedral of San Nicolà, the 18th c. church of Santa Maria Maggiore (marble reredos 8 m high by Antonio Gagini, 1512) and a castle. – Beyond the junction with S.S. 117 the coast road skirts the foot of the **Madonie** hills (*Pizzo Carbonaro*, 1979 m) and comes in 37 km to **Cefalù** (see p. 95).

Beyond Cefalù we take the motorway. – 15 km: junction with the A 19 motorway to Enna and Catania. 2 km S on A 19 is the *Buonfornello* exit, from which we continue on S.S. 113. A short distance along this, on the right, are the remains of the Greek city of *Himera*, founded in 648 B.C. and destroyed by the Carthaginians in 409 B.C. (Doric temple of *c.* 480 B.C.; temple of 6th c. B.C.). The Targa Florio car race (72 km) is held at Buonfornello annually in May. – 13 km: exit for **Términi Imerese** (alt. 113 m; pop. 26,000; Grand Hotel delle Terme, II, 180 b.), finely situated on a promontory. In the lower town is the spa establishment (warm radioactive saline springs, 42 °C – 108 °F), in the upper town the cathedral and the Belvedere Park (on the site of the ancient forum); Museo Civico. 10 km S, on a rocky crag above the *Fiume San Leonardo*, perches the little town of *Cáccamo* (alt. 521 m; pop. 11,000), with a well-preserved 12th c. castle. – 4 km: exit for **Trabia** (pop. 6000), on the coast, with a battlemented castle. – 16 km: exit for *Casteldaccia*, from which we continue on the coast road to *Santa Flavia*, where a road goes off on the right via *Porticello* and *Sant'Elia* to *Capo Zafferano* (14 km; 225 m; lighthouse). From this road a side road (1·5 km) winds steeply up to the remains of **Soluntum** (or *Solus*; Italian *Sólunto*), a Phoenician settlement and later a Roman town, situated on the SE slopes of *Monte Catalfano* (376 m). Particularly notable is the re-erected part of a peristyle belonging to a building known as the Gymnasium. From the top of the hill there are magnificent *views westward of Palermo Bay and eastward, on clear days, as far as Etna.

3 km beyond Trabia on the motorway take the exit for **Bagheria** (alt. 85 m; pop. 34,000; Motel A'Zabara, II, 141 b., SP), notable for its numerous Baroque villas (18th c.). At the end of the Corso Butera, the town's main street, is the Villa Butera (1658: "Certosa", with wax figures in Carthusian habits). A little way E the Villa Palagonía (1715) has an extraordinary collection of grotesque sculptured figures. Still farther E stands the Villa Valguarnera (*view from terrace and from the nearby hill of Montagnola). – 12 km: exit for **Palermo** (see p. 184).

The next part of the circuit, *from Palermo to Trapani*, can be done either direct on the A 29 and A 29d motorways or on the

coast road (S.S. 187), passing through the little port of Castellammare del Golffo and **Erice. Longer, but well worth the extra distance, is the route via S.S. 186 and S.S. 113. For this route leave Palermo by the Porta Nuova and the Corso Calatafimi. – 8 km: **Monreale** (alt. 300 m; pop. 25,000; hotels: Carrubella Park, II, 44 b.; Il Ragno, III, 22 b.; etc.), the see of an archbishop, beautifully situated above the Conca d'Oro.

On the left-hand side of the main street is the **Cathedral with its two towers, the finest example of Norman architecture in Sicily. 102 m long by 40 m wide, in the form of a basilica, it boasts a beautiful choir with interlaced pointed arches of dark grey lava which preserves the structure of a Byzantine church. The main doorway has a fine bronze door by a Pisan artist named Bonannus, with reliefs from scriptural history and inscriptions in early Italian (1186). The left-hand doorway, under a porch of 1569, has a bronze door by Barisanus of Trani (12th c.). In the interior are 18 ancient columns with fine capitals, and its walls are covered with magnificent mosaics, completed in 1182, which cover an area of 6340 sq. m (the largest area of mosaics in Sicily), with scenes from the Old Testament and the life of Christ and the Apostles. In the S transept are the sarcophagi of William I and II, son and grandson of Roger II. In the S aisle is the 18th c. Cappella di San Benedetto (marble reliefs), in the N aisle the Cappella del Crocifisso (1690), with fine wood-carvings of the Passion on the side doors. It is well worth while making the ascent to the roof of the cathedral (172 steps) for the view it affords. – To the right of the cathedral stands the former Benedictine monastery. Of the original building nothing is left but the *cloister (*Chiostro di Santa Maria Nuova*), the largest and finest in the Italian Romanesque style, with 216 columns. The cloister is overshadowed on the S side by a ruined wall of the original monastery.

21 km beyond Monreale on S.S. 186 lies **Partinico** (alt. 189 m; pop. 25,000), dominated by an ancient tower. From here we continue on S.S. 113. – 20 km: **Álcamo** (alt. 256 m; pop. 45,000; hotels: Centrale, IV, 46 b.; Miramare, IV, 33 b.; etc.), a town founded by the Arabs. In the main street is the 17th c. cathedral, with paintings by Borreman (1736–37) and sculpture by Antonio Gagini and his school (also to be seen in the church of San Francesco d'Assisi). In the church of Santa Chiara and the Badia Nuova are stucco figures by Giacomo Serpotta. There is also a 14th c. castle. Above the town rises *Monte Bonifato* (825 m: *view); the climb takes 2 hours. – 15 km: road on right to the remains (3 km W) of the ancient city of **Segesta** or *Egesta* (alt. 305 m), one of the oldest towns in Sicily, founded by the Elymians in pre-Greek times. It was almost incessantly at war with its Greek neighbours, particularly

Sicilian horse-trappings

Selinus (Selinunte); later it became Carthaginian and then Roman, and was
finally destroyed by the Saracens. From
the end of the access road a stepped path
leads up to the *temple, standing in
majestic solitude on a levelled ridge of hill
below the W side of the ancient city.
Begun in 430 B.C. but left unfinished, it is
one of the best preserved temples in Sicily
(61 m long by 26 m across), with 36 Doric
columns still supporting the entablature
and gable. – From the end of the access
road a track winds up to the site of the
ancient city, situated 1·5 km SE on *Monte
Barbaro* (431 m), with remains of fortifications, houses (mosaic pavements)
and a *theatre hewn from the rock.

3 km beyond the turning for Segesta is
Calatafimi (alt. 310 m; pop. 13,000), with
a castle on a hill to the W of the town. – 1
km: minor road (3 km SW) to the Ossario,
a conspicuous monument to Garibaldi
erected in 1892 to commemorate his first
victory over numerically superior Bourbon
forces on 15 May 1860. – 1 km: the road
forks. S.S. 113, to the right, leads to
Trapani (35 km: see p. 286); S.S. 188A,
to the left, runs via *Salemi* (10 km; alt. 442
m; pop. 17,000), with a castle built in the
time of Frederick II in which Garibaldi
proclaimed his dictatorship of Sicily
in 1860 (commemorative column), to
Castelvetrano (another 26 km: see below).

The third part of the circuit of Sicily, *from
Trapani to Syracuse*, is on S.S. 115. – 32
km: **Marsala** (see p. 152). – 19 km:
Mazara del Vallo (alt. 8 m; pop. 37,000;
Hotel Hopps, II, 244 b., SP; etc.), with an
11th c. cathedral (remodelled in the 17th
and 20th c.) founded by Count Roger and

a number of other fine churches and
palaces. – 15 km: *Campobello di Mazara*
(alt. 100 m; pop. 12,000). 3 km SW are the
ancient quarries known as the *Rocche
di Cusa or Cave di Campobello which
supplied the building material for Selinus
(Selinunte). – 8 km: **Castelvetrano** (alt.
190 m; pop. 32,000; hotels: Heus, I, 71 b.;
Selinus, II, 68 b.; etc.), with the churches
of San Giovanni (statue of John the
Baptist by Antonio Gagini, 1512, in choir)
and San Domenico (stucco figures by
Antonio Ferraro, 1577), and marble
(Madonna by Domenico Gagini) and the
16th c. Chiesa Madre (Renaissance doorway). 3·5 km W of the town is the restored
Norman *church of Santa Trinità della
Delia* (12th c.), in Byzantine style on a
centralised plan. – 9 km: road on right
(S.S. 115D) to **Selinunte** (see p. 263). –
37 km: **Sciacca** (or *Sciacca Terme*: alt. 60
m; hotels: Delle Terme, I, 126 b., SP;
Garden, II, 120 b.; Motel Agip, II, 76 b.).

At the W entrance to the town is the *Porta San
Salvatore*. Just beyond it, to the right, stands the 16th
c. *church of Santa Margherita* (N doorway in marble,
1468), and to the left the *Chiesa del Carmine*. NE of
the Porta San Salvatore, at the W end of the Corso
Vittorio Emanuele, is the Gothic *Casa Steripinto*, with
a façade of faceted stones. Near the E end of the Corso
Vittorio Emanuele we come to the *Cathedral*
(Madonna by Francesco Laurana, 1467, in fourth
chapel on right). Beyond this are the *Giardino
Comunale* (view) and the *Terme Selinuntine*, the spa
establishment (sulphur baths), on the site of the
ancient baths. Higher up, on the line of the town walls,
are the remains of the *castle* of Count Luna. – From the
Porta San Salvatore a road runs 7·5 km NE to the limestone hill of **Monte San Calógero** (388 m), with the
Santuario San Calogero on its summit (*view). Below
the monastery are caves with vapour baths (*Le Stufe*:
temperature 34–40 °C – 93–104 °F). – 20 km NE of
Sciacca is the little town of *Caltabellotta* (alt. 750 m;
pop. 7500), dominated by its castle, which has a
cathedral dating from the Norman period.

23 km farther along S.S. 115 a road goes
off on the right to the remains (6 km SW
on Capo Bianco) of the ancient city of
Eraclea Minoa, destroyed in the 1st c. B.C.
– 51 km: *Porto Empédocle*, the port of
Agrigento. – 6 km: road on left to
Agrigento (see p. 49), running between the temples of Zeus and Hera and
then winding its way up to the town. – 32
km: **Palma di Montechiaro** (alt. 160 m;
pop. 20,000), with a handsome Baroque
church. On the hill beyond it, to the right,
is the 14th c. *Castello* (alt. 286 m). –
20 km: **Licata** (alt. 12 m; pop. 40,000;
hotels: Baia d'Oro, II, 144 b.; Al Faro, II,
60 b.; etc.), beautifully situated on the
sloping hillside at the mouth of the river
Salso, an expanding port which is the

Gela Cathedral

principal commercial town on the S coast of Sicily (export of sulphur). Above the town to the W is the 16th c. *Castel Sant'Angelo* (restored). – 11 km: on the coast, to the right, is the 15th c. *Castello di Falconara* (restored). – 22 km: **Gela** (alt. 45 m; pop. 67,000; Hotel Mediterraneo, II, 110 b.; etc.), a port which was formerly called *Terranova di Sicilia* (oil refineries), also frequented as a seaside resort.

To the W of the town are the extensive *cemeteries* of the ancient city (founded by Dorian settlers in 688 B.C.) and the Zona Archeologica di Capo Soprano, with the imposing remains of Greek *defensive walls of the 5th–4th c. B.C. (200 m long, built of regular stone blocks in the lower part and sun-dried bricks in the upper part – the earliest known use of such bricks) and Greek baths of the 4th c. B.C. At the E end of the town near the *Museo Archeologico are the most recent excavations (houses and shops of the 4th c. B.C.). S of the museum, on the Molino a Vento (Windmill) hill, the Acropolis, is the municipal park, with the remains of two Doric *temples* (6th and 5th c. B.C.).

33 km beyond Gela on S.S. 115 is **Vittoria** (alt. 168 m; pop. 45,000; hotels: Italia, II, 53 b.; Sicilia, III, 27 b.; etc), the principal centre of the Sicilian wine trade. In the main square are the neo-classical Teatro Vittorio Emanuele and the church of the Madonna delle Grazie (18th c.). – 8 km: **Cómiso** (alt. 245 m; pop. 27,000), with two 18th c. domed churches, the Chiesa Madre and the Chiesa dell'Annunziata, and a beautiful Fountain of Diana in the Piazza Municipio. – 17 km: **Ragusa** (alt. 512 m; pop. 60,000; hotels: Mediterraneo, II, 174 b.; Ionio, II, 69 b.; San Giovanni, II, 42 b.; Tivoli, III, 54 b.; etc. – Two holiday centres at Camarina, 30 km SW: Village, II, 1684 b., SP; Palace, II, 511 b., SP), a provincial capital, picturesquely situated above the gorge of

the River *Irminio*, with a Baroque cathedral (18th c.) and the splendid Baroque church of San Giorgio (18th c.) in the old part of the town, Ibla, to the E (steep winding streets). From the bypass to the S of the town there are fine *views. – Around the town are deposits of bituminous limestone. 2 km S, on the road to the rising seaside resort of *Marina di Ragusa* (28 km), are large asphalt mines. In recent years oil has been worked here.

15 km beyond Ragusa is **Módica** (alt. 440 m; pop. 50,000; Motel di Modica, II, 67 b.; Hotel Minerva, III, 22 b.), a flourishing town rising up the slopes on both sides of the Modica valley. In the lower town, at the top of a flight of steps, are the churches of San Pietro (18th c.) and Santa Maria di Gesù (*c.* 1478), and adjoining them a former monastery with a cloister. In the upper town stands the imposing 18th c. church of San Giorgio. – 7 km: road on left into the picturesque valley of *Cava d'Íspica*, the rock walls of which contain numerous caves used as dwellings and tombs in the Byzantine period. – 32 km: **Noto** (alt. 158 m; pop. 30,000; hotels: Stella, IV, 32 b.; Eloro, in Pizzuta, to the SE, II, 398 b., SP), attractively laid out in terraces, with Baroque churches and handsome palaces. The present town was built from 1703 onwards to replace the older town of Noto, 11 km SE, which was destroyed by an earthquake in 1693.

On the town's main street, the Corso Vittorio Emanuele, which traverses it from W to E, are three monumental squares. In the first of these, the *Piazza Ércole* (officially the Piazza XVI Maggio), are the Baroque *church of San Domenico* (18th c.) and an ancient statue of Hercules. In the second, the *Piazza del Municipio*, stands the **Cathedral**, with an imposing Baroque façade, the *Palazzo Ducezio* (Town Hall) and the *church of San Salvatore*. In the third, the *Piazza XXX Ottobre*, we find the *church of the Immacolata* (or San Francesco) and the *monastery of San Salvatore*. To the N, 300 m above Via Cavour, is the *Chiesa del Crocifisso*, with a Madonna by Francesco Laurana (1471).

9 km beyond Noto is **Avola** (alt. 40 m; pop. 28,000). The road then crosses the River *Cassibile*, the ancient *Kakyparis*, where Demosthenes and his 6000 Athenians was compelled to surrender to the Syracusans in 413 B.C. Upstream, in the rock faces of the Cava Grande, is a *Siculan necropolis*. – 23 km: **Syracuse** (see p. 277).

The last part of the circuit of Sicily, *from Syracuse to Messina*, is on S.S. 114 (the

"Orientale Sicula"; from Catania also the A 18 motorway), running close to the sea for most of the way. – 14 km from Syracuse the road forks. Straight ahead is the old (and more interesting) road via **Lentini** (alt. 71 m; pop. 35,000; Hotel Carmes, III, 34 b.) to Catania; to the right the new road, S.S. 114, is 18 km shorter and much faster. This road passes large oil refineries and comes in 7 km to the turning for **Augusta**, the principal Italian naval base in Sicily (alt. 14 m; pop. 30,000; hotels: Kursaal Augusteo, III, 75 b.; Megara, III, 21 b.; Villaggio Valtur, in Brucoli, to the N, II, 894 b., SP; etc.). – 63 km: **Catania** (see p. 94).

9 km beyond Catania on S.S. 114 lies the little town of **Aci Castello**, dominated by a picturesque ruined castle on a high crag (alt. 15 m; pop. 9000; hotels: Bahia Verde, in Cannizzaro, I, 254 b., SP; I Faraglioni, I, 123 b., and Eden Riviera, II, 66 b., both in Aci Trezza). Just beyond the town can be seen the seven **Isole dei Ciclopi** (Cyclops' Islands) or *Faraglioni*, traditionally the rocks which the blinded Cyclops hurled after Odysseus' ship ("Odyssey", IX, 537). On the largest of the islands, the *Isola d'Aci*, is a marine biological station. – 7 km: **Acireale** (Sicilian *Iaci*; alt. 161 m; pop. 50,000; hotels: Perla Ionica, II, 978 b., SP; Santa Tecla, II, 602 b., SP; Aloha d'Oro, II, 162 b., SP; Maugeria, II, 68 b.; etc.). On the near side of the town to the right of the road, are the *Terme di Santa Vénera* (warm radioactive water containing iodine, sulphur and salt). From here the town's main street, the Corso Vittorio Emanuele, runs N, with the church of San Sebastiano (Baroque façade) on the right. Beyond this, in the Piazza del Duomo, are the cathedral, the Town Hall (small museum) and the church of Santi Pietro e Paolo. From the municipal park at the N end of the town there are fine views. – 18 km: *Mascali*, a little town which formerly lay farther W but was destroyed by lava in 1928 and rebuilt on its present site. – 15 km: **Taormina** (see p. 280). – 48 km: **Messina** (see p. 155).

Siena

Region: Toscana. – Province: Siena (SI).
Altitude: 322 m. – Population: 67,000.
Post code: I-53100. – Dialling code: 0577.
(i) **EPT**, Via di Città 5;
tel. 4 70 51.
AA, Piazza del Campo 55;
tel. 28 05 51.
Information office at station.
ACI, Via V. Veneto 47;
tel. 4 90 01.
TCI, *Viaggi S.E.T.I.*, Piazza del Campo 56;
tel. 28 30 04.

HOTELS. – *Park*, Via Marciano 16, I, 103 b., SP; *Villa Scacciapensieri*, Via di Scacciapensieri 24, I, 50 b., SP; *Athena*, Via Paolo Mascogni 55, II, 184 b.; *Moderno*, Via Baldassarre Peruzzi 19, II, 123 b.; *Garden*, with annexe, Via Custoza 2, II, 104 b., SP; *Minerva*, Via Garibaldi 72, II, 86 b.; *Continentale*, Via Banchi di Sopra 85, II, 79 b.; *Vico Alto*, Via delle Regioni 26, II, 74 b.; *Castagneto*, Via dei Cappuccini 55, II, 21 b.; *Italia*, Viale Cavour 67, III, 121 b.; *Chiusarelli*, Viale Curtatone 9, III, 86 b.; *La Toscana*, Via C. Angiolieri 12, III, 66 b.; etc. – CAMPING SITE.

EVENTS. – The *Palio, a picturesque procession and horse-race (2 July and 16 August). – Recreation park.

The provincial capital of Siena, situated 70 km S of Florence on three ridges which meet in the middle, is one of the great art centres of Italy, with a profusion of fine architecture and numerous churches and palaces. It has a university, founded in the 13th c., and is the see of an archbishop. From this area comes the brown pigment known as burnt sienna.

HISTORY. – In Roman times *Saena Iulia* was a place of no importance, but under the Franks it became the residence of a count. After the death of Countess *Matilda of Tuscany* in 1115 the town asserted its independence, as did Pisa, Lucca, Florence and other towns. Thereafter it was governed by the Ghibelline nobility, and this brought it into sharp conflict with Florence, a stronghold of the Guelfs. The two towns were constantly at war, vying with one another in power and wealth. After the fall of the Hohenstaufens (1270) *Charles of Anjou* succeeded in establishing his influence in Siena and incorporated it in the Guelf federation of Tuscan towns. In 1348 the town was ravaged by the plague. After a period of internal strife Siena was governed by tyrants, among them *Pandolfo Petrucci* (1487 onwards), known as "Il Magnifico", whom Machiavelli represents as the very model of a despot. In 1555 Siena was occupied by the Spaniards, and in 1559 it was ceded to Duke Cosimo I of Tuscany.

ART. – The heyday of Sienese art was in the 13th and 14th c. The cathedral and many of the palaces are magnificent examples of Gothic architecture. The availability of good brickmaking clay in the area favoured the use of bricks in building. The delicate, graceful Sienese painting of the 13th and 14th c. (*Duccio, Simone Martini, Ambrogio* and *Pietro*

Lorenzetti) surpassed the early painting of Florence. *Jacopo della Quercia* (1374–1438) was one of the founders of Renaissance sculpture, and his influence can still be detected in the work of Michelangelo.

SIGHTS. – The town centre is closed to cars, but access to the hotels is permitted. – In the centre of Siena a spacious semicircular area, the ****Piazza del Campo**, extends in front of the massive Town Hall, the uniform architecture making it one of the finest squares in Italy. The "Palio delle Contrade" is held on 2 July and 16 August (the principal performance). The Palio is a picturesque procession in medieval costumes and a horse-race between the various wards (*contrade*) of the town, the prize for the winners being a banner (Latin *pallium*) bearing the image of the Madonna. The rehearsals in the Campo on 13–15 August are also worth seeing. – On the N side of the square stands the marble *Fonte Gaia*, a copy of Jacopo della Quercia's original masterpiece (1419). Along the S side of the Campo extends the ***Palazzo Pubblico** (Town Hall), a huge Gothic building of travertine and brick (1288–1309); the top floor of the lower side wings was added in 1680. At the left-hand end is the *Torre del Mangia*, built 1338–49 (102 m high; 412 steps; view), and below it the *Cappella di Piazza*, a loggia built after the great plague of 1348, with a Renaissance upper storey added in 1468. The *interior is notable for the numerous frescoes of the Sienese school which reflect the views and attitudes of the proud citizens of Siena in the 14th and 15th c.; particularly interesting is the painting by Ambrogio Lorenzetti in the Sala della Pace, "Good and Bad Government" (1337–43), with a contemporary view of the city. On the first and second floors the *Museo Civico* houses drawings, paintings and other documents on the history of the town. On the third floor is a loggia (view) in which the original sculpture from the Fonte Gaia has been assembled.

From the NW side of the Campo, steps lead up to the *Loggia di Mercanzia* (1417–38), the old commercial tribunal. Here the three principal streets of the town meet: to the N the *Banchi di Sopra*, to the E the *Banchi di Sotto* and to the SW the *Via di Città*, in which stands the beautiful Gothic *Palazzo Chigi-Saracini* (14th c.), now occupied by the Accademia Musicale Chigiana. In Banchi di Sotto is the *University* (on left), and opposite it the *Palazzo Piccolomini*, one of the finest Early Renaissance palaces in Siena, built for Nanni Piccolomini, father of Pope Pius III, after 1469, and now the repository of the extensive State Archives. Situated beyond this, in the Piazza Piccolomini, the elegant *Loggia del Papa* was built for Pius II in 1462.

From Via di Città the Via dei Pellegrini runs W past the *Palazzo del Magnifico* (1508), seen on the left, to the little Piazza San Giovanni, on the SW side of which is the choir of the cathedral, which occupies the highest point in the town. Under this, forming a sort of crypt, is the ***Baptistery** of San Giovanni, with a beautiful but unfinished façade of 1382. It contains a fine *font by Jacopo della Quercia (1427–30), with bronze reliefs by Donatello and others. – From here we can either bear right past the *Archbishop's Palace* or go up the steps to the left to reach the *Piazza del Duomo*.

The ***Cathedral** was begun in 1229, and by 1265 it had been completed as far as the choir, and the dome had already been built; then about 1317 the choir was extended eastward over the baptistery. In 1339 the citizens of Siena resolved to carry out a large-scale rebuilding which would have made the cathedral the largest and finest in Italy; but this project was abandoned as a result of structural defects and the great plague of 1348. The present cathedral has a total length of 89 m and a width of 24 m (across the transepts 51 m). The *façade, in red, black and white marble, was not completed until 1380; the rich sculptural decoration consists largely of reproductions dating from the restoration of the cathedral in 1869, and the mosaics were added in 1877. The campanile dates from the late 14th c.

The Palio, Siena

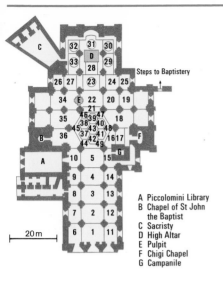

Siena Cathedral

Scenes represented on the PAVEMENT (various dates between 1372 and 1562: partly imitations and copies – originals in Cathedral Museum)

1 Hermes Trismegistus	21 Moses draws water from the rock
2 Coats of arms of Siena (centre), Pisa, Lucca, Florence, Arezzo, Orvieto, Rome, Perugia, Viterbo, Massa, Grosseto, Volterra and Pistoia	22 Dance round the Golden Calf
	23 David and Goliath
	24 Moses
	25 Samson defeats the Philistines
3 Imperial Altar	26, 27 Joshua
4 Fortune	28 Abraham's Sacrifice
5 Wheel of Fortune; four philosophers	29 Wisdom
	30 Moderation
6–15 Sibyls	31 Compassion
16 Seven Ages of Man	32 Justice
17 Faith, Hope, Charity, Religion	33 Strength
	34 Judith and Holofernes
18 Jephthah defeats the Ammonites	35 Massacre of the Innocents
19 Death of Absalom	36 Fall of Herod
20 Emperor Sigismund	37–49 Ahab and Elijah

Map key:
- A Piccolomini Library
- B Chapel of St John the Baptist
- C Sacristy
- D High Altar
- E Pulpit
- F Chigi Chapel
- G Campanile

Steps to Baptistery

20m

The ****INTERIOR**, with its regularly alternating courses of black and white marble, at first produces a rather strange effect. Its unique feature is the marble ****pavement**, with its beautiful graffito figures and scenes, mostly from the Old Testament. (Some of them are copies: originals in the Cathedral Museum.)

Along the cornice in the *nave* are numerous *terracotta busts of Popes* (15th c.). – In the *N aisle* is a masterpiece of decorative sculpture, the *entrance wall* of the Cathedral Library (by Lorenzo di Mariano, the finest sculptor of the Sienese High Renaissance). – In the *N transept* the *Cappella di San Giovanni* has a beautiful doorway by this artist and a bronze statue of John the Baptist by Donatello (1457). – A particularly notable feature is the white marble ***pulpit**, with fine reliefs of New Testament scenes by Niccolò Pisano (1266–68).

From the N aisle we enter the famous ****Cathedral Library** (*Librería Piccolomini*: best light in the afternoon), one of the finest and best preserved creations of the Early Renaissance. It was built in 1495 for Cardinal Francesco Piccolomini (later Pope Pius III) in honour of his kinsman Aeneas Sylvius Piccolomini (Pope Pius II, 1458–64) and decorated by Pinturicchio and his pupils with brilliantly coloured frescoes depicting scenes from the life of Aeneas Sylvius (1502–08).

Opposite the SE side of the cathedral the former *Opera del Duomo* (the "office of works" of the cathedral), is now the **Cathedral Museum**, with material illustrating the constructional history of the cathedral, pictures by Sienese masters, including Duccio di Buoninsegna's ***"Maestà"**, a picture of the Madonna enthroned with angels and saints painted in 1308–11 for the high altar of the cathedral, and embroidered vestments (14th–18th c.). – Opposite the façade of the cathedral are the church and *hospital of Santa Maria della Scala* (13th–14th c.), with frescoes depicting the work of the hospital in the 15th c.

From the Piazza del Duomo the Via del Capitano runs SE past the *Prefecture*, the former Palazzo Reale (on left), and the *Palazzo del Capitano* (on right) to the little Piazza di Postierla, from which Via di San Pietro leads to the ***Palazzo Buonsignori**, a 14th c. brick building now housing the ***Pinacoteca Nazionale**, with an important and representative collection of works of the Sienese school. Among later painters represented in the gallery is the Lombard artist Giovanni Antonio Bazzi, surnamed Il Sodoma (*c.* 1477–1549), notable for his sensitive appreciation of beauty. – Via San Pietro ends in the Prato Sant'Agostino, in which is the *church of Sant'Agostino* (pictures by Perugino, Sodoma and others).

In the Banchi di Sopra, going N from the Loggia di Mercanzia, stands the early Gothic *Palazzo Tolomei* (on left). Beyond this, in Piazza Salimbeni, are the battlemented *Palazzo Salimbeni* and, on the SE side, the **Palazzo Spannocchi**, a fine Early Renaissance building by the Florentine Giuliano da Maiano (begun 1473). – Farther N again (on left) the little *church of Santa Maria delle Nevi* has a beautiful Early Renaissance façade (1471). – To the E, on the edge of the town, is the *church of San Francesco* (1326), with a façade of 1913. Adjoining it are two beautiful cloisters and the **Oratorio di San Bernardino**, the upper floor of which has ***frescoes by Sodoma** and Early Renaissance ceiling decoration. – A short distance SW of the Palazzo Salimbeni is situated the interesting *Museo Etrucso* (Etruscan antiquities).

Piazza del Campo and Palazzo Pubblico, Siena

On the W side of the town is the fortress-like **church of San Domenico**, a rough brick structure in the Gothic style (1293–1391) with a crenellated campanile. St Catherine's Chapel has beautiful *frescoes by Sodoma (1525). In the second chapel to the right of the high altar, which once belonged to the "German nation" of the University, are many tombstones emblazoned with coats of arms belonging to German students of the 16th and 17th c.

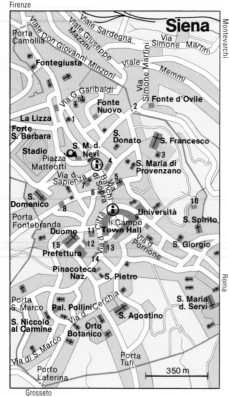

1 Sant' Andrea
2 Porta Ovile
3 Oratorio di San Bernardino
4 Palazzo Salimbeni
5 San Cristoforo
6 Palazzo Tolomei
7 Museo Etrusco
8 Fonte Branda

9 Palazzo Piccolomini
10 Fonti di Follonica
11 Palazzo del Magnifico
12 Cathedral Museum
13 Palazzo Chigi-Saracini
14 Palazzo Piccolomini
   delle Papesse
15 Palazzo Arcivescovile

Below the hill of San Domenico the *Fontebranda*, a picturesquely situated fountain which is mentioned in the records as early as 1081, had a colonnade of three arches built over it in 1242. – A little way E, in Via Santa Caterina, is the **House of St Catherine**. St Catherine of Siena (1347–80), the daughter of a dyer named Benincasa, prevailed on Pope Gregory XI to return from Avignon to Rome in 1377. The best known of her visions was her "mystic marriage" to the Infant Christ, a favourite theme with painters. The rooms in the house, now oratories, contain pictures by Sienese painters of the 15th and 16th c.

From San Domenico we can go either NW along the Viale dei Mille, past the *Stadium*, or N round the Stadium to a beautiful park, the *Passeggio della Lizza*, with a *monument to Garibaldi* (1896). At the W end of the park is the entrance to **Forte Santa Barbara**, built by Duke Cosimo I in 1560, which is now used for open-air performances. In the cellars is a permanent wine exhibition. From the ramparts one can enjoy a charming view of Siena. – A short distance N of the park is the little *church of Fontegiusta* (1484), with a *high altar by Lorenzo di Mariano, one of the finest examples of High Renaissance work of its kind (1519).

SURROUNDINGS. – 23 km NW of Siena on S.S. 2 is **Colle di Val d'Elsa** (pop. 15,000; Hotel Nazionale, III, 42 b.; etc.), situated above the River *Elsa*. It consists of an industrial lower town, *Colle Basso* (alt. 137 m), and the old upper town or *Colle Alto* (223 m), with medieval palaces and a 13th c. cathedral. – From here it is possible either to take S.S. 68 to *Volterra (see p. 324), 27 km W, or to go N to *Poggibonsi* and then W to **San Gimignano (20 km: see p. 255).

Another very interesting excursion is to the large monastery of *Monte Oliveto Maggiore (alt. 273 m), 35 km SE of Siena. One of the most renowned monasteries of the Olivetans (a branch of the Benedictines), it was founded in 1313 by Bernardo Tolomei of Siena. A visit to this great monastic establishment is most rewarding. In the cloister are fine **frescoes of scenes from the life of St Benedict by Luca Signorelli and Sodoma (1505).

The coast at Sorrento

Sorrento

Region: Campania. – Province: Napoli (NA).
Altitude: 50 m. – Population: 15,000.
Post code: I-80067. – Dialling code: 081.
(i) **AA**, Via L. de Maio 35;
tel. 8 78 21 04.
TCI, *Viaggi AVI*, Corso Italia 155;
tel. 8 78 19 84.

HOTELS. – *Parco dei Principi*, I, 373 b., SP; *Cesare Augusto*, I, 220 b., SP; *De la Ville*, I, 215 b., SP; *Ambasciatori*, I, 198 b., SP; *Imperial Hotel Tramontana*, I, 193 b.; *Excelsior Vittoria*, I, 192 b., SP; *Michelangelo*, I, 180 b.; *Riviera*, I, 170 b.; *Capodimonte*, I, 157 b., SP; *President*, I, 148 b., SP; *Flora*, I, 147 b., SP; *Continental*, I, 143 b., SP; *Aminta*, I, 134 b., SP; *Europa Palace*, I, 133 b.; *Royal*, I, 132 b., SP; *Carlton*, I, 131 b., SP; *Belair*, I, 77 b., SP; *Conca Park*, II, 333 b.; *Bristol*, II, 158 b., SP; *Plaza*, II, 135 b.; *Gran Paradiso*, II, 125 b., SP; *Admiral*, II, 113 b., SP; *Eden*, II, 101 b.; *Tirrenia*, II, 99 b.; *Villa Maria*, II, 99 b.; *Cavour*, II, 96 b.; *Bellevue Syrene*, II, 91 b.; *Central*, II, 87 b., SP; *Minerva*, II, 86 b., SP; *Atlantic*, II, 84 b.; *Claridge*, II, 84 b.; *Ascot*, III, 100 b.; *Santa Lucia*, III, 70 b.; *Capri*, III, 70 b.; *La Residenza*, III, 65 b.; *Leone*, III, 62 b.; *Tourist*, III, 60 b.; etc. – YOUTH HOSTEL, Via Capasso 5, 130 b. – CAMPING SITE.

*Sorrento (in the local dialect Surient), the ancient Surrentum, is attractively situated amid luxuriant lemon- and orange-groves on the S side of the *Bay of Naples, on the edge of tufa cliffs 50 m high rising precipitously from the sea. It is the see of an archbishop.

SIGHTS. – Between the *Corso Italia*, Sorrento's long main street, and the sea is the attractive *Museo Correale* (closed Tuesdays), with pictures, porcelain, furniture and local antiquities. On the E side of the old town, in *Piazza Tasso*, stands a marble statue of the poet *Torquato Tasso* (1544–95), who was born in Sorrento. From here a road runs down through a ravine to the *Marina Piccola*, where the boats come in. – From the *Giardino Pubblico*, 0·5 km NW of Piazza Tasso there is an unrestricted view of the sea.

SURROUNDINGS. – To the E of Sorrento extends the very fertile and densely populated **Piano di Sorrento**, enclosed by sheltering hills and slashed by ravines, in Roman times a favourite residence of the great and the wealthy and still a popular holiday resort which attracts large numbers of visitors from far and wide.

A very attractive trip from Sorrento is round the Sorrentine peninsula to Positano. – 6 km SW of Sorrento is **Massa Lubrense** (alt. 120 m; pop. 2000; hotels: Delfino, II, 93 b., SP; Central Park, II, 64 b.; Villaggio Freedom, II, 46 b.; Maria, III, 56 b.; etc.), with the Castello di Santa Maria (224 m) rearing above it. From here it is 2 hours' walk to the *Punta della Campanella*, at the farthest tip of the peninsula. – Beyond Massa Lubrense the road skirts *Monte San Nicola* and comes in another 5 km to **Sant'Agata** *sui due Golfi* (alt. 391 m; hotels: Hermitage, I, 112 b., SP; Iaccarino e la Terrazza, II, 119 b., SP; Due Golfi, II, 112 b., SP; Montana, II, 93 b.; O Sole Mio, II, 86 b.; Delle Palme, II, 76 b., SP; etc.), a pleasant little summer resort. On a hill 1 km NW is the **Deserto** (alt. 455 m), a former monastery which is now an orphanage. From the roof there are fine *views of the bays of Naples and Salerno. – From Sant'Agata it is another 13 km on a beautiful road (the stretch to *Colli San Pietro* being known as the "Nastro Azzurro" or "Blue Ribbon") which passes close to the conspicuous *chapel of Sant'Angelo* (alt. 462 m: **view), to the left of the road, before coming to **Positano** (see p. 176).

La Spezia

Region: Liguria. – Province: La Spezia (SP).
Altitude: 3 m. – Population: 130,000.
Post code: I-19100. – Dialling code: 0187.
(i) **EPT**, Viale Mazzini 45;
tel. 3 60 00.
ACI, Via Costantini 18;
tel. 51 10 98.
TCI, *Turistar*, Piazza Saint Bon 1;
tel. 3 43 73.
Via Veneto 9.
Golfotur, Via G. Galilei 10;
tel. 3 10 21.
Mondadori per Voi, Via Bassa 55;
tel. 2 81 50.

Lerici harbour

HOTELS. – *Jolly*, Via XX Settembre 2, I, 188 b.; *Tirreno*, Piazza Paita 4, II, 155 b.; *Palazzo di San Giorgio*, Via A. Manzoni 60, II, 112 b.; *Astoria*, Via Roma 139, II, 97 b.; *Genova*, Via Fratelli Rosselli 84, II, 49 b.; *Firenze e Continentale*, Via Paleocapa 7, III, 102 b.; *Terminus*, Via Paleocapa 21, III, 84 b.; etc.

The provincial capital of La Spezia, a busy industrial town, lies between Genoa and Pisa on the wide *Golfo **della Spezia, one of the largest and safest natural harbours in the Mediterranean, extending 9 km into the coast and 7 km wide. The surrounding hills offer magnificent views.**

SIGHTS. – The main street of La Spezia is the *Corso Cavour*, where, at No. 39, are the *Biblioteca Civica* (some 80,000 volumes), the *Musei Civici* (local history, natural history) and the *Museo Archeologico Lunense* (Roman antiquities and finds from Luni: see below). – The Corso Cavour runs SE into Via D. Chiodo, which is lined with orange-trees, and near which is the *Giardino Pubblico*, with fine palms and yuccas. From here Viale Mazzini and Viale Italia run NE, separated by a line of palms and flanked on the seaward side by the Passeggiata Morin, from which there are beautiful views of the bay and the Apuan Alps with the shimmering white spoil heaps of Carrara.

Via Chiode leads NE to the Piazza Verdi, with modern office blocks, and beyond this the Piazza Italia, in which stands the new *Town Hall*, and on a terrace above the square the new **Cathedral** (1976). – NW of Piazza Verdi, running along the hillside, is Via 27 Marzo, with the 14th c. *Castello San Giorgio*.

At the SW end of Via Chiodo is the Piazza Chiodo and farther on, beyond a canal the entrance to the **Naval Arsenal**, the largest in Italy, with an important shipyard. The interesting *Shipping Museum* at the entrance contains models illustrating the history of seafaring from the origins to the present day and a large collection of charts.

SURROUNDINGS. – There is a very attractive drive around the N side of the town on the *Giro della Foce*, which follows the slopes of *Monte Castellazzo* (285 m) to the **Passo della Foce** (241 m), with *views of the Gulf of Spezia and the Apuan Alps.

The *coast road is also very beautiful. 11 km W we come to Riomaggiore, the first village in the **Cinqueterre** (see p. 97). 10 km S on the W side of the Gulf of Spezia is **Portovénere** (alt. 10 m; pop. 6000; hotels: San Pietro, II, 59 b.; Belvedere, III, 36 b.; etc.), an old-world little port picturesquely situated on the Bocchetta, the narrow strait, only 150 m wide, between the *Costa dell'Oliva* promontory and the island of *Palmaria*. From the little church of San Pietro (1277) at the southern tip of the promontory there are charming views of the precipitous cliffs of the Cinqueterre to the NW and the bay of Lerici to the E. Above San Pietro are a Genoese castle and the parish church of San Lorenzo (1131).

11 km SE of La Spezia lies the little port and industrial town of **Lérici** (alt. 5 m; pop. 14,000; hotels: Shelley e delle Palme, II, 81 b.; Byron, II, 33 b.; Luisa, III, 34 b.; etc.), which in the Middle Ages, together with Portovénere, was the principal port on the Gulf of Spezia. Beside the church of San Rocco is an unusual Romanesque campanile. On a projecting tongue of land stands a well-preserved 12th c. castle, now a youth hostel. – From Lerici there is a pleasant drive (4 km SE), passing a number of pretty coves and the fishing village of *Fiascherino*, to the picturesquely situated village of *Tellaro* (hotels: Cristallo, II, 62 b.; Il Nido, II, 31 b.; etc.).

16 km E of La Spezia is **Sarzana** (alt. 26 m; pop. 20,000; hotels: Laurina, III, 38 b.; Portanova, III, 33 b.; etc. – Motel Agip, II, 102 b.), founded in 1202 as the successor to the ancient Etruscan city of *Luni* (of which sparse remains can be seen 7 km SE). Remains of 15th c. town walls; Castello (now a prison). The white marble cathedral, in Italian Gothic style (1355–1477), contains a painted crucifix from Luni (by Guillelmus, 1138), the earliest dated panel painting in Italy. To the N of the town stands the picturesque castle of *Sarzanello* (alt. 121 m: view).

Spoleto

Region: Umbria. – Province: Perugia (PG).
Altitude: 305–453 m. – Population: 20,000.
Post code: I-06049. – Dialling code: 0743.
ⓘ **AA**, Piazza Libertà 7;
tel. 2 31 90.

HOTELS. – *Gattapone*, I, 16 b.; *Dei Duchi*, II, 94 b.; *Lello Caro*, III, 68 b.; etc. – *Motel Agip*, III, 114 b. – CAMPING SITE.

EVENTS. – *Festival of the Two Worlds* (music, dancing, theatre) in June and July.

Spoleto, an interesting old town with many fine medieval buildings, is charmingly situated above the left bank of the River Tessino, which here emerges from a narrow valley in the Umbrian Apennines into the plain of Umbria. It is the see of an archbishop.

SIGHTS. – In the long *Piazza del Duomo* on the E side of the town stands the *Cathedral of Santa Maria Assunta, raised to cathedral status in 1067 and restored in the 12th c. It has a stone pulpit on each side of the porch (1491). On the façade is a large mosaic by Solsternus (1207). The interior was remodelled in 1634–44, probably by Bernini. The choir contains damaged *frescoes (Annunciation, Nativity, Death of the Virgin and, in the semi-dome, Coronation of the Virgin) by Fra Filippo Lippi (1466), completed after his death by Fra Diamante (1470). In the S transept is the tomb of Filippo Lippi (1412–69). – On the NW side of the Piazza del Duomo, in the former *Palazzo della Signoría* (14th c.), the *Museo Civico* houses prehistoric and Roman antiquities, medieval sculpture, etc.

A lane in Spoleto

The **Palazzo Comunale** (Town Hall: entrance on S side), approached by a flight of steps at the S end of the Piazza del Duomo, contains an interesting *picture gallery* on the first floor (frescoes by Lo Spagna, etc.). To the N of the Town Hall, in the courtyard of the *Archbishop's Palace*, stands the beautiful Romanesque *church*

of *Santa Eufemia* (10th c.?). – W of the Town Hall we find the spacious Piazza del Mercato, below which, to the S, is the *Arch of Drusus and Germanicus*, half buried in the ground. – On the E side of the Town Hall lies the tree-shaded Piazza Campello. Below the **Rocca**, built in the 14th c. as the residence of the Papal governor and now a prison, the Via del Ponte leads to the *Porta Rocca*, outside which are remains of the old town walls (on left). Continuing past these above the deep ravine of the Tessino, we come to the imposing *Ponte delle Torri, an aqueduct and viaduct (pedestrians only) linking the town with Monte Luco. Built of freestone, with ten arches (230 m long, 81 m high), it was constructed in the 14th c., probably on the foundations of an earlier Roman aqueduct.

In the large *Piazza Garibaldi* in the northern part of the town the Romanesque **church of San Gregorio Maggiore** (1146), has a 16th c. porch and an interesting interior (old frescoes). – From Piazza Garibaldi the *Porta Gàribaldi* leads into the Piazza dellà Vittoria (gardens). Immediately E of the gate are the remains of a *Roman bridge*, the Ponte Sanguinario (24 m long, 10 m high), to which visitors can descend. – From Piazza Garibaldi we cross the Tessino and 100 m beyond the bridge turn right along the river and then left up the hill to reach the *church of San Salvatore** (also known as the *Chiesa del Crocifisso*), on a terrace in the *Camposanto*, which was originally built at the end of the 4th c. within the remains of a Roman temple. A short distance S is the 13th c. *church of San Ponziano*.

SURROUNDINGS. – From the E end of the Ponte delle Torri a road follows the edge of the Tessino ravine (1 km) to the **church of San Pietro** (alt. 388 m), founded in the 5th c. and rebuilt in the 14th, with 11th–12th c. reliefs on the *façade; the four upper scenes are later.

Another road from the E end of the Ponte delle Torri winds its way up the wooded hillside (6 km) to **Monte Luco** (830 m), from which there are magnificent views. Below the summit are a number of hotels and a Franciscan friary.

From Spoleto there is an attractive drive of 123 km to Ascoli Piceno. The road passes through beautiful upland country, much of it forest-covered, and comes in 49 km to **Norcia** (alt. 604 m; pop. 3000; hotels: Europa, III, 114 b.; Posta, III, 60 b.; etc.), the Roman *Nursia*, a little walled town under the W side of the Monti Sibillini which was the birthplace of St Benedict and his sister St Scholastica. In the main square are the Town Hall, the 14th c. church of San Benedetto (built over the remains of the house in which St Benedict was born) and the Prefecture, in a castellated 16th c. building, the Castellina (beautiful courtyard). – The road continues E from Norcia, climbs up to the crest of the ridge, coming in 19 km to the *Forca Canapine* (1543 m), a pass on the boundary between Umbria and the Marche, with magnificent views of the Gran Sasso d'Italia to the SE and the Monti Sibillini to the NE. It then descends with many bends, into the beautiful valley of the *Tronto* and comes in 20 km to **Arquata del Tronto** (777 m). This is the starting point for the ascent (4½ hours, with guide) of *Monte Vettore* (2478 m), the highest peak in the **Monti Sibillini** which are snow-covered until well into the summer (winter sports). It is possible also to drive to the *Forca della Presta* (1540 m), 13·5 km NW (first part of road dust-free), climb to the *Rifugio Zilioli* (2215 m: 3½ hours) and continue from there to the summit (1 hour). – The road continues down the Tronto valley, which at times narrows into a gorge, and comes in another 13 km to **Acquasanta Terme** (alt. 392 m; Hotel Italia, III, 327 b.; etc.), a spa which was already frequented in Roman times (*Ad Aquas*), with warm sulphur springs. Beyond this point the valley begins to open out. 12 km beyond Acquasanta we join the road from Macerata and follow it for another 8 km down the valley to **Ascoli Piceno** (see p. 66).

Subiaco

Region: Lazio. – Province: Roma (ROMA).
Altitude: 408 m. – Population: 10,000.
Post code: I-00028. – Dialling code: 0774.
(i) **AA**, Via Petrarca 18;
tel. 8 53 97.

HOTELS. – *Roma*, III, 56 b.; *Zia Lidia*, III, 34 b.; *Belvedere*, III, 32 b.; etc.

The little town of Subiaco, 70 km E of Rome, is picturesquely situated on a hill above the Aniene valley, dominated by an 11th c. castle which in the past was a frequent residence of the popes.

The Roman *Sublaqueum* grew up on the site of a large villa belonging to Nero, who narrowly escaped being struck by lightning while dining here. The main features of interest in the town, which still preserves its medieval aspect, are the famous Benedictine monasteries.

THE MONASTERIES. – 2 km SE of the town centre on the road to Ienne, situated above the River Aniene (on right), is the large **monastery of Santa Scolastica**, founded by St Benedict about 510 and later named after his sister. In 1052 a second monastery was built here, and later rebuilt in Gothic style; and in 1235 a third, with a Romanesque cloister with mosaic decoration. The present monastic buildings are modern. The church of

Sacro Speco, Subiaco

Santa Scolastica, founded in 975, was completely remodelled in the 18th c. In 1465 two German printers, Arnold Pannartz and Konrad Schweinheim, stayed in the monastery and produced what are probably the earliest Italian printed books.

1·5 km farther E, above the road to Ienne (on left), is the *monastery of San Benedetto or *Sacro Speco* (alt. 640 m), built against a sheer cliff in a magnificent lonely mountain setting. Both the upper and the lower church have 13th c. frescoes. The chapel adjoining the upper church contains a unique early picture of St Francis, who according to the legend, while staying in the monastery about 1218, transformed the thorns grown by St Benedict into the roses which still flourish in the monastery garden. In the cave in which St Benedict lived as a hermit until he moved to Montecassino in 529 is a statue of the saint by a pupil of Bernini.

SURROUNDINGS. – The road continues down the Aniene valley beyond the monastery of San Benedetto to (9 km) the beautifully situated little town of *Ienne* (alt. 834 m). 12 km from there along the *Simbrivio valley* lies the village of **Vallepietra**, in a cirque on the SE side of Monte Autore, from which it is a climb of 1½–2 hours to the *Santuario della Santissima Trinità* (festival on Sunday after Whitsun), situated at an altitude of 1337 m under a vertical rock face 300 m high. From here it is another 2½–3 hours' climb (with guide) to the summit of *Monte Autore* (1853 m), the second highest peak in the wooded **Monti Simbruini** (2156 m); magnificent panoramic views from the top.

Sulmona

Region: Abruzzo. – Province: L'Aquila (AQ).
Altitude: 403 m. – Population: 21,000.
Post code: I-67039. – Dialling code: 0864.
(i) **AA**, Via Papa Innocenzo VII 4;
tel. 5 32 76.

HOTELS. – *Constanza Park*, II, 210 b.; *Artu*, II, 31 b.; *Salvador*, III, 67 b.; etc.

Sulmona lies in a fertile valley between the Gran Sasso massif to the N and the Maiella group, with the Morrone hills in the foreground, to the E. Originally founded by the Paeligni, it was the Roman Sulmo, birthplace of Ovid, who was much attached to his "cool home country, abounding in water". It is the see of a bishop.

SIGHTS. – At the N end of the town stands the **Cathedral** of San Panfilo, with a Romanesque crypt and a Gothic doorway. From here Viale Rossevelt and the *Corso Ovidio*, Sulmona's principal street, lead to the **Palazzo Santa Maria Annunziata** (15th c., Gothic and Renaissance), which houses the *Museo Civico*, with a church of 1710. Farther along the Corso Ovidio we see a *Romanesque doorway*, all that remains of the *church of San Francesco della Scarpa*, destroyed by an earthquake. Opposite it is a beautiful Renaissance *fountain* (1474), fed by an *aqueduct* constructed in 1256.

SURROUNDINGS. – There are alternative routes from Sulmona to **Pescara**: *either* down the Pescara valley via *Popoli* (pop. 5000: castle of the counts of Cantelmi), with a detour to the *abbey of San Clemente a Casauria*, founded by the Emperor Ludwig II in 871 (12th c. church; museum); *or* along the lower slopes of the *Maiella group* (Monte Amaro, 2795 m) via *Campo di Giove* (1064 m: from here ascent of Monte Amaro, 10–12 hours) and *Caramanico Terme* (sulphur springs: ascent of Monte Amaro, 6–9 hours) and thereafter down into the Pescara valley.

There is a very fine drive from Sulmona through the wild *Saggittario gorge* and the rocky gateway of *La Foce* to *Scanno* (alt. 1030 m; pop. 3000), a delightfully situated hill village (traditional costumes), and from there past the *Fonti di Pantano* and down the Sangro valley to *Villeta Barrea*, in a beautiful setting at the W end of the *Lago di Barrea*, an artificial lake 5 km long (60 km: entrance to Abruzzi National Park).

Syracuse/Siracusa

Region: Sicilia. – Province: Siracusa (SR).
Altitude: 5 m. – Population: 110,000.
Post code: I-96100. – Dialling code: 0931.
ⓘ **AA**, Via Maestranza 33;
tel. 6 52 01.
EPT, Corso Gelano 92C;
tel. 6 77 10.
ACI, Foro Siracusano 72;
tel. 6 66 56.

HOTELS. – *Jolly*, Corso Gelano 45, I, 146 b.; *Grand Hotel Villa Politi*, Via M. Politi 2, II, 159 b., SP; *Motel Agip*, Viale Teracati 30, II, 152 b.; *Park*, Via Filisto 22, II, 144 b.; *Panorama*, Via Necropoli Grotticelle 33, II, 90 b.; *Fontane Bianche*, Via Mazzarò 1, II, 84 b., SP; *Aretusa*, Via F. Crispi 75, III, 67 b.; etc.

EVENTS. – Performances of classical plays in the Greek Theatre (alternate years in spring).

*Syracuse, capital of its province and the see of an archbishop, is largely situated on an island off the E coast of Sicily, separated by a narrow channel from the Sicilian mainland, on which are the modern town and the principal remains of the ancient city. The bay of Porto Grande, which cuts deep inland to the S of the town, is perhaps Italy's largest and best natural harbour. The town's situation, its beautiful surroundings and the monuments and relics of its splendid past make Syracuse one of the most fascinating places in Sicily.

HISTORY. – Syracuse (Greek *Syrakusa*, Latin *Syracusae*) was founded on the island of **Ortygia** in the second half of the 8th c. B.C. by settlers from Corinth, and rapidly rose to prosperity. From the 5th c. onwards it was ruled mostly by tyrants, the first of whom were Gelo (485–478) and Hiero I (478–467). Some of Greece's greatest poets, like Aeschylus and Pindar, lived at Hiero's court. In 415 B.C. Syracuse was drawn into the conflict between Athens and Sparta, but an Athenian expedition against the city (415) ended in the total annihilation of the Athenian army and fleet in 413. During the struggle with Carthage, Syracuse rose during the reigns of Dionysius I (406–367) and his successors to become the most powerful Greek city, with a perimeter, according to Strabo, of 180 stadia (33 km) and a population of half a million. Among the eminent men who lived in Syracuse during this period was the mathematician and physicist *Archimedes*. – After the first Punic War, in which Syracuse was allied with Rome, the city went over to the Carthaginian side. Thereupon it was besieged and captured by the Romans (212 B.C.), and Archimedes was killed by a soldier. Thereafter Syracuse shared the destinies of the rest of Sicily but never recovered its earlier importance.

SIGHTS. – The OLD TOWN, with its narrow winding streets and its old houses and palaces – many of them with handsome balconies – lies, as it did in Greek times, on the island of Ortygia. Its busiest traffic intersection is the *Piazza Archimede*, which is surrounded by old palaces. On the W side of the square is the *Banca d'Italia*, with a 15th c. courtyard, and a little way NE the *Palazzo Montalto* (1397), with magnificent Gothic windows. – From here Via Dione runs N to the **Temple of Apollo** (early 6th c. B.C.), which was also dedicated to Artemis (the Roman Diana). The oldest Doric temple in Sicily, it was excavated in 1933 and has recently been partly re-erected.

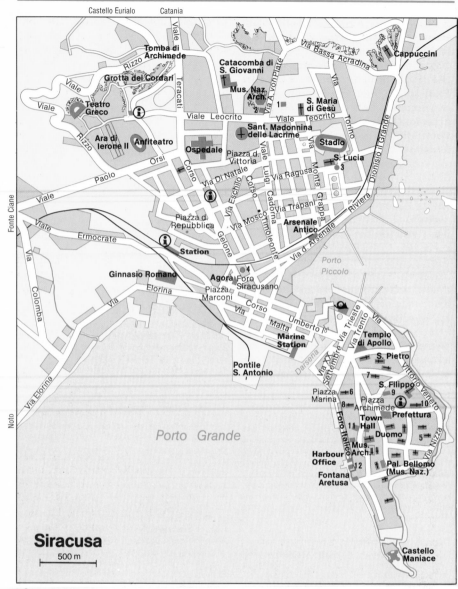

Siracusa

500 m

1 Catacombe di Vigna Cassia	4 War Memorial	7 San Tommaso	10 San Francesco
2 Villa Landolina	5 San Giovanni Battista	8 Chiesa del Collegio	11 Palazzo Beneventano
3 Cappella del Sepolcro	6 Santa Maria dei Miracoli	9 Palazzo Montalto	12 Acquario Tropicale

SW of Piazza Archimede is the elongated *Piazza del Duomo*, with the *Palazzo del Municipio* (Town Hall, 13th c.) and next to it the *Cathedral, built in the 7th c. on the site of a temple of Athena of the 5th c. B.C., enlarged in the 17th c. and provided with a handsome Baroque façade between 1728 and 1757. – Opposite the cathedral is the *Museo Archeologico Nazionale** (closed Sunday afternoons and Mondays), with a large collection of antiquities, mostly of Sicilian origin, ranging in date from prehistoric to early Christian times. Particularly notable items are (Room XIV) the *sarcophagus of Valerius and Adelfia (4th c. A.D.) from the

catacombs of San Giovanni, with carvings of scenes from the Old and New Testaments, and (Room IX) the Landolina Venus (Venus Anadyomene), with a dolphin by her side, a copy (2nd c. A.D.) of a fine Hellenistic work.

From the S end of the Piazza del Duomo Via Picherale continues S to the semi-circular basin of the **Fountain of Arethusa** (*Fonte Aretusa*) with its papyrus plants. The legend of the nymph Arethusa, pusued by the river god Alpheus from Olympia to here, reflects the idea that the Peloponnesian river Alpheus continued flowing under the sea and emerged at this point. – To the N of the Fountain extends the *Foro Italico, a fine seafront promenade with view of the harbour and of Etna. At the S end of the Foro, in a small park, is the entrance to the *Acquario Tropicale, with rare fishes from tropical seas. At the N end of the Foro are the *Porta Marina*, with Hispano-Mauresque ornament (16th c.), and the *church of Santa Maria dei Miracoli* (1501). – A little way E of the Fountain of Arethusa, at the S end of Via Roma, which runs down from Piazza Archimede, is the **Palazzo Bellomo** (15th c.: closed Sunday afternoons and Fridays), with the *Museo Nazionale* (medieval collections and a small picture gallery).

The **Castello Maniace**, a Hohenstaufen stronghold built about 1239 at the southern tip of the island, has a handsome gateway; fine view from the S bastion.

At the N end of the island, W of the Temple of Apollo, is Piazza Pancali, from which there is a bridge over the canal (*Dársena*) to the NEW TOWN on the mainland, with the railway station and the impressive remains of the ancient city. The Corso Umberto I, the main street of the modern town, runs W from the bridge to the large **Foro Siracusano**, on which remains of the ancient *agora* can be seen. To the W are the remains of the *Ginnasio Romano* (Gymnasium), once surrounded by colonnades.

1 km NW of the Foro Siracusano, to the left of the Corso Gelone (the Catania road, S.S. 114), is the Augustan **Amphitheatre** (1140 m long, 119 m across), in the part of the Roman town known as Neapolis. 100 m W of the amphitheatre is the *Altar of Hiero II* (Ara di Ierone II), a gigantic altar 200 m long by 22·5 m broad which originally rose in two tiers to a height of 10·5 m. Here probably was performed the annual sacrifice of 450 oxen. Opposite the altar is the entrance to the **Latomía del Paradiso**, an ancient quarry 30–40 m deep, now covered with a luxuriant growth of vegetation, which was used, like the other *latomie* in Syracuse, as a prison for offenders who were condemned to stone-breaking and also for the confinement of prisoners of war. Keeping left immediately inside the entrance archway along the garden wall, we come to the so-called *Ear of Dionysius*, an S-shaped cave hewn from the rock, 65 m deep, 23 m in height and 5–

11 m wide, contracting towards the top, in which sound is considerably amplified without any recurring echo. It has borne its present name since the 16th c., reflecting the belief that the tyrant Dionysius was thus able to overhear even the whispered remarks of state prisoners confined in the quarry. Farther to the right, under the W wall of the quarry, is the *Grotta dei Cordari*, named after the ropemakers who carry on their trade there. – Immediately E is the *Latomía di Santa Venera*, with a particularly lush growth of vegetation.

Greek Theatre, Syracuse

Immediately W of the Latomia del Paradiso is the *Greek Theatre (5th c. B.C.), with a semicircular auditorium hewn from the rock, the largest in the Greek world (diameter 138·5 m: cf. Athens, 100 m). Two tunnels under the auditorium give access to the orchestra (diameter 24 m, as in Athens). In this theatre Aeschylus (d. 456 B.C.) directed the performance of his "Persians" (c. 472 B.C.), and it is still used for the performance of classical plays (in spring, in alternate – even-numbered – years). From the top of the theatre there is a magnificent *view at sunset of the town, the harbour and the sea. – In the rock face above the theatre is the so-called *Nymphaeum*, a cave which was the terminal point of an ancient aqueduct. From the left-hand side of the Nymphaeum the **Streets of Tombs** (*Via dei Sepolcri*) runs up in a curve for some 150 m, with numerous cavities and tomb chambers of the late Roman period in its walls.

0·5 km NE of the Amphitheatre, to the right of the Catania road (S.S. 114), stands the little **church of San Giovanni alle Catacombe**, the western part of the early medieval cathedral, of which nothing is left but the W front of the present church, with a conspicuous W window, and the 15th c. porch. From the church a flight of steps leads down to the cruciform *Crypt of St Marcian* (4th c., with remains of frescoes) and the adjoining *Catacombs, which are among the most imposing known, far larger than the catacombs of Rome. – SE of San Giovanni, in a small *latomia*, is the *Villa Landolina*, with the tomb of the 19th c. German poet August von Platen in the garden. From here, going N along Via Augusto von Platen, with the entrance to the *Catacombs of Vigna Cassia*, and then 500 m E along Via Bassa Acradina, past the Old Cemetery, we come to a Capuchin monastery and beside it the *Latomia dei Cappuccini, one of the wildest and grandest of the ancient quarries, in which the 7000 Athenian prisoners taken in 414 B.C. were probably confined.

SURROUNDINGS. – 8 km NW of the Foro Siracusano, at the W end of the outlying district of ancient Syracuse, *Epipolae*, on higher ground, is the *fort of Euryalus (*Castello Eurialo*), built between 402 and 397 B.C. at the meeting of the N and S edges of the plateau, one of the best preserved works of fortification that has come down to us from ancient times (view).

A pleasant outing from Syracuse is a boat trip (3–4 hours there and back) from the harbour up the little River *Ciane* (on a hill to the left two columns of the Olympieion, a temple of Zeus of the 6th c. B.C.), between tall stands of papyrus, to the **Fountain of Cyane** (*Fonte Ciane* or *La Pisma*), the "azure spring" into which the nymph of that name was metamorphosed for opposing Pluto when he was abducting Proserpina.

33 km W of Syracuse is the interesting town of **Palazzolo Acréide** (alt. 697 m; pop. 11,000), the ancient *Akrai* (Latin *Placeolum*, Arabic *el-Akrat*), which was founded by settlers from Syracuse in 664 B.C. On the nearby hill of *Acremonte*, the site of the ancient city, is a *Cinta Archeologica* containing the remains of the late Greek theatre (seating for 600), to the W of this the Bouleuterion (Council Chamber), to the SE *latomie* (old quarries) containing Greek and Early Christian tombs, and two tomb chambers known as the Templi Ferali (funerary temples). – From here it is a 15 minutes' walk to the valley of *Contrada dei Santicelli*, near the large cemetery of *Acrocoro della Torre*, to see the *"Santoni", crudely carved cult images in niches in the rock. Most of them represent a seated goddess, presumably Cybele, with Hermes beside her. On the far side of the valley is *Monte Pineta*, with many small tomb chambers. – 34 km NE of Palazzolo Acreide via Ferla is the *Necrópoli di Pantálica, the cemetery of the Siculan town 12th–8th c. B.C.) on the hill to the N, with thousands of small tomb chambers hewn from the rock faces in the Ánapo valley. During the Middle Ages the tombs were used as dwellings. Jewellery and ornaments found in the tombs are displayed in the Museo Nazionale in Syracuse.

Taormina

Region: Sicilia. – Province: Messina (ME).
Altitude: 250 m. – Population: 10,000.
Post code: I-98039. – Dialling code: 0942.
ⓘ **AA**, Palazzo Corvaia;
tel. 2 32 43.
EPT, Corso Umberto I 144;
tel. 2 37 51.
CIT and **TCI**, Corso Umberto I 101;
tel. 2 33 01.

HOTELS. – *San Domenico Palace*, L, 177 b., SP; *Jolly Hotel Diodoro*, I, 202 b., SP; *Excelsior Palace*, I, 125 b.; *Vello d'Oro*, I, 105 b.; *Bristol Park*, I, 99 b., SP; *Méditerranée*, I, 93 b., SP; *Timeo*, I, 93 b.; *Imperial Palace*, II, 136 b.; *Grande Albergo Monte Tauro*, II, 134 b., SP; *Sole Castello*, II, 94 b.; *Presidente Hotel Splendid*, II, 87 b.; *Continental*, II, 80 b.; *Sirius*, II, 69 b.; *Ariston*, III, 207 b.; *Residence*, III, 50 b.; etc. – IN MAZZARÒ: *Grance Albergo Capo Taormina*, 415 b., SP; *Mazzarò Sea Palace*, L, 141 b., SP; *Atlantis Bay*, I, 174 b., SP; *Lido Méditerranée*, II, 110 b.; etc. – CAMPING SITE.

EVENTS. – *Costume Festival* (end of May), with gaily painted Sicilian carts (*carretti*). – *International Film Festival* (July). – *Summer Festival* in Greek Theatre.

The picturesque little town of Taormina, the ancient Tauromenium, enjoys a magnificent ** **situation on a terrace high above the Ionian Sea on the E coast of Sicily. A ruined castle on a rocky crag and the little hill town of Castelmola tower above it, with the majestic cone of Etna in the background. There are many who would claim it to be the most beautiful place in the whole of Sicily.**

The town lies 7 km from the coast. The nearest beaches, at *Mazzarò* (cableway) and *Isola Bella*, are of only moderate quality; the sandy beaches at *San Alessio Sículo* (14 km N) and *Santa Teresa* (20 km N) are to be preferred.

Mazzarò, on the coast below Taormina

SIGHTS. – The road which winds its way up to Taormina from the coast, Via L. Pirandello, terminates at the *Porta Messina*, at the NE end of the town. A little way NE of the gate the *church of San Pancrazio*, occupies the cella of a Greek temple. To the S of the Porta Messina in the Piazza Vittorio Emanuele, stand the Gothic *Palazzo Corvaia* (1372) and the little *church of Santa Catarina*. Behind the church are the remains of a Roman *Odeum*. – From the square the Via del Teatro Greco runs SE to the *Greek Theatre (admission free on Sundays), which was reconstructed in Roman style in the 2nd c. A.D. With a diameter at the top of 109 m, it is the largest theatre in Sicily after the one in Syracuse. It is renowned for its excellent acoustics (performances of classical plays). The **view from the top of the theatre of the precipitous E coast of Sicily, with the gigantic cone of Etna, snow-covered for most of the year, and of the Calabrian coast is one of the most breathtaking in Italy.

From the Piazza Vittorio Emanuele the town's main street, *Corso Umberto I*, flanked by fine old houses, runs SW to the Largo IX Aprile (view), with the *church of San Giuseppe* and the deconsecrated *church of Sant'Agostino*. It then curves N, past the Palazzo Ciampoli (on right), and joins the *Piazza del Duomo*, where stands a beautiful 12th c. fountain. In the small **Cathedral** (13th–16th c.) are a number of fine altarpieces and, to the right of the high altar, a 15th c. Madonna.

On the hillside N of the Piazza del Duomo are the ruins of the Gothic *Badia Vecchia* (14th c.). To the S, on the edge of the terrace, a finely situated *Dominican monastery* is now the Hotel San Domenico Palace (fine cloister); from the tower of the church (destroyed in 1943) there is a beautiful *view. – To the W of the Piazza del Duomo, beyond the *Porta Catania* or *Porta del Tocco*, is the *Palazzo Santo Stefano* (1330), its vaulting supported on a massive granite column. Below the former Dominican monastery, *Via Roma* (fine views) runs E to the *municipal gardens*, in a commanding situation, from which Via Bagnoli Croce continues to the *Belvedere* (magnificent views). From here we can return on Via Luigi Pirandello, passing below the Greek Theatre, to the Porta Messina.

SURROUNDINGS. – From the W end of the town, near the Badia Vecchia, a road winds steeply uphill, with sharp bends, to the *chapel of the Madonna della Rocca* (2 km), from which it is a few minutes' climb to the **Castello di Taormina** on *Monte Tauro* (398 m). Even more attractive is the further stretch of road (3 km) to the village of **Castelmola** (alt. 450 m), perched on a precipitous crag, which commands panoramic *views from its various outlook terraces, but particularly from its highest point near the ruined castle. – A very rewarding excursion from Taormina is the ascent of **Etna** (see p. 109) or the circuit of the mountain by rail.

Táranto

Region: Puglia. – Province: Táranto (TA).
Altitude: 15 m. – Population: 230,000.
Post code: I-74100. – Dialling code: 099.

(i) **EPT**, Corso Umberto 113;
tel. 2 12 33.
ACI, Viale Magna Grecia 108;
tel. 3 59 11.
TCI, *Viaggi Ausiello*, Corso Umberto 49;
tel. 2 30 41.

HOTELS. – *Grand Hotel Delfino*, Viale Virgilio 66, I, 307 b., SP; *Jolly Hotel Mar Grande*, Viale Virgilio 90, I, 145 b., SP; *Palace*, Viale Virgilio 10, I, 121 b.; *Plaza*, Via D'Aquino 46, II, 167 b.; *Bologna*, Via Margherita 4, II, 91 b.; *Imperiale*, Via Pitagora 94, III, 102 b.; *Mater Misericordiae*, Via Lago Trasimeno 4, III, 95 b.; *Miramare*, Via Roma 4, III, 80 b.; etc.

Táranto, which ranks with La Spezia as one of Italy's two principal naval bases, lies on the Mare Grande, the northern bay of the Gulf of Táranto, on the S coast of Italy. This Apulian port is also a considerable industrial and commercial town and the see of an archbishop.

The *old town* is built on a low rocky island between the *Mare Grande* and the *Mare Piccolo*, which runs deep inland on the NE side of the town. From here a bridge leads to the *Borgo*, an industrial suburb (large steelworks) to the NW, which in turn is linked by a swing bridge with the *new town*, situated on a peninsula, with large shipyards. – Táranto is renowned for its honey and fruit. Fishing and the culture of oysters and shellfish also make a contribution to the town's economy.

HISTORY. – The town (Greek *Taras*, Latin *Tarentum*) was founded by Spartan settlers in 708 B.C., and by the 4th c. B.C. was the most powerful city in Magna Graecia. In the time of Augustus it still had a predominantly Greek population, but thereafter it was Romanised. In A.D. 494 it was occupied by the Ostrogoths, and in 540 came under Byzantine rule. Táranto was destroyed by the Saracens in 927 but was rebuilt, and in 1063 was incorporated by Robert

Co-Cathedral, Táranto

Guiscard in the Norman kingdom of southern Italy. Thereafter Táranto shared the destinies of the kingdom of Naples.

SIGHTS. – In the OLD TOWN (*Città Vecchia*), a rectangle of narrow lanes traversed by four parallel longitudinal streets, is the **Cathedral** of San Cataldo (originally built 1072–84; rebuilt in the 18th c., with the exception of the dome and campanile), on the site of the ancient acropolis. It contains eight columns with ancient and *early medieval capitals. To the right of the choir we find the richly decorated Baroque chapel of San Cataldo (crypt). – At the SE corner of the old town stands the **Castello** (15th–16th c.).

From the old town the *Ponte Girévole* (Swing Bridge) leads over the *Canale Navigabile*, one of the few places in the Mediterranean where the ebb and flow of the tide can be observed, into the NEW TOWN (*Città Nuova*), with its wide parallel streets. 100 m beyond the bridge is the palm-shaded square known as *Villa Garibaldi*, on the E side stands the imposing *Palazzo degli Uffici* (1896). On its N side the *National Museum (closed Sunday afternoons and Mondays), one of the most important museums in southern Italy, houses antiquities from Táranto and district, in particular a collection of beautiful Corinthian vases. – To the S, on the Mare Grande, is an avenue of palms, the *Lungomare Vittorio Emanuele III*, with the modern premises of the *Prefecture* and the *Head Post Office*. – To the N of the National Museum, on the Mare Piccolo, the *Institute of Oceanography* (Istituto Talassografico: visitors admitted) has the beautiful municipal park, the *Villa Comunale Peripato*, on its E side.

Tarquinia

Region: Lazio. – Province: Viterbo (VT).
Altitude: 133 m. – Population: 12,000.
Post code: I-01016. – Dialling code: 0766.
ⓘ **AA**, Barriera San Giusto;
    tel. 8 63 84.
    Pro Tarquinia, Piazza Cavour 21;
    tel. 8 60 97.

HOTELS. – *Tarconte*, II, 100 b.; *Motel Aurelia*, IV, 47 b. – CAMPING SITE. – IN LIDO DI TARQUINIA: *Torre del Sole*, II, 37 b., SP; *La Torraccia*, III, 32 b.; etc. – CAMPING SITE.

Tarquinia, an old-world town of many towers, founded in the early medieval period on the territory of ancient Tarquinii and known until 1922 as Corneto, occupies a commanding situation on a limestone plateau above the River Marta, 5 km from the Tyrrhenian Sea and some 20 km N of Civitavecchia.

SIGHTS. – The main square of Tarquinia is the *Piazza Cavour*, at the W end of the town. On the N side of the square a magnificent Gothic palace with a beautiful pillared courtyard, the **Palazzo Vitelleschi** (1436–39), now houses the *Museo Nazionale Tarquiniense*, an important collection of Etruscan antiquities of the 6th–2nd c. B.C. (sarcophagi, vases, jewellery, glass, carved ivories, coins, fragments of large decorative reliefs, etc.; also pictures of the 15th and 16th c.). – Nearby is the **Cathedral** (modernised), with the remains of frescoes.

At the NW tip of the town, near the remains of the Castello, the *church of Santa Maria di Castello* (begun 1121) has Cosmatesque decoration both externally and internally. – In the higher part of the town stands the handsome Romanesque

Painted tomb, Tarquinia

and Gothic *church of San Francesco* (13th c.).

SURROUNDINGS. – On a stony hill 3 km E of Tarquinia are the meagre remains of ancient **Tarquinii**, the most notable of the 12 cities of the Etruscan federation. The town, originally surrounded by a wall 8 km long, was devastated by the Saracens in the 13th c. and razed to the ground in 1307 by the inhabitants of the neighbouring town of Corneto. – Around the old town, particularly on the hill of *Monterozzi* (157 m) to the S, extends the * * **necropolis** of Tarquinia (discovered in 1823), one of the best preserved of Etruscan cemeteries. A tour of the tombs (organised by the museum) takes anything from 1½ to 5 hours. The splendid painted decoration of the tombs gives a picture of the culture, art and religion of the Etruscans.

25 km NE of Tarquinia on the Viterbo road is the little town of **Tuscania** (alt. 166 m; pop. 8000; Hotel Al Gallo, IV, 22 b.), still surrounded by medieval walls and towers. The ancient *Tuscana*, it was known until 1911 as *Toscanella*. A severe earthquake on 6 February 1971 destroyed the old town and damaged the churches outside the town. To the E of the town, on the Viterbo road, are the *Etruscan Museum*, in the former Bishop's Palace, and the Romanesque *church of San Pietro* (8th–10th c.), with a richly decorated façade, a fine interior and an ancient crypt. Nearby, in the valley, the *church of Santa Maria Maggiore* (1050–1206), has an old pulpit and a fresco of the Last Judgment (14th c.) on the wall of the choir.

Terni

Region: Umbria. – Province: Terni (TR).
Altitude: 130 m. – Population: 110,000.
Post code: I-050100. – Dialling code: 0744.
(i) **EPT**, Viale Cesare Battisti 5–7;
    tel. 41 81 60.
    ACI, Viale Cesare Battisti 121C;
    tel. 40 02 39.

HOTELS. – *Valentino*, I, 120 b.; *De Paris*, II, 99 b.; *Plaza*, II, 75 b.; *Allegretti*, II, 70 b.; *Valentino*, III, 93 b.; *Beta*, III, 92 b.; etc. – *Motel Tiffany*, III, 71 b.

The provincial capital of Terni, situated in the fertile valley of the Nera some 100 km N of Rome, is a rising industrial town which since its rebuilding after severe destruction in the Second World War has a predominantly modern aspect.

SIGHTS. – In the centre of the town, in the *Piazza della Repubblica*, stands the *Town Hall*. – To the SW, in the Piazza del Duomo, is the **Cathedral** (13th–17th c.; crypt 10th c.), a short distance S of which are the outer walls of an *amphitheatre* (1st c. A.D.) and the *municipal park*, from where there is an attractive view of the Nera valley.

Some 500 m N of the cathedral is the *church of San Francesco*, with frescoed scenes from the "Divine Comedy" (c. 1400) in the Cappella Paradisi (on right of choir. – NE of the Piazza della Repubblica is the *Palazzo Carrara* houses the **Municipal Museums**, with prehistoric and Roman antiquities and a picture gallery (pictures by Benozzo Gozzoli and others), and the *Municipal Library*.

SURROUNDINGS. – 6 km E of Terni beyond the industrial suburb of *Papigno*, to the right of the Ferentillo road (S.S. 209), are the *Cascate delle Marmore, the falls formed by the River *Velino* at its confluence with the Nera, which are worth seeing only on Sundays and holidays, since at other times almost all the water is diverted to hydroelectric stations and industrial plants (coloured illuminations between May and August). The falls plunge down vertically in three leaps of 20, 100 and 60 m, at some points in a sheer perpendicular drop. The best view is from the *Cascate* tram stop. From here it is possible to cross the Nera on a natural bridge and climb up on a steep path and flights of steps to a series of outlook terraces, joining the road from Terni to Rieti after some 45 minutes' walk.

There is also a very attractive drive (14 km E) to the beautiful **Lago di Piediluco** (alt. 368 m; area 165 hectares), on the N side of which is the charmingly situated village of *Piediluco* (alt. 377 m), with a ruined castle. Half way there, at Le Mármore (alt. 376 m), a road branches off (15 km S) to the *Santuario di Greccio* (alt. 638 m), picturesquely situated in a forest of holm-oaks, a monastery with grottoes and a chapel marking the spot where St Francis celebrated Christmas at a *presepio* (crib, Nativity group) for the first time in 1223.

13 km SW of Terni, commandingly situated on a high crag on the left bank of the Nera, which here forces its way out of the Terni basin through a narrow ravine, is the little medieval town of **Narni** (alt. 240 m; pop. 20,000; Hotel Bellavista dell'Angelo, III, 17 b.). In the centre of the town stands the cathedral, which is mainly 11th c., with a porch of 1497; fine interior. In the nearby Piazza Priora are the beautiful Loggia dei Priori (13th c.) and the Palazzo Comunale (*collection of pictures). Below the town, on the line of the ancient Via Flaminia, are the ruins of the so-called Bridge of Augustus.

Tívoli

Region: Lazio. – Province: Roma (ROMA).
Altitude: 222 m. – Population: 42,000.
Post code: 1-00019. – Dialling code: 0774.
(i) **AA**, Piazzale delle Nazioni Unite 13;
    tel. 2 07 45.

HOTELS. – *Europa e dei Congressi*, in Monte Ripoli, I, 200 b., SP; *Torre Sant'Angelo*, I, 60 b., SP; *Eden Sirene*, III, 39 b.; etc.

The town of *Tívoli, the ancient Tibur, lies 30 km E of Rome in the Sabine Hills, magnificently situated

Fontana dell'Organo, Villa d'Este

on a limestone ridge extending S from Monte Gennaro (1271 m: cableway), above the ravine which the River Aniene has carved through the hills. In Roman Imperial times it was a favourite resort of the great Roman nobles, including Maecenas and the Emperor Augustus himself.

SIGHTS. – At the Porta Santa Croce, the SW entrance to the town, stands the spacious Piazza Boselli. A little way N of this, in the little Piazza Trento, is the entrance to the *Villa d'Este (closed Mondays; son et lumière shows in summer), one of the classic creations of the Renaissance period, designed by Pirro Ligorio for Cardinal Ippolito d'Este (1549). At the beginning of this century it was owned by Archduke Francis Ferdinand of Austria-Este, who was assassinated at Sarajevo in 1914. From the villa and from the beautiful gardens, laid out in terraces with magnificent *fountains and cascades (reduced pressure around midday) and what are said to be the tallest cypresses in Italy, there are attractive views of the Roman Campagna.

From Piazza Trento we can find our way N through narrow lanes to the Cathedral of San Lorenzo (originally Romanesque, rebuilt in 1635). Going E from here along Via San Valerio to the Piazza Rivarola and turning left along the narrow Via della Sibilla, we come to the so-called *Temple of Vesta, a circular structure with Corinthian columns (2nd c. B.C.) which stands on a crag above the Aniene, in the grounds of a hotel. Close by is the so-called Temple of the Sibyl and also the exit from the park of the Villa Gregoriana. To

the E of Piazza Rivarola the Ponte Gregoriano spans the gorge of the Aniene, and beyond the bridge is the main entrance to the park of the *Villa Gregoriana, in the valley of the Aniene. The waters of this river are diverted through the Traforo Gregoriano, a double tunnel (270 m and 300 m long) driven through the W side of Monte Catillo in 1826–35 to prevent the floods which had repeatedly devastated the town. The water emerging from the tunnel forms magnificent *waterfalls with a total drop of 160 m (volume reduced at night to supply a power station). At the end of the tunnel is the Cascata Grande (108 m), of which there are fine views from the upper and middle terraces. Also in the park are the Sirens' Grotto and, at the end of a gallery, the Grotto of Neptune, through which the main channel of the Aniene formerly flowed. From the entrance to the gallery a path zigzags up to the exit near the two temples.

From the entrance to the Villa Gregoriana the Via Quintilio Varo runs round the outside of the park and then along the right bank of the Aniene, past an arch in honour of the Virgin erected in 1955, to the *Via delle Cascatelle, which affords beautiful views of the waterfalls and the town, particularly from the Belvedere outlook terrace and the church of Sant'Antonio.

SURROUNDINGS. – 6 km SW of Tivoli, to the right of the Via Tiburtina, is the **Villa of Hadrian (Villa

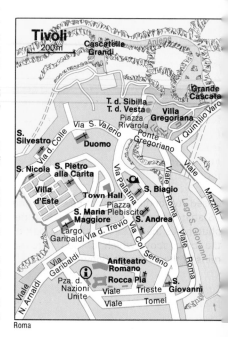

Adriana), a magnificent complex of buildings and gardens covering an area of 185 acres. It dates from the later years of the widely travelled emperor (d. A.D. 138), who sought to reproduce here some of the great buildings of Greece and Egypt. Many of the works of art to be seen in the museums of Rome came from here. The chief charm of the villa lies in its scenic beauty. There is a model of the whole complex in a building at the car park.

Todi

Region: Umbria. – Province: Perugia (PU).
Altitude: 410 m. – Population: 5000.
Post code: I-06059. – Dialling code: 075.
ⓘ Pro Loco, Via Mazzini 2;
tel. 88 24 06.

HOTELS. – Zodiaco, III, 54 b.; Cavour, III, 38 b.

Todi, the ancient Umbrian city of Tuder, occupies a triangular site still partly surrounded by its rings of Etruscan, Roman and medieval walls, on a ridge above the Tiber valley in southern Umbria.

SIGHTS. – In the centre of the town is the Piazza del Popolo surrounded by medieval palaces. On the N side of the square, approached by a flight of steps, stands the late Romanesque **Cathedral** (11th–15th c.), with beautiful choir-stalls of 1530. On the S side is the Palazzo dei Priori or Palazzo del Podestà (13th–14th c.), with an eagle (1339), the arms of Todi, on its façade. On the E side are the 13th c. Palazzo del Popolo and Palazzo del Capitano (small collection of pictures), linked by a later flight of steps.

S of the Piazza del Popolo, in the Piazza della Repubblica, is the Gothic church of San Fortunato (13th–14th c.), approached by a flight of steps with a landing half way up. The façade (unfinished) has a beautiful central doorway (c. 1320). In the fourth chapel on the right is a fresco of the Madonna by Masolino (1432). There are beautiful choir-stalls. In the crypt (on left) is the tomb of the monk Jacopone da Todi (1228–1306), supposed author of the solemn Passion hymn "Stabat Mater dolorosa". To the E of the church lies the picturesque oldest part of the town, above which, to the W, are the ruins of the old castle (view).

On a terrace outside the town walls is the pilgrimage church of *Santa Maria della Consolazione, a domed church

notable for its nobility and beauty, one of the finest creations of Renaissance architecture (by Cola di Matteuccio da Caprarola, 1508; completed 1606).

Trani

Region: Puglia. – Province: Bari (BA).
Altitude: 7 m. – Population: 40,000.
Post code: I-70059. – Dialling code: 0883.
ⓘ AA, Via Cavour 83;
tel. 4 11 26.

HOTELS. – Trani, II, 75 b.; Holiday, II, 72 b.; Miramar, II, 50 b.; Riviera, II, 52 b.; etc.

Trani, the ancient Turenum, beautifully situated on the Adriatic coast between Bari and Barletta, is a very typical Apulian harbour town, the see of an archbishop.

SIGHTS. – To the NW of the harbour entrance, finely situated on an eminence above the sea, stands the *Cathedral (1150–1250), with a Romanesque W doorway (13th c. carving) and beautiful bronze doors (c. 1160) by a local bronze-founder named Barisanus. Above a high archway is a slender campanile (rebuilt). The impressive interior, the only example of an Apulian church with double columns, was restored to its original Romanesque form in 1952–55. The lower church, with fine columns, consists of the Crypt of St Nicholas the Pilgrim (d. 1094), under the transept, which was begun about 1100, and the Crypt of St Leucius (c. 670) under the nave.

On the W side of the harbour we find the Gothic Palace of Simone Caccetta (15th

Trani Cathedral

c.), and a little way S of this the **church of Ognissanti**, with a deep porch, which was formerly a Templars' hospice; above the doorway are Romanesque carvings of the Annunciation and the Tree of Life. – To the W of the cathedral the Castello (1233–49) of Frederick II, is now a prison. – E of the harbour, by the Baroque *church of San Domenico*, are the municipal gardens, with three Roman milestones from the Via Traiana (which ran from Benevento by way of Canosa, Ruvo, Bari and Egnazia to Brindisi). From the W end of the gardens a *view of the harbour and the cathedral can be enjoyed.

SURROUNDINGS. – 22 km SE is **Ruvo di Puglia** (alt. 260 m; pop. 25,000), with a Norman cathedral (12th–13th c.: fine doorway). The Palazzo Iatta contains a fine *collection of vases (6th–3rd c. B.C.) found here. The Palazzo Spada has a beautiful Renaissance courtyard.

The coast, Erice

Trápani

Region: Sicilia. – Province: Trápani (TP).
Altitude: 3 m. – Population: 70,000.
Post code: I-91100. – Dialling code: 0923.
ⓘ **EPT**, Corso Italia 10;
tel. 2 72 73.
ACI, Via Virgilio;
tel. 2 72 92.

HOTELS. – *Nuovo Russo*, Via Tintori 6, II, 48 b.; *Vittoria*, Piazza Vittorio Emanuele, III, 79 b.; etc.

EVENTS. – *Parade of Mysteries* on the night of Good Friday. – *Luglio Musicale Trapanese* (July).

Trápani, situated on a sickle-shaped peninsula on the NW coast of Sicily, and accordingly named Drepanon (="sickle") by the Greeks, was the port of the ancient city of Eryx (Érice), lying inland to the NE, and is still a port of some consequence, shipping salt, wine and tunny meat.

SIGHTS. – Trápani's main street is the *Corso Vittorio Emanuele*; in its eastern half are the 17th c. **Cathedral** of San Lorenzo and the *Chiesa del Collegio* or *Chiesa Nazionale* (1638), which was elaborately adorned with marble and stucco in the 18th c. At the E end of the Corso is the *Old Town Hall* (17th c.: now the registry office), with a magnificent Baroque façade. To the SE the former *church of Sant'Agostino*, with a beautiful rose window, once belonged to the Templars; it is now a concert and lecture

hall. Farther E is the *church of Santa Maria di Gesù* (15th c.).

From the Old Town Hall the Via Torre Arsa runs S to the **Harbour** (attractive seafront promenade) and N to Via Garibaldi, which leads NE to the *Villa Margherita* public gardens and the busy Piazza Vittorio Emanuele. From here the short Via Fardella runs E into the BORGO ANNUNZIATA quarter. In this district is the **Santuario dell'Annunziata** (founded 1332), with a 13th c. *Madonna* (in the Cappella della Madonna di Trapani), richly decked with jewellery and other votive gifts, which is venerated as miraculous (candle procession on 16 August). The old monastic buildings (beautiful cloister) contain the **Museo Nazionale Pepoli** (pictures, sculpture, decorative art, prehistoric and classical antiquities).

SURROUNDINGS. – 15 km NE on a road with numerous steep bends (also accessible by cableway) is **Erice** (alt. 751 m; pop. 1500; hotels: Ermione, I, 58 b.; La Pineta, III, 42 b.), magnificently situated on an isolated hill. Known until 1934 as *Monte San Giuliano*, this was the ancient *Eryx*, much venerated in antiquity, particularly by seamen, as the hill of *Venus Erycina*. The Elymians built a walled town here, of which a few traces remain. The Chiesa Matrice at the Porta Trápani, the W entrance to the town, was restored in 1865 and only the W porch (15th c.) and campanile are old. In the third chapel on the right stands a beautiful statue of the Madonna by Francesco Laurana (1469). – In Piazza Umberto I stands the Town Hall (library, museum). At the E end of the town are the municipal gardens, with a number of medieval towers, and the Castello, built on the site of a temple of Venus, from which there are magnificent * *views – to the SW Trápani and the Ìsole Ègadi can be seen and, occasionally, Cap Bon (175 km) on the African coast. To the S the view frequently extends to the island of Pantelleria and to the E sometimes (particularly in winter) as far as the summit of Etna, 210 km away.

A pleasant trip from Trápani is by boat (daily: $\frac{3}{4}$–$2\frac{3}{4}$ hours) or hydrofoil (several times daily: $\frac{1}{4}$–1 hour) to the İsole Égadi, the main tunny-fishing area. The boats call at the islands of *Favignana* (alt. 302 m; area 19·75 sq. km; hotels: Punta Fanfalo Village, II, 543 b., SP; L'Approdo di Ulisse, II, 176 b.; etc.), *Lévanzo* (298 m; 6 sq. km; Pensione Paradiso, III, 9 b.) and *Maréttimo* (684 m; 12·25 sq. km; only twice weekly).

Trémiti Islands

Region: Puglia. – Province: Foggia (FG).
Area: 3·06 sq. km. – Population: 350.
Post code: I-71040. – Dialling code: 0382.
ⓘ **Ufficio Turistico**, Town Hall, San Nicola; tel. 6 30 02.

BOAT SERVICES. – Regular services daily (in winter once or twice weekly) from *Manfredonia* or *Rodi Garganico*, *Termoli* and *Ortona* to *San Nicola*; from there to *San Domino* as required.

The Trémiti Islands (Isole Trémiti), a beautiful rocky limestone archipelago which has preserved its traditional character unspoiled, lie some 20 km N of the Monte Gargano promontory in the Adriatic. The precipitous coasts with their numerous inlets and sea caves offer ideal conditions for scuba diving.

San Nicola, Trémiti Islands

The most westerly and scenically most attractive of the three major islands is **San Domino** (alt. 116 m; area 2 sq. km; hotels: Eden, II, 181 b,; San Domino, II, 50 b.; etc. Several camping sites), an island with large areas of pine-forest which was used as a place of exile until 1943 and is now becoming an increasingly popular tourist resort. The largest place on the island, *San Domino*, lies above the E coast. There are a number of

interesting caves accessible only from the sea, such as the *Grotta delle Viole* and the *Grotta del Bue Marino*, both with a beautiful play of light. – NE of San Domino is the smaller island of **San Nicola** (alt. 75 m; area 0·5 sq. km), on which is the little walled village of *San Nicola*, capital of the archipelago, with a castle (rebuilt in the 15th c.), the church of Santa Maria (1045), situated on a hill, and the remains of a 9th c. abbey with a beautiful Renaissance doorway and parts of a Romanesque mosaic pavement (11th–12th c.).

To the N, between San Domino and San Nicola, are the island of *Il Cretaccio* and a number of isolated stacks. – The most northerly of the three larger islands is the almost uninhabited **Caprara** or **Capraia** (alt. 53 m; area 0·5 sq. km).

Trento

Region: Trentino. – Alto Adige.
Province: Trento (TN).
Altitude: 193 m. – Population: 95,000.
Post code: I-38100. – Dialling code: 0461.
ⓘ **EPT**, Via San Marco 27; tel. 8 00 00.
AA, Via Alfieri 4; tel. 8 38 80.
ACI, Via A. Pozzo 6; tel. 2 50 72.
TCI, *Calderari e Moggiolo*, Via Manci 13; tel. 8 02 75.

HOTELS. – *Grand Hotel Trento*, Via Alfieri 1, I, 153 b.; *Everest*, Corso Alpini 14, II, 220 b.; *Alessandro Vittoria*, Via Romagnosi 16, II, 100 b.; *Roma*, Via Malpaga 9, II, 95 b.; *Ancora*, Via Manzoni 17, III, 70 b.; *Venezia*, Via Belenzani 70, III, 60 b.; etc. – *Motel Agip*, Via Brennero 168, II, 90 b.

Trento, capital of the province of the same name and the see of an archbishop, lies on the left bank of the Adige in a fertile valley enclosed by high limestone hills, in the southern part of the territory of Tirol which was transferred from Austria to Italy in 1919. With its numerous towers and palaces (many of them with painted façades), it is a town of distinctly Italian character.

HISTORY. – The town (the Roman *Tridentum*) was a place of some importance from an early period by virtue of its commanding situation at the junction of the trading route from Venice up the Valsugana with the road over the Brenner, and was strongly fortified. From 1027 to 1803 it was the residence of a prince-bishop directly subject to the emperor. From 1545 to

Trento

1563 it was the meeting-place of the Council of Trent, which laid down the pattern of the Counter-Reformation. Between 1814 and 1918 it belonged to Austria, thereafter to Italy. In 1948 the province of Trento was combined with the province of Bolzano (which included the German-speaking Alto Adige or South Tirol) to form the autonomous region of Trentino – Alto Adige.

SIGHTS. – In the centre of the town is the *Piazza del Duomo*, which has a beautiful *Neptune Fountain* (1768). On the E side of the square stands the *Palazzo Pretorio* (periodic special exhibitions), with the *Torre Grande* (Clock-Tower). The *Cathedral (11th–12th c.) on the S side was remodelled internally at the beginning of the 13th c. as a pillared basilica in Lombard Romanesque style; the central dome was entirely renewed in 1887–89. The Council of Trent met here from 1545 to 1563. Imposing interior, with frescoes (13th–14th c.) and numerous bishops' tombs (mostly 14th and 15th c.); 16th c. Flemish tapestries in sacristy; rich treasury.

In the choir of the Early Renaissance *church of Santa Maria Maggiore* (1520–33) NW of the cathedral are a beautiful *organ gallery (1534) and a picture of 1563 with likenesses of the members of the Council of Trent, which sometimes met here.

From the Piazza del Duomo *Via Belenzani* runs N. This, the finest street in the town, has a series of handsome palaces and the remains of painting on the façades. Near the N end of the street, on right, is the 16th c. **Palazzo Municipale**, with the 15th c. *Casa Geremia* opposite it. – Via Belenzani joins the main street of the town, *Via Manci*, which has also a number of fine palaces, as well as the beautiful Baroque *church of San Francesco Saverio*. Farther N, in front of the station, is the *Giardino*

Pubblico, with a *monument to Dante* (1896), 17·6 m high, and a monument to *Aldois Negrelli* (1799–1858), an early advocate of the Suez Canal. On the W side of the gardens stands the 12th c. *church of San Lorenzo* (restored).

On the NE side of the town is the *Castello del Buon Consiglio, former residence of the prince-bishops, from 1811 to 1918 a barracks and since then a museum. The 13th c. *Castelvecchio*, built round the massive round tower, was remodelled in Venetian Gothic style from 1475 onwards. The *Magno Palazzo*, a magnificent Renaissance building with arcaded courtyards and important frescoes by Romanino, Dosso Dossi and others, was built in 1528–35, and a linking wing was added in 1686. The Castello now houses the *Museo Nazionale del Trentino*, with pictures (including frescoes of the months in the Torre dell'Aquila), sculpture, period furniture and archaeological and ethnological collections, and the *Museo del Risorgimento*, with relics of the struggle for the liberation of Italy, including mementoes of the "irredentists" (supporters of the reunion of the Trentino with Italy) Cesare Battisti, Chiesa and Filzi, who were executed by the Austrians for treason in 1916.

SURROUNDINGS. – 3 km from Trento, on the *Doss Trento* (307 m) on the right bank of the Adige, is the conspicuous **mausoleum of Cesare Battisti** (1875–1916), from which there are fine views of Trento and the Adige valley.

For an attractive drive into the hills, leave Trento on the Riva road, going NW, and in 3 km turn left into a road which winds its way SW via the commandingly situated village of *Sardagna* (alt. 571 m; also reached by cableway from the banks of the Adige) and *Candriai* (984 m; Hotel Candriai alla Posta, III, 41 b.; etc.), which together with Vaneze forms the commune of Monte Bondone, to the hotel settlement of **Vaneze**

Landslide near Mori (SW of Rovereto)

(1300 m; hotels: Monte Bondone, I, 56 b.; Dolomiti, II, 102 b.; Zodiaco, II, 80 b.; Augustus, II, 67 b.; Alpino, III, 75 b.; etc.), beautifully situated on the slopes of the *Monte Bondone* range and popular both as a summer and a winter sports resort. The highest peak in the range, *Palon* (2091 m), can be climbed in 2 hours, or can be reached by means of two chair-lifts (via *Vason*, 1650 m). There are other chair-lifts on the N side of Monte Bondone (e.g. up *Tre*, 1637 m, and *Montesel*, 1739 m).

For another rewarding ascent, leave Trento on a road which runs N (10 km) to beyond *Lavis* (alt. 206 m; Hotel Bowling, III, 38 b.; etc.); then take the cableway to the summit of *Paganella* (2125 m), with magnificent views, particularly of the nearby Brenta group.

25 km S of Trento is **Rovereto** (alt. 188 m; pop. 30,000; hotels: Rovereto, II, 88 b.; Leon d'Oro, II, 60 b.; Rialto, III, 89 b.; Sant'Ilario, II, 57 b.; etc.). In the centre of the town is Piazza Rosmini, and a little way N of this the handsome Early Renaissance palace now occupied by the Savings Bank, with an arcaded courtyard (restored in its original style 1902–05). Nearby is the Museo Civico (geological collection). In the Castello (14th–15th c.), on higher ground, is a War Museum, with the most extensive collection of First World War mementoes in Italy. To the S of the old town stands a conspicuous circular building, the *Ossario di Castel Dante* (alt. 306 m: view), in which 12,000 dead of the First World War are buried. Above it is a gigantic bell (22·6 tons), cast in 1965 to commemorate the dead of all nations, which is rung every evening at 8.30 or 9.30 p.m.

Treviso

Region: Veneto. – Province: Treviso (TV).
Altitude: 15 m. – Population: 92,000.
Post code: I-31100. – Dialling code: 0422.
ⓘ **EPT**, Via Toniolo 41;
   tel. 4 76 32.
   ACI, Piazza S. Pio X;
   tel. 4 78 01.

HOTELS. – *Carlton*, Largo Altinia 15, II, 142 b.; *Continental*, Via Roma 16, II, 135 b.; *Carletto*, Via Bibano 42, II, 130 b.; *Treviso*, Via Cacianiga 2, II, 118 b.; *Al Fogher*, Viale Repubblica 10, II, 67 b.; *Ca' del Galetto*, II, 34 b.; *Al Cuor*, Piazza Duca d'Aosta 1, III, 112 b.; etc.

The ancient town of Treviso, which was the Roman Tarvisium and later the seat of a Lombard duchy, and is now a provincial capital, lies in the fertile Veneto plain at the junction of the rivers Botteniga and Sile.

It is an old-world town of narrow streets, many of them lined with arcades, and it is still surrounded by well-preserved 15th c. walls and a circuit of canals or moats.

SIGHTS. – In the centre of the town is the picturesque *Piazza dei Signori*, with the **Palazzo dei Trecento** (after 1217),

once the seat of the Great Council of the town. Adjoining it is the *Palazzo della Prefettura*, with the tall *Torre del Comune*. – From the Piazza dei Signori *Via Calmaggiore*, the main street of the town, flanked by handsome 15th and 16th c. houses, runs NW to the Piazza del Duomo. The **Cathedral** of San Pietro, with five domes, was built in the 15th and 16th c. on the site of an earlier Romanesque church (crypt 11th–12th c.); the porch was added in 1836. It contains *pictures by Titian ("Annunciation", 1517) and Paris Bordone and fine frescoes by Pordenone (1519–20). – To the left of the cathedral stands the Romanesque *Baptistery* (11th–12th c.), with 13th c. frescoes.

From the cathedral Via Canova and Via Cavour lead NW to the **Museo Civico** (closed Sunday afternoons and Mondays), with an archaeological collection and an excellent *picture gallery* (frescoes by Tommaso da Modena and pictures by Bellini, Lotto, Pisanello and many other artists).

In Via San Nicolò, at the SW corner of the old town, the Dominican *church of San Nicolò*, a spacious Gothic church built in brick (13th–14th c.) has round piers and an unusual vaulted timber roof. On the high altar is a *"Madonna Enthroned" by Fra Marco Pensaben and Savoldo (1521); tomb of Senator Agostino Onigo (d. 1490), by the Lombardi family; frescoes in chapterhouse by Tommaso da Modena (1352).

At the NE corner of Treviso is the handsome *Porta San Tommaso* (1518). The northern rampart walk which begins here affords beautiful *views of the Alps.

Trieste

Region: Friuli – Venezia Giulia.
Province: Trieste (TS).
Altitude: 2 m. – Population: 280,000.
Post code: I-34100. – Dialling code: 040.
ⓘ **EPT**, Via G. Rossini 6;
   tel. 3 55 52.
   ACI, Via Cumano 2;
   tel. 76 33 91.
   TCI, *Ufficio Centrale Viaggi*,
   Piazza Unità d'Italia 6;
   tel. 6 26 21.
   U.T.A.T., Via Imbriani 11;
   tel. 76 78 31.
   Viaggi Paterniti, Corso Cavour 7/1;
   tel. 6 12 93.

HOTELS. – *Jolly Cavour*, Corso Cavour 7, I, 299 b.; *Savoia Excelsior Palace*, I, 293 b.; *Grand Hotel Duchi d'Aosta*, Piazza Unità d'Italia 2, 96 b.; *Milano*, Via C. Chega 17, II, 163 b.; *Corso*, Via San Spiridione 2, II, 135 b.; *Alla Posta*, Piazza Oberdan 1, II, 101 b.; *Continentale*, Via San Nicolò 25, II, 75 b.; *Colombia*, Via della Geppa 18, II, 59 b.; *San Giusto*, Via Belli 3, II, 56 b.; *Impero*, Via Sant'Anastasio 1, !II, 86 b.; *Adria*, Capo di Piazza 1, III, 76 b.; *Città di Parenzo*, Via degli Artisti 8, III, 72 b.; *Roma*, Via C. Ghega 7, III, 71 b.; etc. – YOUTH HOSTEL, in Grignano, Viale Miramare 331, 100 b.

EVENT. – *International Trade Fair* (end of June to beginning of July).

The port of Trieste lies on the E side of the Gulf of Trieste, framed by the precipitous slopes of a limestone plateau, in the extreme north-eastern corner of the Adriatic.

In Trieste harbour

Trieste is the largest port in the Adriatic. With a greatly increased capacity since its reconstruction after war damage, it has gained considerably in importance compared with the pre-war period as a transhipment point for goods from Central Europe and the Danube region (particularly Austria). There has also been a considerable development of industry (oil refineries), which is promoted by the annual Trade Fair.

HISTORY. – Trieste, the Roman *Tergeste*, was held by Austria from 1382 until 1919. It was made a free port by the Emperor Charles VI in 1719, and from the end of the 18th c., after the construction of an artificial harbour, it captured the trade with the Near East which had been dominated by Venice for more than 500 years. As the last harbour of any size left to Austria Trieste developed into the leading commerial town in the Adriatic, particularly after the construction of the Semmering railway line (1854) and the new port installations to the N of the town (1867–83). After the First World War the town, mainly inhabited by Italians, was assigned to Italy and thus lost its hinterland; but the consequent decline in trade was made good by the large-scale development of industry. Under the Allied treaty with Italy in 1947 the territory immediately bordering on Trieste, with a predominantly Slav

population, was ceded to Yugoslavia and the town itself (in Serbo-Croat *Trst*) together with part of the Istrian peninsula became a free state under the United Nations, divided into two zones. On the basis of a later treaty between Italy and Yugoslavia (5 October 1954) Zone A (area 223 sq. km, pop. 296,000) and the town of Trieste were returned to Italian administration (and finally incorporated in Italy in 1962), while Zone B (area 516 sq. km, pop. 67,000) was assigned to Yugoslavia; the frontier was formally defined in a treaty of 10 November 1975).

SIGHTS. – On the W side of the town lies the **Harbour**, which has no natural anchorage and is exposed to strong NE winds (the *bora*) blowing down from the plateau. To the N the *Porto Franco Vecchio* (Old Free Port) has four piers and a long breakwater; in the middle is the *Porto Vecchio* (Old Harbour), and to the S, beyond the Campo Marzio station, the *Porto Franco Nuovo* (New Free Port) and the industrial zone, with a number of large shipyards.

The largest square in the older part of the town is the *Piazza dell'Unità d'Italia*, on the Old Harbour. On its N side is the *Prefecture* (1905), on the S side the massive palazzo (1882–83) of *Lloyd Triestino*, a shipping line founded in 1832 as the Austrian Lloyd company, and on the E side the **Town Hall** (1874). – The *Tergesteo* building (1842) to the NE now houses the Stock Exchange. In the adjoining Piazza della Borsa is the *Old Exchange* (Borsa Vecchia), a neo-classical building of 1806. – From here the *Corso Italia*, the town's principal traffic artery, lined with modern buildings, runs E to the busy Piazza Goldoni, which is linked with the industrial suburbs to the S by a 347 m long tunnel under the castle hill and another tunnel 1000 m long.

SE of the Town Hall is the broad new Via del Teatro Romano, at the E end of which towers the *Grattacielo* ("Skyscraper"). To the right of this is the **Roman Theatre** (2nd c. A.D.), which was excavated in 1938. Some of the fine marble statues from the stage of the theatre are now in the Museum of History and Art.

On the hill to the S of the Roman Theatre we find the *Castello*. Half way up the hill, on right, is the small Protestant *church of San Silvestro*, and opposite it the Jesuit *church of Santa Maria Maggiore* (1627–82), with a Baroque interior. Close by stands the so-called *Arco di Riccardo*, a gateway which probably dates from the 1st c. B.C. – Beyond this, at Via Catterdrale

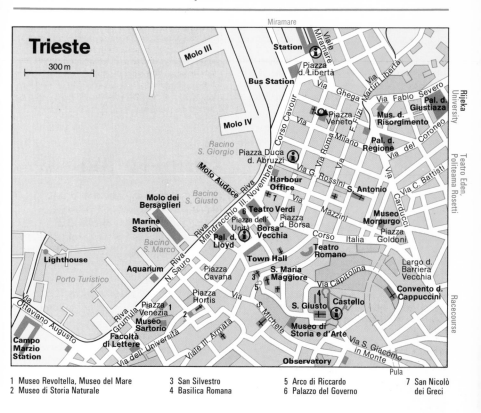

Trieste

300 m

1 Museo Revoltella, Museo del Mare   3 San Silvestro   5 Arco di Riccardo   7 San Nicolò
2 Museo di Storia Naturale   4 Basilica Romana   6 Palazzo del Governo   dei Greci

15, the **Museo di Storia e d'Arte** (Museum of History and Art; closed Mondays) contains antiquities of varying provenance and a number of pictures. In the *Orto Lapidario* is the tomb (1832) of the German classical scholar Johann Joachim Winckelmann (1717–68), who was murdered in Trieste.

At the end of Via Cattedrale the **Cathedral** of San Giusto, on the site of an Augustan temple, was formed in the 14th c. by the joining up of two 6th c. churches and a baptistery: to the right *San Giusto* and to the left *Santa Maria*, their lateral aisles combined to make the central aisle or nave of the cathedral. Fragments of Roman work can be seen in the doorway and campanile (1337–43). In the lateral apses are fine mosaics (7th and 12th c.). – To the left of the cathedral rises a column erected in 1560, and beyond it, on the ancient forum, an Italian *war memorial* (1935). – On top of the castle hill is the **Castello** (15th–18th c.) contains the interesting *Castle Museum* (medieval weapons, furniture, tapestries, etc.: closed in the afternoon and on Mondays). From the Castello and from the *Parco della Rimembranza* on the N side of the castle hill there are fine views.

On the pier to the S of the Piazza dell'Unità d'Italia is the *Marine Station*, and farther along the quay the *Pescheria* (Fish Market), with an interesting *Aquarium*. Beyond this lies the Piazza Venezia, at the E corner of which is the *Museo Revoltella* (closed Mondays), with good modern pictures by Italian artists and some sculpture. To the E, in Piazza A. Hortis, the **Museum of the Sea** (closed Mondays), has numerous ship models (particularly sailing ships). On the SE side of the square are the *Museum of Natural History* (Museo di Storia Naturale: closed Mondays) and the *Municipal Library*.

NE of the Piazza dell'Unità d'Italia, along the quay, stands the *Teatro Verdi*, with the *Theatre Museum* (Tuesdays and Thursdays 12–1). From the pier opposite the theatre, the *Molo Audace*, there are good views of the town and the harbour. Farther along the quay, on right, is the Greek *church of San Nicolò dei Greci*, and farther N again is the *Canale Grande* (1756), the harbour formerly used by sailing ships. At the E end of the canal we come to the neo-classical **church of Sant'Antonio** (1849), Trieste's largest church. To the right of this is the sumptuous Serbian Orthodox *church of San Spiridione*. – A short distance to the E of Sant'Antonio the new Via G. Carducci runs NW from near the castle hill to the *Piazza Oberdan*, the main square of the newer part of the town. Some 500 m N is the Piazza Scorcola, with the lower station of an electric funicular to Poggioreale and Villa Opicina. From Piazza Oberdan the Via Fabio Severo leads past the massive *Palazzo di Giustizia* to the *University* (1939–50).

SURROUNDINGS. – Reached by road from Piazza Oberdan (9 km) or by funicular from Piazza Scorcola is **Poggioreale del Carso** (348 m), on the edge of the karstic plateau to the S of the villa suburb of *Villa Opicina* (Park Hotel Obelisco, I, 56 b., SP; etc.). From the obelisk at Poggioreale station there are magnificent views of Trieste and the sea. A footpath runs NW from the obelisk to the viewpoints of *Vedetta di Opicina* (397 m: 10 minutes) and *Vedetta d'Italia* (305 m: 45 minutes), from which there are extensive prospects in all directions. – 3 km N of Poggioreale is the **Grotta del Gigante**, a stalactitic cave with a huge chamber 240 m long and 136 m high; museum.

Castello di Miramare

2·5 m NW of Trieste, above *Barcola* (alt. 5 m) rises the 68 m high **Victory Beacon** (*Faro della Vittoria*), erected in 1927, from which there are beautiful views (open throughout the day). – 3·5 km farther NW, on a crag above the sea, stands the *Castello di Miramare, built in 1854–56 for Archduke Maximilian of Austria, later briefly emperor of Mexico. Now owned by the State, it houses a historical museum (closed Mondays). From the terrace and the park (bronze statue of Maximilian; open-air theatre) there are magnificent *views of the sea (here protected as a nature reserve, the *Parco Marino di Miramare*, with the interesting flora and fauna of the northern Adriatic). – 7 km along the coast of the Gulf of Trieste is the little port and seaside resort of **Duino** (alt. 53 m; hotels: Europa, in Marina di Aurisina, I, 154 b.; Motel Agip, II, 154 b.; Posta, in Sistina, II, 58 b.; etc.), where Rainer Maria Rilke (1875–1926) wrote his ''Duino Elegies''. The Castel Nuovo (destroyed 1916, rebuilt 1929 onwards; no admission) and the picturesque ruins of the Castel Vecchio are magnificently situated on a projecting crag (fine views). Beyond Duino the village of *San Giovanni al Timavo* (alt. 4 m) has a 15th c. Gothic *church containing the remains of a mosaic pavement belonging to an earlier basilica of the 5th–6th c. At San Giovanni the River *Timavo*, with an abundant flow of water, emerges after an underground course of 40 km from the caves of Skocjan in Yugoslavia, and soon afterwards flows into the sea. – 7 km from Duino is **Monfalcone** (alt. 24 m; pop. 31,000; hotels: Sam, II, 115 b.; Roma, III, 80 b.;

Excelsior, III, 76 b.; etc.), a port and industrial town in the foothills of the karstic plateau. Monfalcone was totally destroyed during the First World War and was rebuilt afterwards, twice its former size. 7 km N of Monfalcone on S.S. 305, finely situated on the slopes of *Monte Sei Busi* (118 m), is the *military cemetery of Redipuglia*, with the graves of 100,000 men who fell in the First World War.

Turin/Torino

Region: Piemonte. – Province: Torino (TO).
Altitude: 239 m. – Population: 1,200,000.
Post code: I-10100. – Dialling code: 011.

(i) EPT, Via Roma 222;
tel. 53 51 81.
ACI, Via G. Giolitti 15;
tel. 57 79.
TCI, Via C. Alberto 57;
tel. 54 01 77.

HOTELS. – *Jolly Ambasciatori*, Corso Vittorio Emanuele 104, I, 336 b.; *Turin Palace*, Via Sacchi 8, I, 225 b.; *Ligure*, Piazza Carlo Felice 85, I, 209 b.; *Jolly Principi di Piemonte*, Via P. Gobetti 15, I, 198 b.; *Sitea*, Via Carlo Alberto 35, I, 195 b.; *Concord*, Via Lagrange 47, I, 188 b.; *Majestic*, Via U. Rattazzi 10, I, 127 b.; *Suisse Terminus*, Via Sacchi 2, I, 122 b.; *City*, Via F. Juvara 25, I, 65 b.; *Villa Sassi*, Via Traforo del Pino 47, I, 22 b.; *Patria*, Via Cernaia 42, II, 184 b.; *Roma e Rocca Cavour*, Piazza Carlo Felice 60, II, 148 b.; *Venezia*, Via XX Settembre 70, II, 133 b.; *Lancaster*, Corso Filippo Turati 8, II, 132 b.; *Genio*, Corso Vittorio Emanuele II 47, II, 122 b.; *Dock Milano*, Via Cernaia 46, II, 119 b.; *Fiorina*, Via Pietro Micca 22, II, 119 b.; *Victoria*, Via Nino Costa 4, II, 116 b.; *Royal*, Corso Regina Margherita 249, II, 115 b.; *Astoria*, Via XX Settembre 4, II, 107 b.; *Luxor*, Corso Stati Uniti 7, II, 102 b.; *Nazionale*, Piazza C.L.N. 254, II, 100 b.; *Plaza*, Via Ilarione Petitti 18, II, 100 b.; *Rex*, Via Pomba 25, II, 100 b.; *San Silvestro*, Corso Francia 1, III, 175 b.; *Bologna*, Corso Vittorio Emanuele 60, III, 104 b.; *Campo di Marte*, Via XX Settembre 7, III, 103 b.; *Dogana Vecchia*, Via Corte d'Appello 4, III, 87 b.; *Italia*, Corso Stati Uniti 9 bis, III, 86 b.; etc. – YOUTH HOSTEL, Via Gatti (corner of Via Alby), 100 b.

RESTAURANTS. – *Villa Sassi*, in Sassi, Via Traforo del Pino 47; *Cambio*, Piazza Carignano 2; *Tiffany*, Piazza Solferino 16; *Al Gatto Nero*, Corso F. Turati 14; etc.

EVENTS. – *Salone dell'Automobile* (International Motor Show) and *Salone del Veicolo Industriale* (Industrial Vehicle Show) in alternate years. – *Salone delle Vacanze, del Turismo e dello Sport* (show devoted to holidays, tourism and sport), in Feb.–Mar. – *Salone della Tecnica*, in autumn. – *Caravan Europa*, in autumn.

Turin, the old capital of Piedmont and the see of an archbishop, lies on the left bank of the Po in a fertile plain which is bounded on the W by the wide arc of the Cottian and Graian Alps, while on the E the Colli Torinesi come right up to the right bank of the river.

Panorama of Turin

The regularity of the city's layout is an inheritance from Roman times; its present aspect was largely shaped by the architects of the Baroque period, chief among whom were *Guarino Guarini* (1624–83) of Modena and the Sicilian *Filippo Juvara* (1678–1736). Many of the long straight streets of Turin are lined with arcades. In recent times many modern buildings have been erected, including some tower blocks. – The city's varied range of industry includes a number of large firms, among them the Fiat and Lancia car plants, factories manufacturing engines and rolling-stock, an electricity corporation, plants producing man-made fibres (Snia, Viscosa), woollen and cotton mills, etc. Turin is also renowned for its vermouths (Martini & Rossi, Cinzano), its chocolate and the sweets called *caramelle*. – Airport at Casalle, 15 km N.

HISTORY. – *Taurasia*, capital of a Celto-Ligurian tribe, the Taurini, became a Roman colony in the time of Augustus under the name of *Augusta Taurinorum*. In the Frankish period it became the seat of a marquis, but the town did not really begin to develop until it passed in 1418 to the main branch of the counts of Savoy. During the War of the Spanish Succession it was besieged by the French but was relieved in 1706 by Prince Eugene of Savoy and Prince Leopold of Anhalt-Dessau. In 1720 it became capital of the kingdom of Sardinia and Piedmont, and after the French occupation (1798–1814) became the centre of the Italian striving towards unity. From 1861 to 1865 it was capital of the kingdom of Italy.

SIGHTS. – The central feature of the older part of the town is the *Piazza Castello*, in the middle of which stands the massive **Palazzo Madama**. The core of the structure is a 13th c. castle built on the remains of the Roman E gate which was enlarged in the 15th c. and embellished by Filippo Juvara in 1718 with the handsome W front, a fine example of Piedmontese Baroque architecture, and the magnificent double staircase. It now houses the *Museo d'Arte Antica* (ground floor and second floor: closed Mondays), with a valuable collection of sculpture in stone and wood, stained glass, pictures and applied art (Duc de Berry's Book of Hours, with Dutch miniatures of c. 1400). On the first floor are the state apartments, richly appointed in 18th c. style.

On the N side of Piazza Castello is the courtyard of the Royal Palace, on the left-hand side of which can be seen the Baroque *church of San Lorenzo* (Guarini, 1687), with an unusual and boldly designed dome. The former **Royal Palace** (*Palazzo Reale*: closed Friday afternoons, Sundays and Mondays) is a plain brick building (1646–58), with the Appartamento di Madama Felicita and 26 sumptuously decorated state apartments (Reali Appartamenti). In the right wing is the *Prefecture*, with the entrance (first door on left) to the former *Royal

Armoury, containing one of the largest collections of arms and armour in Europe; there are many complete suits of armour and other items dating from the 15th–17th c., including the field armour of Prince Eugene of Savoy.

Adjoining the palace on the NW is the **Cathedral** of San Giovanni Battista (1492–98; tower completed 1720). Behind the high altar is the *Chapel of the Holy Shroud* (Cappella della Santa Sindone), a circular structure (by Guarini,

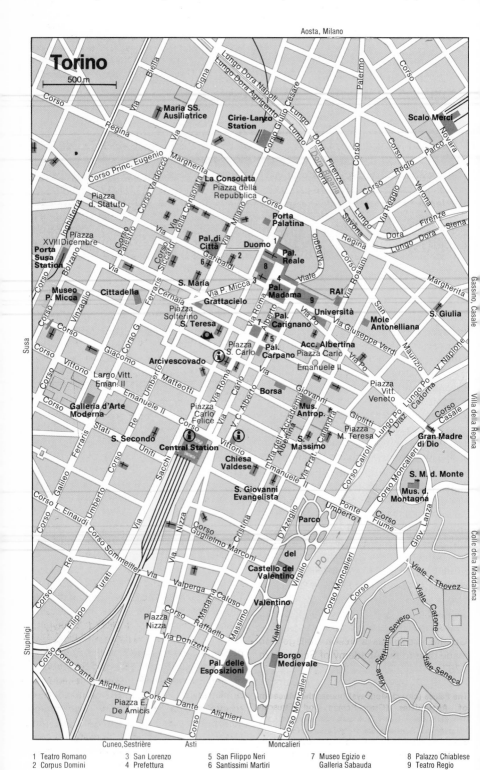

1 Teatro Romano	3 San Lorenzo	5 San Filippo Neri	7 Museo Egizio e
2 Corpus Domini	4 Prefettura	6 Santissimi Martiri	Galleria Sabauda

8 Palazzo Chiablese
9 Teatro Regio

1668–94) containing, in an urn above the altar, the Santa Sindone or Santo Sudario, the linen cloth in which the body of Christ was, according to the legend, wrapped after his descent from the cross. Beside the cathedral are the remains of a *Roman theatre* (1st c. A.D.). – On the S side of the square in which the cathedral stands is the *Palazzo Chiablese*, with the *Film Museum.*

The *Porta Palatina*, NW of the cathedral, the N gate of the Roman town, has two brick towers. – 500 m farther NW, in Via della Consolata, is the **Consolata church**, an unusual pilgrimage church (by Guarini, 1679–1705) formed by the joining up of two Baroque churches and sumptuously rebuilt in 1903–04. Beside it stands a beautiful Romanesque campanile. Adjoining the oval *church of Sant'Andrea*, the front part of the present structure, is the hexagonal Santuario della Consolata, with several round chapels.

From Piazza Castello the narrow Via Garibaldi, part of the old main street (decumanus) of the Roman town, runs NW to the Piazza dello Statuto. The **Palazzo di Città** (Town Hall), on the right-hand side of the street, was built by Francesco Lanfranchi in 1658–65. Almost opposite, on the left, is the *church of the Santi Martiri*, a splendid Baroque building by Pellegrino Tibaldi (1577).

Just S of Piazza Castello is the **Palazzo Carignano** (by Guarini, 1680), meeting-place of the Sardinian parliament from 1848 to 1859 and of the Italian parliament from 1861 to 1864. The establishment of the kingdom of Italy was proclaimed here on 14 March 1861. It now houses, in 30 rooms on the first floor, the *Museo Nazionale del Risorgimento Italiano* (closed Mondays), the largest museum of its kind (mementoes and relics of the campaign for Italian unity and of the two world wars). – Opposite the Palazzo Carignano, to the SW, is the **Palazzo dell'Accademia delle Scienze**, built by Guarini (1679) as a Jesuit college and made over to the Academy of Sciences in 1757.

The Palace (closed Mondays) houses the **Museum of Antiquities** (Greco-Roman and Etruscan material, mainly from Piedmont and Liguria), the ****Egyptian Museum**, one of the finest collections of Egyptian antiquities in the world (numerous statues of pharaohs of the New Kingdom, including Rameses II, papyruses, two tomb chambers from Thebes) and the

***Galleria Sabauda**, a richly stocked picture gallery. The collection includes pictures by the Piedmontese artists Macrino d'Alba and Defendente Ferrari, the Lombards Gaudenzio Ferrari and Sodoma, the Venetians Mantegna ("Madonna with Saints", repainted), Paolo Veronese, Tintoretto, Tiepolo and Canaletto, the Emilians Guido Reni and Guercino, the Tuscans Fra Angelico da Fiesole ("Angels in Adoration", etc.), Lorenzo di Credi (Madonnas) and Piero Pollaiuolo ("Tobias with the Archangel Raphael"), numerous Dutch and Flemish paintings, including works by Jan van Eyck ("St Francis receiving the Stigmata"), Roger van der Weyden, Petrus Christus, Hans Memling, Van Dyck (portraits, including *"Prince Thomas on Horseback", 1634, and *"The Infanta Isabella", 1635) and Rembrandt (a youthful work, "Old Man Asleep"). One room is devoted to the *Gualino Collection*.

E of the Academy of Sciences in Via Maria Vittoria the *church of San Filippo Neri* was begun by Guarini in 1679 and rebuilt by Juvara in 1714; the porch is later. Via Maria Vittoria runs SE to the Piazza Carlo Emanuele II, where there is a marble *monument* (1873) to *Camillo Cavour* (1810–61), a native of Turin, the great statesman who achieved Italian unity, and the *church of Santa Croce* (Juvara, 1718). – To the NW Via Maria Vittoria leads to the Piazza San Carlo, from which Via Santa Teresa (with the Baroque *church of Santa Teresa*) continues to the Piazza Solferino, where stands a 14-storey building. From here Via Cernaia leads to the *Artillery Museum* (closed Mondays, Wednesdays and Fridays), which is housed in the old gatehouse of the Citadel, demolished in 1857, and in which can be seen weapons of many different periods. At the NW end of Via Cernaia stands the 18-storey tower block (1967) of *RAI*, the Italian radio and television corporation (studios also in Via Rossini), and also the *Porta Susa Station*.

The main traffic artery of the city centre is the monumental *Via Roma*, with uniform modern stone façades and arcades, which runs from Piazza Castello to the main station. At the near end, on the right, is the *Torre* (1934), an office building 87 m high. The *Piazza San Carlo*, a symmetrically designed square half way along, was laid out in 1638. On the S side are the *church of Santa Cristina* (1637: to the E), with a façade by Juvara (1718), and the *church of San Carlo* (1619), with a façade in similar style (1836). In the centre of the square stands an imposing *equestrian statue of Duke Emmanuel Philibert* (1838). At the S end of Via Roma lies the Piazza Carlo Felice, with the **Central Station** (*Stazione di Porta Nuova*), in front of which, at right angles to Via Roma, is the Corso Vittorio Emanuele II, a $3\frac{1}{2}$ km long avenue leading to the W. At its intersection with the broad Corso Galileo Ferraris can be seen a conspicuous *monument to Victor Emmanuel*, 38 m high (1899). A little way S along Corso G. Ferraris, on the right, is the **Galleria d'Arte Moderna** (1942: closed Mondays), one of the finest collections of modern art in Italy, with pictures and sculpture of the 19th and 20th c., mainly by Piedmontese artists; there are also some works by foreign (particularly French) artists, and occasional special exhibitions. In the same building is the interesting *Museum of Oriental Art* (closed Mondays), with (among much else) material excavated in Iraq, Iran and Pakistan.

From Piazza Castello the arcaded Via Po runs SE, passing close to the *Accademia Albertina di Belle Arti* (small collection of pictures, etc.), to the *Piazza Vittorio Veneto*, a square in neo-classical style on the banks of the Po (1830). A short distance N of Via Po, in the Villa Montebello gardens, rises the huge **Mole Antonelliana**, begun by Alessandro Antonelli in 1863 as a synagogue, with a tall spire added in 1879–80 (167 m high, with a lift to 85 m: *view). To the E is the massive building of the *University* (1968).

From Piazza Vittorio Veneto the *Ponte Vittorio Emanuele I* crosses the Po to the **church of the Gran Madre di Dio** (1818–31), which was modelled on the Pantheon in Rome and which was erected in thanksgiving for the return of Victor Emmanuel I in 1814. To the NE, on the banks of the Po, are the *Zoological Gardens*. – From the Gran Madre church we go S along Corso Moncalieri and almost immediately turn left into Via Maresciallo Giardino to reach the **Monte dei Cappuccini**, a wooded hill rising above the river (45 m). On top of the hill are a Capuchin monastery founded in 1583, the *church of Santa Maria del Monte* and the interesting *Museo Nazionale della Montagna*, with Alpine maps, photographs, reliefs, models, etc. From near the museum there is a magnificent *view of Turin and the chain of the Alps.

SW of the Monte dei Cappuccini, beyond the *Ponte Umberto I*, is the large **Parco del Valentino** on the left bank of the Po,

together with the *Botanic Garden* (established 1729) and the handsome Renaissance *Castello del Valentino* (before 1638). Towards the S end of the park stands the impressive *equestrian statue of Duke Amadeo of Aosta* (king of Spain 1870–73), erected in 1902. – To the SE, on the banks of the river, are the **Borgo** and **Castello Medioevale** (closed Mondays), a medieval village and castle built for an exhibition in 1884. At the S end of the park is the *Palazzo delle Esposizioni* (1948–52), in which the popular Motor Show and Industrial Vehicle Show are held. – Still farther S, at Corso dell'Unità d'Italia 40, is the *Motor Museum (Museo dell'Automobile Carlo Biscaretti di Ruffia*: closed Mondays), opened in 1960, which gives a comprehensive survey of the development of the motor car, with many veteran and vintage cars.

In the S of the town, beyond the large Piazza d'Armi, is the **Stadio Comunale**, with the *Marathon Tower*, two open-air swimming pools and an indoor pool. – Farther S, in the suburb of *Lingotto*, are the main *Fiat Works* (Fabbrica Italiana Automobili Torinesi, with a work force of 150,000), with a testing track on the roof. A kilometre farther S, in the suburb of *Mirafiori*, are the new Fiat plant (1939), the *Mirafiori Racecourse* and an *airfield*.

SURROUNDINGS. – 10 km NE of Turin, reached on a road which follows the Po to the suburb of *Sassi* (alt. 218 m) and then winds its way up to the top of the hill (or rack railway from Sassi, 16 minutes), is the *Basilica di Superga** (672 m), on the second highest hill in the Colli Torinesi. This large and conspicuous church, built on a centralised plan with a dome 75 m high flanked by 60 m high towers – the masterpiece of the great Baroque architect Juvara –

Basilica di Superga, near Turin

was erected in 1717–31 to commemorate Prince Eugene's victory in 1706 and served as the mausoleum of the royal house of Savoy from 1730 to 1849 (tombs in crypt: closed Fridays). From the terrace in front of the church, in clear weather, there is a *prospect of the Alps; from the forecourt there is a view of Turin. Some distance below the church on the Turin road is the Italia restaurant, from which there is a still more open view.

Another attractive excursion (10 km) is to the **Colle della Maddalena** (715 m; television aerial; several restaurants), the highest of the Colli Torinesi, crowned by the *Faro della Vittoria*, a beacon in the form of a bronze statue (by E. Rubino, 1928) of the goddess of victory carrying a torch, 18·5 m high on an 8 m base; panoramic *views.

Turin is a good base for some magnificent drives into the mountains. Particularly fine is the road to *Sestriere and the Montgenèvre pass* (113 km). – Leave Turin by way of the Fiat works at Montefiori and continue on S.S. 23. – 11 km: **Stupinigi** (alt. 244 m), a magnificent Baroque hunting lodge (by Filippo Juvara, 1729–33) set in a large park which now houses the Museo d'Arte e dell'Ammobigliamento (closed Mondays and Fridays). – 27 km: **Pinerolo** (alt. 376 m; pop. 38,000; Hotel Turismo, III, 106 b.; etc.), a beautifully situated town with an 11th c. cathedral. In the church of San Maurizio is a burial vault of the house of Savoy. Beyond this stands the church of the Madonna della Grazie, from which there is a fine view of Monviso (3841 m). Italian Cavalry Museum. – From Pinerolo a detour can be made to the little town of **Torre Péllice**, a popular summer resort prettily situated in the Pellice valley (alt. 516 m; hotels: Gilly, II, 62 b.; Du Parc, III, 57 b.; etc.), a stronghold of the Waldensians, Protestants who fled from France during the Albigensian wars (1209–29) and sought refuge in the Piedmontese valleys on the E side of the Cottian Alps, where they were able to maintain themselves in spite of frequent persecution. There are now some 25,000 Waldensians, most of them still French-speaking, in the Pellice valley and the lower Chisone valley. Cableway.

Beyond Pinerolo the road to Montgenèvre ascends the *Chisone valley*, towards the main chain of the *Cottian Alps*. – 18 km: *Perosa Argentina* (alt. 614 m; pop. 5000; Hotel Centrale, IV, 19 b.), a little industrial town mainly populated by Waldensians. The road then traverses a gorge and before reaching Fenestrelle passes the large *Agnelli Sanatorium*, on a hill to the right (alt. 1700 m; road, 6·5 km, and cableway). – 16 km: *Fenestrelle* (alt. 1154 m; Hotel Tre Re, IV, 52 b.; etc.), a village with imposing fortifications extending up to the 18th c. *fort of San Carlo*, linked by 4000 steps. – 22 km: **Sestriere** (alt. 2033 m; hotels: *Principi di Piemonte, L, 141 b.; SP; Cristallo, I, 134 b.; Duchi d'Aosta, II, 253 b., with annexe, La Torre, III, 148 b.; Miramonti, III, 68 b.; etc.), on the saddle between the Chisone valley and the valley of the Dora Riparia. This is one of Europe's largest winter sports resorts (heated open-air swimming pool), also popular in summer. Cableways to *Monte Fraitève* (2701 m) to the NW, *Monte Sises* (2658 m; upper station 2597 m) to the SE, *Monte Banchetta* (2555 m) to the E, etc.; chair-lift, many ski-lifts.

Beyond Sestriere the road descends into the valley of the *Dora Riparia*. – 11 km: **Cesana Torinese** (alt. 1350 m; Hotel Chaberton, III, 18 b., etc.), where S.S. 23 joins the road from Turin via Susa. Chair-lift to Sagnalonga (2002 m) and *Colle Bercia* (*Monti della Luna*, 2203 m). Beyond Cesana the road continues to

climb. – 6 km: **Claviere** or *Clavières* (1760 m; hotels: Grande Albergo Claviere, II, 56 b.; Passero Pellegrino, II, 36 b.; Bes, II, 33 b.; Roma, III, 60 b.; etc.), a resort much favoured by winter sports enthusiasts; chair-lift to *La Cloche* (1960 m). Soon after Claviere the road comes to the French frontier. – 2 km: **Col du Montgenèvre** (1854 m; winter sports; several hotels; chair-lifts to 2600 m), formerly an important Alpine pass providing the shortest route between the Po valley and southern France, used by Julius Caesar and the Emperor Barbarossa among many others.

Turin via Susa to the Montgenèvre pass. – Leave on S.S. 25, going W. – 13 km: **Rivoli** (alt. 354 m; pop. 50,000; hotels: Sirena, III, 46 b.; Navicella, III, 40 b.; etc.), an old-world town situated between morainic hills, once a favourite residence of the house of Savoy, with a Baroque palace (by Juvara, 1712), of which only a third was completed (alt. 419 m). Beyond Rivoli the road enters the *Cottian Alps* and runs up the *Val di Susa*, the valley of the Dora Riparia. At the mouth of the valley, on a hill to the left, is the *Sagre di San Michele abbey* (11th–13th c.: alt. 962 m. – 40 km: **Susa** (495 m; pop. 7500; hotels: Napoleon, III, 73 b.; Meana, III, 60 b.; etc.), an old town, beautifully situated between high mountains, which controlled the Montgenèvre and Mont Cenis roads. On the W side of the picturesque old town, on the right bank of the Doria, rises a marble *triumphal arch (13·5 m high) erected in 8 B.C. in honour of the Emperor Augustus by the prefect Cottius, after whom the Cottian Alps are named. NE of the arch stands the cathedral of San Giusto (11th–13th c.), with a beautiful campanile. From here there is a rewarding climb (8–9 hours; also by road to 2205 m) to the summit of *Rocciamelone* (3538 m), with the Santa Maria hut, a pilgrimage chapel (1923) and a large statue of the Virgin (panoramic *views). At Susa the road forks: Montgenèvre to the left, Mont Cenis straight ahead.

The road to Mont Cenis (S.S. 25), constructed by Napoleon in 1803–10, runs uphill, with numerous curves and sharp bends. – 10 km: *Molaretto* (Italian customs). – 9 km: *Passo del Paradiso*, which since 1947 has marked the French-Italian frontier. – 4 km: to the left the *Lac du Mont-Cenis*, in a beautiful setting (alt. 1913 m: hospice and hotel). – 4 km: **Mont Cenis pass** (*Col du Mont-Cenis*, 2084 m), on the old French-Italian frontier.

Beyond Susa the Montgenèvre road (S.S. 24) passes through a gorge formed by the Dora Riparia. – 12 km: *Exilles* (on left), a picturesque village dominated by a massive fortress (17th c.); fine *views. – 11 km: **Ulzio** (*Oulx*: 1067 m; Hotel Commercio, III, 34 b.; etc.), 5 km E of which is the winter sports resort of *Sauze d'Oulx* (1510 m; hotels: Grand Hotel Palace, I, 96 b.; Holiday Debili, II, 80 b.; La Terrazza, II, 68 b.; Splendid, II, 66 b.; Miravalle, II, 69 b.; Stella Alpina, II, 41 b.; Savoia, III, 80 b.; Miramonti, III, 68 b.; etc.); chair-lifts, including one to *Sportinia* (2137 m; Hotel Monte Triplex, III, 41 b.; etc.), to the S. 14 km NW of Sauze d'Oulx is the village of **Bardonecchia**, a popular resort both in summer and winter (1312 m; hotels: Riky Grand Hotel, I, 136 b.; Des Genys Splendid, II, 109 b.; Sommeiller, III, 78 b.; Betulla, III, 63 b.; etc.). It lies near the entrance to the Galleria del Fréjus, the first Alpine tunnel (1861–70), leading to the French town of Modane (rail tunnel, 13·6 km long; road tunnel 12·3 km long under construction). From Bardonecchia there are a number of chair-lifts, including one via *Granges Hippolytes* (1520 m: change lifts) up *Colomion* (2054 m). – 11 km: **Cesana Torinese**, where the road from Turin via Sestriere comes in. – 8 km: **Montgenèvre pass** (1854 m).

86 km NE of Turin, beautifully situated in the foothills of the Alps on the River *Cerro*, is the industrial town of **Biella** (alt. 410 m; pop. 55,000; hotels: Astoria, I, 80 b.; Principe, II, 64 b.; Augustus, II, 60 b.; Coggiola, II, 60 b.; Colibri, II, 43 b.; Michelangelo, III, 18 b.; etc.). In the lower town are the cathedral (originally built 1402, rebuilt 1772; façade 1825), and adjoining an early Romanesque baptistery (11th c.) and the Town Hall, with the tower (11th c.) of a demolished church. In the SW part of the lower town stands the beautiful Renaissance church of San Sebastiano (1504; façade 1882). To the W, above the lower town (funicular), is the picturesque upper town or Piazzo (fine views). – From Biella an interesting excursion on S.S. 144 (13 km), goes N, with beautiful views, past the little spa of *Oropa Bagni* (1060 m) to the magnificent **Santuario d'Oropa** (1180 m; Hotel Miravalle, II, 66 b.), the most popular place of pilgrimage in Piedmont, said to have been founded by St Eusebius in 369. From here a cableway runs up in 6 minutes to the *Rifugio Mucrone* (1820 m), near the *Lago di Mucrone* (Hotel Savoia, II, 62 b.), and in another 4 minutes to *Monte Mucrone* (2335 m; cableway station 2189 m). From the Rifugio Mucrone there is another cableway (12 minutes) up *Monte Camino* (2391 m; mountain hut), from which there are superb *views, including Monte Rosa and the Matterhorn. – From Biella there is also a very attractive circular tour NE to *Trivero* (739 m; Hotel Monte Rubello, III, 38 b.; etc.); then 13 km W on the beautiful * *Strada Panoramica Zegna* (S.S. 232) via *Caulera* and *Bielmonte* (1517 m; winter sports; chairlift up *Monte Marca*, 1618 m) to the *Bocchetto di Séssera* (1382 m); then via *Campiglia* (12 km) back to *Biella* (27 km).

Up the Aosta valley: see p. 58.

Turin to Savona (154 km). – The road passes through the *Monferrato* uplands, famous for their wine, to **Alba** (34 km; alt. 172 m; pop. 30,000; Hotel Savona, II, 170 b.; Motel Alba, II, 88 b.; etc.), which has a Gothic cathedral (beautiful choir-stalls of 1501), fine churches and medieval towers. It then continues through the wine-growing *Langhe* region, where the much sought-after white truffles are harvested in autumn, and down the valley of the *Bórmida di Spigno*, on the edge of the **Ligurian Apennines**, to **Savona** (see p. 215), on the Riviera dei Fiori.

Turin via Acqui to Genoa (181 km). – Leave on S.S. 29 (the Alessandria road), which runs through *Poirino* (alt. 249 m; Hotel Stella d'Oro, IV, 19 b.; etc.). – 56 km: **Asti** (see p. 68). – 9 km: *Piano d'Isola* (130 m). The road now leaves the Tanaro valley and traverses a densely populated upland region (wine-growing). – 20 km: **Nizza Monferrato** (alt. 138 m; pop. 10,000), a little wine-growing town on the River *Belbo*. The road runs over a hill and enters the wide valley of the *Bórmida*. – 19 km: **Acqui Terme** (alt. 164 m; pop. 22,000; hotels: Nuove Terme, I, 89 b.; Ariston, II, 54 b.; Da Alfredo, III, 60 b.; Archi Romani, III, 44 b.; etc.), a spa and centre of the wine trade on the left bank of the Bormida, with a cathedral (consecrated 1067) and the church of San Pietro (*c.* 1015). The mineral springs, containing salt and sulphur, are recommended for the treatment of rheumatic conditions. The hottest spring (La Bollente, 75 °C (167 °F)) is in the Nuove Terme, in the town. From here the Corso Bagni leads over the river (beyond the bridge, on right, remains of an ancient aqueduct) and past a large thermal swimming pool (6500 sq. m) to the Vecchie Terme (hotels: Antiche Terme, I, 128 b.; Pineta, II, 184 b.; Regina, II, 140 b.; etc.). – Beyond Acqui the road continues for a short distance in the Bormida valley and then climbs into the *Ligurian Apennines*, goes

over a hill and descends into the *Orba* valley. – 24 km: **Ovada** (lat. 186 m; pop. 12,000; Hotel Vittoria, II, 47 b.; etc.), at the junction of the *Stura* and the Orba. – 17 km: *Campo Ligure* (alt. 342 m; pop. 4000), formerly called Campofreddo, a picturesquely situated little town and summer resort with a tower which belonged to a 13th c. castle. – 8 km: **Passo del Turchino** (532 m: short tunnel), from which the road runs down into the pleasant valley of the *Leiro*. – 28 km: **Genoa** (see p. 125).

Tuscany/Toscana

ⓘ **EPT Arezzo**, Piazza Risorgimento 116, I-52100 Arezzo (AR); tel. (0575) 2 39 52.
EPT Grosseto, Via Monterosa 206, I-58100 Grosseto (GR); tel. (1564) 2 25 34.
EPT Firenze, Via A. Manzoni 16, I-50100 Firenze (FI); tel (055) 67 88 41.
EPT Livorno, Piazza Cavour 8, I-57100 Livorno (LI); tel. (0586) 3 31 11.
EPT Lucca, Piazza Giudiccioni 2, I-55100 Lucca (LU); tel (0583) 4 69 15.
EPT Massa-Carrara, Piazza II Giugno 14, I-54033 Carrara (MS); tel. (0585) 7 06 68.
EPT Pisa, Lungarno Mediceo 42, I-56100 Pisa (PI); tel. (050) 2 03 51.
EPT Pistoia, Corso Gramsci 110, I-51100 Pistoia (PT); tel. (0573) 3 43 26.
EPT Siena, Via di Città 5, I-53100 Siena (SI); tel. (0577) 4 70 51.

The historic territory and modern administrative region of *Tuscany, with nine provinces and Florence as its capital, covers an area of 22,989 sq. km extending from the ridge of the Tuscan or Etruscan Apennines over the charming Tuscan uplands, with their gently rounded hills, their farms and vineyards and their clumps of slender cypresses, to the Maremma along the Tyrrhenian coast, once unhealthy marshland but now reclaimed for cultivation, and beyond this to Elba and a number of smaller islands off the Tuscan coast.

Most of the 3·5 million inhabitants of Tuscany live in the catchment areas of the industrial conurbations in the Arno valley, between Florence and Livorno and from there N along the coast to Carrara. In this area are concentrated a multiplicity of enterprises, mostly of small and medium

A vineyard in the Arno valley

size, covering an extraordinary range of crafts and industries. The major industries are the working of minerals (iron, lignite, mercury) and marble, but other important activities are engineering, shipbuilding, pharmaceuticals, glass and crystal manufacture, furniture-making, shoe manufacture, textiles and various forms of applied and decorative art.

In the upland areas the predominant activity is agriculture, together with the various industries concerned with the processing of its produce. A leading place among these is taken by the *wine-making* industry. Tuscany is the home of the famous dry dark red wine, Chianti, which is found here in excellent quality. Corn and olives are also grown in large quantities, and in the Arno valley and along the coast there is much market gardening and flower-growing.

A major contribution to the economy is also made by the tourist trade, particularly in the great art centres like Florence, Siena and Pisa, the numerous spas (Montecatini Terme, Bagni di Lucca, etc.) and the resorts on the coast.

HISTORY. – The present territory of Tuscany coincides broadly with that of ancient *Etruria*, occupied by the numerous city states of the Etruscans which flourished between the 9th and 5th c. B.C., forming a kind of federation (the league of 12 towns), which varied in membership and nature from time to time, and extending their power and influence into Campania and the Po valley. Since the surviving

documents in the Etruscan language are confined to inscriptions of a funerary or votive nature or relating to the ownership of property, they tell us little about the advanced culture of the Etruscans, the origins of which are still obscure. Much more informative are the objects recovered from their tombs, which usually imitate the form of houses, and their sculpture and tomb paintings, predominantly depicting scenes from everyday life, which bear witness to a high standard of art and craftsmanship. The Etruscan cities usually occupied strong defensive positions, preferably on isolated rocky plateaux with good views of the surrounding area. Outside the cities lay the extensive necropolises, the finest and most celebrated of which are those of Cerveteri and Tarquinia. As the massive circular tombs of this period show, the Etruscans were familiar with the principle of the false dome and the barrel vault. They were a seafaring people who carried on an active trade with the other peoples of the Mediterranean but were also – if Greek accounts are to be believed – much given to piracy.

The power of the Etruscans began to decline in the 5th c., and by the beginning of the 4th c. the decline was irremediable. More and more of their territory fell into the hands of the Romans, and by about 300 B.C. the whole of Etruria was under Roman control.

After the fall of Rome Tuscany was successively ruled by the Ostrogoths, the Byzantines, the Lombards and the Franks, and in the 11th c. it became part of the county of *Tuscia*. In the 13th c. Florence, now steadily increasing in strength, succeeded in establishing its dominance over the rival cities in the region, particularly Siena and Pisa, and after the defeat of these two towns in the 15th c. asserted its position as the intellectual and political centre of the Duchy of Tuscany, which became a Grand Duchy under *Cosimo I Medici*. In later centuries the region suffered from the effects of the War of the Spanish Succession, from epidemics of plague and from crippling taxation. Under the treaty of Vienna in 1735 Tuscany passed to Francis Stephen of Lorraine, husband of the Empress Maria Theresa. In 1800, as the *kingdom of Etruria*, it was assigned to Duke Luigi of Parma, but in 1807 it was incorporated in the French Empire and ruled by Napoleon's sister Elisa Baciocchi, who took the title of duchess of Tuscany. Her successor Ferdinand II and his son Leopold II of Austria came into violent conflict with nationalist and anti-Austrian forces in the country, and in 1859 Leopold, finding himself without any support, abdicated under protest. In 1861, following a referendum, Tuscany was formally annexed by the *kingdom of Sardinia and Piedmont*, the nucleus of the later united kingdom of Italy.

FEATURES OF INTEREST. – Every visitor to Tuscany will of course want to visit the great art cities of **Florence**, **Pisa** and **Siena**; but there is also much of interest to see along the *Via Aurelia*, which runs S from Pisa via Livorno to Grosseto, now keeping close to the coast, now a little way inland. – On the way down it is well worth making a detour from the rather featureless port and industrial town of **Piombino** (alt. 19 m; pop. 40,000; hotels: Centrale, II, 62 b.; Aurora, III, 55 b.; Collodi, III, 46 b.; etc.) to the village of **Populonia** (alt. 179 m), situated high above the sea on the N side of a promontory, formerly an island, 14 km N of Piombino. This was the Etruscan port of *Pupluna*, with remains of its 2·5 km long circuit of walls and an interesting Etruscan necropolis on the coast below the village. From the castle (14th c.) there are extensive views over the sea.

The provincial capital of **Grosseto** (alt. 12 m; pop. 63,000; hotels: Lorena, I, 104 b.; Bastiani, II, 123 b.; Nuova Grosseto, II, 71 b.; Nalesso, II, 48 b.; Ombrone, II, 20 b.; San Giorgio, III, 63 b.; Maremma, III, 52 b.; Leon d'Oro, III, 51 b.; etc.) is the economic centre of the strip of coastal territory known as the *Maremma*. The main square of the old town, which is still surrounded by a wall with six bastions, is the Piazza Dante, on the W side of which stand the Town Hall and the cathedral (begun 1294; façade restored 1840–45). In the N transept of the cathedral is an "Assumption" by Matteo di Giovanni. Adjoining the cathedral are the interesting Museo d'Arte Sacra and Museo Archeologico. – 6 km NE of Grosseto we come to the sulphur springs of *Terme di Roselle* (alt. 25 m), 6 km farther on are the remains of **Rusellae** (alt. 184 m), one of the 12 principal cities of the Etruscan federation, with sections of its 3 km circuit of walls still standing 7–10 m high.

From the old town of **Abbadia San Salvatore** (alt. 829 m; pop. 9000; hotels: Giradino, III, 77 b.; Italia, III, 47 b.; etc.), some 45 km NE of Grosseto as the crow flies, there is an attractive road (14 km) to the top of *Monte Amiata* (1734 m), an extinct and craterless volcano. From the summit (mountain hut; iron cross 22 m high) there are magnificent *views. The drive *round Monte Amiata from Abbadia San Salvatore (65 km) is also very rewarding.

Udine

Region: Friuli – Venezia Giulia.
Province: Udine (UD).
Altitude: 110 m. – Population: 105,000.
Post code: I-33100. – Dialling code: 0432.

(i) **EPT**, Piazza Venerio 4;
tel. 5 42 05.
ACI, Via Carducci 46;
tel. 20 69 51.

HOTELS. – *Ambassador Palace*, I, 147 b.; *Astoria Italia*, I, 123 b.; *Casa Bianca*, I, 68 b.; *Europa*, II, 143 b.; *Cristallo*, II, 135 b.; *Continental*, II, 90 b.; *La' di Moret*, III, 78 b.; *Da Piero*, III, 65 b.; *Apollo*, III, 64 b.; etc. – *Motel Agip*, Viale Ledra 24, II, 200 b.

The industrial town of Udine, situated at the E end of the N Italian plain, is the capital of the region of Friuli – Venezia Giulia, which was formed in 1947 after the cession of a considerable area of Italian territory to Yugoslavia. It is the see of an archbishop.

HISTORY. – Udine, the Roman *Utina*, was from 1238 to 1752 the residence of the *Patriarchs of Aquileia*, to whom the Emperor Otto II had granted the castle in 983. The town fell under Venetian control in 1420.

View over the roofs of Udine

SIGHTS. – The town contains many old noble palaces, some of them with rather faded painting on their façades. The principal square, at the foot of the castle hill, is the *Piazza della Libertà*, in which stands the **Palazzo del Municipio** (*Loggia del Lionello*), in the style of the

Doge's Palace in Venice (1457, restored 1876). Opposite it is the *Loggia di San Giovanni* (1533), with a clock-tower resembling the one in Venice. On the S side of the square is a tall column bearing the lion of St Mark, and on the N side a statue of the *Goddess of Peace*, commemorating the peace of Campo Formio (1797). On the castle hill, with a fine prospect of the Alps from the tower, is the **Castello**, which now houses the *Municipal Museum* (closed Mondays), with collections of antiquities and pictures.

A short distance SE of the Piazza della Libertà is the **Cathedral**, a Romanesque building, begun in 1236 (interior remodelled c. 1706); it has a hexagonal campanile. Behind it is the little *Chiesa alla Purità*, with frescoes by Giovanni Battista Tiepolo and his son Giovanni Domenico. – NE of the cathedral is the **Archbishop's Palace**, with * frescoes by G. B. Tiepolo and Giovanni da Udine (1487–1564).

In Piazzale XXVI Luglio, in the W of the town, stands the domed *Tempio-Ossario dei Caduti d'Italia* (1936), a mausoleum for 22,000 Italian dead of the First World War.

Umbria

EPT Perugia, Corso Vannucci 30,
I-06100 Perugia (PU);
tel. (075) 2 48 41.
EPT Terni, Viale Cesare Battisti 5–7,
I-05100 Terni (TR);
Tel. (0744) 41 81 60.

The Central Italian region of Umbria, with a population of 776,000, two provinces and its capital Perugia, covers an area of 8456 sq. km straddling the Tiber, whose wide valley is flanked by the foothills of the Apennines. It is bounded on the W by Tuscany, on the E by the Marche and on the S by Latium.

The spacious countryside of Umbria, with its easily accessible hills and its fertile lowlands, has been from time immemorial a prosperous farming region (corn, olives, wine, sugar-beet, tobacco, market gardening; sheep), with flourishing towns like Perugia, Spoleto, Orvieto and Assisi. Only around the towns of Terni, Narni and Foligno, where power is supplied by large hydroelectric stations, has there been any considerable development of industry (chemicals, metal-working); textile manufacture and the production of craft articles have also become established in the Perugia and Spoleto areas.

A pastoral landscape in Umbria

HISTORY. – In ancient times this was the homeland of the Umbrians, and there was also some Etruscan settlement in the region. In 295 B.C. it came under Roman control, and in the reign of Augustus was combined with Etruria to form the sixth region (Regio VI) of the Empire. After the fall of Rome and the subsequent Gothic wars it became part of the Lombard duchy of Spoleto and of the States of the Church. During the Middle Ages, rent by bitter conflicts between the various towns – which enjoyed a large measure of independence – and the ruling families, the region fell into a decline, until the Church succeeded in establishing its authority in the 15th c. In 1869, after a plebiscite, Umbria and its capital Perugia became part of the united kingdom of Italy.

FEATURES OF INTEREST. – Umbria has
a number of towns which stand high among Italy's tourist attractions – in particular **Perugia**, **Assisi** and **Orvieto**. – To the W of Perugia is **Lake Trasimene** (*Lago Trasimeno*; Latin *Lacus Trasimenus*), famous as the scene of Hannibal's victory over the Roman consul Gaius Flaminius in 217 B.C. The lake, lying at an altitude of 259 m, is the largest in the Italian peninsula (area 126 sq. km, circumference *c*. 50 km; greatest depth 7 m) and well stocked with fish. Fed almost solely by rain-water, it is subject to considerable variation of level. – On a promontory on the N side of the lake is the ancient little town of *Passignano sul Trasimeno* (alt. 289 m; hotels: Lido, II, 100 b.; Beaurivage, III, 20 b.; etc.), with an old castle; on another promontory rising above the W side of the lake is *Castiglione del Lago* (alt. 304 m; Hotel La Lucciola, IV, 24 b.), with the ducal castle of the Cornia family.

Urbino

Region: Marche. – Province: Pesaro e Urbino (PS).
Altitude: 451 m. – Population: 8000.
Post code: I-61029. – Dialling code: 4722.
(i) **AA**, Piazza Duca Federico 37;
tel. 26 13.

HOTELS. – *Piero della Francesca*, II, 133 b.; *Montefeltro*, II, 95 b.; *Italia*, III, 72 b.; *San Giovanni*, III, 53 b.; etc. – *Motel La Meridiana*, II, 84 b., SP.

The little town of Urbino, beautifully situated on a steep-sided hill, is notable for its fine Renaissance buildings. It is the see of an archbishop and has a small university.

HISTORY. – Urbino was the Roman *Urvinum Metaurense*. In 1213 it came into the hands of the Montefeltro family, which acquired the ducal title in the 15th c. The court of Duke Federico di Montefeltro (1444–82), a discriminating patron of art and

learning, was recognised to be the most splendid of its day. From 1508 to 1631 the duchy was held by the Della Rovere family; thereafter it was incorporated in the States of the Church.

In the 15th c. the painters *Paolo Uccello, Piero della Francesca, Melozzo da Forlì* and *Giovanni Santi* (Raphael's father) worked in Urbino. The great architect **Bramante** (1444–1514) was born near the town, and probably worked for *Luciano da Laurana*. **Raphael** (1483–1520) and the Baroque painter *Federigo Barocci* (*c*. 1537–1612) were natives of Urbino.

SIGHTS. – In the centre of the town is the *Piazza della Repubblica*, the market square. From here Via Vittorio Veneto leads up to the Piazza Duca Federico, on the N side of which stands the **Cathedral**, rebuilt in 1801 after the destruction of an earlier church by an earthquake in 1789. It contains a number of fine paintings, including in particular works by Federigo Barocci. In the third chapel in the *crypt* (entered from outside the church, under the arcades to the left) is a marble *figure of the dead Christ by Giovanni Bandini.

Urbino Cathedral

The ***Palazzo Ducale**, opposite the cathedral, built by the Dalmatian architect Luciano da Laurana from 1465 onwards, is the most perfectly preserved example of an Italian princely residence of the period. Notable features are the colonnaded courtyard (*c*. 1470) and the staircase. The magnificent state apartments on the first and second floors now house the **Galleria Nazionale delle Marche*, which comprises a museum, a picture gallery (with Raphael's "Mute") and a historical and topographical department.

Opposite the Ducal Palace can be seen the *church of San Domenico* (14th–

15th c.), with a fine doorway by Maso di Bartolomeo (1449–54) and a terracotta relief ("Madonna with Four Saints") by Lucà della Robbia (1449–51). – To the S is the *University* (founded 1671), with a coat of arms above the doorway.

From the Piazza della Repubblica Via Raffaello climbs up towards the NW. At the near end, on the right, is the *church of San Francesco* (14th c.), with a porch and a handsome campanile. Farther up, on the left (No. 57), is **Raphael's Birthplace** (mementoes). – Via Raffaello meets the spacious Piazza Roma, with a *Monument to Raphael* (1897). From the adjoining bastion, *Pian del Monte*, there are excellent views, extending as far as San Marino.

SW of the Piazza della Repubblica, at the end of the short Via Barocci, the *church of San Giuseppe* has a life-size Nativity group by Federico Brandano. Nearby in the *Oratorio di San Giovanni* are paintings by Lorenzo and Jacopo Salimbeni (1416, restored).

SURROUNDINGS. – 20 km SE can be seen the remarkable *Furlo Gorge* (*Gola del Furlo*), enclosed by sheer rock faces. At the narrowest point is the *Galleria Romana del Furlo* or *Forulus* (alt. 177 m), a tunnel 37 m long carrying the Via Flaminia through the rock. It bears an inscription recording that it was cut by the Emperor Vespasian in A.D. 76. Adjoining it is the older *Galleria Piccola del Furlo* (1st c. B.C.), 8 m long.

Varese

Region: Lombardia. – Province: Varese (VA).
Altitude: 383 m. – Population: 85,000.
Post code: I-21100. – Dialling code: 0332.

(i) **EPT**, Piazza M. Grappa 5;
tel. 28 36 04.
  AA, Via Sacco 6;
  tel. 28 46 24.
  ACI, Viale Milano 25;
  tel. 28 51 50.
  TCI, *Viaggi Maccapani*, Corso Roma 4;
  tel. 28 61 00.
  Agenzia Crugnola, Via Magneta 41;
  tel. 28 16 54.
  Viaggi Giuliani Laudi, Via Marconi 10;
  tel. 23 11 39.

HOTELS. – *Palace*, I, 180 b.; *Cristal*, II, 89 b.; *City*, II, 83 b.; *Acquario*, II, 72 b.; *Plaza*, II, 54 b.; *Internazionale*, III, 76 b.; etc. – *Motel Varese Lago*, II, 68 b.

The provincial capital of Varese, attractively situated on hills along the southern edge of the Alps, lies between Lake Como and Lake Maggiore, with the Campo dei Fiori looming above it. Its principal industry is shoe manufacture.

SIGHTS. – The hub of the town's traffic is the Piazza Monte Grappa, with monumental modern buildings and a tower. From here the main street of Varese, the arcaded *Corso Matteotti*, leads to the Piazza del Podestà. A little way E stands the **church of San Vittore**, built in its present form to the design of Pellegrino Tibaldi (1580–1615), with a neo-classical façade (1795) and a campanile (1617–1773) 72 m high. Adjoining the church is a *baptistery* (1185–87).

A short distance W of Piazza Monte Grappa, on the left-hand side of Via Luigi Sacco, the **Palazzo Ducale**, built by Duke Francesco III of Modena in 1768–72 as a summer residence, is now the Town Hall. – Behind the palace is the *Giardino Pubblico* (formerly the palace grounds), beautifully laid out in traditional Italian style (views). In the southern part of the gardens is the *Villa Mirabello*, in which are the **Municipal Museums** (closed Mondays). Of particular interest are the *Museo del Risorgimento* and the fine *Museo Archeologico*, with prehistoric and Roman antiquities (including material from pile dwellings on the Lago di Varese and from Roman tombs).

1·5 km W of the Palazzo Ducale is the **Colle dei Campigli** (453 m), on which are the *Kursaal* and the Grand Hotel Palace. Magnificent views of the Lago di Varese and the western Alps, with Monte Rosa.

SURROUNDINGS. – A little way W of the town we come to the **Lago di Varese**. Near the E end of the lake, above the village of *Gazzada*, is the *Villa Cagnola*, bequeathed to the Vatican by Count Cagnola, with valuable furniture and tapestries and a fine collection of pictures. From the large park there are magnificent* views of the lake and the Alps.

There is an attractive drive from Varese 4 km NW to *Sant'Ambrogio* (alt. 460 m; Hotel Volta, III, 32 b.; etc.) and then another 4 km up the **Sacro Monte** (880 m; Hotel Camponovo, III, 46 b.; etc.), on the summit of which, commanding extensive views, is a pilgrimage chapel. – A still more rewarding trip is to take the road which runs up from Sant'Ambrogio (7 km) to the **Campo dei Fiori** (1032 m: far-ranging views) and continue on foot (8 minutes) to the summit of *Monte Tre Croci* (1083 m), from where there is a famous *view embracing six lakes, the Lombard plain and part of the chain of the Alps. (There are even more extensive views of the Alps from the nearby *Observatory* and from the summit of *Monte Campo dei Fiori*,

1226 m, 1 hour W). – Some 10 km s of Varese, a little way W of S.S. 233 (the Milan road), is the old-world village of **Castiglione Olona** (alt. 307 m). In the Gothic collegiate church and its baptistery are fine *frescoes (1428–35) by Masolino da Panicale, a pupil of Giotto's.

9 km S of Varese, in forest country near the village of *Castelseprio*, are the remains of the Lombard fort of *Sibrium*, with a restored castle. In the adjoining *church of Santa Maria Foris Portas* (7th or 8th c.) **frescoes dating from the 7th and 8th–9th c. were exposed in 1944.

Venetia

(i) **EPT Belluno**, Piazza Stazione 19,
I-32100 Belluno (BL);
tel. (0437) 2 47 81.
EPT Padova, Riviera Mugnai 8,
I-35100 Padova (PD);
tel. (049) 65 18 56.
EPT Rovigo, Corso del Popolo 78,
I-45100 Rovigo (RO);
tel. (0425) 2 54 81.
EPT Treviso, Via Toniolo 41,
I-31100 Treviso (TV);
tel. (0422) 4 06 00.
EPT Venezia, San Marco 71C,
I-30100 Venezia (VE);
tel. (041) 2 63 56.
EPT Verona, Via C. Montanari 14,
I-37100 Verona (VR);
tel. (045) 2 50 65.
EPT Vicenza, Piazza Duomo 5,
I-36100 Vicenza (VI);
tel. (0444) 2 29 27.

The historical region of Venetia, the territory of the old Republic of Venice, lies in the NE of the N Italian plain, extending northward from the lower course of the Po to the Venetian Alps and bounded on the W by Lake Garda and the River Mincio, on the E by the Adriatic coast, a strip of former marshland now occupied by numerous lagoons.

The area is now divided into three administrative regions: in the E *Friuli – Venezia Giulia* (see p. 122); in the N *Trentino – Alto Adige* (see p. 51); and between these two, extending towards the Po and the Adriatic, the region of **Veneto** (formerly *Venezia, Euganea*), the heartland of the old territory of Venetia, with seven provinces (capital Venice) and an area of 18,377 sq. km.

The region of Veneto is notable for its scenic variety and economic diversity. The population of some 4·2 million is concentrated mainly in the larger cities

of the Po plain, which has a highly developed agriculture (grain, particularly maize and rice; wine, fruit, vegetables; cattle-farming), with the associated processing industries (canning, manufacture of foodstuffs, etc.), and much general industrial development (textiles, building materials, metalworking, chemicals, petrochemicals, shipbuilding), promoted by an abundant supply of power (hydroelectric schemes in the Alps, natural gas in the Po plain). The region is also famous for its applied and decorative art, in particular the glass-blowing, embroidery and lace-making of the Venice area and the production of leather goods. – In the mountains and upland regions the holiday and tourist trade has long been an additional source of income, supplementing the traditional pastoral farming. Lake Garda and the area round Cortina d'Ampezzo in the Dolomites attract visitors from far and wide with the beauty of their scenery, and the old cities of Venice, Padua, Verona and Vicenza are among the highlights of any tour of Italy.

FEATURES OF INTEREST. – In northern Venetia, on the River Piave, is the provincial capital of **Belluno** (alt. 294 m; pop. 36,000; hotels: Astor, II, 44 b.; Cappello e Cadore, III, 91 b.; Europa, III, 70 b.; etc.). The cathedral, built from 1517 onwards and restored in 1873, has two beautiful altarpieces in the S aisle; from the campanile, 66 m high, there are fine views. Also in the Piazza del Duomo are the Palazzo dei Rettori (1496), a fine Early Renaissance building which now houses the Prefecture, and the Museo Civico (pictures, bronzes, etc.). – 12 km SE is a winter sports area on the *Nevegal*

Cesarolo, on the River Tagliamento

(chair-lift to Rifugio Cadore, 1600 m; Alpine garden).

There is an attractive road from Belluno (30 km NW) through the magnificent gorge on the River *Cordévole* known as the *Canal d'Agordo* (15 km long) to the little town of **Agordo** (alt. 611 m; pop. 4000; Hotel Milano, III, 54 b.; etc.), ringed by high mountains, a popular walking and climbing centre. In the main square is the picturesque Palazzo Crotta di Manzoni. – From Agordo it is another 18 km N to the S end of the *Lago D'Alleghe* (alt. 966 m), a lake 2 km long formed by a landslide in 1771. On the E side of the lake lies the village of **Alleghe** (979 m; hotels: La Nava, III, 40 b.; Alle Alpi, III, 38 b.; Europa, III, 32 b.; etc.), a popular summer resort and climbing centre. From here there is a pleasant walk on a bridle-path which goes E (3 hours) to the sombre *Lago Coldai* (2146 m); then another 20 minutes over the *Coldai pass* (2190 m) to the *Rifugio Coldai* (2150 m), magnificently situated on the northern slopes of the massive *Monte Civetta* (3218 m), which can be climbed from here in 6 hours (guide necessary). – 3 km NW of Alleghe is the village of **Caprile** (1023 m; hotels: Alla Posta, II, 86 b.; Marmolada, III, 52 b.; etc.), from which an excursion can be made up the *Pettorina valley* to the villages of *Rocca Piétore* (3 km; 1143 m; Hotel Venezia, IV, 24 b.; etc.) and *Sottoguda* (7 km; 1252 m). From Sottoguda it is possible in summer to continue for another 7 km on the old road through the gorge of *Serrai di Sottoguda* to the *Malga Ciapela* (1450 m; hotels: Tyrolia, II, 33 b.; Malga Ciapela, III, 64 b.; Roy, III, 57 b.; etc. – Cableway via the *Forcella Serauta*, 2875 m, to the *Punta di Rocca*, 3309 m) and the *Pian di Lobbia* (1841 m); then 2 km to the **Fedaia pass** (2047 m) and another 3 km along the *Lago di Fedaia* to the *Rifugio Marmolada*; chair-lift to Marmolada glacier and road to Canazei.

18 km NE of Belluno, at the mouth of the *Zoldo valley*, is the little town of **Longarone** (alt. 468 m; hotels: Piave, III, 48 b.; Quattro Valli, III, 42 b.), which was destroyed on 9 October 1963, together with four neighbouring villages, by a flood wave 100 m high when a landslide on *Monte Toc* caused the Lago di Vajont to overflow. Some 2000 people, including 1700 in Longarone, lost their lives in the disaster; the town is being rebuilt on the slopes to the W. From Longarone a road climbs up (sharp bends, tunnels), passing through the wild *Vajont gorge* (4 km long; galleries through rock), to the *Lago di Vajont*, a reservoir formed by a dam 265 m high, now largely drained, and then over the *Passo di Sant'Osvaldo* (827 m) to the summer resort of *Cimolais* (652 m). – 25 km NE of Longarone up the *Piave valley*, which becomes steadily narrower, is **Pieve di Cadore** (alt. 878 m; hotels: Progresso, III, 116 b.; Palatini, III, 112 b.; Belvedere, III, 61 b.; etc.), chief town of the upper Piave region and a popular health and winter sports resort, beautifully situated high above the River Piave. – here dammed to form a lake 8 km long (68 million cu. m). In the main square is a monument to Titian, who was born here; his birthplace (museum) is in a little square with a fountain.

In the S of the Veneto region, on the *Naviglio Adigetto*, lies the provincial capital of **Rovigo** (alt. 7 m; pop. 50,000; hotels: Cristallo, II, 66 b.; Granatiere, II, 52 b.; Corona Ferrea, II, 48 b.; Bologna, III, 26 b.; etc.). In the centre of the town in the elongated Piazza Vittorio Emanuele are a tall column bearing the lion of St Mark, the Loggia dei Notai (Town Hall, with tower; restored) and the Accademia dei Concordi (picture gallery, with paintings of the Venetian school; library). To the W is the cathedral (17th c., restored), and to the N of this the old Castello, to the S a gate-tower of 1138.

At the E end of the region of Venetia is **Portogruaro** (alt. 5 m; pop. 24,000; hotels: Spessotto, III, 50 b.; Trieste, III, 20 b.; etc.), with handsome old arcaded houses, a Gothic town hall (14th–16th c.) and a Romanesque leaning tower (the campanile of the cathedral). The museum contains Roman and Early Christian remains from *Concordia Sagittaria*, the Roman military station of *Concordia*, 2 km downstream, which preserves a Roman bridge and an early medieval baptistery.

28 km NW of Portogruaro, in the Friuli – Venezia Giulia region, is the old provincial capital of **Pordenone** (alt. 24 m; pop. 47,000; hotels: Santin, II, 142 b.; Park, II, 116 b.; Villa Ottoboni, II, 111 b.; Résidence Italie, II, 105 b.; Minerva, II, 62 b.; Montereale, II, 46 b.; Residence, III, 45 b.; etc.), birthplace of the painter Giovanni Antonio de Sacchis, known as *Pordenone* (1484–1539). There are pictures by Pordenone in the Late Gothic cathedral (15th c.) and the Municipal Museum (closed Mondays). The Gothic Town Hall was built between 1291 and 1365.

Venice/Venezia

Region: Veneto. – Province: Venezia (VE).
Altitude: 1 m. – Population: 370,000.
Post code: I-30100. – Dialling code: 041.

ⓘ **EPT**, San Marco Ascensione 71C;
tel. 2 63 56.

Information offices in Piazzale Roma
(tel. 2 74 02) and at station (tel. 2 13 37).
AA, Palazzo Martinengo, Rialto 4089;
tel. 2 61 10.
ACI, Fondamenta Santa Chiara 518A;
tel. 70 03 00.
CIT, Piazza San Marco 48–50;
tel. 8 54 80.

HOTELS. –* *Danieli Royal Excelsior*, Castello 4196, L, 427 b.;* *Bauer Grünwald*, Campo San Moisè 1459, L, 389 b.;* *Gritti Palace*, Campo Santa Maria del Giglio, L, 167 b.;* *Cipriani*, Giudecca 10, L, 160 b., SP; *Europa e Britannia*, San Marco 2159, I, 255 b.; *Carlton Executive*, Santa Croce 578, I, 223 b.; *Luna*, San Marco 1243, I, 220 b.; *Gabrielli-Sandwirth*, Riva degli Schiavoni 4110, I, 190 b.; *Park*, Giardino Papadopoli, I, 180 b.; *Saturnia-International*, San Marco 2399, I,

Gondola race on the Grand Canal

166 b.; *Monaco e Grand Canal*, San Marco 1325, I, 136 b.; *Londra*, Riva degli Schiavoni 4171, I, 118 b.; *Regina e di Roma*, San Marco 2205, I, 112 b.; *Metropole*, Riva degli Schiavoni 4149, I, 117 b.; *Principe*, Lista di Spagna 146, II, 273 b.; *Continental*, Lista di Spagna 166, II, 205 b.; *Bonvecchiati*, San Marco 4488, II, 152 b.; *Cavalletto e Doge Orseolo*, San Marco 1107, II, 146 b.; *Universo e Nord*, Lista di Spagna 121, II, 130 b.; *Austria e de la Ville*, Cannaregio 227, II, 130 b.; *Savoia e Jolanda*, Riva degli Schiavoni 4187, II, 119 b.; *Residence Palace Sceriman*, Lista di Spagna 168, II, 118 b.; *La Fenice e des Artistes*, San Marco 1936, II, 116 b.; *Al Sole Palace*, Santa Croce 136, II, 115 b.; *Terminus*, Lista di Spagna 116, II, 114 b.; *Ala*, San Marco 2494, II, 108 b.; *Concordia*, Calle Larga San Marco 367, II, 106 b.; *Giorgione*, Santi Apostoli 4587, II, 105 b.; *San Marco*, San Marco 877, II, 100 b.; *Nazionale*, Lista di Spagna 158, III, 136 b.; *Rialto*, Riva del Ferro 5147, III, 118 b.; *Gorizia a la Valigia*, San Marco 4696A, III, 101 b.; *Gallini*, San Marco 3673, III, 87 b.; *Dolomiti*, Calle Priuli 72, III, 80 b.; etc. – YOUTH HOSTEL, on Giudecca, Fondamenta Zitelle 86, 320 b.

ON THE LIDO: **Excelsior Palace*, L, 418 b., SP; *Des Bains e Palazzo al Mare*, I, 434 b., SP; *Cappelli's Wagner, Villa Paradiso, Villa Corfu*, II, 243 b.; *Hungaria*, II, 184 b.; *Quattro Fontane*, II, 130 b.; *Biasutti Adria, Urania, Nora*, II, 123 b.; *Riviera*, II, 104 b.; *Helvetia*, II, 90 b.; *Villa Otello*, II, 68 b.; *Centrale*, II, 64 b.; *Sorriso*, III, 75 b.; *Villa Mabapa*, III, 63 b.; etc.

IN MARGHERA: *Vienna*, III, 108 b.; *Mondial*, III, 101 b.; *Lugano-Torretta*, III, 99 b., SP; *Touring*, III, 95 b.; *Adriatic*, III, 83 b.; *Lloyd*, III, 83 b.; etc. – IN MESTRE: *Plaza*, II, 410 b.; *Bologna e Stazione*, II, 199 b.; *Sirio*, II, 190 b.; *Ambasciatori*, II, 167 b.; *Capitol*, II, 160 b.; *Tritone*, II, 129 b.; *President*, II, 95 b.; *Centrale*, III, 175 b.; *Venezia*, III, 171 b.; *Aquila Nera*, III, 78 b.; *Piave*, III, 73 b.; *Ariston*, III, 70 b.; etc. – IN PUNTA SABBIONI: *Lio Grando*, II, 106 b.; etc.

RESTAURANTS. – **Antico Martini*, San Marco, Campo San Fantin 198; **Harry's Bar*, San Marco, Calle de Ca' Vallaresso 1323; *Taverna La Fenice*, San Marco 1938; *Alla Caravella*, Via 22 Marzo 2397; *Alla Colomba*, San Marco, Piscina Frezzeria 1665; *Due Forni*, San Marco 468; *Antica Carbonera*, San Marco, Calle Bembo 4648; *Al Colombo*, San Marco, Campiello del Teatro Goldoni 4619; *Montin*, Dorsoduro, Fondamenta Eremite 1147; etc.

EVENTS. – *Biennale d'Arte* (Art Exhibition), June–Sept. in alternate years. – *Festa del Redentore*, with parade of boats, third Saturday in July. – *Mostra d'Arte Cinematografica* (Film Festival), Aug.–Sept. – *Historic Gondola Race*, first Sunday in Sept. – *Festival of Modern Art*, Sept. – Several church festivals, with gondola races.

**Venice, once the world's most brilliant commercial city and now capital of the Veneto region and the see of a patriarch-archbishop, lies at the very head of the Adriatic, 4 km from the mainland of Italy (rail and road bridge) in the Laguna Veneta, a salt-water lagoon 40 km long and up to 15 km wide which is separated from the Adriatic by a series of narrow spits of land (lidi). It is a town of incomparable attraction with its unique network of canals and its beautiful palaces and churches. – Venice is under constant threat of sinking into the water, and a great variety of plans have been canvassed for saving it.

The town is built on 118 small islands and traversed by something like 100 canals (*canale, rio*), which are spanned by almost 400 bridges, mostly stone-built. Its 15,000 houses, built on piles, form a close-packed huddle of narrow streets and lanes (*calle, salizzada*, etc.), often no more than 1·5 m wide, filled with bustling activity but free from the noise of motor traffic. There is only one *piazza*, St Mark's Square; smaller squares are called *campo* or *campiello*. The quays or embankments are called *riva* or *fondamenta*.

In the past Venice's industry was confined to craft products (particularly glass and lace), boatbuilding, etc., but there has been a considerable development of large-scale industry since the First World War in the suburban district of Mestre. The port is one of Italy's largest, with an annual turnover of some 24 million tons (1976). The industrial port is *Porto di Maghera*, Mestre, and the *Bacino della Stazione Marittima*, SW of the Piazzale Roma, also handles freight traffic, while passenger vessels use the *Canale di San Marco*, near the Doge's Palace.

HISTORY. – In ancient times the Venice area was occupied by an Illyrian tribe, the *Veneti*, who formed a defensive alliance with Rome in the 3rd c. B.C. and rapidly became Romanised. In A.D. 452 the inhabitants of the coastal region fled to the safety of the islands in the lagoon, and in 697 they joined to form a naval confederation under a doge (from Latin *dux*, "leader"). In 811 *Rivus Altus* (Rialto) – i.e. present-day Venice – became the seat of government. In 829 the remains of the Evangelist Mark were brought to Venice from Alexandria, and thereafter Mark became the patron saint of the Venetian republic, which took his name and used his lion as its emblem. The young state prospered as the main channel and entrepôt for trade between Western Europe and the East, occupied the E coast of the Adriatic, conquered Constantinople in 1204 and established itself on the coasts of Greece and Asia Minor. The so-called "Hundred Years' War" with Genoa was decided by the Venetian naval victory off Chioggia in 1380, and in the 15th c. the republic reached the peak of its power, controlling the whole of the eastern Mediterranean and extending its conquests on the Italian mainland as far as Verona, Bergamo and Brescia ("*terra ferma*"). In the 15th and 16th c., too, Venice achieved its finest cultural flowering. – Towards the end of the 15th c., however, the advance of the Turks and the discovery of America and the new sea routes to India brought the beginnings of decline. In the 16th c. the Venetian possessions on the mainland of Italy involved the republic in the conflicts between Austria and Spain on the one hand and France on the other, and the struggle against the Turks ended in 1718 with the loss of all Venice's possessions in the East. In 1797 the French put an end to the city's independence, and under the treaty of Campoformio in that year it was assigned provisionally to Austria. In 1814 it formally became part of Austria, and remained Austrian until it joined the new kingdom of Italy in 1866.

ART. – Venice occupies a special place in the history of art through its relations with the Greek Empire of the East. St Mark's Church is Byzantine in style, as are its earliest mosaics. Gothic, which reached Venice only in the 14th c., took on a different aspect here from the rest of Italy, displaying a lively fantasy and a wealth of decoration and colour. The Early Renaissance style came in only in the second half of the 15th c., producing buildings which cannot compare with those of Tuscany in harmony of proportion, since the façades seek above all to achieve a picturesque effect. Some of the Venetian churches, in particular Santi Giovanni e Paolo and the Frari church, are notable for their numerous fine tomb monuments. The leading architects of the period were *Antonio Rizzo* and *Pietro Lombardi*, who were also sculptors, together with the Florentine *Jacopo Sansovino*, who brought the High Renaissance to Venice, and *Andrea Palladio*, whose influence was felt even by such vigorous exponents of the Baroque style as *Vincenzo Scamozzi* (1552–1616) and *Baldassare Longhena* (1604–82). The sculptors working in Venice included *Alessandro Leopardi* (d. 1522) and, slightly later, *Alessandro Vittoria* (1525–1608). Among 15th c. painters were *Vivarini* and *Jacopo Bellini* (Mantegna's father-in-law), both from Murano, and *Carlo Crivelli*, a native of Venice. Jacopo's son *Giovanni Bellini* (*c.* 1430–1516), with his skill in composition and his love of colour, was the precursor of the great period of Venetian painting. Among his contemporaries were his elder brother *Gentile Bellini* (*c.* 1429–1507), *Vittorio Carpaccio* (*c.* 1455 to after 1523) and *Cima da Conegliano* (*c.* 1459–1518). His greatest pupils were *Girogione* (*c.* 1477–1510, born in Castelfranco), *Palma Vecchio* from Bergamo (*c.* 1480–1528) and the greatest of them all, *Titian* (Tiziano Vecellio, *c.* 1490–1576, born in Pieve di Cadore), who lavished his skill and vigorous imagination equally on representations of the Renaissance delight in life and on highly charged religious scenes and enjoyed high favour as a portrait painter with the Italian princes as well as with Charles V and Philip II of Spain. The contemporaries of these three great masters included such artists as *Sebastiano del Piombo, Lorenzo Lotto, Bonifazio dei Pitati, Pordenone* and *Paris Bordone*. The tradition was carried on by a younger generation which included *Paolo Veronese* (*Caliari*, 1528–88, born in Verona), the *Bassano* family and *Palma Giovane*. A fresh lead was given by *Jacopo Tintoretto* (*Robusti*, 1518–94), whose works, combining vigorous light and colour with the expression of profound spiritual emotion, mark the high point of Venetian Baroque painting. In the 18th c. the two *Canalettos* (*Antonio Canal* and his pupil *Bernardo Bellotto*) and the talented *Francesco Guardi* (1712–93) excelled in the painting of townscapes, *Pietro Longhi* (1702–85) in the depiction of contemporary manners. The last great Venetian painter, heir to a brilliant tradition of 300 years, was the decorative painter *Giovanni Battista Tiepolo* (1696–1770), notable for the glowing colour and spatial effect of his wall and ceiling paintings.

SIGHTS. – At the end of the causeway from Mestre, on the mainland, is the *Piazzale Roma*, with a large parking area and multi-storey garage, and a short distance N, on the *Canale di Santa Chiara*, the **landing-stage** for the city boat services. Opposite, on the N side of the canal, is the modern **Stazione Santa Lucia**. In the short street running NE from the station, the Lista di Spagna, are most of the hotels in the western part of the city.

From the landing-stage there are **motor-boats** (*motoscafi*) to St Mark's Square. The trip along the

Grand Canal takes 25 minutes; the more direct route by the Rio Nuovo 10 minutes. – There are also motor-launches (*vaporetti*) which ply along the Grand Canal to St Mark's Square (30 minutes), taking another 15 minutes to reach the Lido or San Giorgio Maggiore. – The famous **gondolas** (*góndole*) take about an hour to reach St Mark's Square.

The ****Grand Canal** (*Canal Grande*: 3·8 km long, with an average breadth of 70 m and depth of 5 m), Venice's principal traffic artery, starts from the station and traverses the city from NW to SE in a reversed S-curve; it gives an overwhelming impression of the wealth and splendour of Venice in its heyday with a continuous succession of great palaces of the princely Venetian merchants. Every style of architecture from the 12th to the early 18th c. is represented along the Grand Canal. Particularly charming is the Venetian Gothic style with its fantastic arcades; and the Early Renaissance buildings are scarcely less splendid. The posts (*pali*) in front of the steps leading into the palaces, painted in their owners' heraldic colours, serve to protect the gondolas lying at their moorings.

Along the Grand Canal from the Station to St Mark's Square

Left

Chiesa degli Scalzi (church of the Barefoot Friars), a sumptuous Baroque building (1649–89)..

***Palazzo Vendramin-Calergi**, the finest Early Renaissance palace in Venice, completed *c.* 1509. Wagner died here in 1883.

***Ca' d'Oro** ("Golden House"), the most elegant Gothic palace in Venice (15th c.), with the *Galleria Franchetti* (sculpture, bronzes; pictures by Titian, Tintoretto, Mantegna, Signorelli, Van Dyck, etc.: closed).

Fóndaco dei Tedeschi, from the 12th to the 14th c. a hostel and warehouse for German merchants; rebuilt 1506; now *Head Post Office*.

Right

Fóndaco dei Turchi, late Romanesque (13th c.), from 1621 a Turkish warehouse; restored 1861–69; now *Museo di Storia Naturale*.

***Palazzo Pésaro**, the finest Baroque palace in Venice (by Longhena, 1710), with the *Galleria d'Arte Moderna* and the *Museo Orientale* (East Asian art: at present closed).

Pescheria (Fish Market, 1907), with a neo-Gothic market hall.

Erberia (landing-stage for boats bringing in vegetables and fruit: particularly in late afternoon).

***Ponte di Rialto** (from *Rivus Altus*), a marble bridge (by Antonio dal Ponte, 1588–92) 48 m long, with a span of 27·75 m, lined with shops on both sides.

Palazzo Loredan (now Town Hall) and *Palazzo Farsetti* (formerly *Dándolo*), both Romanesque (12th c.).

***Palazzo Grimani**, a masterpiece of High Renaissance architecture by Sanmicheli (16th c.); now the Court of Appeal.

Palazzo Papadópoli, High Renaissance (16th c.).

***Palazzo Corner-Spinelli**, Early Renaissance, in the style of the Lombardis; interior by Sanmicheli, 1542.

***Palazzo Pisani a San Polo**, Gothic (15th c.).

Palazze Mocenigo (three adjoining palaces, the most recent 1580).

Palazzo Tiépolo-Valier (two palaces, 15th and 16th c.).

Venice – the Rialto Bridge over the Grand Canal

Left	Right
Palazzo Contarini delle Figure, Early Renaissance (1504).	*Palazzo Grimani-Giustinian*, High Renaissance (16th c.); adjoining it the San Tomà landing-stage (for the Frari church).
Palazzo Moro-Lin, Late Renaissance (Roman).	
Palazzo Grassi (1745).	*Ca' Fóscari, Gothic (14th c.); now the *University*.
Church of San Samuele, with Romanesque campanile (12th c.).	*Palazzo Rezzónico (by Longhena, (1665–1750), with *Museo del Settecento Veneziano* (applied art, furniture, pictures of 18th c.; ceiling paintings).

Ponte dell'Accademia (previously *Ponte di Ferro*): to right, landing-stage for Accademia.

Palazzo Cavalli-Franchetti, Gothic (15th c., restored 1890).	*Palazzo Contarini dal Zaffo*, in the style of the Lombardis (15th c.).
*Palazzo Corner or *Ca' Grande*, by Jacopo Sansovino (1532); now the Prefecture.	*Palazzo Venier* (Palazzo dei Leoni, 1749), with the *Peggy Guggenheim Collection* (some 300 modern paintings); garden.
Palazzo Contarini-Fasan, Gothic (15th c.), with fine traceried balconies; the so-called "House of Desdemona".	*Santa Maria della Salute, a magnificent domed church (by Baldassare Longhena, 1631–56), built to commemorate the plague of 1630; fine pictures by Titian.
Palazzo Treves dei Bonfili (1680).	
Palazzo Giustinian, Gothic (15th c.); offices of the Biennale d'Arte.	*Dogana di Mare* (Custom House), Baroque (1676–82), in the angle between the Grand Canal and the *Canale della Giudecca*.
San Marco (landing-stage for St Mark's Square).	
Riva degli Schiavoni.	*San Giorgio Maggiore.*

From the Riva degli Schiavoni we cross the Piazzetta and walk past the Doge's Palace into ****St Mark's Square** (*Piazza di San Marco*, or the "Piazza" for short), the hub of the city's life and one of the world's finest squares, giving striking evidence of Venice's past greatness and still serving as a setting for great occasions (concerts, etc.). The square, 175 m long and between 56 and 82 m wide, is paved with slabs of trachyte and marble and lined on three sides by tall arcades housing shops and cafés. The square is particularly beautiful on bright moonlit nights. The innumerable pigeons (*colombi, piccioni*) are supplied with food at the expense of an insurance company. In recent years the square has frequently been flooded.

On the Piazzetta di San Marco

On the N and S sides of the square are the **Procuratie**, formerly the residences of the nine procurators, the highest officials of the Republic. The *Procuratie Vecchie* on the N side were built between 1480 and 1517. The *Procuratie Nuove* on the S

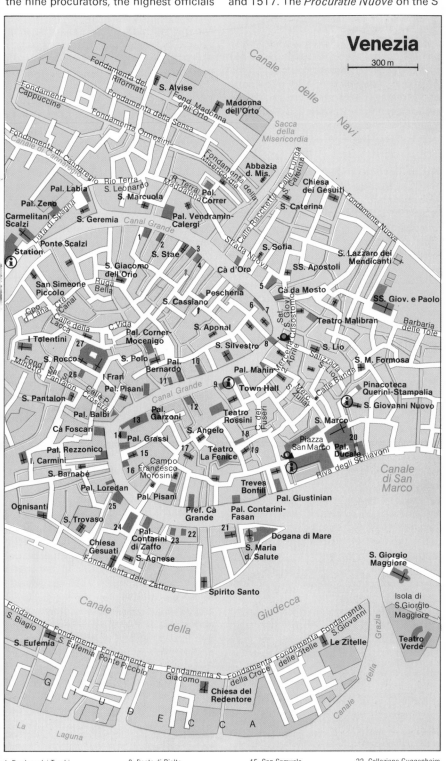

Venezia

300 m

1 Fondaco dei Turchi
2 Palazzo Battagià
3 Palazzo Pésaro
4 Palazzo Corner-Regina
5 Palazzo Valmarana
6 Fabbriche Nuove
7 Fabbriche Vecchie

8 Ponte di Rialto
9 Palazzo Grimani
10 Palazzo Papadopoli
11 Palazzo Cappello
12 Palazzo Corner-Spinelli
13 Palazzi Mocenigo
14 Palazzo Moro Lin

15 San Samuele
16 Palazzo Malipiero
17 Santo Stefano
18 Ateneo Veneto
19 San Fantin
20 Ponte dei Sospiri
21 San Gregorio

22 Collezione Guggenheim
23 Palazzo Mula
24 Accademia di Belle Arti
25 Palazzo Contarini
   degli Scrigni
26 Scuola di San Rocco
27 Archivio Centrale

side were begun in 1584 by Vincenzo Scamozzi and used from the time of Napoleon as a royal palace; they now house the *Museo Civico Correr* (closed Sunday afternoons and Thursdays), an excellent collection illustrating the history and culture of Venice, with pictures by old masters (Bellini, Carpaccio, etc.), and the *Museo Archeologico* (closed afternoons and Mondays), with the ancient sculpture (entrance in Piazzetta, No. 17). Along the W end of the square is the *Ala Napoleonica*, a linking wing added in 1810.

At the SE corner of St Mark's Square rises the* **Campanile of St Mark** (*Campanile di San Marco*), a 99 m high bell-tower rebuilt in 1905–12 after the collapse of the original campanile in 1902; from the top (lift) there are fine *views. The *Loggetta* on the E side of the campanile (by Jacopo Sansovino, 1540) was originally the meeting-place of the Venetian nobles. – Almost opposite the campanile, at the E end of the Procuratie Vecchie, is the Clock-Tower (1496–99), with an arched gateway leading into the Merceria, Venice's principal shopping street (see below). – In front of St Mark's Church are three *flagstaffs* on bronze pedestals (1505), of which there have been many imitations.

St Mark's Church (*Basilica di San Marco*), dedicated to the Evangelist Mark, whose remains are in the high altar, was begun in 830, rebuilt after a fire in 976 and remodelled in the 11th c. in Byzantine style with an Oriental lavishness of decoration. 76·5 m long by 51·75 m wide, it has the form of a Greek cross, with five domes. Externally and internally it is adorned with 500 ancient marble columns, mostly from the East. In the interior the upper parts of the walls and the vaulting are covered with mosaics dating back to the 11th c. Above the main doorway are four *bronze horses* from Constantinople, 1·6 m high (at present in course of restoration: to be replaced by copies), the only surviving example of the four-horse team of an ancient quadriga.

The* INTERIOR of St Mark's is notable for the beauty of its lines and the picturesque and constantly changing vistas which it affords. On the high altar the *Pala d'Oro is a masterpiece of enamel work set with jewels, originally an altar frontal made in Constantinople in 1105 (best side to rear). In the S transept is the valuable **Treasury**. In the *Cappella Zeno* can be seen the handsome tomb of Cardinal Giambattista Zeno (d. 1501). – From the *gallery*

(entrance at main doorway, on left) there is access to the outer gallery and the bronze horses. Adjoining the gallery the *Museo Marciano* houses 15th c. tapestries, pictures, etc.

On the SE side of St Mark's Square, extending to the Canale di San Marco, is the* **Piazzetta**. Near the water's edge, on the *Molo*, where the gondoliers wait for custom, are two *granite columns* from Syria or Constantinople, erected here in 1180, topped by a figure of St Theodore, Venice's earlier patron saint, and the winged lion of St Mark. – On the W side of the square are the* **Old Library** (*Libreria Vecchia*), Jacopo Sansovino's finest work (1536–53), and the *Mint* (*Zecca*), rebuilt by Sansovino in 1536, which houses the celebrated *Library of St Mark*, founded in 1468, with over 500,000 volumes (entrance at No. 13).

Venice – the Campanile and Doge's Palace

The E side of the Piazzetta is occupied by the **Doge's Palace** (*Palazzo Ducale*), said to have been the residence of the Doge since about 814. The oldest part of the present building is the 71 m long S wing on the Molo (1309–40); the 75 m long W wing facing on to the Piazzetta was added in 1424–38. The upper part of the battlemented *façade is decorated with coloured marble in a lozenge pattern; round the ground floor runs a beautiful arcade with free-standing columns, and above this is the *Loggia*, with elegant pointed arches and quatrefoil decoration in Venetian Gothic style. The late Gothic *Porta della Carta* leads into the magnificent *Cortile dei Senatori*, a courtyard which shows a picturesque mingling of late Gothic and Early Renaissance styles.

The* INTERIOR of the palace (purchase of illustrated guide recommended) is reached from the courtyard by way of the *Scala dei Giganti* and the *Scala d'Oro*, which lead to the upper floors, with the *State Apartments*, redecorated after damage by fire in 1574. Notable features of these rooms – magnificent examples of Venetian art of the Late Renaissance and Baroque periods – are the richly decorated and gilded ceilings and the numerous pictures (by Titian, Paolo Veronese, Tintoretto and other artists) glorifying Venice and its doges in historical scenes and allegories.

On the *second floor* the *Sala del Maggior Consiglio* (54 m long, 25 m wide, 15·5 m high) has scenes from the history of Venice on its walls. On the frieze are 76 portraits of doges ranging in date from 804 to 1559, and on the entrance wall is Tintoretto's "Paradise", the largest oil painting in the world (22 m long by 7 m high). From the balcony there are *views of the lagoon, the islands of San Giorgio and Giudecca and the Lido. In the E wing are the *Doge's Private Apartments* (Appartamento Ducale), which escaped damage in the fire.

On the *third floor* are the large *Sala del Senato*, the meeting-place of the Senate, with pictures by Tintoretto, Palma Giovane and other artists, and the *Sala d'Armi*, the armoury of the Republic, with a fine collection of weapons.

From the first floor of the palace visitors can enter the **Prigioni**, dark and dismal cellars with which are associated a *torture chamber* and *place of execution*.

From the Doge's Palace the *Molo* runs E to the *Ponte della Paglia* ("Straw Bridge"), from which there is a good view, to left, of the ***Bridge of Sighs** (*Ponte dei Sospiri*), built about 1595 to link the palace with the Prigioni (erected 1571–97), its name recalling the sighs of the criminals led over the bridge to the place of execution. Beyond this point extends the **Riva degli Schiavoni**, a busy and lively promenade 500 m long with several landing-stages for boats serving the city and the lagoon (including services to the Lido) and extensive views of the harbour and beyond. Beyond the second bridge the Sottoportico San Zaccaria, on left, leads to the nearby *church of San Zaccaria* (15th c.), which contains (to left, on second altar) a *"Madonna Enthroned" by Giovanni Bellini (1505). – On the continuation of the Riva degli Schiavoni are the **Giardini Pubblici** (landing-stage for motor-launches), a beautiful municipal park with the Paradiso café-restaurant and the galleries used for the *Biennale d'Arte*, the international art exhibition held from June to September.

Opposite the Riva degli Schiavoni, to the S (hourly service by motor-launch), lies the little island of **San Giorgio Maggiore**, with the conspicuous monastic church of the same name, a domed structure begun by Palladio in 1565 and completed in 1610. It has handsome Baroque choir-stalls and contains several pictures by Tintoretto. From the 60 m high campanile (entrance from choir) there is the finest *view in Venice. The former monastic buildings (beautiful staircase by Longhena; two cloisters) have been occupied since 1951 by the Fondazione Giorgio Cini, which is concerned with the promotion of research on the cultural history of Venice.

The narrow **Merceria** (*Marzaria*) which leaves the NE corner of St Mark's Square, by the Clock-Tower, and runs NW under various names (Merceria San Zulian, etc.) is the city's principal shopping street, providing a direct link with the Rialto Bridge (500 m). Near its N end is **San Salvatore** (*San Salvador*), the finest High Renaissance church in Venice (by Spavento and Tullio Lombardi, 1506–34), with a Baroque façade added in 1663. – From Merceria San Zulian, beyond the *church of San Giuliano* (San Zulian), Calle della Guerra and Calle delle Bande lead to the **church of Santa Maria Formosa**, which contains (second chapel to the right of high altar) a *"St Barbara" by Palma Vecchio. A little way S of the church is the *Palazzo Stampelia*, with a *collection of pictures* (mainly works by 18th c. Venetians).

From Santa Maria Formosa we go along Calle Lunga and turn into the fourth street on the left (Calle Cicogna) to reach the *Campo Santi Giovanni e Paolo*, with the church of the same name and the famous **statue of Bartolomeo Colloni** (Venetian condottiere, d. 1475), the finest equestrian statue of the Italian Renaissance, modelled by the Florentine sculptor Andrea Verrocchio in 1481–88 and set up here in 1495. The former Dominican *church of Santi Giovanni e Paolo (*San Zan i Polo*), a Gothic brick-built structure (1333–90) is the burial-place of many doges, and contains numerous handsome monuments (the finest being that of Doge Andrea Vendramin, on the N side of the choir). To the left of the church stands the *Scuola di San Marco* (now a hospital), with a richly decorated Early Renaissance façade (1485–95). A little way W the *church of Santa Maria dei Mirácoli*, an elegant Early Renaissance building by Pietro Lombardi (1481–89), is entirely clad in marble both externally and internally.

From the SW corner of St Mark's Square we go along a busy shopping street, the Salizzada San Moisè, with the Baroque church of San Moisè, and its continuation Calle Larga 22 Marzo, passing the Baroque *church of Santa Maria Zobenigo*, to reach the large *Campo Francesco Morosini*. To the E of this square is the *Teatro La Fenice* (1790–92), the largest theatre in Venice (1500 seats); to the S the *Palazzo Pisani a Santo Stefano* (now the Conservatoire), a good example of a wealthy merchant's mansion of the Baroque period.

To the SW is the *Ponte dell'Accademia*, which leads to the **Accademia di Belle Arti**, in premises (rebuilt and modernised) once occupied by the brotherhood and convent of Santa Maria della Carità. The academy's **picture gallery* contains more than 800 pictures, mainly by Venetian artists and including some works of the highest quality, which give an excellent survey of the achievement of the Venetian schools.

Lido di Iesolo

Among the outstanding works in the collection are the brilliantly coloured pictures of Venetian life by *Gentile Bellini* (particularly in Room XX) and *Vittore Carpaccio* (including nine *scenes from the legend of St Ursula in Room XXI); beautiful *religious paintings by *Giovanni Bellini* (particularly in Rooms IV and V); and masterpieces by *Giorgione* (including *'"The Storm", the finest work in the collection, Room V), *Titian* (*'"Presentation of the Virgin", Room XXIV; *'"Lamentation", his last picture, completed by Palma Giovane, Room X), *Paris Bordone* (*'"Presentation of the Ring of St Mark", Room VI), *Jacopo Tintoretto* (particularly the large pictures from the Scuola di San Marco in Room X and other works in Rooms VI and XI) and *Paolo Veronese* (*'"Jesus in the House of Levi", 12·3 by 5·7 m, one of the artist's finest works, Room X). The collection also includes notable pictures by *Mantegna* (*'"St George", Room IV), *Cima da Conegliano, Pietro Longhi, Francesco Guardi, Sebastiano Ricci, Palma Vecchio, Piero della Francesca, Lotto, Tiepolo, Antonio Canaletto* and *Alvise, Bartolomeo* and *Antonio Vivarini*.

From the Accademia landing-stage we can take the motor-launch N to the next landing place, *San Tomà*. A short distance NW is the former Franciscan ***church of l Frari** or *Santa Maria Gloriosa dei Frari*, a brick-built Gothic basilica (1417) with a tall campanile, the largest and most beautiful church in Venice after St Mark's. Like Santi Giovanni e Paolo, it is the burial-place of many famous Venetians. On the high altar is Titian's **'"Assumption"*, the finest work of his early period (1516–18). In the N aisle, beside the tomb of Bishop Jacopo Pesaro, is Titian's **'"Madonna of the House of Pesaro"* (1519–26) and in the sacristy Giovanni Bellini's "Madonna Enthroned" (1488). – The adjoining monastery houses the *State Archives* of Venice, one of the finest collections of the kind in the world. – Nearby stands the **Scuola di San Rocco* (1524–60), with a magnificent Renaissance façade and 56 large *murals by Tintoretto (Biblical scenes, 1560–88). – Across the street from the Scuola di San Rocco the *church of San Rocco* has a

façade of 1771 and some fine pictures by Tintoretto. – From here we cross the Campo San Stin to reach the *Scuola di San Giovanni Evangelista*, with an outer courtyard in the style of Pietro Lombardi (1481) and a staircase by Moro Coducci (d. 1504).

On the long island of **Giudecca**, lying to the S of the main part of the city and separated from it by the *Canale della Giudecca* (300 m wide), is the conspicuous ***church of the Redentore**, formerly belonging to the Franciscans. The finest of Palladio's churches (1577–92), it has two slender round towers to the rear of the central dome and a harmoniously proportioned interior. On the high altar are marble reliefs by Giuseppe Mazza and bronze statues by Girolamo Campagna.

SURROUNDINGS. – From the Riva degli Schiavoni it is a 15 minutes' trip by motor-launch to the **LIDO**, the northern part of the spit of land known as the *Malamocco* which borders the E side of the lagoon. The Lido was once Italy's most famous seaside resort, with numerous hotels, pensions and summer villas. – From the *Santa Maria Elisabetta* landing-stage the Viale Santa Maria Elisabetta runs across the spit (8 minutes' walk) to the **Stabilimento dei Bagni**, with an outlook terrace and a café-restaurant, around which the life of the resort centres in summer. From here it is a 20 minutes' walk S along the Lungomare G. Marconi to a large square in which are the **Casinò Municipale** and the **Palazzo del Cinema** (1937–52), the scene of the Biennale film festival.

From the Lido there is a motor-boat service (and also a car ferry) to the **Punta Sabbioni**, from which a road runs 20 km NE to the large resort of **Lido di Iesolo (alt. 2 m; pop. 6000; hotels: Cesare Augustus, I, 232 b., SP; Las Vegas, I, 184 b., SP; Anthony, I, 120 b., SP; Bellevue, I, 111 b., SP; Gallia, I, 105., SP; Negresco, I, 78 b., SP; Elite, I, 74 b., SP; Le Soleil, II, 216 b., SP; Caravelle, II, 196 b., SP; Tahiti, II, 169 b.; Heron, II, 156 b., SP; London, II, 153 b.; Svezia, II, 152 b.; Aurora, II, 148 b., SP; Alexander, II, 148 b.; Croce di Malta, II, 140 b., SP; Scandinavia, II, 140 b., SP; Adlon, II, 135 b.; Nettuno, II, 133 b.; Cambridge, II, 131 b.; Luxor, II, 128 b.; Astor, II, 125 b.; Casa Bianca al Mare, II, 125 b.; Regent's, II, 122 b., SP; Mariver, II, 119 b.; Capitol, II, 116 b.; Cosmopolitan, II, 116 b.;

Galassia, II, 116 b., SP; Principe-Palace, II, 114 b.; Venezia-Residenza La Villetta, II, 114 b.; Mediterraneo, II, 114 b.; Delle Rose, II, 112 b.; Agora, II, 112 b., SP; Maracaibo, II, 109 b., SP; Oxford, II, 109 b.; Beau Rivage, II, 105 b., SP; Elpiro, II, 104 b.; Imperial Palace, II, 103 b., SP; Rivamare, II, 102 b.; Bettina, II, 100 b.; Byron Bellavista, II, 100 b., SP; Cavalieri, II, 100 b., SP; Majestic-Roscanelli, II, 100 b.; Aquileia, III, 402 b., SP; Eden, III, 242 b., SP; Costa del Sol, III, 219 b., SP; etc.). With its beautiful broad beach Lido di Iesolo ranks with Rimini, Riccione and the Venice Lido as one of the most popular resorts on the Adriatic.

From the Fondamente Nuove on the N side of Venice there is a motor-launch service (landing-stage near church of the Gesuiti: 10 minutes), passing the *cemetery island of San Michele*, to the little town of **Murano** (pop. 8000), on the island of the same name, which has been the main centre of the Venetian *glass industry since the end of the 13th c. 6 minutes' walk from the Colonna landing-stage is the church of San Pietro Martire (1509), which has a beautiful Madonna by Giovanni Bellini (1488) in the S aisle. Beyond this, on the far side of the main canal, stands the cathedral of Sante Maria e Donata (12th c.), with fine columns of Greek marble, a mosaic pavement and a Byzantine mosaic in the apse. Near the cathedral is the Town Hall, with the Museo dell'Arte Vetraria (products of the local glass-making industry, which had its heyday in the 15th and 16th c.). The glass workshops are open only on weekdays.

Another very attractive boat trip is to the picturesque little fishing town of **Burano** (pop. 7000), centre of the Venetian lace-making industry, and the island of **Torcello**, in the lagoon 8 km NE of Venice, with the ancient little town of the same name. Torcello has a beautiful cathedral (Santa Maria Assunta, 7th–11th c.), with a crypt and a Romanesque campanile (view from top), and the octagonal church of Santa Fosca (9th–10th c.: Lagoon Museum).

Near the S end of the Venice lagoon (45 km on S.S. 309, the Strada Romea, from Marghera) lies the interesting island town of *Chioggia (alt. 2 m; pop. 50,000; Hotel Grande Italia, II, 114 b.; etc.), formerly the centre of Venetian salt production, destroyed by the Genoese in 1379 and now Italy's largest fishing port. With its narrow streets of old houses, picturesque in decay, its canals and its bustling life and activity, it is a popular resort of artists. In the main street, the Corso del Popolo, are the cathedral (rebuilt by Longhena), with a 60 m high campanile (14th c.), and the little Gothic church of San Martino (1392). – A bridge 800 m long leads from the old town of Chioggia to **Sottomarina** (alt. 2 m; hotels: Vittoria Palace, II, 255 b.; Ritz, II, 150 b.; Capinera, II, 86 b.; Real, III, 122 b.; Bristol, III, 120 b.; etc.), a popular bathing resort with a good beach.

Chioggia – a bird's eye view

Verona

Region: Veneto. -- Province: Verona (VR).
Altitude: 59 m. – Population: 270,000.
Post code: I-37100. – Dialling code: 045.
(i) **EPT**, Via C. Montanari 14;
tel. 2 50 65.
ACI, Via della Valverde 34;
tel. 3 41 35.
TCI, *Mondadori per Voi*, Piazza Brà 24;
tel. 2 26 70.

HOTELS. – *Due Torri*, Piazza Sant'Anastasia 4, L, 160 b.; *Colomba d'Oro*, Via C. Cattaneo 10, I, 86 b.; *Grand Hotel*, Corso Porta Nuova 105, I, 81 b.; *Accademia*, Via Scala 12, II, 147 b.; *Nuovo San Pietro*, Via Santa Teresa 1, II, 112 b.; *Milano*, Vicolo Tre Marchetti 11, II, 92 b.; *Firenze*, Corso Porta Nuova 88, II, 84 b.; *Europa*, Via Roma 8, II, 79 b.; *San Luca*, Vicolo Volto San Luca 8, II, 70 b.; *Giulietta Romeo*, Vicolo Tre Marchetti 3, II, 55 b.; *Italia*, Via G. Mameli 64, III, 82 b.; *Touring*, Via Q. Sella 5, III, 75 b.; *Rossi*, Via delle Coste 2, III, 68 b.; *Piccolo*, Via Camuzzoni 3, III, 62 b.; *Trieste*, Corso Porta Nuova 57, III, 60 b.; *De' Capuleti*, Via del Pontiere 26, III, 60 b.; etc. – CAMPING SITE.

RESTAURANTS. – *Tre Corone*, Piazza Brà 16; *Re Teodorico*, Piazzale Castel San Pietro; *Pedavena*, Piazza Brà 20; *12 Apostoli*, Corticella San Marco 3; *Bragozzo*, Via del Pontiere 13.

EVENT. – *Operatic Festival* in Amphitheatre (July–Aug.).

The historic old town of *Verona, now a provincial capital, is an important centre of communications, lying as it does at the point where the River Adige emerges from the Alps into the N Italian plain. The main part of the town is situated below the Alpine foothills of the Altipiano dei Lessini on a peninsula enclosed on two sides by the rapidly flowing Adige and linked with the districts on the left bank by ten bridges. Verona is the largest town on the old mainland territory of Venice (the "terra ferma"), a city of picturesque streets and squares, rich in art and architecture.

Verona is also a considerable commercial centre, handling the produce (particularly fruit and vegetables) of the province's fertile irrigated soil.

HISTORY. – Verona, which still preserves the name of the prehistoric settlement on this site, became a Roman colony in 89 B.C. and thereafter developed into a town of considerable importance, as the remains of its amphitheatre and other buildings testify. In the 6th c. the Ostrogothic king Theodoric (d. 526) made it one of his royal residences, together with Pavia and Ravenna. During the Frankish period Charlemagne's son Pepin reigned here as king of Italy, and later the Saxon and Hohenstaufen emperors found the town,

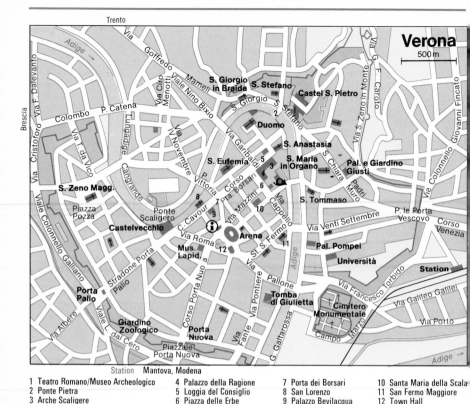

Verona
500 m

1 Teatro Romano/Museo Archeologico   4 Palazzo della Ragione   7 Porta dei Borsari   10 Santa Maria della Scala
2 Ponte Pietra   5 Loggia del Consiglio   8 San Lorenzo   11 San Fermo Maggiore
3 Arche Scaligere   6 Piazza delle Erbe   9 Palazzo Bevilacqua   12 Town Hall

situated at the end of the road over the Brenner, a convenient base from which to control Italy. From the middle of the 13th c. Verona was ruled by the Ghibelline family of Della Scala (the Scaligers), but in 1387 they were expelled by the Viscontis. In 1405 the town passed into the hands of Venice. During the Austrian period (1814–66) Verona became a fortress town, forming with Peschiera, Mantua and Legnago the famous defensive "quadrilateral".

ART. – Verona is notable for its fine Romanesque churches (11th c.), but it was also a considerable artistic centre in the Renaissance period, particularly in the field of architecture. Its leading architects were the Dominican monk *Fra Giocondo* (*c.* 1433–1515) and *Michele Sanmicheli* (1484–1559). Sanmicheli sought to embellish his works of fortification by the use of classical architectural forms, erected numerous splendid buildings and built the bastioned town walls (1527 onwards).

SIGHTS. – The central feature of the old town is the elongated *Piazza delle Erbe*, one of the most picturesque squares in Italy, on the site of the Roman forum (now a fruit and vegetable market). In the centre of the square is the *Capitello* (16th c.), a canopy borne on four columns, formerly used for the election of the Signori and the Podestà. To the N of it is the *Market Fountain* (1368), with the "Madonna Verona", an ancient marble statue (restored). At the N end of the square the *Marble Column* bears the lion of St Mark, the emblem of Venetian authority. At the NE corner stands the *Casa Mazzanti*, originally built by the Scaligers; like many houses in the town, it is adorned with Renaissance frescoes. On the N side of the square is the Baroque *Palazzo Maffei* (1668), and to the left of this the *Torre del Gardello* (1370). The *Casa dei Mercanti* at the corner of Via Pellicciai was rebuilt in 1878 in its original form (1301). Opposite it rises the 83 m high *Torre del Comune* (lift to top: view).

The short street to the left of the Torre del Comune runs E into the *Piazza dei Signori* (a name recalling the rule of the

The Adige at Verona

Scaligers), surrounded by palaces. In the centre is a monument to Dante (1865). The **Palazzo della Ragione** (Town Hall), on the S side of the square, was begun in 1193 but much altered in later centuries. The main front is Renaissance (1524). In the courtyard are a Gothic grand staircase (1446–50) and the entrance to the Torre del Comune. – Farther on, beside a battlemented tower, is the *Tribunal*, formerly the Palazzo del Capitano with a Renaissance doorway by Michele Sanmicheli, converted in 1530–31 from a Scaliger palace. On the E side of the square we find the *Palazzo del Governo* (Prefecture), originally another Scaliger palace, rebuilt in the 16th c. (doorway by Sanmicheli, 1532). On the N side stands the *Loggia del Consiglio, one of the finest Early Renaissance buildings in Italy (by Giovanni and Bartolomeo Sanmicheli, 1486–93), crowned by statues of famous citizens of Verona in antiquity.

The passage between the Prefecture and the Tribunal leads to the *church of Santa Maria Antica*, with a Romanesque campanile. Adjoining it are the imposing Gothic *Tombs of the Scaligers (*Arche Scalígere*), with the ladder (*scala*) which was the heraldic emblem of the family frequently recurring in the elaborate wrought-iron railings. Above the church door are the sarcophagus and a copy of an equestrian statue of Can Grande della Scala (d. 1329); to the left are seen the mural monument of Giovanni (d. 1359) and the sarcophagus of Mastino I (d. 1277). Within the railings, under a canopy, are the sarcophagi and equestrian statues of Mastino II (d. 1351) and Can Signorio (d. 1375).

To the N, at the end of the Corso Sant'Anastasia, on the river, is the Dominican **church of Sant'Anastasia**, a brick-built Gothic structure (1290–1323, 1422–81) with a magnificent interior (richly decorated altars of the 15th–18th c.). – From here it is a short distance NW to the **Cathedral**, a 12th c. Romanesque basilica with a 15th c. Gothic nave. Adjoining it is a campanile on a Romanesque base, designed by Sanmicheli but not completed until 1927. On the beautiful main doorway of the cathedral are figures of Charlemagne's two paladins Roland and Oliver (*c*. 1139–53). Within the church, on the first altar on the left, is an "Assumption" by Titian (*c*. 1525),

at the end of the S aisle the Gothic tomb of St Agatha (1353) in a Renaissance framework (1508) and to the left of the cathedral is a Romanesque cloister (1123), with an Early Christian mosaic pavement on a lower level.

From here we continue towards the river and cross the *Ponte Garibaldi* to the left bank, then turn right through the gardens and the *Porta San Giorgio* to reach the *church of San Giorgio in Braida (16th c.), with a beautiful dome and fine altarpieces of the Veronese and Brescian schools (on the high altar "The Martyrdom of St George", a masterpiece by Paolo Veronese).

Returning to the right bank of the Adige, we go upstream along the *Lungádige Panvinio* (views) and then turn left past the *church of Sant'Eufemia* into the Corso Porta Borsari, which runs SW from the Piazza delle Erbe. At the far end is the *Porta dei Borsari*, one of the Roman city gates (A.D. 265). – Beyond this the Corso Cavour, once the main street of Verona, is flanked by handsome old palaces. On the left (No. 19) is the imposing *Palazzo Bevilacqua* (by Sanmicheli, 1530), with the Romanesque *church of San Lorenzo* (*c*. 1110) opposite it. At the end of the street, on the banks of the Adige, stands the **Castel Vecchio**, built by the Scaligers in 1354–55; from the platform of the keep (Mastio) there are extensive views. The castle now houses the *Museo di Castelvecchio* (Roman sculpture; applied art; excellent picture gallery, with works of the 15th–16th c. Veronese school). Below the castle the Adige is spanned by the fine *Ponte Scaligero* (14th c.; restored 1949–51 after wartime destruction).

To the S of Corso Cavour, linked with it by a number of short streets, is the spacious *Piazza Brà* (from Latin *pratum*, "meadow"). On the N side of the square, near the end of Via Mazzini, is the *Palazzo Malfatti*, by Sanmicheli. Opposite it stands an equestrian statue of Victor Emmanuel II (1883). – The Roman **Amphitheatre** (*Arena*), one of the largest of its kind, on the E side of the square, was built in the reign of Diocletian (*c*. A.D. 290). Of the outer wall only four arches on the N side have survived. With its 43 rows of seating it can accommodate some 22,000 spectators; from the top rows there are fine views. The overall length of the structure was 152 m, its height 32 m. In July and August a famous operatic festival is held in the Arena.

On the S side of the Piazza Brà is the **Palazzo Municipale** or Town Hall (1836–38; semicircular extension built after the last war). To the right the long building of the *Gran Guardia* was the old guard-house (1614), and adjoining this the *Portoni della Brà*, an old gateway and tower. Close by are the *Museo Lapidario Maffeiano* and the *Teatro Filarmonico* (opera).

Passing through the Portoni, we follow the wide *Corso di Porta Nuova* (or Corso Can Grande) to the *Porta Nuova* (by Sanmicheli), beyond which is the principal railway station, the *Stazione di Porta Nuova*. – From the Porta Nuova we follow the tree-lined avenue which runs round inside the old walls to the magnificent **Porta del Palio** (by Sanmicheli, mid 15th c.). From here we go E along the wide Stradone di Porta Palio and then turn left into Via Aurelio Saffi to reach the former Franciscan *church of San Bernardino* (15th c.), with a large arcaded courtyard (gravestones, remains of frescoes). The Cappella Pellegrini (begun by Sanmicheli before 1554) has fine Renaissance decoration. – To the N of San Bernardino is the large *church of San Zeno Maggiore** (11th–12th c.), perhaps the finest Romanesque building in northern Italy, with a beautiful main front flanked by a slender Romanesque campanile (1045–1178) and the battlemented defensive tower (14th c.) of a former Benedictine abbey. The doorway has Romanesque reliefs with Biblical and other scenes. The interior boasts an unusual timber roof (14th c.) and beautiful Romanesque capitals. In the aisles are frescoes of the 12th–14th c. In the choir is a marble figure, ascribed to the 13th c., of St Zeno, bishop of Verona (d. 380), whose reliquary is in the crypt (which dates back to the 11th c.). On the high altar is a *"Madonna with Saints" by Mantegna (1456–59) and on the N side of the church an elegant *cloister* (partly Romanesque, partly Gothic).

In the Campo di Fiera, near the Adige in the southern part of the town, visitors are shown, in a *cloister* built in 1899, a medieval trough which purports to be the coffin of Juliet Capulet, Shakespeare's heroine.

From the Piazza delle Erbe Via Cappello, with the **Casa di Giuletta** (Juliet's house, with her balcony), and its continuation Via dei Leoni (on left, the Roman *Arco dei Leoni*) runs SE to the **church of San Fermo Maggiore**, with a Romanesque lower church (11th–12th c.) and a Gothic upper church, its façade beautifully decorated with marble. It contains a number of notable monuments and pictures by Pisanello and others. –

Performance of an opera (Verdi's "Aida") in the Arena Verona

Immediately beyond the church is the *Ponte delle Navi*, from which there is a fine view up-river of the Castel San Pietro.

Beyond the bridge, going NE along the Interrato dell'Acqua Morta and then turning right into Via Carducci, we come to the *Palazzo Giusti* (1580) and the **Giardino Giusti**, with beautiful old cypresses (delightful views from the terrace). – Farther N is the **church of Santa Maria in Órgano**, originally founded in the Lombard period and rebuilt in Renaissance style in 1481, with an unfinished façade designed by Sanmicheli (1592). The choir has stalls with intarsia work by Fra Giovanni (1499). – Farther along the hillside, under the commandingly situated *Castel San Pietro*, is the **Roman Theatre**, with remains of the stage wall; built in the reign of Augustus, it was excavated between 1904 and 1913. Above the theatre in the former *Convento di San Girólamo*, the church of which is built into the seating of the theatre, the *Museo Archeologico* contains prehistoric and Roman material, old views of the town, etc.

Below the Roman theatre, to the NW, is the Roman **Ponte di Pietra** (rebuilt after wartime destruction). – A short distance N is the Romanesque **church of Santo Stefano**, a very ancient building (originally 5th–8th c.) with two unusual ambulatories round the choir (8th c. capitals); the choir itself contains an episcopal throne of 1008.

SURROUNDINGS. – Above the town to the N stands the *pilgrimage church of the Madonna di Lourdes* (1964). – One trip which should not be missed is the 25 km drive W to * *Lake Garda (see p. 122).

16 km SW of Verona, on the River *Tione*, is **Villafranca di Verona** (alt. 54 m; pop. 23,000; hotels: Roveda, II, 80 b.; San Pietro, III, 35 b.; etc.), with a ruined castle (1202), part of the "Serraglio", the frontier fortifications of Verona, which extended to Valeggio, 9 km W.

Another attractive excursion from Verona (45 km N) is to the beautiful **Monti Lessini** and *Giazza* (German *Glietzen* or *Jätzen*; alt. 758 m), the only one of the "*Tredici Comuni*" (Thirteen Communes) inhabited by the descendants of settlers from Bavaria and Tirol, and where German is still spoken.

15 km E of Verona is the little medieval town of *Soave, renowned for its white wine (alt. 40 m; pop. 6000; Hotel Soave, IV, 32 b.), with battlemented town walls and towers, handsome palaces and an old castle (restored).

Vesuvius/Vesuvio

Ⓘ **EPT Napoli**, Via Partenope 101, I-80100 Napoli (NA); tel. (081) 40 62 89.

Rearing abruptly out of the plain some 15 km SE of Naples on the shores of the bay, **Vesuvius has been since the 17th c. the only volcano on the European mainland which is still intermittently active.

The height of Vesuvius varies from time to time, since every eruption of any violence alters the shape of the summit; at present it is 1277 m high. The crater now has a circumference of 1400 m, a maximum diameter of 600 m and a depth of 216 m; before the last major eruption in 1944 the circumference was 3400 m. – NE of the main crater, and separated from it by the deep sickle-shaped valley known as the *Atrio del Cavallo* (alt. *c.* 800 m), is *Monte Somma* (1132 m), a relic of the caldera of an older volcano which had a diameter of 4 km.

Vesuvius first emerged in the Quaternary in the form of an island. In antiquity it was regarded as extinct until the violent eruption on 24 August in the year A.D. 79 which destroyed Pompeii, Herculaneum, Stabiae and a number of smaller places. Between that date and 1139 there were 15 eruptions, after which the volcano appeared to be quiescent, and woodland and scrub spread right up to the rim of the crater. In 1631, however, it came back to life with a fearsome eruption. The last eruption was on 20 March 1944, when the funicular from Ercolano (then known as Resina) up the mountain was destroyed. Since then Vesuvius – as is normally the case for a few years after a major eruption – has remained inactive apart from a number of fumaroles. – The ash cone and the more recent lava flows are almost devoid of vegetation, but the older weathered lavas form a fertile soil for the growth of oaks and chestnuts at medium heights and of fruit and vines (Lacrima Christi wine) below 500 m.

For the ASCENT OF VESUVIUS, leave the Naples–Salerno motorway at the *Ercolano* exit and take the *Strada Vesuviana*, which winds its way uphill between lava flows. In 7 km it comes to the *Albergo Eremo* (III, 34 b.), where a short side road goes off to

View of Vesuvius from Naples harbour

the **Observatory** (alt. 608 m), founded in 1844, with a small *museum*. – In another 3 km the road forks. To the left is a private road running up the N side of Vesuvius to the *Colle Margherita* (3 km), from which it is a 20 minutes' climb on foot to the rim of the crater (guide compulsory). The road continuing straight ahead comes in 1·5 km to the lower station (753 m) of a chair-lift, which takes 5–6 minutes to reach the upper station (1160 m), from which there is a fascinating walk round the crater (1 hour: guide compulsory). In clear weather the** views are magnificent.

Another toll road runs from *Torre Annunziata* NE (2 km) to **Boscotrecase** (alt. 92 m; pop. 22,000; hotels: Vesuvio, III, 33 b.; Principe, III, 28 b.), then another 10 km NW, past the *Nuova Casa Bianca* restaurant and up the SE slopes of Vesuvius, with numerous bends and for the last stretch on an unguarded road, to an altitude of some 1200 m, from which it is a 15 minutes' walk to the edge of the crater.

Viareggio

Region: Toscana. – Province: Lucca (LU). Altitude: 2 m. – Population: 55,000. Post code: I-55049. – Dialling code: 0584.
ⓘ **AA**, Viale Carducci 10;
tel. 4 22 33.
Information office at station;
tel. 46 33 82.
TCI, *Turitalia*, Viale Margherita 11.
Viaggi Vet, Viale Margherita 48.

HOTELS. – *Grand Hotel e Royal*, I, 231 b., SP; *Principe di Piemonte*, I, 221 b.; *Astor e Residence*, I, 129 b.; *Palace*, I, 124 b.; *De Russie e Plaza*, I, 83 b.; *Excelsior*, II, 154 b.; *Marchionni*, II, 110 b.; *Riviera Golf*, II, 88 b.; *Belmare*, II, 76 b.; *Liberty*, II, 74 b.; *Garden*, II, 73 b.; *Stella d'Italia*, II, 65 b.; *Bristol*, II, 64 b.; *Derna Mare*, II, 64 b.; *Kursaal*, III, 72 b.; *Turismo*, III, 58 b.; *Flamingo*, III, 56 b.; *Frank*, III, 52 b.; *Bonelli*, III, 52 b.; *Bella Riviera*, III, 50 b.; etc.

EVENT. – **Carnival** (Feb.), with a splendid* parade of colourful floats.

Viareggio, situated at the S end of the Riviera della Versilia between La Spezia and Pisa, is the leading seaside resort on the W coast of Italy, with a beautiful sandy beach, and thanks to its mild climate is also a popular winter resort. It is renowned for its carnival parade.

SIGHTS. – The life of the resort centres on the palm-shaded *Piazza d'Azeglio* and the seafront promenades to the N, Viale Manin and Viale Carducci. – At the S end of the town is the northern **Molo** (pier), 200 m long, with views of the coast extending from the Gulf of La Spezia to Livorno, and of the nearby Apuan Alps. Going E from the Molo along the *Canale Burlamacca*, coming from the Lago di Massaciuccoli, and past two small harbours for the shipment of marble, we come to the *station*.

SURROUNDINGS. – There are pleasant walks to the **Pineta di Ponente** or *Pineta Comunale*, a wood of umbrella pines 10 km long which begins a little way E of Viale Carducci, and the **Pineta di Levante** (formerly the *Tenuta Borbone*), to the S of the town.

6 km E of Viareggio, near *Torre del Lago Puccini* (alt. 2 m; hotels: Parco Nazionale, I, 190 b., SP; National Park, II, 48 b.; Da Pina, III, 40 b.; etc.), is the Villa Puccini, where the composer Giacomo Puccini (1858–1924) and his wife (d. 1930) are buried. Between the villa and the large Lago di Massaciuccoli open-air performances of Puccini operas are given in summer. – To the E of Torre del Lago Puccini is the *Pineta di Migliarino*.

Carnival, Viareggio

Vicenza

Region: Veneto. – Province: Vicenza (VI).
Altitude: 39 m. – Population: 120,000.
Post code: I-36100. – Dialling code: 0444.
ⓘ **EPT**, Piazza Duomo 5;
tel. 2 29 27.
   ACI, Piazza San Biagio 1;
tel. 2 87 57.
   TCI, *Mondadori per Voi*, Corso Palladio 117;
tel. 2 67 08.

HOTELS. – *Jolly Campo Marzio*, Viale Roma 27, I, 54 b.; *Jolly Stazione*, Viale Milano 92, II, 104 b.; *Continental*, Via G.G. Trissino 89, II, 86 b.; *Internazionale*, Ponte Alton 1, II, 84 b.; *City*, Viale Verona 12, II, 35 b.; *Cristina*, Corso San Felice 32, II, 42 b.; *Adele*, Via G. Medici 36, III, 100 b.; *Vicenza*, Via

dei Nodari 5, III, 53 b.; *Giardini*, Via Giuriolo 10, III, 51 b.; etc. – *Motel Agip*, Via degli Scaligeri 68, II, 126 b.

EVENTS. – *Settembre Vicentino* (performances of classical plays in the Teatro Olimpico), in Sept.

The provincial capital of Vicenza, the Roman Vicetia, lies NW of Padua on the edge of the fertile Po plain, straddling the River Bacchiglione at the point where it is joined by the Retrone. It is enclosed between the foothills of the Alpine uplands reaching down from the N and the volcanic chain of the Monti Bérici.

ART. – The old town, still partly enclosed by its walls, is renowned for its numerous palaces of the 15th–18th c., most notably those built by the Vicenza-born **Andrea Palladio** (1518–80), the last great master of the High Renaissance, whose grand style, based on his study of ancient architecture, provided a model for the whole of the Western world. His principal successors were *Vincenzo Scamozzi* (1552–1616) and *Ottone Calderari* (1730–1803). The leading painter of the 15th c. Vicenza school was *Bartolomeo Montagna* (c. 1450–1523), a native of Orzinuovi, whose works can be seen in the picture gallery of the Museo Civico and in several churches in the town.

SIGHTS. – In the heart of the old town is the *Piazza dei Signori*, with two columns dating from the Venetian period, the slender *Torre dell'Orologio*, 82 m high (built in 1174 for defensive purposes by a noble family) and several café-restaurants. – On the SE side of the square stands the **Basilica Palladiana** (1549–1614), Palladio's masterpiece, with open colonnades of two storeys surrounding the earlier *Palazzo della Ragione* (Town Hall) in Gothic style. On the first floor is a hall 52 m long with a wooden vaulted roof (renewed after wartime destruction). In front of the W end of the basilica is a marble statue of Palladio (1859). – At the NW corner of the square the *Loggio del Capitanio* (now part of the Town Hall), was formerly the residence of the Venetian governor; it was begun by Palladio in 1571 but only half finished (rich stucco decoration). To the right is the *Palazzo del Monte di Pietà*, with the *church of San Vincenzo* (1620).

From the Basilica Palladiana the Via Garibaldi runs SW to the *Piazza del Duomo*, on the NW side of which stands the **Cathedral**, a Gothic structure with a façade of white and red marble (15th c.) and a fine interior. Under the cathedral are the foundations of three earlier churches. – On the SW side of the Piazza del Duomo

Bassano del Grappa
San Marco, Giardino Querini, Aracoeli

Station, Basilica di Monte Berico

1 Palazzo Angaran
2 Palazzo Da Schio
3 Palazzo Valmarana

4 Loggia Valmarana
5 Palazzo Breganze
6 Casa Pigafetta

the *Bishop's Palace* has a neo-classical façade of 1819. In the courtyard (1543), on the right, is an elegant Early Renaissance hall by Tommaso Formentone (1494).

A little way NW of the Piazza dei Signori is the main street of Vicenza, the *Corso Andrea Palladio*, lined with palaces. Half way along this street we find the handsome **Palazzo del Comune** (by Vincenzo Scamozzi, 1588–1662) and 100 m NE of this the Gothic *Palazzo Da Schio*, known as the Ca' d'Oro ("Golden House"), with the Baroque *church of San Gaetano* adjoining it. A little way N is the Baroque **church of Santo Stefano** (by Guarini, early 18th c.), which has a *"Madonna Enthroned" by Palma Vecchio in the N transept. From here Via Santo Stefano runs NE to the Gothic **church of Santa Corona** (13th c.), which has a *"Baptism of Christ" by Giovanni Bellini (c. 1501: fifth altar on left).

At the NE end of the Corso Andrea Palladio, in the *Palazzo Chiericati*, one of Palladio's finest buildings (before 1566), is the **Museo Civico** (closed Sunday afternoons and Mondays). On the ground floor are archaeological collections, on the first floor a *picture gallery* containing major works by painters of the Vicenza school (Bartolomeo Montagna, Giovanni Buonconsiglio, etc.), Venetian masters and others. – Opposite the museum is the *Teatro Olimpico** (damaged by an earthquake shock in 1976), which was begun by Palladio in 1580 and completed by Vincenzo Scamozzi in 1585. Built of wood and stucco, this is a Renaissance

adaptation of the ancient type of theatre. The auditorium, with seating for 1000, rises in semi-oval tiers; the magnificent stage wall offers vistas through three openings of streets contrived to secure the effect of perspective.

From the middle section of the Corso Andrea Palladio the Via Fogazzaro (at No. 16, on right, the *Palazzo Valmarana*) runs NW to the **church of San Lorenzo**, a brick-built Romanesque and Gothic structure (1280–1344) with a slender campanile and a beautiful main doorway; fine interior, with the tomb of Bartolomeo Montagna (on left).

At the SW end of the Corso Palladio are a number of handsome palaces, including the *Palazzo Bonin* (No. 13, on the N side) and the *Palazzo Zileri Dal Verme* (No. 42, on the S side). – The Corso ends in Piazza Castello, in which is the *Porta Castello*. To the left, on the shorter side of the square, the unfinished *Palazzo Porto-Breganze*, was probably designed by Palladio and built by Vincenzo Scamozzi about 1600.

SURROUNDINGS. – From the *Villa Roi*, on the southern outskirts of the town, the *Portici di Monte Berico* (1746), a series of arcades 650 m long, lead up to the **Basilica di Monte Berico** or *Madonna del Monte* (also reached by road, 1·3 km, from the Porta Lupia). This pilgrimage church was built by the Bologna architect. A. Borella in 1668; it has a centralised plan modelled on the Rotonda (see below). In the chapel to the right of the high altar is a *"Lamentation" by Bartolomeo Montagna (1500). From the square in front of the church there are magnificent views of the city and the Pre-Alps (including Monte Pasubio and Monte Grappa). – At the bend in the Portici a road runs E, and 2 minutes

Basilica di Monte Berico, Vicenza

along this a footpath goes off on the right and runs past the *Villa Valmarana* (with mythological *frescoes by G. B. Tiepolo, 1737) to reach in 10 minutes the famous *Rotonda, a square structure crowned by a dome which was begun by Palladio about 1567 and completed by Scamozzi between 1580 and 1592. (The Villa Valmarana and the Rotonda can also be reached by road from the Strada della Riviera Berica, which skirts the E side of Monte Berico.)

Viterbo

Region: Lazio. – Province: Viterbo (VT).
Altitude: 293–354 m. – Population: 55,000.
Post code: I-01100. – Dialling code: 0761.
(i) EPT, Piazza dei Caduti 16;
tel. 3 00 92.
ACI, Via A. Marini 16;
tel. 3 19 33.

HOTELS. – *Mini Palace*, II, 72 b.; *Tuculca*, II, 28 b.; *Terme Salus*, III, 150 b., SP; *Leon d'Oro*, III, 75 b.; *Tuscia*, III, 69 b.; etc.

The provincial capital of Viterbo is attractively situated at the foot of the Monti Cimini, some 80 km NW of Rome. Noted in the past as the "city of beautiful women and beautiful fountains", it still preserves its old Lombard walls, handsome and historic buildings and picturesque old-world nooks and crannies. It suffered much damage during the last war, but this has now been repaired.

HISTORY. – The town was presented to the Pope by Pepin the Short in the 8th c. At the end of the 11th c. it became a free city, but in 1396 was again incorporated in the States of the Church.

SIGHTS. – The central feature of the town is the *Piazza del Plebiscito*, on the W side of which stands the **Palazzo Comunale** (begun 1247; porch 15th c.). In the courtyard, from which there is an attractive view of the western part of the town, is an elegant 17th c. fountain. – From the Piazza del Plebiscito the Via di San Lorenzo runs S to the little Piazza del Gesù, with the *church of San Silvestro*, and the Piazza della Morte, which has another charming fountain, the *Fontana a Fuso*. – Continuing W over a bridge and past the 15th c. *Palazzo Farnese* (on right: beautiful courtyard), we come to the Piazza San Lorenzo, with the fine **Cathedral** of San Lorenzo (12th c.; Gothic campanile; façade of 1570). To the right of the cathedral we see the **Palazzo Papale** (1266), with a Gothic loggia, which has been the Bishop's Palace since

the 15th c. In its huge hall three conclaves met for the election of a pope in the 13th c.

SE of the Piazza della Morte lies the picturesque *San Pellegrino quarter, which has preserved many medieval houses, particularly in the Piazza San Pellegrino, with the *Case degli Alessandri*.

From the Piazza del Plebiscito the busy *Via Cavour* runs SE to the Piazza Fontana Grande, with the town's largest fountain, the *Fontana Grande* (1279). – From here Via Garibaldi continues E to the *Porta Romana* (1653). To the left of the gate is the *church of San Sisto*, a Lombard building of the 9th c. with a fine apse which was increased in height in the 12th c. – Going N from the Porta Romana outside the town walls, we come to the former monastic **church of Santa Maria della Verità** (13th c.; restored after the last war), with a beautiful Gothic cloister. The monastic buildings now house the *Museo Civico* (Etruscan sarcophagi and other material, medieval pictures, etc.). Farther N, inside the town walls, is the **church of Santa Rosa** (rebuilt from 1840 onwards), with the mummified body of the saint (d. 1261). Every year on 3 September, the eve of her feast-day, the saint's statue is borne on an 18 m high tower from the Porta Romana to the church – a ceremony first introduced in 1664.

NW of Santa Rosa, in the Piazza San Francesco, the Gothic **church of San Francesco** contains the tombs of Pope Clement IV (d. 1268) in the N aisle (on right) and Pope Hadrian V (d. 1276) in the S aisle (on left). Adjoining the Piazza San Francesco on the W is the Piazza della Rocca, with a fountain which is ascribed to Vignola and the remains of the *Rocca* (1457), which suffered severe destruction during the Second World War. Farther W again, outside the *Porta Fiorentina* (1768), lies the beautiful *Giardino Pubblico.*

SURROUNDINGS. – 3 km NE of Viterbo, in the suburb of **La Quercia**, is the pilgrimage church of the *Madonna della Quercia* (1470–1525), a handsome Renaissance building with a fine interior. In the adjoining Dominican monastery are two beautiful cloisters with fountains of 1508 and 1633. – 2 km E of La Quercia in **Bagnaia** (alt. 441 m), is the *Villa Lante (15th–16th c.), once the summer residence of the ducal family of that name. In the park are an elegant casino by Vignola, beautiful fountains and fine holm-oaks. – 9 km N of Viterbo is the Roman theatre of *Ferentum* (Italian *Ferento*: 1st c. A.D.).

In the Park of Monsters, Bomarzo

5 km W of Viterbo we come to the little spa establishment of **Bagni di Viterbo** (alt. 258 m). 1 km NE of this, on a flat-topped hill of travertine with a fine view of Viterbo and the Monti Cimini, is the sulphur spring known as the *Bullicame* (alt. 298 m), a pool of clear blue water surrounded by a low wall, constantly effervescing with bubbles of gas. The water of the spring, which is mentioned by Dante ("Inferno", XIV, 79), is still used for medicinal bathing.

One trip which will appeal to children as well as to adults is to the little town of **Bomarzo** (alt. 263 m), picturesquely situated on a high crag above the Tiber valley 23 km NE of Viterbo. In the town is a palace of the Orsini family (16th c.), part of which now serves as the Town Hall. From the terrace in front of the church there is a superb view of the Tiber valley. Outside the town, on the slopes of the hill, is the *Parco dei Mostri* ("Park of Monsters"), a beautiful terraced park with a whole series of monstrous beasts, grotesques and figures of divinities hewn from the local rock in the 16th c.

Volterra

Region: Toscana. – Province: Pisa (PI).
Altitude: 531 m. – Population: 13,000.
Post code: I-56048. – Dialling code: 0588.
(i) **Pro Volterra** and **EPT**, Piazza Priori 16;
tel. 8 61 50.

HOTELS. – *Nazionale*, II, 80 b.; *Etruria*, III, 38 b.

SOUVENIRS. – Articles made of alabaster.

The medieval town of *Volterra, magnificently situated on a hill in the Tuscan uplands between Livorno and Siena, was one of the 12 cities of the Etruscan confederation, under the name of Velathri, when it was three times its present size. In the 3rd c. B.C. it became the Roman municipium of Volaterrae. A free city during the medieval period (to which its finest buildings belong), it

passed under Florentine control in 1361. – Volterra is noted for its alabaster industry, which provides employment for about a third of the population.

SIGHTS. – The central feature of the town is the *Piazza dei Priori*, surrounded by medieval palaces. On the W side of the square the handsome **Palazzo dei Priori** (1208–54), now the Town Hall, has Renaissance coats of arms and two lions on the façade. On the first floor is the frescoed Sala del Consiglio, on the second floor the *Galleria Pittorica*, with a small but good collection of pictures. Opposite the Town Hall is the *Palazzo Pretorio* (13th c.).

Behind the Town Hall, to the W, stands the **Cathedral**, consecrated in 1120 and enlarged in Pisan style in 1254, with a fine interior. Opposite it is the *Baptistery of San Giovanni*, an octagonal structure on a centralised plan (1283). – A little way S, in the circuit of Etruscan *town walls* (7280 m long), is the **Porta all'Arco**, from which there are extensive views. The best preserved section of the walls is 1 km NW below the church of Santa Chiara.

In the eastern part of the old town, at Via Minzoni 11, the *Museo Etrusco Guarnacci houses a rich assemblage of Etruscan material from the town and surrounding area. Particularly notable is its collection of over 600 ash-urns, mostly of alabaster, dating from the late Etruscan period (4th–1st c. B.C.), with curiously

Etruscan gate, Volterra

The Balze, Volterra

foreshortened figures of the dead persons on the lids. – To the E of the museum is the **Citadel** (now a prison), consisting of the irregularly built *Rocca Vecchia* (the "Femmina" or "Woman": 14th c.) to the E and the *Rocca Nuova* (the "Maschio" or "Man": 15th c.) to the W.

Leaving the Piazza dei Priori on Via Ricciarelli, we continue NW past the churches of *San Lino* and *San Francesco* to the *Porta San Francesco*; then past the remains of the Pisan-style façade of the *church of Santo Stefano* (on right) and the *church of Santa Chiara* (on left) to the *church of San Giusto* (18th c.). Between San Giusto and the *Badia San Salvatore*, a Camaldolese abbey founded in 1030, is a deep ravine known as the **Balze* formed by landslides and erosion, which engulfed an older church, some of the monastic buildings and sections of the Etruscan

walls in the 17th c. and is steadily growing wider and deeper.

From the Porta San Francesco we follow the Via Volterrana and in 100 m turn right into Viale Francesco Ferrucci, which runs along the N side of the town walls to the **Roman theatre, probably dating from the time of Augustus, which has been excavated in recent years. The stage of the theatre (which could seat over 5000 spectators) is particularly well preserved.

SURROUNDINGS. – Outside the town, 1 km NE of the centre, stands the monastic **church of San Girólamo** (15th c.), notable for its pictures and its terracotta altarpieces by Giovanni della Robbia.

Volterra to Massa Maríttima (64 km). – Take the road which runs 9 km SW to *Saline di Volterra* (alt. 72 m; Hotel Africa, IV, 13 b.), noted for its salt-works, which supply the whole of Tuscany; then S over the bare uplands of the **Colline Metallífere** (*Poggio di Montieri*, 1051 m), a district of great mineral wealth. – 13·5 km: *Pomarance* (alt. 367 m; pop. 4000; Hotel Il Gioiello, IV, 13 b.), with a large palace of the Counts of Larderel. – 10·5 km: **Larderello** (alt. 390 m; Hotel La Perla, III, 40 b.), lying off the main road on slopes of *Monte Cérboli* (691 m), with the large boric acid works belonging to the Larderel family. The volcanic water vapour which issues from the ground in jets (*soffioni*) deposits the boric acid and other chemicals which it contains in underground reservoirs (*lagoni*) and supplies the motive power for the turbines of an electric power station. The columns of steam can be seen from a long distance away. – From Larderello the road continues past ancient mines (copper pyrites and argentiferous galena) and comes in 31 km to **Massa Maríttima** (alt. 400 m; pop. 7000; hotels: Il Girifalco, III, 33 b.; Duca del Mare, III, 30 b.; etc.), one of the principal towns in the *Maremma*, with a Mining College. The main square of the town is the handsome Piazza Garibaldi, with the principal public buildings. The **Cathedral of San Cerbone (13th c.) has a font by Giroldo da Lugano and (in the crypt) the reliquary of San Cerbone (by Goro di Gregorio da Siena, 1324). In the Romanesque Palazzo Comunale (13th c.) is a five-part altarpiece by Ambrogio Lorenzetti (*c.* 1330). Other features of interest are the Palazzo Pretorio and (in the "Città Nuova") the massive ruins of the 14th c. Fortezza dei Senesi.

Practical Information

Yacht harbour, San Remo

Safety on the Road. Some Reminders for the Holiday Traveller

When to Go

The best times of the year for travelling in Italy are spring (from the end of March to the middle of June) and autumn (from mid September to mid November). At the height of summer the most popular places are the coastal and the hill resorts, which accordingly tend to be overcrowded with visitors at this season. Particularly in the south and in the towns it can become unbearably hot in summer. It should be remembered, too, that during the *Ferragosto* (Assumption) holiday in mid August many museums, restaurants and shops are closed. Towards the end of September the *scirocco*, a warm, moist SE wind can be disagreeable, particularly on the coast and in Tuscany. – In winter the most popular resorts are the skiing areas in the Italian Alps.

Weather

Since Italy extends up to the chain of the Alps in the north but is bathed by the Mediterranean in its central and southern regions, and in addition is broken up by ranges of hills, it is subject to a great diversity of weather conditions. In the north, where the influence of the continental climate of the European mainland is still strongly felt, the summers are warm and the winters are cold, with little rain. Farther south the moderating influence of the sea increases in strength: the summers have little rain, and most of the rain falls during the winter months, which are not unduly cold.

For a fuller account of the Italian climate, see pp. 22–23 of Introduction.

Time

Italy is on Central European Time (one hour ahead of Greenwich Mean Time, six hours ahead of New York time). From early April to the end of September summer time (2 hours ahead of GMT, seven hours ahead of New York time) is in force.

Travel Documents

British and USA citizens require only a **passport** (or the simpler visitor's passport) to enter Italy. **No visa** is required for a stay of up to three months. This applies also to citizens of Australia, Canada, Ireland, New Zealand and many other countries.

British, USA and other national **driving licences** are valid in Italy, but must be accompanied by a translation, obtainable free of charge from the AA, offices of the Automobile Club d'Italia at the Italian frontier and within Italy, and the Italian State Tourist Office. Motorists should also take their car's **registration document**. Foreign cars must display an oval *international distinguishing sign* of the approved type and design. Failure to comply with this regulation is punishable by a heavy on-the-spot fine. **Insurance** is compulsory. It is very desirable to have an *international insurance certificate* ("green card"): although this is not a legal requirement for citizens of EEC countries, Italy prefers visitors to be able to produce a green card when required. Local car rental agencies provide tourists with all the necessary documents. *Warning triangles* are required for all vehicles.

It is desirable also to take out *baggage insurance* cover.

British visitors, like other EEC citizens, are entitled to receive **health care** on the same basis as Italians (including free medical treatment, etc.). You should apply to the Department of Health and Social Security, well before your date of departure, for leaflet SA30 which gives details of reciprocal arrangements for medical treatment and contains an application form for a certificate of entitlement (Form E111). Fuller cover can be obtained by taking out insurance against medical expenses; and non-EEC nationals and USA citizens will of course be well advised to secure insurance cover.

Customs Regulations

Visitors to Italy can take in, without liability to duty, clothing, toilet articles, jewellery and other personal effects (including two cameras and a small movie camera with 10 rolls of film each), and camping equipment and sports gear, together with reasonable quantities of food for the journey. In addition visitors can take in the usual allowances of duty-free alcohol, tobacco and perfume (varying for EEC nationals, USA visitors, other European citizens and overseas residents).

On leaving Italy visitors can take out items they have acquired during their visit up to a maximum total value of 1,000,000 lire. For the export of antiques and modern objets d'art permission must be obtained from the Export Department of the Ministry of Public Education; if export is permitted an appropriate tax will be payable.

Currency

The unit of currency (which circulates also in San Marino) is the Italian **lira** (plural *lire*).

There are *banknotes* for 500, 1000, 2000, 5000, 10,000, 20,000, 50,000 and 100,000 lire and *coins* in denominations of 5, 10, 20, 50, 100, 200 and 500 lire. Small change is sometimes in short supply, and various tokens and vouchers, or even postage stamps or sweets may be offered instead.

There are no restrictions on the import of foreign currency into Italy; but since there may sometimes be a strict control on the export of foreign currency it is desirable to declare any large sum on the appropriate form (Modula V 2) when entering the country. No more than 200,000 lire per person of Italian currency can be taken in. – The export of foreign currency without declaration is permitted only up to the value of 200,000 lire per person. No more than 200,000 lire of Italian currency can be taken out. – It is advisable to take money in the form of travellers' checks or to use a credit card. The principal credit cards are widely accepted.

Postal Rates

Letters (up to 20 g) within Italy 200 lire.

Postcards within Italy 150 lire.

Travel in Italy
Motoring

The Italian *road system* is extensive and is generally good. It consists of motorways, national highways (trunk roads), provincial roads and secondary roads.

Practically all the major towns, particularly in northern Italy, are served by **motorways** (*autostrade* are numbered and prefixed with the letter A), which are mostly toll roads. Among the motorways of most importance to visitors are those from Varese or Como via Milan, Genoa and Pisa to Livorno or Florence; from

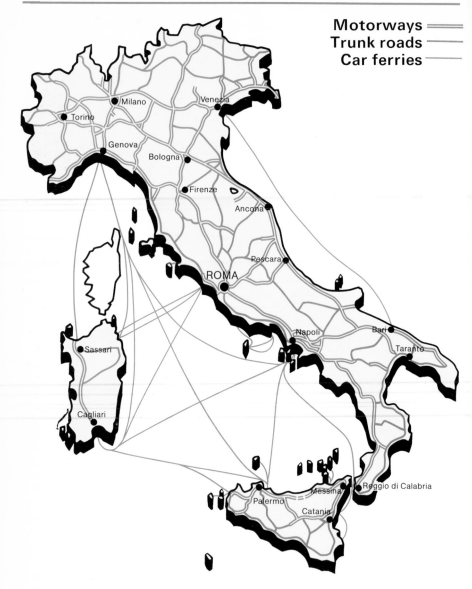

Motorways ══════
Trunk roads ─────
Car ferries ─────

Milan via Parma, Bologna and Florence to Rome, and from there to Naples; and from Bologna to Ravenna or via Rimini, Ancona, Pescara and Bari to Taranto. The motorway from the Brenner (Italian-Austrian frontier) via Bolzano, Trento and Verona links up with the Milan–Bologna motorway at Modena. There is also an important W–E link from Milan via Verona, Padua and Venice to Trieste.

The **national highways** (*strade statali* are numbered and prefixed with the letters S.S.), most of them well built and maintained, also serve important trunk routes. Many of them have names as well as numbers (e.g. Via Aurelia, Via Emilia), and these are often more generally known than the numbers. The provincial .roads (*strade provinciali*), which are un-

numbered, are also of good quality. Local connections are provided by the secondary roads (*strade secondarie*).

Road signs and markings are almost entirely in line with international standards.

Highway code. – As in the rest of continental Europe traffic goes on the right, with overtaking on the left. *Seat belts* must be worn when driving. – *Motorcycle trailers* are prohibited in Italy.

Priority belongs to main roads only if they are marked with the priority sign (a white or yellow square, corner downwards, in a red or black and white frame): otherwise, even at roundabouts (traffic circles), traffic coming from the right has priority. On mountain roads the ascending vehicle has priority. *Vehicles on rails* always have priority.

Drivers moving from one lane to another, even for the purpose of passing, or pulling in to the side of the road must give warning of their intention by the use of their direction indicators. The *horn* must be sounded before passing, outside built-up areas, and before intersections, side roads, blind curves and other danger spots; after dark the headlights should be flashed instead. – In towns of any size the use of the horn is prohibited (indicated by a sign showing a horn with a bar through it or by the words "zona di silenzio"). – On roads or streets with good lighting only sidelights may be used. In tunnels and galleries low-beam headlights must be used. Full-beam headlights may be used only outside built-up areas. Foglights must be used in pairs, together with sidelights. They may only be used in fog or falling snow. Special care is required on account of the numerous cyclists riding without lights or rear reflectors. – On *zebra crossings* pedestrians have absolute priority.

Strict *driving discipline* should be observed by foreign motorists, and the directions of the traffic police (*polizia stradale*) should be exactly complied with. On-the-spot fines for traffic offences are high. A receipt must be obtained. There are heavy penalties (imprisonment and fine) for driving under the influence of drink.

If you are involved in an *accident* you must stop. If the accident involves personal injury medical assistance must be sought for the injured person, and the accident must be reported to the police. Make sure that all essential particulars are noted, especially details concerning third parties, and get the names and addresses of witnesses. It is a good idea to take photographs of the scene, showing the other vehicles involved, their number plates and any background which might help at later enquiries. Fill in the "European accident statement" which you will have received along with your "green card". – Notify your insurance company, by letter if possible, within 24 hours of the accident. If a third party is injured the insurance company or bureau whose address is given on the back of your green card should be notified. – If your car is a total write-off the Italian customs authorities must be informed at once, since otherwise you might be required to pay the full import duty on the vehicle.

The **speed limit** within built-up areas is **50 km p.h./31 m.p.h.** Outside built-up areas the speed limits for private cars vary according to engine capacity, as follows:

Capacity	Nat. highways	Motorways
Up to 600 cc	80 km p.h./50 m.p.h.	90 km p.h./56 m.p.h.
Up to 900 cc	90 km p.h./56 m.p.h.	110 km p.h./69 m.p.h.
Up to 1300 cc	100 km p.h./62 m.p.h.	130 km p.h./80 m.p.h.
Over 1300 cc	110 km p.h./69 m.p.h.	140 km p.h./87 m.p.h.

The same limits apply to cars with trailers. Motorcycles of under 150 cc are not allowed on motorways.

WARNING:
Infringements of these regulations can result in fines of up to £400 ($930) plus a term of imprisonment.

Car Ferries

SERVICE	FREQUENCY	COMPANY
Mainland – Elba		
Piombino – Elba	Daily	Navarma
	Daily	Torremar
Mainland – Sardinia		
Civitavecchia – Cagliari	Daily	Tirrenia
Civitavecchia – Golfo Aranci	Daily	Ital. State Railways
Civitavecchia – Olbia	Daily	Tirrenia
Genoa/Civitavecchia – Porto Torres	3 times weekly	Tirrenia
Genoa – Olbia/Arbatax	Several times weekly	Tirrenia
Livorno – Olbia	Daily	TTE
Naples – Cagliari	Twice weekly	Tirrenia
Mainland – Lipari and Pontine Islands		
Naples – Lipari Islands (Stromboli, Panarea, Renella, S. Marina, Lipari)	Twice weekly	Siremar
Naples – Pontine Islands (Capri, Ischia, Ponza)	Daily	Caremar
Mainland – Sicily		
Genoa/Livorno – Palermo	3 times weekly	Grandi Traghetti
Genoa/Naples – Palermo	4 times weekly	Tirrenia
Naples – Catania/Syracuse	Weekly	Tirrenia
Naples – Palermo	Daily	Tirrenia
Naples/Reggio Calabria – Catania/Syracuse	3 times weekly	Tirrenia
Reggio Calabria – Messina	Daily	Ital. State Railways
Villa S. Giovanni – Messina	Daily	Ital. State Railways
Sicily – Sardinia		
Palermo – Cagliari	Weekly	Tirrenia
Trapani – Cagliari	3 times weekly	Tirrenia
Sicily – Lipari Islands		
Palermo/Messina – Lipari Islands	Weekly	Siremar
Sicily – Malta		
Catania/Syracuse – Malta	3 times weekly	Tirrenia

There are also ferry services from the Italian mainland to Corsica (also from Sardinia), Spain, the Balearics, Tunisia (also from Sicily), Yugoslavia, Greece and Turkey.

Information and booking: see next page.

Warning

Visitors to Italy should keep a careful eye on their property and take sensible precautions against theft, particularly in the larger towns. Handbag snatching and the theft of other portable articles of value such as cameras, binoculars, watches and jewelry, as well as more substantial items, including suitcases, are a constant hazard, and particular care should be taken in public places especially shops, cafés and gas stations; even a car slowing down at traffic lights is a possible target for attack. Cars may be broken into, robbed or stolen if left unattended; trailers and minibuses are particularly vulnerable, but even touring coaches and hired cars with Italian registration are not immune.

Air Services

Italy is linked with the international network of air services by a number of airports, the most important of which are Rome-Fiumicino, Milan and Venice. Direct flights from the United Kingdom, Ireland and USA are operated by Alitalia, British Airways, British Caledonian, Aer Lingus, TWA and Pan American.

There are direct connections (in some cases with intermediate landings) from London to Alghero, Bari, Bologna, Brindisi, Cagliari, Catania, Genoa, Milan, Naples, Palermo, Pisa, Rimini, Rome, Turin, Venice and Trieste; from Manchester to Milan and Rome; from Birmingham to Milan; from Glasgow to Milan; and from Dublin to Rome; from New York to Milan and Rome; from Chicago to Milan and Rome; from Los Angeles to Rome; from Washington to Milan and Rome; from Boston to Milan and Rome; and from Boston to Rome.

There are also numerous *charter flights* to the principal Italian airports during the main holiday season.

The Italian national airline, **Alitalia**, flies both international and Italian domestic routes. Domestic services are also flown by *ATI – Linee Nazionali*, *Itavia* and *Avio Ligure*; services to Sardinia are flown by *Alisarda*.

Rail Services

The Italian railway system, roughly half of it electrified, has a total length of some 16,000 km. Most of it is run by the **Italian State Railways** (*Ferrovie Italiane dello Stato*, FS), but there are also a number of privately run lines, the timetables of which are included in the published timetables of the State Railways.

The State Railways have information bureaux in the larger Italian towns. – International tickets are valid for two months, and allow the journey to be broken as often as desired. Tickets for Italian domestic services are valid for one day for journeys of up to 250 km, two days for journeys of 251–450 km and an additional day for each additional 200 km or part thereof, with a maximum of six days; the journey can be broken as often as desired.

Reduced fares. – Return fares (up to 250 km; between a provincial and a regional capital no limit) 15% reduction; day returns (up to 50 km) and 3-day returns (up to 250 km) 15% reduction; circular tickets (minimum 100 km; valid 30 days, when issued outside Italy 60 days); "travel-at-will" tickets, *biglietti libera circolazione* (obtainable only outside Italy, at certain frontier stations and at a number of major stations within Italy; valid for 8, 15, 21 or 30 days over the whole Italian railway system); kilometric tickets (3000 km) 20% reduction; (reduced-price railcards (valid 3, 6 or 12 months, giving a reduction of 40% on all fares); party tickets (10–24 persons 20% reduction, 25 and over 30% reduction); family tickets (minimum 4 persons; adults 30% off, children 65% off); inter-rail pass (for young people from 10 to 23); rail inclusive tours. – *Children* under 4 travel free; children over 4 and under 12 pay half fare.

Motorail

Visitors travelling by car can shorten the journey to Italy by using one of the car sleeper services from stations in north-western Europe: e.g. Boulogne–Lille–Milan, Paris–Milan, Schaerbeek (Brussels)–Milan, 's Hertogenbosch–Domodossola–Genoa–Milan, 's Hertogenbosch–Chiasso–Milan. Information from Belgian National Railways, 167 Regent Street, London W1 (745 5th Ave., New York, NY); French Railways, 179 Piccadilly, London W1 (610 5th Ave., New York, NY); German Federal Railways, 10 Old Bond Street, London W1 (630 5th Ave., New York, NY).

There are also motorail services within Italy: Milan to Rome, Bari, Brindisi and Villa San Giovanni; Turin to Rome, Bari and Villa San Giovanni; Genoa to Rome; Bolzano to Rome; Bologna to Bari; Rome to Bari and Villa San Giovanni. Some of these services run only in summer. Information from Italian State Railways, 10 Charles II Street, London SW1 (666 5th Ave., New York, NY).

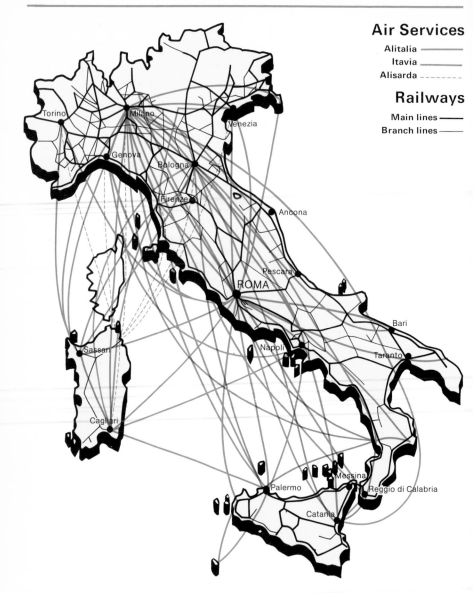

Air Services

Alitalia ————
Itavia ————
Alisarda ‑ ‑ ‑ ‑ ‑

Railways

Main lines ————
Branch lines ————

Buses

Bus services play a major part in public transport, particularly in the more thinly populated uplands regions. They are mostly run by Italian State Railways, together with a number of private companies.

European Bus Services

Euroways (a consortium of four major international travel companies) run a two-day bus service from London to Italy (London–Dover–Paris–Lyons–Turin–Genoa–Milan–Bologna–Florence–Rome). Information and booking: Euroway (tel. 01–462 7733); Express

Coaches Ltd, 8 Park Lane, Croydon, CR9 1DN; National Travel Passenger Enquiries, Victoria Coach Station, London (tel. 01–730 0202).

Europabus (the coach system of the European Railways) runs many long-distance services to Italy and within Italy: e.g. Geneva–Chamonix–Courmayeur–Aosta–St Vincent–Turin; Vienna–Caorle–Lido di Iesolo–Venice; Venice–Padua–Ravenna–Bologna–Florence; Rome–Naples–Pompeii–Sorrento–Positano–Amalfi. Information from British Rail, Hudson Place, London SW1 (tel. 01–834 2727).

Sailing

Boats (with or without motor) can be brought into Italy either by land or by sea without customs documents for a stay not exceeding 6 months. Boats with engines over 3 h.p. (equivalent to a capacity of 98 cc. for a two-stroke engine) must be insured, and there are heavy penalties for failure to observe this requirement. Boats with engines must carry a number plate. A driving licence is not required for craft not exceeding 5 m, with engine not above 20 h.p. and sails not more than 14 sq. m; sailing boats (with auxiliary engine) for sailing within 20 miles of the coast; boats with engines not exceeding 3 BRT inboard or outboard, and not above 20 h.p. for navigation within 20 miles of the coast. Foreigners carrying an "ability document" from their country of origin may sail the craft for which they are qualified.

Information. – *Federazione Italiana Motonautica* (Italian Motorboating Federation), Via Cappuccio 19, I-20123 Milano (tel. 02–87 44 10 and 86 14 92); *Federazione Italiana Vela* (Italian Sailing Federation), Porticciolo Duca degli Abruzzi, I-16126 Genova (tel. 010–29 83 18).

Language

The Italian language is a direct continuation of Latin, to which it is closer than any other of the Romance languages, and has preserved something of the rotundity and monumentality of the Latin oratorical style. Numerous dialects developed, largely in consequence of the earlier political fragmentation of Italy, and among these *Tuscan* became accepted as the standard language, created by the great writers of the 13th and 14th c., particularly Dante. The language of the educated Florentine ranks as the purest form of Italian.

In the larger towns and the main holiday resorts the staff of hotels, restaurants, shops, etc., usually have some English.

Pronunciation. – The stress is usually on the second-last syllable. Where it falls on the last syllable this is always indicated by an accent (perché, città). Where it falls on the third-last syllable an accent is not officially required except in certain doubtful cases, but is sometimes shown as an aid to pronunciation (e.g. in place-names in this Guide). – *Consonants: c* before *e* or *i* is pronounced *ch*, otherwise *k; g* before *e* or *i* is pronounced like *j*, otherwise hard as in "go"; *gn* and *gl* are like *n* and *l* followed by a consonant *y* (roughly as in "onion" and "million"); *h* is silent; *qu* as in English; *r* is rolled; *s* is unvoiced (as in "so") at the beginning of a word before a vowel but has a *z* sound between vowels and before *b, d, g, l, m, n* and *v; sc* before *e* or *i* is pronounced *sh; z* is either *dz* or *ts*. – *Vowels* are pronounced in the "continental" fashion, without the diphthongisation normal in English; *e* is never silent. The vowels in a diphthong are pronounced separately (ca-usa, se-i).

Numbers

0	zero	21	ventuno
1	uno, una, un, un'	22	ventidue
2	due	30	trenta
3	tre	31	trentuno
4	quattro	40	quaranta
5	cinque	50	cinquanta
6	sei	60	sessanta
7	sette	70	settanta
8	otto	80	ottanta
9	nove	90	novanta
10	dieci	100	cento
11	undici	101	cento uno
12	dodici	153	centocinquantatre
13	tredici	200	duecento
14	quattordici	300	trecento
15	quindici	400	quattrocento
16	sedici	500	cinquecento
17	diciasette	600	seicento
18	diciotto	700	settecento
19	diciannove	800	ottocento
20	venti	900	novecento
		1000	mille
		5000	cinque mila
		1,000,000	un milione

Ordinals

1st	primo (prima)
2nd	secondo
3rd	terzo
4th	quarto
5th	quinto
6th	sesto
7th	settimo
8th	ottavo
9th	nono
10th	decimo
20th	ventesimo/ vigesimo
100th	centesimo

Fractions

$\frac{1}{2}$	un mezzo (mezza)
$\frac{1}{4}$	un quarto
$\frac{1}{10}$	un decimo

Everyday expressions

Good morning, good day!	Buon giorno!
Good evening!	Buona sera!
Goodbye!	Arrivederci!
Yes, no	Si, no
I beg your pardon	Scusi!
Please	Per favore
Thank you (very much)	(Molte) grazie
Not at all! (You're welcome!)	Prego
Excuse me (e.g. when passing in front of someone)	Con permesso!
Do you speak English?	Parla inglese?
A little, not much	Un poco, non molto
I do not understand	Non capisco
What is the Italian for . . . ?	Come si dice . . . in italiano?
What is the name of this church?	Come si chiama questa chiesa?
The cathedral	Il Duomo
The square	La piazza
The palace	Il palazzo
The theatre	Il teatro
Where is the Via . . . ?	Dov'è la via . . . ?
Where is the road (motorway) to . . . ?	Dov'è la strada (l'autostrada) per . . . ?
Left, right	A sinistra, a destra
Straight ahead	Sempre diritto
Above, below	Sopra, sotto
When is (it) open?	Quando è aperto?
How far is it?	Quanto è distante?
Today	Oggi
Yesterday	Ieri
The day before yesterday	L'altro ieri
Tomorrow	Domani
Have you any rooms?	Ci sono cámere líbere?
I should like . . .	Vorrei avere . . .
A room with bath (shower)	Una cámera con bagno (doccia)
With full board	Con pensione completa
What does it cost?	Qual'è il prezzo? Quanto costa?
All-in (price)	Tutto compreso
That is too dear	È troppo caro
Bill, please! (to a waiter)	Cameriere, il conto!
Where are the lavatories?	Dove si tróvano i gabinetti?
Wake me at six	Può svegliarmi alle sei
Where is there a doctor (dentist)?	Dove sta un médico (dentista)?
A hospital	Un ospedale
A pharmacy	Una farmacia
First aid	Pronto soccorso

Road signs

Alt!	Stop
Attenzione (attenti) al treno, alle mine	Caution – train, blasting
Caduta sassi (massi)	Beware of falling rock
Deviazione	Diversion
Divieto di sosta	Stopping prohibited
Incrocio	Road intersection
Lavori in corso	Road works
Passaggio al livello	Level crossing
Rallentare	Slow
Sbarrato	Road closed
Senso proíbito	No entry
Senso único	One-way street
Svolta pericolosa	Dangerous bend
Tenere la destra	Keep to the right

Tránsito interrotto	No thoroughfare
Veícolo al passo	Dead slow
Velocità non superiore ai 15 km/h	Speed limit 15 km p.h.
Vietato (proíbito) il tránsito – per tutti i veícoli pesanti	No entry – for heavy vehicles

Travelling by train

All aboard!	In carrozza!
Arrival	Arrivo
Change (trains)	Cambiare treno
Departure	Partenza
Fare	Prezzo, importo
Guard	Capotreno
Halt	Fermata
Line	Binario
Luggage, baggage	Bagagli
No smoking	Vietato fumare
Platform	Marciapiedi
Porter	Portabagagli, facchino
Smoking compartment	Fumatori
Station	Stazione
Stop	Sosta
Ticket	Biglietto
Ticket-collector	Conduttore
Ticket-window	Sportello
Waiting room	Sala d'aspetto

At the post office

Address	Indirizzo
Air mail	Posta aérea
Express	Espresso
Letter	Léttera
Mail-box	Buca delle léttere
Postcard	Cartolina
Poste restante	Fermo posta
Postman	Postino
Registered letter	Léttera raccomandata
Stamp	Francobollo
Telegram	Telegramma
Telephone	Teléfono

Geographical, architectural, etc., terms

Abbazia	Abbey
Albergo	Inn, hotel
Arcivescovado	Archbishop's palace
Bacino	Basin; dock
Badia	Abbey
Baluardo	Rampart, bastion
Basílica	Basilica (referring either to the architectural form of a church or a Roman secular building or to the special ecclesiastical status of a particular church)
Battistero	Baptistery
Belvedere	Belvedere, viewpoint
Biblioteca	Library
Borgo	Small town, village; quarter (of town)
Borsa	Exchange
Broletto	Town hall
Campo	Field, ground, camp
Campo santo	Cemetery
Casa	House
Cascata	Waterfall, cascade

Castello	Castle
Cava	Quarry, mine
Certosa	Charterhouse, Carthusian house
Chiesa	Church
Chiostro	Cloister
Cima	Summit, peak
Cimitero	Cemetery
Colle	Hill
Corso	Street (usually a main street)
Cortile	Courtyard
Duomo	Cathedral
Faro	Lighthouse, beacon
Fiume	River
Fonte	Spring, fountain
Giardino	Garden
Gola	Gorge, defile
Golfo	Gulf, bay
Grotta	Cave, grotto
Isola	Island
Lago (*plural* laghi)	Lake
Latomía	Stone-quarry (*hist.*)
Loggia (*plural* logge)	Loggia
Lungomare	Seafront avenue, promenade
Mare	Sea
Mercato	Market
Molo	Breakwater, pier, quay
Monte di pietà	(Municipal) pawnshop
Museo	Museum
Museo cívico	Municipal museum
Museo lapidário	Museum of inscriptions, etc., on stone
Naviglio	Canal, waterway
Orto	Garden, orchard
Ospedale	Hospital
Palazzo	Palace
Passeggiata	Walk, promenade
Passo	Pass; strait
Piana, piano	Plain, plateau
Piazza	Square
Piazzale	Square (often on the outskirts of a town)
Pinacoteca	Picture gallery
Pineta	Pinewood
Podestà	Mayor
Ponte	Bridge
Porta	Gate, door
Porto	Port, harbour
Prefettura	Prefecture
Rifugio	Mountain hut
Rio	Stream, river
Rione	Quarter (of a town)
Rocca	Fortress, castle; rock
Santuario	Sanctuary, shrine
Scala	Staircase
Scalo	Wharf, landing-place; port of call
Spiaggia	Seashore, beach
Stagno	Pond, pool
Strada	Road, street
Tempio (*plural* templi)	Temple
Tenuta	Estate, holding, farm
Terme	Baths (thermal, Roman)
Torre	Tower
Torrente	(Mountain) stream
Traforo	Tunnel
Vescovado	Bishop's palace
Via	Street, road
Viale	Avenue
Vico	Narrow street, lane; village, hamlet
Vícolo	Alley, passage
Zecca	Mint (for coining money)

Accommodation

Hotels and Pensions

The hotels in the higher categories in large towns and holiday centres offer the usual international standards of comfort and amenity, but in the more remote areas the accommodation available will often be of a more modest standard. The Italian Automobile Club (ACI) and the AGIP oil company have built numbers of *autostelli* and *motels*. In the larger towns and in spas and seaside resorts there are numerous pensions (*pensioni*) or guesthouses.

The **hotels** (*alberghi*, singular *albergo*) are officially classified in five categories (luxury, I, II, III and IV), the **pensions** in three (I, II and III). Hotel tariffs vary considerably according to season, and are substantially higher in large towns and popular holiday areas than in the rest of the country.

The rates given in the following table (in lire) are based on information given in the Italian State Tourist Office's list of hotels, "Alberghi d'Italia". Given the current rate of inflation, increases in the rates are to be expected.

Category	Single room Rate for 1 person	Double room Rate for 2 persons
Hotels		
L	15,000–80,000	24,000–100,000
I	10,000–45,000	12,000– 70,000
II	6000–25,000	10,000– 33,000
III	5000–15,000	6000– 25,000
IV	3000–12,000	4000– 20,000
Pensions		
PI	6000–18,000	10,000– 25,000
PII	4000–13,000	6000– 20,000
PIII	3000–10,000	4000– 15,000

Information on *holiday villages, apartments* and *bungalows* and on *holidays on the farm* can be obtained from the Italian State Tourist Office.

Youth Hostels

Youth Hostels (*ostelli per la gioventù*) provide accommodation at very reasonable prices, particularly for younger visitors. Priority is given to young people under 30 travelling on foot. If the hostel is full the period of stay is limited to 3 nights. Advance booking is advisable during the main holiday season and for groups of more than five. Hostellers are not allowed to use their own sleeping bags: the hire charge for a sleeping bag is included in the overnight charge. Foreign visitors must produce a membership card of their national youth hostel association.

Information: *Associazione Italiana Alberghi per la Gioventù*, Palazzo della Civiltà del Lavoro, Quadrato della Concordia, I-00144 Roma-EUR (tel. 5 91 37 02 and 5 91 37 58).

Camping and Caravanning

Italy has large numbers of good **camping sites**, most of them in the Alto Adige and the Aosta valley, on the North Italian lakes and on the coasts of the Adriatic, Tyrrhenian and Ligurian Seas. Lists of camping sites are published by the Italian State Tourist Office and the Federazione Italiana del Campeggio. Campers who prefer to find a site for themselves should seek permission from the owner of the land.

Information: *Centro Nazionale per Campeggiatori Stranieri*, Casella Postale 649, 1-50100 Firenze (tel. 8 87 96 41).

Food and Drink

Gastronomically Italy takes a high place among the countries of Europe. Its cuisine is notable both for its variety and its excellence. – Lunch is usually served in Italian restaurants from 12 noon onwards, though in Rome and the southern parts of the country it tends to be taken considerably later. Dinner is rarely eaten before 7, and 8 o'clock is widely regarded as the "normal" time.

Apart from the numerous pasta dishes, served in infinite variety and with a wide range of different sauces or dressings, the Italian menu includes numerous excellent fish dishes. Much use is made of olive oil in cooking. The famous Italian pizza was originally made of bread dough spread with tomatoes and herbs – a simple, cheap and tasty form of bread which is sold in slices; the numerous variations with cheese, salami, ham, mushrooms, artichoke hearts, etc., developed later with increasing prosperity, particularly in northern Italy and under the influence of tourism. The standard drinks with all meals are wine and water. Beer is found everywhere, both the light Italian beer and foreign brands (*birra éstera*), particularly German, Danish and Dutch.

Breakfast is a meal of little consequence to the Italians. The hotels, however, have mostly adapted to northern European habits and provide bread, butter and jam – plus eggs, sausage or cheese if required – to accompany the morning cup of coffee. *Lunch* usually consists of several courses. Spaghetti and other forms of pasta (and in the north rice dishes) are merely a substitute for soup – hence the term *primo*, "first course" – and not a main dish. They are often preceded by an *antipasto* (hors d'œuvre). The pasta is followed by the *secondo* (second course), a meat or fish dish, and this in turn is often followed by cheese and fruit or a sweet of some kind. Lunch always ends with a cup of *espresso* (strong black coffee), which some connoisseurs prefer *corretto* – "corrected" by the addition of grappa (Italian brandy) or cognac. The morning cup of coffee is usually *cappuccino* (with foaming hot milk). The evening meal is usually a substantial one.

> **WARNING: Meals in hotels and restaurants**
>
> Legislation introduced in March 1980 provides for a special numbered receipt to be issued indicating the cost of various services obtained and the total charge after adding VAT.
>
> The consumer must ensure that this receipt (*ricevute fiscale*) is issued as spot checks outside restaurants will be made – both the restaurateur and the **consumer** will be liable to an on-the-spot fine if the receipt cannot be produced.

Reading an Italian Menu
(lista, carta)

The table. – Table-setting *coperto*; spoon *cucchiaio*; teaspoon *cucchiaino*; knife *coltello*; fork *forchetta*; plate *piatto*; glass *bicchiere*; cup *tazza*; napkin *tovagliolo*; corkscrew *cavatappi*. – Breakfast *prima colazione*; lunch *pranzo*; dinner *cena*.

Hors d'œuvre (antipasti): anchovies, sardines, olives, artichokes, mushrooms, radishes, sausage, ham, eggs, salads of seafood or with mayonnaise, etc. – *Soups:* *brodo* broth; *consommé* consommé, clear soup; *minestra* soup with pasta, vegetables, etc.; *minestrone* thick vegetable soup; *stracciatella* broth with beaten eggs; *zuppa di (pesce*, etc.) (fish, etc.) soup. – *Pasta (farinacei):* *agnolotti* a kind of ravioli with meat stuffing; *cannelloni* large rolls of pasta; *capellini* long thread-like spaghetti; *cappelletti* "little hats", a form of ravioli with various stuffings; *fettuccine* egg noodles; *gnocchi* a form of ravioli; *lasagne* broad strips of pasta, often green; *maccheroni* maccaroni; *panzotti* small packets of pasta with cheese and spinach stuffing; *pasta asciutta* the general term for all kinds of pasta; *ravioli* ravioli; *rigatoni* short macaroni; *spaghetti* spaghetti; *vermicelli* vermicelli (threadlike spaghetti). – *Risotto* risotto; *riso* rice. – *Polenta* boiled maize flour (solid when cold). – *Pizza.* – *Eggs (uova):* *alla coque, al guscio* soft-boiled; *sode* hard-boiled; *al piatto* fried; *frittata* omelette. – *Bread (pane):* *panini* rolls; *grissini* thin sticks of rusk-like bread.

Fish (pesce) and seafood (frutti di mare). – *Acciughe* anchovies; *anguilla* eel; *aragosta* lobster; *aringa* herring; *baccalà* dried cod; *calamari* cuttlefish; *carpa, carpone* carp; *céfalo* mullet; *cernia* grouper; *cozze* mussels; *dátteri* date-shells; *déntice* dentex; *fritto misto mare* mixed fried fish; *gamberetti* shrimps; *gámberi* prawns; *gamberoni* large prawns; *granchi* crabs; *luccio* pike; *merluzzo* hake; *moscardino* curled octopus; *múscoli* mussels; *nasello* hake; *orata* gilt-head bream; *óstriche* oysters; *pescatrice* frogfish; *pesce pérsico* perch; *pesce spada* swordfish; *pesce ragno* greater weever; *polpo* octopus; *razza* skate; *riccio marino* sea-urchin; *rombo* turbot; *salmone* salmon; *sarde* pilchards; *sardine* sardines; *scampi* scampi; *sfoglia, sógliola* sole; *sgombro* mackerel; *spígola* bass; *storione* sturgeon; *tonno* tunny; *triglia* red mullet; *trota* trout; *vóngole* palourdes; *zuppa di pesce* fish soup. – *Lumache* snails. – *Rane* frogs' thighs.

Meat (carne). – Animals: *abbacchio* spring lamb; *agnello* lamb; *bue* ox; *capretto* kid; *coniglio* rabbit; *maiale* pig; *manzo* bullock; *montone* ram; *porchetto, porcello* sucking pig; *vitello* calf (older). – *Cuts of meat: animelle* sweetbreads; *cervello* brain; *bistecca* steak; *coda* tail; *coscia* haunch, leg; *cuore* heart; *costoletta, costata* cutlet; *fégato* liver; *filetto* fillet; *lingua* tongue; *lombata* loin; *ossobuco* shin of veal; *paillard* veal fillet; *petto* breast; *piccata* sliced veal; *piede, piedino* foot; *polmone* lung; *rognoni* kidneys; *scaloppa* scallop, schnitzel; *spezzatino* veal goulash; *testa, testina* head; *trippa* tripe; *zampone* pig's trotter. – *Methods of cooking: arrosto* roast; *bollito* boiled; *bollito misto* mixed boiled meat; *cibreo* ragout; *ben cotto* well done; *ai ferri* grilled; *al girarrosto* roasted on the spit; *alla griglia* grilled; *all'inglese* underdone; *lesso* boiled; *pasticcio* pie; *polpette* rissoles; *al sangue* rare; *stracotto, stufato, stufatino* steamed, stewed. – *Salame* slicing sausage; *salsiccia* small sausage. – *Ham: prosciutto crudo* raw; *cotto* boiled; *coppa* cured shoulder of pork; *pancetta* stomach of pork. – *Affettato* cold meat. – *Game (selvaggina): camoscio* chamois; *capriolo* roe-buck; *cervo* deer (venison); *cinghiale* wild pig; *fagiano* pheasant; *faraona* guinea fowl; *lepre* hare; *pérnice, starna* partridge; *piccione* pigeon; *tordo* thrush. – *Poultry (pollame): ánitra* duck; *gallinaccio, dindo, tacchino* turkey; *oca* goose.

Vegetables (verdure, legumi) and garnishings (guarnizioni). – *Aspáragi* asparagus; *barbaforte* horse-radish; *bróccoli* broccoli; *carciofi* artichokes; *cardoni* cardoons; *cavolfiore* cauliflower; *cávolo* cabbage; *cavolini di Bruxelles* Brussels sprouts; *cipolle* onions; *crudezze* raw vegetable salads; *fagioli* haricot beans; *fagiolini* French beans; *fave* broad beans; *finocchio* fennel; *funghi* mushrooms; *lenticchie* lentils; *melanzane* aubergines; *patate* potatoes; *peperoni* peppers; *piselli* peas; *pomidori, pomodori* tomatoes; *ráfano* (horse-)radish; *ravanelli* small radishes; *sédano* celery; *spinaci* spinach; *zucchini* courgettes. – *Insalata* salad. – *Sauces: salsa al burro* butter sauce; *salsa alle noci* walnut sauce (made of ground walnuts and cream); *salsa bolognese* tomato sauce with meat; *salsa napoletana* tomato sauce; *salsa verde* parsley sauce with oil, egg, spices and capers; *maionese* mayonnaise; *pesto alla genovese* green basil sauce with pine nuts, parmesan cheese and garlic. – *Condiments: aceto* vinegar; *aglio* garlic; *burro* butter; *mostarda* candied fruit in mustard sauce; *olio* oil; *pepe* pepper; *sale* salt; *sénape* mustard; *sugo* gravy, juice.

Desserts (dessert, dolce). – *Bavarese* a mousse of cream and egg; *budino* pudding; *cassata* tart, cake; *frittata* omelette; *gelato* ice; *macedonia* fruit salad; *panettone* sweet cake; *torta* tart; *zabaglione* egg-flip with wine. – *Fruit (frutta): anguria, cocomero* watermelon; *arancia* orange; *ciliege* cherries; *fichi* figs; *frágole* strawberries; *frutta secca* dried fruit; *lamponi* raspberries; *limone* lemon; *mándorle* almonds; *mela*

Cassata siciliana

apple; *melone* melon; *néspola* medlar; *noci* walnuts; *pera* pear; *pesca* peach; *pistacchi* pistachios; *pompelmo* grapefruit; *popone* melon; *prugne* plums; *uva* grapes; *uve secche* raisins. – *Cheese (formaggio): Bel Paese* (soft); *Brancolino* (goat's-milk); *Gorgonzola* (blue-veined); *Mozzarella* (moist curd cheese); *Parmigiano* (parmesan); *Provolone* (mellow); *Pecorino* (ewe's-milk); *Ricotta* (soft, unsalted); *Romano* (ewe's-milk); *Stracchino* (with mould but without blue veins).

Table wine (vino da pasto) is served in carafes. – *Nero, rosso* red; *bianco* white; *secco* dry; *asciutto* very dry; *abboccato, amabile* slightly sweet; *dolce, pastoso* sweet; *vino del paese* local wine; *un litro* a litre, *mezzo litro* half a litre, *un quarto* a quarter litre; *un bicchiere* a glass. – Older wines and wines of high quality are served in the normal way in corked and labelled bottles.

Other popular drinks *(bevande)* are *birra* beer, *acqua minerale* mineral water, *aranciata* orangeade, *limonata* lemonade, *succo (di . . .) . . .* juice and *spremuta (di . . .)* freshly pressed fruit juice.

The Wines of Italy

1 Piedmont, Aosta valley, Liguria
Barbera d'Asti: ruby-red, dry.
Barbera d'Alta: ruby-red, dry.
Barbera del Monferrato: deep red, dry to slightly sweet, semi-sparkling.
Nebbiolo d'Alba: deep ruby-red, dry or slightly sweet, semi-sparkling.
Moscato d'Asti (various kinds): straw-coloured to golden yellow, sweet.
Barolo: garnet-red, dry, full and fragrant.
Gattinara: garnet-red, dry.
Carema: garnet-red, soft, velvety and full-bodied.
Barbaresco: garnet-red, dry, full-bodied.

2 Lombardy
Moscato dell'Oltrepò Pavese: light yellow, aromatic.
Barbera dell'Oltrepò Pavese: ruby-red, dry.
Pinot dell'Oltrepò Pavese: greenish yellow, dry, aromatic.
Riesling dell'Oltrepò Pavese: light yellow, dry.
Valtellina: deep red, dry to very dry.

3 Trentino – Alto Adige
Santa Maddalena: ruby-red to garnet-red, full, velvety.
Lagarina (dark red): deep red, full, soft, velvety.

The Wine-Growing Regions of Italy

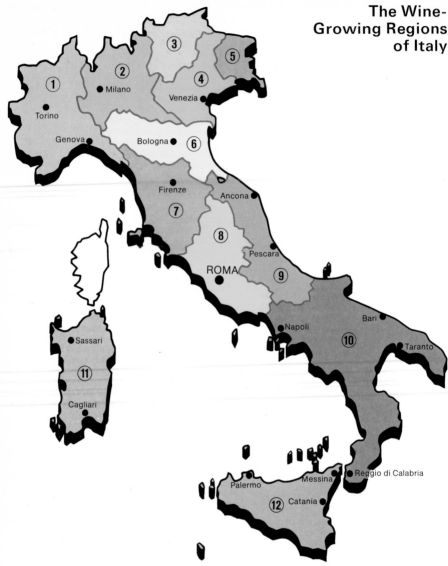

Terlaner: greenish yellow to golden yellow, dry, fresh.
Cabernet: ruby-red, dry, full.
Teroldego: light red to ruby-red, dry.

4 Venetia
Valpolicella: ruby-red to garnet-red, dry to semi-sweet, full-bodied, well rounded.
Bardolino: light red, dry, well rounded.
Soave: straw-coloured to greenish yellow, dry, well rounded.

5 Friuli – Venezia Giulia
Grave del Friuli: red and white, made from different varieties of grape.
Isonzo: white, several kinds made from Tokay, Malvasia, Riesling or Weissburgunder grapes; red, several kinds made from Merlot or Cabernet grapes.

6 Emilia-Romagna
Lambrusco: ruby-red, semi-sparkling; several kinds, dry to sweet.
Albano di Romagna: straw-coloured to golden yellow, dry to semi-sweet.
Sangiovese di Romagna: ruby-red, dry, well rounded.

7 Tuscany
Chianti: ruby-red to garnet-red, dry, well rounded.
Vernaccia di San Gimignano: light yellow, dry, well rounded.

8 Umbria, Latium
Colli Albani: straw-coloured, dry to slightly sweet.
Frascati: straw-coloured, soft, velvety, semi-sweet to sweet (several varieties).
Est Est Est (Montefiascone): straw-coloured, full, slightly sweet.
Orvieto: light yellow to straw-coloured, dry.

9 Marche, Abruzzi
Verdicchio dei Castelli di Jesi: straw-coloured, dry, well rounded.
Montepulciano d'Abruzzo: deep ruby-red, dry, soft.
Bianchello del Metauro: straw-coloured, dry, fresh.

10 Campania, Apulia, Calabria, Basilicata
Ischia: red and white, several kinds.
San Severo: straw-coloured, fresh and well rounded; ruby-red, dry, full-bodied.

The Barolo vineyards, Serralonga d'Alba

Locorotondo: greenish yellow to straw-coloured, dry, pleasant.
Rossa Barletta: ruby-red, dry, well rounded.

11 Sardinia
Cannonau: ruby-red, dry to slightly sweet, pleasant.
Monica di Sardegna: light ruby-red, dry, aromatic.
Nuragus: light straw-coloured, dry, soft.

12 Sicily
Etna: red and white, several kinds.
Marsala: the famous dessert wine, amber-yellow, full-bodied, dry or sweet.

The Language of the Wine Label

There is hardly any part of Italy where wine is not produced on a greater or lesser scale. There are innumerable local wines, usually drunk only in the immediate area where they are grown and as a rule excellent of their kind; for they are mostly still made by the old natural methods, since any special method of treatment is not worth anyone's while. In addition to these wines for everyday drinking there are also wines of high quality which fully repay the additional effort put into their production.

Under the Wine Law of 1963 – not yet fully in force in all regions – Italian wines must satisfy specified requirements to qualify for certain statutory designations.

Denominazione semplice, the lowest grade, is the mark of a good table wine. No specific standards of quality are prescribed.

Denominazione di origine controllata, the next grade, means that the wine comes from an officially recognised wine-growing area and meets defined quality standards. Such wines must bear a special DOC label.

Denominazione controllata e garantita, the highest grade, is granted only to wines of fine quality made by particular producers. Such wines must be bottled by the producer or some other recognised agency and must carry a State seal guaranteeing the bottling.

The names on the wine label are not necessarily very informative about the nature of the wine: they may be place-names or varieties of grape, but they are often invented names or brand-names. It is not uncommon to find red and white wines of quite different characters being sold under the same name.

Manners and Customs

Visitors to Italy, or any other foreign country, can do much to establish friendly relations with the inhabitants of the country by tactful behaviour and a readiness to adjust to local manners and customs. Those who observe the forms of politeness which come naturally to Italians of all classes will always find a ready and courteous response: brusqueness and impatience, on the other hand, will always create an unfavourable impression on even the humblest of Italians, with their strong sense of human equality. – The former strict rules about dress are now much relaxed; but appropriate clothing should always be worn in churches. – Particularly in large cities and in the south visitors should keep a watchful eye on their property and take sensible precautions against theft. it cannot be stressed too strongly that all valuables should be removed from a parked car, even if it is parked in a supervised car park or a lock-up garage.

If you lose traveller's checks or a bank card or credit card you should inform the bank or other agency concerned immediately by telegram so that they can stop payment.

Guides (*guide,* singular *la guida*) can be obtained through the local tourist information office, and are often to be found waiting for visitors at the main tourist sights. With the information and the plans given in this Guide, however, a guide can usually be dispensed with. Visitors who want to engage a guide should enquire about his charge and in case of doubt ask to be shown the official tariff (*la tariffa*).

Tipping. – The tip (*mancia*) to a chambermaid, porter, etc., should be at the rate of at least 500 lire per day or per service. For a cloakroom attendant or the person who opens up a church a tip of 200 lire is adequate; rather more (200–500 lire), according to circumstances and the time involved, for someone who accompanies you to a particular place or switches on the light in a dark building. Services which are unsolicited and undesired need not be remunerated.

Bathing Beaches

See map, p. 347

See map, p. 347

1 Duino
A small rocky beach with gravel and concreted areas. Nearby are the shingle beaches, each 200 m long, of *Sistiana* (to the SE) and *Le Ginestre*. There is a well-kept little shingle beach on the W side of Pantano Bay.
Unsuitable for children.

2 Grado
A beach of clean white sand 3 km long and up to 70 m wide, with a very gentle slope. To the W is another sandy beach, less well kept.
Good for children.

3 Lignano
A very well-kept beach of fine sand, 4 km long, with a gentle slope, at *Sabbiadoro*; and good sandy beaches at *Riviera* and *Pineta*.
All the Lignano beaches are good for children.

4 Bibione
Beach of fine sand, 8 km long and up to 300 m wide, with a very gentle slope; certain parts well maintained.
Good for children.

5 Caorle
Sandy beach, fully 2 km long, reasonably well kept, at *Spiaggia di Ponente*. To the NE of this is the 2 km long beach of *Spiaggia di Levante*. To the SW, beyond the mouth of the Livenza, is a sandy beach 3 km long, not yet developed.
All beaches suitable for children.

6 Eraclea Mare
Sandy beach, 6 km long and up to 100 m wide in places; parts untidy and undeveloped.
Not all suitable for children.

7 Lido di Iésolo
Beach of fine sand 16 km long and up to 200 m wide in places, gently sloping, almost all well kept.
Good for children.

8 Lido di Venezia
An old-established and famous resort with a gently sloping beach of fine sand fully 4 km long and up to 300 m wide; of variable quality, untidy in places, but all suitable for children.

9 Chioggia
Beach of fine sand over 6 km long and up to 500 m wide, with a very gentle slope, at *Sottomarina*. Reasonably well kept.
Good for children.

10 Volano
Well-kept, flat sandy beach fully 1 km long.
Good for children.

11 Lido delle Nazioni
Gently sloping beach of fine sand 3 km long and up to 100 m wide.
Good for children.

12 Lido di Pomposa
Narrow beach of fine sand 2 km long, usually overcrowded.
Not much room for children.

13 Porto Garibaldi
Well-kept, gently sloping beach of fine sand fully 1 km long and up to 100 m wide.
Good for children.

14 Lido degli Estensi
Well-kept, gently sloping beach of fine sand over 2 km long and up to 150 m wide.
Good for children.

15 Marina Romea
Gently sloping beach of fine sand 2·5 km long and up to almost 100 m wide; untidy in places.
Suitable for children.

16 Marina di Ravenna
Gently sloping sandy beach almost 4 km long and 50 m wide; only parts well kept.
Suitable for children.

17 Milano Maríttima
Gently sloping beach of fine sand 3 km long and 60 m wide; very well kept.
Good for children.

18 Cervia
Well-kept, gently sloping beach of fine sand 1·5 km long and 60 m wide.
Good for children.

19 Cesenático
Well-kept, gently sloping beach of fine sand, fully 2 km long and 100 m wide, at *Zadina Pineta*. To the S of this are *Spiaggia di Ponente* and *Spiaggia di Levante*, respectively 1 km and 2 km long and up to 150 m wide; both well kept, with a gentle slope and fine sand.
All three good for children.

20 Bellaria
Well-kept, gently sloping beach of fine sand 2·5 km long and up to 50 m wide.
Suitable for children.

21 Igea Marina
Well-kept beach of fine sand fully 3 km long and up to 50 m wide.
Little room for children.

22 Rimini
An old-established resort with a very well-kept, gently sloping beach of fine sand almost 4 km long and up to 120 m wide. Continuation to the NW to *Torre Pedrera* (7 km) and SE to *Miramare* (3 km); both well kept but much narrower.
All suitable for children.

23 Riccione
Beach of fine sand over 6 km long and up to 150 m wide; most of it well kept and with a gentle slope.
Suitable for children.

24 Misano Adriático
Sandy beach fully 2 km long and up to 70 m wide; most of it gently sloping and well kept.
Suitable for children.

25 Cattólica
Well-kept beach of fine sand 3 km long, gently sloping; narrow and always overcrowded.
Little room for children.

The beach, Carrara; in the background the Alpi Apuane

26 Pésaro
Beach of fine sand fully 1 km long at *Spiaggia di Ponente* (to NW); also beach of fine sand 2·5 km long at *Spiaggia di Levante* (to SE); both flat and well kept.
Suitable for children.

27 Fano
Beach of fine sand 500 m long at *Spiaggia di Ponente* (to NW); also beach 200 m long at *Spiaggia Arzilla*; and gravel beach 1 km long at *Spiaggia Sassonia* (to SE).
All well kept and suitable for children.

28 Senigallia
Well-kept sandy beach 5 km long and up to 75 m wide at *Spiaggia di Levante* (to SE); also beach 1 km long and up to 50 m wide, less well kept at *Spiaggia di Ponente* (to NW).
Both gently sloping and suitable for children.

29 Numana
Small and very narrow gravel beach of *Numana Alta*, steeply sloping; well kept. To the S is another steep gravel beach 2 km long.
Not really suitable for children.

30 Porto Recanati
Shingle beach, steeply sloping, 2·5 km long and up to 50 m wide; reasonably well kept.
Care required with children.

31 Civitanova Marche
Well-kept sandy beach to S, 2·5 km long and up to 50 m wide; also sandy beach to N, 1 km long and up to 50 m wide; both steeply sloping.
Care required with children.

32 Grottammare
Flat sandy beach, fairly narrow, 3·5 km long; not well kept.
Suitable for children.

33 San Benedetto del Tronto
Well-kept beach of fine sand SE of harbour, 2 km long and more than 100 m wide. Suitable for children.
Smaller and narrow beach NW of harbour not so well recommended.

34 Alba Adriática
Gently sloping beach of fine sand 2·5 km long and 100 m wide; condition varies.
Good for children.

35 Roseto degli Abruzzi
Narrow sandy beach, gently sloping, 4 km long; condition varies.
Suitable for children.

36 Silvi Marina
Gently sloping sandy beach 5·5 km long and almost 100 m wide; condition varies.
Suitable for children.

37 Pescara
A total of 6 km of beaches of fine sand, average width 50 m, gently sloping; mostly well kept.
Good for children.

38 Ortona
Small beach of fine sand within town, *Lido Saraceni*. Narrow but clean beach of sand and shingle, 2 km long, at *Riccio*, 5 km NW of Ortona.

39 Marina di Vasto
Gently sloping beach of fine sand fully 5 km long and up to 100 m wide; condition varies.
Suitable for children.

40 Rodi Gargánico
Gently sloping sandy beaches to W (3 km long, up to 50 m wide) and E (1 km long, up to 50 m wide) of town; little maintenance.
Suitable for children.

41 Vieste
Apart from the narrow *Spiaggia del Castello*, 2 km long, to the S of the town, the beaches are unattractive.

42 Trani
Picturesque sandy bay, with a narrow flat beach, *Spiaggia di Colonna*.
Suitable for children.

43 Rosa Marina
Well-kept sandy beach fully 2 km long and up to 40 m wide.
Suitable for children.

44 Marina di Ostuni
Rocky coast 1 km long with an artificially constructed bathing beach. For good swimmers.
Not so suitable for children.

45 San Cataldo
Narrow sandy beach 4 km long; well kept.
Suitable for childrn.

46 Gallípoli
Sandy beach to S of town 1·5 km long and up to 40 m wide; parts of it well kept.
Suitable for children.

47 Porto Cesáreo
Beach to S of town, fully 1 km long and up to 50 m wide; condition varies.
Suitable for children.

48 Marina di Castellaneta
Steeply sloping sandy beach, narrow, 3·5 km long; little maintenance.
Not really suitable for children.

49 Copanello
Well-kept sandy beach 500 m long and up to 40 m wide.
Suitable for children.

50 Soverato
Well-kept, gently sloping sandy beach 1·5 km long and over 100 m wide.
Very good for children.

51 Cefalù
Well-kept sandy beach, narrow, 500 m long; steep in places.
Not particularly suitable for children.

52 Vulcano
Small beach of black sand in the harbour.
Not particularly suitable for children.

53 Lípari
Small beach of black gravel at *Canneto*.
Not suitable for children.

54 Lido Mortelle
On a sandy beach 10 km long and up to 50 m wide; condition variable.
Good for children.

55 Taormina
Unattractive beaches in surrounding area. Small and charmingly situated beach of gently sloping shingle at *Isola Bella*, below the town.
Not particularly suitable for children.

56 Nicotera
Small steeply sloping beach of sand and gravel; little maintenance.
Not particularly suitable for children.

57 Capo Vaticano
Several quiet little bays with narrow sandy beaches; little maintenance.
Not particularly suitable for children.

58 Tropea
A total of 6 km of steeply sloping sandy beaches, average width 30–50 m; condition varies.
Suitable for children.

59 Praia a Mare
Well-kept, steeply sloping beach of sand and gravel, 7 km long and over 100 m wide.
Suitable for children.

60 Maratea
Several beautiful gravel beaches, many of them belonging to hotels and well maintained.
Suitable for children.

61 Sapri
Well-kept gravel beach 1 km long, narrow.
Suitable for children.

62 Marina di Camerota
Small but wide sandy beach, very gentle slope; little maintenance.
Suitable for children.

63 Castellabate
Sandy beach, 2 km long and 50 m wide, mostly well kept, at *Santa Maria*; also sandy beach 1 km long and up to 50 m wide at *San Marco*.
Suitable for children.

64 Paestum
Paestum lies on a stretch of coast with a beach of fine sand fully 50 m wide extending without interruption for 18 km, mostly with a very gentle slope; condition variable.
Good for children.

65 Vietri sul Mare
Small steeply sloping beach of sand and gravel.
Not particularly suitable for children.

66 Maiori
Narrow beach of sand and gravel almost 1 km long; well kept.
Suitable for children.

67 Minori
Small steeply sloping beach of sand and gravel; well maintained.
Good for children.

68 Amalfi
Small beaches; little maintenance.
Not particularly suitable for children.

69 Positano
Small, well-maintained, beaches of sand and gravel, *Spiaggia Grande* and *Spiaggia del Fornillo*; also a rocky beach at *La Scogliera* for good swimmers.
Not particularly suitable for children.

Bathing Beaches in Italy

70 Capri
Artificially constructed bathing station, *Marina Piccola*; also a small and very narrow beach, *Marina Grande*.
Not suitable for children.

71 Forío
Several small sandy bays with narrow, steeply sloping beaches; condition variable.
Not particularly suitable for children.

72 Lacco Ameno
Small and narrow beach, *Lido di San Montano*, beautifully situated; very well kept. Thermal swimming pool.

73 Casamícciola Terme
Small sandy beach; well kept.

74 Ischia
Narrow sandy beach between Porto and Ponte; flat, well kept.
Not particularly suitable for children.

75 Pontine Islands
Several small bays with good beaches. Excellent conditions for scuba diving.

76 Sperlonga
Small beach of fine sand in the town, and a number of small bays with gently sloping beaches in the surrounding area.
Suitable for children.

77 Terracina
More than 10 km of narrow flat sandy beach; well maintained in places.
Suitable for children.

78 San Felice Circeo
Good bathing in small sandy bays. A narrow beach of fine sand extends NW to Sabaudia.
Suitable for children.

79 Anzio
Flat sandy beach almost 1 km long, 50 m wide.
Suitable for children.

80 Monte Argentario
Rocky coast. For good swimmers only.

81 Marina di Grosseto
Some 15 km of fine sand, almost 100 m wide, in a beautiful setting.
Good for children.

82 Castiglione della Pescaia
Well-kept, gently sloping beach of fine sand 5 km long, 50–80 m wide.
Good for children.

83 Punta Ala
Well-kept sandy beach over 1 km long; beautiful scenery.
Good for children.

84 Follónica
Narrow, steeply sloping beach of fine sand 3 km long; condition varies.
Little room for children.

85 Porto Azzurro
Small narrow beaches round the town, not well kept and overcrowded.

86 Capolíveri
Several remote sandy bays in the surrounding area, many of them difficult to reach.

87 Marina di Campo
Several charming little bays with good sandy beaches.
Suitable for children.

88 Procchio
Narrow beach of fine sand almost 1 km long; well kept.
Suitable for children.

89 San Vincenzo
Narrow sandy beach 5 km long, with gentle slope; little maintenance.
Suitable for children.

90 Castiglioncello
Rocky beach 5 km long with small artificial sandy bays; well kept.
Not particularly suitable for children.

91 Tirrenia
Flat beach of fine sand 5 km long and up to 100 m wide.
Good for children.

92 Viareggio
Gently sloping beach of fine sand more than 6 km long and up to 120 m wide; well kept.
Good for children.

93 Lido di Camaiore
Well-kept flat beach of fine sand 2–3 km long and almost 100 m wide.
Good for children.

94 Marina di Pietrasanta
Well-kept, gently sloping sandy beach 4 km long and almost 100 m wide.
Good for children.

95 Forte dei Marmi
Well-kept flat beach of fine sand, 4 km long and almost 100 m wide.
Good for children.

96 Marina di Massa
Flat sandy beach more than 10 km long and up to 100 m wide; very well kept.
Good for children.

97 Lérici
1 km of sandy beach in several flat bays; mostly well maintained.
Suitable for children.

98 Sestri Levante
Narrow beach of sand and gravel 3·5 km long, much of it steeply sloping; condition variable.
Not particularly suitable for children.

99 Lavagna
Narrow beach of gravel and stone fully 4 km long, mostly on a gentle slope; condition variable.
Not particularly suitable for children.

100 Chiavari
Narrow beach of stone and gravel over 1 km long; well kept.
Not particularly suitable for children.

101 Santa Margherita
Small narrow beach of gravel and stone.
Not really suitable for children.

102 Portofino
Rocky coast; for good swimmers only.
Unsuitable for children.

103 Varazze
Narrow beach of sand and gravel fully 2 km long; then rocky coast.
Suitable for children.

104 Celle Ligure
Two flat bays, each with a beach of sand and gravel almost 1 km long and up to 40 m wide.
Suitable for children.

105 Albisola
Gently sloping sandy beach fully 1 km long and up to 60 m wide.
Suitable for children.

106 Spotorno
Narrow, steeply sloping beach of sand and gravel 2 km long; well kept.
Not particularly suitable for children.

107 Noli
Very narrow, steeply sloping beach of sand and gravel 1 km long; well kept.
Not particularly suitable for children.

108 Finale Ligure
Well-kept, gently sloping sandy beach 3 km long and up to 50 m wide.
Good for children.

109 Pietra Ligure
Narrow, gently sloping beach of sand and gravel 5 km long; condition variable.
Suitable for children.

110 Loano
Narrow artificial sandy beach almost 2 km long, steeply sloping; well kept.
Not particularly suitable for children.

111 Alassio
Narrow beach of fine sand 3 km long, gently sloping; usually overcrowded.
Little room for children.

112 Laigueglia
Narrow beach of fine sand 3 km long, gently sloping; well kept.
Suitable for children.

113 San Bartolomeo al Mare
More than 1 km of concrete esplanade with stretches of gravel; well kept.
Not particularly suitable for children.

114 Diano Marina
Narrow, gently sloping beach of fine sand 2 km long; well kept.
Suitable for children.

115 Imperia
Beach of sand and gravel 2 km long at *Oneglia*; also sandy beach 500 m long at *Porto Maurizio*; both reasonably well kept and suitable for children.

116 Arma di Taggia
Narrow, gently sloping sandy beach 1 km long; reasonably well kept.
Suitable for children.

117 San Remo
Sandy beach 2 km long, mostly narrow but well kept; then gravel and rocky coast.
Not particularly suitable for children.

118 Ospedaletti
Beach of gravel and rock 1 km long, steeply sloping; well kept.
Not particularly suitable for children.

119 Bordighera
Narrow, steeply sloping gravel beach 3 km long; well kept.
Not particularly suitable for children.

120 Costa Rei
Gently sloping beach of fine sand 7 km long and 50 m wide; condition variable.
Good for children.

121 La Caletta
Several kilometres of wide, gently sloping sandy beach, not yet developed.
Good for children.

122 Costa Smeralda
Many beautiful well-kept sandy bays in sheltered situations.
Good for children.

123 Baia Sardinia
Several small sandy bays, mostly well kept.
Good for children.

124 Santa Teresa di Gallura
Several gently sloping sandy bays; well kept.
Good for children.

125 Alghero
More than 4 km of fine sand at *Lido San Giovanni*, part of it well maintained.
Good for children.

Spas   See map, p. 350

1 Pré-Saint-Didier (Aosta)
Alt. 1004 m.
Slightly radioactive spring (36 °C – 97 °F) containing arsenic and iron.

2 Saint-Vincent (Aosta)
Alt. 575 m.
Alkaline spring containing iodine, bromine, sodium bicarbonate and sulphur.

3 Bognanco (Novara)
Alt. 670 m.
Alkaline water containing sodium bicarbonate and sulphur.

4 Crodo (Novara)
Alt. 505 m.
Springs containing lime, sulphur and sulphur bicarbonate.

5 Craveggia (Novara)
Alt. 885 m.
Acidulous chalybeate spring (at present in course of reconstruction).

6 San Pellegrino Terme (Bergamo)
Alt. 400 m.
Alkaline spring (26 °C – 79 °F) containing sodium bicarbonate and sulphur.

7 Boario Terme (Brescia)
Alt. 221 m.
Alkaline spring containing sodium chloride, lime and sulphur and colloidal water with catalytic and hypotonic effect.

8 Vetriolo Terme (Trento)
Alt. 1500 m.
Springs containing iron and arsenic.

9 Lévico Terme (Trento)
Alt. 506 m.
Spring containing iron and arsenic.

10 Roncegno (Trento)
Alt. 505 m.
Cold spring containing iron and arsenic.

11 Recoaro Terme (Vincenza)
Alt. 445 m.
Alkaline springs containing iron and bicarbonates.

12 Arta Terme (Udine)
Alt. 443 m.
Spring containing lime and sulphur.

13 Vinadio (Cuneo)
Alt. 904 m.
Hyperthermal spring containing sulphur.

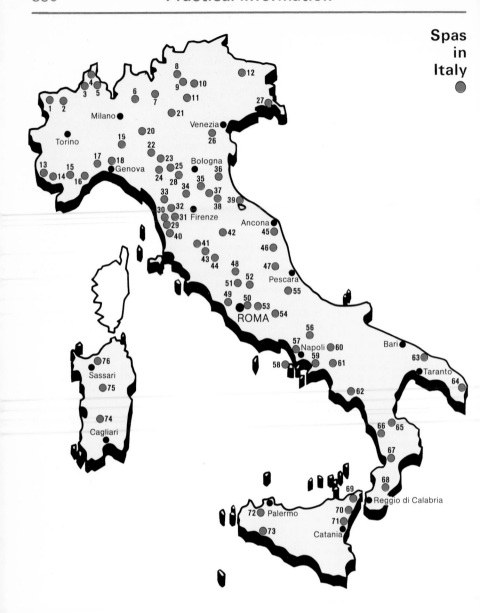

Spas in Italy

14 Valdieri Terme (Cuneo)
Alt. 1368 m.
Springs (69 °C – 156 °F) containing sulphur, iodine and bromine.

15 Lurisia (Cuneo)
Alt. 660 m.
Radioactive springs.

16 Garessio (Cuneo)
Alt. 621 m.
Water with low mineral content.

17 Acqui Terme (Alessandria)
Alt. 156 m.
Hot spring (75 °C – 167 °F) containing iodine and sulphur and cold spring containing sodium chloride.

18 Castelletto d'Orba (Alessandria)
Alt. 200 m.
Springs containing magnesium, sulphur and iron.

19 Sálice Terme (Pavia)
Alt. 167 m.
Spring containing iodine and water containing sulphur.

20 Miradolo Terme (Pavia)
Alt. 72 m.
Springs containing sulphur, salt and magnesium.

21 Sirmione (Brescia)
Alt. 68 m.
Radioactive spring (60 °C – 156 °F) containing sulphur.

22 Salsomaggiore Terme (Parma)
Alt. 160 m.
Springs containing sodium chloride, iodine and bromine.

23 Tabiano Bagni (Parma)
Alt. 166 m.
Springs containing lime and sulphur

24 **Sant'Andrea Bagni** (Parma)
Alt. 190 m.
Springs containing magnesium, lime and sulphur and water containing sodium chloride.

25 **Monticelli Terme** (Parma)
Alt. 112 m.
Water containing iodine; mud treatment.

26 **Àbano/Montegrotto** (Padova)
Alt. 14 m.
Radioactive water containing salt, iodine and bromine; mud treatment.

27 **Grado**
Alt. 1 m.
Sea-water treatment, sand baths.

28 **Sassuolo** (Modena)
Alt. 70 m.
Alkaline water containing iodine and sulphur.

29 **Uliveto Terme** (Pisa)
Alt. 8 m.
Earthy alkaline spring containing bicarbonates.

30 **San Giuliano Terme** (Pisa)
Alt. 10 m.
Earthy spring (41 °C – 106 °F) containing bicarbonates and sulphur.

31 **Monsummano Terme** (Pistoia)
Alt. 23 m.
Alkaline thermal water (34 °C – 93 °F) containing sulphur.

32 **Montecatini Terme** (Pistoia)
Alt. 29 m.
Radioactive springs containing chloride sulphate and alkalis, and springs containing sulphur.

33 **Bagni di Lucca** (Lucca)
Alt. 150 m.
Springs of varying temperature and radioactivity (54 °C – 129 °F) containing lime and sulphates.

34 **Poretta Terme** (Bologna)
Alt. 395 m.
Water containing iodine and sulphur.

35 **Riolo Terme** (Ravenna)
Alt. 98 m.
Water containing sulphur, iron and sodium chloride.

36 **Castel San Pietro Terme** (Bologna)
Alt. 75 m.
Water containing iodine and sulphur.

37 **Brisighella** (Ravenna)
Alt. 115 m.
Water containing sulphur and iodine.

38 **Castrocaro Terme** (Forlì)
Alt. 68 m.
Water containing iodine and lithium and water containing sodium chloride and magnesium.

39 **Riccione** (Forlì)
Alt. 6 m.
Slightly radioactive water containing sulphur.

40 **Casciana Terme** (Pisa)
Alt. 100 m.
Earthy alkaline water (36 °C – 97 °F) containing sulphates.

41 **Rapolano Terme** (Siena)
Alt. 334 m.
Spring (39°C – 102 °F) containing sulphur.

42 **Fontecchio** (Perugia)
Alt. 33 m.

43 **Chianciano Terme** (Siena)
Alt. 550 m.
Alkaline water containing sodium bicarbonate and sulphur and acidulous water containing sulphur.

44 **Sarteano** (Siena)
Alt. 573 m.
Earthy spring (24 °C – 75 °F) containing sulphates and bicarbonates.

45 **Aspio Terme** (Ancona)
Alt. 33 m.
Springs containing bromine and iodine.

46 **Tolentino** (Macerata)
Alt. 228 m.
Spring containing sulphur, bromine and iodine.

47 **Acquasanta Terme** (Ascoli Piceno)
Alt. 411 m.
Spring (38·6 °C – 101 °F) containing salt and sulphur.

48 **Acquasparta** (Terni)
Alt. 320 m.
Springs containing bicarbonates and lime.

49 **Stigliano** (Roma)
Alt. 150 m.
Springs containing sulphur (up to 56 °C – 133 °F).

50 **Bagni di Tívoli** (Roma)
Alt. 70 m.
Alkaline water containing iodine and sulphur and hyperthermal water containing iodine.

51 **Sangémini** (Terni)
Alt. 340 m.
Water containing lime and bicarbonates.

52 **Cotilia** (Rieti)
Alt. 409 m.
Spring containing sulphur.

53 **Fiuggi** (Frosinone)
Alt. 747 m.
Water of low mineral content.

54 **Ferentino** (Frosinone)
Alt. 393 m.
Water containing sulphur.

55 **Caramánico Terme** (Pescara)
Alt. 650 m.
Spring containing sulphur, bromine and iodine and water of low mineral content.

56 **Telese** (Benevento)
Alt. 50 m.
Earthy spring containing sulphur.

57 Agnano (Napoli)
Alt. 14 m.
Alkaline water containing iodine and sulphur.

**58 Ischia – Lacco Ameno – Porto d'Ischia –
Casamícciola – Forío** (Napoli)
Alt. 2 m.
Radioactive springs, water containing sodium
chloride and springs (75 °C – 167 °F) containing
chlorine, bromine and iodine; mud baths.

59 Castellammare di Stabia (Napoli)
Alt. 6 m.
Springs containing sulphur and iron.

60 Villamáina (Avellino)
Alt. 570 m.
Earthy alkaline water containing sulphur.

61 Contursi Terme (Salerno)
Alt. 180 m.
Springs (up to 50 °C – 122 °F) containing sulphur,
bromine and iodine.

62 Montesano (Salerno)
Alt. 850 m.
Water of low mineral content.

63 Torre Canne (Brindisi)
Alt. 4 m.
Springs containing bromine and iodine.

64 Santa Cesarea Terme (Lecce)
Alt. 67 m.
Water containing sulphur, iodine and lithium.

65 Spezzano (Cosenza)
Alt. 320 m.
Water containing salt, bromine and iodine.

66 Terme Luigiane (Cosenza)
Alt. 167 m.
Springs (45 °C – 113 °F) containing sulphur,
bromine and iodine.

67 Sambiase/Lamézia Terme (Catanzaro)
Alt. 220 m.
Radioactive water (39 °C – 102 °F) containing
sulphur.

68 Antonimina (Reggio Calabria)
Alt. 350 m.
Spring containing sulphates and chlorides.

69 Castroreale Terme (Messina)
Alt. 30 m.
Water containing sulphur and sodium bicar-
bonate.

70 Ali Terme (Messina)
Alt. 9 m.
Springs containing sulphur, bromine and iodine.

71 Acireale (Catania)
Alt. 161 m.
Radioactive water containing sulphur and sodium
chloride.

72 Castellammare del Golfo (Trapani)
Alt. 60 m.
Spring containing sulphur and sulphates.

73 Sciacca (Agrigento)
Alt. 36 m.
Hyperthermal water (56 °C – 133 °F) containing
sulphur.

74 Terme di Sárdara (Cagliari)
Alt. 95 m.
Springs (60 °C – 140 °F) containing sodium
bicarbonate.

75 Terme Aurora (Sassari)
Alt. 254 m.
Hyperthermal springs containing salt and sulphur.

76 Casteldoria (Sassari)
Alt. 167 m.
Hyperthermal springs (75 °C – 167 °F) containing
bromine and iodine.

Winter Sports
See map, p. 353

The winter sports areas in the Italian Alps
have long enjoyed an international reputation. In the Western Alps the principal
area is the **Aosta valley**, on the frontiers
with France and Switzerland, running to
the SE of the Mont Blanc massif –
conveniently reached from Turin. The
best-known resorts are Courmayeur and
Breuil-Cervinia.

Another popular winter sports region lies
E of Lake Como and N of Bergamo.
Livigno, on the W side of the Ortles
group, is a great tourist attraction with its
dependable covering of good snow and
its advantages as a customs-free area.

Particularly well equipped with winter
sports facilities and other amenities is the
area known as **Dolomiti Superski**, to
which such old-established resorts as
Cortina d'Ampezzo and San Martino di
Castrozza belong, as well as the Val
Gardena, the Val di Fassa and the Val
d'Ega. The most striking peak is Marmolada (3342 m), which offers facilities
for skiing even in summer. An excellently
coordinated system of lifts and cableways
brings more than 600 km of downhill
trails within easy reach.

There are also various smaller skiing
resorts on the S side of the Resia and
Brenner passes.

There are popular skiing areas, almost
exclusively frequented by Italians, in the
Apennines, W of Bologna, in the Ancona
area and N and S of Pescara, and also in
Calabria, on the slopes of Etna and in
Sardinia.

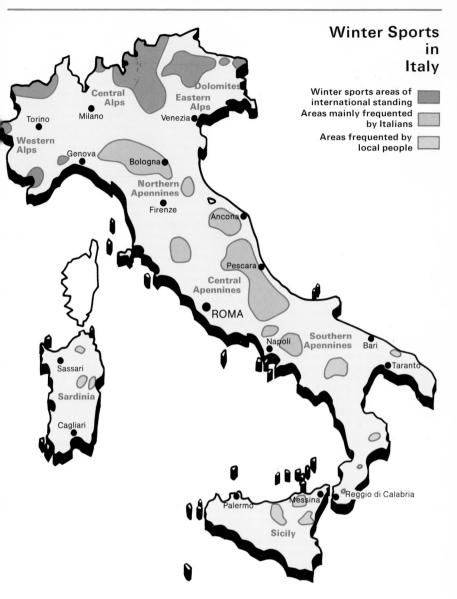

Folk Traditions

Although the process of assimilation to the American and northern European lifestyle and the trend towards uniformity of taste are well advanced in Italy as in other countries, the old traditions, costumes and folk music have nevertheless managed to survive in many parts of the country. Despite all external influences many of the old traditional festivals have preserved their distinctive character – both secular celebrations (often going back to pagan origins) and religious festivals. Some local festivals commemorating historical events which had fallen into oblivion have been revived in recent years under the stimulus of the developing tourist trade and have found

the local people very ready to take up the old traditions and join in the ceremonies, if only for the sake of the celebrations themselves. In addition to such major secular festivals as the Palio in Siena and the Giostra del Saracino in Arezzo there are a whole host of small events of mainly local concern – village festivals, fishermen's festivals, vintage and harvest celebrations, etc. – which give visitors an opportunity of seeing something of the traditional customs and way of life of ordinary people.

An important part is played in Italian life by the various **religious festivals**, which are usually celebrated with much more spontaneity then in northern Europe and frequently take on the character of folk celebrations. Particularly notable are

Historic costumes in the Piazza della Signoria, Florence

the numerous processions on the occasion of Corpus Christi, Assumption and Holy Week. On Good Friday the richly decked Santo Sepolcro (Holy Sepulchre) which is displayed in all churches attracts large numbers of worshippers. In northern Italy the Christmas tree is becoming a regular feature of the Christmas celebrations, but in the south the *presepio* (crib, Nativity group) retains its almost exclusive role as the symbol of Christmas. Children usually receive their presents at Epiphany (6 January). The carnival is now celebrated in only a few places (e.g. in Viareggio and San Remo); but some traditional features still survive from earlier times, like the *mamutones* (fools, jesters) in Sardinia, witches in Alto Adige and the "burning of Winter" in northern Italy.

The old traditional **costumes** are still often worn at the various festivals which take place throughout the year, particularly in the country areas. At any time of year, therefore, it is possible to see people wearing the old traditional dress in the Abruzzi, Sardinia and many parts of Calabria and Piedmont. The local costumes of Italy show a remarkable variety. In the Valle d'Aosta the peasants wear dark-coloured and rather severe costumes reminiscent of French models, while in the Alto Adige with its German-speaking population the traditional dress shows

Austrian and Bavarian features, including leather trousers and the typical Tirolean hat. In central and southern Italy the variety, opulence and vivid colours of the local costumes are sometimes almost overwhelming, and a diversity of influences – Yugoslav, Greek and even Oriental – can be detected. The women's costumes on Sardinia frequently include a veil.

On festive occasions visitors may have an opportunity, too, of hearing some of the old traditional tunes which in everyday life tend to be crowded out by the hit tunes of the day, usually of Anglo-Saxon origin. **Music** is an essential element in Italian life, and this is particularly true of singing. A passer-by will frequently hear the voice of some amateur singer from the courtyard of a house, through an open window or on a canal in Venice; and the cliché of the baker singing as he makes his pizzas has a foundation in reality. It is no accident that Italy is known as the land of *bel canto* and the home of opera. Although the famous Neapolitan *canzoni* ("O sole mio", "Torna a Surriento", "Tu ca' nun chiange", "Na sera e maggio", etc.) can hardly be called folk songs in the proper sense of the term, they do represent a curious and typically Italian combination of folk music, pop song and musical composition. Genuine Neapolitan folk music is performed to high standards of musicianship by such groups as the Nuova Compagnia di Canto Popolare; and a great body of Italian folk music has been collected and recorded by the Ricordi firm of music publishers in Milan, the Italian Radio Corporation (RAI) and the Accademia di Santa Cecilia, the National Musical Academy in Rome. The catalogue published by these institutions lists over 5000 titles.

Italian **folk music** uses a number of characteristic instruments, often centuries old. Among wind instruments, in addition to the reed pipe and the fife (*piffero*) there are the triple-piped *launeddas* and the *firlinfoeu*, resembling Pan pipes. Various kinds of bagpipes, such as the *zampogna*, are played by shepherds in the Abruzzi and Sardinia. Guitars and mandolines are also popular, as is the concertina, particularly in the country, where it often provides the music for a *ballo liscio*.

In earlier times **dancing**, often of ritual or religious significance, played an important part in Italian life. Although many of the old dances have not survived the centuries, a few, like the *ballo tondo* – a round dance, popular particularly in Sardinia, with some similarity to the Catalan *sardana* – have been preserved. The martial *danze delle spade* (sword dances) have also survived, and are danced with particular verve and vigour by the *spadonari* of Venaltio (17 May), Giaglione (5 April) and San Giorgio Canavese. The most popular Italian folk dances, however, are undoubtedly the Neapolitan *tarantella* and the *saltarello*, which both have love as their theme, representing its awakening and development by a whole range of symbolic movements, usually to a lively and rousing rhythm.

Calendar of Events

February	
San Remo	Italian Festival of Popular Songs
2 February	
Rome	Festa de la Candelora (Candlemas: processions)
Carnival	
Viareggio, San Remo, Pisa, Turin and some other towns on the Riviera	Colourful parade and celebrations
Venice	Historical gondola parades
Friday before Shrovetide	
Verona	Gnocco (Festival of Bacchus)
19 March	
Many places	San Giuseppe (St Joseph's day)
March–April	
Rome	Festa della Primavera (Spring Festival)
1 April	
San Marino	Installation of Regents
Palm Sunday	
Many places, particularly Rome and Florence	Blessings of palms, with procession
Wednesday before Easter	
Many places, particularly Rome	Mercoledì Santo (lamentations, Miserere)
Maundy Thursday	
Many places, particularly Rome and Florence	Washing of the Feet, Burial of the Sacraments
Good Friday	
Many places, particularly Rome and Florence	Adoration of the Cross
Easter Saturday	
Many places, particularly Rome and Florence	Lighting of the Sacred Fire
Easter Day	
Rome	Papal blessing "Urbi et Orbi"
Florence	Scoppio del Carro ("Explosion of the Cart" in the cathedral)
End of April	
Taormina	Costume festival and parade of floats
1 May	
Florence	Gioco del Calcio (historical ball-game)
May	
Florence	Maggio Musicale (musical festival)
Beginning of May	
Cagliari	Sant'Elisio (costume festival)
First Saturday in May	
Naples	San Gennaro (feast of St Januarius)

8 May Bari	Festival of St Nicholas (procession of fishing boats)
Second Sunday in May Camogli (Liguria)	Sagra del Pesce (fishermen's festival: frying of fish in giant pan)
15 May Gubbio (Umbria)	Corsa dei Ceri (procession with candles)
26 May Rome	San Filippo Neri
Last Sunday in May Gubbio (Umbria)	Palio (shooting with crossbows)
Ascension Florence Sassari (Sardinia)	Festival of the Crickets Cavalcata Sarda (mounted procession)

Floral decorations for Corpus Christi, Genzano di Roma

Corpus Christi Many places, particularly Orvieto (Umbria)	Processions
June–September Venice	Biennale art exhibition
First Sunday in June Pisa	Gioco del Ponte (Bridge Festival: historic boat races)
Mid June Many places	Corpus Domini (Ascension processions)
Mid June to mid July Spoleto (Umbria)	International Festival of Music, Dancing and Drama

23–24 June Rome	Vigilia di San Giovanni Battista (St John's Eve: fireworks, eating of snails, song competition)
29 June Rome	Santi Pietro e Paulo (feast of SS. Peter and Paul)
July Genoa–Nervi	International Ballet Festival in park of Villa Gropallo
2 July Siena	Palio delle Contrade (horse-race, historical parade). Also held on 16 August
15 July Rome	Festa Noiantri (folk dancing and singing; mass spaghetti eating)
16 July Naples	Feast of Santa Maria del Carmine
Third Saturday in July (night to Sunday) Venice	Festival of Redentore on Grand Canal
July and August Verona	Operatic Festival in Roman amphitheatre
Beginning of August Assisi	Perdono (Forgiveness) Festival
August Venice	Nocturnal Festival on Grand Canal
August and September Venice	Film Festival
First Sunday in August Ascoli Piceno (Marche)	Quintana
14 August Sassari (Sardinia)	Festival of Candles
15 August Many places	Assumption (processions and fireworks)
16 August Siena (Toscana)	Palio delle Contrade (horse-races and processions in medieval costume)
25 August to 20 September Stresa (Piedmont)	Settimane Musicali (musical festival)

First Sunday in
September
Arezzo — Giostra del Saracino
Venice — Historical regatta on Grand Canal

5–7 September
Naples — Madonna della Piedigrotta Folk Song Festival

7 September
Florence — Rificolone (nocturnal festival with lanterns)

8 September
Loreto (Marche) — Nativity of the Virgin
Recco (Liguria) — Nativity of the Virgin (large firework display, eating of *focaccia*)

Second Sunday in September
Foligno (Umbria) — Quintant (tournament, with tilting at the ring)
Sansepolcro (Tuscany) — Crossbow contest

13 September
Lucca (Tuscany) — Luminara di Santa Croce

Mid September
Ravenna — Dante celebrations
Asti (Piedmont) — Palio race

19 September
Naples — Liquefaction of St Januarius's blood

1 October
San Marino — Installation of Regents

22 November
Many places — Santa Cecilia (St Cecilia's day)

10 December
Loreto (Marche) — Santa Casa (procession)

25 December
Rome — Papal blessing "Urbi et Orbi"

Mid December to mid January
Many places — Christmas cribs (Nativity groups)

Various church festivals feature prominently in the annual programme, in particular church consecration festivals and patronal festivals (in almost every place of any size). In addition there are pilgrimages and performances of Passion plays in many places.

Public Holidays	
1 January	New Year's Day
6 January	Epiphany
25 April	Liberation Day (1945)
Easter Monday	
1 May	Labour Day
Ascension	
Corpus Christi	
2 June	Proclamation of Republic (celebrated on following Saturday)
15 August	*Ferragosto* (Assumption: family celebrations; the climax of the Italian holiday season)
1 November	All Saints
4 November	National Unity Day (celebrated on following Saturday)
8 December	Conception of the Virgin
25 and 26 December	Christmas

Shopping and Souvenirs

It is still possible to find in Italy an astonishingly wide range of traditional arts and crafts. All over Italy there are good shoes, leather articles and textiles (particularly woollens), and in some places also well-designed silver jewellery. In the Alto Adige visitors will be tempted by the famous wood-carving of Val Gardena, and in northern Piedmont by the charming local pottery. Cremona is noted for the making of violins, Venice for its glass, its lace and its copper ware, Tuscany for articles of alabaster, woodworking and pottery. The south of Italy produces iron and copper wares, corals, porcelain, pottery and terracotta, occasional furniture, textiles, embroidery and carpets.

Some visitors may like to take home Italian confections like *panettone* and candied fruit, or a bottle or two of Italian wines and spirits.

Warning: Visitors may well be offered watches, jewellery, etc., by street vendors at what appear to be very low prices. Such goods are almost invariably worthless; gold and silver assay stamps are frequently forged.

Information

Italian State Tourist Office

(*Ente Nazionale Italiano per il Turismo,* ENIT)

Head office:
Via Marghera 2,
I-00185 **Roma**;
tel. (06) 4 95 27 51.

United Kingdom:
201 Regent Street,
London W1R 8AY;
tel. (01) 439 2311.

United States of America:
500 North Michigan Avenue,
Chicago, Illinois 60611;
tel. (312) 644 0990–1.

630 Fifth Avenue, Suite 1565,
New York, N.Y. 10111;
tel. (212) 245 4822–4.

360 Post Street, Suite 801,
San Francisco, California 94109;
tel. (415) 392 6206–7.

Canada:
Store 56, Plaza, 3 Place Ville Marie,
Montreal, Quebec;
tel. 866 7667.

There are ENIT offices at the main frontier crossings into Italy and in the ports of Genoa, Livorno and Naples. Within Italy tourist information is provided by the Regional Tourist Offices (*Assessorati Regionali per il Turismo*) in regional capitals, provincial tourist offices (*Ente Provinciali per il Turismo*), spa administrations (*Aziende Autonome di Cura*) and local tourist offices (*Aziendi Autonome di Soggiorno e Turismo*).

Touring Club Italiano (TCI)
Head office:
Corso Italia 10,
I-20100 **Milano**;
tel. (02) 80 87 51.
Branch offices in Bari, Rome and Turin.

Automobile Club d'Italia (ACI)
Head office:
Via Marsala 8,
I-00185 **Roma**;
tel. (06) 49 98.

Branch offices in all provincial capitals, in major tourist centres and at the main frontier crossings.

Club Alpino Italiano (CAI)
Via Ugo Foscolo 3,
I-20121 **Milano**;
tel. (02) 80 25 54.

Diplomatic and Consular Offices in Italy

United Kingdom
Embassy
Via XX Settembre 80A,
I-00187 **Roma**;
tel. (06) 4 75 54 41 and 4 75 55 51.

Consulates
Via San Lucifero 87,
I-09100 **Cagliari**;
tel. (070) 66 27 55.

Palazzo Castelbarco,
Lungarno Corsini 2,
I-50123 **Firenze**;
tel. (055) 21 25 94, 28 41 33 and 28 74 49.

Via XII Ottobre 2,
I-16121 **Genova**;
tel. (010) 56 48 33–36.

Via San Paolo 7,
I-20121 **Milano**;
tel. (02) 80 34 42.

Via Francesco Crispi 122,
I-08122 **Napoli**;
tel. (081) 20 92 27, 66 33 20 and 68 24 82.

Via Marchese di Villabianca 9,
I-90143 **Palermo**;
tel. (091) 25 33 64–66.

Via Rossini 2,
I-34132 **Trieste**;
tel. (040) 6 91 35.

Corso M. d'Azeglio 60,
I-10126 **Torino**;
tel. (011) 68 78 32 and 68 39 21.

Accademia 1051,
I-30100 **Venezia**;
tel. (041) 2 72 07.

United States of America
Embassy
Via Veneto 119A,
I-00187 **Roma**;
tel. (06) 46 74.

Consulates
Lungarno Amerigo Vespucci 38,
I-50100 **Firenze**;
tel. (055) 29 82 76.

Piazza Portello 6,
I-16100 **Genova**;
tel. (010) 28 27 41 55.

Piazza Repubblica 32,
I-20124 **Milano**;
tel. (02) 6 52 84 15.

Piazza della Repubblica,
I-80122 **Napoli**;
tel. (081) 66 09 66.

Via Baccarini 1,
I-90143 **Palermo**;
tel. (091) 5 32 35.

Via Roma 9 (4th floor),
I-34100 **Trieste**;
tel. (011) 54 36 00 and 54 36 10.

Canada

Embassy
Via Zara 30,
I-00198 **Roma**;
tel. (06) 8 44 18 41–46.

Consulate
Via Vittor Pisani 19,
I-20124 **Milano**;
tel. (02) 65 26 00 and 6 57 04 51–55.

Airlines

Alitalia,
251–259 Regent Street,
London W1;
tel. (01) 734 4040.

666 5th Ave.,
New York, NY;
tel. 212 582 8900.

Via L. Bissolati 6–10,
I-00187 **Roma**;
tel. (06) 46 88.

Desks at all Italian airports and international airports in other countries.

British Airways,
Via Bissolati 48,
I-00187 **Roma**;
tel. (06) 47 99 91.

Offices or agencies in Alghero, Bari, Bologna, Catania, Codroipo, Florence, Genoa, Messina, Milan, Naples, Nuoro, Palermo, Sassari, Turin, Udine, Venice and Verona.

Pan American,
Pan American Building,
East 45th Street,
New York, NY;
tel. 212 973 4000.

Trans World Airlines,
605 3rd Ave.,
New York, NY;
tel. 212 557 3000.

Italian State Railways

10 Charles II Street,
London SW1;
tel. (01) 930 6722.

765 Route 83, Suite 105,
Chicago, Ill., USA.

5670 Wilshire Boulevard,
Los Angeles, Ca., USA.

668 Fifth Avenue,
New York, NY, USA.

2055 Peel Street, Suite 102,
Montreal, Canada.

111 Richmond Street West, Suite 419,
Toronto, Canada.

Emergency Calls

Make sure you always have some telephone tokens (*gettoni*) handy!

Dial the following numbers for police, ambulance or breakdown assistance anywhere in Italy:

Police and ambulance
(Pronto soccorso)   **113**

ACI breakdown service
(Soccorso stradale)   **116**

International telephone dialling codes for subscriber trunk dialling

From the United Kingdom to Italy
    010

From the United States to Italy **01139**

From Italy to the United Kingdom
    0044
From Italy to the United States **01139**
From Italy to Canada   **01139**

(The initial zero of the local dialling code should be omitted.)

Remember that Italian public telephones are operated by the insertion of a 50 or 100 lire coin or a telephone token (*gettone*) obtainable from tobacconists, news-stands and bars with a telephone.

Abbreviations for tourist information offices, etc.

AA   *Azienda Autonoma di Soggiorno (Cura)*
Local tourist information office (spa administration)

ACI   *Automobile Club d'Italia*

CIT   *Compagnia Italiana Turismo*
(The official Italian travel agency)

ENIT   *Ente Nazionale Italiano per il Turismo*
Italian State Tourist Office

EPT   *Ente Provinciale per il Turismo*
Provincial tourist information office

Pro Loco   Local tourist information office

TCI   *Touring Club Italiano*